Right-Wing Populism in America

Right-Wing Populism in America

TOO CLOSE FOR COMFORT

Chip Berlet • Matthew N. Lyons

THE GUILFORD PRESS
New York   London

To Lorraine Hansberry and Earl B. Dickerson

©2000 The Guilford Press
A Division of Guilford Publications, Inc.
72 Spring Street, New York, NY 10012
www.guilford.com

This book is printed on acid-free paper.

Last digit is print number: 9   8   7   6   5   4   3   2   1

Library of Congress Cataloging-in-Publication Data

Berlet, Chip.
    Right-wing populism in America : too close for comfort /
Chip Berlet, Matthew N. Lyons.
        p.   cm.—(Critical perspectives)
    Includes bibliographical references and index.
    ISBN 1-57230-568-1 — ISBN 1-57230-562-2 (pbk.)
    1. Conservatism—United States. 2. Right-wing
extremists—United States. 3. Populism—United States
I. Lyons, Matthew Nemiroff. II. Title. III. Series.
JC573.2.U6 B47   2000
320.52′0973—dc21   00-037636
                                                      CIP

Right-Wing Populism in America is the latest volume in the Guilford series
"Critical Perspectives," edited by Douglas Kellner.

ACKNOWLEDGMENTS

JOINT THANKS

Thanks to our editors Douglas Kellner and Peter Wissoker for believing that our original manuscript could be turned into a book; and to William Meyer and all the people at The Guilford Press for their efforts in making it a reality.

Various drafts of the manuscript were read for comments by Martin Durham, Jean V. Hardisty, Carol Mason, Abby Scher, and Holly Sklar. We thank them for their critical insights while taking responsibility for any factual errors or analytical shortcomings.

This book was originally to be published by the South End Press under the title *Too Close for Comfort*. We thank them for their work, especially our original editor, Sonia Shah, and their courtesy in releasing the manuscript.

MATTHEW

Thanks to Chip for suggesting that we write a book together, and for his patience, open-mindedness, and good humor throughout the process.

Special thanks to John Goetz: our discussions and shared political work over seventeen years inform my contribution to this book throughout.

I am grateful to the many people who read and commented on various portions of the manuscript, among them Amy Ansell, Debbie Balser, Lourdes Benería, Tom Burghardt, Cathy Gelbin, John Goetz, Jewell Handy Gresham, Victor Grossman, Scott Henstrand, Sasha Lilley, David Lyons, Sandra Lyons, Elspeth Meyer, Matt Meyer, Betsy Mickel, John Milich, Leo Nemiroff, Mili Nemiroff, Dair Obenshain, John Riley, Larry Roberts, Beth Ruck, Meg Starr, Art Strum, and Rossanna Wang. Bob Lederer offered lengthy, detailed comments and suggestions on several chapters. Terry Schleder's enthusiasm for each new chapter draft helped me stick to the task.

A number of people, in addition to those listed above, helped me develop ideas, steered me to relevant sources, or offered useful advice and support regarding various aspects of the book project. Thanks to Mimi Abramovitz, Electa Arenal, Regina Arnold, Samer Atout, Russ Bellant, Fred Clarkson, Clinton Cox, Monisha Das Gupta, Sandi DuBowski, Bonnie Duran, Catherine Hill, Steve Hubbell, Dennis King, Tom Lampert, Tia Lessin, Fouad Makki, Mike Morgan, Michael Novick, Lucy Oppenheim, Suzanne Pharr, Riti Sachdeva, John Stoltenberg, Serena Sundaram, and Jamie Walker. Thanks to laurie prendergast for all the conversations and shared projects.

Many of the ideas I brought to this book were formed, tested, and strengthened in political organizations and study groups. I am grateful particularly to the members of the *Settlers* study group, the Ithaca Coalition Against War in the Gulf/Solidarities Action & Education, Action Against Rape and Misogyny, and Resistance in Brooklyn. My thinking about history benefited greatly from a dialectics study group based on course materials from the former Sojourner Truth Organization. Thanks to all who developed that course and all who took part.

Thanks to those who offered helpful criticism and bibliographic advice on two earlier unpublished essays, *Parasites and Pioneers: Antisemitism in White Supremacist America* and *Tracing the Roots of Conspiracy Thinking*, that formed part of the basis for the analysis presented here: Eric Acree, Lisa Albrecht, Evelyn Annuß, David Elliott, Fadya El-Rayess, Thomas Ferguson, Sander Gilman, J. K. Langford, Fouad Makki, Rod Malpert, John Milich, Ann Peters, Robert Schmidt, Mab Segrest, Paul Seidman, Barbara Smith, Kizer Walker, and Katie Welch.

My analysis benefited from participating in the Blue Mountain Working Group gathering in November 1994, and from preparing a background report for that gathering, *Business Conflict and the Right in the United States.* A later version of that study appeared in *Unraveling the Right: The New Conservatism in American Thought and Politics*, edited by Amy E. Ansell (Boulder, CO: Westview Press, 1998).

Research for this book depended on the help of staff members at several libraries, particularly the Cornell University Library, the New York Public Library, and the University of New Mexico Libraries in Albuquerque. The staff of Planned Parenthood Federation of America's Public Policy Institute, Political Research Associates, and the Women's Project also provided valuable help and support.

The writings of Moishe Postone, Alexander Saxton, and Thomas Ferguson provided some of the key analytical tools I apply to right-wing populism. Isaac Deutscher, W. E. B. Du Bois, Muriel Rukeyser, and Lorraine Hansberry changed the way I look at the world.

Thanks to my friends and colleagues in Ithaca, Berlin, New York City, Albuquerque, Boston, New Jersey, Chicago, Minneapolis, and points beyond who supported, encouraged, taught, questioned, and argued with me over these past eight years. Thanks for more than I can put into words to the members of the Lyons and Nemiroff extended families, especially to Mili and Leo, Jewell, Emily, Jeremy, and to my parents, Sandy and David.

CHIP

Thanks to Matthew, who started by writing a thoughtful critique of my first published efforts at describing right-wing populism, and became a full partner in writing this book over an eight-year period of research, struggle, laughter, and mutual support.

For over twenty years I have worked under the guidance of Jean V. Hardisty, director of Political Research Associates (PRA), where the culture of cooperation and the document archives have made my work possible. My research into the political Right has also been greatly influenced and assisted by my colleagues Sara Diamond, Holly Sklar, the late Margaret Quigley, and Fred Clarkson. Early research was carried out under the auspices of the Public Eye network, with assistance from Sheila O'Donnell, Russ Bellant, Eda Gordon, and others.

Conversations over many years (and with much wine) with family friends Herman Sinaiko and Susan Fisher were crucial to shaping my understanding of the social and psychological dynamics of conspiracist scapegoating. Carol Mason spent time at the PRA library exploring apocalyptic themes in antiabortion rhetoric and she generously shared her original research and analysis on that subject with me. In a similar manner, I have had extended conversations with Kevin Coogan, James Danky, Paul de Armond, Lin Collette, Evan Harrington, Aaron Katz, Dennis King, Erin Miller, Adele Oltman, Meg Riley, Al Ross, and Ariane van Buren.

I have drawn material from articles I either cowrote or coresearched with the following authors: Russ Bellant, Joel Bellman, Reena Bernards, Eda Gordon, Nancy Katz, Dennis King, Juliette Kayyem, Margaret Quigley, and Holly Sklar. When appropriate, I have cited the article. Some especially cogent passages penned by Ms. Quigley are directly credited to her.

I participated in several symposia as an advisor to the PBS television series *With God on Our Side* hosted by Cal Skaggs and the staff of Lumiere Productions. I learned much from the other participants: Michael Cromartie, Frances Fitzgerald, John C. Green, Susan Harding, George Marsden, William Martin, and Leo Ribuffo.

The Center for Millennial Studies (CMS) and its director, Richard Landes, hosted several conferences where I benefited from thoughtful and challenging presentations. Conversations with the following attending scholars were especially enlightening: Victor Balaban, Michael Barkun, Brenda Brasher, Paul Boyer, Andrew Gow, Philip Lamy, Stephen O'Leary, Lee Quinby, David Reddles, and Damian Thompson. Thanks also to the CMS staff, especially Beth Marie Forrest, Aaron Katz, and David Kessler.

A number of academics shared specific insights, suggestions, and encouragement, including: Amy Ansell, Robert Antonio, Kathleen Blee, Betty Dobratz, Raphael Ezekiel, Abby Ferber, Peter Fritzsche, Jerome Himmelstein, Janice Irvine, Valerie Jenness, Linda Kintz, Burt Klandermans, Lauren Langman, Brian Levin, Jack Levin, Clarence Lo, Carol Mason, Gerry O'Sullivan, Abby Scher, Stephanie Shanks-Meile, and David Norman Smith.

A series of retreats that were started at the Blue Mountain Conference Center in upstate New York, taking place over several years and in several states, involved many people and many spirited discussions that informed my work. I especially benefited from the ideas of the convener, Suzanne Pharr, and my colleague Loretta Ross with whom I served as a co-coordinator of the Blue Mountain Working Group. My thanks extend to all the participants, especially Robert Bray, Mandy Carter, Fred Clarkson, Marghe Covino, Gary Delgado, Deanna R. Duby, Suzanne Goldberg, Kerry Lobel, Lance Hill, Leni Marin, David Mendoza, Scot Nakagawa, Skipp Porteous, Tarso Ramos, Suzanne Shende, Barbara Simon, Frieda Takamura, Deborah Toler, and Urvashi Vaid.

Conversations with a number of other journalists and activists were also important to my political analysis, and I thank Terry Allen, Anne Bower, Ward Churchill, Liz Galst, Ross Gelbspan, Alan Hunter, Dan Junas, Martin A. Lee, Kate Porterfield, Diana Reynolds, Nan Rubin, Jerry Sloan, and Peter Snoad. Sometimes gatherings produce serendipitous learning. Eric Ward of the Northwest Coalition for Human Dignity has coordinated several such public and private symposia. Marlene Gerber Fried and Betsy Hartmann have staged annual conferences on abortion rights and reproductive freedom at Hampshire College. Students at the University of Illinois invited me to spend a week studying and lecturing on campus. I reread the work of Girard on scapegoating with new interest after a discussion with faculty at Bucks County Community College. A symposium sponsored by Group Regards Critiques at the University of Lausanne, Switzerland, broadened my perspective on globalism and ethnonationalism.

The staff of PRA over two decades has carried out research and created an archive that makes my work possible: Francine Almash, Nikhil Aziz, Pam Chamberlain, Susie Chancey-O'Quinn, Francine Davis, Judith Glaubman, Liza Goldman Huertas, Anoosh Jorjorian, Aaron Katz, Chris McGee, Erin Miller, Vanessa Mohr, Geetha Nadiminti, Mark Umi Perkins, Jesse Ward Putnam, Margaret Quigley, Mitra Rastegar, Peggy Shinner, and Peter Snoad. The interns and volunteers at PRA also contributed to the research effort, and I thank them all, singling out Miranda Balkin, Jeremy Dittmar, and Jon Reed.

A number of journalists, researchers, and activists have helped me with specific research, sent me documents, or swapped information with me: Steve Askin, Dan Barry, Bill Berkowitz, David Cantor, Johan Carlisle, Cara

DeGette, Sandi DuBowski, Rick Eaton, Mary Eich, Rachel Rosen DeGolia, Sally Greenberg, Kit Gage, Brian Glick, John Goetz, Howard Goldenthal, Charles Haber, Gordon Hall, Steven Hassan, Jane Hunter, Leslie Jorgenson, Ernie Lazar, Richard Lobenthal, Jim McNamara, Mimi Morris, Hollis Mosher, cullen nawalkowsky, Mark Potok, Jean E. Rosenfeld, Al Ross, Andrew Rowell, Mark Rupert, Adele Stan, Ken Stern, Mike Weber, A. J. Weberman, Louis Wolf, Leonard Zakim, Leonard Zeskind, and Larry Zilliox, among others too numerous to list or too circumspect to be named. Acquisition and translation of documents from Europe was accomplished by Sabine Freizer, Chris Muntiu, and Margaret Quigley, as well as several file ferrets who prefer to remain anonymous.

Three participants in the Patriot movement, Leroy Crenshaw, Ed Brown, and Scott Stevens, spent time explaining their views to me in detail. I remain unconvinced, but appreciate their courtesy.

I relied on the staff and librarians at Americans United for Separation of Church and State, the Burlington Public Library, the Center for Millennial Studies, the Data Center, People for the American Way, the Simon Wiesenthal Center, the State Historical Society of Wisconsin, the University of Oregon Knight Library Special Collections, the University of Wyoming American Heritage Center, and the Library of Congress. I was assisted in online research by Devin Burghart, Mark Pitcavage, Michael Pugliese, and Hank Roth. The Data Center's *Culture Watch* newsletter saved hundreds of hours of research.

Along the way I have had mentors who graciously shared their insights and suggestions over coffee (or martinis), including Ann Mari Buitrago, Earl B. Dickerson, Frank Donner, Gabrielle Simon Edgcomb, George Seldes, and I. F. Stone.

Throughout our life together my family has tolerated outlandish requests, improbable situations, and sporadic threats as I carried out my work. They have my eternal gratitude.

AUTHORS' NOTE

We used a division of labor in writing this book. Matthew is the primary author of Chapters 1 through 8; Chip is the primary author of Chapters 9 through 16. The Introduction and Conclusions are coauthored.

Supplementary materials to this book, such as a categorized version of the Bibliography, are available at

http://www.publiceye.org/tooclose/more.htm

CONTENTS

INTRODUCTION

Right-wing politics in the United States has taken many forms since the end of the Cold War. The rise of the armed citizens militias accompanied electoral support for Patrick Buchanan's xenophobic economic nationalism. Christian evangelical groups at times dominated the Republican Party while the Promise Keepers filled stadiums with praying men. Major politicians denounced undocumented immigrants and poor single mothers while libertarian antigovernment attitudes flourished. On talk radio, discussions of black helicopters, secret teams, and sinister elites envisioned a massive global conspiracy. Some boldly asserted that President Clinton assisted drug smugglers, ran a hit squad that killed his political enemies, and covered up the assassination of his aide Vincent Foster. In 1995 a powerful homemade bomb—delivered in a rental truck driven by a fresh-faced American neonazi named Timothy McVeigh—destroyed the Murrah Federal Building in Oklahoma City. The blast killed 167 persons (including 19 children in an onsite day care center), and injured over 650 more. One rescue worker died. Violence from the Far Right continued, targeting abortion providers, people of color, gay men and lesbians, and Jews.

In this book we show how all of these phenomena involve some form of right-wing populism—a concept we think is crucial to understanding not just the U.S. political Right, but also our history as a nation. Right-wing populist movements often defy conventional explanations of "extremism" because they combine attacks on socially oppressed groups with grassroots mass mobilization and distorted forms of antielitism based on scapegoating. We will trace right-wing populism from its roots in the colonial period up to the present, and show how it has been interwoven with this country's central institutions, structures, and political traditions.

One of the most visible right-wing populist movements from the mid-1990s to the present has been the armed citizens militias. As the militant cutting edge of a much larger "Patriot" movement, the militias collected weapons, conducted paramilitary training, advocated armed self-defense against what they saw as an increasingly repressive federal government, and warned of a vast elite conspiracy to subject the United States to a tyrannical "New World Order."[1]

Militias and Patriot groups were complicated—bringing together hard-core neonazis with a much wider array of right-wing antigovernment activists. The movement was pervaded by conspiracy theories historically rooted in antisemitism; and by arcane constitutional doctrines that implicitly rejected women's suffrage, citizenship rights for people of color, and the abolition of slavery. Yet many supporters seemed unaware of (or indifferent to) the history or politics of these oppressive ideas. Most of the militias disavowed ethnic bigotry, and some of them included a handful of Jews and people of color as members. Here was a movement that seemingly blurred the line between hate ideology and inclusiveness, and that mixed reactionary scapegoating with progressive-sounding attacks on economic injustice, political elitism, and government repression.

As is true for the militias, members of other recent right-wing populist movements have often spoken or acted in ways that challenged outsiders' expectations. Despite a history of close collaboration between law enforcement agencies and paramilitary rightists, sections of the neonazi–Klan movement undertook armed combat against the U.S. government beginning in the 1980s. Although the Right has regularly championed private enterprise and business interests, ultraconservative leader Patrick Buchanan denounced multinational corporations and "unfettered capitalism." Despite its traditional superpatriotism, large sections of the Right opposed the U.S.-led war on Iraq in 1990—1991, and the U.S.-led bombing of Yugoslavia in 1999. Although the Christian Right was virulently antifeminist and staunchly Eurocentric, major sections of that movement urged women to become politically active and to develop leadership skills, or made genuine efforts to build alliances with conservative Black, Latino, and Asian organizations.

This type of political complexity is not new. We will place the Christian Right, the Buchananites, and the militias in a long line of right-wing populist movements such as Father Coughlin's movement in the 1930s, the anti-Chinese crusade of the 1880s, and the Ku Klux Klan. Right-wing populist movements often borrow political slogans, tactics, and forms of organization from the Left, but harness them to rightist goals. They attract people who often have genuine grievances against elites, but channel such resentments in ways that reinforce social, cultural, political, or economic power and privilege.

Historically, right-wing populist movements have reflected the interests of two different kinds of social groups, often in combination:

1. Middle-level groups in the social hierarchy, notably middle- and working-class Whites, who have a stake in traditional social privilege but resent the power of upper-class elites over them, and,
2. "Outsider" factions of the elite itself, who sometimes use distorted forms of antielitism as part of their own bid for greater power.

The original Ku Klux Klan of the late 1860s, for example, represented an alliance between some lower- and middle-class southern Whites (outraged that Black emancipation and Reconstruction had eroded their social privilege), and southern planters (who sought to win back some of the power they had lost to northern capitalists in the Civil War). The Klan combined racist terrorism against Black people and their allies with demagogic antielite rhetoric about northern "military despotism."

While the original Klan is generally remembered today as an "extremist" movement, its politics reflected traditions considered mainstream. For example, Jacksonianism in the early nineteenth century (on which the modern-day Democratic Party is founded), is typically thought of as a progressive reform movement that championed "the common man" and helped to democratize the U.S. political system. Yet the Jacksonian political reforms, such as Pennsylvania's 1838 Constitution, disenfranchised Black men while giving the vote to poor White men. The Jacksonians spearheaded the murderous forced expulsion of American Indians, as in the 1838 Trail of Tears, when thousands of Cherokees died after being driven from their homes at gunpoint. And the Jacksonians denounced "the money power" of federal central banking as an evil conspiracy, yet upheld class inequality. Like many of the movements discussed in this book, Jacksonianism represented an alliance between lower-class Whites and certain factions of the elite. When the Klan emerged a few years later as the first truly right-wing populist movement, its constituency, doctrine, and rhetoric were largely Jacksonian.

Right-wing populist movements are subject to the same basic dynamics as other social movements, and their members are, for the most part, average people motivated by a combination of material and ideological grievances and aspirations. Despite widespread popular rhetoric, it is neither accurate nor useful to portray right-wing populists as a "lunatic fringe" of marginal "extremists." Right-wing populists are dangerous not because they are crazy irrational zealots—but because they are not. These people may be our neighbors, our coworkers, and our relatives.

This introduction presents some of the basic conceptual tools we will use in the book. We explain the concept of populism and the many forms it can take, including right-wing populism. This leads into a discussion of major right-wing populist themes, notably producerism, demonization, scapegoating, conspiracism, apocalypticism, and millennialism. We then outline our view of right-wing populist movements as social movements with a contradictory relationship to the established social and political order, which is followed by an overview of subcategories within the Right, from conservatism to fascism. We conclude by outlining some of the key issues developed in the following chapters, such as right-wing populism's relationship to White supremacy and male dominance.

POPULISM

There is much confusion over the term *populism*. Margaret Canovan, in one of the few in-depth studies of the subject, mapped populism onto two main branches—agrarian and political—with seven overlapping subcategories.[2] Although we do not use her typology in this book, it shows how many different kinds of political movements and phenomena have been labeled as populist. Canovan's categories look like this:

Agrarian populism includes:

- Commodity farmer movements with radical economic agendas such as the U.S. People's Party of the late 1800s.
- Subsistence peasant movements such as eastern Europe's Green Rising movement after World War I.
- Intellectuals who wistfully romanticize hard-working farmers and peasants and build radical agrarian movements like the late-nineteenth-century Russian narodniki or the U.S. back-to-the-land movement in the 1960s.

Political populism includes:

- Populist democracy, including calls for more political participation, such as the use of referenda; recent examples include the general perspective of columnists Jim Hightower and Molly Ivins.
- Politicians' populism marked by vague appeals for "the people" to build a unified coalition such as used by Ross Perot in his presidential campaigns in the 1990s.
- Reactionary populism such as the White backlash against civil rights that was harvested by George Wallace in the 1960s and 1970s and reseeded to some extent by Patrick Buchanan in the 1990s.
- Populist dictatorship such as that established by Juan Peron in Argentina in 1945–1955 or envisioned by some U.S. neonazi groups.

Across this wide range of categories there are only two universal elements, Canovan argues: all forms of populism "involve some kind of exaltation of and appeal to 'the people,' and all are in one sense or another antielitist."[3] We take these two elements—celebration of "the people" plus some form of antielitism—as a working definition of populism. A populist movement—as opposed, for example, to one-shot populist appeals in an election campaign—uses populist themes to mobilize a mass constituency as a sustained political or social force. Our discussion of populism will focus mainly on populist movements.

Michael Kazin calls populism a style of organizing.[4] Populist movements can be on the right, the left, or in the center. They can be egalitarian or authoritarian, and can rely on decentralized networks or a charismatic leader. They can advocate new social and political relations or romanticize the past. Especially important for our purposes, populist movements can promote forms of antielitism that target either genuine structures of oppression or scapegoats alleged to be part of a secret conspiracy. And they can define "the people" in ways that are inclusive and challenge traditional hierarchies, or in ways that silence or demonize oppressed groups.

REPRESSIVE POPULISM AND RIGHT-WING POPULISM

We use the term *repressive populist movement* to describe a populist movement that combines antielite scapegoating (discussed below) with efforts to maintain or intensify systems of social privilege and power. Repressive populist movements are fueled in large part by people's grievances against their own oppression but they deflect popular discontent away from positive social change by targeting only small sections of the elite or groups falsely identified with the elite, and especially by channeling most anger against oppressed or marginalized groups that offer more vulnerable targets.

Right-wing populist movements are a subset of repressive populist movements. A *right-wing populist movement*, as we use the term, is a repressive populist movement motivated or defined centrally by a backlash against liberation movements, social reform, or revolution. This does not mean that right-wing populism's goals are only defensive or reactive, but rather that its growth is fueled in a central way by fears of the Left and its political gains. The first U.S. populist movement we would unequivocally describe as right wing was the Reconstruction-era Ku Klux Klan, which was a counterrevolutionary backlash against the overthrow of slavery and Black people's mass mobilization and empowerment in the post-Civil War South. Earlier repressive populist movements paved the way for right-wing populism, but did not have this same backlash quality as a central feature.

The term "right wing" requires some attention. We do not accept the conventional definition of right wing as meaning "conservative or reactionary," because many of the movements we consider right-wing populist have advocated some form of social change, not simply preserving or restoring old institutions and relations. Conventional classifications of populist movements on a right–left spectrum are often misleading as well. Compare the Jacksonians and the Know Nothings, two pre-Civil War repressive populist movement. The Jacksonians are often remembered as left-leaning, because of their antielite positions discussed above, while the Know Nothings are generally considered right-wing, because they were anti-Catholic and anti-immigrant. Yet the Jacksonians advocated and practiced a far more virulent and murderous form of ethnic oppression than did the Know Nothings.

And, in sharp contrast to the Jacksonians, the Know Nothings opened up important new opportunities for women's political activism.

Sociologist Sara Diamond has offered a simple but nuanced definition: "To be right-wing means to support the state in its capacity as *enforcer* of order and to oppose the state as *distributor* of wealth and power downward and more equitably in society."[5] This accurately describes many movements generally regarded as rightist, and has the advantage of cutting through claims that the Right consistently opposes "big government." But Diamond's definition does not cover all cases. Some rightist movements, such as Father Coughlin's Social Justice movement in the 1930s and George Wallace's American Independent Party in the 1960s, have advocated downward redistribution of wealth and power—not to everyone, but to certain groups below the elite. And some right-wing movements, such as the Ku Klux Klan of the late 1860s or various Patriot/militia groups in the 1990s, have rejected the state altogether and have sought to overthrow it, in the process rejecting and disrupting the state's order–enforcement role.

Terms such as "left" and "right" are difficult to define, in part, because they are relative rather than absolute: they take on meaning in relation to the range of political actors in a particular historical situation. We use the concept of backlash in our working definition of right-wing populism partly to highlight this relational character.

CHARACTERISTICS OF RIGHT-WING POPULISM

Producerism

One of the staples of repressive and right-wing populist ideology has been *producerism,* a doctrine that champions the so-called producers in society against both "unproductive" elites and subordinate groups defined as lazy or immoral. The Jacksonians were the first major U.S. movement to rely on producerism. Their vision of the producing classes included White farmers, laborers, artisans, slave-owning planters, and "productive" entrepreneurs; it excluded bankers, speculators, monopolists—and people of color. In this way, producerism bolstered White supremacy, blurred actual class divisions, and embraced some elite groups while scapegoating others.

After the Jacksonian era, producerism was a central tenet of the anti-Chinese crusade in the late nineteenth century. Kazin points out that as it developed in the nineteenth century,

> the romance of producerism had a cultural blind spot; it left unchallenged strong prejudices toward not just African-Americans but also toward recent immigrants who had not learned or would not employ the language and rituals of this variant of the civic religion. . . . Even those native-born activists who reached out to immigrant laborers assumed that men of Anglo-American

origins had invented political democracy, prideful work habits, and well-governed communities of the middling classes.[6]

In the 1920s industrial philosophy of Henry Ford, and Father Coughlin's fascist doctrine in the 1930s, producerism fused with antisemitic attacks against "parasitic" Jews. Producerism, with its baggage of prejudice, remains today the most common populist narrative on the right, and it facilitates the use of demonization and scapegoating as political tools.[7]

Demonization and Scapegoating

Gunning down children in a Jewish community center in Los Angeles makes sense if you think Jews run the world and are thus responsible for all that is wrong in the country as a whole and your life in particular. Shooting a postal worker who is a person of color makes sense if you think lazy people of color are conspiring with the Jewish-controlled Zionist Occupational Government to rob the hard-working taxpayer. The gunman accused of committing both these acts in California in 1999 is Buford O'Neal Furrow, Jr. He emerged from a neonazi milieu where Christian Identity is the dominant religious philosophy. Christian Identity argues that Jews are in league with Satan and that Blacks and other people of color are subhuman. The battle of Armageddon prophesied in the Bible is envisioned by Christian Identity as a race war. This is an extreme example of demonization, but it is hardly new. An earlier example happened during the depression of 1837–1843 when there was a wave of attacks against Catholic immigrants to the United States. Catholics were demonized in popular culture as lazy and treacherous and the resulting scapegoating generated violence. Jean Hardisty argues that the contemporary Right has frequently relied on "mobilizing resentment" as an organizing process.[8]

Demonization of an enemy often begins with marginalization, the ideological process in which targeted individuals or groups are placed outside the circle of wholesome mainstream society through political propaganda and age-old prejudice. This creates an us–them or good–bad dynamic of dualism, which acknowledges no complexity or nuance and forecloses meaningful civil debate or practical political compromise.

The next step is objectification or dehumanization, the process of negatively labeling a person or group of people so they become perceived more as objects than as real people. Dehumanization often is associated with the belief that a particular group of people is inferior or threatening. The final step is demonization, the person or group is framed as totally malevolent, sinful, and evil. It is easier to rationalize stereotyping, prejudice, discrimination, scapegoating and even violence against those who are dehumanized or demonized.[9]

In *The Origin of Satan*, Elaine Pagels points out that today,

Many religious people who no longer believe in Satan, along with countless others who do not identify with any religious tradition, nevertheless are influenced by this cultural legacy whenever they perceive social and political conflict in terms of the forces of good contending against the forces of evil in the world.[10]

Casting enemies in the role of evil demons is hardly original to Christians or to the Bible. "Nothing is more common in history than the change of the deities of hostile nations into demons of evil," says Paul Carus, who notes that Beelzebub, a Phoenician god, "became another name for Satan," for the early Jews. In fact, the word Satan means "enemy."[11]

Scapegoating in the form of the ritualized transference and expulsion of evil is a familiar theme across centuries and cultures. In Western culture the term "scapegoat" can be traced to an early Jewish ritual described in the book of Leviticus in the Bible. As Gordon W. Allport explains:

> On the Day of Atonement a live goat was chosen by lot. The high priest, robed in linen garments, laid both his hands on the goat's head, and confessed over it the iniquities of the children of Israel. The sins of the people thus symbolically transferred to the beast, it was taken out into the wilderness and let go. The people felt purged, and for the time being, guiltless.[12]

The word scapegoat has evolved to mean a person or group wrongfully blamed for some problem, especially for other people's misdeeds. "Psychologically," Richard Landes explains, "the tendency to find scapegoats is a result of the common defense mechanism of denial through projection."[13] People redirect frustrated aggression or guilt over their own misconduct, onto the scapegoat.[14] But scapegoating does not necessarily work the same way at the personal level, such as within a family, as it does at a societal level, where in Susan M. Fisher's words "the scapegoated group serves more as a metaphor." Nor does scapegoating by large groups and social movements indicate mass mental dysfunction.[15]

We use the term *scapegoating* to describe the social process whereby the hostility and grievances of an angry, frustrated group are directed away from the real causes of a social problem onto a target group demonized as malevolent wrongdoers. The scapegoat bears the blame, while the scapegoaters feel a sense of righteousness and increased unity. The social problem may be real or imaginary, the grievances legitimate or illegitimate, and members of the targeted group may be wholly innocent or partly culpable. What matters is that the scapegoats are wrongfully stereotyped as all sharing the same negative trait, or are singled out for blame while other major culprits are let off the hook.[16]

Scapegoating often targets socially disempowered or marginalized groups. At the same time, the scapegoat is often portrayed as powerful or privileged. In this way, scapegoating feeds on people's anger about their own disempowerment, but diverts this anger away from the real systems of power and oppression. A certain level of scapegoating is endemic in most societies, but it more readily becomes an important political force in times of social competition or upheaval. At such times, especially, scapegoating can be an effective way to mobilize mass support and activism during a struggle for power.

Conspiracism

Conspiracism is a particular narrative form of scapegoating that frames the enemy as part of a vast insidious plot against the common good, while it valorizes the scapegoater as a hero for sounding the alarm. Like other forms of scapegoating, conspiracism often, though not always, targets oppressed or stigmatized groups. In many cases, conspiracism uses coded language to mask ethnic or racial bigotry, for example, attacking the Federal Reserve in ways that evoke common stereotypes about "Jewish bankers." Far-right groups have often used such conspiracy theories as an opening wedge for more explicit hate ideology.

On a local level, Herman Sinaiko observes, "The most decent and modest communities have people in their midst who are prone to scapegoating and who see the world as run by conspiracies. A healthy community is organized in a way that controls them and suppresses their tendencies." But there are times when "the standards and control mechanisms are weakened, and these people step forward and find their voice and an audience."[17] This dynamic is common to the Far Right; for example, conspiracy narratives scapegoating Jewish bankers flourished in the economically devastated farm belt in the 1980s.

Mark Fenster describes how broader groups of people who are not necessarily caught up in far-right bigotry can still use conspiracism to construct a theory of power that fails to recognize how real power relations work in modern society. He argues that the phenomenon "should not be dismissed and analyzed simply as pathology," and suggests that "conspiracy theory and the contemporary practices of populist politics require a cultural analysis that can complement an ideological and empirical 'debunking.'"

According to Fenster,

> just because overarching conspiracy theories are wrong does not mean that they are not on to something. Specifically, they ideologically address real structural inequities, and constitute a response to a withering civil society and the concentration of the ownership of the means of production, which together leave the political subject without the ability to be recognized or to signify in the public realm.[18]

Certainly, real conspiracies exist: plotting in secret is one of the ways in which power is exercised (and resisted). The U.S. political scene has been littered with examples of illegal political, corporate, and government conspiracies such as Watergate, the FBI's Counterintelligence Program (COINTELPRO) of spying and dirty tricks against dissidents, the Iran–Contra scandal, and the systematic looting of the savings and loan industry. But as Bruce Cumings argues,

> if conspiracies exist, they rarely move history; they make a difference at the margins from time to time, but with the unforeseen consequences of a logic outside the control of their authors: and this is what is wrong with "conspiracy theory." History is moved by the broad forces and large structures of human collectivities.[19]

Conspiracism differs in several ways from legitimate efforts to expose secret plots. First, the conspiracist worldview assigns tiny cabals of evildoers a superhuman power to control events; it regards such plots as the major motor of history. Conspiracism blames individualized and subjective forces for political, economic, and social problems rather than analyzing conflict in terms of systems, institutions, and structures of power.

Second, conspiracism tends to frame social conflict in terms of a transcendent struggle between Good and Evil that reflects the influence of the apocalyptic paradigm.

Third, in its efforts to trace all wrongdoing to one vast plot, conspiracism plays fast and loose with the facts. While conspiracy theorists often start with a grain of truth and "document" their claims exhaustively, they make leaps of logic in analyzing evidence, such as seeing guilt by association or treating allegations as proven fact.[20]

Conspiracist attacks can be directed either "upward" or "downward." *Antielite conspiracism* (or *antielite scapegoating*) targets groups seen as sinister elites abusing their power from above. *Countersubversive scapegoating* targets groups portrayed as subversives trying to overturn the established order from below or from within.

Antielite conspiracism has deep roots in U.S. political culture. In some versions, antielite scapegoating attacks groups who do not really dominate society (such as Jews or Catholics); in other cases, it targets subgroups within the elite power structure (such as bankers, the Trilateral Commission, the Central Intelligence Agency, or the World Trade Organization). What these versions share, and what especially defines antielite conspiracism, is that the scapegoat is seen as a subjective, alien force that distorts the normal workings of society. Thus, despite its "radical" veneer, antielite conspiracism shares the mainstream assumptions that the United States is fundamentally democratic, and that any injustice results from selfish special interest groups, not from underlying systems of power and oppression.

U.S. elites, meanwhile, have long propagated fears of subversive conspiracies: bloodthirsty slaves plotting mass murder, disloyal immigrants undermining U.S. institutions, labor unionists spreading criminal anarchy, or godless Reds bent on global dictatorship. Whether cynical constructs or projections of the elite's own nightmares, such images have been used to demonize antioppression struggles by playing on people's fears of disorder, violence, invasion, and moral collapse.

As Frank J. Donner noted, propaganda based on a myth of the enemy "other" has helped to justify antidemocratic activities by state security forces and their allies, including spying, harassment, judicial persecution, forced removal, and physical violence. And, Donner argued, "In a period of social and economic change during which traditional institutions are under the greatest strain, the need for the myth is especially strong as a means of transferring blame, an outlet for the despair [people] face when normal channels of protest and change are closed."[21] In these ways, countersubversive scapegoating has played an important role in this country's system of social control, bolstering elite privilege and power.

Apocalyptic Narratives and Millennial Visions

The poisoned fruit of conspiracist scapegoating is baked into the American apple pie, and its ingredients include destructive versions of apocalyptic fears and millennialist expectations. This is true whether we are studying Christian-based right-wing movements consciously influenced by biblical prophecy, or more secularized right-wing movements for which Bible-based apocalypticism and millennialism have faded into unconscious—yet still influential—metaphors.[22]

Apocalypticism—the anticipation of a righteous struggle against evil conspiracies—has influenced social and political movements throughout U.S. history.[23] Early Christian settlers saw America as a battlefield for a prophetic struggle between good and evil. Starting in the 1620s, witch hunts swept New England for a century.[24] Many of the insurgent colonists who brought about the American Revolution invoked apocalyptic and millennial themes, as did the Antimasons and Jacksonians who denounced banks in the 1830s. Apocalypticism infused the evangelical Protestant revival that contributed to the Ku Klux Klan's rise in the 1920s and influenced both fascist and nonfascist rightists during the Great Depression of the 1930s. Today, apocalypticism remains a central narrative in our nation's religious, secular, political, and cultural discourse.[25] Numerous authors have noted that the contemporary Christian Right is significantly motivated and mobilized by apocalyptic and millennialist themes.[26] Yet as Richard Landes observes, apocalyptic activities rarely "receive more than a passing mention in 'mainstream' analyses."[27]

In its generic sense, the word apocalypse has come to mean the belief in an approaching confrontation, cataclysmic event, or transformation of epochal proportion, about which a select few have forewarning so they can make appropriate preparations. Those who believe in a coming apocalypse might be optimistic about the outcome of the apocalyptic moment, anticipating a chance for positive transformational change; or they might be pessimistic, anticipating a doomsday; or they might anticipate a period of violence or chaos with an uncertain outcome.[28] Christian apocalyptic fervor appears, often at seemingly random dates, throughout Western history.[29] A major U.S. episode of Christian millennialist fervor occurred among the Millerites in the 1840s, some of whom sold their worldly belongings and pilgrimaged to a mountaintop to experience the Rapture that they hoped in vain would sweep them up into God's protective embrace.[30] The apocalyptic tradition also exists in Judaism, Islam, and other religions.[31]

Apocalypticism is the principal source for what Richard Hofstadter called the "paranoid style" in American politics. According to Damian Thompson:

> Richard Hofstadter was right to emphasise the startling affinities between the paranoid style and apocalyptic belief—the demonisation of opponents, the sense of time running out, and so on. But he stopped short of making a more direct connection between the two. He did not consider the possibility that the paranoia he identified actually derived from apocalyptic belief.[32]

The process of demonization, a consistent factor in scapegoating, takes on special features during periods of apocalyptic fear or millennial expectation. Apocalyptic thinking meshes readily with producerism, since the good (and often Godly) people are counterposed against the traitorous elites and their lazy and sinful allies.

Millennialism is a specific form of apocalyptic expectation.[33] Most contemporary Christian fundamentalists believe that when Christ returns, he will reign for a period of 1,000 years—a millennium. Yet not all contemporary Christians promote apocalyptic demonization. Within Christianity, there are two competing views of how to interpret the apocalyptic and millennial themes in the Bible, especially the book of Revelation. One view identifies evil with specific persons and groups, seeking to identify those in league with the Devil. A more optimistic form of interpreting apocalyptic prophecy is promoted by those Christians who see evil in the will to dominate and oppress.[34] Apocalyptic thinking, in this case, seeks justice for the poor and weak. The two interpretations represent a deep division within Christianity. The dangerous form of millennialism comes not from Christianity per se, but from Christians who combine biblical literalism, apocalyptic timetables, demonization, and oppressive prejudices.

Christian apocalypticism and millennialism are based on many sources in the Bible, including the Old Testament books of Daniel and Ezekiel, and the New Testament Gospel of Matthew. The primary biblical source, however, is the book of Revelation, the last book of the Christian New Testament. Many Christians on the political Right who are looking for the "signs of the End Times" adopt a particular demonizing way of interpreting prophecy in the book of Revelation.

In this view, a powerful and charismatic agent of the Devil—the Antichrist—comes to earth along with his ally—the False Prophet. They appear disguised in the form of widely respected political and religious leaders. Promising peace and prosperity, these leaders launch a popular campaign to build a one-world government and a one-world religion. Many Christians are fooled, but a few recognize that these leaders are the prophesied Antichrist and the False Prophet, and thus actually Satanic traitors. Agents of the Antichrist try to force devout Christians to accept the Mark of the Beast (sometimes the number 666) which would mean they reject Christ. A wave of political and religious repression sweeps the world, with devout Christians rounded up and persecuted for their beliefs. Christians with this view read the book of Revelation as a warning about a government conspiracy and betrayal by trusted political and religious leaders in the End Times. A secular version of this narrative appears in conspiracy theories about liberal collectivists building a global new world order through the United Nations.

These apocalyptic themes buttress the producerist narrative in right-wing populist movements. This is the narrative of Pat Robertson's 700 *Club* TV broadcasts, the newsletter of Beverly LaHaye's Concerned Women for America, and scores of other Christian Right media outlets. As the year 2000 approached a number of apocalyptic and millennial social movements surged in excitement and activism. Some were religious, such as the Promise Keepers; some were secular, such as the armed militias. These social movements sought to influence public policy, social conduct, and cultural attitudes, sometimes coming into conflict with the established order and state power.

SOCIAL MOVEMENTS AND SOCIAL STRUCTURES

While they may express apocalyptic fervor or millennialist expectation, mass political and social movements are composed of people motivated by a sense of grievance—legitimate or illegitimate—who mobilize to seek redress of their grievances through a variety of methods often including, but seldom limited to, the electoral process.[35] These grievances flow from social, cultural, and economic tensions that combine and vary over time. Most participants in these groups and movements try to organize others using rational strategies and tactics—even if their claims seem bizarre or conspiracist and their goals are illegitimate and prejudiced—and in defense of disproportionate access to power, wealth, and privilege.[36]

Our view of social movements is hardly unique. As Christian Smith observes,

> The 1970s saw a major break in the social-movement literature with earlier theories—e.g., mass society, collective behavior, status discontent, and relative-deprivation theories—that emphasized the irrational and emotional nature of social movements. . . . There was at the time a decisive pendulum-swing away from these "classical" theories toward the view of social movements as rational, strategically calculating, politically instrumental phenomena.[37]

While these newer and more complex social movement theories have shaped some popular discussions of liberal and radical social change movements, they have been less successful in changing the public discourse about right-wing movements.

We see two common pitfalls in contemporary discussions of right-wing populist movements. On one side, many liberals and moderate conservatives routinely portray such movements as paranoid fringe phenomena fundamentally at odds with the political mainstream. A standard premise is that the U.S. political system has an essence of democracy and freedom—a vital center of pragmatism, rationality, and tolerance—but that this essence is threatened by extremists from the left and right. This centrist/extremist model, as we call it, obscures the rational choices and partially legitimate grievances that help to fuel right-wing populist movements, and hides the fact that right-wing bigotry and scapegoating are firmly rooted in the mainstream social and political order. Centrist/extremist theory is the dominant model used by government agencies, mass media, and major human relations groups to portray right-wing movements. It is based to a large degree on the pessimistic studies of populism by Daniel Bell, Seymour Martin Lipset, Earl Raab, and others.

Centrist/extremist theory does not stand up to the field work done by social scientists who have studied members of right-wing (and left-wing) movements and groups and found them no more or less mentally unbalanced, politically dysfunctional, or "fringe" than their neighbors.[38] Nor does centrist/extremist theory allow us to recognize the frequent direct linkages—ideological, organizational, and economic—between right-wing and mainstream political forces.

Centrist/extremist theory fosters a dangerous complacency about mainstream politics and institutions. It has often been used to rally support for moderate versions of oppressive politics—for example, to attack Republicans and bolster the Democratic Party, even as Democratic leaders embrace traditionally right-wing positions. In addition, because it logically relies on government crackdowns to protect us from the "irrational zealots," centrist/extremist theory fuels the growth of state repression, and can serve as a rationale for aiding repressive government surveillance operations.[39]

On the other side of the coin, some left-leaning people have portrayed sections of the insurgent Right, especially the militias, as positive expressions of grassroots discontent, and as legitimate allies against the state and the elite.[40] In addition, some liberals and leftists have echoed right-wing conspiracy theories about the U.S. government and big business.[41] These positions romanticize populist activism and overlook the immediate and long-term dangers posed by right-wing movements. They also help blur the dividing line between an analysis of systemic and institutionalized oppression and conspiracist scapegoating, which is often rooted in and facilitates ethnic bigotry.

In contrast to both centrist/extremist doctrine and the left-romanticist view, we see right-wing populist movements as having a complex relationship with the established power structure: both rooted in it and distinct from it, opposing it in some ways yet bolstering it in others. Such movements often have close links with economic and political elites, yet they are not simply ruling-class puppets, but rather autonomous social forces with their own agendas and mass appeal. Right-wing populist movements often help to strengthen social oppression, yet they are themselves fueled by popular discontent at elite privilege and power.

The contradictions within right-wing populism point to tensions and complexities in the larger social order. We describe the U.S. political system as *pluralist*, meaning that a certain range of political debate and conflict between different political organizations, factions, and tendencies is accepted as legitimate, and civil liberties are protected to a degree. Yet we do not believe that this system has lived up to its image as a democracy, because most political and economic power is held by a tiny wealthy elite. [42] In our view, class hierarchy, racial and national oppression, male dominance, and other systems of social control have always been central to U.S. society.

At the same time, the social power structure is not divided neatly between oppressors and oppressed. Because there are many different intersecting lines of power, the majority of people occupy contradictory positions in society: they are oppressed in some ways but hold varying degrees of relative privilege in other ways. Such privilege brings social, political, or economic benefits that give many people a tangible stake in the very system that keeps them down. Even elite forces, while sharing basic interests, are internally divided. As business conflict theorists have argued, factional divisions within the elite play a major role in political life.[43] In some situations, both intraelite conflict and people's contradictory status can foster a kind of double-edged politics: a dissatisfaction with the people in charge, coupled with a desire to preserve or strengthen certain social inequalities. This double-edged politics often finds expression in repressive populist movements.

MAPPING THE RIGHT

Since the 1970s, the political center of gravity in the United States has moved dramatically to the right. This shift is often identified with the Republican Party of Ronald Reagan and Newt Gingrich, but the Democratic Party, too, has largely embraced traditional right-wing positions regarding "welfare reform," "crime," "illegal aliens," and a host of other issues. The right turn has been driven by both elite policymakers and a range of mass-based political movements, from the electoral activism of the Christian Coalition to the insurrectionism of citizen militias.

We use various terms to describe specific gradations of right-wing politics, populist and otherwise. The *Reactionary Right* seeks to turn the clock back toward an idealized past. *Conservatism* emphasizes stability and order, and generally some combination of cultural traditionalism and "free-market" economics. *Ultraconservatism* goes beyond the conservative defense of the established order while stopping short of demands to fully eliminate pluralist institutions. The *Christian Right* is motivated by religious interpretations of cultural, social, and economic issues, and has branches that otherwise fall into all the other sectors of the Right, including the Hard Right and the Far Right. See Appendix A.

The *Hard Right* takes an inflexible approach to politics and rejects pluralist discourse in principle or in practice. Hard rightists may be either elitist or mass activist in their organizing, and may include both ultraconservatives and far rightists. The *Far Right* squarely rejects the existing political system, and pluralist institutions generally, in favor of some form of authoritarianism.

Fascism, in our usage, is the most virulent form of far-right populism. Fascism glorifies national, racial, or cultural unity and collective rebirth while seeking to purge imagined enemies, and attacks both revolutionary socialism and liberal pluralism in favor of militarized, totalitarian mass politics.[44] There are many definitions of fascism, and the term is often misused. Fascist movements are a product of the twentieth century, and first crystallized in Europe in response to the Bolshevik Revolution and the devastation of World War I. In the United States, fascist movements have blended European ideological imports with homegrown repressive populist traditions, and first became a significant political force during the Great Depression of the 1930s.

Today, in addition to the openly fascist organizations of the neonazi Right, fascist groupings (and more broadly, fascistic tendencies) play a significant role in larger right-wing populist movements. Certain fascistic tendencies can be detected in the militias, the Buchananites, and in the most militant authoritarian sectors of the Christian Right.

Although the role of fascism in right-wing movements needs to be addressed, it is frequently overstated, and it would be a serious mistake to regard a "fascist takeover" as the main threat of right-wing populism. The danger associated with right-wing populism comes not only from its real or potential bids for power, or even from its day-to-day violence, bigotry, and scapegoating, but also from its interactions with other political forces and with the government.

The 1990s saw a dangerous interplay, for example, between right-wing paramilitarism and state repression. The government's response to the militias following the 1995 Oklahoma City bombing made it clear that antidemocratic initiatives do not only come from hard-right political movements. President Bill Clinton exploited fears of the Right to promote sweeping "counterterrorism" legislation that represented a serious attack on civil liberties. This in turn bolstered widespread fears of state repression, some of which militia groups were able to exploit. (The Terrorism Prevention and Effective Death Penalty Act, signed by Clinton in April 1996, was promoted based on claims that the militia movement bombed the Oklahoma City federal building, and claims that TWA Flight 800 bound for Paris was sent into the sea by a terrorist bomb. Both claims were false. All credible evidence suggests that Timothy McVeigh, convicted in the Oklahoma City bombing, was a neonazi trying to move the less militant and largely defensive militia movement into more aggressive insurrectionist action, and that Flight 800 was downed by a mechanical flaw.)

Here and in many other instances, we see a dynamic tension between right-wing populist movements, including the insurrectionist Far Right, and mainstream electoral politics. Such movements help pull the entire political spectrum to the right and make mainstream forms of brutality and injustice look more acceptable by comparison.

CORE ISSUES AND THEMES

This book traces the development of repressive and right-wing populist movements from colonial times to the present. It shows how repressive popular movements involving aggressive White supremacy, demagogic appeals, demonization, conspiracist scapegoating, antisemitism, hatred of the Left, militaristic nationalism, an apocalyptic style, and millennialist themes have repeatedly been at the center of our political conflicts, not on the fringe.

The following chapters examine distinctive features of the U.S. social order—particularly the combination of racial oppression and mass-based participatory politics—that have fostered such movements and, in turn, have been shaped by them. We trace many other sources and currents of right-wing populist ideology and conspiracist scapegoating, including anti-immigration nativism, hatred of Catholics and Jews, Anglophobia (fear or hatred of Britain), and regionally based resentments against an "Eastern Establishment." Many of these discussions show how the producerist narrative has been used to frame grievances in ways that target scapegoats and generate conspiracy theories.

Several chapters address the central role of gender politics in some repressive populist movements, including both women's subordination through discrimination, sexual violence, and the glorifying of the "traditional family," and also the political mobilization of women as supposed guardians of virtue. Since World War II, the scapegoating and suppression of lesbian, gay, bisexual, and transgender people has also become a major right-wing populist theme.

The book traces the pivotal role of intraelite factional conflicts in many repressive and right-wing movements. We discuss how 1930s efforts to fight right-wing populism with state repression rebounded disastrously against liberals and leftists in the Cold War. Later chapters examine right-wing populism's resurgence in recent decades as a backlash against social liberation movements, economic dislocations, and the relative decline of U.S. global power.

Throughout, we argue that the scapegoating and conspiracism of right-wing populism—exploiting antielite resentments but inextricably rooted in social inequality and oppression—is not on the margins of U.S. political traditions, but is too close for comfort.

1

REBELLIOUS COLONIZERS
Bacon's Rebellion and the American Revolution

BACON'S REBELLION

In July, 1676, as the leader of a rebellion in the colony of Virginia, Nathaniel Bacon issued a "Declaration of the People." Writing exactly 100 years before a more famous Virginian penned a more famous declaration, Bacon set forth his reasons for defying the authority of Governor William Berkeley. The document charged the governor with imposing "great unjust taxes upon the Commonality," appointing unqualified personal favorites to public office, monopolizing the beaver trade and, to protect that trade, favoring the Indians and failing to defend the colonists against their attacks.[1]

Bacon's Rebellion highlighted a quarter-century of intense unrest in Virginia, during which working people rose up repeatedly against the privileged colonial elite.[2] The colony was deeply polarized between oppressors and oppressed. In the Tidewater region, where most settlers were concentrated, one-half of the economically active population were European indentured servants, who were recruited—sometimes by force—to work for a fixed number of years in exchange for ship-passage and subsistence in Virginia.[3] These European bond laborers worked under similar conditions (and often side by side) with African bond laborers, who at that time formed a small part of the colonial population. During this period there was relatively little difference in status between the two groups of unfree workers. Both African and European bond laborers repeatedly sought freedom through escapes and occasionally direct resistance against their masters. Other rebellious groups included landless free workers and small farmers, whose economic vulnerability often forced them into debt. Such groups resented the power of the big planters, who monopolized much of the land, controlled the colonial government, and often used public office for personal gain.

Not only was the Virginia colony internally divided, but it also faced conflict with the indigenous people it had driven out. Governor Berkeley approached American Indians with a strategy of divide and conquer. Britain's victory in the war of 1644–1646 had reduced members of neighboring Indian nations to the status of British subjects, to be used as a frontier buffer and as allies in wars against other Native nations. The empire-builders' long-term interests called for orderly, controlled expansion of European settlement. As J. Sakai notes, "The Indian nations held, if only for a historical moment, the balance of power in North America between the rival British, French and Spanish empires. Too much aggression against Indian territories by English settlers could drive the Indians into allying with the French."[4]

Many frontier farmers disliked the governor's policy. They were vulnerable to Native counterattacks and were taxed to pay for military defenses they regarded as inadequate. Nathaniel Bacon, a young planter recently arrived in the colony, drew a large following among frontier settlers by denouncing Berkeley's "pro-Indian" stance and calling for a total war of extermination against all Indians without distinction. The rebellion began when Bacon defied the governor's orders and organized a military expedition against neighboring Indians, which culminated in the massacre of almost an entire village of Occaneechee allies. In Wilcomb Washburn's words, "Bacon and his men did not kill a single enemy Indian but contented themselves with frightening away, killing, or enslaving most of the friendly neighboring Indians, and taking their beaver and land as spoils."[5]

But Bacon did not base his rebellion only on a hard-line anti-Indian policy. He also rallied broad support among lower-class colonists who wanted to end their economic misery and political disenfranchisement. After marching to Jamestown and confronting the governor, Bacon's forces became associated with a series of antielite reforms passed by the new colonial assembly in June, 1676, including a law allowing property-less freemen to vote. As the conflict deepened, both sides sought popular support where they could: Governor Berkeley offered freedom to indentured servants of the rebels if they would join his army; Bacon responded with the same offer not only to the European servants, but also to the African bond laborers held by loyalists. The rebels burned the capital city of Jamestown and at one point even captured the governor, but Bacon's sudden death from illness a few months later precipitated the movement's collapse.

A number of historians have cited Bacon's Rebellion as an early example of grassroots activism in the cause of liberty. Sidney Lens, in *Radicalism in America*, describes it as "the first revolt of the common people—small farmers, impoverished freemen, even some white indentures—against the authority of a royal governor and his privileged class." Theodore W. Allen, in *The Invention of the White Race*, argues that the rebellion's most important feature was that "in Virginia, 128 years before William Lloyd Garrison was born, laboring-class African-Americans and European-Americans fought side by side for the abolition of slavery."[6] While there is some truth in both of these descriptions, they cannot be separated from the demand for genocidal warfare against American Indians, which was one of the rebellion's central aims.

Theodore W. Allen has described Bacon's Rebellion as a pivotal event leading to "the invention of the white race" and of the U.S. system of racial oppression. By showing the potential power of united resistance by European and African bond laborers, Allen argues, the rebellion scared the colonial elite into creating a more effective system of social control. In the half-century that followed, the colonial elite drove a wedge between the two laboring groups: reducing Africans from the ambiguous status of bond-service to permanent, hereditary slavery, and elevating Europeans over them with a system of legal and social privileges based on skin color and ancestry. The process created both "Black" and "White" as social categories. In this way the ruling elite ensured that it could more fully exploit the plantation labor force, and created a social buffer group with a stake in helping to control those at the bottom of the hierarchy. Viewed in relation to this process, Allen argues, Bacon's Rebellion stands out as a revolutionary struggle in which "Afro-American and European-American proletarians made common cause . . . to an extent never duplicated in the three hundred years since."[7]

This analysis is crucial but one-sided. White supremacy indeed developed in the seventeenth century as a system that bolstered elite power, but it was as much about conquering land as it was about controlling labor. The expulsion and mass killing of Native peoples were as central to the formation of racial oppression as was the enslavement of kidnapped Africans. And the anti-Indian conquest was well underway in 1676. British settlers may not yet have defined American Indians as a separate race, but they did generally treat them as malevolent, heathen savages and, often, as fair game for slaughter.

Because Allen regards the European conquest of indigenous peoples as peripheral to the process by which White supremacy was created, he regards the anti-Indian "phase" of Bacon's Rebellion as peripheral to the main event: "a civil war against the Anglo-American ruling class."[8] But these dimensions must be treated together as parts of one contradictory whole. The same applies to the rebellion's later period, when Bacon recruited both African and European workers by offering them freedom. Allen oversimplifies when he characterizes this stage of the rebellion as an attempt to end bond-servitude. We think it more accurate to say that a tactical maneuver by the rebel leaders created an opportunity that bond laborers, both African and European, were ready to exploit. At no time did the rebels repudiate their efforts to enslave those Indians they did not kill.

Most leaders of the rebellion, including Bacon himself, were members of an "outsider" faction of the planter class, who resented the dominance and special privileges enjoyed by the inner circle around Governor Berkeley. They appealed to popular grievances because they needed lower-class support in order to gain power. To a large extent, however, they succeeded in channeling these grievances into anti-Indian violence or forms of anti-elitism that served their own interests, such as plundering the estates of wealthy people loyal to the governor.

Bacon's Rebellion was a confused, contradictory upheaval. Yet the general pattern of its contradictions—plebian resentment coupled with intra-elite conflict, and egalitarianism for a limited group coupled with expansionist, murderous attacks against non-European peoples—set a pattern of repressive populist politics that would be repeated again and again.

THE AMERICAN REVOLUTION

The American Revolution provides another example of such contradictions. As in Bacon's Rebellion, an outsider faction of the upper class joined with lower-class European Americans in an effort to wrest power from the King's appointed representatives. In 1776, as in 1676, the rebels fought not simply for an end to excessive taxes and arbitrary government, but also for greater freedom to attack American Indians and expand slavery. Yet the Revolution was better organized and enjoyed a more extensive base of support, reflecting the fact that colonial society had developed dramatically since Nathaniel Bacon's day. By 1776, a color line was firmly in place, and slave labor had become a larger and more crucial component of the economy than a century before. The settler population had grown rapidly and was poised for a big push westward across the Appalachian mountains, and the colonial elite was more stable, interconnected, and articulate.

Unlike Bacon's Rebellion, which "produced no real program of reform, no revolutionary manifesto, not even any revolutionary slogans,"[9] the colonial Revolutionary movement was infused with the new language of Enlightenment humanism, natural rights, and a belief that government is a social contract between rulers and the people. Thomas Paine's best-selling pamphlet *Common Sense*, published in January 1776, denounced belief in the divine right of kings and called for a popularly elected republic.[10] Thomas Jefferson's Declaration of Independence, adopted by the Continental Congress in July 1776, anchored resistance to British rule in the ideals of equality, liberty, popular sovereignty, and the right of "the People" to overthrow tyranny.

Today it is widely acknowledged that the leaders of the American Revolution excluded women, Black people, and American Indians when they declared that "all men are created equal." Many patriots at the time embraced this contradiction, treating human rights as a limited commodity that could only be enjoyed by a select group if others were excluded and subordinated. In this view, as Joan Gunderson has commented, "Independence was a condition arrived at by exclusion . . . by *not* being dependent or enslaved." Thus a male head of the household was independent by contrast with his dependent wife and children; thus White patriot writers expressed outrage that Britain had reduced them to "slavery"—on the grounds that slavery was intended only for Blacks.[11]

Our description of the Revolution as a repressive populist movement focuses on two points. First, by equating tyranny with the British crown, the struggle for U.S. independence promoted a form of antielite scapegoating that deflected discontent away from inequities within colonial society. Second, the drive for independence was also a drive to expand and intensify the system of White supremacy. People of color were not simply "left out" of the Revolution—they were among its major targets.

Colonial Class Conflict

Like Bacon's Rebellion, the independence movement drew on widespread plebian demands for greater economic and political power.[12] In the 1760s and 1770s, tenant-farmer uprisings in New York and New Jersey, the antielite Regulator movement in North Carolina, and lower-class street activism in cities such as Boston and Philadelphia expressed a widespread and deep-seated hostility to established centers of wealth and privilege. Lower-class Whites demanded more representation and popular access to government, more equitable taxes, fairer land distribution, and other political and economic reforms. In the Hudson Valley, 2,000 tenant farmers proclaimed themselves "Levelers" in 1766 and took up arms against the big landlords; two regiments of British troops were needed to crush the uprising. Rebellious small farmers in New Jersey argued that royal grants of land were illegitimate since they were made without consent of the indigenous people who held true title to the area.[13]

Although propelled by lower-class unrest, the drive for independence was spearheaded by a section of the colonial elite. In the short term, the demand for independence offered this upper-class patriot bloc a means to channel popular anger away from itself and onto the British government. In the long term, independence enabled the colonial elite to expand its own wealth and power without external restraints. Wealthy colonists were far from united on the issue; indeed, the American Revolution involved a colonial civil war between rebels and loyalists, each led by a faction of the colonial elite.

Upper-class patriots were not entirely successful in deflecting lower-class White resentment. Despite leaders' efforts to contain them, popular mobilizations against British rulers repeatedly spilled over into attacks on property and elite privilege. During and after the Revolutionary War, poor farmers rioted repeatedly against tax collectors and court seizure of their lands for debt. Most New York tenant farmers sided with the British, whom they hoped would redistribute the huge estates of proindependence landlords.[14] Nevertheless, the movement for cross-class unity against Britain succeeded in winning broad popular support, not simply because of elite manipulation, but also because many European American farmers, artisans, and laborers shared a stake in U.S. independence.

Trade and Westward Expansion

Up until 1763, conflicts between Britain and the colonists had been limited by a shared enmity toward France, Britain's main rival for control of the North American continent. But four years after the British conquest of Quebec in 1759, France ceded all claims to land in continental North America. Not only did this remove the colonists' primary need for protection by the British Empire, but it also gave Britain the imposing tasks of managing vast new lands and pacifying French-Canadian and Native populations. To finance these projects and pay off its war debt, the British government imposed a series of new taxes on the Anglo-American colonists, while simultaneously tightening restrictions on settler expansion and trade. These measures directly precipitated the movement for independence.

Trade was especially important for the northern colonies. Officially, British companies were guaranteed control of most manufacturing and trade within the empire, but this control was enforced only sporadically for most of the colonial period. New England merchants, such as Thomas Hancock and his nephew John Hancock, president of the Continental Congress in 1776, grew rich from smuggling. Smugglers sold North American manufactured goods abroad, imported products from outside the British Empire, and competed with British shippers in the highly profitable triangle trade of finished goods, West Indian sugar, and enslaved Africans. Rum production was the chief source of hard currency for Massachusetts, and the colony's "West Indian trade employed some ten thousand seamen, to say nothing of the workers who built, outfitted, and supplied the ships."[15] Increasingly, such competition threatened British capital and government revenues, and Britain fought back with new efforts at restriction. Eric Williams, in *Capitalism and Slavery*, argues that

> The attempt to render the [Sugar Duties] Act [of 1764] effective and stamp out smuggling led directly to the American Revolution. It was this that John Adams had in mind when he stated that he did not know why the Americans "should blush to confess that molasses was an essential ingredient in American independence."[16]

Westward expansion was another point of growing conflict.[17] Constant efforts by settlers to buy, swindle, or steal Indian lands repeatedly led to wars that were expensive and disruptive for the British government. In an effort to keep peace with the Indians, Britain enacted the Royal Proclamation of 1763, which closed the territories west of the Appalachians to colonial settlement. This ban, widely ignored, was reinforced by the Quebec Act of 1774; that Act extended Quebec's boundaries southward to the Ohio River and nullified land claims in the region by other colonial governments. Colonial rebels labeled the Quebec Act "intolerable" and the Continental Congress demanded its repeal.

The colonists' outrage at the expansion of Quebec (with its French civil law and Roman Catholic Church) also reflected widespread Protestant hostility to Catholic France, and had millenialist undertones. First the French and then the British were placed in an apocalyptic and millennial framework by insurgent colonists. According to Robert Fuller,

> The long-standing identification of the pope with the Antichrist made Catholic France an easy target for the clergy's efforts to explain the cosmic significance of the colonies' enemies. No sooner had the colonists helped achieve victory over the French Antichrist than they discovered that the Anglican Church was itself steeped in the Antichrist's deceit, and by association, so was King George III.[18]

The restrictions of 1763 and 1774 directly challenged the colonial landed elite, especially in the South. The southern "slavocracy"—including the families of George Washington and Thomas Jefferson—had established itself by getting huge grants of land at little or no cost, and was outraged that its "liberty" to continue grabbing Indian land might be cut off, especially at a time when its taxes were being raised. Tobacco growers depended on westward expansion, because tobacco rapidly depleted the soil. At the time of the Revolution, tobacco was not only enslaved Black workers' primary product, but also accounted for more than half of the colonies' total exports.[19] In addition, southern and northern land speculators such as Patrick Henry, Benjamin Franklin, and Washington had acquired enormous wealth by reselling cheap western lands to settlers. As these men found their commercial ventures restricted, their desire for political independence grew.

The triangle trade (importing enslaved Africans) and westward expansion (killing Indians and taking their lands) primarily benefited merchants, big landowners, and other members of the elite. Yet many less affluent settlers, too, had a stake in these practices. As J. Sakai argues, all strata and sectors of colonial society depended on slave labor:

> the fisherman whose low-grade, "refuse fish" was dried and sold as slave meal in the Indies; the New York farmer who found his market for surpluses in the Southern plantations; the forester whose timber was used by shipyard workers rapidly turning out slave ships; the clerk in the New York City export house checking bales of tobacco awaiting shipment to London; the master cooper in the Boston rum distillery; the young Virginia overseer building up his "stake" to try and start his own plantation; the immigrant German farmer renting a team of five slaves to get his farm started; and on and on. While the cream of the profits went to the planter and merchant capitalists, the entire settler economy was raised up on a foundation of slave labor, slave products, and the slave trade.[20]

Westward expansion, too, benefited not only plantation owners and land speculators. The reason speculation was so profitable was that thousands of settlers eagerly sought land as a way out of hardship to prosperity and higher status. After about 1760, immigration to the colonies rose sharply due to a population explosion and crop failures in Europe, among other factors. This increased the pressure for cheap land just as Britain was tightening restrictions on the expansion into the West.[21] In a series of backcountry rebellions from the 1760s to the 1790s, militant small farmers laid claim to so-called wilderness land. They declared that only those who worked and "improved" the land had a right to it, and they denounced both absentee landlords and American Indians as unproductive. These rebellions, some of which physically attacked Native communities, laid the foundations for what would become producerist ideology.[22]

While frontier land and Indian nations represented easier targets, millions of acres of farmland would have been available east of the frontier if the big estates were broken up. In a few areas such as the Hudson Valley, where tenant farmers challenged wealthy landlords, the American Revolution seized loyalist estates and redistributed them in a slightly more equitable way.[23] To an overwhelming extent, however, the Revolution deflected popular aspirations away from the possibility of radical land reform and focused on the supposedly empty land to the west. Rather than tax the rich to pay their troops, the proindependence forces offered western land as standard payment for those who enlisted in the Continental Army or state militias. In the South, soldiers fighting for liberty from Britain were also paid in slaves captured from loyalists.[24]

Indian nations feared the massive land grab that would result from settler independence. Seeking to survive the conflict, some American Indians tried to stay neutral, while others sided with the colonial rebels. Faced with continued settler provocations, however, most eventually joined with the British.[25] This choice did not reflect naive trust in Britain, whose brutal war practices had included the "gift" of smallpox-infected blankets to Indians during negotiations in 1763, but rather the recognition that a cautious, measured invasion is less bad than an unrestrained one. General Washington, commander of the Continental Army, offered support for this judgment in 1779 when he sent Major General John Sullivan to attack the Iroquois and instructed him "to lay waste all the settlements around . . . that the country may not be merely *overrun* but *destroyed*."[26] Similar scorched earth campaigns, part of a consistent military strategy, devastated the Cherokees, the Shawnees, and other indigenous nations.[27]

Slavery and Antislavery

People of African origin faced a more complex situation.[28] As part of the political ferment leading up to the Revolution, a growing number of Whites began to question the morality and the usefulness of slavery. Antislavery pamphlets circulated widely in the colonies, and many Revolutionary leaders opposed slavery to varying degrees and from a variety of motives. This sentiment found expression in a number of legal changes after independence, including the beginnings of emancipation in the North, legalization of private manumissions in the Upper South, a ban on bringing slaves into the northwestern territories, and steps toward ending the importation of enslaved Africans.[29] Such developments have led some historians to argue that the American Revolution marked a substantial, though tragically incomplete, advance for the antislavery cause.[30]

The Revolutionary movement's antislavery current was real and unprecedented. But in gauging its significance, it is not enough to acknowledge the cautious, timid nature of antislavery reforms in this period, or even to note that many of the Founding Fathers did not like slavery largely because they wanted an all-White republic.[31] If the independence movement challenged slavery in some limited ways, to a far greater extent, in practical terms, it actively worked to bolster and expand the institution. Efforts to keep African people enslaved and to crush their resistance were in fact central to the Revolutionary movement.

Enslaved Blacks in British North America had a long history of resistance and, as Peter H. Wood notes, tended to increase their resistance activities "during periods when the white community was distracted."[32] Thus as conflict between colonists and British authorities escalated in 1765–1775, Black people throughout the colonies stepped up their challenges to slavery, including several attempted insurrections. In 1774–1775, Blacks in Massachusetts and Virginia offered to help British officials put down colonial rebels in exchange for freedom.[33]

Black resistance terrified White revolutionists, especially in the South, where about ninety percent of Blacks lived. Rather than acknowledge Black people as conscious actors seeking freedom, colonists blamed slave unrest on British propaganda and conspiratorial manipulation. From Georgia to Maryland, fear of British-inspired slave revolts became one of the key factors rallying Whites to the cause of independence. In many areas, patriot militias were charged with two tasks: to fight British troops and to suppress or recapture disobedient Blacks.[34]

Beginning in November 1775, British generals, acting from military pragmatism rather than moral principle, offered freedom to the slaves of rebel slaveowners. In response, thousands of Blacks escaped to join the British military forces, and Blacks building harbor fortifications in Charleston went on strike.[35] A majority of Lord Dunmore's loyalist army in Virginia in the winter of 1775–1776 consisted of Black escapees bearing the words "Liberty to Slaves" across their uniforms. In some cases enslaved Blacks greeted the approach of British troops by seizing their masters and turning them over to the British. Many free Blacks, too, joined the British cause.[36]

General Washington wrote in December 1775 that if Dunmore "is not crushed before spring, he will become the most formidable enemy America has; his strength will increase as a snowball by rolling." Partly to counteract the British appeal, several states (mostly in the North) began recruiting free and enslaved Blacks, promising freedom to the latter in exchange for military service. Approximately 4–5,000 people of African origin served in the Continental Army. The number who served with the British forces was several times higher.[37]

British authorities sought to exploit Black rebelliousness while avoiding any real upheaval in the slave system. They mistreated and even re-enslaved many Black escapees.[38] Yet they also created an opportunity for many Black people to free themselves from their immediate oppressors, and helped thousands of them resettle in Britain, Nova Scotia, and Sierra Leone after the war. Other escapees fled to British Florida, joined Indian nations, or established free "maroon" communities beyond White control. An extraordinary number of enslaved Blacks, perhaps 80–100,000 out of a total slave population of 500,000, liberated themselves at least temporarily during the upheavals of war.[39] Some Black loyalists continued fighting long after the peace treaty was signed in 1783. As late as 1787, sizable guerrilla forces were raiding plantations and encouraging slave resistance in Georgia and South Carolina, including one unit of about 100 men who called themselves "the King of England's soldiers."[40] It was in quelling such bids for freedom that the final battles of the American Revolution were fought.

These points help place the Revolutionary era's antislavery measures in perspective. Few Black people—3.5 percent of the nation's total in 1790—lived in states that accomplished or initiated emancipation in the 1770s and 1780s (Pennsylvania and the New England states), and several of these states kept substantial numbers of Blacks in bondage for decades. In New York, slavery expanded significantly in the 1790s and, after the legislature approved gradual emancipation in 1799, many enslaved New Yorkers—perhaps as many as two-thirds—were sold into the South rather than freed.[41] Douglas Egerton argues that, in the South, where the vast majority of enslaved workers were held, "white independence from Britain only fastened slavery more securely . . . by placing control of the plantation regime in the hands of the indigenous elite." Bounties of land and slaves awarded to veterans helped spread the institution westward and broaden the number of White people who owned slaves.[42]

The U.S. Constitution, written in 1787 (on the heels of Black loyalist clashes with the Georgia militia), further strengthened slavery. For example, it guaranteed federal support to "suppress insurrections," required that runaway slaves who crossed state lines be surrendered to their owners, and barred Congress from prohibiting the African slave trade until 1808. During the twenty years leading up to that date, the United States imported more kidnapped Africans than were brought in during any other two decades in history.[43]

One of the first federal laws passed under the new Constitution was the Naturalization Law of 1790, which limited naturalized citizenship to "free white person[s]." Although later modified to allow certain non-European peoples access to naturalization, this racist clause would not be fully expunged from U.S. law until 1952.[44]

In addition to targeting people of color directly, the Revolutionary movement used fears of Indian and Black resistance to bolster its critique of British "tyranny." In *Common Sense*, Paine—who earlier had advocated Black emancipation—denounced the British government as "that barbarous and hellish power, which hath stirred up the Indians and Negroes to destroy us."[45] A few months later, the Declaration of Independence, in its list of accusations against King George III, charged that "He has excited domestic Insurrections [slave revolts] amongst us, and has endeavored to bring on the Inhabitants of our Frontiers, the merciless Indian Savages, whose known Rule of Warfare, is an undistinguished Destruction, of all Ages, Sexes, and Condition."[46]

Here is a classic example of repressive populist scapegoating. Not only did this passage hide the colonists' own murderous aggression and project it onto their victims, but it also treated people of color as passive beings manipulated from the outside. Thus the founding document of the United States of America harnessed a racist stereotype to a classic conspiracist image: the plot by a power-hungry elite, controlling a primitive, violent horde, to dominate freedom-loving people. As Colin Calloway notes, the myth that all Indians had fought for the British justified an indiscriminate rush to take over their lands as "spoils of war," and the Declaration's "image of Indians as vicious enemies of liberty became entrenched in the minds of generations of white Americans."[47] In addition, blaming King George for Black and Native resistance represented the germ of Anglophobia, particularly the scapegoating of Britain for home-grown conflicts and crises, which became an important theme in later repressive and right-wing populist politics.

Jefferson's original draft of the Declaration carried anti-British scapegoating even further. In a clause deleted by the Continental Congress, Jefferson the slaveowner blamed King George not only for inciting slave insurrections but also, incredibly, for slavery itself:

> he has waged cruel war against human nature itself, violating it's most sacred rights of life & liberty in the persons of a distant people who never offended him, captivating & carrying them into slavery in another hemisphere, or to incure miserable death in their transportation thither. . . . He is now exciting those very people to rise in arms against us, and to purchase that liberty of which *he* had deprived them, by murdering the people upon whom *he* also obtruded them; thus paying off former crimes committed against the *liberties* of

one people, with crimes which he urges them to commit against the *lives* of another.[48]

One wonders if Jefferson recognized the absurdity of portraying colonial slaveowners as innocent victims who had slavery "obtruded" upon them.[49] Though absolving colonists of responsibility, the passage was cut from the Declaration because many congress members objected to any statement that called slavery into question.

Gender

Gender as well as race was an important theme in anti-British scapegoating. Although patriots often depicted Liberty as a woman, they also frequently used negative stereotypes of femininity in their attacks on Britain. Samuel Adams castigated a womanly Britain "absorbed in luxury and dissipation" as well as "vanity and extravagance." There were many variations on the theme of Britain as a corrupt, violent old woman: "a cruel Beldam, willing like Lady Macbeth, to 'dash their brains out'"; a monstrous mother "red with the blood of her children"; or, in fact, no mother at all, but a "vile imposter—an old abandoned prostitute—crimsoned o'er with every abominable crime, shocking to humanity!"[50]

In the view of many revolutionists, Britain's corrupt, feminine qualities stood in sharp contrast with the healthy, masculine simplicity of colonial life in frontier America. Independence signaled manhood, and the end of dependence on maternal protection and guidance. As Paine put it in *Common Sense*, "Is it the interest of a man to be a boy all his life?" To submit to British control was to be emasculated, as in James Otis's claim that abolishing the colonial assemblies was like "circumcising all the male colonists."[51]

While reviling Britain as wickedly feminine (and excluding women from their political vision), the men of the Revolution depended on women's help in securing independence. Through organizations such as the Daughters of Liberty, White women were recruited as auxiliaries to the patriot cause, who took part in crowd actions, helped enforce boycotts of British goods, and fed and nursed the troops. The campaigns after 1763 to boycott British goods and increase domestic production placed special emphasis on home manufacturing, especially spinning and weaving. Thus in many ways, the supposedly masculine virtue of independence rested in large part on women's productive activity.[52]

Long-term socioeconomic trends were closing off the limited opportunities colonial White women had enjoyed to work outside the home and to learn skilled trades through apprenticeships. Limited legal rights for women to hold property, make contracts, act as "attorneys-in-fact," petition officials, and even vote in some local elections, were curtailed in most states, as legal codes were redrawn after independence.[53] Yet participation in the patriot movement, and the overall social upheaval that accompanied the war for independence, encouraged many middle- and upper-class White women to play more vocal and assertive roles in society. Quiet voices during the Revolution itself, such as Abigail Adams's private admonition to her husband John to "Remember the Ladies" when fashioning a new legal system, were followed in the 1780s and 1790s by "an outpouring of public writing by and about women," such as Judith Sargent Murray's essays asserting women's intellectual competence and need for education.[54]

Responding to these claims in the years after independence, the new republican ideology recognized White women's domestic activity as important for society as a whole. As historians Mary Beth Norton and Linda K. Kerber argue, though the new doctrine still excluded women from a direct voice in political life, it granted them an important indirect role "in [a woman's] obligation to create a supportive home life for her husband, and particularly in her duty to raise republican sons who would love their country and preserve its virtuous character."[55] The concept of the "republican mother" as upholder of civic virtue contrasted with the symbolic evil mother identified with the British government.

Republican motherhood helped expand White women's education, as necessary preparation for the new civic responsibility of women. But the doctrine was an unstable compromise, because it sought to link White women to the public political sphere while keeping them at arm's length from it. And it accommodated White women's growing assertiveness only in exchange for their loyalty to the established social order, including not only gender hierarchy but also class and racial oppression. In this respect, republican motherhood reinforced White women's status as subordinate members of the privileged racial caste.

CONCLUSION

Many of the tensions that fueled the American Revolution persisted even after independence was secured. Unlike the American Revolution, Shays' Rebellion in 1786–1787 was not a repressive populist movement, as it did not attack oppressed groups or use scapegoating. It was a populist revolt against real elites by economically strapped farmers in Western Massachusetts, and it was crushed swiftly. Led by Revolutionary War veteran Daniel Shays, armed bands stopped court proceedings and demanded economic and judicial reforms, such as an end to foreclosures and to imprisonment for debt. In September 1786 Shays and several hundred followers marched on mid-state Springfield, forcing the adjournment of a state Supreme Court session. When Shays led some 1,200 men in a January 1787 assault on a federal arsenal in Springfield, he was routed and pursued north, where his forces were defeated and he fled across the nearby border into Vermont.

The revolt, however, forced the state legislature of Massachusetts to pass laws offering some relief to those in debt due to the harsh economic times. Shays' Rebellion also provided arguments for persuading anti-Federalists to accept the centralized authority of the Constitution during the state ratification process, which began in 1787.

Federalism and the Constitution were soon put to the test with the 1794 Whiskey Rebellion in western Pennsylvania. When some 7,000 protestors against a new federal excise tax on whiskey marched on Pittsburgh, President Washington sent militias from four states to put down the uprising. This too was a populist revolt in a power struggle with real elites, rather than a repressive populist movement.[56]

The struggle for U.S. independence rallied thousands of people seeking relief from social, economic, and political oppression. By disrupting established institutions and traditions of obedience, the Revolution created an opening in which many social groups challenged and sometimes transformed their allotted roles. In its propaganda, especially the Declaration of Independence, the movement proclaimed the principles of equality, inalienable rights, popular sovereignty, and the legitimacy of resisting tyrannical authority—principles that would provide inspiration for antioppression movements across the nineteenth and twentieth centuries.

The central tragedy of the American Revolution is that, with few exceptions, it deflected people's legitimate grievances and aspirations away from a fuller examination of the oppressive structures and elite groups within colonial society. The British monarchy provided a scapegoat for the system of elite rule. Crushing most Black people's own bids for freedom, and accelerating the plunder and killing of Indians, bolstered the relative privilege of lower-class Whites and thus helped reconcile them to their own relative subordination. It is the combination of these dynamics that made the struggle for U.S. independence a repressive populist movement. And like other repressive populist movements, the Revolution left unresolved the internal social tensions that had fueled it. As the new republic expanded and changed, people continued to seek outlets for their grievances—against those both above and below them—and elites continued looking for ways to deflect popular discontent.

2

THE REAL PEOPLE

Antimasonry, Jacksonianism, and Anti-Catholic Nativism

In this chapter we will look at three movements that developed between the 1820s and the 1850s: Antimasonry, Jacksonianism, and anti-Catholic nativism. All were populist, all relied on conspiracist scapegoating, and all reinforced antidemocratic structures in some ways while challenging them in others. The Antimasonic movement tried to destroy the secretive Order of Freemasons, claiming it was an elite plot that threatened Christian morality and republican government. In the process the movement helped to invent the modern political witch-hunt, but also called attention to real inequities in U.S. society. The nativists vilified and assaulted immigrants, especially Irish Catholics, and tried to reduce their citizenship rights. But nativist parties also promoted a broad range of social reforms, from free public services to workers' cooperatives to expanded rights for women and people of color. The Jacksonians are usually remembered as champions of "the common man," who welcomed poor immigrants and helped remove property qualifications so that White men of all classes could vote and run for office. Yet, they also championed aggressive White supremacy and expansionist nationalism and channeled popular hatred of monopolies and banks to the benefit of a new rising sector of capitalist entrepreneurs.

Simplistic histories of "right-wing extremism" have distorted our image of this period. They have focused on the nativists (and to a lesser extent the Antimasons) as forerunners of the modern Right, while treating the Jacksonians as egalitarian reformers. Two influential books in this vein—*The Politics of Unreason* by Seymour Martin Lipset and Earl Raab (1970) and *The Party of Fear* by David H. Bennett (1988)—do not even mention the Jacksonians' racist policies toward Black people and American Indians.[1] But the Jacksonians' producerist ideology, which denounced parasitic elites while applauding the enslavement, forced removal, and mass killing of non-Europeans, directly foreshadowed right-wing populism.

Another factor in this skewed portrait is that the Antimasonic and anti-

Catholic movements had strong ties to evangelical Protestantism, while the Jacksonian movement did not. Some writers, such as Lipset and Raab, have portrayed Protestant evangelicals as backward-looking conservatives or reactionaries who felt threatened by the modern world. Lipset and Raab argue further that "organized traditional evangelical religion" was under siege from forward-looking secular liberals, whom they identify with the Jacksonians.[2] These are distortions, however. Evangelicals profoundly influenced U.S. culture and politics in this era, but their impact was as much to transform social institutions as it was to uphold traditional morality. Evangelicals included a number of Protestant denominations—especially Congregationalists, Baptists, Methodists, and Presbyterians—that emphasized salvation through faith, personal conversion, and the authority of scripture. The evangelicals were moral crusaders who engaged in large-scale campaigns to proselytize, combat drinking, and strengthen public observance of the Sabbath. But a large minority of evangelicals, in the North at least, championed a broad range of social and political causes. Some of these causes were repressive, such as anti-Catholic nativism, but others were liberatory, notably antislavery and feminism—key freedom struggles that most Jacksonians opposed.

The United States experienced a series of major economic, social, and political changes in the first half of the nineteenth century. These upheavals fostered a wide variety of hopes, fears, and demands, and the movements examined in this chapter gained support because they spoke to such concerns. One of these upheavals was the cotton boom. The invention of spinning and weaving machines increased British demand for the fiber, and Eli Whitney's cotton gin, which removed the seeds mechanically, made large-scale cotton growing profitable for the first time. Expanded cotton production increased demand for slave labor, thereby strengthening the entire slave economy, which for a time some had thought might disappear. Demand for new cotton lands also fueled the drive for westward expansion into American Indian and, later, Mexican territory. By the 1820s, a vast "cotton kingdom" stretched across the Deep South.[3]

Many enslaved Black workers resisted their oppression in a variety of ways, including flight, sabotage, and self-defense. Slave revolts—notably Denmark Vesey's aborted 1822 insurrection in South Carolina, and Nat Turner's Virginia uprising in 1831—terrified slave owners. From the late 1820s on, militant abolitionists, including free Blacks and their White allies, became an increasingly visible force in the North, and the Underground Railroad became an elaborate network helping thousands of enslaved Blacks escape to freedom. Antislavery activism fueled growing political conflict between the North, where slavery was gradually abolished, and the South, where it was increasingly entrenched.

Despite this sectional conflict, cotton produced by slave workers was crucial for the North's economic development as well. Cotton exports to

Europe enriched New York and other port cities. Cotton plantations provided an important market for food products grown in the Midwest (known then as the Northwest). Most of all, cotton provided the raw material for New England textile mills, which led the country's industrialization. By 1860 the United States was the number two manufacturing nation in the world.[4]

Also crucial for economic growth was the transportation revolution. Widespread construction of canals, steamboats, roads (and later railroads) dramatically expanded regional and national commerce. Increasingly, production for the market replaced production for direct use on farms and in households. Factories replaced craft workshops run by masters and apprentices. The beginnings of a factory system spurred formation of labor unions and "Workingmen's" parties among White workers. Banks proliferated, providing credit and issuing paper notes that circulated as money. Beginning with the Panic of 1819, the booms and busts of modern business cycles became a regular feature of U.S. life. According to Thomas Ferguson, inequality of wealth increased more sharply than at any other time in U.S. history.[5]

The country's economic growth helped to attract growing numbers of European immigrants, mostly poor and working class, including 4.3 million newcomers between 1840 and 1859. Over 40 percent of these immigrants came from Ireland, where English colonial policies resulted in mass starvation.[6] In the United States, which had been overwhelmingly Protestant at the time of independence, Irish and German Catholics formed a religious minority whose presence became increasingly controversial.

The role of White women was central in the early industrial labor force, as New England farm women shifted from spinning and weaving at home to working at the fast-growing textile mills as wage workers. Yet the decline of household-based manufacturing effectively narrowed women's approved sphere. While slave women worked on plantations and lower-class Whites on farms and in factories, middle-class women were now expected to confine themselves to homemaking and child-rearing (with servants performing much household labor). A new cult of domesticity or "true womanhood" portrayed the home as a private haven from the harsh, competitive world of the labor market and public life. White middle-class (and to some extent working-class) women were cast as protectors of moral purity and subjected to new rigid standards of feminine respectability. At the same time, a growing minority of women (monied and poor, White and Black) reinterpreted or defied such strictures by taking part in a variety of public social and political causes, including the emerging women's rights movement.[7]

Populist politics in this era was also shaped by changes in the electoral system. Political contests in the early republic were an elite affair: voting was mostly restricted to property-owning males, many important officials were either appointed or elected indirectly, and candidates were chosen by legislative caucuses. By the late 1820s, however, much of this had changed.

Most states removed property and tax restrictions on the vote for White men and replaced the old system of voice voting with printed ballots. Presidential electors, once chosen by state legislatures, were now popularly elected in all but a few states, as were a growing number of lesser officials. In the 1830s, the nominating convention replaced legislative caucuses as the standard way for parties to choose presidential candidates. These and other changes helped to bring about the modern system of political parties based on mass constituencies and broad coalitions.[8] In addition, improvements in communication and transportation, along with the growth of inexpensive newspapers and other forms of mass media, facilitated popular organizing.[9] All three of the movements examined in this chapter benefited from change and instability in the political system. The Antimasons, and especially the Jacksonians, helped define the new type of mass party in the late 1820s, and the nativists achieved their greatest electoral successes during the growing sectional crisis of the 1850s, when the established parties were divided and widely criticized.

ANTIMASONRY

The Antimasonic movement flourished across much of the Northeast and Midwest in the late 1820s and early 1830s. The movement began in western New York, a region known as the "burned-over district" because of its many heated religious revivals, and gained support in other areas where evangelicalism was strong. The Antimasonic Party became a major force in New York, Pennsylvania, Massachusetts, Rhode Island, Vermont, Ohio, and Michigan Territory, electing numerous legislators, members of Congress and Vermont's governor from 1831 to 1835. The movement declined in the mid-1830s after it had succeeded in temporarily decimating Freemasonry. Antimasons invented the political nominating convention, brought large numbers of new voters into the electoral process, and contributed to the development of mass-based political parties.

Modern Freemasonry is a fraternal order with secret rituals established in England in the eighteenth century and then brought to Britain's North American colonies. In the early nineteenth century, the Masonic Order cultivated a male subculture based on elitist fellowship, cosmopolitanism, religious tolerance, and Enlightenment liberalism. By the 1820s, Freemasonry had spread throughout the United States and had attracted perhaps 100,000 members, mainly upper-class men or those with upward aspirations. Paul Goodman notes that, in the face of competitive individualism, geographic mobility, and cultural flux, "Freemasonry offered businessmen and professionals instant access to a circle of friends, much like themselves, who affirmed their importance." At the same time, "Masonry was a visible, artificial, in a sense, impersonal network, whereas older community-based elite networks and newer upper-class ones were informal, half-hidden. This exposed Masonry to notice, suspicion, and envy."[10]

In Continental Europe, Freemasonry became associated with anti-clerical, republican doctrines. In Europe, the Catholic Church and traditional oligarchies promoted Antimasonry as part of a reactionary backlash against the Enlightenment and the French Revolution. Masonic lodges and individual Masons in the fraternal societies of Freemasonry were first accused of being the Devil's disciples in the late 1700s.[11] The original allegation of a conspiracy within Freemasonry to control the world traces back to British author John Robison, a professor of Natural Philosophy at the University of Edinburgh, who wrote a 1798 book, *Proofs of a Conspiracy*. The full title explains the basic premise: *Proofs of a Conspiracy—against All the Religions and Governments of Europe, carried on in the secret meetings of Freemasons, Illuminati, and Reading Societies.*[12]

Robison influenced French author Abbé Augustin de Barruel, whose first two volumes of his eventual four-volume study, *Memoirs Illustrating the History of Jacobinism*, beat Robison's book to the printer.[13]

The Enlightenment rationalist ideas of the Illuminati were, in fact, brought into Masonic lodges, where they played a role in a factional fight against occultist philosophy.[14] Both Robison and Barruel discuss the attempt by Bavarian intellectual Adam Weishaupt to spread the ideas of the Enlightenment through his secretive society, the Order of the Illuminati, organized in 1775–1776. Weishaupt, a professor of canon law at the University of Ingolstadt in Germany, was a critic of the church, especially the doctrinaire Jesuits. In 1784 a new, more conservative, Bavarian government with strong ties to the church began to suppress the Order of the Illuminati, fearing it was a breeding ground for revolution. In 1787 the government threatened recruiters with death, and the Order was officially disbanded.[15]

Weishaupt, his Illuminati society, the Freemasons, and other secret societies are portrayed by Robison and Barruel as bent on a conspiracy using front groups to spread their influence and to eventually establish world domination.[16]

A few New England Protestant clergy imported this conspiracy theory in 1798–1799 as part of a Federalist Party scare against foreign and domestic radicals. But Federalists George Washington (himself a Mason) and President John Adams rejected the attack on Freemasonry, and it won little support.[17]

But when Antimasonry reemerged in the United States in the 1820s, it differed sharply from the European version. Rather than an oligarchic campaign against subversive radicals, this was a grassroots-based movement that saw Freemasonry as an upper-class, "aristocratic" threat to republican government and values. Like their European counterparts, many U.S. Antimasons denounced Freemasonry's religious inclusiveness as fostering immorality. These critics, however, were mostly Protestant evangelical reformers, not adherents of a medieval church hierarchy. Freemasonry's European opponents rejected core progressive political principles, such as liberty and equality. But in the United States many supporters of Antimasonry—such as Thaddeus Stevens, Charles Sumner, and William Lloyd Garrison—were also or later became committed abolitionists.[18]

Paul Goodman has described the Antimasons' ideology as "Christian republicanism" because of the way it fused religious and political concerns. Republican doctrine, as handed down by the Founding Fathers, emphasized the concept of "virtue," meaning "the ability to subordinate individual self-interest to the public good."[19] Many believed that republican virtue depended on Christian morality to restrain human passions. In a period when the growth of commercialism, secularism, and class inequality seemed to threaten republican virtue, Freemasonry offered a ready scapegoat. Antimasons declared that the secret order ruthlessly promoted its members' interests over the public good, that Masonic rituals were idolatrous and anti-Christian, that Masons encouraged drunkenness and indecency, and that their use of fancy titles betrayed an aristocratic craving for power.

A degree of truth bolstered Antimasonry's choice of targets. Although Freemasonry did not represent the elite as a whole, it did include many affluent and powerful men. Masons disproportionately held key posts in government, the press, and the courts, and often helped each other advance in business and politics. And while the 1820s Antimasonic movement came to embrace grandiose conspiracy theories, it began as a legitimate and focused protest against genuine crimes by Masons.[20] William Morgan, a disaffected Mason in western New York, announced plans in 1826 to publish an exposé about the secret order. Local Masons responded by trying to steal the manuscript and to destroy the publisher's offices, then kidnapped Morgan and probably murdered him. His body was never found. A number of well-placed Masons, including judges, sheriffs, prosecutors, and other officials, took part in a cover-up to shield the culprits. Many Masons ignored, ridiculed, or threatened those who pressed for an investigation. Local critics concluded, reasonably, that Masons had conspired to violate the administration of justice and equality before the law. Not trusting the many Freemasons who held public office, protesters began to field candidates in 1827 and founded the Antimasonic Party the following year. The movement soon spread to other states.[21]

As it grew, Antimasonry took on an absolutist quality. Applying the principle of guilt by association, the new party denounced all Freemasonry as inherently evil and pledged to destroy it. Antimasons charged that Masonic oaths automatically placed obedience to the secret order before the rule of law and morality. With little or no evidence, they accused Freemasons of numerous murders, of enforcing loyalty with gruesome penalties, of preying on women outside the families of fellow Masons. They portrayed Freemasonry as a superpowerful force whose "insidious influence extended to every transaction in society."[22] Eventually, some members of the movement also borrowed from the European myth of an international Illuminati plot to destroy civilization.

Antimasons saw themselves as defending core republican principles against a tyrannical threat, but their crusade itself attacked basic civil liberties such as freedom of speech and freedom of association. They urged states to revoke the charters of Masonic lodges and passed laws in several states banning Masonic oaths. In a foreshadowing of twentieth-century countersubversive surveillance practices, they called for states to compile detailed records of Masonic members, meetings, activities, and funds. Operating as private citizens, Antimasons conducted their own surveillance, which they used to expose Masons holding public office. Their campaign of intimidation sometimes included physical threats, vandalism, and attempted arson. Masons, it should be noted, sometimes responded with harassment and physical attacks of their own.[23]

But Antimasons also had a populist reform agenda. They opposed licensed monopolies and imprisonment for debt, advocated equal universal education and more equitable property taxes—all salient antielite demands of the time. Their attack on "aristocracy" did not simply target Freemasonry but also the various ruling cliques in the states where they were active: in New York, this was the "Albany Regency" that controlled the Democratic Party; in Massachusetts, the Boston Brahmins at the head of the National Republican Party. The Antimasons criticized Freemasonry for excluding women, and, in a period when women's right to engage in public activism was still deeply controversial, Antimasons appealed for women's support and welcomed them to their conventions. And many declared that slavery, like Freemasonry, must be attacked decisively in the name of republican equality.[24]

Historians have disagreed about Antimasonry's class base. Older accounts linked the movement to poor farmers, renters' grievances against wealthy absentee landlords, and disadvantages the transportation revolution imposed on some rural groups. More recent detailed studies have tended to portray the bulk of Antimasonic activists as middle-class, prosperous, and upwardly mobile.[25] Paul Goodman argues that, in New England, many self-made manufacturers steeped in evangelical morality were drawn to temperance, antislavery, and Antimasonic movements. They "found in perfectionist reform movements a mode of resolving the conflict between equal-rights norms and republicanism and the emerging system of social stratification and competitive individualism."[26]

Goodman also notes that in industrial Lynn, Massachusetts, Antimasons "constructed a broad-based coalition that combined shoe bosses and shoe workers," preempting the growth of a Workingmen's party. "By focusing on the aristocratic dangers of Freemasonry, Antimasons diverted cordwainers [shoe workers] from other manifestations of class inequality, a pressing concern in view of the propensity of some shoemakers, men and women, to organize trade unions." While the Antimasonic movement echoed some working-class reform demands, it generally opposed workers' efforts to organize along class lines. The *Boston Advocate*, a major Antimasonic newspaper, accused labor unions of mirroring Masonic conspiratorial tactics.[27]

By targeting Freemasonry, the Antimasonic movement helped call attention to political and social inequality in U.S. society but deflected attention away from the systemic forces that fostered such inequality. Antimasons believed that the threat came from a conspiracy to "break the rules" of the U.S. republic. In fact, these rules themselves provided the framework for a system of inequality and oppression. But while the Antimasons engaged in political persecution against their opponents, they did not concentrate their attacks against socially oppressed groups. For this reason, we consider them a borderline example of a repressive populist movement. Like other Protestants of the period, Antimasons sometimes defamed Catholics or Jews, and as noted they sometimes criticized labor unions. But Catholics, Jews, and labor unionists were marginal targets of Antimasonic propaganda, and we have found no claims that Antimasons ever attacked them physically.

In later decades, the Illuminati conspiracy myth was resurrected and harnessed to a reactionary or right-wing populist agenda, but this must not be lumped together with the Antimasonry of 1826–1835. Despite their reputation as paranoid bigots, the early Antimasons left a record far cleaner than that of their revered contemporaries, the Jacksonians.

JACKSONIANISM

Like Antimasonry, the Jacksonian movement began in the 1820s and, like it, tapped a broad reservoir of populist antielitism. The movement attracted western debtor farmers who resented the power of eastern banks, southern backwoodsmen challenging the political dominance of rich planters, and urban artisans in the Northeast who confronted industrialization and growing class conflict. This lower-class upsurge, however, was not only co-opted and exploited by politically skillful members of the elite. It was also fused with aggressive racism and demands for military conquest. Jacksonianism dominated U.S. politics from the 1828 elections until 1860.

Andrew Jackson won the 1828 presidential election by building a new coalition from the fragments of the old Republican and Federalist parties. Key to Jackson's support was a "states' rights" alliance between southern planters and sections of the northern elite, especially in New York. Against the National Republicans, who advocated a strong federal role in the economy and domestic policy, states' rights proponents stood for a weak federal government. They included southerners who feared northern "interference" with slavery, and the Albany Regency in New York, which opposed federal aid to transportation projects after New York had built the Erie Canal on its own. In the lead-up to the 1828 elections, pro-Jackson politicians around the country organized the Democratic Party as the first modern political machine, with an elaborate hierarchy of party committees and well-funded propaganda directed at a mass audience.[28]

Anchoring this coalition was Andrew Jackson himself, a prototype of the charismatic populist leader. Like Nathaniel Bacon, Jackson was a frontier planter, a rich man who could present himself as a friend of the people. Lawyer and land speculator, slaveowner and slave trader, Jackson romanticized White farmers and workingmen while regarding the old upper classes as corrupt. He warned repeatedly of conspiracies by Washington politicians or foreign agents. As president he fought and won a bitter "war" against the Bank of the United States, symbol of entrenched financial power. He believed that his role as first executive gave him a special direct communion with the popular will.

Jackson won national hero status as a military commander during and after the War of 1812, fighting both British troops and American Indians. During the 1813–1814 campaign against the Creeks of Mississippi, Jackson referred to his Indian opponents as "cannibals," "savage dogs," and a threat to White "female innocence." At the battle of Horseshoe Bend, Jackson's troops (with the help of Cherokee allies) surrounded a party of 800 Creek men, women, and children and killed virtually all of them. "His soldiers cut long strips of skin from the bodies of the dead Indians and used them for bridle reins; they also cut the tip of each dead Indian's nose to count the number of enemy bodies."[29] In 1818, without authorization, Jackson invaded Spanish Florida, ostensibly to stop the Seminoles from raiding Georgia settlements and providing sanctuary to Blacks fleeing enslavement. The next year, the United States acquired Florida from Spain, and Jackson was appointed military governor. Over the decade from 1814 to 1824, Jackson used threats, bribery, and possibly forgery to engineer nine treaties with the Cherokees, Chickasaws, Choctaws, Creeks, and Seminoles, resulting in huge cessions of land to Whites.[30]

Jackson and the Democratic Party spearheaded a policy of mass killing and systematic removal to eliminate all Native people east of the Mississippi. As president, Jackson encouraged illegal efforts by southern states to extend control over remaining Indian lands and open them up to settlers and speculators, and he refused to enforce treaties, laws, and a U.S. Supreme Court order protecting Native rights. In 1830, President Jackson signed the Indian Removal Act, under which some 70,000 people were forced to migrate west of the Mississippi.[31] Perhaps one-third of them died on the way to Oklahoma—from violence, hunger, disease, and other hardships. The Seminoles of Florida fought a guerrilla war against removal for eight years, and were regarded as a particular threat because their confederacy was a haven for Black refugees from slavery. Jackson ordered search-and-destroy missions targeting Seminole women in an effort to exterminate their nation completely. But in 1842, after a massive commitment of money and troops, the U.S. government gave up and let the survivors stay in the Florida swamps.[32]

In 1845, three years after the Florida war ended, a Democratic newspaper editor coined the term "Manifest Destiny" to describe what was commonly viewed as the United States' God-given right to seize all of North America.[33] In 1845–1848, largely at the behest of expansionist slaveholders, the Democratic-controlled U.S. government annexed Texas, then went on to conquer the northern half of Mexico.

In *The Rise and Fall of the White Republic*, Alexander Saxton contrasts the Jacksonian stance on race and class issues with that of their main opponents, the National Republicans, later reincarnated as the Whigs. The elitist National Republicans/Whigs "accepted and revered class hierarchy"; they promoted an ethic of deference by which each class knew its place. "Within this spectrum of difference racial difference could be viewed, not as overriding all others, but simply one among many." Whig leaders tended to regard people of color as childish inferiors to be manipulated in a paternalistic way, and who could sometimes be used to counterbalance challenges from lower-class Whites. Whigs tended toward a more cautious version of expansionism than the Democrats. They favored "civilizing" Native peoples, not massacring and deporting them, and leaned toward either gradual emancipation of slaves or silence on the question for the sake of national unity.[34]

If, in Saxton's terms, National Republicans/Whigs were "hard" on class but "soft" on race, Jacksonians were the reverse. They combined an inclusive class ideology of White male egalitarianism with the hard racism of exclusion, terror, and suppression toward people of color. This spoke particularly to those lower-class Whites who feared an upper-class alliance with people of color against them.[35]

Thus Jacksonians not only applauded and promoted efforts to extend the franchise to all White males but also worked to take the vote away from Black men. Before New York's "Reform Convention" of 1821, for example, both White and Black men faced the same property and residence requirements for voting. The convention voted to abolish nearly all suffrage restrictions on White men, but increased property requirements for Black voters so that only a handful retained the franchise. This New York convention was led by Martin Van Buren, Jackson's ally and successor in the White House and a key architect of the Democratic Party. In Pennsylvania, another state with a large free Black population, the 1838 convention disenfranchised all Black men while abolishing property qualifications for Whites. Connecticut, North Carolina, Tennessee, and other states made similar changes, and the constitution of every new state admitted to the union from 1819 to 1865 restricted voting to Whites only.[36]

Jacksonianism provided a key prop to slavery, linking southern planters to a mass political base that included many northern Whites. Jacksonian hard racism infused the armed slave patrols of mostly poor Whites who terrorized Blacks in the South and the White mobs that played an analogous, if less organized, role in northern cities. Faced with growing abolitionist activism and Nat Turner's 1831 uprising, the proslavery power structure intensified its repression and scapegoating of opponents. Jacksonians denounced abolitionism as a conspiracy by northern capitalists to undermine White workers' status and to increase competition from Black workers. Anti-abolitionist mobs in New York, Cincinnati, Philadelphia, and other northern cities attacked Black communities, killing dozens and forcing thousands to flee for their lives. Many northern states barred Black people from entering their territory or required them to post a prohibitively large bond as guarantee of good behavior. Northern Whites' terrorism and pervasive discrimination against free Black people helped slaveowners by discouraging enslaved Blacks from running away to the North.[37]

The emerging White labor movement often helped to enforce racial oppression. Although an important minority of White workers supported abolitionism, the majority opposed it, and few if any recognized enslaved Blacks as part of a U.S. working class, or their struggle for freedom as a labor struggle. White labor activism included not only strikes and other challenges to elite power but also widespread campaigns to drive Black workers out of skilled trades and many other occupations. Arguing that the "white slavery" of wage workers was worse than chattel slavery, many White labor leaders cultivated warm relations with militant defenders of slavery and states' rights such as John C. Calhoun.[38]

Much of Jacksonianism's producer ideology came from the growing White labor movement. In the 1820s and 1830s, Workingmen's parties operated briefly in a number of cities, but most of these groups were soon drawn, with some ambivalence, into the Jacksonian coalition. The Workingmen's movement primarily represented independent artisans. During this period, when small factories were just beginning to supplant traditional workshops, the line was still fluid between the small business owner and the skilled worker. Many wage workers could reasonably hope to become entrepreneurs.[39] Rather than class politics, the Workingmen's movement promoted solidarity among "producers," encompassing all employees and employers involved in "useful" pursuits. Excluded were "parasitic" lawyers, bankers, brokers, and a few other privileged groups, on the one hand, and people of color, on the other. Unity among producers—"the real people," as Andrew Jackson called them—quickly became a central theme for the Jacksonian coalition of White farmers, artisans, planters, and entrepreneurs.[40]

Jacksonianism focused on rallying producers at the very moment when the cult of domesticity was excluding "true" women from the sphere of productive labor. In this sense, Jacksonianism did not simply omit women from the circle of White equality but rather defined that circle in opposition to women. As Paula Baker has noted, extension of the franchise to all White men showed White women that "their disenfranchisement was based solely on sex."[41] The Jacksonian notion of equality and the concept of true womanhood also came together in the demand for a "family wage," that is, a wage that would enable a male worker to support a family so that his wife and children would not have to enter the labor market. This demand, first put forward by White male labor activists in the 1830s, "asserted the social right of the working class to the ideal of family and gender roles embodied in the 'cult of true womanhood.'" White labor activist Seth Luther argued that White equality depended on a family wage system to keep women out of the male sphere of factories: "we know . . . that the *wives* and *daughters* of the rich manufacturers would no more associate with a *factory girl* than they would with a *negro slave*."[42] In contrast to the Antimasonic and nativist movements, both of which challenged strictures on women in certain ways, the Jacksonians consistently upheld women's subordination.

Producerism appealed to Jacksonians in part because it meshed well with their emphasis on minimal government. When the Jacksonians talked about economic equality, they meant equal opportunity to compete in the marketplace. In their view, "monopolies" and other injustices did not result from concentrations of wealth or market power but rather from special, government-created privileges, such as corporate charters. (At this time, each charter was enacted as a separate legislative act.) Similarly, Jacksonian "agitation for land reform was expressed, not as an indictment of landlords who had monopolized the soil, but by the demand that the law should be changed to give the potential settler free access to the public lands."[43]

Antimonopoly efforts focused above all on banks, prime examples of chartered privilege. The number of banks had grown enormously since the early 1800s; they played a key economic role in financing business growth and westward expansion. Often they were also the most tangible representatives of the ruthlessness and inequity of contemporary economic development—especially along the frontier, where credit was most scarce and financial practices most unscrupulous. During the Panic of 1819, bank foreclosures engendered tremendous resentment in frontier farming country, where banks were referred to as "horse leeches" and "vultures." The banking system came under attack not only from Jacksonians but also from independent Workingmen's groups and Antimasonic parties.[44]

Beginning in 1832, President Jackson launched a campaign to destroy the Bank of the United States. Chartered by Congress in 1816 and headquartered in Philadelphia, the U.S. Bank served as the depository for federal funds and a powerful central regulator of the country's financial system.

Jackson opposed renewal of the U.S. Bank's charter and eventually destroyed the Bank by transferring federal funds to a number of state banks. He denounced the Bank as an institution of artificial privilege, robbing the "humble members of society" through secret manipulation. "It is to be regretted," Jackson declared in his 1832 bank veto message, "that the rich and powerful too often bend the acts of government to their selfish purposes." With its system of paper money, the U.S. Bank promoted a "spirit of speculation injurious to the habits and character of the people" and an "eager desire to amass wealth without labor." Martin Van Buren, then Jackson's Secretary of State, warned that banks threatened "the manly virtues" by seeking "to substitute for republican simplicity and economical habits a sickly appetite for effeminate indulgence."[45]

As Michael Rogin points out, the threats the Jacksonians identified with the U.S. Bank—the rise of acquisitiveness, the loss of independence, and subjection to distant institutions—were not due to some sinister cabal, but in fact were inherent in the growth of unrestrained market capitalism itself, a system that the Jacksonians glorified. Yet, the Bank War reflected genuine conflicts within the country's economic elite. Many of Jackson's advisers had ties to state banks, some of which opposed the U.S. Bank's restriction of credit and other regulatory practices. In particular, Van Buren headed the Albany Regency political machine, which had numerous ties to New York City's financial community.[46] Bray Hammond notes that

> in the federal Bank Philadelphia retained an impressive stronghold of her former primacy. It was the Bank in Philadelphia in whose Wall Street office the revenues of the port of New York were received on deposit. Those revenues, paid by New York business men, were larger than those of all other American ports together, but they passed into the control of directors who were mostly Philadelphians. New York's jealousy in this matter was no empty question of first place in an honorific sense but a lively question of whose pockets the profits were going into.[47]

At the same time, the Bank War enabled the Jackson administration to rally populist mass support by exploiting and redirecting the antielite arguments of political opponents. In New York, both the Antimasons and the independent *Working Men's Advocate* had been waging an antimonopoly campaign against the Regency's ties with state-chartered banks, and both pointed out that these institutions would benefit from destroying the U.S. Bank. Lee Benson argues further that the language with which Jacksonians attacked the U.S. Bank—"this Beast with seven heads and horns; this dragon, this Hydra-headed monster," and so on—closely resembled the distinctive propaganda Antimasons had previously used against both Freemasonry and state banks.[48] Such phrasing could also be interpreted by apocalyptic Christians as a reference to satanic collusion.

Destruction of the U.S. Bank did nothing to help the "humble members of society," but it benefited many state and private bankers, and it helped make New York City the financial capital of the young North American empire.[49] This exploitation of popular antielitism was characteristic of the Jacksonian movement. While denouncing artificial privilege, many Democratic leaders themselves held office in monopolistic companies or used government power to aid specific entrepreneurial interests. Despite the Jacksonians' reputation as advocates of the common people, they instituted no laws to shorten the working day, improve labor conditions, or provide aid to the lower classes during economic slumps. Andrew Jackson became the first president to use federal troops to break a strike.[50]

One concrete basis for the Jacksonians' image as advocates for the poor and humble—in addition to their stand on voting rights—was their opposition to anti-Catholic nativism, especially with regard to the Irish. The Democratic Party energetically recruited Irish Catholics, the most downtrodden immigrant group. At a time when nativist discrimination made Irish exclusion from the White racial caste seem a real possibility, Democratic leaders welcomed them into what Thomas Hart Benton called the "Celtic-Anglo-Saxon race."[51] As a fast-growing community strategically concentrated in northern cities, and providing much of the labor power for early industrial development, the Irish were important to the Jacksonian aim of building a broad base of support in the emerging White working class.

Noel Ignatiev notes that the Democratic Party was central to the process whereby "the Catholic Irish, an oppressed race in Ireland, became part of an oppressing race in America." Guided by Jacksonianism, veterans of Ireland's radical anticolonial struggles were transformed into militant defenders of White supremacy. A special twist on the Jacksonian formula was to denounce abolitionism as an English plot to undermine the United States. In 1841, when sixty thousand people in Ireland signed an appeal urging Irish Americans to join the struggle against slavery, the response was overwhelmingly hostile. Yet there were also dissenters, notably the members of the San Patricio (Saint Patrick) Battalion, Irish Americans who fought on the side of Mexico against the U.S. invasion of 1846–1848, in part motivated by opposition to slavery.[52]

ANTI-CATHOLIC NATIVISM

Anti-Catholicism was inherited from sixteenth- and seventeenth-century Britain, where it grew out of the revolt against feudalism, nationalist opposition to Spain and France, and colonial conquest of Ireland. Hostility to Catholics was strong in Britain's North American colonies. After independence, a majority of state constitutions barred Catholics—and Jews—from political office. On the national level, the Federalist Party's repressive Alien and Sedition Acts of 1798–1801 largely targeted radical immigrants from Catholic Ireland and France.

Organized anti-Catholic nativism was a major force from the 1830s to the eve of the Civil War, peaking in the mid-1850s with the Know Nothing Party. Protestant evangelicals played a major role, as they had in Antimasonry, although many nonevangelicals also embraced anti-Catholicism. The nativist movement was strongest in the North and in cities with large Catholic immigrant populations; native-born workers and middle-class people both rallied to the cause. Because the United States of the early 1800s was overwhelmingly Protestant and steeped in anti-Catholic prejudices, many people reacted with fear and hostility as, first, thousands and then millions of Catholic foreigners came to stay. Nativists denounced the newcomers as paupers, criminals, and drunks. They accused them—especially during the depression of 1837–1843—of stealing jobs and undercutting wages. They claimed that the immigrants' European backgrounds made them unfit for electoral politics—an ignorant mass easily controlled by party bosses.[53] Evangelicals condemned Catholic newcomers for breaking the Sabbath and opposing temperance crusades. Many antislavery activists singled out Irish immigrants as pawns of the slavocracy.

The stereotype of Irish Catholics as brute savages—filthy, violent, drunken Papist idolators—was rooted in the system of racial oppression that British rule had imposed in Ireland. In the White supremacist hierarchy of nineteenth-century U.S. life, Irish people temporarily held a racially ambiguous position—above Indians, Blacks, and Mexicans but below native-born Whites. "In the early years," Noel Ignatiev notes, "Irish were frequently referred to as 'niggers turned inside out'; the Negroes, for their part, were sometimes called 'smoked Irish,' an appellation they must have found no more flattering than it was intended to be." Unlike Black people, however, Irish Catholics had access to key privileges reserved for Whites: the presumption of liberty, the rights (threatened but never suspended) of immigration and naturalization, and (for men) the right to vote.[54] Thus, anti-Irish oppression functioned as a second-tier division within the White racial caste.

Nativists condemned "Papism" as fake Christianity: an idolatrous perversion that mocked Holy law and promoted drunkenness, gambling, greed, and lawlessness. Ignoring the anticolonialist republican tradition that many Irish brought to the United States, nativists called Catholicism an authoritarian religion incompatible with democratic government. They denounced Catholics as foreign agents secretly plotting to take over the country and deliver it to the despotism of the Pope or European monarchs. In the early 1850s, rumors that Irish Catholics planned to massacre Protestants sparked panic in many areas.[55] These claims were made more plausible by the long-standing argument that Catholics were agents of Satan because the Pope was the Antichrist.

Anti-Catholic propaganda also emphasized sexual corruption and violence as central to the hidden evil design. Pornographic anti-Catholic books and articles—circulated under the guise of religious righteousness—"exposed" convents as dens of prostitution, rape, and infanticide. To nativist Protestants, themselves steeped in deeply repressive attitudes toward sex, the Catholic vow of celibacy was an "unnatural" doctrine that masked female promiscuity and superpotent, predatory manhood: nuns who bared their breasts to every male visitor; priests who fathered scores of children and had to be given concubines to keep them from attacking women on the street.[56]

If "Papist" men were the more frightening threat, women were sometimes the easier target of anti-Catholic violence. One of the first large-scale attacks targeted the Ursuline Convent in Charlestown, Massachusetts, whose school for girls offered an alternative to the strict Puritanism of the local public schools. Several years of increasingly frenzied propaganda against the convent culminated in August 1834, when a mob of hundreds of men stormed the building and burned it to the ground, forcing the nuns and children to flee into the night.[57]

Nativists began organizing political parties in the 1830s, and they won significant electoral support during the 1837–1843 depression. "Native American" and American Republican parties operated in a number of cities, including New York, Philadelphia, New Orleans, Boston, Newark, St. Louis, Charleston, Baltimore, and Richmond. An estimated 60 per cent of their supporters were former Whigs and 40 percent were former Democrats (who resented Catholics' growing influence within the Jacksonian party). The nativist parties called on the government to curtail immigration, bar Catholics from holding public office, reduce immigrant voting by extending the naturalization period from five to twenty-one years, and maintain Protestant religious teaching in public schools. In 1844, with Whig support, these parties elected six members of Congress, the mayors of New York and Boston, and a majority of the New York city council. But, following the return of prosperity and then the beginning of war with Mexico in 1846, most of the nativist parties soon collapsed.[58]

This collapse did not happen in the Philadelphia area. An 1844 dispute over required use of the Protestant Bible in the Philadelphia public schools led to days of rioting between nativists and Irish Catholics, with troops eventually called in to quell the nativists. Twenty people were killed. The riots, and the immigrants' readiness to defend themselves, chilled nativist sentiment among upper-class Philadelphians. As Ignatiev comments, "while the city's elite loved the Protestant virtues of thrift, sobriety, the sabbath, and the wage system, they loved order more," and violent ethnic conflict between Whites threatened such order.[59] But the Native American Party made a strong showing in the elections that fall, especially in Protestant working-class districts, and it remained an important force into the 1850s.

Strongest and most enduring of the first-generation nativist parties, the Philadelphia party put forward a broad-ranging reform agenda that belies the image of all nativists as "conservative." The Native American Party helped to invent the primary system and successfully pushed for direct election of many local officials, such as police commissioners and members of the school and health boards. It also advocated direct election of the president, vice president, judges, and other officials. In the early 1850s, the party called on municipal governments to provide their citizens with extensive services free of charge, including libraries, schools, washing houses, baths, lectures, "useful amusements," and even free legal aid for the poor. In an era of rampant laissez faire, the party supported public regulation of housing, factory construction, and street railways.[60]

Such positions put the nativists at odds with the Jacksonians' demand for minimal government. But they echoed Jacksonian rhetoric when they spoke up for "the productive classes" or "the real people, the mechanics and working men," against "the aristocracy." And Philadelphia nativists enthusiastically supported the Democratic-led war against Mexico. They backed the Wilmot Proviso, which would have banned slavery from any lands conquered in the war, but they called for annexing all of Mexico, in order to "sweep away this degenerate and feeble race, redeeming the land that they pollute."[61]

The Native American Party blamed cheap foreign labor for hurting native-born workers and called for a "capitation tax" to discourage immigration. But the Philadelphia party also supported workers' right to strike and attacked capitalists for squeezing excessive profits out of their employees. One faction of the party called for increased taxes on corporate wealth. Although opposing the abolition of private property, Philadelphia nativists promoted ideas for workers cooperatives developed by the French socialist Louis Blanc, and applauded the 1848 French Revolution for overthrowing both "feudal despotism" and "a commercial and moneyed oligarchy."[62]

The Philadelphia party, and the nativist movement generally, also welcomed women's activism—an unusual and controversial step in this period. In 1844, four years before the Seneca Falls Women's Rights Convention, Philadelphia nativists established a political newspaper staffed and financed solely by women—perhaps the first such publication in the country. Here and in other cities, nativist women held mass meetings, formed organizations, made speeches, circulated petitions, and even formed a women's militia unit. Many women's groups combined nativism with temperance work. Nativists often publicized the hardships of women factory and domestic workers, and sometimes called for shorter hours, more equitable wages, and wider opportunities for working-class women. Anti-Catholic women blended the traditional paternalistic claim of women's moral and spiritual superiority with a feminist claim that women were responsible human beings able to think and act for themselves. Nativist men often welcomed women activists, not as fully equal partners but as important "co-laborers." As Jean Gould Hales argues, the nativist movement embraced the cult of true womanhood but helped to expand the boundaries of women's accepted sphere by encouraging women to carry their role as moral educators outward from the home into the public arena.[63]

In the mid-1850s, nativism returned stronger than ever. The vehicle was the Order of the Star Spangled Banner, a nativist secret society dubbed the Know Nothings because members were instructed to say "I know nothing" when outsiders asked them about the order. Based in New York, between 1852 and 1854 the order spread throughout the country and recruited hundreds of thousands of members. In 1853–1854, the Know Nothings won a series of surprise electoral victories by backing candidates secretly. In the Massachusetts 1854 elections they captured the governorship, all U.S. House seats, and over 99 percent of the state legislature. By 1855, running open candidates under the American Party ticket, they controlled most of New England and were the major anti-Democratic party in the Mid-Atlantic states, California, and most of the South.[64]

An 1855 book written for the movement asked, "Shall TRUE AMERICANS govern themselves, or shall foreigners, unacquainted with our laws and brought up under monarchical governments, rule? Shall those who are temporally and spiritually subject to a foreign prince be our legislators, and change our laws as they are directed by the Pope of Rome?"[65]

Yet, by the fall of 1857 the Know Nothings had collapsed as a national organization. Several factors contributed to the Know Nothings' meteoric rise and fall. Famine in Ireland and revolution in Germany drove record numbers of immigrants to the United States between 1846 and 1855. By the early 1850s, the newcomers' increased electoral strength began to be felt, mainly through the Democratic Party. Also during this period, the Catholic Church hierarchy began to lobby against compulsory use of the Protestant Bible in public schools and for use of Catholics' school taxes to support parochial schools. Many nativists saw these moves as an attack on public education. Meanwhile, sharp economic fluctuations, rapid growth of the railroads, and mechanization of industry brought dislocation and insecurity to many, especially working-class people. Above all, sectional conflict over slavery was beginning to tear apart the political system, fracturing and discrediting both the Democrats and the Whigs. Widespread disgust with party machines and corrupt bosses fostered dozens of third parties in state and local races.[66]

The Know Nothings declared they would sweep out the professional politicians and return government to the people. Beyond that, the substance of their politics varied widely. In the South, the Know Nothings stressed nationalism and preservation of the Union. This stance rallied most former Whigs, whose party was virtually dead in much of the region by 1854, and some moderate Democrats, who opposed their party's states' rights intransigence. In many southern states, too, the Know Nothings dropped Catholic-bashing in favor of a broader antiforeignism, with which they tried to divert attention from slavery.[67]

In sections of the North, however, Know Nothings emulated the Philadelphia Native American Party by combining anti-Catholicism with economic and social reform. In Massachusetts, the Know Nothing landslide of 1854 had solid working-class support and put an unprecedented number of White working men into public office. The new nativist state government deported hundreds of impoverished immigrants back to Europe and appointed a legislative committee to investigate supposed evildoings in convents and Catholic schools. But the same government also increased school spending, promoted basic utilities, and improved regulation of such areas as banking, insurance, and railroad safety. Several new laws expanded women's rights regarding divorce, property, and child support. And Massachusetts Know Nothings also passed the nation's first school desegregation laws, banning the exclusion of any child based on race, color, or even religion.[68]

The Know Nothing Party collapsed as quickly as it had risen. Supporters and potential supporters were alienated by the organization's secrecy (objectionable especially to former Antimasons), by the failure to pass major anti-immigrant legislation, by professional politicians who quickly took control of the party, and by the violence nativists used in many cities to keep immigrants from voting. In 1855–1856, the party split between those northern Know Nothings who opposed expansion of slavery and southerners who demanded a proslavery, or at least neutral, platform. After 1856 most northern Know Nothings were absorbed into the new Republican Party.

CONCLUSION

Jacksonianism, anti-Catholic nativism, and to a lesser extent Antimasonry represented three different kinds of repressive populist politics. They each gained mass support by offering simple explanations and remedies for genuine problems and conflicts and by combining conspiracist scapegoating and persecution with social or political reforms. In different ways, each addressed the sense of political disempowerment, cultural dislocation, and economic hardship or injustice that many people experienced during this time of great upheaval. Each played an important role in shaping the U.S. political system and political culture—not as marginal opponents of a supposedly democratic mainstream but as central actors.

As these three movements demonstrate, conspiracist ideology in the United States comes from many sources and has taken many forms. In the wake of the Nazi genocide, the Jewish conspiracy myth has sometimes been treated as the basic model for conspiracy thinking. This can be misleading when we look at the United States. Although U.S. culture inherited antisemitic stereotypes from Europe, political movements did not scapegoat Jews on a significant scale until the late nineteenth century. But conspiracism in the Jacksonian era offers striking parallels with antisemitism. The attack on Freemasons echoes descriptions of the Jew as a bloodthirsty, power-hungry threat to Christian morality. The Jacksonian dichotomy between "productive" entrepreneurs and "parasitic" bankers is almost identical to a basic tenet of modern antisemitism: that the abstract, parasitic power of money (embodied in the Jewish banker) threatens the concrete authenticity of productive activity (embodied in non-Jewish workers, farmers, and industrial capitalists). Other aspects of the hatred of Jews are mirrored in the nativist image of Catholics as agents of a foreign power secretly plotting to take over the country, as tools of Satan, and as rapists and prostitutes whose sexual corruption takes monstrous forms. When antisemitism did become an important tool of political movements later in U.S. history, it resonated and interacted with these distinct ideological traditions.

Mass anti-Jewish scapegoating was still in the future, but White racial oppression was in the present. On this question, the three movements diverged sharply. Although many Antimasons embraced abolitionism, Antimasonry as a movement did not take a strong position one way or another on White supremacy. Jacksonianism, however, made race politics central: it stood for the hard racism of forced removal and terrorist subordination, while welcoming all Europeans to share in—and help enforce—White privilege. By contrast, nativist anti-Catholicism was split on the question of slavery but united in its aim to exclude some European immigrants from full membership in White society. Such exclusion represented a fundamental challenge to the Jacksonians' inclusive vision of the White racial caste. In this contest, nativism lost and Jacksonianism won. Not until the early twentieth century would another effort be mounted on this scale to strip White privilege from some Europeans, and that effort too would eventually fail. Here is the reality behind the myth that the nativists were extremist bigots while the Jacksonians were egalitarian reformers: ethnic discrimination against Europeans stands out because it violates the basic rules of U.S. society, while White supremacy has become so entrenched that it can be treated as invisible.

Jacksonian principles lived on after the Jacksonian coalition itself was broken and defeated. As Alexander Saxton argues, the Republicans came to dominate national politics by combining Whiggish and Jacksonian themes, linking northern capitalists with an expanded popular base. Like the Whigs, the Republicans stood for an active federal role in economic development through protective tariffs, public works, and a national banking system. But they borrowed several key points from the Jacksonian program. First, they embraced the concept of "free banking," under which anyone could set up a bank if properly qualified rather than depending on the favoritism of a special charter from the legislature. This meant that the corporation, once the symbol of monopoly and artificial privilege, could now be identified with equal opportunity. Second, while deploying a certain amount of anti-Catholic rhetoric to satisfy their nativist constituents, the Republicans supported mass immigration, which provided industrialists with many workers vulnerable to harsh exploitation. Third, the Republicans championed inexpensive western homesteads and the concept of Free Soil.[69]

The Free Soil movement called for a ban on slavery in the western territories. Although the movement attracted some abolitionist support, most Free Soilers did not challenge slavery in the South and sought to exclude *all* Black people, slave or free, from the West. David Wilmot, Democratic congressman from Pennsylvania who laid the groundwork for the Free Soil Party, declared in 1846: "I would preserve to free white labor a fair country, a rich inheritance, where the sons of toil of my own race and color can live without the disgrace which association with negro slavery brings upon free labor." Such a proposal to benefit White homesteaders implied not only anti-Black racism but also further extermination of American Indian nations. Free Soil, in Ignatiev's words, "marked the emergence into the light of day of the inner tensions of Jacksonianism. The hunger of the free Northern population for land in the West collided with the demand of the slavocracy for more territory."[70]

Through Republicanism, which absorbed the Free Soil Party, northern capitalists exploited this conflict in order to wrest federal power from southern planters, the main barrier to their plans for industrial growth and national expansion. In the process they appealed directly to Jacksonian racial exclusivism. Lyman Trumbull, Republican leader and Senator from Illinois, declared in 1858: "We, the Republican party, are the white man's party. We are for free white men, and for making white labor respectable and honorable, which it can never be when negro slave labor is brought into competition with it."[71] The Republicans eclipsed the Know Nothings, in part, because this program to exclude Black people was a more solid basis for mass organizing than the nativist program to exclude Catholic European immigrants. The Republicans' comparatively quick political rise cut off southern planters from a large part of their mass base—and brought on the Civil War.[72]

3

A GREAT MONGREL MILITARY DESPOTISM

The First Ku Klux Klan and the Anti-Chinese Crusade

The Civil War (1861–1865) unleashed a radical challenge to White supremacy, which in turn brought a counterrevolutionary backlash. This struggle centered in the South, where newly emancipated Black people sought political equality through Radical Reconstruction governments. Here terrorist groups such as the Ku Klux Klan (KKK) led a mass movement to restore White rule on a new basis. The counterrevolutionary drive to "redeem" the South received help from another repressive populist movement—the western-based campaign to ban Chinese immigration and drive Chinese workers from the labor market. Rooted in the Jacksonian tradition, both the Klan movement and the anti-Chinese crusade denounced tyrannical elites while focusing most of their energy on racist pogroms.

The North began the Civil War simply trying to preserve the Union—and, as Frederick Douglass observed, to keep slavery in it.[1] Yet, by the end, the war had become a crusade to abolish slavery. Military necessity pushed Lincoln's government to take this radical course. In 1863 the government enacted the Emancipation Proclamation—which applied only to those slaves in Confederate-controlled areas, but committed the U.S. government to abolition—and began to recruit Black soldiers. The growing mass struggle of southern Blacks influenced this shift, as they resisted overseers, proclaimed their support for Lincoln, and escaped to the Union armies. The Emancipation Proclamation strengthened their resistance. In what W. E. B. Du Bois rightly termed a general strike, hundreds of thousands of enslaved workers left the plantations, bringing whole sections of the Confederate economy to a standstill, and transferred their labor power to the Union armies, both as workers and as soldiers. Two hundred thousand black soldiers and sailors played a key role in defeating the Confederacy. Thousands of poor Whites from the upland South, hostile to the rich planters, also resisted the Confederacy, many of them with guns.[2]

Pressure for the complete abolition of slavery came from Christian activists, many of whom saw the Civil War struggle in apocalyptic and millennial terms. The lyrics to "The Battle Hymn of the Republic" were not simply empty metaphors for those who literally expected their eyes to see the glorious day of the coming of their Lord. There were even published tracts claiming the end-times struggle would culminate in the new millennium, slated for 1866; but, while most Christians dismissed these claims as excessive, many still saw the struggle against slavery in cosmic terms that they had no trouble translating into political pressure.[3]

Pro-Confederate sentiment in the North influenced the U.S. government's decision to seek Black support. New York City was a major center of rebel sympathy. On the eve of the Civil War, a bloc of New York merchants advocated secession for their city so that it could continue to trade with the South. Mayor Fernando Wood publicly endorsed the proposal. During the war, a steady campaign of proslavery and White supremacist activism culminated in New York City's "Draft Riot" of July 1863, which was spearheaded by working-class Irish Americans, and described by Eric Foner as "the largest civil insurrection in American history apart from the South's rebellion itself." It was also one of the most brutal: scores, perhaps hundreds, of Black people were slaughtered in the streets and in their homes. The pogromists raised the Confederate flag only ten days after the Battle of Gettysburg, which capped a Confederate invasion of neighboring Pennsylvania.[4]

The mix of grievances that sparked the Draft Riot—a conscription law that discriminated against the poor and increased federal power, the employment of Black workers in "White" occupations, the wealth of the city's Republican elite, and the abolitionist Emancipation Proclamation—was classically Jacksonian. But as an act of irregular, terrorist warfare on an unprecedented scale, which picked up where the regular Confederate armies left off, the Draft Riots in the North also foreshadowed the KKK's new form of racist violence that would soon spread across the South.

Slavery had been at the heart of White supremacy in North America for two centuries. The distinction between free labor and slave labor had helped keep lower-class Whites loyal to the social and economic system. Thus, the abolition of slavery, coupled with a mass rising by Black people, not only weakened the southern planter class as never before but also called into question the whole racial order—and presented the possibility of an alliance between Black and White workers against powerful elites. For a fragile moment, racism against Blacks was widely discredited by its association with the secessionist cause, that is, with treason against the United States. Between 1867 and 1877, in the period of Radical Reconstruction in the former Confederacy, a society free of racial oppression seemed possible.[5]

For a time, at least, the Republican Party abandoned its original self-conception as "the white man's party." Under Republican leadership, the United States adopted the Fourteenth Amendment to the Constitution, enacted in 1868, which proclaimed a nonracial definition of citizenship and equality before the law, and the Fifteenth Amendment, enacted in 1870, which extended voting rights to male citizens of color. Although these and related measures did not establish even formal equality for everyone (in particular, they left women's legal subordination intact), they did significantly expand the scope of "inalienable rights" under the official U.S. creed. The new concept of equality not only bolstered dramatic changes in the South but also spurred the abolition of many, though not all, racially discriminatory laws in the North.[6]

But the campaign against racial oppression proved only temporary. Many Whites had come to support abolitionism because of its identification with the Union cause, but this shift toward antiracist consciousness was tentative, inconsistent, and unstable.[7] In succeeding decades a series of counteroffensives reconstituted racial ideology and racial oppression on a new basis. These counteroffensives included the two movements examined in this chapter as well as a new wave of conquest against American Indians in the West.

Radical Reconstruction's driving energy in the South came from the former slaves and free Blacks who organized Union Leagues, established schools, churches, and community groups, occupied land, formed labor unions, conducted strikes, and attempted to defend their new freedom with weapons. As Du Bois argued in his pioneering study of Reconstruction, the end of slavery represented "the greatest revolution in labor that had happened in America for a hundred years," and southern Blacks' attack on racial oppression offered White workers a radical counterexample of what a labor movement could and should be.[8] A limited but important group of southern Whites, most of them from the lower classes, broke ranks and joined southern Blacks in their struggle for political equality.

But northern Republican leaders, tied to big business and deeply ambivalent about the Black political mobilization they had helped unleash, largely determined the scope of Reconstruction. Radical Republicans such as Thaddeus Stevens and Charles Sumner advocated civic equality for Black people as a matter of principle. But a majority of the party's leaders supported Radical Reconstruction only as a tactical maneuver, a means to consolidate their national control and implement their program of industrial development. Black electoral support in the South offered them an important counterweight to a powerful Democratic opposition that included President Andrew Johnson, Lincoln's successor, as well as powerful northern business interests that wanted quick reconciliation with the South.[9] At the same time, the bulk of the Republican business leadership feared Black people in motion as a threat to its own power, which was tied to White supremacy, private property, and class privilege.

Thus, Republican leaders sought to channel and control the Black uprising. Reversing President Johnson's initial policy of restoring Whites-only politics in the southern states, the Republican-controlled Congress established Radical Reconstruction governments that were elected by all adult males, with Black elected officials playing a significant role for the first time in U.S. history. These governments, supported by a coalition of Blacks and Whites, passed a series of reform measures, such as free public education, medical and legal services for the poor, expanded property and divorce rights for women, improved public works, protections for labor, and more progressive tax structures. While many inequities persisted, southern Blacks temporarily held a degree of political power along with their White allies.

But to make Reconstruction reforms a lasting reality required economic and military power, and here Congress blocked the way. Seizing the big plantations and redistributing them to poor Blacks and Whites alike was necessary to free Blacks from economic servitude and to break the hold of White solidarity that gave the planter class its mass base. But most Republican leaders rejected such an attack on property relations. Instead, they sent Union troops to force tens of thousands of Black people off the land. To combat rising White supremacist violence required a strong military presence. But Black Army units were demobilized and most federal troops withdrawn from the South in 1866, and in most cases state militias proved completely inadequate to defend the Reconstruction governments. Thus, the Republican leadership's constraints on Reconstruction set it up for bloody defeat.

In the West, the Republican Party continued the Jacksonian program of anti-Indian genocide. In the Sand Creek Massacre of 1864, for example, militia units of the Republican-dominated Colorado Territory killed and mutilated over 100 peaceful Cheyennes, who were encamped under promises of safety. General William T. Sherman embodied the Republicans' dual stance on race. In 1864–1865 he led the army that broke the back of the Confederacy in Georgia, and he authorized a radical, if temporary, program of land grants for Blacks along the Georgia and Carolina coasts. Yet, in 1866, directing military forces in the West, he advised General Ulysses S. Grant, "We must act with vindictive earnestness against the Sioux, even to their extermination, men, women and children." Borrowing from the scorched-earth tactics he had used in Georgia, Sherman supervised annihilation of the bison (buffalo), which provided the economic basis for the Plains Indians' survival. After 1866, Black regiments of the U.S. Army were not stationed in the South to defend Reconstruction governments, but instead were in the West to fight Indian nations. Though unwilling to countenance large-scale land redistribution in the South, the Republican Congress made newly conquered western territory cheaply available to settlers under the Homestead Act of 1862, and awarded 100 million acres of western land to railroad companies, free of charge.[10]

While the South stagnated economically during Reconstruction, railroads spearheaded economic development in the North and West. The railroads laid down 30,000 miles of track between 1865 and 1873, stimulating the growth of coal, iron, and machine industries, and establishing a national market that spanned the continent. Railroad companies spurred on the army as it stripped western American Indians of their lands and forced them onto reservations. In the West, White farmers soon brought vast new areas into cultivation, while lumber and mining companies expanded operations, all linked by rail to urban markets. Railroads, increasingly concentrated, were by far the largest and most powerful business sector. They and other big companies routinely used bribery to manipulate government officials of both major parties. In return, they received massive public subsidies. By the late nineteenth century, for example, federal, state, and local grants had enabled the railroads to acquire almost one-tenth of all land in the United States. Despite such government favors, the corporation, which laissez-faire Jacksonians had criticized as a form of special privilege, was now heralded as the embodiment of free enterprise.[11]

Industrialization brought industrial class conflict. More and more, wage laborers replaced independent artisans. High unemployment, low wages, and brutal conditions fueled a new militancy. Many workers formed unions during the economic boom of 1866–1873, and in 1866 some of them united to form the National Labor Union (NLU), the first national labor federation, which lasted until 1872. The NLU was followed by the Knights of Labor, founded in 1869, the American Federation of Labor (AFL), founded in the 1880s, and many independent unions. The first significant Marxist organizations in the United States also developed during the Reconstruction period, including the Workingmen's Party of the United States (later renamed the Socialist Labor Party), which had about 2,500 members in 1876.[12]

THE FIRST KU KLUX KLAN

The mass activism of Black people and the limited but real gains they achieved through Reconstruction provoked a massive racist counterattack.[13] Across the South, White men used murder, torture, rape, beating, and arson to drive Black people back into subjugation and to restore White rule and planter control through the Democratic Party. The Ku Klux Klan is only the most notorious organization in this terrorist wave; similar groups operated under such names as the Knights of the White Camelia, the Red Shirts, the Southern Cross, and the White League. The Klan formed in late

1865 or early 1866 in Pulaski, Tennessee. By 1868, it had branches in every southern state. Also known as the Invisible Empire, the KKK was a secret society whose members typically wore hoods and launched their terrorist raids at night. The Klan developed an elaborate hierarchy on paper, but in practice it functioned in a completely decentralized manner. It included White men from all social classes: planters, merchants, professionals, small farmers, artisans, and poor Whites.

The Klan targeted Black men and women who exercised leadership, voted Republican, taught school, possessed firearms, sought economic independence from Whites, or otherwise refused to be subservient. Also targeted were "carpetbaggers" (northern Whites living in the South, many of them Union Army veterans) and especially "scalawags" (southern Whites who supported Black political rights). Although racist terror organizations operated throughout the South, the Klan itself was active primarily in the upland and piedmont areas of the Deep South and in the border states, where Blacks were less concentrated and less able to defend themselves. The full extent of Klan violence is not recorded; however, Philip S. Foner estimated that over 1,500 Black people were murdered in 1868–1871 in Georgia alone.[14]

Before emancipation, slaveowners' desire to protect their property had, to a degree, limited White violence against Black people. The end of slavery removed this constraint. At the same time, violence took on new importance for the racial caste system. As Martha Hodes has noted, now that the legal division between slavery and freedom was gone, White supremacists had to find new ways to draw the line between White and Black. One way was to establish "stricter racial definitions, which would come to fruition in the late nineteenth century with a codified 'one-drop rule,'" under which a person was considered Black if he or she had any trace of African ancestry. Another way to strengthen the color line was to intensify violent restrictions on Blacks in the political, economic, and social spheres.[15]

White supremacists were especially anxious to restrict Black men—not only because of their new electoral power and moves toward economic independence but because of their potential threat to White men's sexual control over White women. Under slavery, as Hodes has argued, "voting had connoted manhood and citizenship, which in turn had represented patriarchal power. That power entailed control by white men over black men and women, as well as over white women." During Reconstruction, White supremacists claimed that allowing Black men to vote would lead to social integration, and this would inevitably give Black men sexual access to White women.[16] In the slave South, contrary to myth, Whites had often tolerated sex between White women and Black men. After the Civil War, however, the White South became increasingly concerned to prevent and punish such unions. By the 1890s the myth of the Black rapist had become the overarching rationale for lynching thousands of Black people—including many Black women and men who were not even accused of sexual assault.[17]

The Ku Klux Klan often portrayed its mission as defense against rape—the metaphorical rape of the South by Reconstruction governments as well as Black men's physical rape of White women. Klansmen helped cement the unwritten rule by which a Black man could be killed for having any personal contact with a White woman. Sometimes they castrated Black men instead of killing them. White women, especially if they were poor, could also be raped, beaten, or killed for sexual contact with Black men. At the same time, it was standard practice for Klan nightriders to rape and sexually abuse Black women. As Kathleen M. Blee notes, "The Klan avowed horror of miscegenation but practiced it, as did antebellum white plantation masters, as a tactic of terror." Klansmen also frequently used sexual torture against scalawags, both male and female, as special punishment for traitors to the South.[18]

Like other repressive populist movements we have examined, the KKK represented a population that saw its position threatened from below and above—in this case, by Black "insubordination" from below and northern military occupation from above. Unable to comprehend Black people as autonomous human beings acting in their own interests, White supremacists blamed plots by Yankee Republicans for fomenting Black political assertiveness. Freed of this foreign interference, southern Blacks would supposedly become docile and contented once again, as they had been under slavery. Philadelph Van Trump, Democratic Senator from Ohio and a leading defender of the Klan, described the carpetbagger as a "demon of discord and anarchy; his infernal schemes and intrigues with the negroes have thrown a whole people into utter and hopeless despair." He portrayed the Klan as a self-defense organization with a mission comparable to that of Robin Hood.[19]

As a mass-based paramilitary network for enforcing racial oppression, the Reconstruction-era Klan was rooted in the antebellum slave patrols and other organs through which rank-and-file White men aided the elite in keeping down people of color. In certain respects, however, the Klan represented a new kind of repressive populist politics. First, unlike the slave patrols or the prewar Jacksonians, the Klan was not simply defending or intensifying the racial status quo. Rather, it was reacting to a large, organized, sustained movement for Black liberation that had won some important reforms and a measure of political power. In our view, this backlash character stamped the Reconstruction-era Klan movement as the United States' first significant *right-wing* populist movement. To take the point a step further, the Klan was not simply an oppositional pressure group but rather an extralegal counterrevolutionary force literally at war with the established government. In the United States no other significant right-wing movement would adopt this insurgent strategy until sections of the neonazi movement did so in the 1980s.

The Klan, and the wider movement to "redeem" the South, also introduced a new ideological theme into U.S. politics. This was the theme of collective rebirth after a nearly fatal crisis—what Roger Griffin has labeled a myth of "palingenesis," from the Greek word meaning rebirth. In the twentieth century, as Griffin has emphasized, palingenesis has been central to the ideology of fascism, whose "mobilizing vision is that of *the national community rising phoenix-like after a period of encroaching decadence which all but destroyed it.*"[20] (This also replicates a prophetic theme from apocalyptic Christian narratives of the final battle between good and evil.) In the United States up until 1860, no part of the White racial caste had experienced a crisis such as Griffin describes. But the reimposition of racial oppression in the South, after total military defeat and the "barbarism" of Radical Reconstruction, seemed to White supremacists a phoenixlike rebirth indeed. Since Reconstruction, this palingenetic myth has provided White supremacists a model for interpreting and addressing other crises in the racial order. That is part of the reason the Ku Klux Klan, unlike many other racist organizations of the nineteenth century, has been revived again and again. And in the twentieth century the Klan myth of collective rebirth helped prepare the ground for the spread of fascist doctrines.

Nathan Bedford Forrest, former Confederate general and the Ku Klux Klan's Grand Wizard, officially disbanded the Invisible Empire in 1869, claiming that its original purposes had been "perverted." This decree had little effect on local Klan chapters, but it absolved Forrest's headquarters of responsibility for a movement it could not control. Some Republicans, Black and White, successfully fought back against the Klan.[21] In a few states Republican governors used martial law to curtail Klan violence, though Democrats exploited such moves to portray themselves as the upholders of liberty. In 1870 and 1871, Congress passed a series of Enforcement Acts that dramatically expanded federal power to protect citizens' rights, even to the point of military intervention. Applied in some states, such as in South Carolina, these acts helped eradicate the Klan itself by about 1872. But such federal intervention was sporadic, and racist terror continued under other names. In many areas, bands of White men roamed the streets threatening and killing Blacks who tried to vote. Using such tactics, racist Whites overthrew one Republican state government after another. In the spring of 1877, the last two southern Republican governments, in Louisiana and South Carolina, fell when federal troops were withdrawn to barracks as part of an agreement that gave Republican candidate Rutherford B. Hayes the U.S. presidency in a disputed election. Reconstruction was over.

White supremacist "redemption" of the South did not fully wipe out the economic, social, and political gains that Black people had made. It required a second racist counteroffensive in the 1890s to impose "Jim Crow" legal segregation and fully exclude Black men from voting and holding office. But the defeat of Radical Reconstruction was a crucial turning point, when antiracist politics was smashed and White loyalty recemented. Northern business forces, their national industrialization program securely under way, turned away from racial equality and ceded control of the South to the White planters. Klan-type violence was no longer a form of insurgency but rather a tool for defending the status quo.

WHITE LABOR AND THE ANTI-CHINESE CRUSADE

In keeping with its Jacksonian heritage, most of the White labor movement opposed Radical Reconstruction. Out of some 230 White labor newspapers formed between 1863 and 1873, only one, the *Boston Daily Evening Voice*, supported political and economic equality for Black people.[22] Nearly all of the unions affiliated with the National Labor Union excluded Black workers from membership; many conducted strikes to protest the hiring of Blacks. White labor leaders praised President Johnson as a friend of labor and denounced Radical Reconstruction as a stratagem by Republican agents of Wall Street. As David Roediger notes, few White workers "appreciated how much African-Americans, who had by far the most experience of any Americans with regimenting systems of mass labor and of successful resistance to them, had to teach white labor."[23]

The founding of the National Colored Labor Union (NCLU) in 1869, representing Black workers in a wide range of industries and in twenty-one states, North and South, forced White labor to modify its policy as a defensive measure. Thus, the NLU welcomed a small group of NCLU delegates to its 1869 and 1870 conventions and urged "our colored fellow members to form organizations in all legitimate ways." But at the same time, the NLU, ignoring the life-and-death struggle taking place in the South, called on Black workers to abandon the Republican Party and to accept the racist exclusionism of White union locals. After the 1870 convention, Black workers withdrew from the NLU.[24]

As Du Bois argued, White labor's stance had profound implications for working-class organizing in the United States. "The South, after the war, presented the greatest opportunity for a real national labor movement which the nation ever saw or is likely to see for many decades." Yet, with few exceptions, White labor failed "to see in black slavery and Reconstruction, the kernel and meaning of the labor movement in the United States." Most White workers turned their backs on this opportunity not simply because of indoctrination by elites but because racial oppression offered even the poorest of Whites concrete and immediate social privileges over Black people, from better schools to better police treatment to "public deference and titles of courtesy."[25]

Failure to support Reconstruction directly contributed to a long series of strategic defeats for White labor, beginning with the Great Railroad

Strike of 1877. In July of that year, only a few months after the end of Reconstruction, railroad workers and strike supporters shut down virtually all freight trains outside of New England and the South. The strike was violently suppressed by a combination of local troops, private "citizen militias," and federal soldiers—including units recently withdrawn from their role in defending southern Reconstruction governments.[26] Like the NLU leadership a few years before, some White participants in the uprising expressed tentative solidarity with workers of color. In St. Louis, where a general strike controlled the city for several days, White workers initially welcomed Blacks at demonstrations and even as members of the strike executive committee before shifting toward a more familiar Whites-only policy. In San Francisco, however, White workers quickly vented their hatred of the Central Pacific Railroad by murdering Chinese and torching their buildings.[27]

The 1877 crackdown opened a sixty-year period of bloody antilabor repression in which the forces of big business killed hundreds and injured thousands of union activists. Hired guards and middle-class vigilantes had virtual carte blanche to intimidate or shoot strikers; they were backed up by local police, state militias, and the U.S. Army. Courts routinely convicted labor organizers on vague conspiracy charges and began to issue preemptive injunctions barring union activity. Big corporations dominated or even owned many towns across the country, exercising dictatorial power over the workers who lived there.[28] With the help of public officials, business leaders used laissez-faire doctrine to block virtually all moves toward government regulation as attacks on freedom.

The red scare became a standard antilabor tactic, as police agencies and the procorporate press blamed strike activity on foreign radicals supposedly manipulating gullible American workers. Such scapegoating reached a peak with the 1886 Haymarket Affair, when a bomb killed six Chicago police officers shortly after a nationwide strike to demand the eight-hour day. The press responded with a frenzy of hate mongering, as police conducted brutal raids and arrested thousands of workers. Eight anarchists, seven of them immigrants, were convicted of the crime simply because of their political views. Four of them were hanged.[29]

In this climate of growing repression, White labor organizations did not always exclude Black workers as they had before the Civil War. Even after Reconstruction's defeat, Black workers retained more mobility than they had as slaves, could be used to defeat White-only strikes, and had demonstrated their readiness to organize unions with or without White allies. Thus, White unions tended to make pragmatic decisions, based on immediate self-interest, about whether or not to admit Black workers. Although it brought some important moments of White–Black solidarity, this approach rarely challenged White supremacy itself or confronted the specific forms of oppression Black people faced.[30]

The Knights of Labor pursued such a pragmatic policy. They were a broad organization of skilled and unskilled workers that briefly grew to 700,000 members in the mid-1880s, including over 60,000 Black workers. Between one-third and one-half of the Knights' southern membership was Black. The organization fostered interracial cooperation in numerous strikes and demonstrations, but kept most Black members in segregated locals and helped bar them from skilled trades. During the 1890s, as their organization declined and southern racist terror intensified, the Knights became openly anti-Black; by 1894 they called for deporting all Black people to Africa.[31]

A related example was the Populist movement of the 1880s and 1890s. The Populists included hundreds of thousands of southern and western farmers, White and Black, who challenged the growing economic pressure from merchants, railroad freight companies, and banks. The People's, or Populist, Party received one million votes in the 1892 presidential contest while electing three governors and several members of Congress. Black support was crucial to the movement in the South, but with few exceptions the unity White Populists sought was self-centered and based on the superficial claim that White and Black farmers shared the same oppression. Yet the specter of Populist White–Black cooperation, whether opportunistic or principled, helped spur a renewed racist backlash across the South in the 1890s. Lynch mobs killed hundreds as new state constitutions took the vote away from Blacks, and from many poor Whites as well. At the national level, the Populists were destroyed in 1896 by being lured into a disastrous electoral alliance with the Democrats.[32]

Embodying the transition between the preindustrial and industrial eras, both the Knights of Labor and the Populists were rooted in Jacksonian producer ideology but moved beyond it in certain ways. The Knights had a heterogeneous organization, including "local and national bodies of skilled craftsmen, industrial unions, cooperatives, [and] mixed assemblies of wage earners, farmers, professionals, and small proprietors."[33] Like the NLU before them, both the Knights and the Populists upheld the Jacksonian focus on "parasitic" bankers and placed great emphasis on currency reform. (Like a growing number of their contemporaries, some Populists equated the money power with Jews, though this was marginal to the movement's political focus.)[34] But the Knights also engaged in bitter struggles against railroad and industrial capitalists, while the Populists demanded nationalization of the railroads as part of their thoroughly un-Jacksonian call for government intervention to break up concentrated economic power. Both the Knights and the Populists also took limited but important steps to organize women and advocate women's rights.[35]

In one respect, however, the Knights and all White-led labor organizations of the post-Civil War decades, as well as the Populists, solidly upheld the Jacksonian tradition: they all supported racist exclusion of Chinese immigrants. The Chinese exclusion crusade paralleled and reinforced the attack on Reconstruction—thus, the National Colored Labor Union was the only union of the period to welcome Chinese workers.[36] The anti-Chinese crusade gained support throughout the country, but it was centered in the West, and especially in California.[37]

By the time of Reconstruction, California already had a complex history of racial oppression. Before U.S. annexation in 1848, Mexican ranchers of mixed Spanish, Indian, and African descent had ruled over the native California Indians and lower-caste Mexicans. Beginning with the gold rush of 1849, tens of thousands of European American men poured into the new territory, terrorizing Mexicans and American Indians alike and seizing control of the land.[38] "Free-Soil" provisions of the 1849 state constitution barred Black people from California. Chinese immigrants, who also came to California seeking gold, became a highly exploited, low-paid labor force. Chinese workers built the Sierra Nevada section of the transcontinental railroad, which was completed in 1869 at the cost of thousands of lives. By the 1870s, Chinese men constituted 20–25 percent of California's wage workers and were heavily represented in railroad construction, cigar, shoe, and textile manufacturing, farming, fishing, and service work. Relatively few Chinese women immigrated; most of them were brought to the United States as sexual slaves for the use of Chinese and White men.[39]

Chinese immigrants, regarded as "unassimilable aliens" by Whites, faced many forms of legal discrimination. In particular, they were barred from U.S. citizenship. Even after 1870, when Congress amended the Naturalization Law to allow people of African descent as well as Whites to become naturalized citizens, Asians and other people were still excluded. As early as the 1850s, White workers began forcing Chinese out of jobs and calling for a ban on Chinese immigration. Some small manufacturers who were struggling to compete with the big companies that employed low-paid Chinese workers supported these attacks.[40]

Hatred of the "Heathen Chinee" provided an important form of cultural unity for the many European Americans and European immigrants that came together as White people on the West Coast. Whites sometimes equated the Chinese with Blacks as "nagurs"; sometimes with American Indians as "new barbarians." But, unlike Blacks and American Indians, the Chinese were also stereotyped as crafty schemers who possessed uncanny, almost magical, powers and as vampires or parasites. Henry George, a leading theoretician of Chinese exclusion, called them "long-tailed barbarians, who have no interest in this country, and whose earnings do not add to its wealth." When a bubonic plague scare in San Francisco led to the quarantining of Chinatown in 1900, a labor newspaper wrote, "The almond-eyed Mongolian is watching for his opportunity, waiting to assassinate you and your children with one of his many maladies."[41]

Sexual stereotyping was a major preoccupation for Whites. Henry George wrote that the Chinese "practice all the unnameable vices of the

East." Whites stereotyped Chinese men as effeminate, for example, in the 1902 pamphlet *Meat vs. Rice: American Manhood vs. Asiatic Coolieism: Which Shall Survive?* by Sam Gompers (president of the American Federation of Labor) and Herman Guttstadt. In the disproportionately male frontier society of the West, Chinese men were often relegated to "women's" work—laundry, food service, and domestic work. At the same time, in a contradictory way, they were regarded as sexual predators who lured or forced innocent White girls into prostitution. White writers equated Chinese women with prostitutes and claimed they were "debauched" and not "decent." Colville's *San Francisco Gazeteer* of 1856 described Chinese women as "the most degraded and beastly of all human creatures."[42]

In the years after the Civil War and Black emancipation, the Chinese figured in debates about what the country's new racial order should look like. Republicans mingled abolitionist egalitarianism with Whiggish racial paternalism. In 1867 George C. Gorham, soon to be the nominee for California governor from the Union Party, a Civil War coalition of Republicans and prowar Democrats, voiced the egalitarian sentiment that was then at a high point:

> The same God created both Europeans and Asiatics. No man of whatever race has any better right to labor, and receive his hire therefor, than has any other man. . . . I am as emphatically opposed to all attempts to deny the Chinese the right to labor for pay, as I am to the restoration of African slavery whereby black men were compelled to labor without pay.[43]

Gorham was a lobbyist for the Central Pacific Railroad, one of the largest employers of Chinese workers in the state. A less high-minded rationale for welcoming Chinese labor, propounded by Central Pacific Director Charles Crocker, among others, called for establishing the Chinese as a permanent supply of cheap labor on a large scale, whose temporary members would be continually replaced by new arrivals. The supposedly obedient Chinese would discourage labor organizing and strikes by Whites. At the same time, their presence would raise White workers into supervisory roles such as foremen, managers, and even capitalists. One writer argued that Chinese house servants would elevate White women by relieving them of household toil.[44]

True to the Jacksonian tradition of hard racism, Democrats advocated total exclusion. Like southern opponents of Reconstruction, California Democrats after the Civil War identified themselves with a White populace threatened by elites above and people of color below. Indeed, the Democrats directly tied the anti-Chinese theme to their attacks on Radical Reconstruction. With explicit racism against Blacks considered suspect because of its association with secession, hatred of Chinese helped relegitimize overt White supremacy.[45] The Democrats swept the 1867 elections in California, contributing to the party's dramatic resurgence across the North and West. During the campaign that year, the Democrats' San Francisco *Examiner* wrote of "the self-styled Union or Mongrel party":

> Take away the Chinese, negro-suffrage, and negro-brotherhood plank from their platform, and they become simply a plunder-league, banded together to rob the Government and use its powers for the aggrandizement of special interests and favored classes. . . . The Democracy are . . . for a white man's government, constitutionally administered, against a great Mongrel military despotism, upheld by a union of the purse and the sword, and sought to be perpetuated through negro and Chinese votes.[46]

In this respect, anti-Chinese racism in the West was interconnected with Ku Klux Klan racism in the South. But, while the Klan represented an alliance of White men from all classes led by rich planters, the anti-Chinese campaign was predominantly a working-class movement. In the late 1870s, the crusade gave rise briefly to the Workingmen's Party of California (not to be confused with the national Workingmen's Party). The California Workingmen called for progressive taxation, large-scale welfare programs for the needy, destruction of the "land monopoly," and expulsion of "cheap Chinese labor as soon as possible and by all means in our power." They elected over one-third of the delegates to the 1878 constitutional convention against a combined slate of Republicans and Democrats. In California and many other areas of the West, anti-Chinese racism became the major organizing tool for building a White labor movement. The union label, for example, was invented as a certificate on cigars, indicating that they had been made by White workers, as part of a campaign to force Chinese out of the cigarmaking industry. The campaign included a successful effort to break a strike by Chinese cigarmakers, belying the frequent claim that Chinese workers were servile while White workers stood up to employers.[47]

The White labor movement across the country supported the campaign to bar Chinese from immigration and the job market. From its inception in the 1880s, the American Federation of Labor, dominated by "craft" unions representing only skilled workers and composed overwhelmingly of White men, championed Chinese exclusion. Samuel Gompers, longtime AFL president, rose to prominence through the anti-Chinese Cigar Makers' International Union. However, even labor organizations considered more progressive than the AFL supported anti-Chinese measures. The Knights of Labor barred Chinese from its ranks; in 1885–1886, workers affiliated with the Knights conducted numerous physical attacks on Chinese, including a massacre of twenty-eight Chinese miners in Rock Springs, Wyoming Territory. The Socialist Labor and Populist parties endorsed Chinese exclusion. The American Railway Union of the early 1890s, headed by future Socialist Party presidential candidate Eugene Debs, was a Whites-only organization that called for an immediate ban on immigration by "Chinese and similar classes."[48]

By 1876, both the Democrats and Republicans had anti-Chinese clauses in their national platforms. In 1882, Congress passed the Chinese Exclusion Act, which barred Chinese laborers from immigrating and was extended to all Chinese two years later. Widespread pogroms and expulsions followed in 1885–1886, forcing Chinese to flee communities up and down the West Coast. Only San Francisco's Chinatown was too well defended for the mobs to attack.[49] Elsewhere, however, periodic anti-Chinese violence continued for years. Chinese exclusion set a pattern that was soon repeated with other Asian immigrants. Between 1882 and 1934, Japanese, Koreans, Indians, and Filipinos were all brought in as low-paid workers, then scapegoated and terrorized, and eventually barred from further immigration. A total ban on immigration from mainland Asia remained in effect from 1924 until 1943, and significant numbers of Asian immigrants were not permitted until 1965.[50]

Anti-Chinese racism also helped lay the groundwork for the violent nativism that was just beginning to target eastern and southern European immigrants in the 1880s and that culminated in the immigration restriction law of 1924. The *Los Angeles Times* declared in 1893:

> If we can keep out the Chinese, there is no reason why we cannot exclude the lower classes of Poles, Hungarians, Italians and some other European nations, which people possess most of the vices of the Chinese and few of their good qualities, besides having a leaning towards bloodshed and anarchy which is peculiarly their own.[51]

As discussed later, in Chapter 5, this viewpoint gradually gained mass support with the help of new "scientific" theories proclaiming the racial superiority of northern and western Europeans.

CONCLUSION

The Ku Klux Klan and the anti-Chinese crusade spearheaded efforts to strengthen the U.S. system of racial oppression after the Civil War, a critical juncture when White dominance was being widely challenged. Building on the Jacksonian tradition of producerist populism, these movements used large-scale terrorism and scapegoating to crush Black people's bid for political equality and to stop Chinese people from immigrating or working in most jobs. Both efforts reinforced the established social hierarchy, yet both successfully challenged elite power. The multiclass Klan forced northern Republican capitalists, the strongest faction of the elite, to change their plans for the South and helped southern planters, a weaker elite faction, to win back some of the power they had lost in the Civil War. The anti-Chinese crusade, based overwhelmingly among White workers, cut big business off from an important source of cheap labor. These movements refute claims that racist violence and bigotry are simply imposed on society from above. White workers and farmers had the power to defy elite wishes; yet, most of them failed to exercise this power in genuinely radical fashion—by joining with workers of color to attack White supremacy in its moment of vulnerability.

4

BARBARIANS
AND PLUNDER LEAGUES

Theodore Roosevelt and the Progressives

The post-Civil War movements we considered in the previous chapter, the Ku Klux Klan and the anti-Chinese crusade, were both based outside the Northeast, hostile toward northern big business and the Republican Party, and more or less oriented toward the Democrats. Now we will shift our focus in the other direction. During the so-called Progressive Era of roughly 1900–1916, the Republican Party—northeastern-centered and widely identified with the northern capitalist elite—became the primary forum for a new type of authoritarian mass politics based in the urban middle class. Like repressive populism, this initiative sought to unify and mobilize "the people" and combined economic and political reforms with strident White and male supremacy, cultural conformism, and hatred of the Left. In place of antielitism, however, its rallying mission was an ominous new concept of national duty based on warnings of spiritual and physical decline. The focal point and leader of this movement was Theodore Roosevelt.

The emergence of the United States as a modern industrial society brought major economic, demographic, and cultural upheavals that shaped political life. Industry replaced railroads as the business community's driving force, as manufacturing grew rapidly while railroads became less profitable after the 1890s. An unprecedented wave of mergers between 1897 and 1905 contributed to the rise of big industrial companies. By 1904, 318 firms controlled 40 percent of all U.S. manufacturing.[1] Banks increased their investments in industry and helped to organize many corporate mergers. In 1901 the banker J. P. Morgan assembled the U.S. Steel Corporation, the first billion-dollar corporation, which controlled 60 percent of the nation's iron and steel production. Through U.S. Steel and myriad other holdings in industry, finance, utilities, mining, and railroads, the House of Morgan controlled the largest economic empire the United States had ever seen. Working on a scale almost as large, the Rockefeller interests branched out from the enormous Standard Oil Company to control the National City Bank and several other important New York banks.[2]

Despite the growth of corporate empires, as Gabriel Kolko points out, the U.S. economy remained chaotic, irrational, and unpredictable. Explosive growth brought instability and wide swings between prosperity and depression. Mergers did not stop competition, and even huge firms such as U.S. Steel, Standard Oil, International Harvester, and AT&T saw their market shares drop significantly in the 1900s. Eastern financiers faced growing rivalry from banks further west. In a halting and haphazard way, various businesses began to favor government action to bring more order and control to the economy.[3]

Economic growth also pushed big business to seek raw materials, markets, and investment opportunities overseas, especially in Latin America and Asia. Having conquered the last independent American Indian nations, the United States continued its expansion westward and southward. During the late nineteenth century, the United States seized a series of Pacific Islands—including Hawaii, which was annexed in 1898—to serve as naval refueling stations and plantation colonies. Also in 1898, the United States defeated Spain in a brief war and annexed Puerto Rico, Guam, and the Philippines while dominating a newly independent Cuba. In 1900, U.S. troops joined a pan-European force to suppress the Boxer Rebellion in China, whose markets the United States coveted.

Industrialization enormously increased the amount of goods produced, yet widened the gap between rich and poor. It uprooted millions of people from their former ways of life as farmers, artisans, and shopkeepers, and transformed them into industrial workers, white-collar workers, and professionals. It brought large-scale factory production and large-scale bureaucratic organization, and dramatically enlarged cities.

Industrialization also affected the country's ethnic hierarchy. Native-born Whites and so-called old immigrants from Germany, Britain, Ireland, and Scandinavia dominated the skilled trades. Most Blacks, American Indians, Mexicans, and Asians were forcibly restricted to agriculture, service work, and in some cases mining—not until World War I would they be admitted to factory work in significant numbers. "Neither the family farms of the Midwest nor the plantations of the South," writes George Fredrickson, " . . . had the capacity to generate the kind of massive labor surplus needed for rapid industrial growth."[4] So-called new immigrants from southern and eastern Europe—Slavs, Italians, Jews, Hungarians, and others—supplied many of the new workers needed for low-skilled jobs in factories and mines. The wave of new immigrants began in the 1880s, surpassed the continuing influx of old immigrants by 1896, and remained high until 1914, when it was interrupted by the beginning of World War I in Europe. New immigrants formed the core of the expanding industrial workforce.

Southern and eastern Europeans faced systematic economic and social

discrimination and periodic violence. Increasingly, they were labeled as racially inferior. The new immigrants' racial status was not firmly established,
and eventually they would be integrated into the White racial caste. But for
several decades southern and eastern Europeans formed an ambiguous middle stratum of the racial order, between the native-born Whites and old European immigrants above them, and the American Indians, Blacks, Asians,
and Mexicans below. The latter groups still bore the main burden of White
supremacist oppression: continued plundering and forcible breakup of com-
munally owned Native lands, violent anti-Asian campaigns on the West
Coast, and lynch law against Black people in the South and Mexican people
in the Southwest. In this murderous period, the most influential Black
leader was Booker T. Washington, head of the Tuskegee Institute, who advocated cautious "self help" and accommodation to White supremacy.
More radical Black leaders, such as Ida B. Wells and W. E. B. Du Bois,
worked for social and political equality.

Industrial class conflict helped make socialism an important force in
U.S. politics for the first time. The Socialist Party was formed in 1901. At
its peak before World War I, the party included 100,000 members, elected
two members of Congress and hundreds of state and local officials, and published scores of newspapers around the country. Eugene Debs, Socialist
Party presidential candidate, received 900,000 votes in 1912, about 6 percent of the total. The party brought together people of various ideological
persuasions: former Populists in the Southwest, German Marxists in Milwaukee, Christian socialists, militant labor activists, and others.

Some Socialists, such as Victor Berger and Morris Hillquit, regarded
old-stock White male craftsmen as the "real American workers." They
aligned themselves with the elitist American Federation of Labor, which
mostly excluded women, workers of color, and new immigrants. Radical Socialists such as Debs and Bill Haywood advocated the organization of all
workers, with no exclusion by skill level, race, nationality, or sex. This position often ignored the specific realities of racial, ethnic, and gender oppression, but posed a fundamental challenge to the AFL. The Socialist Party's
left wing overlapped with the Industrial Workers of the World (IWW),
founded in 1905. The IWW ("Wobblies") organized tens of thousands of
the most exploited workers, from migrant laborers in the West to new-immigrant factory women in the East. The IWW's militant actions were guided
by anarcho-syndicalism, which advocated the general strike as the chief
weapon for the revolutionary overthrow of capitalism.

Industrialization and urbanization brought many women into the paid
labor force, including domestic service, factory jobs, teaching, nursing, and
secretarial work. By 1900, 41 percent of single women worked outside the
home, and women played an important role in many labor struggles.
Women's social and political organizations also expanded. The National
American Woman Suffrage Association, first headed by Elizabeth Cady

Stanton and Susan B. Anthony, grew from 13,150 members in 1893 to 75,000 in 1910, and helped win the vote for women in a number of states and municipalities. Larger still was the Women's Christian Temperance Union (WCTU), founded in 1874, which advocated prohibition as well as women's suffrage and other reforms. The WCTU considered civic activism a necessary extension of women's domestic role; by 1900 it had 200,000 members.[5] Alongside these White-dominated organizations, which often accepted or promoted racism, the National Association of Colored Women, formed in 1896, challenged both White and male supremacy and was one of the most effective Black organizations of the period. Its members numbered 50,000 by 1915.[6] The cult of domesticity was in crisis. The movement of women, especially White women, into the public sphere was blamed for shrinking families, a decline of traditional values, a rise in the divorce rate, the spread of prostitution, and various other real or imagined problems.

PROGRESSIVISM

Progressivism arose around 1900 in response to the tensions of rapid economic and social change. The Progressive movement aimed to rationalize the market economy, ameliorate working-class suffering and preserve a productive labor force, and stave off more radical change by softening some of the worst features of laissez-faire capitalism. Many Progressives sought an expanded government role in the economy to establish consumer protections, shorter working hours, safety on the job and in housing, workers' compensation, unemployment insurance, old-age pensions, and various other reforms. Progressives also sought to reform the electoral system through such measures as the secret ballot, voter initiative and referendum, and the direct election of U.S. senators.

Much of the support for Progressivism came from middle-class people trying to adapt to the new era of big industry and an increasingly bureaucratized society. As Robert L. Allen notes, many middle-class reformers wanted to re-create the small-proprietor ethos and frontier individualism of a preindustrial era, yet admired modern bureaucratic rationality and industrial efficiency. "Torn between these opposing tendencies, the old middle class in effect sacrificed its independence, while integrating itself as a ´white collar´ elite within the new corporate social order which it helped bring into being."[7]

Reform-minded business leaders also supported the Progressive movement. Some big industrialists were concerned that frequent industrial accidents and deaths, fourteen-hour days of mindless work, and filthy, overcrowded housing hurt workers' productivity, thus reducing profits.[8] Some looked to government regulation to help stabilize the marketplace or to provide specific competitive benefits. For example, northern textile manufacturers supported national child labor legislation because they were losing ground to southern mills that relied heavily on low-paid child workers.[9]

Some Progressive initiatives directly aimed to block grassroots mobilization. The National Civic Federation (NCF), founded in 1900, brought together big-business representatives with conservative trade unions in an effort to maintain an obedient workforce and fight radical labor organizations such as the IWW. Many NCF business leaders also set up company welfare policies for their employees, including housing, health care, insurance, and pensions—often offered on condition of not joining a union.[10] Many electoral reforms increased the obstacles to third parties and dramatically reduced voter turnout, for example, new poll taxes, naturalization rules, and residency, voter registration, and educational requirements.[11]

Progressivism encompassed a range of organizations and political tendencies. Except for the brief period of the 1912 presidential campaign, Theodore Roosevelt did not lead a Progressive organization of his own, but he gave voice to a distinct ideological current within the larger Progressive movement. This current was defined by romanticist, palingenetic nationalism. Romanticism concerns itself with national culture, origins, and upward development, and with a spiritual essence that unifies a people. It emphasizes authenticity of feeling, closeness to nature, and youthful vitality. Some forms of romanticism glorify masculinity and combat. Palingenesis, as we noted in the preceding chapter, means collective rebirth after a period of severe decline. Palingenetic nationalism warns against cultural, physical, or political degeneration and demands unified patriotic action to purge all sources of decay.[12]

Theodore Roosevelt called for an activist state not only to soothe economic misery, rationalize the market, and blunt class conflict but also to fulfill a national mission—the White race's mastery of the earth. Although he never fully abandoned liberal individualism, Roosevelt regarded individual interests as subordinate to national duty. He warned of a spiritual decadence that all White Americans must combat. He believed that men must be warriors and women must be mothers, and proclaimed a virtual cult of violence as a purifying, masculine force. The youngest man ever to be president of the United States, and the first charismatic occupant of the White House since Lincoln, Roosevelt presented himself as a model of energy, virility, and heroism and as a strong leader directly in touch with the popular will who could discipline labor and capital alike in the service of the nation as a whole. As rancher, conservationist, and honorary "Chief Scout Citizen" of the Boy Scouts, Roosevelt embraced frontier symbols as part of a credo he called the "new nationalism." His call for collective spiritual rebirth invoked a romanticized past but pointed toward a rather different future.

Roosevelt's efforts to re-create nineteenth-century warrior heroism reflect the Progressive movement's unstable melding of past and present, country and city, East and West. "I have been fulfilling a boyish ambition of

mine," he wrote his sister in 1884 from Dakota Territory, "playing at frontier hunter in good earnest."[13] Roosevelt was a wealthy, patrician-born New
York intellectual who glorified the harsh physical existence of the frontier
and who drove himself to become a westerner—a "real" man. The Rough
Riders, a cavalry regiment he helped to organize and lead during the Span-
ish-American War, became a popular symbol of American unity because
they brought together rugged western cowboys and upper-class Easterners.
Even ex-Confederates cheered the flag when the Riders traveled through
the South on their way to Cuba. In reality, only a few of the Riders came
from the East, and mounted cavalry proved virtually useless for combat in
Cuba. On one occasion, the inexperienced Riders were saved from annihilation by veteran Black soldiers, whom Roosevelt later falsely accused of cow-
ardice under fire.[14] But the legend of Roosevelt's charge up San Juan Hill
catapulted him within three years to governor of New York and then vice
president of the United States. He succeeded to the White House a few
months later in 1901, when President William McKinley was assassinated.

Roosevelt remained popular throughout his career. In 1904, he was reelected president with 56.4 percent of the popular vote, the highest percentage any presidential candidate had received since 1820. After leaving office
in 1909, he made an unsuccessful bid for the 1912 Republican nomination
against incumbent President Taft, then formed the Progressive Party so he
could run in the general election. His defection guaranteed Democrat
Woodrow Wilson's victory. But Roosevelt received 27.4 percent of the
vote, well above Taft's total and by far the strongest showing of any third-
party presidential candidate in U.S. history.

EXTENDING MANIFEST DESTINY

Like many of his contemporaries, Roosevelt was a zealous and unapologetic
proponent of global White supremacy, of Manifest Destiny extended overseas. He wrote in *The Strenuous Life* in 1901:

> Of course our whole national history has been one of expansion. . . . That the
> barbarians recede or are conquered, with the attendant fact that peace fol-
> lows their retrogression or conquest, is due solely to the power of the mighty
> civilized races which have not lost the fighting instinct, and which by their ex-
> pansion are gradually bringing peace into the red wastes where the barbarian
> peoples of the world hold sway.[15]

Propelled by such beliefs, Roosevelt vigorously supported the U.S.
conquest of the Philippines. Following the war with Spain, the United
States spent three years crushing Philippine independence forces led by
Emilio Aguinaldo. Roosevelt was president during the last phase of the con-

quest. It was a war against an entire people, in which U.S. troops systematically destroyed villages, tortured and murdered civilians, and burned crops. Hundreds of thousands of Filipinos were killed. As one U.S. military officer put it: "We exterminated the American Indians, and I guess most of us are proud of it, or, at least, believe the end justified the means; and we must have no scruples about exterminating this other race standing in the way of progress and enlightenment, if it is necessary."[16]

There were sharp debates over the Philippine war but, except for a few Black leaders such as W. E. B. Du Bois (and many Black soldiers in the Philippines who deserted or even joined the Philippine guerrilla forces), critics did not call its racist underpinnings into question. Even the so-called Anti-Imperialist League, which many prominent politicians and businessmen supported, opposed annexation of the Philippines on the ground that bringing a large dark-skinned population under U.S. sovereignty threatened racial purity and democratic institutions. Roosevelt wanted no such limits on U.S. power. "To grant self-government to Luzon under Aguinaldo," he declared, "would be like granting self-government to an Apache reservation under some local chief."[17] Like every generation of Americans that has fought in Asia since that time, Roosevelt was translating the new experience of industrial-era conquest overseas into the familiar idiom of Indian killing.

Roosevelt also projected U.S. power southward into Latin America. In 1903, to construct a canal giving U.S. fleets ready passage between the Atlantic and Pacific, Roosevelt forced Colombia to accept secession by its northwestern province of Panama. Panama then ceded to the United States permanent control over a ten-mile-wide Canal Zone. Roosevelt argued that this violation of Colombian sovereignty was in the "interest of civilization." In 1904, as part of this same civilizing mission, he announced a policy that became known as the Roosevelt Corollary to the Monroe Doctrine. The original doctrine held that the European powers should stay out of Latin America; the new corollary declared that the United States would act as police officer to stop "chronic wrongdoing" in the region.[18] A long series of self-serving military interventions in the Caribbean region followed.

Toward Black people, Teddy Roosevelt retained some of the old Whiggish/Republican paternalism. Some of his overtures to the "better class" of Blacks, such as inviting Booker T. Washington to dine at the White House, outraged many Whites. But Roosevelt refused to challenge Black people's oppression in any significant way. He praised White rule in Africa for leading Blacks out of "savagery," and he denounced slavery primarily because it had brought large numbers of Africans to North America, where they had threatened to "supplant" Whites. At the 1912 Progressive Party convention, Roosevelt supported the exclusion of Black delegates from the South and helped block a resolution demanding equality for Black people.[19]

RACE SUICIDE AND GENDER RENEWAL

If Roosevelt and many of his fellow Progressives were confident that White Americans had a mission to rule over other peoples, they also worried that Whites might be losing their fitness to do so. Modern circumstances— such as commercialism, labor radicalism, mass immigration, and women's growing autonomy—were endangering the European American's traditional strength and virtue. Yet, Roosevelt's response—that White men and women must do their duty as part of a coordinated national effort to revitalize the race—tended to undermine traditional individualism in favor of a centralized organizational approach. "Social efficiency," he argued, depended on "love of order, ability to fight well and breed well, [and] capacity to subordinate the interests of the individual to the interests of the community."[20] The principles of this creed were expressed in two projects that Roosevelt endorsed enthusiastically: race-suicide propaganda and the Boy Scouts of America.

The race-suicide controversy arose from fears that native-born White women, especially upper- and middle-class women, were not having enough babies. A strong nation bent on expansion needed big families to provide workers and soldiers. The declining birthrate among native-born Whites, critics charged, was coupled with a high birthrate among lower-class immigrants from southern and eastern Europe. This combination threatened the nation with moral, cultural, and racial decline. The campaign against race suicide blended nativism and sexism, but with special emphasis on the latter. Women, specifically middle- and upper-class women, "became the scapegoats," Linda Gordon notes, because "traditional religious and moral scruples and belief in the system's economic need for population growth would not yet allow seeking remedy by urging birth control upon the poor."[21]

Concern about the birthrate became a rationale for criticizing various changes in women's roles. Race-suicide warnings were used to attack not only the sins of birth control and women's sexual autonomy but also feminist activism, for encouraging women to be independent, as well as women's higher education and work outside the home, both of which supposedly made women less fit for motherhood. Such attacks reasserted the cult of domesticity in its most restrictive form but placed much less emphasis than before on child-rearing and homemaking; now breeding as a purely biological function became the true purpose of a woman's life. In Gordon's words, "as an ideology motherhood was becoming more animal-like and less human."[22]

For Roosevelt, who as president became a leading proponent of race-suicide theory in 1905, having babies was the female equivalent of the male obligation to fight. "I put the veteran of the great war ahead of every man in the country; but I put ahead even of him the good mother, the mother who has done her duty and brought up well a family of children." To Roosevelt, the White woman who avoided having children was a "criminal against the race . . . the object of contemptuous abhorrence by healthy people." He delivered one of his first public addresses on race suicide to the National Congress of Mothers, a body whose very existence symbolized the new treatment of motherhood as a matter of public, national policy.[23]

Proclaiming motherhood a duty was one of several ways in which Progressivism helped draw women into the national civic culture. Some aspects of this process were emancipatory, such as the advancement of women's suffrage, eventually incorporated into the U.S. Constitution with the ratification of the Nineteenth Amendment in 1920. Others aspects, however, simply reshaped women's subordination—for example, so-called protective labor legislation, which mandated shorter hours and improved conditions for women workers (but not men). By 1917, 39 states had adopted such measures. Although supported by some women's rights advocates, these laws were based on paternalistic claims about women's alleged weakness and "periodic semi-pathological state of health," as well as fears that wage labor would have a masculinizing effect on women or seduce them away from marriage and motherhood. Protective laws were used to bar women from higher-paid, traditionally male occupations and push many women back into the home and domestic subordination—results applauded by the AFL unions. From the standpoint of business owners, as Mimi Abramovitz argues, protective legislation helped strike a balance "between the endless use of cheap female (and child) labor to keep profits up and the ever-present need for women's reproductive labor at home to maintain the working class as a whole." In the process, the laws "vest[ed] more patriarchal power in the state."[24]

Attacks on women's desire for independence and wider economic opportunities drew on the deep-rooted belief that individual autonomy was for men only.[25] But Roosevelt was concerned about the lack of a sense of national duty among males as well. Thus, he endorsed the work of so-called character builders—Progressive activists who worked to develop conventional strength and virtue in teenage and preteenage boys of the middle class. As David Macleod notes, "Boys—like women—were cultural surrogates, expected to remain loyal to traditional values while men's lives changed."[26] The Boy Scouts of America (BSA) arose as a primary vehicle for this project.

The Boy Scouts were a concept imported from Britain. Military reconnaissance veteran Lord Baden-Powell had founded the Scouts as a make-believe version of his colonial warfare experiences in South Africa and India. His project won strong support from a British upper class worried about working-class discontent and declining imperial power. Baden-Powell instructed his Scouts to accept the social status quo, reject socialism, and serve the empire. In the United States, the BSA was founded in 1910 in response to widespread fears that middle-class males were growing up undisciplined or, worse, effeminate. Character builders pointed to many sources of weakness: the softness of urban life and white-collar work, excessive female influence in the home and in the school (women had just begun to enter the teaching profession in large numbers), forms of Christianity that preached the supposedly feminine message of self-denial, masturbation, and mental overstrain. The Boy Scouts were tailor-made for this array of problems: they removed boys from the debilitating control of women and from the city into an all-male outdoor world re-creating the frontier, and they avoided sexuality and intellectualism by channeling boys' energy into disciplined physical activities. "Ironically, like most Progressive reformers, character builders sought the values of preindustrial life by the methods of the new organizational society."[27]

Roosevelt, appointed to the honorary post of Chief Scout Citizen, declared that the BSA would "make boys good citizens in time of peace, and incidentally . . . fit them to become good soldiers in time of war." Not wishing to alienate opponents of war, BSA officials cautiously asserted that the Boy Scouts were not military but taught "the military virtues such as honor, loyalty, obedience, and patriotism." After World War I broke out in Europe in 1914, the BSA's reluctance to join the rising militaristic wave led Roosevelt briefly to denounce the organization as "part of the wicked and degrading pacifist agitation of the past few years." After that, BSA officials disavowed any antiwar sentiment, embraced superpatriotism, and many scoutmasters instituted military drills.[28]

The rise of the United States as an aggressive expansionist power gave meaning to the Boy Scouts in more ways than one. Not only did Boy Scouting help prepare middle-class males for their national duty to be soldiers, who would help bring "peace" to "the barbarian peoples," but Scouting itself was defined as a civilizing process that recapitulated racial development. Echoing romanticist conceptions of human progress,[29] character builders and the BSA embraced theories that boyhood was developmentally linked with savagery, adolescence with barbarism, and adulthood with civilization. In this view, character building paralleled imperialism, which psychologist G. Stanley Hall described as "the ethnic pedagogy of adolescent races."[30]

The belief that Scouting was a civilizing process among young savages fit well with the BSA's efforts to re-create life on the frontier, which the historian Frederick Jackson Turner had recently described as the "meeting point between savagery and civilization." Frontier romanticism had played an important role in Roosevelt's life since his years in Dakota Territory, and also figured prominently in the conservationist movement, which influenced federal government policy under Roosevelt's administration. "The leaders of the Roosevelt conservation movement," writes G. Edward White, "combined a faith in technocratic efficiency with a delight in the image of a nontechnological, nonurban, noncorporate, nonelitist—in short, a noneastern—society."[31]

While John Muir, founder of the Sierra Club, led a branch of conservationism that called for preserving pristine wilderness, Rooseveltian conservationists such as Gifford Pinchot, head of the Forest Service, called for the "wise use" of natural resources. In their vision, an expert elite working through the government would regulate use of lands, waters, and forests to ensure long-term industrial development—that is, a stable environment for profit making. The major timber companies supported Pinchot's efforts to maintain forests for long-term harvesting. But Pinchot, Roosevelt, and their colleagues presented conservation policy to the public as part of an effort to defend yeoman farmers and oppose monopolies. Their work appealed to traditionalist middle- and upper-class groups that revered the small entrepreneur and saw conservation as an antidote to industrialism and commercialism.[32]

MEDIATING INDUSTRIAL CONFLICT

Roosevelt's conservation policy typified his approach to the economic order in general—use federal government power to stabilize and rationalize the existing economic hierarchy while cultivating an image as someone who stood up to big business. He denounced "predatory wealth" and "bad trusts," meaning trusts established through unfair or corrupt methods. Although he repeatedly stated that he wanted to regulate monopoly power, not abolish it, a few well-publicized antitrust actions by his administration gave him an image as a "trust buster." Yet, Roosevelt was in fact intimately tied to big-business interests, especially the Morgan corporate empire, through members of his administration as well as the Oyster Bay Roosevelt clan to which he belonged. In almost all cases, notes Philip H. Burch Jr., "Roosevelt's 'bad trusts' were basically 'non-Morgan trusts,' such as the Rockefeller-controlled Standard Oil Co., the Harriman-dominated Union Pacific Railroad, and the American Tobacco Co. . . . Conversely, Roosevelt's 'good trusts' usually turned out to be big Morgan-controlled companies, such as the U.S. Steel Corp. and International Harvester Co." J. P. Morgan associates George W. Perkins and Willard Straight were major backers of Roosevelt's Progressive Party in 1912; indeed, Kolko argues that "the party's fortunes were based almost entirely on the desires of the Morgan interests."[33]

To a large extent, Roosevelt's approach to industrial conflict followed the lead of the National Civic Federation, at least two of whose members sat in his cabinet.[34] Bitterly hostile to socialism and to labor unions advocating militant class struggle, Roosevelt, like the NCF, was willing to work with the AFL and other conservative unions. This was the U.S. elite's first serious attempt to control the working class through *corporatism*, a formalized system of "social partnership" between representatives of different classes and economic sectors, sanctioned by the state. Corporatism uses top-level, consensus-oriented bargaining and tends to hide political conflict and inequalities of power.[35]

President Roosevelt used government power to bolster the NCF's corporatist approach during the important anthracite coal strike of 1902. In a move supported by NCF leaders, Roosevelt pressured both employers and strikers to submit to an arbitration commission, which awarded strikers limited gains in wages and hours while condemning the principle of a union shop. This departure from the government's usual resort to naked antilabor repression strengthened the NCF's own mediation efforts and helped the AFL while weakening union activism.[36]

The NCF social partnership was fragile and short-lived. Many employers, centered in the rival National Association of Manufacturers, rejected NCF corporatism. Many NCF business leaders themselves were only willing to negotiate with labor when it benefited them directly. The AFL's ability to represent and control workers was sharply limited because it included only a small part of the paid labor force—6 percent in 1905. Most AFL unions excluded unskilled workers, new immigrants, and women. In the 1910s, organizing efforts by these groups challenged the AFL's claim to speak for labor and forced it to bend exclusionary rules in specific cases. But, in the long run, the AFL's stopgap measures to contain working-class militancy were inadequate. This led business leaders to abandon corporatism for more openly repressive strategies, especially after World War I.[37]

The AFL sought to bolster its dominance among workers by calling for immigration restriction. Echoing the claims of certain patricians such as Republican Senator Henry Cabot Lodge of Massachusetts, the AFL denounced southern and eastern Europeans, like Asians, as an unassimilable threat to White America's racial purity, and called for sharp limits on their entry into the United States. Some Socialists, with official Socialist Party backing from 1910 on, embraced AFL racism and nativism.[38] But calls for immigration restriction brought the AFL into conflict with business forces in the NCF. Big industry now wanted European labor more than it feared immigrant radicalism, and had established rigid segregation of nationalities as part of a system of divide and rule at many workplaces.[39]

Roosevelt supported a literacy test and certain other limits on European immigration on the grounds that immigrants contributed to radicalism and urban poverty. But he did not view southern and eastern Europeans as racially separate and inferior. Rather, he declared, all immigrants of European origin were being blended in a racial melting pot: "We are making a new race, a new type, in this country."[40] Nor, despite some personal prejudice, did Roosevelt engage in public anti-Catholic or antisemitic scapegoating, and he sometimes denounced religious bigotry. In 1912, Roosevelt's Progressive Party advocated expanding immigrant education and protecting newcomers against exploitation. In part, Roosevelt was siding with the NCF employers against the restrictionist AFL. In part, too, he was appealing to the large bloc of new-immigrant voters who had been brought into the Republican Party in 1896, when presidential candidate McKinley replaced traditional Republican nativism with cultural pluralism. Like Andrew Jackson, Roosevelt combined an aggressive commitment to White supremacist expansion with a relatively inclusive concept of Whiteness. In exchange for inclusion and equal treatment, however, European immigrants must become Americanized. They must give up their names, languages, cultural traits, and any political views that clashed with U.S. patriotic loyalty.[41]

Roosevelt went beyond NCF corporatism by advocating a more powerful role for the state. He formed the Progressive Party in 1912 because of a split with the Republican Party's laissez-faire conservatives. The new party's platform called for occupational health and safety regulation; the eight-hour day in certain industries; a minimum wage for women; unemployment, health, and old-age insurance; and federal mediation of labor disputes. Yet, the platform made no mention of unions' right to organize. The AFL, which claimed that social welfare laws such as unemployment insurance and a minimum wage usurped union functions, backed Woodrow Wilson in 1912. Most corporate leaders, too, balked at the extent of Roosevelt's welfare policies, except for a few key Progressive Party supporters such as J. P. Morgan associate George W. Perkins.[42]

The Progressive Party's welfare proposals were partly intended to take votes away from the Socialist Party, whose presidential candidate, Eugene Debs, ended up receiving over 900,000 votes in 1912. This also helps to explain Roosevelt's radical-sounding attack on "the plunder league of the professional politicians who are controlled and sustained by the great beneficiaries of privilege and reaction," and the Progressives' planks advocating women's suffrage, direct primaries and election of senators, and the initiative, referendum, and recall. But in another sense, social welfare legislation, with government experts who would make labor unions largely superfluous, fit with Roosevelt's larger vision of a strong state. Roosevelt's slogan "new nationalism," which he borrowed from Progressive writer Herbert Croly and first used in 1910, expressed this vision. New nationalism combined Roosevelt's general emphasis on subordinating individual interests to national duty with the specific claim that U.S. global expansion required a centralized, regulated form of monopoly capitalism. During the 1912 campaign, while Woodrow Wilson called for dismantling trusts, Roosevelt and the Progressive Party emphasized the need to maintain "the concentration of modern business" under government supervision. "If we are to compete with other nations in the markets of the world," Roosevelt declared at the party's nominating convention, "as well as to develop our own material civilization at home, we must utilize those forms of industrial organization that are indispensable to the highest industrial productivity and efficiency."[43]

Lest its radical pretensions be taken too seriously, the Progressive Party cited Imperial Germany as an ideal example of expanded state power.[44] Germany at that time was a semiauthoritarian monarchy with a weak parliament, in which power rested on a partnership between the big industrialists and the Prussian Junkers, a military-oriented landed aristocracy. By closely coordinating government and business, Germany had achieved a dynamic, powerful economy, rivaling Britain for preeminence in Europe. It combined antisocialist repression with welfare legislation such as social insurance programs and workplace health and safety laws.

CONCLUSION

Teddy Roosevelt's brand of mass politics influenced right-wing populism, although he himself did not lead a right-wing populist movement. His supporters mounted no grassroots challenge to elites; Roosevelt's own rhetorical attacks on "bad trusts" were just weak echoes of populist antielitism, and he spoke plainly for regulating and rationalizing big business, not dismantling it. But, like Andrew Jackson before him, Roosevelt was a charismatic leader who embraced expansionist racial nationalism while challenging the status quo in certain respects. In an echo of the Reconstruction-era Ku Klux Klan, he declared that Whites must undertake a collective renewal in the face of grave threats to the race, and he sought to mobilize people who felt squeezed between big business above and radical insurgents below. And Roosevelt's Progressivism included several other themes that would help shape right-wing populist politics in the twentieth century, such as the emphasis on national duty before individual interests. He blended an elite-based hatred of labor radicalism with radical-sounding welfare measures borrowed from the Left, and promoted a top-down corporatist approach to relations between labor and capital. He raised women's subordination to the level of a national mission, and distilled male supremacist ideology into the duty to "fight well and breed well."

Roosevelt's Progressivism paralleled a new breed of right-wing mass movements that formed across Europe between 1880 and 1914. While the traditional European Right had emphasized deference to the old upper classes, these new populist movements relied on charismatic politics and mass activism. They stressed a romanticist version of nationalism that glorified self-sacrifice, and they warned of cultural and physical degeneration that must be reversed. Although fiercely anti-Marxist, these movements advocated social and economic reform and criticized established ruling groups to varying degrees. Some of them promoted strong-state corporatism as a "third way" between capitalism and socialism. These movements included *Action Française* in France; the syndicalists, futurists, and National Association in Italy; the Black Hundreds in Russia; the German Workers Party in Austria; and a host of "*volkish*" groups in Germany. They directly foreshadowed the European fascist movements that developed after World War I.[45]

Both Roosevelt's Progressivism and the European protofascists were responses to the growth of socialism, imperialist conquest, and the tensions and dislocations caused by rapid industrial change. Both largely attracted middle-class people navigating between big business and labor radicalism and between old and new social orders. Both blended modernizing impulses with preindustrial nostalgia. Roosevelt used frontier heroism and closeness to nature to bolster a new vision of centralized, technocratic, White supremacist power—much like the German nationalists' "blood and soil" ideology that helped shape Nazism. Worried that modern society was weakening masculine vigor and nationalist commitment, Roosevelt celebrated violence as a spiritual purifier. The futurists, who later cofounded the Italian Fascist Party, echoed Roosevelt when they declared, "We want to glorify war, the only hygiene of the world."[46]

But Roosevelt's politics and the European protofascists' also differed sharply in key ways. Unlike the European movements, Roosevelt's following was diffuse and organized through conventional institutions. He and his supporters did not try to build a disciplined political organization, nor did they use paramilitary tactics against opponents. Roosevelt did not scapegoat Jews or "parasitic" financiers, as many (but not all) European protofascists did. And while the European movements fundamentally rejected parliamentary institutions and pluralist doctrines, Roosevelt's Progressives did not. Although he endorsed political repression in many cases, Roosevelt did not try to silence all political debate, suspend or rig elections, place all institutions under centralized control, or found a quasireligious cult of personality. European protofascists were at war with Enlightenment liberalism, whereas Roosevelt's Progressives were content to modify it from within.

5

100 PERCENT AMERICANISM

World War I–Era Repression
and the Second Ku Klux Klan

World War I (1914–1918) and the Russian Revolution of 1917 permanently altered the international context for right-wing populist movements. Across Europe, these two events precipitated the birth of fascism, the most virulent form of repressive populism. During the Russian Civil War of 1918–1921, counterrevolutionaries slaughtered tens of thousands of Jews as part of their effort to smash the so-called Jewish–Bolshevik conspiracy. In Italy, Hungary, Germany, and other European countries where the revolutionary Left was strong, demobilized soldiers formed the nucleus of fascist movements, which represented a new kind of counterrevolutionary politics. Fascists glorified the camaraderie of battle, despised parliamentary government, and blended anticommunism, national or racial bigotry, and antielite scapegoating. In 1922 the first fascist-led government came to power, in Italy.

The United States experienced these events at a distance, but here, too, war and the threat of revolution sharply increased ultrapatriotic jingoism, racist and nativist attacks, and the demonization and repression of leftists. Mass roundups of radicals, especially foreign-born radicals, accompanied widespread massacres of Black and Mexican people. The hatreds that motivated these assaults were tightly interwoven—in practice they were often interchangeable, for example, when Mexicans were denounced simultaneously as "greasers," revolutionaries, and German spies.

The war in Europe cut off U.S. industry's supply of immigrant labor while also raising demands on production. As a result, northern industrialists began to waive the color bar and recruit Black workers from towns in the South. Over 400,000 Blacks moved to northern cities in 1916–1918 alone; by 1930 one million Blacks had moved North, in what has been called the Great Migration. Smaller numbers of Chicano, Mexican, and Caribbean people also began to move to the northern United States for industry, service, and farming jobs. Almost ten million women entered the paid labor force during the war; after 1918, many White women moved into the rapidly growing clerical sector.[1] In 1920, after decades of struggle, women won the right to vote nationwide with the ratification of the Nineteenth Amendment.

Despite deep inequities and brief recessions, the United States experienced overall prosperity and expansion between 1914 and 1929. Many people saw their incomes rise, and a large minority had access to a booming new market in consumer products. The automobile, the radio, Hollywood movies, recorded music, and mass advertising became fixtures of U.S. society for the first time. Protestant fundamentalism originated at this time, partly as a reaction against the new popular culture. Fundamentalists interpreted the Bible literally, attacked liberal or "modernist" versions of Christianity, and emphasized a rigid and patriarchal moral code.

The war also brought to a head a crisis in the nation's racial structure. Eastern and southern European ethnic groups—Italians, Jews, Poles, Hungarians, Russians, Serbs, Finns, Greeks, and others—held an unstable middle position in the racial hierarchy—above Asians, Latinos, Blacks, and American Indians, but below native-born Whites and old Christian immigrants from northwestern Europe. The new immigrants formed a strategic core of the industrial workforce, yet many Whites feared them as cultural outsiders and potential revolutionaries. The dilemma was: should southern and eastern Europeans be admitted to full membership in the privileged racial caste, or should race privilege be reserved for those of northwest European "Nordic" descent? In the short term, Nordic supremacy gained ground, as laws of the early 1920s virtually banned new arrivals from eastern and southern Europe. But the more inclusive system of White supremacy soon began to reassert itself. As Black and Mexican workers started to replace them on the bottom rungs of industry, the new ethnic groups from Europe were gradually "Americanized"—made White—over the next two decades. This gave them a greater cultural and material stake in U.S. capitalism and undercut their radical tendencies.

The Ku Klux Klan, refounded in Georgia in 1915, embodied the deeply repressive politics of this period. By the early 1920s it had become a national movement with millions of members organized in both the all-male KKK and the Women's Ku Klux Klan (WKKK). The Klan contributed to and benefited from the antileftist backlash, and its doctrine of White Protestant nationalism helped popularize and strengthen Nordic supremacy. A standard view of the 1920s Klan attributes its rise to "nativist intolerance, fundamentalist frustration with the libertinism of the Roaring Twenties, and the general anti-modernist urge of the heartland."[2] But recent scholarship has challenged this picture. The Klan was primarily an urban movement that attracted more mainstream Protestants than fundamentalists, targeted genuine problems such as political corruption or organized crime as well as ethnic scapegoats, and blended nostalgia with forward-looking appeals. And while it defended traditional social hierarchies in many ways, the Klan often challenged elite interests, sometimes made common cause with socialists, and even welcomed outspoken advocates of women's rights. This combination was key to the Klan's popularity, and marked it as the first major right-wing populist movement of the twentieth-century United States.

RED SCARE, BLACK SCARE, BROWN SCARE

The wave of repression that peaked in 1917–1920 was a key factor shaping the Ku Klux Klan's rise. After the United States entered World War I in April 1917, a mass campaign for "100 per cent Americanism" brought bitter attacks on anyone suspected of disloyalty. In an early sign of the new climate, hundreds of women's suffrage activists picketing the White House were arrested for trivial infractions, many of them receiving lengthy sentences and harsh treatment. German Americans were prime targets of suspicion, vigilante attacks, and government repression during the war.[3] But the crackdown on leftists lasted much longer. Faced with an array of radical forces that opposed the war and renewed their efforts after the armistice, political and business elites used the crisis atmosphere to forge a permanent national security apparatus dedicated to rooting out radical subversion. Patriotic and veterans organizations cheered on the government-led crackdown. Demonization of reds was closely tied to demonization of immigrants and people of color.

In 1917–1918, the U.S. government passed a series of laws—the Espionage Act, the Sedition Act, the Alien Act—that harshly penalized criticism of the war or other expressions of disloyalty. These laws remained in effect until the official end of hostilities in 1921. Nineteen states passed criminal syndicalism laws that permanently outlawed radical dissent.[4] The war also helped centralize intelligence activities in federal hands. Complementing the existing network of local police "red squads" and private detective agencies, several federal agencies rapidly expanded their domestic spying: the Justice Department's Bureau of Investigation (renamed the Federal Bureau of Investigation [FBI] in 1935), army and navy intelligence divisions, the Post Office, and the State Department. Despite some rivalry, these offices coordinated their efforts and worked closely with vigilante groups, such as the American Protective League, and large corporations to ferret out spies, draft resisters, labor activists, and critics of the war.[5] Meanwhile, the federal government's Committee on Public Information (CPI) mobilized writers, artists, speakers, filmmakers, and college professors in a massive propaganda campaign to bolster the war effort. The CPI portrayed strikers as equivalent to military deserters and labeled immigrants who failed to assimilate as "deliberate colonists of a foreign empire, and enemies of the American republic."[6]

Many leading Socialists were sentenced to long prison terms for criticizing the war, which the Socialist Party condemned as "a crime against the people of the United States," "instigated by the predatory capitalists." Thousands of native-born Socialists joined the war effort and abandoned the party, but southern and eastern Europeans—radicalized by the upheavals in Europe and repression in the United States—rallied to the party's foreign-language federations. By 1919, these federations constituted 52 percent of the Socialist Party's 109,000 members.[7] This ethnic shift intensified the attacks against the party. Even more harshly targeted was the revolutionary Industrial Workers of the World, which brought together some of the most oppressed native-born White workers with European immigrants and a few Black, Latino, and Asian workers. The IWW proclaimed that "it is better to be a traitor to a country than a traitor to your class." Local police and vigilantes declared open season on the union. In Arizona they drove 1,300 suspected Wobblies from the state at gunpoint; in Butte, Montana, vigilantes lynched IWW organizer Frank Little, an American Indian. A federal court in Chicago convicted 101 IWW leaders of sabotaging the war effort, and thousands more were arrested under state laws.[8]

Germany surrendered to the Allies in November 1918. But the birth of the Soviet state in November 1917 and the Communist International (Comintern) in March 1919 presented new menaces. The United States sent 12,000 troops to Archangel and Vladivostok as part of an Allied anti-Bolshevik invasion force; many troops remained until 1920. In the United States, a number of Socialists, the vast majority of them eastern European, split off to form two small Communist parties. Although U.S. Communists remained politically isolated for years, they were a handy scapegoat for the tremendous strike wave of 1919, in which four million workers walked off the job. That same year, anarchist groups were blamed (perhaps falsely) for a series of highly publicized bomb attacks. Immigrants were heavily represented in all of these leftist groups, and the Red Scare now encompassed a broad attack on southern and eastern Europeans.

Especially vulnerable to repression were millions of non-U.S. citizens, who could be deported if they advocated or belonged to an organization that advocated revolt or sabotage. In the Palmer Raids of November 1919 and January 1920, named for Attorney General A. Mitchell Palmer, agents of the Bureau of Investigation, the Immigration Service, and local police rounded up thousands of suspected radical "aliens."[9] Most arrestees were held incommunicado, many for long periods without arrest warrants; hundreds were tortured with beatings, intense heat, food deprivation, and death threats. However, lack of evidence and widespread public opposition forced their eventual release.[10]

Future FBI Director J. Edgar Hoover played a central role in the Palmer Raids as head of the Bureau of Investigation's antiradical General Intelligence Division. In addition to bringing bureaucratic efficiency to the Bureau, Hoover promoted the specter of a worldwide communist conspiracy that threatened not only capitalism but all morality and civilized order.

Such demonization became common during the Red Scare. Radicals, as Frank Donner writes, "were attacked as godless, bestial, dirty, and depraved practitioners of 'free love,' lusting to 'nationalize' American womanhood like their Bolshevik counterparts in Russia."[11]

The American Legion embodied the image of patriots defending America against the vast communist conspiracy. Founded by army officers in early 1919, the Legion paralleled the many European veterans groups formed at that time, which supplied members for fascist parties and counter-revolutionary militias. Legionnaires eagerly assaulted leftists, broke strikes, and drove Wobblies out of town. But, while the Legion praised Mussolini's work in Italy, unlike the fascists in Europe it defended existing institutions without trying to seize power or impose monolithic control.[12]

In the United States, the Christian fundamentalist movement emerged in the early twentieth century as a backlash against the principles of the Enlightenment, modernism, and liberalism.[13] No surprise, then, that the fear of a global subversive communist menace was influenced by Christian apocalyptic millennialism. In his 1994 book *Red Hunting in the Promised Land*, Joel Kovel reviews at length the influence of the Catholic Inquisition and Protestant Puritanism on U.S. anticommunism.[14] The threat of communism—represented as the "Red Menace"—became the main focus of apocalyptic conspiracism. According to Frank Donner:

> The root anti-subversive impulse was fed by the Menace. Its power strengthened with the passage of time, by the late twenties its influence had become more pervasive and folkish. Bolshevism came to be identified over wide areas of the country by God-fearing Americans as the Antichrist come to do eschatological battle with the children of light. A slightly secularized version, widely-shared in rural and small-town America, postulated a doomsday conflict between decent upright folk and radicalism—alien, satanic, immorality incarnate.[15]

Antisemitism gained strength during the Red Scare. Although Jews had been widely scapegoated as greedy bankers since the late nineteenth century, the image of the conspiratorial Jewish radical now found wide currency as well. Influenced by the propaganda of czarist Russian exiles, many newspapers, officials of the State Department, the military, the American Red Cross, the YMCA, and President Wilson himself all echoed the claim that Bolshevism was "led by Jews." Prescott F. Hall of the Immigration Restriction League called Bolshevism a "movement of Oriental Tartar tribes led by Asiatic Semites against Nordic *bourgeoisie*." Police spies constantly reported that it was mainly "the lower type of Russian Jews" and other foreigners who attended radical meetings.[16]

But Russian Jews and other Europeans were not the only ethnic groups targeted during the Red Scare. The United States and other western governments feared the Bolshevik government in part because it endorsed revolutionary action by oppressed peoples throughout the world against capitalism, colonialism, and racial oppression. U.S. intelligence agencies made it a priority to monitor and disrupt radical activism by Blacks, Mexicans, and Japanese, as well as Irish, Indian, and Egyptian anticolonial organizations working in the United States. The government particularly sought to block these groups' efforts to collaborate with one another or with White American radicals.[17]

Mexican radicalism was a prime worry for U.S. elites because of the Mexican Revolution (from 1910 to roughly 1920) just across the border. Not only did radical-nationalist and collectivist sentiment within this upheaval threaten large U.S. investments in Mexico. Mexican revolutionaries in exile, such as the anarchists of the Mexican Liberal Party (PLM), also helped to organize Mexican and Chicano workers within the United States and forged ties with North American radicals. Mexican revolutionary troops under Francisco "Pancho" Villa raided U.S. border towns. Some Mexican revolutionaries even called for an uprising by people of color in the southwestern United States to establish independent Chicano, Black, and American Indian nations. Faced with this threat from the south, the U.S. military invaded Mexico twice during the revolution, in 1914 and 1917. The United States repeatedly jailed the PLM's Ricardo Flores Magón, who was ultimately murdered by U.S. prison guards. In the southwestern United States, anti-Mexican propaganda intensified into a "brown scare," as U.S. authorities and vigilantes killed hundreds, if not thousands, of Mexicans and Chicanos.[18]

Other people of color, too, were targeted. In California, anti-Japanese racism "rose to unprecedented heights during the election of 1920," when voters tightened a law barring Japanese from owning land.[19] Black veterans were often singled out for lynching after the war. African Americans' northward migration, too, sparked murderous panic among Whites. In 1917 over forty cities saw racial clashes in which Whites attacked Blacks, who often fought back. Pogromists in East St. Louis killed 39 Blacks, injured hundreds, and burned hundreds of homes; nine Whites were also killed. Two years later, anti-Black terrorism exploded in Chicago, Washington, DC, and some twenty other cities and towns. Much of the White public blamed African Americans for the violence; their acts of self-defense became proof that outside radicals were fomenting "Negro subversion," since many assumed Blacks were incapable of organizing resistance themselves. A 1920 Justice Department document stated: "The reds have done a vast amount of evil damage by carrying the doctrine of race revolt and the poison of Bolshevism to the Negroes. . . . This business has perhaps been the most contemptible and wicked performance of our American revolutionary fanatics."[20]

Self-defense against lynch mobs was one facet of the largest upsurge in Black activism since Reconstruction. During and after World War I, the new urban Black communities in the North—especially Harlem—became centers of cultural and political ferment. A broad range of new organizations bluntly condemned White supremacy and pressed for Black rights, dignity, and self-determination. These new forces included Black labor organizations such as the National Brotherhood Workers of America, active in twelve states; the socialist magazine the *Messenger*, edited by A. Philip Randolph and Chandler Owen; and the left-nationalist African Blood Brotherhood, which later merged into the Communist Party. The National Association for the Advancement of Colored People (NAACP), founded in 1909 with an emphasis on education and legal reform, temporarily embraced militant tactics such as strikes and gained tens of thousands of new members in both the North and the South.[21] By far the largest Black organization was the Universal Negro Improvement Association (UNIA), led by Jamaican immigrant Marcus Garvey. Hundreds of thousands joined the UNIA behind its program of Black pride, economic advancement through Black business enterprises, solidarity among colonialized peoples, and repatriation to Africa to help establish a unified, independent African nation. The UNIA included socialist and feminist minority constituencies.[22]

Opponents vilified militant Black organizations as Bolshevist mouthpieces supposedly promoting both "racial hatred" and "social equality" (meaning racial intermarriage). Federal agencies infiltrated and harassed Black groups, exploited and encouraged conflicts among them, and sought any available means to shut them down. Their most prominent success was Garvey's 1923 conviction for mail fraud; he was imprisoned in 1925 and deported to Jamaica three years later.[23]

The U.S. Left was not prepared to cope with the sustained persecution it received in 1917–1920. In the wake of the Palmer Raids, the IWW was virtually destroyed, the Socialist Party drastically reduced in numbers, the Communist and Communist Labor parties driven underground. The anarchists Emma Goldman and Alexander Berkman and hundreds of other leftists had been deported to Russia; Eugene Debs and thousands more were in prison. Black political organizations disintegrated or moved to the right: the NAACP retreated from militant activism while Garvey formed ties with the Klan and other White racial nationalist groups, which praised the UNIA's emphasis on racial purity. With the radical threat broken, political repression loosened its grip, but the effect remained. In this stifling political climate, a struggle continued over who should be included in the privileged sector of the country's racial hierarchy.

NORDIC SUPREMACY VERSUS WHITE SUPREMACY

Nordic supremacist ideology in the United States was the product of the White Protestant intellectual elite. Since the 1890s or earlier, the mass influx of southern and eastern Europeans had spurred patrician scholars to re-think the established notion that all Europeans belong to a superior race. In doing so, they borrowed heavily from intellectual developments in Britain, France, and Germany. European race theorists maintained that precise an-thropological research and physical measurements proved the validity of the racial hierarchy. Social Darwinists claimed that struggles for social domi-nance expressed humanity's biological evolution, in which the fittest would naturally come out on top. And eugenicists argued that humans should practice selective breeding in order to improve their racial stock.

U.S. racial theorists who drew on these ideas did not develop a single, fully unified ideology, but most of them advocated certain basic principles: first, that heredity, rather than environment, determines not only a person's physical characteristics but also intelligence, cultural tendencies, and moral outlook; second, that, on the basis of these hereditary qualities, humans are divided into a number of races that may be ranked as superior or inferior; third, that interbreeding between superior and inferior races always pro-duces offspring who are as low as—or, according to some writers, even lower than—the inferior parental strain; and, fourth, that Europeans include several races, of which Nordics are the best and most valuable.[24]

Madison Grant offered one of the most systematic and influential ver-sions of the new race theory in his best-selling *The Passing of the Great Race* (1916). He divided Europeans into three races, or "subspecies": Nordic or Baltic, Mediterranean or Iberian, and Alpine. These three European races to-gether formed one "species" of the genus *Homo*. In Grant's schema, non-Eu-ropeans, including all Jews, belonged to separate species.[25]

To Grant and his fellow Nordicists, the Alpine, Mediterranean, and Jewish immigrants posed a serious threat to the United States' Nordic "old stock." "The man of the old stock is being crowded out of many country dis-tricts by these foreigners just as he is today being literally driven off the streets of New York City by the swarms of Polish Jews. These immigrants adopt the language of the native American, they wear his clothes, they steal his name and they are beginning to take his women." Unless the trend were reversed, the melting pot would swallow up the higher race in "a population of race bastards in which the lower type ultimately preponderates." African Americans, however, could remain, provided they were segregated. "Ne-groes," Grant declared, "are never socialists or labor unionists and as long as the dominant imposes its will on the subservient race and as long as they re-main in the same relation to the whites as in the past, the Negroes will be a valuable element in the community."[26]

Nordic supremacist views did not remain confined to Yankee upper-crust circles. Although specific terminology varied, the belief that many Eu-ropeans were racially distinct from and inferior to Nordics was disseminated through popular magazines such as *The Saturday Evening Post* and *The Atlantic Monthly*. By the 1910s, this belief had become commonplace at all levels of

European American society. As early as 1885, an Iowa laborer put anti-immigrant resentment in racial terms with the comment that "the Bohemians [i.e., Czechs] will get a job in preference to a white man." The St. Paul District Attorney argued in court against granting citizenship to Finns because "a Finn . . . is a Mongolian and not a 'white person.'" A midwestern coal miner complained: "I tell ye, sir, the Italians and Hungarians is spoil'n' this yere country for white men." A U.S. senator from North Carolina labeled southern Italians "the degenerate progeny of the Asiatic hordes which, long centuries ago, overran the shores of the Mediterranean."27

Today it is easy to see that classifying Europeans into different races was a biologically arbitrary move, a way to rationalize social oppression. This is also true of the race categories that now prevail in the United States—White, Black, Asian, etc.—although it may be more difficult to see that from inside the system. But race-categories are not simply ideological fabrications, because they also describe and structure people's concrete experiences within society. This was equally true of the non-White label for Finns, Hungarians, Czechs, and other Europeans in 1920. The non-White classification, a simplified version of the elite's racial theories, took hold in the popular consciousness because it described something real—the fact that the immigrant groups were culturally distinct from older-stock European Americans and did not share many of the social and economic privileges associated with Whiteness. Once this ideology took hold, it began in turn to shape material reality, notably through changes in the immigration laws and, indirectly, in the development of publicly sanctioned sterilization programs for the "unfit."

The Nordicists' concept of fitness excluded everyone regarded as physically, mentally, or morally degenerate. Such people, of course, were heavily represented among the lower races. Racism and discrimination against disabled people thus reinforced each other. A French work by Anatole Leroy Bearlieu, translated into English in 1895, claimed that Jews, for example, were "often misshapen; few races have so many men who are deformed, disabled, or hunch-backed, so many who are blind, deaf mutes, or congenital idiots." A 1912 intelligence test of immigrants at Ellis Island found that "83 percent of the Jews, 80 percent of the Hungarians, 79 percent of the Italians, and 87 percent of the Russians were 'feeble minded.'"28 One of the major problems with race mixing, eugenicists believed, was that it raised the incidence of such conditions in the "higher race."

The eugenic solution to this alleged problem was controlled breeding. The state, argued Madison Grant, must establish "a rigid system of selection" through sterilization of the unfit. "This is a practical, merciful and inevitable solution of the whole problem and can be applied to an ever widening circle of social discards, beginning always with the criminal, the diseased and the insane and extending gradually to types which may be called weaklings rather than defectives and perhaps ultimately to worthless racial types."29

Between 1895 and 1913, many states enacted marriage restriction laws, most of which targeted people regarded as insane, epileptic, or mentally deficient. Apparently these laws were not strongly enforced. However, between 1905 and 1922, fifteen states passed laws allowing institutionalized persons to be sterilized involuntarily. During this period, at least 3,233 such sterilizations were carried out, most on people labeled insane. The California law included the prisoner shown to be "a moral or sexual degenerate or pervert" among those targeted. By 1931, twenty-eight states had sterilization laws, and the rate of operations had risen substantially. By 1941, 38,087 institutionalized persons had been legally sterilized.[30] The U.S. example strongly influenced Nazi Germany's 1933 eugenic sterilization law, under which an estimated 3.5 million people were sterilized, and many U.S. eugenicists strongly supported Nazi policies of "racial hygiene" during the 1930s.[31]

Since most of the categories targeted for sterilization in the United States ("feeble-minded," "insane," "criminal," etc.) reflected strong cultural and class bias, it seems safe to assume that non-Nordic groups were hit disproportionately. Until 1927, a slight majority of those legally sterilized were male. During the next five years, two-thirds were female, and thereafter women continued to receive the bulk of sterilizations. Eugenicists, like the "race-suicide" propagandists before them, tended to regard women simply as breeders. As one eugenicist stated in 1917, "in my view, women exist primarily for racial ends."[32]

Eugenic ideology pervaded U.S. society after the Red Scare. In the 1920s, eugenics was a required subject at many U.S. universities, and the field received heavy financial backing from corporate foundations and wealthy individuals. Public fairs often included "fitter family" contests in which "judges reviewed human pedigrees to determine the most eugenically positive families, just as the best cattle, chickens, and pigs competed for blue ribbons."[33]

Immigration restriction paralleled controlled breeding as a strategy for improving the racial stock. Between 1891 and 1907, a series of federal immigration laws excluded people for mental deficiency, a history of mental illness, epilepsy, and "crimes of moral turpitude."[34] But advocates of immigration restriction also pushed for a more explicitly racial policy. As discussed previously, Chinese immigration was barred in the 1880s. Japanese immigration was sharply limited in 1907, and the 1917 immigration law excluded laborers from most other Asian countries.[35] Meanwhile the Immigration Restriction League, founded in 1894 and based among the New England elite, lobbied for exclusion of the non-Nordic European immigrants. Their first success came during the war, in 1917, when Congress required that immigrants be able to read and write. This measure targeted southern and eastern Europeans, who were believed to have high illiteracy rates. In the wake of the Red Scare, restrictionists went even further. A temporary law in 1921 limited immigration from any European country to 3 percent of the number of its nationals who were listed as U.S. residents in the 1910 census. The 1924 Immigration Act changed the limit to 2 percent of nationals resident in 1890, which drastically reduced the immigration quotas for eastern and southern European countries. The Italian quota fell from 42,000 to about 4,000, and the Polish from 31,000 to 6,000. The same law barred immigration by all "aliens ineligible for citizenship," which included all Asians except for Filipinos (who as colonial subjects were eligible for U.S. citizenship until that privilege was revoked in 1934).[36]

Nordic supremacist arguments dominated the immigration debates that led to the 1924 laws. For the first time southern and eastern Europeans faced large-scale exclusion based on their status as non-Nordics. The AFL, the American Legion, and the Ku Klux Klan had all lobbied for the 1924 Immigration Act, which passed both houses of Congress by large margins. Big business had long opposed immigration restriction because it wanted the readily exploitable labor new immigrants provided. But by the early 1920s, the migration of African Americans to northern cities, combined with mechanization, reduced industry's demand for European workers, so corporate leaders, too, endorsed racial restrictions. However, agricultural and other business interests blocked efforts to restrict immigration from Mexico. Mexicans were exempted from the literacy provision of the 1917 Immigration Act until economic recession reduced demand in 1921. Western agribusiness forestalled efforts to include quota limitations on Mexican immigration in the 1921 and 1924 acts.[37]

Although Nordicists won the battle over immigration policy, they were not able to consolidate Nordic supremacy as a permanent replacement for White supremacy. Southern and eastern Europeans still had access to naturalized citizenship as White persons.[38] And, as we discuss in the next chapter, over time they were able to become full members of the White racial caste through Americanization.

THE SECOND INVISIBLE EMPIRE

The Ku Klux Klan, perhaps more than any other organization, brought together this period's broad range of political hatreds. The Klan's rebirth in 1915 followed some two decades of intense anti-Black terrorism across the South and widespread glorification of the original Klan. Prominent White historians such as future president Woodrow Wilson and popular novelists such as Thomas Dixon portrayed Reconstruction as a time of barbaric rule by Blacks and carpetbaggers, a time when the Klan nobly defended civilization and White womanhood. D. W. Griffith's groundbreaking and enormously popular film *Birth of a Nation* (1915) dramatized Dixon's *The Clansman* (1905) and brought the racist myth of the Klan to millions of viewers.[39]

The film's success, which helped to establish Hollywood moviemaking as a major industry, also encouraged William Simmons, a former Methodist preacher experienced in fraternal orders, to refound the Invisible Empire in Georgia.

Another precipitating event was the Leo Frank case, which ended with the first antisemitic lynching in U.S. history. Frank was a Jewish businessman from New York living in Atlanta who was falsely convicted after one of his employees, a fourteen-year-old girl named Mary Phagan, was found raped and murdered in 1914. During Frank's appeal, to which several rich northern Jews contributed money, a statewide vilification campaign developed, which drew on images of the Jewish "white slaver" as well as fear of Jews stimulated by the 1914 depression. Tom Watson, a Populist turned reactionary, spearheaded the campaign. In his newspaper, he called Frank the "lecherous Jew . . ., the lascivious pervert guilty of the crime that caused the almighty to blast the Cities of the Plain" and wrote that "the black man's lust after the white woman is not much fiercer than the lust of the licentious Jew for the Gentile." Watson also urged that "another Ku Klux Klan may be organized to restore Home Rule."[40] In August 1915, Frank was lynched by a group calling itself the Knights of Mary Phagan, who burned an enormous cross on Stone Mountain overlooking Atlanta two months later. In November 1915, Simmons led fifteen men in a ceremony on Stone Mountain to found a new "Invisible Empire, Knights of the Ku Klux Klan, Inc." The burning cross, which was featured in Dixon's novel and Griffith's film but, according to Wyn Craig Wade, was not used by the original Klan,[41] became one of its symbols.

Initially the new KKK was little more than a fraternal order that borrowed the glory and ritual of the original Klan. The wartime crusade against disloyalty gave the Klan a political purpose. Klansmen "began harassing prostitutes around military bases, threatening people who seemed insufficiently fired by wartime zeal, and bullying laborers 'infested with the I.W.W. spirit.'"[42] In 1918 they kidnapped labor leaders and threatened would-be strikers at the Mobile shipyards and Birmingham mills. The Klan's Red Scare mission led it to strengthen its emphasis on secrecy and mystery.[43] Still, by early 1920, the Klan included only a few thousand members in Georgia and Alabama.

In the period immediately after the Left's crushing defeat, culminating in the Palmer Raids, the Knights of the Ku Klux Klan rose to national prominence. The 1920s has been described as "an entrepreneurial riot," and the Klan was in on the salesmanship boom from the beginning.[44] Just as the Wilson administration forcefully combined propaganda and repression during the war, the Klan combined mass marketing and vigilantism to powerful effect in 1920–1922. In June 1920, some five months after the Palmer Raids, Imperial Wizard Simmons commissioned the Southern Publicity Association (SPA) to be the Klan's new "Propagation Department." The SPA, consisting of Edward Young Clarke and Elizabeth Tyler, had promoted the Salvation Army, the YMCA, and the Red Cross. Clarke and Tyler quickly set up an efficient organizational structure based on local recruiters, or "Kleagles," who worked on commission. Within a year, the SPA had hired 1,100 Kleagles, and within fifteen months the Klan had grown from 3,000 to about 100,000 members, each of whom contributed $10 for membership, plus fees for robes and other items.[45]

Clarke and Tyler's Kleagles recruited at showings of *Birth of a Nation*, at Protestant churches, and in fraternal orders, especially Masonic lodges. They varied their appeal depending on local circumstances. Unlike its Reconstruction-era predecessor, the new Klan was not only White supremacist but also anti-Catholic, antisemitic, against "Foreign Labor Agitators," and for 100 percent Americanism. In the same decade that launched Protestant fundamentalism, the Klan also championed religious piety. It defended "traditional values" against the growing independence of young women and men and the rising commercialization of sexuality in movies, advertising, magazines, and songs. It claimed to uphold prohibition—inscribed in the Constitution since 1919—when millions of citizens were ignoring it. Local Klan groups would opportunistically use any of these and other themes as the focus of their organizing drives.

During this early growth period the Klan perpetrated widespread violence. Most of its vigilante activity was concentrated in five southern and southwestern states—Georgia, Alabama, Florida, and especially Texas and Oklahoma—which were the first areas of its rapid expansion, although scattered Klan terrorism took place in all regions.[46] In the fall of 1920, Klansmen paraded through southwestern towns to warn Blacks against voting. The Klan assaulted Blacks, Catholics, Jews, and immigrants for failing to be subservient, especially, in the case of Black men, for "insulting a white woman." Sometimes Klan violence also targeted White Protestants, for bootlegging, adultery, gambling, "petting parties," and other moral offenses. A widely reprinted September 1921 New York *World* exposé detailed 152 Klan attacks, including forty-one whippings, twenty-seven tar-and-featherings, and four murders. But a half-hearted congressional investigation that fall merely gave the Klan lots of favorable publicity.[47]

By 1922 the Klan had grown into a national movement. Peak membership estimates vary from one-and-a-half million to five million or more. President Warren Harding joined in 1921 in a special White House ceremony led by Imperial Wizard Simmons.[48] The Klan was strongest in the Midwest; it briefly dominated Indiana politics and had important influence in such far-flung states as Texas, Oregon, Colorado, Georgia, and Maine. In 1923, the Women of the Ku Klux Klan was founded and soon included hundreds of thousands of members. Hiram Evans, who succeeded William Simmons as Imperial Wizard of the KKK after a power struggle in 1922, tried to reduce Klan violence and urged more emphasis on conventional political chan-

nels. The order helped to elect some sixteen U.S. senators, eleven governors, and an unknown number of congressional representatives and local
officials from both major parties. But the Invisible Empire was unable to sustain its size or power. Blacks, Catholics, Jews, and many others organized
against the Klan, with tactics ranging from public ridicule to antimask laws,
and from boycotts of Klan merchants to mass physical attacks on Klan gatherings. Internal conflicts, lack of a clear long-term program, and leadership
scandals also severely weakened the Klan. Indiana Grand Dragon D. C.
Stephenson, in particular, was convicted of murder in 1925 for the kidnapping, rape, and fatal torturing of a White woman.[49] After 1925 the Klan
declined rapidly, although it retained a southern core of support.

Until fairly recently, most accounts of the 1920s Klan have tended to
portray it as small-town, "white trash" parochialism and religious fundamentalism run amok. These accounts describe Klan members as economic and
historical "losers" frightened by the modern world and cities and the foreigners who congregated in them, venting their frustrations and longings on
imaginary enemies. In the same vein, such accounts describe the Klan's
vigilantism and racial and religious bigotry as forms of social deviance and
political pathology.

But this characterization of the 1920s Klan has increasingly come under attack.[50] A growing body of research, especially a number of detailed local studies published since the late 1970s, have suggested a different, more
complex, picture. The Klan, these studies have argued, was centered in big
cities; a majority of Klan members were longtime city dwellers, came from a
broad range of class backgrounds, and belonged to mainstream Protestant
denominations. The new scholarship has stressed diversity of members,
goals, and tactics within the Klan movement. Several historians have argued
that most Klansmen avoided vigilante violence and were not primarily motivated by racial or religious bigotry. In Indiana, for example, little direct violence—and no lynchings—took place during the Klan's reign.[51] In Leonard
J. Moore's words,

> The idea that the Klan existed primarily to suppress ethnic minorities fails to
> explain why the Klan became most popular in states where members of these
> groups lived in the smallest numbers [for example, in Indiana], and why,
> when the Klan gained political power in these states, it all but ignored the lo-
> cal populations of ethnic minorities that did exist.[52]

In many areas, these authors contend, the Klan gained support primarily because it addressed popular local concerns such as law enforcement, especially prohibition, and moral and civic reform. "The Klan, it seems, could
direct itself to popular desires for new school buildings, clean government,
and crime-free streets as easily as it could represent popular prejudices."[53]
In the Klan's vision, such local concerns were integral to the White
Protestant traditions and values that must be protected.[54]

The point here is not to dismiss the Klan's hideous record of bigotry and terrorism but rather to contextualize it. As Shawn Lay concludes in one recent study,

> it is clear that the biased stereotype of the Invisible Empire as an irrational movement that lay outside the major currents of American political and social life must for the most part be discarded. Not only does this traditional view unfairly depict the millions of average citizens who joined or supported the Klan, but it obscures the racism and bigotry that have traditionally pervaded United States society. Far from being a historical aberration, the Ku Klux Klan reflected the hopes, fears, and guiding values of much of the American public in the 1920s.[55]

The Knights of the Ku Klux Klan were part of a broader movement to defend White Protestant dominance and repel socialism and anarchism. During and shortly after World War I, many sections of this movement used physical violence against ethnic and political opponents. The Klan itself used terrorism extensively in the South and Southwest from 1917 to 1922; in other areas it reaped the fruits of violence perpetrated by other sections of the movement. By the 1920s, with many ethnic and political opponents defeated or shut out, open violence at least partially receded in favor of threats, boycotts, whisper campaigns, and electoral organizing. At the same time, White fears of external threats partially gave way to a focus on purifying White Protestant America itself. While the eugenicists tried to purify the dominant group racially through controlled breeding, the Klan portrayed itself as purifying it morally.

The recent scholarship highlights populist features of the 1920s Klan that belie a strictly conservative defense of the established order. First, antielitism often figured prominently in local Klan activities. Although business and professional leaders took part in the Klan in many communities, in many others the secret order denounced the local political establishment for failing to control street crime, enforce prohibition, maintain public works, or other misdeeds. Second, the Klan reflected both antimodern impulses, such as its efforts to enforce traditional sexual morality, and modern ones, such as its use of mass marketing techniques and the new film industry in recruitment. Third, the Klan movement combined patriarchal and quasifeminist tendencies. The WKKK, the male Klan's autonomous female affiliate, often turned the movement's conventional image of womanhood into a call for expanding White Protestant women's social, economic, and political rights.

While the Klan's relationship with local elites varied, it often presented itself as a vehicle for "the plain people" to find a greater role in politics, and those in power often felt threatened by the secret order. "By 1922 almost all major southern urban dailies, which typically served as the spokespieces of entrenched political and economic interests, openly opposed the Klan." In Indiana, the Klan's "most powerful adversaries were businessmen's organizations such as the Rotary Club and the Chamber of Commerce." In Georgia's U.S. Senate race of 1920, the Klan backed former Populist Tom Watson, whom the American Legion denounced as a "Bolshevist." In Canon City, Colorado, the Klan sponsored a successful "Progressive" slate; the Klan labeled the town's elite a tool of the papal conspiracy but also criticized its economic conservatism and failure to spend money to improve sewers, streets, and schools. In El Paso, Texas, the Klan mainly represented middle-class Anglos against both the business establishment and the Mexican working class. In Eugene, Oregon, "many Eugene Klansmen were salesmen or relatively young owners or managers of local businesses, who had a stake in a developing economy." The Klan offered them "a means to challenge what they perceived as entrenched economic and political interests." In Salt Lake City, Utah, "a group of non-Mormon businessmen apparently constituted the main force behind the establishment of the KKK, viewing the secret society as a promising means of challenging Mormon mercantile power."[56]

The Klan's relations with organized labor also reflected its antielitist tendencies. The Klan staunchly opposed "foreign labor radicals" and took part in strikebreaking and antiunion activities in Oklahoma, Kansas, and West Virginia.[57] But sometimes Klansmen sided with strikes by White workers, including, in 1922, railroad strikers in La Grande, Oregon, and in Kansas. The La Grande klavern set up a committee to investigate "four klansmen who are strikebreakers and who are teaching negroes and japs to take places of strikers."[58] At the 1924 United Mine Workers convention, Klansmen joined with leftists in an unsuccessful bid to increase rank-and-file power over union officials. In 1927 some Colorado Klansmen even aided an unsuccessful miners strike led by the declining IWW.[59] Although the Colorado Federation of Labor, like several other AFL affiliates, condemned the KKK, many Colorado Federation members joined the Klan, which also enjoyed substantial support among labor unionists in Indiana, Pennsylvania, Louisiana, Alabama, and Wisconsin.[60]

Klan ties with organized labor must be viewed in relation to the racism and nativism that pervaded the White labor movement. As in the past, most AFL unions excluded or segregated workers of color. The AFL's Texas affiliate often helped employers break Chicano strikes. The East St. Louis Central Trades Council had helped to incite that city's 1917 anti-Black pogrom, and even AFL organizer William Z. Foster—future Communist Party leader—scapegoated and threatened Black workers after the defeat of the 1919 steel strike.[61] Similarly, the Klan's electoral alliance with the Socialist Party in Oregon in 1922 and Wisconsin in 1924 reflected continued racism and nativism among Socialists as much as Klan members' support for economic reform.[62]

But there is no question that many Klan members did not fit the common stereotype of marginal, hopelessly ignorant, backward reactionaries.

For example, according to a 1924 *Outlook* magazine poll of Pennsylvania and New Jersey Klan members, almost one-quarter of respondents supported the nationalization of railroads and coal mines. (Only 5 percent opposed such measures.) More surprisingly, 38 percent favored, and only 2 percent opposed, a federal antilynching law. And over 40 percent supported (3 percent opposed) "equal social, legal, and industrial rights for women."[63]

One of the 1920s Klan's most striking features is the degree to which it accommodated feminist demands.[64] On the one hand, the 1920s KKK was a fraternal organization that claimed to admit only "real men" and that continued the traditional Klan emphasis on protecting "pure American womanhood."[65] On the other hand, several factors pushed the Klan movement to modify its traditional stance: women's large-scale participation in the suffrage and temperance movements, their increasing economic independence through wage work, and the passage of the Nineteenth Amendment in 1920 recognizing women's right to vote. By 1922, White Protestant women objected to being excluded from the Klan as if they were no better than Blacks, Jews, or Catholics. Several Klan-oriented women's organizations were consolidated in the Women of the Ku Klux Klan, founded in June 1923.[66]

The WKKK drew on the fruits of women's organizing over several decades. The Women's Christian Temperance Union, although not limited to White Protestants, had scapegoated Catholics and immigrants as the cause of alcohol problems since the 1890s. The women's suffrage movement, too, had moved far from its original close association with the antislavery and antiracist cause. As early as 1869, suffragist leader Elizabeth Cady Stanton had urged: "American women of wealth, virtue and refinement, if you do not wish the lower orders of Chinese, Africans, Germans and Irish, with their low ideas of womanhood to make laws for you . . . demand that woman, too, shall be represented in the government." By the turn of the century, such racist and nativist arguments had become routine, and the National American Women's Suffrage Association refused to denounce lynching or racial injustice, despite repeated criticisms from Black women suffragists. Many Klanswomen, including the WKKK's first Imperial Commander, Lulu Markwell, had been active in the temperance and suffrage causes.[67]

Like the male KKK, the WKKK used white robes and masks, emphasized ritual, and adopted a militaristic, hierarchical structure. While some chapters functioned merely as social auxiliaries to the KKK, many Klanswomen asserted the autonomy of their organization and resisted efforts by male Klan leaders to control it. Women took an active part in Klan demonstrations and boycotts of Jewish and Catholic-owned businesses. In Indiana, Klanswomen formed a statewide "poison squad"—a tightly organized network for spreading malicious rumors against those targeted by the Klan. Following a 1924 Klan riot in Wilkinsburg, Pennsylvania, a large group of

Klanswomen reportedly paraded through town armed with heavy riot clubs.[68]

Both the KKK and the WKKK were ambivalent about women's status, but in different ways. The men's Klan most often took a paternalistic line toward White Protestant women, treating them as helpless victims of Black, Jewish, Catholic, and White Protestant men. When the Indiana KKK attacked gambling, prostitution, and alcohol, it consistently claimed to be protecting wives from their husband's economic recklessness or drunken violence. If women were the transgressors, as in cases of adultery, they could be punished with particular sadism. Klansmen sought to keep women in secondary, supporting roles to men. Yet, KKK publications repeatedly endorsed efforts to strengthen women's rights, such as the National Women's Party campaign to elect women to Congress, and once praised women's entry into the wage labor force as the awakening of "women's economic freedom."[69]

The WKKK took this quasifeminism a step further. Klanswomen reinterpreted the idealized, patronizing Klan symbols associated with "pure American womanhood" to point out gender inequality. For example,

> Klanswomen described the home as a place of labor for women, the site of "monstrous and grinding toil and sacrifice." The life of a homemaker, the WKKK insisted, was held in "low esteem" by the larger society and women received too little credit for their efforts. It also pictured marriage as a double-edged sword for women—at once women's crowning glory and the burden they bore. . . . Even motherhood . . . the WKKK described as women's *work*. . . . One kleagle encouraged Klanswomen mothers to campaign collectively for an eight-hour day for the job of mothering.[70]

Klanswomen interwove these sentiments with racial and religious bigotry. They accused Black men of seeking to marry White women, Jewish-owned movie houses and dance halls of spreading sexual immorality, and Catholic priests and nuns of kidnapping, raping, and torturing Protestant girls. Bishop Alma Bridwell White of the fundamentalist Pillar of Fire church, a suffragist who urged passage of the Equal Rights Amendment, was also a leading Klan advocate. She spread lurid stories of Jewish and Catholic sexual predators and proclaimed that the Catholic Church was the world's main force opposing women's suffrage and equality.[71]

Male supremacist ideology remained dominant within the 1920s Klan movement as a whole. But the movement's disturbing mixture of pro- and antifeminism in a right-wing racist framework is comparable to Oswald Mosley's British Union of Fascists of the 1930s, in which veterans of Britain's women's suffrage movement sparred with hearth-and-home traditionalists.[72] Similar dynamics could be seen more recently in sections of the U.S. Far Right, for example in the Aryan Women's League and a neonazi publication entitled *The Radical Feminist* (later, *The Rational Feminist*), which was based in Florida in the 1980s and 1990s. These examples highlight the tendency of right-wing populist movements—both fascist and nonfascist—to co-opt elements of progressive politics by reframing them within an oppressive framework.

CONCLUSION

Like Theodore Roosevelt's Progressivism, the 1920s Ku Klux Klan can be usefully compared to parallel developments in Europe. Such comparison helps clarify the Klan's politics and the role of right-wing populism in the United States during that period. In many ways, the Klan resembled the European fascist movements that arose at the same time. Both the Klan and the fascists responded to industrial-era social change with a combination of nostalgia and forward-looking appeals. Both used mass marketing, propaganda, and elaborate ritual to mobilize a broad following into a hierarchical organization. Both developed largely as a backlash against the Left and against supposed moral and cultural decay within society at large. Both promoted social oppression but appropriated some elements of antielitism and liberatory politics, such as feminism and labor activism. And, at least in some cases, both used violence and intimidation against political opponents and scapegoats.

Because of these similarities, as well as the Klan's later history, many people have described the 1920s Klan as a fascist movement. But, while the fascists rejected parliamentary pluralism, the Klan remained loyal to the U.S. republic. Fascists wanted to sweep away the old political systems in favor of a dictatorial "new order" in which loyalty to the national community replaced any concept of individual rights or competing interests. The Klan manipulated political institutions where it could but made no moves to seize complete power or remake society in totalitarian fashion. Like Roosevelt's Progressives, the 1920s Klan found a pluralist political system built on deeply undemocratic foundations and functioned comfortably within it.

As background to these differences between the Klan and European fascists, a few points are worth noting briefly. Unlike the European countries where fascism thrived, the United States was not devastated or traumatized by World War I: it entered the fighting late, had relatively few casualties, and fought no battles on home soil. The United States emerged from the conflict not only on the winning side but also as the strongest economic power on earth. Superpatriots raised no cries of national humiliation, urging traitors to be thrown out of power. And, while the leftist upsurge in the United States was strong enough to provoke intense repression, it never approached the revolutionary force that horrified and mobilized nationalists across continental Europe. Unlike most of Europe, the United States had a stable republic with broad popular support and a set of institutions well able to suppress or co-opt social conflicts. Not until the Great Depression of the 1930s would this system start to unravel.

6

THE INDUSTRIALIST AS PRODUCER

Henry Ford's Corporate Empire

While the Ku Klux Klan was gathering millions of supporters, Henry Ford was sponsoring the biggest antisemitic propaganda campaign the United States had ever seen. The *Dearborn Independent*, a weekly newspaper owned by Ford and distributed largely through his auto dealerships, ran a series of anti-Jewish articles from 1920 to 1927. Many of the articles were later collected in a book entitled *The International Jew*, which became a classic of twentieth-century antisemitism. The German Nazis admired the work, and several generations of fascists on both sides of the Atlantic have been influenced by Ford's version of the global Jewish conspiracy myth.

Many historians have treated Henry Ford's antisemitism as an embarrassing side issue in his life, or as a quirky throwback to his boyhood on a farm and imagined roots in the agrarian Populist movement.[1] Actually, hatred of Jews was integrally tied to Ford's industrial philosophy, and his rapport with fascist politics extended far beyond antisemitism. Like the German Nazis and many other fascists, Ford regarded himself as a champion of productive industry, threatened by parasitic financiers from above and subversive labor organizers from below. He worked hard to destroy working-class independence within the Ford Motor Company, first through paternalism but increasingly through physical terror. He regarded Black people as racially inferior to Whites and immigrants as culturally inferior to native-born Americans. He glorified both modern technology and traditional farm life, and his village industry experiments provided a model for deurbanization plans in Nazi Germany. While preaching the sanctity of the family, he used bureaucratic power not only to reinforce male dominance but also to probe workers' home lives and reshape families to meet company requirements. And he cultivated an image as a charismatic, action-oriented leader who cut across ideological lines and could draw support from both the Right and the Left. These policies echoed those of European fascists and helped lay the basis for U.S. fascist politics in the 1930s. Ford developed a kind of right-wing populist politics without a mass movement or political organization.

THE INTERNATIONAL JEW

Ford purchased the *Dearborn Independent* in November 1918. The anti-Jewish articles began in May 1920, appeared regularly until December 1921, and continued appearing thereafter in periodic bursts until 1927, when the paper was closed down. Ford auto dealers were urged to sell a subscription with every Model T car. Estimates of the readership vary from 250,000 to close to one million. Klan publications often reprinted the antisemitic articles. Some half-million copies of the four-volume collection, *The International Jew*, were sold in the United States, and it was also translated into numerous languages and distributed all over the world. With the help of the Nazis, the book became a best-seller in Germany.[2]

U.S. antisemitism in this period was widespread and institutionalized. For several decades, Jews had routinely been barred from jobs, housing, and hotels. As some Yiddish-speaking immigrants or their children began to rise out of the working-class ghettos into small business and white-collar work, systematic discrimination increased. In the 1920s, many colleges and universities established quotas to limit the number of Jewish students. Discrimination sharply limited Jews' entry into the middle class, and excluded them almost entirely from corporate management and university faculties.[3] In these ways, reflecting Nordic supremacist doctrine, Jews were systematically denied some of the privileges accorded to Whites. This affected the older and more Americanized German Jewish community as well as the eastern European newcomers. Systematic discrimination both strengthened and was strengthened by widespread anti-Jewish propaganda, especially during and after the Red Scare.

The articles in *The International Jew* were largely based on an earlier antisemitic work, *The Protocols of the Elders of Zion*. A forgery first published in 1903 in Russia and generally attributed to the czar's secret police, the *Protocols* purport to be the account of secret meetings by leaders of world Jewry conspiring to take over the world.[4] Here was scapegoating on an immense scale—tracing war, collectivism, tyranny, financial speculation, social disorder, global government, and revolution all to a single demonic plot. Following the Russian Revolution, czarist émigrés brought the forgery to other European countries and the United States, claiming that it was an authentic explanation of the Bolshevik Revolution. Boris L. Brasol, who in the United States organized the Union of Czarist Army and Navy Officers, commissioned an English translation of the *Protocols* and presented it to U.S. officials. The New York office of the army's Military Intelligence Division helped Brasol's group circulate the forgery.[5] Ford's representatives received a copy of the *Protocols* in 1920.[6]

The *Dearborn Independent* printed excerpts from the *Protocols* and applied them to contemporary U.S. society. The press, the theater, bootleg liquor, the burgeoning film industry, and the "abandoned sensuousness" of jazz— all were part of a calculated Jewish effort to spread propaganda and corrupt Gentile morals, according to the *Independent*. It was Jewish profiteers who had engineered World War I and pushed the United States into the conflict. Secret societies that had previously been scapegoated in the United States— the Illuminati and the Masons—were revealed to be merely fronts for Jewish interests. All reflected the workings of the covert world government of "All-Judaan." Jews were able to rule covertly because of special racial characteristics: "commercial and masterful genius" and "a racial loyalty and solidarity the like of which exists in no other human group."[7] Yet, Ford's newspaper insisted that it was promoting fairness, not antisemitism: "it is usually understood that . . . humanity ought to be shown toward the Jew. There is just as great an obligation upon the Jew to show his humanity toward the whole race." The paper trivialized antisemitism by claiming that Jews were just as ruthless as their opponents: "society is as helpless before the well-organized extortions of certain financial groups, as huddled groups of Russian Jews were helpless against the anti-Semitic mob."[8]

Ford's newspaper offered the standard antisemitic claim that Jews were parasites, not producers, and that Jewish financiers were the real exploiters, fundamentally at odds with Gentile "creative industry":

> That which we call capital here in America is usually money used in production, and we mistakenly refer to the manufacturer, the manager of work, the provider of tools and jobs—we refer to him as the "capitalist." . . . There is a power yet above him—a power which treats him far more callously and holds him in a more ruthless hand than he would ever dare display to labor.[9]

Jews were both economic exploiters and revolutionaries, Ford's paper claimed, evidenced by the "fact" that Jewish bankers had financed the Bolsheviks.

> The real struggle in this country is not between labor and capital; the real struggle is between Jewish capital and Gentile capital, with the I.W.W. leaders, the Socialist leaders, the Red leaders and the labor leaders almost a unit on the side of the Jewish capitalists.[10]

Another striking feature of the *Independent's* anti-Jewish campaign was its Anglophobia. Since before the Civil War, Britain's dominant position in the world economy had led some U.S. economists and currency reformers to portray British financiers as sinister manipulators. By the 1890s, this theme had merged with antisemitism in the image of the English Rothschild banking family.[11] Ford's newspaper took it almost for granted that Jews controlled Britain, which suggests this claim was commonly accepted in the 1920s United States. World Jewry could rely on

> the British fleet which guards from hindrance the progress of all-Jewish world economy, or that part of it which depends on the sea. In return, All-Judaan assures Britain an undisturbed political and territorial world rule. All-Judaan has added Palestine to British control.[12]

Ironically, British leaders such as Winston Churchill and the self-described "ardent Zionist" Lord Balfour, both of whom were often labeled as pawns of the Jews, had themselves blamed Bolshevism on a Jewish plot.[13]

The International Jew series paralleled the work of Nesta H. Webster, who synthesized conspiracy theories concerning Jewish elites and the Illuminati Freemasons in *World Revolution: The Plot against Civilization* (1921) and *Secret Societies and Subversive Movements* (1924).[14] While much of her work stressed non-Jewish secret elites, antisemitic stereotyping runs throughout it. Webster helped write the original *London Morning Post* series that introduced *The Protocols of the Elders of Zion* to a wide British audience.[15] In the 1930s and early 1940s Elizabeth Dilling and many other rightists applied many of Nesta Webster's themes to Roosevelt and the New Deal, portraying communism as Jewish and Roosevelt as an agent of the conspiracy, or, in some versions, as a secret Jew himself.[16]

Conspiracist hatred of Jews, John Higham argues, did not then have the intellectual respectability that Nordic supremacy had achieved. Thus, Ford's antisemitic articles encountered sharp criticism not only from Jewish organizations but also from non-Jewish liberals, church groups, and many political leaders. In 1927, under the pressure of a libel suit, Henry Ford ceased publication of the *Independent* and publicly apologized to the Jewish people, blaming the articles on his newspaper staff. However, he made little effort to block continued circulation of *The International Jew* until 1942, when the United States was at war with Nazi Germany.[17]

Long after the *Independent* closed shop, the Ford empire maintained close ties with antisemites and fascists. *Independent* editor William J. Cameron, one of Ford's top assistants, went on to head a far-right organization called the Anglo-Saxon Federation, which was founded in 1930. The Federation advocated British Israelism, the doctrine that Anglo-Saxons were the descendants of the lost tribes of Israel: they, not Jews, were the true Chosen People. Cameron helped fuse British Israelism with racial and conspiracist antisemitism to create Christian Identity, a doctrine that many U.S. neonazis embraced in the 1980s and 1990s. The Ford payroll also included Heinz Spanknoebel, who founded a Detroit chapter of the Teutonia Society, and Fritz Kuhn, who later headed the German-American Bund.

Both of these were pro-Nazi organizations. In 1937, Ford security chief Harry Bennett, unsuccessfully trying to thwart a labor organizing drive, recruited the country's most prominent fascist, Father Charles Coughlin, to form a company union called the Workers Council for Social Justice, Inc. In 1938, Henry Ford accepted the Nazi government's prestigious Supreme Order of the German Eagle. He was the first American to receive the decoration.[18]

The extent of Henry Ford's ties with German Nazism is disputed. Adolf Hitler praised Ford repeatedly. Learning in 1923 that Ford might run for president, Hitler declared: "I wish that I could send some of my shock troops to Chicago and other big American cities to help in the elections. . . . We look to Heinrich Ford as the leader of the growing Fascist movement in America." In 1924, the vice president of the Bavarian Diet testified in court that Ford had funded Hitler's party. Various versions of this claim have often been repeated. However, Ford biographer Carol Gelderman argues that the claim is unsubstantiated and—in a more subjective judgment—that it would have been "totally out of character for Ford to act secretly."[19]

But Ford's relationship with fascism went beyond direct organizational ties or his newspaper campaign against the "international Jew"; it was embodied in the workings of his corporate empire as a whole. To understand this, we need to look more broadly at Henry Ford's beliefs, the development of the Ford Motor Company, and the treatment of its employees.

THE FORD EMPIRE

Automobile production in the United States increased tenfold between 1910 and 1915 and continued to rise sharply after that.[20] In 1910, the country had one passenger car registered for every forty-four households; by 1930, the figure was one for every 1.3 households.[21] Economist Douglas F. Dowd has described the automobile industry in this period as the "hot center" of the economy's dynamic sector. Its expansion "meant the expansion of industries directly (metals, machinery, paints, leather, rubber and glass) and indirectly (petroleum, highway, residential housing and service station construction, etc.) connected to the automobile."[22]

From the 1910s until the late 1920s, Henry Ford and the Ford Motor Company led this industrial explosion. By the early 1920s, half of all cars sold in the United States were Fords.[23] As David L. Lewis writes, "During the 1920s Henry Ford developed America's first vertically integrated . . . industrial empire," controlling all stages of production from extraction of raw materials, through refining, production of components, rail and water transport, to final manufacture of cars, trucks, tractors, and airplanes.[24] In the space of less than two decades, Henry Ford rose from a talented engineer to one of the richest and most powerful men in the world.

Ford Motor achieved its dominant position through a series of dramatic and innovative steps. In the 1910s, when many manufacturers regarded the automobile as a luxury product for a select market, Ford began mass producing the Model T as a simple, no-frills vehicle accessible to workers and farmers. To speed production and increase efficiency, the company introduced the conveyor belt assembly line and other forms of mechanization. Against standard business practice, Ford Motor repeatedly lowered prices on the Model T in the face of rising demand, from $950 in 1909 to $260 in 1924.[25] And in 1914 Ford doubled the wages of many of its workers by introducing a standard wage of five dollars a day.

It is difficult to exaggerate Henry Ford's enormous fame and popularity during this period. During the 1920s Ford received more publicity than any other American except Calvin Coolidge, who received attention only because he was president from 1923 to 1929. "The conservative *New York Times*, which omitted many of the reports and rumors concerning Ford, ran an average of 145 stories per year on the industrialist throughout the 1920s."[26] Henry Ford was regarded as a folk hero of industrial progress, efficiency, and abundance. In 1915, "enthusiastic crowds at the San Francisco ´Palace of Transportation´ rioted in their eagerness to see a working replica of Ford's new Highland Park assembly line."[27] In 1927, when Ford Motor unveiled its new Model A automobile, an estimated 10 million people jammed U.S. showrooms during the first 36 hours.[28] Henry Ford's corporate prestige was augmented by his personal image as self-made, plain-speaking, antielitist, and unpredictable.

During the 1910s, Ford had established a political reputation as unorthodox but generally left of center. In 1915–1916, with World War I raging in Europe but the United States still neutral, Ford loudly opposed military preparedness and personally led a peace delegation to Europe. After the United States entered the war in 1917, Ford supported President Wilson's liberal internationalism; in 1918 he ran for the Senate as a Democrat and a proponent of the League of Nations. In its first year (1919) Ford's *Dearborn Independent* criticized the Red Scare repression and supported women's suffrage, public ownership of railroads, telephones, and telegraphs, and a variety of other progressive reforms.[29] Although the beginning of the "international Jew" series in 1920 marked a shift in Ford's politics, it neither branded him as a reactionary in the public mind nor appreciably hurt his popularity. In 1923, with his anti-Jewish views by then well known, a national poll by *Collier's* magazine nonetheless listed Ford as the front-runner for president, fourteen percentage points ahead of incumbent Warren G. Harding. "Ford for President" clubs sprang up across the country. His principal base of support was in the left-leaning Progressive Party, successor to Theodore Roosevelt's party of 1912. A gathering of Progressives and other liberals from fifteen states endorsed Ford for president in November 1923. The movement, however, collapsed the following month when Ford declared he would support Calvin Coolidge, who had succeeded Harding as president on his death in August 1923.[30]

Ford's comments on the presidential race revealed his willingness to abandon an electoral system of government. In a 1923 interview he said: "I can't imagine myself today accepting any nomination. Of course I can't say what I will do tomorrow. There might be a war or some crisis of the sort, in which legalism and constitutionalism and all that wouldn't figure, and the nation wanted some person who could do things and do them quickly." "Shouldn't wonder," he told the interviewer, "if industry would eventually absorb the political government." This from a man who declared elsewhere that industry must be "more or less of a friendly autocracy."[31]

With journalists publicizing his views to an eager mass audience during the 1910s and 1920s, Henry Ford expounded his principles of prosperity. High wages and low prices, he declared, were good for business, because they ensured the manufacturer a stable, high-quality workforce and enabled people to buy the products. This was a startling departure from prevailing business practices and marked the rise of the new consumer society. "An underpaid man," Ford argued, "is a customer reduced in buying power." Frank Costigliola notes: "Along with such industrial leaders as Owen Young [chair of General Electric and RCA] and Alanson B. Houghton [congressmember and ambassador], Ford urged a consumption ethic. In 1919, Ford advertisements urged: 'Buy a Ford—SAVE the difference.' By 1923 the message had changed to: 'Buy a Ford—SPEND the difference.'"[32]

Ford's industrial philosophy brought together the antisemitism of the *Protocols* and the U.S. producerist tradition. This convergence was particularly striking in the 1926 book *Today and Tomorrow*, which Ford coauthored with journalist and economist Samuel Crowther.[33] Although the book counterposed good manufacturers and bad financiers in terms similar to the *Dearborn Independent*, and warned that "certain hereditary groups" had manipulated the world's gold supply for centuries, it contained no overt references to Jews.[34] This reticence served several purposes. First, it enabled Ford to keep the charge of antisemite at arm's length, as he also did the following year when he pretended that the "international Jew" series had been written without his knowledge. Second, the use of coded language to refer to Jews intensified the aura of mystery and power surrounding the Jewish conspiracy—here was a plot so dangerous it could only be hinted at. In recent decades the LaRouchites and others have taken such coded antisemitism to elaborate lengths. Third, the absence of overt hatred of Jews highlighted the distinctly homegrown tradition of producerism.

There is a clear American flavor in Ford and Crowther's praise for the dignity of manual labor and self-advancement, blurring of class boundaries, celebration of the "pioneer spirit" of innovation and industrial progress, and disdain for things and practices European. The Jacksonians would have applauded; the czarist reactionaries who wrote the *Protocols* would have squirmed. The high wage–low price policy was to Ford and Crowther a uniquely American contribution. In Europe and elsewhere, they saw capital and labor as tragically locked in conflict. Only in the United States, they claimed, was it recognized that "the owner, the employees, and the buying public are all one and the same" and that high wages and low prices were in the interest of all. "The man who possesses health, strength, and skill," they declared, "is a capitalist"—a definition that placed Henry Ford on the same level as the assembly line worker. Manhood itself was impossible without hard work: "A criminal is a non-producer, but when he has been caught and sentenced, it is very wasteful to continue him as a non-producer. He can surely be turned into a producer *and probably into a man*" [emphasis added].[35]

Ford, who considered himself a worker first and foremost, had contempt for the idle rich. Elsewhere he remarked that

> every manufacturer should be able to go into the shop and with his own hands make the thing that he wants to manufacture. If he cannot do this, he is no manufacturer at all. . . . His workingmen are the real manufacturers, and he is but a parasite that lives upon them.[36]

Ford and Crowther argued that "business—that is, the whole material side of life—is threatened by two classes of people who think they are in opposition, but who actually have a common cause—the professional financier and the professional reformer. . . . The professional financiers wrecked Germany. The professional reformers wrecked Russia."[37] Here was a thinly veiled reference to the Jew as banker and Bolshevik.

"Manufacturing is not to be confused with banking," insisted Ford and Crowther. The industrialist, they protested, was really an innocent victim caught in the middle of class struggle:

> In the violent period of the union labour movement, the employer was always referred to as the capitalist. The whole trouble was that the employer was not a capitalist, but was under the thumb of capitalists. In those years, most business was conducted on borrowed capital, which gave the capitalist a super-control of industry. The manufacturer, standing between hostile labour and rapacious capital, had a hard time getting anything done. Pressed from above for interest and dividends, pushed from below to grant more money for less work, he had small chance to give service. And all the time he had to bear the abuse that was being heaped upon the capitalist.[38]

Here Ford and Crowther used "capitalist" to mean banker or speculator, contradicting their equation of capitalist and worker noted above. In both cases, the point was the same: workers should identify with, and be loyal to, the industrialist and direct their class hostility against "the money power." Fortunately, "no money trust today controls the American worker, or the creator—the men who with hand or brain serve society in a productive way."[39]

While he built on a long U.S. tradition, Ford shared with European fascists the idea that workers and productive manufacturers should rally against the evil parasites exploiting them both. In addition, German Nazis often appealed to "the workers of hand and brain," meaning industrial workers and white-collar employees, as part of their claim that Aryan racial unity must transcend class differences.[40]

Ford's banker bashing was not an arbitrary choice of scapegoats. It reflected genuine tensions within the economic elite and the shifting industrial economy. Most leading auto companies relied on bank loans to expand, which often made them subject to a high degree of outside control. General Motors, for example, was run by a syndicate of eastern bankers from 1910 to 1916. During the economic slump of 1920–1921, control passed to the DuPont chemical company and the J. P. Morgan banking empire. In contrast, Ford Motor's expansion was financed almost entirely through sales revenues. New York bankers, many of whom considered Henry Ford mentally unstable, repeatedly tried to gain control of his company through purchase offers and by offering loans in exchange for a role in choosing company officers. Ford steadfastly resisted these attempts. The pressure on Ford's independence reached a peak in 1920–1921. In order to buy out minority stockholders and gain complete control of the company, Ford had finally borrowed $75 million from a group of eastern banks. The sudden drop in sales during 1920 threatened Ford Motor's independent survival, but the company held on by cutting costs and forcing dealers to pay for car shipments regardless of demand. It was during this crisis that Ford's newspaper launched the series on "the international Jew."[41]

Conflicts between bankers themselves may have contributed to Ford's antisemitic propaganda campaign. Thomas Ferguson has noted that "J. P. Morgan Jr. quietly encouraged Henry Ford's circulation of the notorious *Protocols of the Elders of Zion* in the early 1920s" at a time when the House of Morgan's dominance of investment banking was being challenged by a number of smaller firms, many of them led by Jews or seen as led by Jews.[42]

Ford's role as a champion of the emerging consumer economy ("Buy a Ford—SPEND the difference") may also have fueled his hostility toward finance capital. "I do not believe in bank accounts for boys," he declared in 1919; it was better that they should "invest in a mechanism if they have a mechanical bent and invest in good books if they like to read." Such statements, reports David L. Lewis, "horrified the banking community," with its traditional interest in promoting thrift. But this apparent conflict between banking and consumerism was at most temporary and brief. Over the course of the 1920s, commercial banks themselves began to provide consumer loans on a large scale.[43]

Ford's hostility to labor unions requires no special explanation—it reflected the basic clash of interests between owners and workers, all claims of producer unity notwithstanding. A union provides workers with a counterweight to the owners' control over the labor process, and Ford insisted on absolute control. This was not unusual. Business and industry, then as now, generally restricted or kept out unions wherever they could, and the 1920s was a particularly difficult period for the labor movement. Antiunionism did not always take the antisemitic form that Ford gave it, as in one 1923 interview: "You probably think the labor unions were organized by labor, but they weren't. They were organized by these Jew financiers. The labor union is a great scheme to interrupt work. It speeds up loafing. It's a great thing for the Jew to have on hand when he comes around to get his clutches on an industry."[44]

Yet, it was not financiers, but workers, Jewish and non-Jewish alike, who bore the brunt of Ford's antilabor policies.

Absolute control of labor was integral to the mechanized assembly system that Ford instituted in the 1910s. Before that time, auto assembly was the job of skilled mechanics who performed many different complex operations. With the moving assembly line system, management subdivided tasks wherever possible into simple, repetitive movements for maximum efficiency and speed. This drastically reduced the worker's sphere for independent thought, creativity, and initiative. Management took over these mental functions and used them to dictate every aspect of work. The worker became, as Karl Marx wrote fifty years before, the "mere living appendage" of the machine.[45] In Henry Ford's own words, "A business is men and machines united in the production of a commodity and both the men and the machines need repairs and replacements. . . . Machinery wears out and needs to be restored. Men grow uppish, lazy, or careless."[46]

Despite such statements, Ford usually denied the dehumanizing nature of mass assembly production. "The function of the machine," he and Crowther wrote, "is to liberate man from brute burdens, and release his energies to the building of his intellectual and spiritual powers for conquests in the fields of thought and higher action. The machine is the symbol of man's mastery of his environment."

Not only was repetitive work safe, but "it seems to produce better physical and mental health than non-repetitive work." And, in any case, "if the men did not like the work, they would leave."[47]

At first they did leave—by the thousands. The annual turnover rate for 1913 was 380 percent. At that time workers *could* leave the new mass assembly system, because other auto companies still used the older production methods. This option was soon closed off, as competition from Ford Motor caused other companies to copy its innovations. During 1913, the Industrial Workers of the World began an organizing drive among Ford workers. With the five-dollar day, announced in January 1914, Ford temporarily preempted unionizing efforts and ensured that throngs of workers would line up for jobs. The high wage policy not only helped provide a consumer market for Ford cars but also induced employees to accept disempowerment in the workplace.[48]

Thus, the rise of mass production, in which Ford and his company played a leading role, was not only a technological change but also a political one. It involved a shift of power on the shop floor from workers to owners. Intensified discipline and dehumanization were the reality behind Henry Ford's celebration of productive labor. In his eyes, those who refused to submit to this regime—by "loafing" or becoming "uppish"—joined the ranks of nonproducers, who were led by Jews. This was a plausible attempt by Ford to construct an ideological rationale for his own class power—just as plausible, for example, as the equally dubious claim that anyone can succeed in the United States through individual hard work. Today, Ford's view is judged irrational or paranoid not because it was incoherent but because it lost out to other ideologies that defend economic inequality.

In many respects Ford Motor treated its employees comparatively well—for a time. In 1914, the company not only started paying most of its workers five dollars a day, but also shortened the workday from nine hours to eight and established a system of job security for all employees. Further wage hikes and time reductions followed over the next fifteen years, although inflation and raises at other companies eroded Ford's advantage in this area. The major Ford plants at Highland Park and River Rouge were (for the time period) bright, well ventilated, and relatively safe. Company schools, grocery stores, and doctors provided workers a variety of free or inexpensive services.[49] Black workers were hired in far greater numbers and on a more egalitarian basis with Whites than at any other auto manufacturer. A company policy instituted in 1914 stated that no worker should be refused a job or dismissed on account of physical disability, and all jobs were classified and assigned according to the physical skills required.[50]

Beginning in the 1920s, however, Ford's "friendly autocracy" became less friendly. Workers were forbidden to talk or sit down on the job. Job security was abolished in 1920, and employees were often fired for petty offenses, such as buying a sandwich a few seconds before the lunch bell. Speedups, which sometimes caused workers literally to collapse from exhaustion, were instituted periodically. Starting in the late 1920s, the service department under Harry Bennett became an elaborate secret police network within the company. By the late 1930s, the department included about 800 toughs, many of them veterans of organized crime, who roamed the factories policing workers, brutally attacking and sometimes killing union organizers. About 10 percent of the workforce served as spies and informers for the department. The National Labor Relations Board called Ford's policy "a regime of terror and violence directed against its employees." This system was not broken until 1941, when Ford workers shut down the enormous River Rouge plant and forced the company to sign a contract with the United Auto Workers (UAW).[51]

Long before Harry Bennett's "regime of terror," however, Ford Motor used authoritarian methods not only to control the labor process but also to reshape workers' home lives. Workers had to meet a set of conditions in order to receive the five-dollar-day wage. Married men had to be "living with and taking good care of their families." Single men had to be "of proven thrifty habits." Women, and men under age twenty-two, had to be "the sole support of some next of kin or blood relative." At first women were excluded entirely from the five-dollar-day wage; Ford reversed this when feminists protested, but few women at Ford Motor actually received the higher wage. Married women were not hired unless their husbands were unable to work. Gamblers, alcoholics, and drug addicts were ineligible for the five-dollar day, as were employees who conducted any kind of outside business. All employees had to show what they did with wages left over after food, shelter, and clothing.[52]

To determine who was eligible for the five-dollar day, the company's sociology department investigated all workers in their homes. They instructed workers and their families about hygiene, personal habits, shopping, home management, and the use of savings banks. Most employees were quick to comply with the company's directives rather than be denied the higher wage.[53]

Ford claimed to be lifting working-class families out of slum life, but the workers and their families had no say in shaping the policies. Even the Detroit Board of Commerce, presumably not a champion of industrial democracy, concluded that Ford's system was despotic and should be administered by the workers themselves.[54]

Part of Ford Motor's goal with its social engineering policies, as Martha May notes, was to cultivate "a specific form of family structure" among its workers:

> Ford believed that only a specific form of family relationship—one in which the husband provided for a non-income-earning wife—would insure the stability of his labor force. . . . Ford appeared to sanction only the most "middle-class" form of family life, or what seemed to be the middle-class form of life to him, where a husband earned enough to protect the home as a sanctuary and a refuge.[55]

Many labor unionists since the Jacksonian era had argued that the adult male worker should be paid a "family wage" high enough to "keep his wife and children out of competition with himself." At the turn of the century, this principle became standard among Progressive movement reformers. The principle's corollary was that women could or should be excluded from wage labor, since they supposedly drove down wages and would all be-

come wives anyway. Thus, the family wage doctrine reinforced sexist no-
tions of true manhood and womanhood and helped keep women economically dependent on men. To a degree, Ford Motor's efforts to reshape
workers' families according to its own dictates also resembled Italian and
German fascist policy, which glorified the family as inviolate but subjected
it to extensive bureaucratic pressure and intrusion in the name of national
duty.[56]

Ford's social engineering also focused on the "un-American" practices
of immigrant workers. "When first we raised the wages to five dollars a
day," Ford and Crowther wrote in 1926, "we had to exercise some supervision over the living of the men because so many of them, being foreign
born, did not raise their standards of living in accord with their higher incomes." Sociology department investigations into workers' personal habits
weighed more heavily on immigrants than on native-born White workers.
For example, the company "had to break up the evil custom among many of
the foreign workers of taking in boarders—of regarding their homes as
something to make money out of rather than as a place to live in."[57]

To help the company Americanize its foreign-born workers, Ford established an English School in 1914, which all immigrant employees were required to attend. This school became a model for Americanization programs across the country. Not all of its methods were especially subtle:

> The first thing that foreign-speaking employees learned in the Ford school
> was how to say, "I am a good American." Later the students acted out a panto-
> mime [in which] a great melting pot (labeled as such) occupied the middle of
> the stage. A long column of immigrant students descended into the pot from
> backstage, clad in outlandish garb and flaunting signs proclaiming their father-
> lands. Simultaneously from either side of the pot another stream of men
> emerged, each prosperously dressed in identical suits of clothes and each car-
> rying a little American flag.[58]

Throughout the 1910s and 1920s, many industrialists and middle-class
reformers promoted Americanization. By 1920, twenty-eight states sponsored programs for educating immigrants, and fifteen states banned foreign
language instruction in basic school subjects.[59] But Americanization was
not just a consciously directed crusade. The everyday pressures of the workplace and the marketplace, as well as the rapidly expanding advertising and
film industries, also pushed immigrants to assimilate.

Americanization taught immigrants to abandon the habits, family structures, traditions, and loyalties of agricultural and handicraft societies in favor of industrial discipline, "rationality," and wage labor. It meant learning
to be a "good citizen"—and to reject the "un-American" doctrines of socialism, communism, and anarchism. In defiance of Nordicist efforts to exclude
southern and eastern Europeans, Americanization helped immigrants to

take on the social and material privileges of Whiteness—to become White. And, in keeping with Ford Motor's direct economic interests, it meant joining in the new consumer economy. As Stuart Ewen and Elizabeth Ewen note, "The promise of the 'melting pot' was inextricably tied to the consumption of American goods." In Stephen Fox's words, advertising in this period "projected a WASP vision of a tasteless, colorless, odorless, sweatless world. Ethnic minorities cooked with vivid spices—even garlic!—and might neglect toothpaste, mouthwash, deodorants, and regular bathing. Advertising would show these minorities how to cleanse themselves."[60]

Ford's paternalism extended not only to immigrants but also to African Americans. In the 1910s and 1920s, Black workers were just beginning to break through the color bar that had kept them out of nearly all areas of factory labor. Most auto manufacturers confined Blacks to the dirtiest, hardest, and most difficult jobs. Racism emanated from employers and White workers alike. Ford Motor hired more Black workers than any other company; by the late 1920s, 10–12 percent of the 100,000 employees at Ford's River Rouge plant were Black. Perhaps more noteworthy, the company stood alone as "the only major company that was willing to force its white employees to work with Negroes in all departments and occupations."[61] At Ford Motor and, with rare exceptions, at no other auto company, Blacks worked on the assembly lines, as machine and press operators, mechanics, electricians, tool and die makers, and foremen supervising racially mixed or all-White crews. This was not true equality—even at the Rouge, Blacks were concentrated in the least desirable jobs, and they were virtually excluded from all other Ford plants—but it came closer to equality than any other large industrial company did before World War II.[62]

Ford's newspaper declared that "the destiny of the white race and the black race in this continent is to live together in the same economic system, and together they will resist all attempts to destroy the white man's civilization which is the black man's best security."[63] Blacks, Ford believed, were racially inferior to Whites but were entitled to certain rights, such as economic opportunities and decent, but segregated, housing. Whites should use paternalism rather than force: "Dominance is an obligation. The whole solution of the race question as of every other, lies in the stronger serving the weaker, the abler serving the less developed. . . . The superior racial stream was equipped for the service of the other, not for exploitation and suppression."[64] Ford viewed Black people as docile, hard-working, and loyal by nature. The "strange unrests and convulsions" among Blacks following World War I were the work of radical Jewish conspiracies: Black people were "being tampered with by influences cleverer than anything [they] could devise."[65]

For many years, the company's relatively open policies toward Blacks won it a high reputation in Detroit's Black community. Ford employees and their families formed about 25 percent of this community in the 1930s.

Ford developed close ties with the local Black business and professional elite, relying on local Black leaders, especially certain ministers, to recommend workers who would conform to company standards. Without such a recommendation, it was nearly impossible for a Black person to get a job with Ford Motor. This system, under which Black people flocked to churches favored by the company, led some Black leaders to voice concern about Ford's domination of the Black church. The local chapters of the NAACP and the Urban League also had close ties to Ford and remained hostile to labor unions long after their national organizations had endorsed multiracial unions such as the UAW. In 1941, a substantial number of Black workers opposed the UAW's organizing drive at Ford.[66]

Ford Motor's paternalistic relationship with Detroit's Black community anticipated the Ford Foundation's efforts during the 1960s to promote moderate civil rights organizations and keep the Black liberation movement within "responsible" channels. As Robert L. Allen and others have argued, the Ford Foundation's work spoke softly but complemented the big stick of local and federal police repression against Black revolutionaries, such as the FBI's COINTELPRO operations.[67] Similarly, Ford Motor's paternalism toward Blacks in the 1920s complemented its repressive policies toward labor militancy.

Another distinctive aspect of Ford's ideology was his romanticist attitude toward nature and rural life. Ford considered big cities "pestiferous." "He contrasted the ´unnatural,´ ´twisted,´ and ´cooped-up´ lives of city dwellers with the ´wholesome´ life of ´independence´ and ´sterling honesty´ that a farm environment offered." Celebrating traditional country life, Ford collected antiques, organized old-fashioned dances, restored old buildings. He was also an avid hiker, stressed exercise, banned tobacco and alcohol in the company, and avoided caffeine, most meat, and other rich foods. He commissioned experiments in the nutritional uses of the soybean.[68]

Ford's glorification of nature, fitness, and the countryside was also linked to antisemitism. To Ford, cities were breeding grounds for Jews and the immorality they propagated. The *Dearborn Independent* blamed Jews for undermining traditional values by promoting alcohol, creating jazz music, and corrupting organized sports. "The Jews are not sportsmen," it declared.[69]

Henry Ford's nostalgia for an idyllic rural past may seem in conflict with his role in revolutionizing modern industry, but there is an underlying unity here. As Moishe Postone argues, modern antisemitism does not glorify tradition at the expense of modernity in general. Rather, it celebrates "concreteness" in both traditional and modern forms.[70] In this schema, the Jew represents the abstract power of finance against concrete productivity, both old and new. Jewishness is seen as artificial, impersonal, dishonest, rootless, and diseased. Against this threat, farming, industrial production, physical health, closeness with nature, and the "honest" face-to-face relations of rooted small-town life all represented the concrete authenticity

Ford sought to defend. Not for nothing did Ford and Crowther describe business as "the whole material side of life."

Here, again, Ford's philosophy mirrored German Nazi doctrine. For decades, German romanticists and nationalists had promoted hiking, camping, folk singing, nudism, and environmental consciousness. Rooted in this tradition, the Nazi cult of "blood and soil" declared that racial health depended on closeness to nature, forests, and rural life. But Nazi plans to build up a yeoman farmer class, couched in images of ancient Germanic tribes, were coupled with the rapid development of industrial and technological power.

Ford brought together the concrete aspects of country and city, tradition and modernity, in his efforts to promote village industries. "Factory and farm should have been organized as adjuncts of one another, and not as competitors," his newspaper declared. Ford's idea was to build small water-powered factories where farmers could work when their labor was not required on the land. During the 1920s, Ford Motor organized at least nine such plants, with workforces ranging from a few dozen to 2,500 employees. According to Ford biographer David L. Lewis, Ford's village industries inspired the governor of East Prussia in Nazi Germany to call for "the scattering of small plants over his province. Each factory was to be the nucleus of a village and each working family therein was to be given a plot of land nearby." Nazi cabinet members such as Alfred Rosenberg and Walther Darré advocated similar deurbanization plans. Yet Ford's idea also influenced Franklin Roosevelt's New Deal administration during the 1930s, indicating the industrialist's wide-ranging influence. Federal Emergency Relief Administration director Harry L. Hopkins proposed putting hundreds of thousands of urban laborers to work in small towns, partly on farms and partly in factories.[71]

CONCLUSION

Through his vast corporate empire as well as his publications, Henry Ford fused conspiracist antisemitism from the *Protocols* with homegrown ideological traditions. He adapted Jacksonian producerism to the era of assembly line production and mass consumption. His Anglophobia had its roots in nineteenth-century writings and, before that, in the American Revolution. Although he avoided Theodore Roosevelt's cult of violence and military conquest, Ford echoed Roosevelt in many other ways: he fought organized labor with a combination of physical terror and top-down reforms, advocated paternalism toward Blacks and immigrants, centralized women's subordination by using corporate policy to intervene in family structures, and romanticized nature and traditional country life. Ford wove all of this together with a public cult of personality and an authoritarian system of rule within the company. Only by examining Ford's industrial philosophy and policies as a whole, rather than his antisemitic propaganda campaign alone, can we understand the full scope of Ford's affinity with, and influence on, fascist movements in the United States and abroad.

Although Ford's politics overlapped with those of the Ku Klux Klan on many points, there were also striking differences, beyond the fact that the Klan was a political mass movement and Ford's apparatus was not. Ford was more obviously right-wing than the 1920s Klan in his consistent male supremacy and repudiation of labor unions. He was less obviously right-wing regarding Black people and non-Jewish European immigrants. In Alexander Saxton's terms, Ford's soft racism (cultural assimilation for immigrants and paternalistic inclusion for Black workers) contrasted with the Klan's hard racism (immigration restriction, hostility toward all non-Nordic ethnic groups, and anti-Black terror). Right-wing populism mixes reactionary and progressive-sounding appeals; Ford and the Klan represented different variations on this theme.

7

DRIVING OUT
THE MONEY CHANGERS

Fascist Politics in the New Deal Era

The stock market crash of October 1929 opened the Great Depression, which spread around the world and lasted through the 1930s. The Depression was the deepest crisis for U.S. capitalism in the twentieth century. Industrial output fell by half, banks closed by the thousands, and unemployment climbed to 25 percent or more. Mass want reached upward from the poor and workers into large sections of the middle class. While hunger spread, food crops and slaughtered livestock were left to rot because it was unprofitable to sell them. In the fall of 1931, Soviet representatives in New York received 100,000 applications for jobs in the USSR.[1]

Organized responses to the crisis ran the political gamut. On the left, the Communist Party (CP) achieved its greatest support and influence; its version of Marxism became temporarily respectable. Communists and, to a lesser extent, Socialists and Trotskyists played important roles in militant workers struggles that vastly increased union membership and forced big business to recognize organized labor in major industries. Left-liberal third parties gained strong support in several states. Pressure from these movements influenced President Franklin Delano Roosevelt's "New Deal" policies. At first, the Roosevelt administration tried to revive the economy with a system of state-sponsored cartels that heavily favored big business. But after two years the administration moved to the left. It forged unprecedented links with organized labor and oversaw important social welfare reforms, such as the Social Security Act and the National Labor Relations Act. While the New Deal failed to end the Depression or substantially reduce unemployment, it offered short-term help to millions, stabilized the economic order, and transformed the dominant conception of government's role in society. These measures helped make Roosevelt one of the most popular— and one of the most hated—presidents in U.S. history.

Not all popular-based responses to the Depression were on the left. In

1934–1935, Louisiana demagogue Huey P. Long spearheaded the "Share Our Wealth" mass movement that combined leftist and rightist features. Hard-right organizations also proliferated, which used scapegoating to rally people hurt by the national collapse. Such groups blended racism and antisemitism with attacks on the New Deal, organized labor, and the Left. Many hard rightists were influenced by fascist movements in Europe, especially the German Nazi Party, which came to power in 1933. In 1940–1941, hard rightists joined with others in a large movement to oppose U.S. entry in World War II as part of the Allies.

During the 1930s and 1940s, critics applied the fascist label to many different right-wing groups, as well as to business organizations, Huey Long's movement, and the Roosevelt administration itself. Some of this usage was appropriate; most was not. As we have argued, fascist movements are a particularly deadly form of right-wing populism. Fascists call for national, racial, or cultural unity and collective rebirth after a period of crisis. All "alien" groups and ideas must be purged, and all individual and special interests must be subordinated to a new order of totalitarian mass politics. Fascists promote conspiracist antielitism and, often, vaguely collectivist schemes, but they reject the socialist principles of workers' solidarity and class struggle, and often cut deals with established elites while retaining political autonomy. Fascists seek to organize a cadre-led mass movement to seize state power. Often, fascists glorify violence, practice political terrorism and street fighting, and promote mass killing. Few 1930s U.S. organizations fit this profile. The largest right-wing populist movement that shifted into fascism was headed by Father Charles E. Coughlin, a fervent early Roosevelt supporter who moved to the right as the New Deal moved left.

This chapter examines the rise of fascist movements and their relationship with other political forces during Franklin Roosevelt's presidency. In Chapter 8, we will discuss the antifascist repression of the 1930s and 1940s, and how it paved the way for the antileftist witch-hunts of the Cold War years. The same chapter also traces the business community's bitter factional conflict over the New Deal, which has influenced right-wing populist politics for over half a century.

THE FIRST NEW DEAL

President Roosevelt took office in the worst depths of the Depression, when fiscal panic had forced thirty-eight states to close their banks. The New York Stock Exchange, the Chicago Board of Trade, and several other important markets were also closed. In an atmosphere of national desperation, Roosevelt's First New Deal (1933–1935) brought together a loose, unstable coalition behind an emergency relief and recovery program. Supporters of the First New Deal included many of Roosevelt's future right-wing opponents, such as Father Coughlin and conservative businessman Robert E. Wood, who later headed the America First Committee.

During the First New Deal, Roosevelt echoed producerist rhetoric about a conspiracy of bankers. In his inaugural address, he said that "the money changers have fled from their high seats in the temple of our civilization. We may now restore that temple to the ancient truths." (Coughlin had used this same metaphor in a national radio address a few months earlier.)[2] In November 1933, FDR wrote one adviser: "As you and I know . . . a financial element in the larger centers has owned the Government ever since the days of Andrew Jackson . . . The country is going through a repetition of Jackson's fight with the Bank of the United States—only on a far bigger and broader basis."[3]

Roosevelt's attack on the "money power" won broad support. The years of depression, the 1933 banking crisis, and a recent Senate investigation of Wall Street had made financiers a target of national outrage. Most hated was J.P. Morgan & Co., the monarch of Wall Street, which for years had functioned as a virtual wing of the U.S. government and which embodied the most exclusive White Protestant elitism. Along with workers and farmers, many industrialists, too, demanded an end to the deflationary policies identified with international banks, especially Morgan. They endorsed Roosevelt's decision to increase the money supply by taking the dollar off the gold standard. At the same time, many non-Morgan bankers saw these attacks as an opportunity to weaken their most powerful competitor. Morgan was the chief victim of several banking laws passed during this period, especially the 1933 Glass–Steagall Act, which separated investment banking from commercial banking.[4]

Another cornerstone of the First New Deal was the National Recovery Administration (NRA), created in 1933. The NRA established a set of codes regulating production, prices, wages, and hours in every major industry, drawn up by big business in nominal consultation with workers, consumers, and the government. It was a corporatist experiment explicitly modeled after the plans of Theodore Roosevelt, FDR's cousin, for government-supervised monopolies. On paper, NRA codes protected labor's right to collective bargaining, but big corporations dominated NRA-regulated industries. They "used their powers to stifle competition, cut back production, and reap profits from price-raising rather than business expansion."[5]

The broad coalition behind the First New Deal quickly fragmented once the immediate sense of emergency had passed. Important sections of the business community broke with Roosevelt, including the U.S. Chamber of Commerce, the National Association of Manufacturers, and the powerful du Pont empire.[6] Father Coughlin increasingly criticized the New Deal and began his slide into fascism. In May 1935, the Supreme Court declared the NRA unconstitutional.

THE LIBERTY LEAGUE

du Pont and Morgan interests dominated the American Liberty League, formed in 1934. Many of the League's leaders had been active in the Democratic Party and in the fight to repeal prohibition, and included two former presidential candidates: Alfred E. Smith and Morgan lawyer John W. Davis. The League criticized the New Deal in conservative terms, as an attack on free enterprise and even as a fascist effort to imitate Benito Mussolini's corporatist policies in Italy. Yet, League members quietly aided rightist antisemitic initiatives and explored the possibility of an alliance with the Ku Klux Klan.[7]

Liberty Leaguers may even have attempted to organize a coup d'etat against Roosevelt. In 1934, Smedley Butler, a well-known retired Marine Corps major general, told the Special House Committee on Un-American Activities that he had been asked to head a veterans' army in a "march on Washington" similar to Mussolini's March on Rome. Butler said that the plotters would force Roosevelt to appoint an "acting president" who would hold real power, and, if Roosevelt refused, he would be deposed in favor of Butler. The coup was to be financed by Morgan and other powerful financial interests; guns would be supplied by a du Pont-owned company. Should Butler decline to take part, General Douglas MacArthur would be recruited for the job. According to Butler, the plotters claimed wide support within the American Legion and the Veterans of Foreign Wars, and indicated that the Liberty League was connected with the plan.[8]

Most press accounts derided Butler's story, which was denied by those he had named as accomplices in the plot. No charges resulted. Many parts of the report remain unproven, and some historians have treated it with great skepticism. Robert F. Burk, for example, argues that "At their core, the accusations probably consisted of a mixture of actual attempts at influence peddling by a small core of financiers with ties to veterans organizations and the self-serving accusations of Butler against the enemies of his pacifist and populist causes." But the congressional committee, which found corroboration for many of Butler's statements, concluded in its report: "There is no question that these attempts were discussed, were planned, and might have been placed in execution when and if the financial backers deemed it expedient."[9]

If Liberty Leaguers did in fact try to seize power by force in 1934, their effort highlights the difference between a conspiracy among wealthy elites and a mass-based fascist movement. As John L. Spivak commented:

> The takeover plot failed because though those involved had astonishing talents for making breathtaking millions of dollars, they lacked an elementary understanding of people and the moral forces that activate them. . . . The con-

spirators went about the plot as if they were hiring an office manager; all they needed was to send a messenger to the man they had selected.[10]

This shortcoming was in keeping with the Liberty League's whole elitist approach. The organization's image as a mouthpiece for the rich severely hurt its political effectiveness.

Meanwhile, Roosevelt faced growing demands to confront economic inequality. The year 1934 saw general or near general strikes led by Marxists in San Francisco, Minneapolis, and Toledo, and a nationwide textile strike involving almost half-a-million workers. Left-liberal electoral campaigns such as Upton Sinclair's End Poverty in California movement and Minnesota's Farmer–Labor Party gained broad support. And Huey Long, with a program to dramatically redistribute wealth, was amassing a nationwide following in the millions and threatening to split the Democratic Party.

HUEY LONG'S "SHARE OUR WEALTH" MOVEMENT

Huey Long has often been called a fascist. While we do not agree with that characterization, in some ways Long's career contributed to the growth of fascist politics during the 1930s. Like the First New Deal, which he opposed, Long's movement blurred the lines between Left and Right. He combined charismatic leadership, a populistic critique of economic injustice, and repressive, even dictatorial, politics. Born and raised in an area of northern Louisiana with strong left-wing Populist and Socialist Party traditions, Long rose to the governorship in 1928 by denouncing the oil companies, railroads, and utilities. When he moved on to the U.S. Senate in 1932, he retained firm control over the Louisiana state government.

Long dramatically expanded public services in Louisiana, which was one of the nation's poorest, least developed states. The state government under Long built roads, bridges, and public buildings, expanded school and university facilities, opened night classes for adults, provided school buses and free textbooks, expanded public health care, and founded a major medical school. Long also abolished the poll tax, reduced property tax assessments and exempted low-income families, and instituted an income tax and an occupational tax on oil refining. But Long's state policies have rightly been described as "business progressivism"—a program to develop basic infrastructure, restrict the tax burden on employers, and keep labor cheap to promote economic growth. To appease the oil companies, for example, Long cut the occupational tax by 80 percent. He did little to help workers or labor unions, opposed old-age pensions, and provided no unemployment relief or pensions for mothers.[11]

Long was a ruthless machine politician. He rigged elections, bought off or intimidated opponents, used the state police and militia to suppress dissent, and reduced the legislature and supreme court to rubber-stamp bodies. He was a brilliant public speaker, with a colorful plebian style, who skillfully used mass communication techniques such as sound trucks and radio. He once claimed that Louisiana was a "perfect democracy"—because its government responded directly and perfectly to the people's will. This plebiscite notion of democracy, implying an organic unity between the leader and the masses, contributed to his cult of personality. Many poor Whites regarded Long with an "almost religious adulation." He bolstered his charisma with pageantry and physical monuments glorifying his regime.[12]

Although Long's demagoguery reminded critics of fascism, unlike 1930s hard rightists he usually avoided public scapegoating and bigotry. He did not attack Jews or Catholics, but rather worked closely with members of both groups, especially Catholics, an important Louisiana constituency. He was not especially anticommunist and did not promote conspiracy theories. And, in sharp contrast to other southern politicians, he generally—though not always—avoided race baiting against Black people. When, in 1934, KKK head Hiram Evans announced plans to campaign against Long in Louisiana, Long vowed, "that Imperial bastard will never set foot in Louisiana," and if he did, he would leave with "his toes turned up." When asked about Adolf Hitler, Long once replied, "Don't compare me with that so-and-so. Anybody that lets his public policies be mixed up with religious prejudice is a plain God-damned fool."[13]

But Huey Long was hardly a principled opponent of bigotry. The national organizer for his Share Our Wealth Society was Gerald L. K. Smith, who had briefly worked with the pro-Nazi Silver Shirts and who would later go on to become one of the country's most notorious antisemites. While working for Long, Smith once declared that in stirring up the people he might "duplicate the feat of Adolph [sic] Hitler in Germany." Long's professed efforts to help Black people were usually expedient or condescending, and he did nothing to enfranchise Black voters, oppose discrimination, or end racist violence. After his death, *The Crisis*, the journal of the National Association for the Advancement of Colored People, summed it up succinctly: "Of the late Senator Huey P. Long, Negro Americans may say that he was the only southern politician in recent decades to achieve the national spotlight without the use of racial and color hatred as campaign material. . . . But when this is said, his story, so far as Negroes are concerned, is done."[14]

Long offered Franklin Roosevelt valuable support in the 1932 presidential campaign. Yet, Long's relations with the Roosevelt administration were strained almost from the beginning. Although he supported a number of Roosevelt's bills, especially spending and currency inflation measures, he also criticized the New Deal for catering to the wealthy and powerful. Many of his charges proved accurate. He denounced the Emergency Banking Act for helping only big national banks. The NRA wage and price codes, he accurately predicted, would be written by industrialists. "Every fault of socialism is found in this bill," he declared of the measure establishing the NRA, "without one of its virtues." He criticized Social Security as inadequate and, because it would be administered by the states, discriminatory against Blacks. In the Senate, Long had a loose affinity with the bipartisan "progressive" bloc of western and Midwestern senators, such as Burton K. Wheeler of Montana, George W. Norris of Nebraska, Robert M. La Follette, Jr., of Wisconsin, and Gerald P. Nye of North Dakota.[15] These progressives eventually broke with FDR in the late 1930s, but Long did so in the summer of 1933.

Huey Long presented himself as a left-wing critic of a vacillating New Deal. "Whenever this administration has gone to the left I have voted with it, and whenever it has gone to the right I have voted against it." The cornerstone of his political challenge to Roosevelt was the Share Our Wealth plan, unveiled in early 1934. Though the plan's details varied slightly over time, in essence Long proposed that every family be provided a start-up allowance of $5,000 and guaranteed an annual income between $2,000 and $2,500. These payments would be funded by taxing personal fortunes above a few million dollars and annual income beyond approximately $1 million. Supplemental proposals included government support for students, farmers, and veterans, old-age pensions, and limits on work hours.[16]

The Share Our Wealth plan criticized concentrated wealth in all forms. The plan drew no illusory dichotomy between parasitic finance capital and productive industrial capital. It was not "an attempt to direct attention away from real problems; it did not focus resentment on irrelevant scapegoats or phony villains. . . . Long was, in a crude way, describing one of the basic causes of the Depression: the insufficient distribution of purchasing power."[17]

But the plan was economically unworkable: there was nowhere near enough liquifiable wealth to cover the proposed family payments. Long's admission that Share Our Wealth would require a huge administrative apparatus contradicted his opposition to the growth of central bureaucracy. Furthermore, the plan's apparent radicalism masked a traditionalist and conservative core. It romanticized the family as the basic unit of society, and made no provision for single adults.[18] And Share Our Wealth did not challenge capitalism as an economic system. Long's "targets of attack were distant Wall Street financiers and men of great wealth like the Rockefellers, not local employers or small town bankers, merchants and landlords—the élites who constituted the economic and social power structure at the local level."[19]

In January 1934, Long founded the Share Our Wealth Society, and began making weekly national radio broadcasts to promote his plan. His newspaper, *American Progress*, averaged a circulation of 300,000 copies, with a few issues reaching 1.5 million. Gerald L. K. Smith, the society's national organizer, was described by H. L. Mencken as "the greatest rabble rouser seen on earth since Apostolic times." By July 1935 the society claimed seven million members. Some 27,000 Share Our Wealth clubs were formed nationwide. Support was strongest in the South but was also pronounced in New York, the Midwest, and even the West, a region Long never visited. The Share Our Wealth Society was loosely organized, without any clear direction for activity at the local level. Long's use of radio and his general political style fostered an aura of direct communication between the leader and the masses. It did not encourage grassroots activism or a disciplined structure.[20]

Long could have posed a serious challenge to Roosevelt in the 1936 elections. According to a 1935 poll conducted for the Democratic National Committee, 10.9 percent of the U.S. population supported Long as a third-party presidential candidate in 1936. The poll showed that Long was equally strong in urban and rural areas, that he drew support from all regions (though less from mid-Atlantic and northeastern states than elsewhere), and that his supporters were disproportionately low-income voters, the vast majority of whom had voted for Roosevelt in 1932. Speculation about an alliance between Long and other dissident leaders, such as Father Coughlin and Dr. Francis E. Townsend of the Old Age Revolving Pension Plan, sharpened the electoral threat. Apparently Long hoped to win enough votes to produce a Republican victory, which would deepen the Depression and usher Long into the White House in 1940.[21] But Long's career ended abruptly in September 1935, when he was shot and killed in the Louisiana capitol building, under circumstances that have never been clearly explained.

Huey Long, arguably the most capable rival President Roosevelt ever faced, left a contradictory legacy. His work helped focus national attention on economic inequality as a cause of the Depression—and helped pull the Roosevelt administration to the left—while avoiding any major appeals to bigotry or scapegoating. Yet, Long also promoted simplistic solutions that mixed radical words with conservative content, and used charismatic direct appeals to a mass audience. It was the Hard Right that would inherit much of this legacy, though it never produced a populist leader of comparable skill. Smith laid claim to the Share Our Wealth movement, but soon abandoned the wealth redistribution theme in favor of conspiracist attacks on communists and international bankers. Smith and other hard rightists continued to revere Huey Long and cited his assassination as the fruit of a Jewish–communist–New Deal plot.[22]

THE SECOND NEW DEAL

In mid-1935, partly responding to Long's movement and other challenges, the Roosevelt administration shifted to the left and initiated the Second

New Deal. The First New Deal had set up temporary relief measures to soften the Depression's impact. The 1935 Social Security Act—though riddled with gaps and inadequacies—created a permanent system of federal social services, including unemployment insurance, retirement benefits, and public assistance for disabled and poor people. The 1935 National Labor Relations Act (the Wagner Act) guaranteed workers the right to unionize and bargain collectively, and set up the National Labor Relations Board to conduct union elections and prevent business from using unfair labor practices. Other measures identified with welfare-state liberalism included a law to break up public utility holding companies, tax reforms, minimum-wage laws, and experiments in Keynesian deficit spending to stimulate the economy.[23]

Roosevelt forces shifted from banker bashing to class rhetoric against the rich in general. At a 1936 Roosevelt rally in Pittsburgh, Pennsylvania, Governor George H. Earle thundered against

> the Mellons, who have grown fabulously wealthy from the toil of the men of iron and steel, the men whose brain and brawn have made this great city; Grundy, whose sweatshop operators have been the shame and disgrace of Pennsylvania for a generation; Pew, who strives to build a social and economic empire with himself as dictator; the du Ponts, whose dollars were earned with the blood of American soldiers; Morgan, financier of war.[24]

Roosevelt won the 1936 election with over 60 percent of the vote—the biggest presidential landslide in U.S. history. The 1936 victory consolidated the New Deal electoral coalition that included organized labor, European ethnic groups in northern cities, Southern Whites, and African Americans. Despite the anticapitalist rhetoric, the New Deal also lined up key support from a number of major industrialists and bankers, including many with strong ties to the eastern elite (see Chapter 8).

In large part, the New Deal moved leftward as a defensive response to mass working-class insurgency.[25] Beginning in 1933, millions of workers began to organize—especially the low-skilled immigrant and second-generation workers in core industries whom the American Federation of Labor (AFL) had long excluded. Workers demanded not just economic gains but above all an end to management's dictatorial power in workplaces and company towns. Communists, Socialists, Trotskyists, and other radicals in the factories provided key leadership. In 1935, under pressure from this rank-and-file upheaval, eight AFL member unions formed the Committee for Industrial Organization (CIO), dedicated to organizing workers on an industrywide basis, regardless of skill or trade. The CIO, renamed the Congress of Industrial Organizations after being expelled from the AFL in 1937, coordinated successful organizing drives in the auto, steel, textiles, electrical, food processing, and many other industries. The breakthrough came with the 1936–1937 wave of sit-down strikes, in which tens of thousands of workers occupied their factories so that scab labor could not be used. Most famous was the forty-four-day sit-down strike in Flint, Michigan, that forced General Motors to recognize the United Auto Workers in February 1937.

Most CIO unions did little to organize women workers, and often failed to live up to their commitment to represent and organize all workers equally regardless of race. But the CIO weakened AFL-type exclusionary policies, and forced the AFL to adopting a watered-down version of industrywide organizing. Organized labor grew from 3.7 million members in 1935 to almost 9 million in 1940. For the first time, the union movement had won a lasting role in the nation's major industries, though it was a reformist, bureaucratic union movement that increasingly discouraged rank-and-file militancy. Along with New Deal relief and patronage systems, organized labor carried forward the process of integrating working-class southern and eastern Europeans into White society by increasing their stake in the U.S. economic and political system.[26]

The Roosevelt administration provided organized labor important breathing space it had never before enjoyed. For several years the federal government refused to send troops against any union initiative. The CIO and part of the AFL staunchly supported the New Deal, and unions became closely tied to the Democratic Party apparatus in many cities. In 1936, the CIO was the top contributor to Roosevelt's reelection campaign, with $770,000 in contributions.[27] Yet, Roosevelt repeatedly stood by as employers violated the Wagner Act and as Democratic state governors used national guard troops to break strikes, and in 1941 the president used the army to crush a major strike in the aircraft industry. Like the labor bureaucracy itself, the Roosevelt administration wanted to keep working-class activism within "responsible" limits that would not threaten the basic economic system.

Designed to reform the economy in limited ways, many New Deal reforms primarily served to soften poverty's worst features. "The minimum wage law of 1938," writes Howard Zinn, "which established the forty-hour week and outlawed child labor, left many people out of its provisions and set very low minimum wages (twenty-five cents an hour the first year). But it was enough to dull the edge of resentment." And, even as it improved many people's lives, the New Deal often bolstered social hierarchies. In a time when employed women were widely blamed for men's unemployment and other ills, the Social Security Act reinforced strictures on female autonomy by penalizing single women and those who worked outside the home.[28] Many New Deal programs condoned or enforced racial discrimination. Roosevelt, who endorsed the bloody suppression of Puerto Rico's proindependence movement in 1937, refused to publicly support an antilynching bill; no federal civil rights legislation was passed during his administration.[29]

But to many supporters, as well as right-wing opponents, the New Deal seemed like a major break with the past. Roosevelt appointed more Blacks, women, Catholics, and Jews to office than had any previous president, and sections of his administration upheld nondiscriminatory policies. By cultivating an alliance with organized labor and establishing the principle that the federal government has a role in meeting basic human needs, the Roosevelt administration laid the foundations of a modern welfare state. Some praised FDR as a hero; others vilified him as an agent of the Jewish–Bolshevik conspiracy.

THE HARD RIGHT: ULTRACONSERVATIVES AND FASCISTS

There were probably hundreds of hard-right organizations in the 1930s. A few won a sizable following; many were little more than a central office or an individual with a mailing list of supporters, or a loose association of street thugs clustered around a charismatic leader. Hard rightists of the 1930s hated Marxism, organized labor, and the New Deal; what set them apart from conservative groups such as the American Liberty League was their hostility to pluralist discourse and especially their focus on explicit White supremacy and conspiracist antisemitism. Some hard rightists specialized in propaganda while others built disciplined organizations, engaged in paramilitary training, or used physical violence against their opponents. Most opposed U.S. support for the Allies in World War II, and some openly praised the Hitler and Mussolini regimes.

The Protocols of the Elders of Zion and *The International Jew* were standard hard-right texts. Hard-right propaganda denounced FDR as a would-be communist dictator and racial equality and desegregation as "communistic" goals that would bring, in Elizabeth Dilling's words, "a complete surrender of individuality, blending and inter-marriage." Blacks were routinely portrayed as an immediate physical (often sexual) threat, while Jews were usually depicted as the hidden wire-pullers, such as the rich Jew who hired Black men to rape White women, or the radical Jew who fomented communist rebellion in the Black community.

Many hard rightists sought to re-create a pre-New Deal traditional order. Such groups advocated a laissez-faire form of capitalism and sharp restrictions on federal government power. Many of them embraced anti-immigrant and anti-Catholic nativism, sometimes coupled with Protestant fundamentalism. In contrast to these ultraconservatives, as we will call them, fascists wanted a strong authoritarian state and sweeping changes in society and the economy. Although more likely than ultraconservatives to regard Jews as a separate race, many fascists advocated solidarity among all Christians of European descent, including Protestants and Catholics, immigrants and native-born Whites. Between these ideological poles, a number of essentially ultraconservative groups borrowed fascist trappings and ideas.

Representing the Hard Right's ultraconservative wing were the Knights of the Ku Klux Klan, no longer the national mass movement they had been in the early 1920s but still powerful in the Deep South. As before, the Klan stood for White Protestant nationalism against Blacks, Jews, Catholics, and immigrants. But in the 1930s the New Deal, the labor movement, and the Communist Party also became prime targets. The Klan's antielitism, ties with labor, and quasifeminism had withered since the 1920s, making the organization a consistent defender of the traditional social order. In southern states, the Klan worked with local police and businesses to terrorize union activists who demanded equal pay for equal work, especially Black workers and farmers. Although wary of "un-American" influences, many Klansmen (especially in the North) praised German Nazism as a kindred movement. In 1934 the Klan's *Kourier* magazine observed that "the spark that fired Hitler and other German nationalists to build a new Germany may easily have been ignited by the example of the American Ku Klux Klan." In August 1940 New Jersey Grand Dragon Arthur H. Bell addressed a joint rally of Klansmen and German-American Bund members. But with the prospect of war with Germany growing, public outcry prompted Imperial Wizard James Colescott, national head of the Klan, to repudiate the event.[30]

An equally violent, northern offshoot of the Klan called the Black Legion, which used black robes and hoods instead of white, flourished briefly in Michigan and neighboring states. At its peak in 1936, the Black Legion may have had as many as 40,000 members, who were primarily unskilled workers. Its militaristic hierarchy and murderous assaults on labor organizers imitated European fascist parties as well as the Klan.[31]

Gerald B. Winrod was a Protestant fundamentalist minister whose Defenders of the Christian Faith, founded in 1925, stressed Protestant moralism, biblical prophecy, and a small-business ideology of individual success. Initially Winrod denounced fascism and argued that Mussolini might be the Antichrist, but in 1933–1934 he began targeting "Jewish Bolshevism" and praising Nazi Germany. This shift also led him to tone down his attacks on Catholicism. "By 1939, [Winrod] was protesting the persecution of priests by the Spanish Republic, favorably quoting Father Coughlin, and urging Catholics and Protestants to cooperate in 'patriotic Americanism.'" But while he defended fascist dictatorship abroad, Winrod still advocated minimal central government for the United States.[32]

The Defenders had no formal membership structure. Winrod's *Defender Magazine* achieved a circulation of over 100,000 by 1937, and he himself garnered 52,000 votes in the 1938 Kansas Republican primary for U.S. senator, placing third in a four-way race. Winrod reported that the states with the most subscribers were Pennsylvania, California, and Illinois, with subscription rates in Michigan, New York, Ohio, Kansas, and North Carolina also strong. His choice of speaking venues, and the advertisements in the *Defender*, indicate a predominantly small-town and rural, lower-middle-class readership.[33]

If Winrod's Defenders was an ultraconservative group with fascist overlays, William Dudley Pelley's Silver Legion stood for actual fascism. Pelley was the son of a Methodist preacher who became a fiction writer and spiritualist. He founded the Silver Shirts, as his group was commonly known, immediately after Hitler's January 1933 appointment as German chancellor. The Silver Shirts were active mainly on the Pacific Coast and in the Midwest; they achieved a peak membership of about 15,000 in 1934, but declined to 5,000 by 1938. *Liberation*, their weekly magazine, had a peak circulation of about 50,000 in 1933. The Silver Shirts focused mostly on propaganda and pageantry, with relatively little actual violence. There were disputed reports in 1934 that the San Diego unit bought weapons and ammunition from soldiers for use against an expected communist revolution. Although they avoided openly anti-Catholic propaganda, the Silver Shirts were predominantly Protestant and included a number of clergymen as well as ex-Klansmen. One sample of members identified by occupation was "almost evenly divided between the working class (skilled craftsmen and low-level clerks as well as laborers) and the solid middle class (including teachers, clergy, and small businessmen)," with a sizable sprinkling of lawyers, doctors, and corporate executives.[34]

Pelley's program for society, "the Christian Commonwealth," borrowed heavily from Edward Bellamy's utopian novel *Looking Backward*. Pelley envisioned the country as one enormous, centrally planned corporation, with inheritance virtually prohibited and all income determined by one's civil service ranking. Banks, money, advertising, labor unions, and private law practices would be abolished. Women could seek high-level appointments on an "absolute equal footing" with men, but marriage and motherhood would be their primary roles. Blacks, American Indians, and immigrants would form separate castes and be made voteless wards of the Commonwealth. Jews, too, would be disenfranchised and ghettoized in one city per state.[35]

Pelley was convinced that his was an apocalyptic struggle with the forces of darkness. An example of this variation on the demonic theme appeared as a chart in Pelley's publication, *Liberation*, in 1938:[36]

Anti-Christ	Christ
Judaism	Christianity
materiality	spirituality
modernism	fundamentalism
leftist	rightist
Jewish socialism	individualism

Jewish communism	constitutionalism
Protocols of Zion	U.S. Constitution enforced
Communist Manifesto	"Bill of Rights"
democracy	constitutional republic
Communism	Americanism
internationalism	National patriotism
Jewish subversion	American vigilantism
War	**Peace**

Various immigrant fascist groups expressed solidarity with compatriot regimes and movements in Europe. The most important of these groups was the Friends of New Germany and its successor, the German-American Bund, founded in 1936. Fritz Julius Kuhn, who assumed command in 1936, overcame the group's endemic factionalism, turned the debt-ridden organization into a moneymaker, and gave the Bund a higher profile through increased pageantry, sensationalism, and leadership cultism. Kuhn also built up the *Ordnungsdienst* (security service), the Bund's paramilitary wing.[37]

In public, Kuhn claimed that the Bund's active membership was 20,000, with 100,000 sympathizers and affiliates, although at one point he told government agents privately that the Bund had only 8,299 members (plus an unstated number in affiliated groups). The Bund's ability to draw 22,000 people to its "Pro-American Rally" in New York City in February 1939 gives some indication of its strength. It consisted predominantly of German nationals and naturalized U.S. citizens. A large proportion of members were skilled workers or artisans. The largest concentration of members was in New York City and New Jersey.[38]

While applauding Nazi rule in Germany, the German-American Bund had essentially defensive aims in the United States. The Bund struggled between trying to insulate Germans from the corrosive effects of supposedly Jewish-dominated, materialistic U.S. culture, and trying to Americanize itself in order to win greater support, influence, and political security. Bundists looked back with horror at the 100 percent Americanism crusade during World War I, which tried to suppress every expression of Germanness. They denounced the melting pot as a Jewish invention and called on Germans to remain culturally and racially pure. At this time, the Nazi-controlled German Foreign Institute (DAI) of Stuttgart disseminated propaganda in the United States promoting "minority group rights" and cultural pluralism—by which it meant ethnic and racial segregation. The DAI's leading scholar on the United States, Heinz Kloss, "welcomed the coming of the New Deal because of its stressing of minority and racial diversity."[39]

Nazi cultural pluralism took an added twist when Hitler's government declared that American Indians were members of the Aryan race. The Bund made serious (but virtually fruitless) efforts to recruit Indians as members.

In 1937, Pelley, calling himself "Chief Pelley of the Tribe of Silver," promised American Indians that he would free them from reservations and place Jews in reservations instead. The emblem of the tiny American National-Socialist Party was "an American Indian, arm outstretched in salute, poised against a black swastika."[40] These moves combined White Americans' traditional parasitic use of the American Indian as political symbol, as in the Boston Tea Party, with German Nazism's romanticist cult of nature and of "savagery" as the antithesis of corrupt Jewish civilization. (Hitler was an avid fan of Karl May's novels, in which noble Indians figured prominently.) U.S. fascist groups also made common cause with the right-wing American Indian Federation (AIF) against the Roosevelt administration's 1934 Indian Reorganization Act, which replaced naked colonialism with more sophisticated federal control through elected tribal governments. The AIF, which advocated full assimilation of Americans Indians into White society, opposed the 1934 act as communistic.[41]

The Hard Right also included several small Black organizations. These groups emphasized solidarity between African Americans and imperial Japan against White domination, but also endorsed Nazi Germany. Robert O. Jordan's Ethiopian Pacific League received funds from an associate of Japan's Black Dragon Society. Estimates of League membership ranged from 500 to 5,000. Other Black profascist groups included David Erwin's Pacific Movement of the Eastern World and the Colored American National Organization. Presumably relations between White and Black hard rightists were not especially cordial, but Jordan's group collaborated to a degree with two of the most violent White fascist organizations, the Christian Front and Christian Mobilizers.[42]

Women played an active role in many hard-right groups.[43] Elizabeth Dilling was an influential writer, publishing such books as *The Red Network* and *The Roosevelt Red Record*. In the late 1930s and early 1940s, Dilling and other profascist women led a large network of "mothers" groups that opposed U.S. participation in World War II. Some of these women, such as Cathrine Curtis and Lyrl Clark Van Hyning, sought to increase women's power and autonomy, though they did not challenge male dominance directly. But, unlike the early 1920s, when large-scale feminist activism significantly influenced the Klan movement, feminism was weak in the 1930s, and most hard rightists in that decade defended women's subordination or took it for granted. Dilling denounced women's equality as a Marxist goal and a "robbery" of the "God-given instinct" to be a traditional wife and mother.[44] Eleanor Dennis expressed a similar sentiment in a 1936 letter to her husband, pro-Nazi author Lawrence Dennis:

> When this reaches you, you will be in Deutschland, in Berlin right in the heart and pulse beat of that wonderful nation where men are he-men and women are so womanly. . . . Be nice to all the Germans for me and specially

to those brave women who are making babies for Hitler being slaves so happily and willingly to their men.[45]

Critics of the Hard Right during the 1930s often portrayed it as a vast, coordinated network, an antidemocratic conspiracy masterminded from abroad or bankrolled by the rich. For example, Albert E. Kahn, in a book entitled *High Treason: The Plot Against the People*, described the Hard Right as "a huge fifth column apparatus," "cooperating with or directly supervised by the Axis Propaganda Ministries and Military Intelligence Agencies." Kahn added that "from the beginning, the machinations of the fifth columnists were directly aided by some of the wealthiest and most powerful men in the United States."[46]

Such statements mixed fragments of truth with exaggeration. Certainly, Hitler's government took an active interest in promoting pro-Nazi sentiment within the United States. Nazi propaganda agencies supplied the U.S. public with millions of magazines, pamphlets, books, and flyers through rightists such as Pelley and Winrod as well as such bodies as the German Library of Information and the German Tourist Information Office. But to the extent that the Hard Right was a political movement rather than just a publishing house, it was not subject to control from Berlin. Even the German-American Bund, which Kahn described as an "army of trained Nazi spies and propagandists," actually endured tense, sometimes hostile, relations with Hitler's regime. Although the Nazis had helped sponsor the Friends of New Germany and similar groups in the early years, they found them to be more of an embarrassment than an asset and severed most ties with them in 1935. Bund leader Fritz Kuhn pretended to be in close touch with Berlin in order to bolster his own prestige.[47]

Nor, as many liberals and Communists claimed, was the Hard Right primarily a tool of big business, though some wealthy capitalists aided sections of the Hard Right to a degree. Many specific charges of business involvement are plausible but vague or unsubstantiated. Winrod, for example, "is said to have obtained contributions from two wealthy Oklahoma oil men"—perhaps in response to a CIO organizing drive among oil field workers. Governor George H. Earle of Pennsylvania blamed the Black Legion on "the money changers and the great industrialists behind the Republican Party leadership"—specifically, the du Ponts and "the munition princes of the American Liberty League." Yet, a Michigan Federation of Labor investigation found no evidence that Detroit industrialists (including the du Pont-controlled General Motors) supported the Black Legion.[48]

Gerald L. K. Smith was one hard-right leader who did receive substantial backing from a number of business executives, including Henry Ford. Smith's Committee of One Million, founded in 1936, may have amassed hundreds of thousands of supporters. Smith was an effective union buster, and many employers paid him to break strikes.[49] Although his bigotry and scapegoating later intensified, in the late 1930s Smith held on to a degree of respectability by emphasizing anticommunism while soft-peddling hatred of Jews and conspiracy theories. Like Winrod, Smith was essentially an ultra-conservative who glorified individualism, patriotism, Christianity, and small government. Glen Jeansonne claims that Smith hoped for a revolution that would enable him to seize dictatorial power, but adds that "He had little idea what he would do with power."[50]

Even if we assume that anti-New Deal business executives bankrolled actual fascists, this does not mean they wanted a fascist takeover but simply that rightist attacks on labor, communists, Jews, Blacks, and Roosevelt complemented their agenda. From a pragmatic business standpoint, a fascist government's ability to impose order, smash working-class militancy, and divert popular grievances through scapegoating must be weighed against its volatile populist tendencies and hunger for absolute power. In Germany and Italy, the strongest sectors of big business threw their support to fascism when the government and the political center were in shambles and Marxist revolution seemed a real threat. In the United States the crisis never got anywhere near that point.

The power of fascist politics in the 1930s United States did not rest on Berlin spymasters or a capitalist conspiracy, but rather on fascism's ability to attract mass support as an autonomous movement. Profound disunity among hard rightists weakened this threat. Personal rivalries and turf wars, disorganization, inept leadership, and lack of a shared positive program plagued the movement. Despite frequent contact and overlap between hard-right groups, efforts to build a stable coalition failed. Yet, fascism's potential popularity was real: Father Coughlin, one of the few hard-right leaders with a well-developed fascist ideology and program, attracted millions of supporters. His movement, which began as a wing of the New Deal coalition and ended by glorifying Hitler, shows that fascism could appeal to people well beyond the Right's conventional boundaries.

FATHER COUGHLIN'S MOVEMENT

Charles E. Coughlin was known as the radio priest. In the early 1930s his radio sermons, broadcast over thirty stations, drew up to an estimated 40 million listeners and brought Coughlin more mail than anyone else in the United States, including the president. "Commercial radio was less than six years old when Coughlin began broadcasting in 1926. The first radio network, the National Broadcasting Company, began operations that same year. Coughlin was exploiting a system of communication whose potential conventional politicians had not yet begun to appreciate."[51]

Ironically, a Ku Klux Klan cross burning on his church lawn in Royal Oak, Michigan, helped spur Father Coughlin to begin broadcasting his sermons. Soon letters and contributions began pouring in. At first he concentrated on religious themes, but by 1930 the broadcasts had become almost entirely political in character. Coughlin denounced the Klan, prohibition, and birth control; he attacked communism and, as the Depression deepened, targeted "predatory capitalism" and "concentrated wealth." He supported FDR's 1932 campaign and praised the new administration extravagantly during its first year. Coughlin's support was a factor to be reckoned with. "When in a broadcast late in 1933, for example, he casually suggested that his listeners write Franklin Roosevelt to express their gratitude for his inspired leadership, the White House mail room was inundated with hundreds of rapturous letters."[52]

Coughlin focused on currency reform as the key to ending the Depression. In 1933–1934 he presented a series of proposals for increasing the money supply—revaluate gold, remonetize silver, issue currency based on "real wealth" rather than precious metals—and called for a government bank to take currency control away from the private bankers who headed the Federal Reserve. These proposals, especially the proposal to remonetize silver, helped draw Coughlin together with members of the progressive bloc in Congress. In June 1933, ten senators, including Huey Long, and seventy-five representatives urged Roosevelt to name Coughlin an adviser to a major international economic conference in London.[53]

Coughlin was not a fascist at this point, but his views contained the seeds of fascism. At least as early as 1933, his treatment of economic issues, and his double-edged attack on bankers above and communist subversives below, placed him squarely in the producerist tradition. Like Andrew Jackson and Henry Ford, Coughlin considered the "manufacturers of money" and the "producers of real wealth," including industrialists, to be fundamentally different from each other. According to Coughlin, "The object of [the financialist] is to make money out of money, caring only for profits. The object of [the industrialist] is to make things—shoes, plows, stoves, typewriters, automobiles—out of raw materials. He is essentially a producer. The financialist is essentially a parasite."[54]

This perspective blurred actual class divisions. Consider, for example, his description of the 1933 Detroit banking crisis:

> On the one side tenaciously clinging to the past were the speculative bankers, the credit inflationists, the gamblers with other peoples' money.
> Opposing them were the battalions of the exploited—the deceived investors, the small depositors, the anxious industrialists, the hard pressed merchants, the laborer and the farmer.[55]

Under capitalism, Coughlin asserted, it was "just and ethical" to charge interest "for some productive enterprise." "Usury, however, is identified with exploitation, with injustice, with the rental of money for non-productive enterprises." Such statements implied that productive enterprise did not involve injustice or exploitation of employees. It was usury, Coughlin argued, that led toward the "suicide of capitalism."[56]

In a period that saw a huge upsurge in labor militancy, Coughlin could not entirely ignore the division between workers and industrialists. But he urged both groups to recognize that their "natural" enemy lay elsewhere. In March 1934 he declared:

> Today capital and labor are in a strained and unstable state. . . . Both are victimized by financial interests who know little of the problems of the industrialist and care less for the tears of the laborer. . . . Both are bloodsucked by speculators in the stock market and profiteers on Wall Street.[57]

However, he continued a few months later, "Capital, intended by nature to remain faithful to labor, has gone forth to dwell with the prostitute of finance who manufactures money." "I am not excoriating you industrialists. . . . You, too, have been victimized. But I do castigate you because, like parrots, you have repeated the sophistry of your bankers. . . . Today your only redemption is for capital to join labor instead of perpetuating its harlotry with finance."[58]

In the context of the liberalism Coughlin then espoused, such ideas seemed intended to bolster reformist tendencies within the business community. But they could be easily redirected into a fascist program to replace labor activism ("unproductive" strikes against one's "natural" allies) with scapegoating—as Coughlin himself soon discovered.

Coughlin's references to financiers whoring and sucking blood echoed classic stereotypes of Jews. In the early 1930s, Coughlin was not the unrestrained hater of Jews that he became by 1938 and later, but antisemitism was organically connected with his producerist philosophy. In his pro-New Deal period, Coughlin often self-consciously praised Jews while reinforcing stereotypes about them. For example, he distinguished between good Jewish principles and bad Jewish deeds:

> It is a notorious fact that the Rothschilds clinging to the Egyptian heresy, disparaging the teachings of their forebears, despising the precepts of their great leader, Moses, mocking the doctrines of the Talmud and the precepts of the Old Testament, these Rothschilds reestablished in modern capitalistic life the pagan principle of charging interest on non-productive, or destructive debts. . . . The horrible, hated word spelled "W-A-R" was the secret of their success.[59]

Whether because of their own "heresy" or Christian persecution against them (as Coughlin argued elsewhere), it was the Rothschilds, personifying "the international Jew," who allegedly formulated the idea "of gold as a medium of control"—the root of all economic woes.[60] Over the next few years, Coughlin's attacks on Jews slowly became more explicit and frequent.

In November 1934, declaring that capitalism and communism "are both rotten!" Coughlin announced the formation of the National Union for Social Justice (NUSJ) to be an "organized lobby of the people" against "the mighty lobbies of wealth." The Union's sixteen principles included freedom of conscience and education, "a just, living, annual wage" for everyone who was able and willing to work, "a Government owned Central Bank" to replace the Federal Reserve, tax reform, and the right to organize labor unions. One NUSJ plank called for nationalizing the banks and public utilities. Coughlin later "clarified" this to mean government regulation of these institutions, not expropriation. The Union welcomed members "irrespective of race, of color, of creed or of profession."[61]

For the first year, the NUSJ was little more than a mailing list. Coughlin initially declared that political meetings "were entirely outmoded" because radio broadcasts and letters allowed direct communication between him and his followers—a notion similar to Huey Long's organicist "perfect democracy." Late in 1935, however, a loose system of local chapters began to take shape. Since Coughlin's speeches were not broadcast in the South, nor west of the Rockies before 1935, the NUSJ had little support in these regions, but it grew rapidly in the rest of the country. There are no reliable membership figures, though Coughlin claimed there were 8.5 million members in April 1935.[62]

Coughlin presented the NUSJ largely as a counterweight to the American Liberty League's laissez-faire conservatism. He declared that "Capitalism is doomed and is not worth trying to save." Yet he remained fiercely hostile to "international communism"—"the irrational revolt against the irrational plutocracy of the international banker." He advocated some form of "socialized" or "state capitalism" in order to ensure broad distribution of goods and services.[63] Coughlin urged that, in place of hourly wages, workers be awarded "partnership in the profits of the business" and that "representatives of labor should have a voice in the management of business." His aim was not to abolish capitalist property relations but rather to bring about "a wide distribution of property ownership." German Nazi leader Josef Goebbels had made a similar point in 1925, when he represented the Nazi Party's "left" wing. Goebbels wrote that "the working classes can be made free materially and spiritually by increasing the number of property owners up to the last possible point."[64]

By this time there were growing tensions between Coughlin and the Roosevelt administration. In April 1934, during the battle over silver remonetization, Treasury Secretary Henry Morgenthau, Jr., revealed that Coughlin's office was a major investor in silver. Coughlin denounced Morgenthau, who was Jewish, as a tool of Wall Street and defended silver as a "gentile" metal. In January 1935, a Coughlin radio address helped defeat Roosevelt's effort to bring the United States into the World Court and highlighted the radio priest's isolationist views. Increasingly, Coughlin criticized the New Deal for serving finance capital and failing to reduce unemployment.[65]

In 1935, there was much speculation about an alliance between Coughlin and Huey Long, whose programs, constituencies, and antielitist appeals overlapped to some extent. (Long supported most of Coughlin's currency reform proposals, though he considered them secondary to wealth redistribution; Coughlin refused to endorse the Share Our Wealth Plan, but he favored taxation to reduce economic inequality.)[66] After Long's assassination in September 1935, Coughlin forged an uneasy alliance with Dr. Townsend, the old-age pension advocate, and Gerald L. K. Smith behind the presidential candidacy of William Lemke on the Union Party ticket. Although Coughlin promised to deliver nine million votes (his estimated radio listenership), Lemke polled less than 900,000. Roosevelt was reelected in a landslide victory. "In making Roosevelt their chief target of attack," writes Jeansonne, "the trio of crusaders erred badly. It would have been better to identify Wall Street or big business as the enemy—but these too were the opponents of Roosevelt and thus aligned with Townsend, Smith, and Coughlin."[67]

The 1936 presidential campaign pushed Coughlin into a harsher form of demagoguery and reduced his following to a more fanatical core. The August 1936 NUSJ convention was a pageant of frenzied hero worship, as delegates repeatedly likened Coughlin to Christ. In 1937 Coughlin declared that his great mistake the preceding year was to believe that democracy could work. Though in 1935 he had explicitly identified the National Union with liberal politics, his rightward shift was now clear.[68] His relationship with organized labor offers a case in point. In 1935 Coughlin had energetically supported the Automotive Industrial Workers Association (AIWA), which although more cautious than the larger United Auto Workers was still a legitimate labor union. However, he abandoned the AIWA when it conducted its first major strike in the fall of 1935. He maintained friendly relations with officials of the AFL, who represented the labor elite, but denounced the CIO as communistic when the AFL expelled it in 1937. That same year Coughlin announced the formation of a Workers Council for Social Justice at Ford Motor—in practice, an adjunct to Ford's terrorist suppression of independent worker organizing. In an important shift away from the NUSJ's original nondiscrimination policy, the "Workers Council" explicitly barred Jews and other non-Christians. It quickly folded for lack of support.[69]

In March 1938, borrowing an idea from Mussolini's followers, Coughlin proposed that the U.S. government be restructured as a "Corporate State" in which Congress members would be elected by functional groups such as autoworkers, farmers, and capitalists rather than by districts. Political parties would be abolished. In July, his newspaper, *Social Justice*, began publishing *The Protocols of the Elders of Zion*, although Coughlin continued to deny that he was antisemitic and urged that the "mass of Jews . . . join with us in opposing the Jew money changers as well as the Gentile money changers." In November, he defended the Nazis' *Kristallnacht* pogrom as an attempt to prevent a communist takeover of Germany.[70]

Also in 1938, Coughlin established the Christian Front, a body much closer than the amorphous NUSJ to a disciplined fascist organization. The new organization's membership was concentrated in New York and other northeastern cities with large Catholic populations. Christian Fronters openly advocated violence and often attacked Jews on the street. "The Christian Front organization is not a debating society," Coughlin proclaimed in June 1939, "it is an action society. . . . We will fight you in Franco's way . . . we'll fight you, and we'll win." In January 1940, the FBI arrested seventeen Christian Front members in New York on charges of plotting to overthrow the government, and seized a cache of weapons. FBI Director J. Edgar Hoover claimed that the group also planned the mass killing of Jews. Charges against some of the seventeen were dismissed. Other members were acquitted.[71]

Coughlin's following was smaller than it had been during his pro-New Deal years, but it was still formidable. In 1938, an estimated 3.5 million people listened to his radio speeches regularly. In two surveys conducted that year, about 25 percent of those polled said that they approved of Father Coughlin; as late as April 1940, he retained the support of 17 percent of those surveyed. In 1941, *Social Justice*'s weekly sales were estimated at 300,000 copies and its circulation at one million readers. The size of the Christian Front is difficult to establish. Presumably its officials exaggerated greatly when they claimed 200,000 members, but an alternative estimate of 1,200 seems much too low. In New York City alone, between fifty and seventy meetings were reportedly held each week in the spring and summer of 1939, and the mayor's office discovered that 407 city police officers had joined the front.[72]

From 1938 onward, Coughlin defended Axis aggression, often in Anglophobic terms. *Social Justice* excused Japanese attacks against China as simply an imitation of British empire building. Coughlin opposed U.S. intervention in the conflict in a speech entitled "Shall America Fight for Britain in Asia?" He praised Neville Chamberlain's appeasement policy toward Hitler and condemned Winston Churchill. Even after Pearl Harbor, *Social Justice* continued to denounce Britain, label Roosevelt a communist, and blame the war on the Jews. The newspaper urged that Douglas MacArthur be appointed commander-in-chief.[73]

Such views provoked intense protests against Coughlin. In late 1939, the National Association of Broadcasters cut off Coughlin's access to radio.

In April 1942, four months after Pearl Harbor, the Post Office suspended second-class mailing privileges for *Social Justice*, and Attorney General Francis Biddle announced that the paper violated the Espionage Act. Under pressure from the church hierarchy as well as the government, Coughlin withdrew from his political activities.[74]

Coughlin was the only U.S. fascist leader of the 1930s to enjoy mass support. Detailed survey data from 1938 shed light on the demographics of his following. Catholics were more than twice as likely as Protestants to say they approved of Coughlin. Among Protestants, Lutherans (probably German Lutherans, for the most part) registered the most favorable responses to Coughlin. His support was strongest among the lowest economic strata and also among farmers and Catholic white-collar workers. Men's responses were slightly more favorable than women's. Wisconsin, Minnesota, Missouri, and the Plains states, along with New England, gave him the highest approval ratings, as did people who lived in small towns and rural areas. But Coughlin's base seems to have changed as his politics moved rightward from about 1935 on. Middle-class support declined, and Coughlin increasingly relied on northeastern city-dwellers and Irish Catholics.[75]

Coughlin's strong blue-collar support may seem ironic, given his open hostility to the industrial union movement. Alan Brinkley suggests, based on fragmentary evidence, that Coughlin's working-class popularity was centered primarily "among those who worked relatively autonomously outside the factory environment," for whom industrial unionism had little appeal, and among older, more assimilated, immigrant groups—Germans, Irish, second- and third-generation Poles—and Anglo-Saxon Protestants, who were more likely than newer immigrants "to hold skilled jobs, to belong to craft unions, and to view themselves as part of the 'labor aristocracy.'"[76]

Coughlin promoted a consistent fascist doctrine, not ultraconservatism with fascist trimmings. "He did not warn against the danger of a strong state but demanded extensive government economic and social intervention," including authoritarian corporatist structures for stifling class conflict.[77] He presented himself as a leader directly in tune with the people's will and began to develop a disciplined, paramilitary organization. Coughlin's was a White multiethnic movement in which Klan-style nativism had no place. At the same time, he rooted his attacks on Jews, bankers, and Bolsheviks in the well-established American producerist ideology, which for years gave his populist antielite scapegoating an aura of depth and thoughtfulness.

Coughlin's mass appeal rested first and foremost on his skill at radio propaganda. Another key element, however, was his ability to cut across political boundaries in ways that a William Dudley Pelley or even a Gerald L. K. Smith could only dream of. Coughlin's early role in the New Deal coalition as a self-identified liberal fueled his tremendous popularity. He lost more than half of that support when he broke with Roosevelt, but that still left him with a sympathetic base numbering in the millions. Since Coughlin's fundamental views did not change, many who were attracted when he called himself a liberal may have continued to identify with the same elements in his politics.

THE ANTI-INTERVENTION MOVEMENT

In the late 1930s and early 1940s there was one other arena in which fascists gained a mass forum by bridging political divisions: the movement to oppose U.S. intervention in World War II. The anti-intervention (or "isolationist") movement encompassed a wide range of political forces, some of which supported fascism and many of which did not. This diversity offered many hard rightists an opportunity to break out of their political ghetto. Fascist participation in the movement left nonfascist anti-interventionists open to both legitimate criticism and unfair guilt by association.

There is a popular conception that those who wanted the United States to join the Allies were principled antifascists while their opponents were essentially Nazi sympathizers. The reality was more complex than that. To the U.S. government, stopping fascism was always secondary to extending its own political and economic sphere of influence. Throughout the 1930s, the Roosevelt administration pursued a policy of conciliation toward fascist expansion in Europe and Africa and Japanese imperialist expansion in East Asia—until its own strategic interests became threatened. During the European war, U.S. strategy was to watch Germany and the Soviet Union weaken each other as long as possible, then move in. "As late as April 1943, Soviet forces were fighting 185 Nazi divisions while the U.S. and British Empires were together fighting 6."[78] The Roosevelt administration made almost no effort to save Jews from Nazi genocide, barred many Jewish refugees from entering the United States, and refused to bomb the gas chambers at Auschwitz or the railroad lines that led to them. In the Pacific, the U.S. strategy was even harsher: the United States conducted a war filled with racism and atrocities as bad as, if not worse than, those of the Japanese themselves. This policy culminated in the nuclear bombing of Hiroshima and Nagasaki after the Japanese government had indicated it was prepared to surrender.[79]

Certainly many in the United States regarded joining the Allies as essential for opposing fascism and dictatorship. But others pointed out weaknesses and inconsistencies in this position. Many African Americans regarded the Allies' supposed "war for democracy" as hypocritical. The *Pittsburgh Courier*, a leading Black newspaper, declared in March 1939 that the war would be fought over "the right to EXPLOIT the darker peoples of the world" and that the Allies' "meaning of democracy is for WHITE PEOPLE only, and just a FEW of them."[80]

Leftists were divided over the war. The Trotskyist Socialist Workers

Party opposed U.S. involvement and denounced the war as imperialist on both sides, though it supported defense of the USSR and non-imperialist nations such as China. The Socialist Party took an anti-interventionist position but included a large pro-Allied minority faction. The Communist Party stance oscillated with policy dictates from Moscow. The CP advocated a broad antifascist alliance in 1935–1939, switched to an anti-interventionist position during the German–Soviet nonaggression treaty of 1939–1941, then reversed itself again when the Nazis invaded the USSR in June 1941. It then urged that the United States join the Allies and, after Pearl Harbor, demanded complete loyalty to the government's war effort.[81]

The bulk of anti-interventionist sentiment before Pearl Harbor came from three overlapping sources: ethnic groups disproportionately sympathetic to the Axis or hostile to Britain, particularly German, Irish, and Italian Americans; liberals such as agrarian progressive Senator Gerald P. Nye of North Dakota and United Mine Workers president John L. Lewis; and conservative business executives such as Robert E. Wood of Sears, Roebuck, who headed the America First Committee.[82] Much of the anti-interventionist sentiment was centered in the Midwest, and much of it involved Anglophobia, or hostility to the British Empire.

Liberal anti-interventionists such as Nye and Lewis supported New Deal reformism but disagreed with Roosevelt over foreign policy. Although not anticapitalist, they opposed the dominance of urban big business and finance, which they regarded as the main beneficiaries of war and overseas expansion. They believed the United States could best build an egalitarian, prosperous economy by not depending on Europe or Asia for markets or resources. Many of them also feared that involvement in war would trigger a disastrous growth of government power and decline of political freedom— as happened during the World War I Red Scare.[83]

Conservative anti-interventionists such as Wood generally represented business interests that opposed the New Deal. Strongest among midwestern firms such as Wood's own Sears, Roebuck, these anti-interventionists mistrusted the globalism of the British Empire and the U.S. Eastern Establishment, and feared entanglement in Europe's problems. Wood worried that U.S. involvement in World War II could aid communism and Nazism and mean "the end of capitalism all over the world." He opposed alliance with Britain: "We are weakening our defense by trying to bolster up a decadent system and nation. Nature's law is survival, and if a race is not strong enough to survive unaided, it will perish." Instead, he urged that the United States concentrate on developing and controlling the "virgin continent" of Latin America.[84]

Anti-New Deal business executives guided and financed the America First Committee (AFC), formed in the summer of 1940, which quickly became the most prominent anti-intervention organization. The AFC's original statement of principles declared that "American democracy can be preserved only by keeping out of the European war" and "'aid short of war' weakens national defense at home and threatens to involve America in war abroad." By December 7, 1941, the AFC had about 800,000 to 850,000 members organized in 450 chapters and subchapters, with the Midwest providing the largest contingent. Other anti-intervention groups included the No Foreign War Committee, which was active for a few months in 1940–1941; the National League of Mothers of America, which claimed four million members before it splintered in April 1941; and We the Mothers Mobilize for America, which claimed 150,000 members.[85]

Like these other anti-interventionist organizations, the America First Committee was a magnet for profascists, forcing the leadership to make repeated gestures disavowing fascism and antisemitism. The AFC removed Henry Ford from the leadership in late 1940, barred Gerald L. K. Smith from membership, and protested efforts by the German-American Bund to recruit on its behalf.[86] Nevertheless, fascists and fascist sympathizers were members and leaders of many AFC chapters, and often shaped the tenor of AFC events. Garland L. Alderman, Secretary of the fascist National Workers League, chaired the Pontiac, Michigan, AFC chapter. AFC organizer Don Lohbeck became Gerald L. K. Smith's office manager. S. A. Ackley moved from the AFC to lead the Chicago branch of the Anglo-Saxon Federation. Laura Ingalls (later convicted of failing to register as a German agent) frequently spoke at AFC events. Walter Schellenberg, a high-ranking officer in the German SS, sat on the speakers platform at an AFC rally in Madison Square Garden on March 22, 1941. The Committee also worked with antisemitic journalists, such as Japanese agent Ralph Townsend of *The Herald*, and accepted contributions from antisemites.[87]

The aviator Colonel Charles A. Lindbergh was the AFC's most popular speaker. Lindbergh, who accepted a medal from Hitler's government in 1938, favored an alliance with Germany. He rationalized Nazi aggression by asserting "the right of an able and virile nation to expand—to conquer territory and influence by force of arms as other nations have done at one time or another throughout history." "If the white race is ever seriously threatened," he argued, "it may then be time for us to take our part for its protection, to fight side by side with the English, French, and Germans. But not with one against the other for our mutual destruction."[88] In September 1941, he created a furor by declaring on an AFC platform in Des Moines that "the three most important groups which have been pressing this country toward war are the British, the Jewish, and the Roosevelt administration."[89]

Lindbergh's comment in Des Moines echoed Nazi propaganda such as the 1940 book *War! War! War!* by "Cincinnatus," which blamed "World Jewry, Roosevelt and the British-Jewish Empire" for dragging the United States toward war, and emphasized Jews' supposed dominance of England. This book was promoted by the German embassy and disseminated widely as part of an effort to prevent Roosevelt's reelection in 1940. Throughout the late 1930s and early 1940s, the Nazi government waged an extensive secret propaganda campaign to help the anti-interventionist cause. German agent George Sylvester Viereck directed much of this effort. Viereck's published propaganda brought together writings by German propaganda agencies (under pseudonyms such as James Burr Hamilton), U.S. fascists such as Lawrence Dennis, and nonfascist anti-interventionists such as Senator William E. Borah of Idaho and Representative Stephen A. Day of Illinois.[90]

To lend a greater aura of legitimacy to his message, Viereck purchased anti-intervention speeches reprinted from the *Congressional Record*, often by the hundreds of thousands. A number of senators and representatives provided him with congressionally franked envelopes, so he did not have to pay to mail the reprinted speeches. He then distributed these materials to various organizations, from the AFC to Winrod's Defenders of the Christian Faith, to send out to their mailing lists. Viereck's practices were revealed in the fall of 1941. No charges were filed against Congress members, but Viereck and his associate George Hill, assistant secretary to Representative Hamilton Fish of New York, were convicted of serving as unregistered foreign agents.[91]

Many nonfascist anti-intereventionists ultimately discredited themselves when they allowed fascists to join or hold office in their organizations or speak at their events, when they contributed articles to Germanophile publications alongside fascist writers such as Lawrence Dennis, or when they knowingly or unknowingly aided a Nazi-sponsored propaganda campaign. But in the meantime, they provided fascists a veneer of legitimacy and access to a wide audience, enabling them to spread their bigotry and lies more effectively than before. This does not necessarily mean that they agreed with the fascists. It indicates a mixture of willful ignorance, opportunism, and some varying measure of ideological sympathy. The ideological sympathy was strong and explicit in the case of Charles Lindbergh, and probably substantial in the case of business leaders such as Robert Wood. In the case of progressive isolationists such as Gerald Nye, who had often been to the left of the Roosevelt administration through the 1930s, ideological sympathy with fascism was presumably weak—at least to begin with. But Nye's politics moved sharply to the right in the 1940s, and anti-intervention coalition work probably contributed to that process. In 1942 Nye described Nazi propagandist Ralph Townsend as "a loyal and patriotic American citizen." By the 1944 elections he was portraying himself as the target of a plot by New Dealers, Jews, communists, and eastern journalists.[92]

The United States' declaration of war following the Japanese attack on Pearl Harbor on December 7, 1941, did not end anti-interventionist activism, but it effectively destroyed anti-interventionism as a mass political movement. The America First Committee dissolved, and its leaders pledged their support to the war effort. Many ultraconservatives remained politically active and took part in the anticommunist crusade that followed World War II. But postwar efforts by Coughlin and others to revive fascist activism quickly collapsed,[93] and fascist politics remained mostly dormant until formation of the Liberty Lobby network in the late 1950s.

CONCLUSION

Fascism was the main form of mass-based right-wing populism in the United States during the 1930s. Inspired by political developments in Europe, U.S. fascists blended ideas from the Hitler and Mussolini regimes with homegrown traditions such as producerism and White supremacy. The result was a major shift in U.S. politics: for the first time since Reconstruction, a large right-wing movement called for overthrowing the government.

Contrary to some portrayals, 1930s fascism was a cluster of political movements, not a vast conspiracy orchestrated from Berlin or from corporate boardrooms. The extent of 1930s U.S. fascism has often been exaggerated, but fascism's interconnections with other political forces were important. The fascist label does not rightly apply to Huey Long's Share Our Wealth movement or the American Liberty League's clumsy machinations; yet, both contributed to a climate of authoritarian demagoguery and contempt for pluralist institutions. Right-wingers who were antisemitic or opposed U.S. involvement in World War II often stopped short of fascist political goals, but many of them borrowed doctrines from fascism or lent it legitimacy through collaboration.

Fascists tried to destroy the New Deal. They hated its acceptance of industrial unionism and willingness to work with Marxists, its ties with multinational capital and the Eastern Establishment (discussed in the next chapter), and its small but visible steps beyond the racist and antisemitic consensus of the 1920s. But fascism also shared features with the New Deal itself. Both rejected the laissez-faire form of capitalism and recognized that the economic crisis demanded active government intervention. In its first years, the New Deal experimented with a system of government-sponsored economic cartels that reminded observers of Mussolini's corporatism, and pushed banking and monetary reform measures that echoed fascism's scapegoating of finance capital. During this early period, Roosevelt's most enthusiastic supporters included the nascent fascist Father Coughlin, who continued to endorse many of the same principles after his move to the right. Later, FDR's administration upheld an antisemitic visa policy that shut the door on hundreds of thousands of Jews desperately trying to flee Hitler. As we will discuss in the next chapter, Roosevelt also oversaw a major expansion of state repression, including the racist mass imprisonment of Japanese Americans in concentration camps.

Like New Deal liberalism, 1930s fascism derived much of its appeal from the economic and social crisis that led people to search for new doctrines and bold solutions. Throughout the decade, rightists could point to European fascist states as models of apparent strength and national revival. But fascism and the Hard Right also suffered from many weaknesses in the 1930s: disunity, feeble organization, ideological conflict, and lack of skilled leadership and a clear program. And as Jürgen Kocka argues, "From the outset the US was simply not as vulnerable to right-wing attacks as Germany without the long years of economic distress which Germans had experienced before the depression even began, without the handicap of a delayed, then half imported parliamentary democracy, without the blow of a lost war."[94] In depression-era Germany, former liberals in the middle class and big business abandoned their shaky alliance with Social Democratic reformism, embraced right-wing populism, and eventually threw in their lot with the Nazis.[95] By contrast, New Deal liberalism offered concrete new benefits to organized labor, much of the middle class, and an important sector of the business community. Fascists could only chip away at this support base. In addition, the New Deal successfully co-opted the Communist Party, effectively neutralizing the only serious potential for an organized, large-scale revolutionary threat. This, in turn, limited the demand for a counterrevolutionary force.

Fascism's weakness and failure to win state power in the 1930s do not mean it had no effect on society. Physical violence and threats left their scars on targeted groups; union busting seriously hurt the labor movement in some areas. Some fascist political themes would influence the postwar Right. And, as our next chapter relates, the authoritarian liberal reaction against fascism fed the growth of the national security state and helped lay the groundwork for the Cold War repression of the late 1940s and the 1950s.

8

FROM NEW DEAL
TO COLD WAR

Political Scapegoating and Business Conflict
from the 1930s to the 1950s

U.S. politics moved sharply to the right as World War II ended and the Cold War began. Franklin Roosevelt's administration had chiefly faced opposition from the Right. But under Harry S. Truman, who succeeded Roosevelt as president in 1945, the federal government increasingly concerned itself with supposed threats from the Left. In this chapter we will trace two threads of political conflict from the Roosevelt era to the Cold War Red Scare. The overall anticommunist campaign during the Cold War pitted a broad coalition of forces, from ultraconservatives to liberals, against the Marxist Left and its allies. As we will argue, many 1930s antifascists unwittingly helped to lay the groundwork for this Red Scare by falsely portraying the Hard Right as an alien conspiracy and by promoting the growth of state repression. These events offer important lessons for current-day opponents of right-wing populism.

The early Cold War Red Scare is commonly remembered as "McCarthyism"—after Wisconsin's Republican Senator Joseph R. McCarthy—a term that, from today's perspective, connotes reckless and unfounded accusations that someone is a communist. But McCarthyism, which targeted liberals and even conservatives in both major parties, was a specific right-wing tendency within the overall anticommunist drive. As we will argue in the second part of this chapter, McCarthyism was rooted in the 1930s battles over the New Deal and reflected a factional fight within the economic and political elite. Through McCarthy and his allies, anti-New Deal business leaders and politicians made a comeback power bid against the more moderate elite faction, centered in the Eastern Establishment. We will trace the outlines of this intraelite struggle, which has continued to influence right-wing politics for half a century.

In the 1930s, as we have seen, many critics falsely portrayed the Hard

Right and the anti-intervention movement as a vast coordinated fascist conspiracy. At the same time, they often uncritically glorified the Roosevelt administration and the U.S. government. This simplistic analysis led many liberals and leftists to support government repression against the Hard Right, in what Leo Ribuffo has called the "Brown Scare." (Adolf Hitler's storm troopers in Germany were known as the Brown Shirts.) The Brown Scare, Ribuffo argues, "set precedents for suppression that liberals and radicals would later regret during the Cold War."[1]

THE BROWN SCARE

During the Franklin Roosevelt era, ultraconservatives and fascists faced opposition from both private organizations and government agencies. The most prominent independent antifascist group was the Friends of Democracy, founded in 1937 and headed by Reverend Leon M. Birkhead, who helped to defeat Gerald Winrod's 1938 senatorial bid. The Non-Sectarian Anti-Nazi League, founded by Samuel Untermeyer in 1933, organized a boycott of goods from Nazi Germany. The American Council Against Nazi Propaganda published *The Hour*, edited by Albert E. Kahn and Albert Perry. Leftist parties, Jewish organizations such as the Anti-Defamation League, and labor unions were all active in antifascist campaigns. These and other groups organized demonstrations, held educational events, and published literature to expose and confront the Hard Right.

One particularly dramatic confrontation took place on February 20, 1939, at Madison Square Garden in New York City. While the German-American Bund hosted 22,000 people at an indoor "Pro-American Rally," complete with a huge portrait of George Washington flanked by swastikas, 50,000 antifascists protested outside. Almost 2,000 police were required to keep protesters from storming the hall. The Socialist Workers Party (SWP) initiated the antifascist gathering. Most participants in the protest were Jews; a contingent from Marcus Garvey's Universal Negro Improvement Association also took part.[2]

In contrast to such direct action tactics, many antifascists looked to the government to stop the fascist threat. The first publicized federal response came in March 1934, when the House of Representatives created a Special Committee on Un-American Activities, with Democrats John McCormack from Massachusetts and Samuel Dickstein from New York as cochairs. Dickstein had fled to the United States with his parents to escape anti-Jewish pogroms in Europe. He saw the committee as a way to eradicate Nazism in the United States. McCormack and Dickstein concentrated their main attention on the Friends of New Germany and, to a lesser extent, the Silver Shirts. They also investigated communists to a limited degree, as well as Smedley Butler's report of a right-wing coup plot. The committee's well-publicized hearings helped force the Friends of New Germany to disband and regroup as the German-American Bund. Although the committee was dissolved in January 1935, its recommendations led to the Foreign Agents' Registration Act of 1938 (the McCormack Act), requiring foreign-sponsored propagandists to disclose their patrons, and helped shape the Smith Act of 1940, which we will discuss shortly.[3]

In May 1938 the House appointed a second Special Committee on Un-American Activities, under Democrat Martin Dies from Texas. Although liberals had pushed to revive the committee as a way to target the Right, committee members were more interested in red-baiting the Left. "In the first few days [of hearings], witnesses branded as communistic no less than 640 organizations, 483 newspapers, and 280 labor unions." Dies was a segregationist on friendly terms with the Ku Klux Klan; he regarded the New Deal as a breeding ground for communists—and accepted Gerald L. K. Smith as a credible witness to that effect.[4]

As a secondary concern, the Dies Committee also investigated some hard-right groups. These probes served two functions. First, they helped win liberal support—or at least neutralize liberal opposition—to the committee's work. Well-timed investigations of the Bund in 1939, and the Klan in 1942, helped persuade the House of Representatives to extend the life of the committee, which was not made permanent until 1945. Second, portraying fascism as a German-controlled "fifth column" enabled committee members to draw an arbitrary line between "American" and "un-American" forms of right-wing politics. Thus, the committee exaggerated the role of the German-American Bund within the Hard Right, falsely portrayed the Bund as a nest of German spies and agents of a centralized "Nazintern" (Nazi International), and focused on Bund members' alleged personal immorality—such as the claim by one witness that Bund youth camps fostered homosexuality.[5]

In his effort to delineate his own politics from the un-American Left, on the one hand, and the un-American Right, on the other, Dies explained that "nazi-ism, fascism, and communism are pagan philosophies," whereas "Americanism is a philosophy of government based upon the belief in God as the Supreme Ruler of the Universe." He argued: "It is as un-American to hate one's neighbor [if] he has more of this world's material goods as it is to hate him because he was born into another race or worships God according to a different faith."[6] This sentiment did not prevent Dies from urging Ku Klux Klan Imperial Wizard James Colescott at a committee hearing a few years later to lead his organization "back to the original objectives of the Klan."[7]

The Dies Committee philosophy was supported by the American Legion. Legionnaires clashed with Bundists physically in several cities in 1938, but overall they were much more concerned about exposing un-Americans of the Left than the Right. A number of state and local governments, too, investigated and passed measures against people they called subversives. These countersubversive actions drew on antifascist sentiment but primarily targeted leftists. The Bund, once again, was the chief right-wing target as the organization most easily classified as alien. In 1939, for example, New York State passed a statute that was aimed at the Bund, banning public use of paramilitary uniforms or drill by private organizations. A 1935 New Jersey law banning racial or religious hate speech was used against nine Bund members in 1940, but was struck down by the state's Supreme Court as unconstitutional. From 1938 on, Bundists faced frequent police surveillance, tax probes, liquor license suspensions, and other forms of official pressure. In 1939 Bund leader Fritz Kuhn was imprisoned on a larceny conviction for mismanaging funds; later his citizenship was revoked, and he was deported to Germany after the war.[8]

Although his politics differed sharply from those of Martin Dies, President Roosevelt, too, took steps to investigate supposed subversive activities in the Right and the Left. In the process, he helped transform the FBI into a permanent, large-scale political police force—something more threatening to civil liberties than any congressional investigation. In 1934, reversing a 1924 ban on countersubversive probes, Roosevelt secretly directed the FBI to investigate fascist organizations on a limited basis. In August 1936, once again in secret, the President authorized FBI director J. Edgar Hoover to survey foreign-directed communist and fascist activities. With FDR's tacit approval, Hoover used this authorization as a broad mandate to investigate any activities in the United States he deemed subversive. In September 1939, after the outbreak of war in Europe, Roosevelt publicly instructed the Bureau to investigate "matters relating to espionage, sabotage, and violations of the neutrality regulations," which Hoover again reinterpreted as a general mandate to gather political intelligence on dissidents.[9]

Over the years, Hoover reported regularly to the White House about fascist groups and, after 1939, nonfascist anti-interventionists, as well. According to Frank Donner, however, "Hoover apparently saw nothing wrong with Nazism on either political or humanitarian grounds." He exchanged information with Nazi police officials for many years and maintained ties with the German-dominated International Police Commission (Interpol) until three days before Pearl Harbor.[10] Although he investigated fascists in the United States, his primary concern remained surveillance of the Left.

Anticommunism intensified in the United States after the Hitler–Stalin Non-Aggression Pact of August 1939. "In a shift reminiscent of the twenties, the images of savagery and ruthlessness associated with Nazis were absorbed into the [Red] Menace."[11] In June 1940 Congress passed the Alien Registration Act (the Smith Act), which free speech law expert Zechariah Chafee, Jr., termed "the most drastic restrictions on freedom of speech ever enacted in the United States during peace." Sedition provisions of the Smith Act banned speech advocating the violent overthrow of the U.S. government or insubordination in the armed forces. The law also required the mass registration and fingerprinting of foreigners.[12]

Roosevelt endorsed the Smith Act. Congressional liberals went along with it—in the House, only four members voted no and forty-five abstained. Representative Dickstein hoped that the law would be used against hard rightists. His wish was borne out in the Mass Sedition Trial of 1942–1944, in which the government attempted and failed to convict a number of prominent fascists and ultraconservatives as members of a Berlin-directed conspiracy, under both the Smith Act and the Espionage Act of 1917. But the chief targets of the act's sedition provisions were Marxists, beginning with eighteen members of the Socialist Workers Party, convicted in 1942 as part of a move to smash the Trotskyist-led radical wing of the Teamsters union. The Communist Party, which applauded the use of the Smith Act against rightists, also hailed this attack on its leftist rivals. Six years later, the CP's own top leadership would be jailed en masse under the same law.[13]

Meanwhile, the Roosevelt administration and its allies promoted FBI surveillance as a kinder, gentler alternative to more obviously repressive measures such as the Smith Act. "To many liberals, the notion of dealing with Communists by measures short of outright repression held a strong appeal. It would be wrong to jail them, but to identify and watch them seemed unobjectionable." Surveillance, it was hoped, would also undercut reckless red-baiting by distinguishing secret communists from true liberals. "The marketplace of public discourse would be improved and cleansed, so the argument ran, if the offerings were properly labeled."[14]

Hoover was fundamentally hostile to New Deal liberalism but was also dependent on Roosevelt's patronage. By leaking selected FBI files to the Dies Committee, Hoover both helped to publicize the communist threat and undermined administration efforts to keep intelligence matters within the executive branch. Still, Hoover also feared the committee as a potential rival and was careful to limit its access to FBI information.[15]

The FBI expanded enormously during World War II, from 898 agents in 1940 to 4,886 in 1945. It began conducting wiretaps, expanding on a limited authorization by Roosevelt in 1940. It amassed an extensive network of informers by establishing "contact programs" with the American Legion, which supplied some 60,000 informers, and with many other civic groups, from the Daughters of the American Revolution to the Boy Scouts. Shortly after the outbreak of war in Europe in 1939, Hoover established a Custodial Detention Index of persons with "German, Italian, and Communist sympathies" for possible imprisonment during war or a national emergency. Attorney General Francis Biddle banned it in 1943 as unreliable and illegal, but Hoover retained the index under a different name. To shield such operations from external oversight, Hoover instituted a system of secret report-writing and filing procedures.[16] By the beginning of the Cold War, the FBI had a long head start in the job of exposing radicals, real and imagined.

Although it tried to squelch the FBI's Custodial Detention Index—which presumably included large numbers of White people—the Roosevelt administration herded some 110,000 Japanese Americans into concentration camps based on nothing more than their national origin. Two-thirds of those imprisoned were U.S. citizens. Building on decades of anti-Asian racism, hate mongering against "Japs" intensified after Pearl Harbor. Rumors of sabotage or spying by Japanese Americans proliferated on the West Coast. California's liberal Attorney General Earl Warren, who later became U.S. Supreme Court Chief Justice, joined the clamor. With Orwellian logic, Warren declared that the lack of such sabotage or spying was "the most ominous sign in our whole situation," since it meant that Japanese Americans were waiting for a signal from Tokyo to launch an uprising. The mass imprisonment, which lasted from 1942 to 1945, forced Japanese Americans to abandon or sell at token prices property worth hundred of millions of dollars. This enabled White competitors to seize control of Japanese businesses, including highly productive farms.[17]

While public officials, from Roosevelt on down, were the principal culprits behind the growth of the repressive state apparatus, antifascists outside the government bore a measure of responsibility as well.[18] Clearly, it was important for people to expose and confront the Hard Right, and many organizations and individuals took on this challenge with energy and commitment. In the process, however, some antifascists fed dangerous illusions and helped to legitimize repressive forces they could not control. Frequent references to right-wing groups as "un-American" tools of Berlin obscured the domestic roots of fascism and ultraconservatism and the oppressive nature of U.S. society, and played into the Dies Committee's self-serving embrace of the center.

Criticizing nonfascist anti-interventionists was a trickier question. Groups such as the America First Committee were rightly castigated for their extensive ties with fascists, but some antifascists clouded the issue by using unsubstantiated charges and reckless guilt-by-association tactics. A prime example was Avedis Derounian's 1943 best-seller, *Under Cover: My Four Years in the Nazi Underworld of America—The Amazing Revelation of How Axis Agents and Our Enemies Within Are Now Plotting to Destroy the United States.* Derounian, who wrote under the pseudonym John Roy Carlson, included much useful information in his book, but untangling it from the "reconstructed" dialogue, loose claims, and inaccuracies is often difficult. Like some other antifascists, he portrayed the fascist "enemy within" in sensationalistic, conspiracist terms, making it easier for repressive forces to treat leftists the same way.[19]

The Communist Party's complicity in the Brown Scare reflected its rightward shift. In the early 1930s, the CP had equated the First New Deal with fascism. Though burdened by sectarian dogmatism, the CP during this period combined genuine revolutionary commitment, workplace organizing, and a major focus on fighting White supremacy. But, starting in 1935, with the Communist International's new Popular Front strategy of reformism and broad antifascist alliances, the CP embraced the New Deal and the CIO, where its members played a major role as labor organizers. To win favor with liberals, the CP retreated from active revolutionary politics and stressed its patriotism with the dubious slogan "Communism is Twentieth Century Americanism." As its membership became more and more middleclass, the party increasingly downplayed grassroots labor and antiracist activism while cultivating bureaucratic influence within unions and other organizations. After Pearl Harbor, the CP demanded strict loyalty to the Roosevelt administration's war effort. It helped to suppress strikes, opposed civil rights struggles, and endorsed the mass imprisonment of Japanese Americans—and then publicly expelled all Japanese American party members to prove its patriotic loyalty.[20]

The most dangerous part of the Brown Scare was that many liberal antifascists, together with the Popular Front CP, placed their faith in the U.S. government's repressive power. They urged the government to ban hard rightists' organizations, silence their propaganda, and throw them in jail. This demand unwittingly helped to establish new government instruments— the Un-American Activities Committee, the Smith Act, the FBI—which, all too soon, were turned with much greater force against radicals and even liberals themselves.

THE COLD WAR RED SCARE

The United States' wartime alliance with the Soviet Union helped keep anticommunism in check until after the Allied victory in 1945. But, as the Cold War opened, Communists were again increasingly portrayed as an internal Red Menace, the number one threat to democracy, freedom, and all human decency. From 1947 on, there was a broad consensus—stretching from hard rightists such as Gerald L. K. Smith to liberals such as Hubert H. Humphrey—in favor of driving radical leftists and their supporters out of public life. "Communists in America," declared Attorney General J. Howard McGrath in a 1949 speech, "are everywhere—in factories, offices, butcher stores, on street corners, in private businesses. And each carries in himself the germ of death for society."[21] Cold War witch-hunts brought a pervasive climate of fear and major setbacks for organized labor, communities of color, and gay men and lesbians.

The U.S. Communist Party was a small but significant political force in the mid-1940s. Its approximate membership stood at 63,000 in 1945 and reached 70,000 some two years later. About half of all party members in 1945 belonged to labor unions. Communist-aligned leaders represented 18 unions within the CIO, or 1,370,000 unionists, about one-fourth of the

CIO's total membership, including the 500,000-strong United Electrical, Radio, and Machine Workers (UE). The CP also had a strong presence among middle-class professionals such as teachers, lawyers, entertainers, social workers, and writers. Surrounding the Party were scores or hundreds of "mass organizations," which formed a distinct subculture while also connecting the CP to wider circles of leftists and liberals.[22]

From 1946 onward, Republicans and Democrats engaged in a sort of anticommunist bidding war. In 1947, under pressure from a Republican-controlled Congress, President Truman (a Democrat) established the Attorney General's list of subversive organizations and initiated a loyalty program within the federal civil service. This began the purge that soon spread throughout the public and private sectors. In 1948 Truman's Justice Department prosecuted the first in a series of trials against leaders of the Communist Party, who were convicted under the Smith Act for conspiracy to advocate the violent overthrow of the government and were sentenced to prison terms of between three and five years.

While some liberals, led by former Vice President Henry Wallace, urged peaceful coexistence with the USSR and tolerance for Communists at home, most liberals—including many who had participated in the Brown Scare—supported Truman's combination of anticommunism and mild reformism. In his 1946 book, *The Plotters,* Avedis Derounian denounced communism along with the Hard Right; his colleague L. M. Birkhead endorsed the Cold War and the Attorney General's list.[23] After Truman's 1948 reelection and the crushing defeat of Wallace's presidential bid on the Progressive Party ticket, only a few scattered liberals remained vocal critics of the growing anticommunist consensus.

After World War II, the government's repressive instruments were put fully at the service of the Red Scare. The House Committee on Un-American Activities (dubbed HUAC) was made permanent in 1945. The Senate established a counterpart body, the Senate Internal Security Subcommittee, in 1951, as well as Joe McCarthy's Subcommittee on Investigations in 1953. These bodies, which were dominated by ultraconservatives of both major parties, had wide latitude to conduct investigations, subpoena witnesses, and conduct hearings without regard to courtroom rules of due process. Witnesses called by the committees were routinely fired from their jobs and could be imprisoned for contempt of Congress if they refused to confess and "name names."

To the Smith Act and other existing anticommunist laws, Congress added a series of new ones. The Internal Security Act of 1950 (the McCarran Act) authorized the internment of suspected subversives in concentration camps without trial or hearing if the president or Congress declared a national emergency. The Subversive Activities Control Act of 1950 barred foreigners who advocated "the economic, international, and governmental doctrines of world communism or . . . of any other form of totalitarianism." Mass detentions at Ellis Island resulted. The Immigration and Nationality (McCarran–Walter) Act of 1952 gave the government new powers to deport or bar noncitizens and to strip naturalized citizens of their citizenship and deport them for political reasons. McCarran–Walter also awarded the Immigration and Naturalization Service (INS) sweeping new powers of search, interrogation, and arrest to be used against "illegal aliens."[24]

The FBI, consolidating and strengthening the "internal security" powers it had amassed under President Roosevelt, stood at the center of the anticommunist purge. By the late 1940s, FBI Director Hoover had achieved a position of virtual autonomy, not least through the potential for blackmail that he possessed.[25] Under Truman's loyalty program, the FBI processed some 4.7 million fingerprints and loyalty forms for federal employees and applicants between 1947 and 1953. Using agents and a large network of informers, the Bureau conducted wide-ranging surveillance against suspected radicals and infiltrated leftist and liberal organizations. The FBI frequently passed information about suspected radicals to their employers. It also channeled extensive propaganda to the public through reporters, government officials, and private organizations.[26] Many other federal, state, and local agencies, company security officers, and veterans groups also hunted out subversives. Loss of employment was the most pervasive threat, but real and suspected Marxists were also evicted from public housing and frequently denied passports, unemployment benefits, and in some cases Social Security payments. The anti-red crusade weakened and isolated all of the leftist parties. It destroyed most of the CP-affiliated mass organizations and smashed the party's strong ties with the labor movement.[27]

The Red Scare reinforced an aggressive postwar campaign by employers against organized labor. During the massive strike wave of 1945–1946, Truman used his power to break the miners' and railroad workers' strikes and asked Congress for authority to draft any workers "on strike against their government." In 1947 a Republican-controlled Congress passed the antilabor Taft–Hartley Act. Truman, who was trying to win back labor support, saw his veto overridden but later used the act nine times to prevent strikes. Taft–Hartley required all labor officials to sign an oath that they were not communists. The act also shredded many of the rights organized labor had won during the 1930s, making it impossible for labor unions in many situations to wage an effective struggle without breaking the law.[28]

During the war, the FBI had collected fingerprint dossiers on some 37 million workers employed on war contracts, and in the postwar years over 12.6 million workers—one-fifth of the paid labor force—faced loyalty–security investigations. The FBI and other agencies routinely used the results of such probes to aid employers against unions.[29]

Meanwhile the labor movement conducted its own internal anticommunist purge. In the late 1940s, CP-friendly activists were forced out of leadership positions in several CIO unions. In 1949–1950 the CIO expelled or forced out eleven CP-aligned unions representing some one million workers. Newly created rival unions and existing ones such as the United Auto Workers raided the purged organizations for members. A combination of red-baiting and racism by antileftist unions helped destroy the CIO's drive to organize the South, known as "Operation Dixie."[30] In 1955 a seriously weakened CIO merged with the more conservative AFL to form the AFL-CIO.

Gay men and lesbians, too, were heavily targeted during the early Cold War. Where the Dies Committee had once helped link the German-American Bund with homosexuality, witch-hunters now focused on parallels between the demonic homosexual and the demonic communist. Both were seen as hidden traitors and corrupters who undermined the country's moral fabric, destroyed families, and emasculated America in its hour of peril. Hundreds, if not thousands, of federal government employees were fired or forced to resign, and many others were denied employment, because of "sexual perversion." The number of annual military discharges for homosexuality doubled from the late 1940s to the early 1950s. State and local governments and private employers conducted similar purges. Local police forces staged periodic crackdowns against lesbians and gays; newspaper editors often printed the names of people arrested in bar raids; vigilante attacks proliferated. The FBI and other federal agencies, together with local police, conducted extensive surveillance of gays and lesbians and those who associated with them.[31]

In the early 1950s, homophobia also helped to destroy the National Union of Marine Cooks and Stewards (MCS), one of the eleven leftist unions that had been forced out of the CIO. The MCS was a West Coast CP-influenced union that had one of the best records of antiracism and multiracial solidarity in the labor movement and that included a high proportion of gay men in both rank-and-file and leadership positions. To a large extent, "queens" in the MCS were able to stake out a position of dignity and positive self-assertion within a context of working-class solidarity. In the face of persecution, the MCS won strong support from San Francisco's Black community, including a federation of Black Baptist ministers. Nevertheless, the Coast Guard, employers, and rival unions used a combination of gay-baiting, racism, and anticommunism to drive the union off the ships.[32]

Guilt-by-association tactics had once made all conservative and liberal anti-interventionists look like secret Nazi collaborators; now the taint of un-Americanism clung to anyone who challenged economic, political, or social inequality. Cold War red-baiting devastated Black and Chicano civil rights groups. Had it not been for the witch-hunts, writes Manning Marable, "the democratic upsurge of black people which characterized the late 1950s could have happened ten years earlier."[33] Numerous reform organizations, from the NAACP to the American Civil Liberties Union to the Mattachine Society, a pioneering gay-rights group, consumed themselves in internal antired purges meant to prove their loyalty, much as the CP had purged itself of Japanese American members in 1942.[34]

The growth of state repression, too, had far-reaching effects. The Immigration and Naturalization Service, with expanded powers of search and arrest under the McCarran–Walter Act, conducted "Operation Wetback" in 1954. This was a mass deportation of Mexicans largely designed to reduce an "oversupply" of undocumented workers during the 1953–1954 recession. In a virtual military campaign against Mexican people, the INS subjected citizens and noncitizens alike to searches, detentions, and expulsions. Labor organizers, of course, were specially targeted.[35] Meanwhile, state governments administering the New Deal's Aid to Dependent Children (ADC) program created special investigative units to spy on ADC families and search their homes without warning and at all hours. Investigators looked for any evidence, however specious, of a "substitute father" who would automatically disqualify the family from receiving aid.[36]

The shift of official ideology from antifascism to anticommunism created a circumstance whereby fascists were more acceptable than communists, provided they were discreet about certain aspects of their politics. Both the State Department and the courts determined that immigration restrictions against those advocating "totalitarianism" did not apply to former Nazis or other fascists. James Carey, a red-baiting labor leader in the CIO, declared, "In the last war we joined with the Communists to fight the Fascists. In another war we will join the Fascists to defeat the Communists."[37] In Europe, the Truman administration recruited thousands of former Axis war criminals and collaborators for use against the Soviet bloc. Such recruitment complemented the administration's support for right-wing dictators such as China's Chiang Kai-shek and the United States' own brutal counterinsurgency operations against nationalist uprisings in Puerto Rico and the Philippines.[38]

RED-BAITING THE RED BAITERS

The Truman administration's zealous anticommunism at home and abroad did not shield it from right-wing attacks. From the beginning, Truman and his domestic allies faced a war within a war: an ultraconservative drive to red-bait the hawkish Cold War liberals and Eastern Establishment conservatives who were leading the global anticommunist crusade. The roots of this conflict traced back to the mid-1930s, when Franklin Roosevelt's Second New Deal reconfigured factional alliances within the business community. Anti-New Deal corporate interests failed to dislodge Roosevelt from the White House in 1936 and 1940; they failed to stop the United States from joining the Allies in 1941. During the early Cold War, Senator Joseph McCarthy and other ultraconservative politicians rallied many of the same forces against the same opponents, but failed to reverse the New Deal's reforms or unseat its backers.

McCarthyism was "a purge within the state," not a mass populist movement.[39] Although it won support from broad constituencies and exploited popular resentments against elites, McCarthy's drive involved no mass organizing and did not depend on grassroots activism. As Michael Rogin notes, "McCarthy became prominent in the vacuum of popular apathy and moderation, not on a wave of radical mass mobilization."[40] But McCarthy's brand of antielite conspiracism—blending elements of producerism, regional prejudice, Anglophobia, homophobia, and anti-intellectualism—has directly influenced a long series of right-wing populist movements, from the John Birch Society in the 1960s to the followers of Patrick Buchanan in the 1990s. And McCarthy contributed to another shift in ultraconservative politics: unlike many of his 1930s predecessors, McCarthy avoided open ethnic bigotry. In this he helped initiate a broad right-wing move from open biological racism toward subtler cultural racism.

NATIONALISTS VERSUS MULTINATIONALISTS

The Second New Deal, initiated in 1935–1936, created a sharp split among business interests.[41] While the majority of capitalists opposed FDR's left turn, as Thomas Ferguson has shown, the Second New Deal brought together "a new power bloc of capital-intensive industries, investment banks, and internationally oriented commercial banks." This bloc included the Rockefellers' Standard Oil of New Jersey and several other major oil companies, General Electric, IBM, Mead Paper, RCA, Pan Am, tobacco companies such as R.J. Reynolds, and retailers Edward A. and Lincoln Filene. They were joined by major banks such as Brown Brothers Harriman, Dillon Read, Goldman Sachs, Lehman Brothers, A. P. Giannini's Bank of America, and the Rockefeller-controlled Chase National Bank.[42]

The pro-New Deal bloc, which has been dubbed "internationalist" or "multinationalist," initially included only a fraction of the business class, but it was the dynamic core of that class and reflected key trends within the business community. For generations, most industrial production had been labor-intensive, which meant that profits depended on keeping wages and benefits to a minimum. This fueled business owners' intense hostility toward labor activism. But capital-intensive firms, which had grown rapidly since World War I, were under comparatively little pressure to keep labor costs low. In the 1930s, they could be relatively flexible about making concessions to the increasingly militant labor movement. Under pressure from below, many of them accepted measures such as the Wagner Act, minimum-wage protections, and the Social Security Act, which provided a limited income cushion to working- and middle-class people.

Roosevelt's shift in trade policy also galvanized support from many of these companies. Since the late nineteenth century, the U.S. government and the majority of industrialists had stood for high tariffs in order to protect the country's growing industries from foreign (especially British) competition. But by the 1930s, a growing number of the capital-intensive firms had become competitive or dominant internationally; thus, they wanted low tariffs to boost trade and open up new markets. They responded enthusiastically to another key part of the Second New Deal: a series of reciprocal tariff agreements to reduce trade barriers, which marked a sharp departure from the government's previous economic protectionism. Pro-New Deal industrialists were joined by many major banks, which favored free trade and had tiny labor costs compared to other industries. In addition, a 1935 law establishing long-term oil price controls strengthened many oil companies' support for Roosevelt.

The multinationalists had outposts in various regions of the U.S. and included an important sprinkling of Jews and Catholics, but mainly represented the cutting edge of the White Protestant "Eastern Establishment," which was centered in New York City and which dominated the most prestigious universities, policy foundations, and newspapers, as well as the foreign service. The multinationalists saw their interests tied to Europe and emulated Britain, whose empire was their model of a globally managed economy. This orientation buttressed their support of the Allies during World War II.

Thomas Ferguson and Joel Rogers note the importance of the multinationalist bloc in the 1930s:

> By intervening in support of the Second New Deal's meliorative social policies, this bloc spared Roosevelt the choice—then being forced on leaders of other countries with fewer capital-intensive and internationally oriented big businesses—between socialism and the termination of a constitutional regime. Their support permitted Roosevelt to emerge as the guardian of all the millions, and to initiate a set of policies that delivered unprecedented benefits to the general population while satisfying a leading segment of American business.[43]

In the face of the Second New Deal, the majority of business forces rallied to the Republican Party, yet remained divided. Republican moderates spoke for a section of the Eastern Establishment led by the Morgan bank, which opposed the Roosevelt administration's social welfare programs but largely shared its trade and foreign policy outlook. In the 1940s and 1950s, the gap between these forces and the multinationalist bloc would largely disappear.

The Republican Right represented a more intransigent faction of anti-New Deal businesses. This "nationalist" bloc included many old manufacturing industries such as textiles, steel, and shoes, which were labor-intensive and thus especially vulnerable to labor unions, and countless private or family-controlled firms, large and small, steeped in laissez-faire individualism and hostile to the federal government. Also included were companies that favored protectionist policies because they could not compete internationally, or which were oriented toward domestic markets or U.S.-dominated regions such as Central America. Examples of such firms included the nationally oriented Sun Oil Company, owned by the Pew family, and the Midwest-based retailer Sears, Roebuck, whose board chair, Robert Wood, headed the America First Committee in 1940–1941. The nationalist bloc's most powerful member was the DuPont chemical company, which favored protectionism because technologically it lagged behind Germany's I.G. Farben chemical trust, and which at that time also had dominant interests in General Motors and U.S. Rubber.

Most business nationalists were hostile to any form of strong state that would restrict their entrepreneurial freedom at home. Yet they tended to be more sympathetic to the economic nationalism of fascist Germany and Italy than to free-trading England. Along with many fascists, they saw the New Deal as proof of a sinister alliance between international finance capital and communist-controlled working-class organizations to destroy free enterprise. Such views, rooted in the antibanker producerist tradition, were easily translated into conspiracy theories centered on Wall Street, Jewish bankers, and Britain.[44] Thus, some business nationalists directly promoted profascist politics. In the late 1930s, Gerald L. K. Smith's wealthy funders were concentrated in nationalist-oriented industries, such as William B. Bell, president of the American Cyanamid chemical company; J. Howard Pew, president of Sun Oil; the heads of national oil companies Quaker State, Pennzoil, and Kendall Refining; and automakers Henry Ford and John and Horace Dodge. Both Bell and Pew were executive committee members of the National Association of Manufacturers (NAM) and had been active in the American Liberty League.[45]

In contrast to the eastern elite's vision of global economic coordination, business nationalists favored unilateral, predatory U.S. expansion southward into Latin America and especially westward across the Pacific into Asia. Henry Ford's publicist, Samuel Crowther, became a representative for business nationalism in the 1930s; he castigated British dominance of world markets and condemned Britain's classic free-trade theorist Adam Smith while praising the German mercantilist Friedrich List. (Crowther, whose writings were promoted by the protectionist Chemical Foundation, also praised the chemical industry's development of new products such as artificial rubber as the key to U.S. economic self-sufficiency.)[46] In the 1930s and early 1940s, the nationalists opposed involvement in European conflicts, though many of them regarded Japan as a serious rival for control of China.

Many business nationalists endorsed the anti-interventionist movement in 1940–1941. Midwestern business nationalists dominated the American First Committee. In addition to Robert Wood, other business nationalists active in the anti-intervention movement included textile magnate William Regnery, Ernest Weir of the National Steel Corp., *Chicago Tribune* owner Robert R. McCormick, and meat-packing executive Jay Hormel.[47]

World War II strengthened the multinationalist faction. The war, which finally ended the Depression that relief and recovery programs could not solve, helped transform the New Deal into an enduring system. Large-scale federal spending to fuel economic prosperity, close ties between federal agencies and big business, and limited concessions to a bureaucratized labor movement were all part of the war effort. The war put millions of U.S. troops in Europe and deepened U.S. ties with Britain. When the Axis powers surrendered, the United States had unrivalled military, economic, and political dominance within the capitalist world. U.S. multinationalists oversaw creation of the United Nations, headquartered in New York City; the World Bank and International Monetary Fund, both based in Washington, DC; and an international financial system tied to the U.S. dollar.

CONTAINMENT VERSUS ROLLBACK

The conflict between multinationalist and nationalist elite factions continued into the Cold War, but the terms of conflict shifted. During the tumultuous FDR years, multinationalists had accepted limited concessions to organized labor and a wartime alliance with the USSR. But after the war, with economic stability restored and the Axis destroyed, multinationalists moved toward the right. From 1946 on, they generally favored a policy of "containment" both abroad and at home. The Truman Doctrine of 1947, which called for containment of communist forces around the world, was based on a belief that the Soviet Union was an expansionist threat, but one that could either be defeated through attrition or forced to abandon its dreams of conquest. Containment also describes the analogous domestic policy: to block the labor movement's growing size and power and make it abandon its focus on class struggle.[48] This meant targeting the labor movement's militant leftist wing while favoring the rise of a more conservative labor bureaucracy, which would be more cooperative with management to maintain a stable workforce.

Broadly speaking, business multinationalists accepted or favored Keynesian policies of active government intervention in the economy, including social welfare programs for the sake of social peace, foreign aid to develop international markets, and big military budgets to subsidize high technology industries and support large troop commitments abroad. Multinationalists controlled the most powerful business organizations: the Business Advisory Council, the Committee for Economic Development (CED), and the Council on Foreign Relations. The multinationalist outlook guided both the Truman administration and the moderate wing of the Republican Party.

Before Pearl Harbor, most nationalists had been anti-interventionists, and some military isolationism persisted after the war. But after the Chinese Revolution in 1949, they increasingly demanded a policy called "rollback"—a drive to fully destroy international communism. Rather than collective security, they wanted unilateral attack; rather than expensive ground forces and foreign aid, they wanted quick, cheap, often high-tech measures such as airpower and nuclear weapons. In addition, they regarded U.S. communists not simply as agents of Russian expansionism but as members of a global conspiracy, in which, as McCarthy put it, "the Communists within our borders have been more responsible for the success of Communism abroad than Soviet Russia."[49] Rollback is also a useful label for their aim to destroy the domestic communist threat by entirely smashing the labor movement and the New Deal, and by rooting out the subversives who supposedly infested Hollywood, the Ivy League, the State Department, and Wall Street. The nationalist-oriented NAM helped write the harshly anti-labor Taft–Hartley Act; the multinationalist CED had wanted a milder law.[50]

During the Cold War, business nationalists' base was in the Midwest and, increasingly, in the newly industrializing Sunbelt. They controlled the NAM and, at least to a large extent, the U.S. Chamber of Commerce. Business nationalists were represented by the right wing of the Republican Party and by sections of the Democratic Party, especially in the West and—on some issues—the South.

The split between multinationalists and nationalists was often bitter, but it was not fundamental. There was back-and-forth movement and shadings between the two factions, and collusion as well as conflict. In the 1930s, members of both camps had formed close economic ties with German industries that helped build the Nazi war machine.[51] During the early Cold War, the Central Intelligence Agency (CIA) was dominated by patrician Ivy Leaguers in top positions, but it gravitated toward the rollback doctrine. And while multinationalists were threatened by the nationalists and intensified their red-baiting to cover their right flank, they also used business nationalists in a game of good cop–bad cop. The specter of an even harsher crackdown by the Right gave the multinationalists greater leverage in disciplining the labor movement and keeping most of it loyal to the strike-breaking Truman administration. Both elite factions actively fueled the Cold War witch-hunts.

McCARTHYISM

If U.S. elites had all shared the same conception of anticommunism after World War II, "McCarthyism" would not be a word today, and the Red

Scare of those years might be as unremembered as the Red Scare of 1917–1920. But, in promoting the witch-hunts, business multinationalists provided an opening to their right-wing opponents. To business nationalists and ultraconservatives, real anticommunism entailed not just rollback abroad but also purging all elements of the New Deal system. Shortly after the CIO's red-baiting 1949 convention, the business-nationalist U.S. Chamber of Commerce proclaimed, "In spite of a partial house-cleaning, the CIO has never rid itself of its Marxist economics. Virtually every important speech and publication . . . is replete with class consciousness, hatred for employers." In 1950, an Arizona employer quoted a 1944 *Chicago Tribune* editorial, which had warned, "The people who support the New Deal ticket this November are supporting the Communists and building up the day when they plan the Red Terror sweeping down upon America. A New Deal vote is an invitation to murder." Representatives of the FBI and military intelligence, too, denounced liberalism—or as the FBI's J. Edgar Hoover called it, "pseudo liberalism"—as a breeding ground for communists.[52]

To the ultraconservatives and business nationalists, the enemy was a vast communist conspiracy of overt radicals, effete cosmopolitan intellectuals, and members of the Anglophile Eastern Establishment, such as the State Department. Alger Hiss, a former State Department official accused in 1948 of spying for the Soviets and eventually convicted of perjury in 1950 on dubious evidence, epitomized the image of the upper-class, Ivy League-educated New Dealer as a subversive security threat. Secretary of State Dean Acheson, who refused to "turn his back" on a convicted Hiss, was another prime target. The *Chicago Tribune* called Acheson "a striped-pants snob" who "ignores the peoples of Asia and betrays true Americanism to serve as a lackey of Wall Street bankers, British lords, and Communistic radicals from New York."[53] Homophobic language was common in right-wing denunciations of liberal elites.

President Truman's upset reelection over Republican Thomas Dewey in 1948 enraged the Right. When the Chinese Communists came to power in 1949—in the same year that the Soviet Union exploded its first atomic bomb—right-wing claims of State Department treachery reached new levels. China became a rallying cry for rollback advocates seeking to wrest political power from the New Dealers and the multinationalists. It was the furor over the "loss" of China that set the stage for McCarthy.

On the surface, the debate was about a ludicrous claim: that a handful of communist agents in and around the State Department had manipulated events to bring about the largest-scale revolution in the history of the world. But below this conspiracist fantasy lay a genuine conflict between the multinationalists' vision of a well-managed global system modeled after the British Empire and oriented toward Europe and the nationalists' desire for unilateral, predatory expansion southward into Latin America and westward across the Pacific into Asia.

After the Chinese Revolution drove Chiang Kai-shek's reactionary government onto Taiwan, rollbackers began promoting Chiang's plan to reconquer the Chinese mainland with U.S. help. They were supported by General Douglas MacArthur, commander of U.S. occupying forces in Japan and a longtime hero of the anti-New Dealers.[54] MacArthur and the China Lobby in the United States called for U.S. air and naval support for Chiang's planned invasion. The China Lobby was a major source of conspiracy theories about communist influence in the State Department and among government advisers at the Institute for Pacific Relations. Bankrolled by Chiang's government, the China Lobby was headed by Alfred Kohlberg, a textile manufacturer who owned factories in China, and who was assisted by William Goodwin, former associate of Father Coughlin and Gerald L. K. Smith. Beginning in 1949, the China Lobby received support from major Republican politicians and newspapers, nationalist businessmen, and some right-wing Democrats.[55]

It was in this context that McCarthy seized on the internal Red Menace as his ticket to fame and power. His crusade began in early 1950 with an attack on "subversives" within the State Department, the "Communists and queers who have sold 400,000,000 Asiatic people into atheistic slavery." In these attacks, and his denunciations of the Institute for Pacific Relations' Owen Lattimore as "the top Russian espionage agent," McCarthy followed a script laid out by rollback nationalists in general and the China Lobby in particular. He was supplied with documentation for his claims by Kohlberg, members of MacArthur's staff, and J. Edgar Hoover, among others.[56]

The outbreak of the Korean War in June 1950 shifted the center of foreign policy debate even further to the right. Temporarily departing from his policy of containment, President Truman endorsed MacArthur's attempt, as commander of United Nations forces in the war, to roll back communism by conquering North Korea, a move that ended disastrously as Chinese troops swept southward in response. The Korean War also boosted McCarthy's sagging fortunes by promoting a siege atmosphere and bringing U.S. troops into direct combat with communist forces.

McCarthy denounced as communists "the whole group of twisted-thinking New Dealers [who] have led America near to ruin at home and abroad."[57] His prime target was the multinationalist Acheson, "the Great Red Dean" whose "primary loyalty in international affairs seems to run to the British Labor Government, his secondary allegiance to the Kremlin." McCarthy also investigated communist plots in such multinationalist strongholds as the International Information Agency, the Voice of America, the United Nations, and Harvard University. In 1953 he attempted to investigate the CIA but was stopped by President Dwight Eisenhower.[58]

McCarthy received support from business nationalists such as Robert Wood of Sears, Roebuck; independent oil barons H. L. Hunt, Clint Murchison, Hugh Roy Cullen, and Sun Oil's Pew family; Lammot du Pont; Charles

M. White of Republic Steel; textile manufacturer and right-wing publisher William Regnery.[59] The big Republican newspaper publishers—Hearst, Scripps–Howard, Gannett, and Robert R. McCormick's *Chicago Tribune*—applauded McCarthy, which was key to his ability to shape public opinion. But, except for Texas, where independent oil was strong and generally hostile to Rockefeller-type multinational oil, McCarthy found relatively little backing in the South. Southern elites, though ultraconservative, were not only Democratic Party regulars but traditionally tied to British cotton markets and free trade policy.[60]

McCarthy was aided by FBI Director Hoover's desire for monopoly control over all government intelligence functions at home and abroad. The FBI's close cooperation with McCarthy and the other witch-hunting congressional committees was partly an effort to discredit the CIA, military intelligence, and other rivals. Like McCarthy, Hoover had close connections to Texas oil millionaires Murchison and Sid Richardson, and he also had long-standing ties with chemical industry figures, including A. Mitchell Palmer, his former boss at the Justice Department.[61]

David Caute describes McCarthy's political style as "notable for its crude, below-the-belt, eye-gouging, bare-knuckled partisan exploitation of anti-Communism, usually on the basis of half-truths, warmed-over 'revelations,' and plain lies. McCarthy was also the man with the briefcase full of incriminating documents—this appealed to a country much enamored of factuality, of the cult of hard fact." His attacks on the eastern upper crust— "the bright young men who are born with silver spoons in their mouth"— tapped a well of conservative antielitism among midwestern farmers, small businesspeople, Catholics, and some (primarily nonunionized) workers.[62]

The split between containment advocates and rollbackers spread to the middle-class women's movement, where two factions emerged in the League of Women Voters. This conflict helped set the stage for the John Birch Society and was the training ground for activists such as Phyllis Schlafly.[63]

Cold War liberals hated and feared McCarthy, but they had little ground on which to challenge him since they themselves had helped usher in his anticommunist crusade.[64] As I. F. Stone wrote in early 1954:

> If Communists are some supernatural breed of men, led by diabolic master minds in that distant Kremlin, engaged in a Satanic conspiracy to take over the world and enslave mankind—and this is the thesis endlessly propounded by American liberals and conservatives alike, echoed night and day by every radio station and in every newspaper, the thesis no American dare any longer challenge without himself becoming suspect—then how fight McCarthy?[65]

It was mainly Cold War liberal intellectuals such as Daniel Bell, Richard Hofstadter, and Seymour Martin Lipset who formulated centrist/extremist theory during this period. They drew parallels between McCarthyism and the Left and portrayed themselves as guardians of the rational, democratic center against both extremes.[66]

Moderate Republicans found McCarthy's tirades useful as long as they were directed against a Democratic administration. Red-baiting and rollback helped the Republicans win control of the White House and Congress in 1952. Once in power, President Eisenhower and his administration exploited rollback rhetoric but did not abandon containment or New Deal policies. Eisenhower and Republican moderates blocked right-wing efforts to cut back Social Security, dismantle the Tennessee Valley Authority, and repudiate the United Nations, NATO, and other international commitments.[67]

McCarthy and his allies continued to attack the State Department, exposing the deep split between nationalist and multinationalist wings of the Republican Party. With the signing of a truce agreement in Korea in July 1953, the tensions that had strengthened McCarthy's position began to abate. Hoover cut off FBI assistance to McCarthy in the late summer of 1953, fearing that the senator's crude smear tactics might discredit the FBI. McCarthy's attacks on the U.S. Army in 1954 finally went too far, and the Senate voted to condemn him (a move less severe than the censure initially proposed). The motion against McCarthy was introduced by Vermont Senator Ralph Flanders, who had close ties with the eastern elite, and was quietly promoted by a group of establishment businessmen headed by Paul Hoffman of Studebaker and Philadelphia banker Howard Peterson. In the 67 to 22 Senate vote, eastern Republican senators supported the motion while western and midwestern Republicans opposed it.[68] This vote ended McCarthy's political crusade; he died from alcoholism three years later.

McCarthy's fall did not end the Red Scare, but it ended the loud red-baiting of major federal officials by members of Congress. Claims that treason had infected Washington at the highest levels were dropped from mainstream political debate, though they were still voiced by ultraconservative organizations such as the Christian Anti-Communism Crusade, H. L. Hunt's Life Line Foundation, and, after 1958, the John Birch Society. Nor did ultraconservatives halt the New Deal policies of expanding social welfare and government spending as a motor of economic prosperity.

Yet, business nationalists remained an important political force. Although frustrated by continued Eastern Establishment control within both major parties, the nationalists had helped to shift the entire spectrum of political debate to the right. They had seriously weakened organized labor with the Taft–Hartley Act. Foreign policy in the following decades, under Republicans and Democrats alike, included selective rollback policies, mainly against Third World nationalist reform movements falsely labeled as communist, within a framework of global containment of communism. U.S. foreign policy priorities increasingly shifted toward the Third World, and more specifically Asia. And, while business nationalists' support for huge military budgets meant a retreat from their original commitment to cheap government and low taxes, it also meant vast subsidies for aerospace production in the nationalist-oriented Sunbelt states.[69]

FROM BIOLOGICAL TO CULTURAL RACISM

McCarthyism also marked a shift in ultraconservatism's racial and ethnic politics. By the 1950s, southern and eastern European ethnic groups were quickly gaining full access to White privilege. The doctrine of Nordic supremacy, which defined these groups as racially inferior, no longer reflected the material divisions within U.S. society and was widely discredited by its association with Nazism. Remnants of Nordic supremacist ideology, especially antisemitism, persisted, but they no longer dominated racial discourse as they had a generation earlier. Leo Ribuffo notes that "much as centrist liberals advertised their respectability by ostracizing domestic Communists, prominent conservatives advertised their respectability by ostracizing conspiratorial anti-Semites."[70]

Meanwhile, Black and Mexican Americans were moving from the countryside to the cities, from farm and service labor into industry, and, to a much smaller extent, into white-collar and professional work. Economic discrimination remained severe; between 1945 and 1960, the gap widened between Whites and Blacks in unemployment and income. Yet, rapidly growing communities of color in major cities, especially where Black people could vote (outside the South), were a political force to be reckoned with. Despite red-baiting's crippling effects, Black and Chicano organizations helped to pressure President Truman to undertake limited civil rights initiatives, such as desegregating the armed forces, and chipped away at discrimination in a series of court victories, such as the Supreme Court's historic *Brown v. Board of Education* ruling in 1954. Even in the South, efforts to attract industry with a stable "law-abiding" climate contributed to a sharp decline in racist lynchings.[71]

Yet racism remained strong. The federal government had forced the Ku Klux Klan to dissolve in 1944 for nonpayment of taxes, but violent Klan groups quickly revived. Gerald L. K. Smith was more isolated than before the war, but he developed a huge direct-mail operation and, in 1945–1949, "spoke to more and larger audiences than any other American of that time."[72] In 1948, when the Democrats included a civil rights plank in their national party platform, many southern Democrats formed the breakaway States' Rights Democratic Party (the "Dixiecrats"), with Strom Thurmond as their presidential candidate. The Dixiecrats denounced civil rights proposals as communist-originated maneuvers to "excite race and class hatred."[73]

Among witch-hunters, McCarthy stood somewhere between Mississippi Senator John Rankin's naked antisemitism and racism and Harry Truman's cautious civil rights politics. McCarthy—who was himself a Catholic—avoided ethnic and racial scapegoating and worked closely with Jews such as his investigative aide Roy Cohn and China lobbyist Kohlberg. Yet, in a time when many readily associated "un-American" ideas with "un-American" people, McCarthy's red-baiting had a clear anticosmopolitan tone. David Caute comments that "McCarthyism was the umbrella held out to all Americans, a repudiation of the Other (the alien) even when the Other was the Self."[74] This combination of appeal and threat resonated strongly with ethnic groups that felt vulnerable to scapegoating. For example, many Jewish organizations anxiously denounced Ethel and Julius Rosenberg—executed in 1953 for supposedly passing atomic bomb secrets to the USSR—in order to dissociate Jews from the taint of disloyalty and subversion. In the 1917–1920 Red Scare, antisemitism had been used to exclude Jews; now it served more as a lever to induce their ideological obedience.[75]

McCarthyism also reflected the beginnings of an important trend in ultraconservative politics: a partial shift from open biological racism, which ranked people on the basis of genetic ancestry, to a more sophisticated cultural racism, which extended limited opportunities to people of color if they pledged loyalty to the dominant values of White America, including anticommunism. The 1952 Immigration and Nationality (McCarran–Walter) Act, for example, preserved sharply discriminatory national quotas but abolished racial bars on immigration and citizenship. For the first time in U.S. history, Japanese-born people living in the United States could become citizens. McCarren–Walter also permitted 30,000 Chinese to enter the United States. This provision, designed for people fleeing the 1949 Chinese Revolution, placed anticommunist solidarity before racial exclusivism.[76]

But ultraconservative "color-blindness" could be harshly punitive. The New Deal had softened the colonial dominance of American Indians by creating elected tribal governments under federal control. In the 1950s, congressional Democrats and Republicans both reacted against this system as part of the anti-New Deal backlash. A 1953 House resolution claimed that they wanted "to end [the Indians'] status as wards of the United States, and to grant them all of the rights and privileges pertaining to American citizenship." Stated more bluntly, the new policy was the "termination" of tribal communities and the renewed breakup of Native land holdings. The Klamath of Oregon and the Menominee of Wisconsin, both of whom owned valuable timber areas, were among a number of tribes formally dissolved. Federal services to many Indian reservations were cut off, forcing

further land sales and producing severe hardship. Under the Urban Reloca-
tion Program, begun in 1950, thousands of American Indians were removed
to distant cities and deliberately isolated from their communities and
cultures.[77]

BANKERS, REDS, JEWS, AND SATAN

The main antisemitic subtext of McCarthyism was enforcing obedience
among Jews, who were suspected of having dual loyalties. At the same time,
there was a sector of the Right that linked anticommunism with more open
and nasty forms of antisemitism.

John Beaty's 1951 book *The Iron Curtain over America* is an example. The
false and fantastic thesis of the book concerns the descendants of the
Khazars, whose tiny ruling oligarchy centuries ago converted to Judaism
and then dispersed across Europe.[78] According to Beaty and other authors,
the Asiatic racial descendants of the Khazars founded and controlled the
Russian Communist Party as a step toward destroying western Christian civilization. A related and equally false corollary is that many Jews in the
United States are descendants of the Khazars and thus likely candidates for
enlistment by foreign Khazarite Jewish communists as subversives and
spies.[79]

Praise for the Beaty book came from a slew of retired generals and admi-
rals. Senator William A. Langer, former chairman of the Senate Judiciary
Committee, wrote: "I think it ought to be compulsory reading in every public school in America."[80] Linking Godless communism to the Antichrist was
an easy step for the more zealous right-wing Christian activists of the
1950s. Typical of this genre is *One World a Red World*, a pamphlet by Kenneth
Goff that claims to link Stalin and the "new world-order" to the Antichrist
and the Mark of the Beast. Goff warns that "the dream of the ´One-
Worlders´ may look good on paper but it all adds up to the age-old plan of
Satan to produce a Christless Millennial Reign—that man himself can be
God."[81] Goff, a former communist organizer, turned to Christianity and
then to White supremacy, writing a 1958 pamphlet, *Reds Promote Racial War*,
that claimed biblical support for segregation and that communists promoted racial strife.[82]

In 1962 the antisemitic four-page semimonthly newspaper *Common Sense*
published by Conde McGinley hit a circulation high of 90,000 with its message of the "Zionist Invisible Government" plotting to establish a "World
Government" under a "Red Dictatorship" led by "Asiatic Marxist Jews," a
racialized version of the Khazar myth.[83] The newspaper of the Louisiana
chapter of the White segregationist Citizen's Councils promoted books
and published articles with the same theme.[84] The warnings of a "Zionist
Occupational Government" popularized in the 1970s and 1980s by the

Posse Comitatus, Christian Identity, Aryan Nations, and other Christian Patriot groups are the heirs to this premise.

CONCLUSION

The anticommunist crusade of the early Cold War never really ended, but after the mid-1950s it gradually lost its overwhelming dominance of public life. A series of Supreme Court decisions in 1955–1958 curbed some of the worst civil liberties abuses connected with the Red Scare, for example, gutting the Smith Act. The FBI, however, not only continued its antileftist activities but intensified them. In 1956 it initiated its Counterintelligence Program (COINTELPRO) against the Communist Party, marking a shift from surveillance and infiltration to more aggressive forms of disruption and harassment. COINTELPRO was later extended to many other political targets.[85]

The Cold War Red Scare built directly on the foundation laid by the Brown Scare. By treating the 1930s Hard Right as an "un-American" fascist conspiracy rather than a set of political movements rooted in U.S. society, many critics of the Right contributed to sensationalism and demonization that were easily redirected against the Left. Brown Scare tactics such as guilt by association and smears such as sexual "perversion" were translated and magnified in the Red Scare. Cold War conservatives and liberals who denounced the Right and the Left as evil mirror images of each other sketched the outlines of centrist/extremist theory, which has dominated discussions of social movements for decades.

The Brown Scare depended not only on a false image of the Hard Right but also on the false belief that the U.S. state apparatus can be trusted with repressive powers. The laws, congressional probes, and political police powers that liberal antifascists hoped would be used against the Hard Right boomeranged forcefully against leftists, workers, people of color, gay men and lesbians. Far from being means to free the United States from hatred and fear, these institutions became tools to safeguard and reinforce systems of oppression.

Although the term McCarthyism is often used to describe the Red Scare as a whole, McCarthyism actually represented a distinct current within it. Business conflict analysis is crucial for understanding Senator McCarthy's role in the 1950s Red Scare. The Cold War liberals who developed centrist/extremist theory tended to regard him as a mouthpiece for uneducated lower-class hysteria, but this cannot explain McCarthy's close ties with wealthy and powerful elite figures. On the other hand, to view his campaign simply as a cruder version of President Truman's red-baiting or as a zealous Republican attack on the Democrats does not explain why McCarthy targeted high officials from both parties both before and after Republican Dwight Eisenhower's election to the White House. And to treat McCarthy simply as a power-hungry opportunist fails to explain the strong resonance his version of conspiracist antielitism has struck for generations of ultraconservatives and right-wing populists. When the John Birch Society attacked the United Nations, when Barry Goldwater's presidential campaign denounced the Rockefellers and free trade, when Lyndon LaRouche attacked the CIA and the British monarchy, and when Patrick Buchanan criticized the "unfettered capitalism" of transnational corporations, they were invoking McCarthy's legacy. And many of them also spoke for the descendants of 1950s business nationalists.

9

THE PILLARS OF
U.S. POPULIST CONSPIRACISM
The John Birch Society and the Liberty Lobby

The John Birch Society and the Liberty Lobby are the two pillars of the Hard Right that evolved in the late 1950s and grew in the 1960s.[1] Both groups blend populism, nativism, and conspiracism in the classic model of producerism. Like all producerist movements the Birch Society and the Liberty Lobby consider the "real" patriotic Americans to be hard-working people in the middle class and working class who create goods and wealth while fighting against "parasites" at the top and bottom of society who pick their pockets.[2]

These and other "Americanist" and "Patriot" movements promoted a brand of xenophobic nationalism that implicitly embraced White northern European cultural standards in confronting the ideas of increasingly diverse immigrant groups and increasingly secular liberal voting blocs.[3] Building on earlier antielite conspiracist campaigns, such as McCarthyism, the rightwing populism of the Birch Society and the Liberty Lobby targeted the government and other "insiders,"[4] but the two organizations differed in their interpretations of the alleged conspiracy and the steps they advocated to combat it.

Pre-World War II rightist movements were largely discredited in the public mind after the war, so with the emergence of the Cold War, rightwing movements adjusted their style. In addition, during the early 1950s, according to Abby Scher, "a majority of the grassroots anti-Communist activists were women."[5] Women had long played a role in conservative and reactionary movements, justifying their political activism as defending hearth and home, but World War II had expanded opportunities for women in many ways. Scher's analysis of one early 1950s group, the Minute Women of the U.S.A., reveals it to be primarily middle class and concerned with exposing communist subversion, defending constitutional limits, and stopping the internationalists from diluting U.S. sovereignty. These themes set the stage for the predominantly male John Birch Society and Liberty Lobby that inherited the conspiracist anticommunism of the McCarthy period and disseminated grandiose claims about the extent of the alleged conspiracy.

The John Birch Society maintains that internationalist "insiders" with a collectivist agenda (claimed to have been behind both Moscow communism and Wall Street capitalism) are engaged in a coordinated drive to destroy national sovereignty and individualism. JBS members are primarily elitist, ultraconservative, and reformist. The Society's published conspiracist theories do not center on scapegoating Jews and Jewish institutions, nor do they center on biological racism. In a more subtle form of racism and antisemitism, the Birch Society promotes a culturally defined White Christian ethnocentrism as the true expression of America. Echoing historic producerist themes, the group's ideology is suffused with implicit racism and antisemitism, but the latter are not explicitly articulated as principles of unity. The Society's conspiracist narrative may be traced back to John Robison's 1798 book alleging an Illuminati Freemason conspiracy. The Society's roots are in business nationalism, economic libertarianism, anticommunism, Eurocentrism, and Christian fundamentalism.[6]

The Liberty Lobby's conspiracist narrative asserts that the secret elites are Jews (descended through non-European bloodlines) who manipulate Blacks and other people of color to destroy national unity and popular will, seen as deriving its strength from a racially separate organic tribalism. The Lobby is primarily populist, fascist, and insurgent. It promotes conspiracist theories that center on scapegoating Jews and Jewish institutions and on biological racism as the basis for White supremacist xenophobia. However, by using coded rhetoric, and appeals to racial separatism that extol Black nationalist groups, the group attempts, with some success, to mask its core White supremacist views and antisemitism. The Liberty Lobby relies on historic antisemitic conspiracist sources that trace back to the *Protocols* and its many progeny. Its roots are in isolationism, small business resentment of large corporate interests, and eugenicist White racial nationalism.

The Birch Society and the Liberty Lobby both use populist rhetoric, but Birchites distrust the idea of the sovereignty of the people and stress that the United States is a republic, not a democracy—which they dismiss as a "mobocracy." This perspective explains how the Society can criticize the alleged secret elites and yet retain an elitist point of view: Birchites want to replace the "bad" elites with "good" elites—presumably their allies.

Both groups use conspiracist scapegoating, a common feature of right-wing populism. As is common with producerism, the Birch Society and the Liberty Lobby are especially scornful of those who organize on behalf of impoverished and marginalized communities, especially progressive social change activists.[7]

While both the Lobby and the Society have genuinely grassroots constituencies, they played a role in providing foot soldiers for business conflict. As we have seen, political conflicts of the 1930s, 1940s, and

1950s were strongly influenced by the clash between a rising pro-New Deal, pro-free trade multinationalist faction of business and a weaker anti-New Deal nationalist faction. During the 1960s the multinationalist faction endorsed limited concessions to antioppression movements as a way to maintain or restore social stability and expand its own political base.[8]

THE JOHN BIRCH SOCIETY

Robert Welch introduced the idea of the John Birch Society in Indianapolis when he convened on December 9, 1958, a meeting of twelve "patriotic and public-spirited" men.[9] The first chapter was founded only two months later, in February 1959. The core thesis of the Society was contained in Welch's initial Indianapolis presentation, transcribed almost verbatim in *The Blue Book* of the John Birch Society and subsequently given to each new member.[10] According to Welch, both the U.S. and Soviet governments were controlled by the same furtive conspiratorial cabal of internationalists, greedy bankers, and corrupt politicians. If left unexposed, the traitors inside the U.S. government would betray the country's sovereignty to the United Nations for a collectivist new world order managed by a "one-world socialist government."[11] The Birch Society incorporated many themes from pre-World War II rightist groups opposed to the New Deal, early 1950s anticommunist movements such as the Minute Women, and had its base in the middle class and business nationalist sectors.

Welch was born in 1899 and worked "in the candy manufacturing business all of his adult life," for many years as the vice president for sales and advertising of the James O. Welch Company, founded by his brother. He was on the board of directors of the ultraconservative National Association of Manufacturers (NAM) for seven years starting in 1950, and chaired the NAM's Educational Advisory Committee for two years. It was at the NAM, during the height of the Red Menace hysteria, that Welch honed his Americanist philosophy. Welch toured the country, chairing meetings on the state of American education, and produced a 32-page brochure, "This We Believe About Education," that concluded that in America "parents—and not the State—have the ultimate responsibility for the education of their children." Two-hundred thousand copies of the brochure were distributed by the NAM.[12] While an otherwise unremarkable pamphlet, it further advanced the theme that federal and state governments and professional teachers had usurped parental prerogatives, perhaps with a hidden agenda of social engineering.

Welch served as vice chairman of the Massachusetts Republican Party finance committee in 1948 and unsuccessfully ran for lieutenant governor in the 1950 Republican primary. Welch supported the ultraconservative Taft over the more moderate Eisenhower for president by running as a Massachusetts Taft delegate to the 1952 Republican convention.[13] In 1952 he wrote *May God Forgive Us*, a study alleging "subversive influences" by government officials and their allies aimed at shaping "public opinion and governmental policies to favor the Communist advance."[14] The book was published by the ultraconservative Henry Regnery Company, which in 1954 also published Welch's *The Life of John Birch*, which told the story of a fundamentalist missionary in China who became an intelligence agent for General Claire Chennault's Flying Tigers. Birch was killed by Chinese communist soldiers while he was on a mission at the end of World War II.[15] In February of 1956 Welch started publishing a magazine, *One Man's Opinion*, and in January 1957 he left the candy business to devote his energies to "the anti-Communist cause."[16]

Many of the founders and early leaders of the John Birch Society had ties to the National Association of Manufacturers, which during this period was controlled by medium-sized and family-controlled businesses.[17] The Birch Society was squarely in the business nationalist anti-New Deal tradition in its fierce opposition to the United Nations, foreign aid, the income tax, and the welfare state, and in its alternation between isolationist and rollback positions in military affairs.[18]

Welch saw collectivism as the main threat to Western civilization, observing that "both the Greek and the Roman civilizations did perish of the cancer of collectivism, and the civilization of Western Europe is doing so today."[19] This view was shared by many conservatives of the day, and had been developed after World War II by conservative intellectuals such as Friedrich A. Hayek.[20] The ingredient that Welch added was an "uncompromising conspiracy theory of world events, one that blamed domestic rather than foreign enemies for the spread of communism," as Diamond noted.[21] Although criticizing Oswald Spengler for intellectual snobbery, Welch agreed with Spengler's idea of a "cyclical theory of cultures," detailed in Spengler's *Decline of the West*. Welch, however, argued that the cycle of dominance for western European civilization was being prematurely put at risk by a conspiracy promoting collectivism.[22]

According to the JBS theory, liberals consciously encourage the gradual process of collectivism; therefore, JBS reasoning goes, many liberals and their allies must actually be secret traitors whose ultimate goal is to replace the nations of Western civilization with a one-world socialist government. "There are many stages of welfarism, socialism, and collectivism in general," wrote Welch, "but communism is the ultimate state of them all, and they all lead inevitably in that direction."[23] A core tenet of the Birch Society is that the United States is a republic, not a democracy, and that collectivism has eroded that distinction. That this distinction was largely just a semantic one—used to divert attention from the essentially repressive elitism of Welch and the Birchite philosophy—was a theme taken up by Lester DeKoster, a conservative Christian who warned of the Birch Society's antidemocratic agenda in his monograph *The Citizen and the John Birch Society*.[24]

The Birchites' concern that collectivism, statism, and internationalism would be ushered in through a subversive communist conspiracy prompted them in 1959 to undertake a "Get US out of UN!" campaign (the slogan is a pun), which alleged that the "real nature of [the] UN is to build One World Government (New World Order)."[25] In 1962 the attacks on the United Nations became a major theme for Birchite publications and activism.[26] Behind much of the Birchite concern over collectivism was opposition to communism not only on economic, ideological, and pragmatic geopolitical grounds but also on religious grounds, in that communism was seen as a godless conspiracy. The influence of apocalyptic fundamentalist Christian beliefs on Birchite doctrine is often obscured by the group's ostensibly secular orientation. But, Welch himself at one point put it in biblical apocalyptic terms: "This is a *world-wide* battle . . . between light and darkness; between freedom and slavery; between the spirit of Christianity and the spirit of anti-Christ for the souls and bodies of men."[27]

Welch's self-published magazine, renamed *American Opinion*, became the official Birch Society publication in 1959, as new chapters began to be added.[28] In January 1960 the organization had 75 chapters and 1,500 members, and then by September there were 324 chapters and some 5,300 members.[29] In March 1961, according to Welch, there was "a staff of twenty-eight people in the Home Office; about thirty Coordinators (or Major Coordinators) in the field, who are fully paid as to salary and expenses; and about one hundred Coordinators (or Section Leaders as they are called in some areas), who work on a volunteer basis as to all or a part of their salary, or expenses, or both."[30] Estimates of Society membership by the end of 1961 ranged from 60,000 to 100,000.[31] The actual membership figures are shrouded in secrecy and often disputed. J. Allen Broyles argues that by 1966 the actual active membership was more like 25,000–30,000,[32] but this estimate seems low, especially given that active participants are usually just a fraction of the paid membership in most groups.

No matter what the actual membership, the Birch Society pioneered new ways to organize grassroots lobbying, combining educational meetings, petition drives, and letter writing campaigns. One early campaign against the second Summit Conference between the United States and the Soviet Union generated over 600,000 postcards and letters, according to the Society.[33] A June 1964 Birch campaign to oppose Xerox Corporation's sponsorship of certain television programs considered favorable to the UN produced 51,279 letters from 12,785 individuals.[34]

Much of the early Birch conspiracist narrative reflected an ultraconservative business nationalist critique of business multinationalists who were seen as exercising complete control over the world economy through groups such as the Council on Foreign Relations (CFR). The CFR, as viewed through the lens of conspiracy theorists, is a puppet of the Rockefeller family. Dan Smoot's (1962) *The Invisible Government* added several other policy groups to the list of purported conspirators, including the

Committee for Economic Development, the Advertising Council, the Atlantic Council (formerly the Atlantic Union Committee), the Business Advisory Council, and the Trilateral Commission.[35] Smoot had worked at FBI headquarters in Washington, DC, before leaving to establish an anticommunist newsletter, *The Dan Smoot Report*.[36] For Smoot, the shift from countersubversion on behalf of the FBI to countersubversion in the private sector was an easy one; his basic premises remaining the same. In Smoot's concluding chapter of *The Invisible Government*, he wrote, "Somewhere at the top of the pyramid in the invisible government are a few sinister people who know exactly what they are doing: They want America to become part of a worldwide socialist dictatorship, under the control of the Kremlin."[37]

In a 1966 speech, Welch coined the term "The Insiders" to denote the leaders of the conspiracy.[38] The Birch Society seems unable to make up its mind if the Insiders are continuing the same collectivist plan launched by the Illuminati Freemason conspirators. During the late 1980s and early 1990s the Birch Society leadership downplayed the connection, while in the late 1990s the Society book list began including titles seeking to prove the link to the Illuminati Freemason conspiracy. Many Birch Society members, and founder Welch himself, expressed support for this thesis. According to the theory, there is an unbroken ideologically driven conspiracy linking the Illuminati, the French Revolution, the rise of Marxism and communism, the Council on Foreign Relations, and the United Nations. Of course, not all Birch Society members agreed with everything that Welch or the Society propounded. Welch's famous book *The Politician* caused a stir even among loyal Birch members, many of whom were shocked by Welch's assertion that President Dwight D. Eisenhower was "a dedicated conscious agent of the communist conspiracy."[39]

The Birch Society's influence on U.S. politics hit its peak around the time of the failed 1964 presidential campaign of Republican candidate Barry Goldwater, who lost in a landslide to incumbent President Lyndon Johnson who carried 44 states with 61 percent of votes, at the time, the largest margin in U.S. history. While Welch had supported Goldwater over Nixon even for the 1960 Republican nomination, the membership was split on the question, with about one-third supporting Nixon.[40] A number of Birch Society members and their allies were Goldwater supporters in 1964, and some were even delegates to the 1964 Republican convention.[41]

Business nationalists provided most of the capitalist backing for Goldwater's 1964 presidential campaign, which offered them yet another vehicle for attacking the Rockefellers and other Eastern Establishment leaders (the sinister cabal of "secret kingmakers" described in Phyllis Schlafly's campaign paperback, *A Choice Not an Echo*). The Goldwater campaign denounced federal desegregation efforts, New Deal programs, the UN, and low tariffs. The 1964 campaign was the only time in U.S. history that the vast majority of top corporate leaders supported the Democratic presidential candidate.[42]

Advertisements warning about the communist menace (placed by the JBS in major daily newspapers) generated 500 letters per day to the Society headquarters in 1963, but there were many targets. In 1964 the John Birch Society conducted a major organizational effort seeking to "Impeach Earl Warren." The Society also sought to restore prayer in public schools, repeal the graduated personal income tax, stop "Communist influences within our communications media," and end the "trend of legislation by judicial fiat," meaning that states' rights should supersede federal laws and Supreme Court decisions. What was specifically spurring the Society's campaign against liberal Chief Justice Warren however, was the Society's avowed opposition to federal assistance to the goals of the civil rights movement.[43]

The Birch Society's "Support Your Local Police" campaign, launched in the mid-1960s, opposed the use of federal officers to enforce civil rights laws.[44] "The Communist press of America has been screaming for years . . . to have local police forces discredited, shunted aside, or disbanded, and replaced by Federal Marshals or by similar agents and personnel of a *national federalized* police force," one article complained.[45]

The Birch Society opposed the civil rights movement, mainly because it was seen as a "fraud" created by communists, and Birch members were urged to "Show the communist hands behind it."[46] According to a 1967 personal letter from Welch to retired General James A. Van Fleet, inviting him to serve on the Birch Society's National Council:

> Five years ago, few people who were thoroughly familiar with the main divisions of Communist strategy saw any chance of keeping the Negro Revolutionary Movement from reaching decisive proportions. It was to supply the flaming front to the whole "proletarian revolution," as planned by Walter Reuther and his stooge, Bobby Kennedy.[47]

Despite its opposition to civil rights, throughout this period the JBS had a handful of Black conservative members who consistently supported its opposition to the liberal civil rights movement—based on philosophical grounds involving states' rights, economic libertarianism, and suspicions of communist subversion of the civil rights movement. While the JBS discouraged overt and conscious displays of racism, at the same time it promoted policies that had the direct effect of buttressing racist oppression. Whether or not White supremacy was the conscious intent of some Birch Society leaders, the group's stance was very different from the conscious ideological racism of far-right hate groups.

The degree of political racism expressed by JBS leaders was similar to that of many mainstream Republican and Democratic elected officials of the time. This level of mainstream racism should not be dismissed lightly, as it was often crude, treating Black people in particular as second-class citizens, and assuming that most Blacks had limited intelligence and little ambition. In Alan Stang's book published by the JBS, *It's Very Simple: The True Story of*

Civil Rights, Rev. Martin Luther King, Jr., is portrayed as an agent of a massive communist conspiracy instructed to agitate among otherwise happy Negroes to foment revolution, or at least promote demands for more collectivist federal government intrusion.[48]

The same impetus to moderate the most overtly bigoted elements is evident among Birchites' varying levels of personal and political antisemitism. When crude antisemitism was detected in JBS members, their membership was revoked.[49] The most celebrated incident involved Birchite leader Revilo P. Oliver, who moved over to work with Willis Carto and the Liberty Lobby after being forced to resign from the Birch Society for making antisemitic and White supremacist comments at a 1966 Birch Society rally.[50]

The Birch Society promoted the 1971 book *None Dare Call It Conspiracy* by Gary Allen, an example of producerism. The book included a graphic chart showing the middle class being squeezed between the ruling elite "insiders" above (the Rothschilds, Rockefellers, and Council on Foreign Relations), and the rabble below ("naive radicals" of the Left, such as the Students for a Democratic Society, the Black Panthers, the Yippies, the Young Socialist Alliance, and Common Cause).[51] Allen included a dubious discussion of the Rothschilds and other Jewish banking interests as part of a sketch of a much larger conspiracy involving financial and political elites and the Council on Foreign Relations. Allen explicitly rejected the idea that by focusing on the early role of the Rothschilds in investment banking he was promoting a theory of a Jewish conspiracy:

> Anti-Semites have played into the hands of the conspiracy by trying to portray the entire conspiracy as Jewish. Nothing could be farther from the truth. The traditionally Anglo-Saxon J. P. Morgan and Rockefeller international banking institutions have played a key role in the conspiracy. But there is no denying the importance of the Rothschilds and their satellites. However, it is just as unreasonable and immoral to blame all Jews for the crimes of the Rothschilds as it is to hold all Baptists accountable for the crimes of the Rockefellers.[52]

Nicely put, perhaps, but Allen used insensitive and loaded language about the "cosmopolitan" nature of the "international bankers," and he slipped in comparing Jews to Anglo-Saxons, mixing issues of race, ethnicity, and religion. He seemed sincere in rejecting overt and conscious antisemitism and did not seem to be cloaking a hidden hatred or distrust of Jews; yet he included a hyperbolic and inaccurate assessment of the role of the Rothschilds, Warburgs, and other Jews compared to the non-Jewish banking interests that grew along with industrial capitalism. The problem was unintentional but still real.

The stereotype of a Jewish establishment was clearer in some of Allen's other work, but, as Mintz explained, "A conspiracist unimpressed by anti-

Semitism could construe the material differently from a confirmed sociological anti-Semite, who could find a codification of his fears and anxieties."[53] In 1974 Allen updated the scenario in *Rockefeller: Campaigning for the New World Order*, articulating the antiglobalist theme of much conspiracism later echoed in the Patriot and armed militia movements.[54] Allen's work is championed by the John Birch Society.

Like Allen, the Birch Society promoted conspiracist theories linking international bankers and certain Jewish financial elites. Welch and the Society buttressed claims of the Illuminati conspiracy by citing Nesta Webster, and used the works of Antony C. Sutton to buttress claims of a Wall Street banking conspiracy.[55] Yet, as Mintz observed about the work of Allen, persons unaware of the history of antisemitism could easily miss the antisemitic stereotyping in the work of Webster or see nothing problematic in Sutton's inclusion of names such as Rothschild, Warburg, Schiff, and Baruch in his lists of secret manipulators. Sutton strenuously objects to his work being linked in any way to antisemitism.

The Birch Society view of the alleged financial conspiracy does not reveal it to be controlled or significantly influenced by Jews in general, or a secret group of conniving Jews; nor is there evidence of a hidden agenda within the Society to promote suspicion of Jews. The Society always struggled against what it saw as objectionable forms of prejudice against Jews, but it can still be criticized for having continuously promoted mild antisemitic stereotyping. The Birch Society's viewpoint more closely resembled mainstream stereotyping and bigotry than the naked race hate and genocidal antisemitism of neonazi or Ku Klux Klan groups. When the Society undertook to distribute any historic tract about the conspiracy, it was usually a simple reprint of Robison's *Proofs of a Conspiracy*.

The Birch Society helped to transform earlier, more blatant, biological forms of ethnocentric White racism and Christian nationalist antisemitism into less obvious cultural forms. This evolutionary leap forward was in contrast to the intentional White supremacist bigotry and open loathing of Jews that had typified much of the Old Right prior to World War II. Throughout its existence, however, the Society has promoted open and intentional homophobia as well as sexist antifeminist themes.

The Society's anticommunism and states' rights libertarianism were based on sincere principles, but both may have been utilized as a cover by segregationists and White supremacists determined to organize themselves anyway. How much official Birchite doctrine was consciously (or unconsciously) ignored is difficult to determine in individuals or chapters. That the Birch Society clearly attracted members with a bigoted (even fascistic) personal agenda is undeniable, and these more zealous elements used the Society as a recruitment pool from which to draw persons toward a more neofascist or neonazi stance. As Birch members assisted in building grassroots support for Goldwater's Republican presidential bid in 1964, critics of the Society highlighted the group's more unsavory elements as a way to discredit Goldwater, who was labeled an "extremist." For the Birch Society, however, Goldwater was a compromise candidate. Internal records from 1964 reveal Birch Society misgivings about the political reliability of Goldwater. Newspaper articles from the Birch Society archives show various Goldwater quotes that conflicted with Birchite dogma heavily underlined and sporting rows of question marks. At the same time, however, a racist and antisemitic attack on Goldwater by the White supremacist *Thunderbolt* is labeled "Poison," with a bold pen stroke.

After Goldwater was soundly drubbed in the 1964 general election, and Richard Nixon won a three-way presidential race in 1968, Welch tried earnestly to recruit another politician to take up the Birchites' torch—namely, former Alabama Governor George Wallace. "It is the ambition and the intention of Richard Nixon, during the next eight years, to make himself the dictator of the world," warned Welch in a November 11, 1968, postelection letter to Wallace, who as the third-party candidate had drawn 13.5 percent of the vote. "The people of this country are ready for an anti-Communist crusade behind some political leader who really means it," wrote Welch, urging Wallace to embrace the Birch Society's platform.[56]

The more pragmatic conservatives and reactionaries who had been fund-raising and organizing specialists during the Goldwater campaign would form the core of what became known as the New Right. Although many New Right and new Christian Right activists were groomed through the Birch Society, the group's conspiracist obsession, passionate and aggressive politics, and its labeling by critics as a radical right extremist group tainted by antisemitism and racism were all seen as impediments to successful electoral organizing. The Birch Society became a pariah. The faltering finances and reputations of the organization were further stung in the 1970s when the Birch Society lost a defamation lawsuit brought by Chicago civil liberties attorney Elmer Gertz, whom the JBS had red-baited.

In the late 1970s the New Right coalition of secular and Christian conservatives and reactionaries emerged as a powerful force on the American political landscape, and helped elect Ronald Reagan to the presidency in 1980 and 1984. The eclipsed Birch Society saw its influence dwindle even further after Reagan took office, and further still after Birchites attacked Reagan's policies as too liberal.

The Society also apparently turned to a fund-raising scheme of dubious propriety. A donor seeking to make tax exempt gifts to the Society in 1983 was instructed to make the checks out to two nonprofit groups, Summit Ministries of Colorado and the San Antonio Academy of Texas. Both institutions bought substantial advertising in Birch Society publications.[57] This scheme appears to have been a systematic one enabling supporters to make donations to tax-exempt groups while really channeling the funds into the coffers of the Society.

By founder Robert Welch's death in 1985, the Birch Society had shrunk to less than 50,000 members. There then ensued an internal struggle over who would grab the reins of power. The victors quickly alienated Welch's widow, who denounced the new leadership from her retirement home in Weston, Massachusetts. Magazine subscriptions, often a close indicator of relative membership, fell from 50,000 to fewer than 20,000.

A study of the 1987 Birch subscription list by Charles Jeffrey Kraft revealed that the highest per capita Birch membership was clustered in the Rocky Mountain states. The top dozen states by percentage of membership (ranging from 45 to 15 per persons per 100,000 population) were South Dakota, Idaho, Montana, North Dakota, Utah, Nebraska, Wyoming, Washington, Colorado, Arizona, Oklahoma, and Georgia. In the 1980s and 1990s many of these states would see disproportionately high activism by hard-right populist groups such as the Posse Comitatus and armed citizens militias.

The greatest number of members lived in California (2,648), Texas (1,232), Florida (1,154), Georgia (949), Washington (873), New York (773), Ohio (726), Tennessee (694), Indiana (635), Wisconsin (604), Colorado (590), and Pennsylvania (586). The Birch membership was found to be "disproportionately well educated and upper income status," with a "high incidence of physicians and dentists."[58]

The collapse of communism in Europe and the end of the Cold War might have signaled the end of the Birch Society, but the UN role in the Gulf War and President Bush's call for a New World Order unwittingly echoed Birch Society claims about the goals of the internationalist One World Government conspiracy.[59] As growing right-wing populism sparked new levels of cynicism regarding politicians, and economic and social fears sparked rightist backlash movements, the Birch Society positioned itself as the group that for decades had its fingers on the pulse of the conspiracy behind the country's decline. In 1989 Birch Society leadership cashed in by selling its prime office buildings in Belmont, Massachusetts, relocating to Appleton, Wisconsin, and investing the funds from the sale of its real estate in improving its magazine and rebuilding its membership.

Between 1988 and 1995 the Birch Society at least doubled, and perhaps tripled, its magazine subscribers to over 55,000.[60] Birch organizers in the 1990s were especially active in organizing against federal land use regulations and expansion of the national park system.[61]

THE LIBERTY LOBBY

The idea for a Liberty Lobby in Washington, DC, was first announced by founder Willis Carto in 1957, but the organization was not fully functional until 1961. At first glance, the Liberty Lobby seems to be what it claims to be—a patriotic populist organization seeking to restore constitutional safe-guards and national sovereignty. A careful inspection of the group's rheto-ric and history, however, reveals that depiction to be a clever cover for a far-right agenda.[62]

In materials promoting the group, the underlying producerist and conspiracist themes of right-wing populism are clearly evident.[63] In 1997 the Lobby's web page declared that the organization was "Dedicated to shining a light of truth on corruption in Government, media, and the secret powers that govern our planet." Focus sections on the web page included Congress, The Media, Immigration, and New World Order.

The Liberty Lobby's newspaper, the *Spotlight*, is described on the *Spot-light's* website as follows:

> The *Spotlight* is the world's largest-circulation POPULIST weekly, with over 250,000 readers in all 50 states and in 57 countries.
>
> Since 1975, The *SPOTLIGHT* has expertly exposed government corrup-tion, media distortion, insider scandals, corporate rip-offs of consumers and stockholders, investor scams and the various ways elitists scheme to unduly exercise their influence over the average productive citizen who obeys the law, pays the taxes and is of REAL value to mankind.
>
> Every day, the U.S. Government betrays its own citizens—often to the tune of BILLIONS of DOLLARS!! Yet, the mainstream media, liberal and es-tablishment oriented, either suppresses or slants the TRUTH to justify their one-world-oriented, often mean-spirited actions.
>
> But with The *SPOTLIGHT*, these stories—and the often insidious, awful truth behind them—are truly in the *Spotlight* for all but the willfully ignorant or the stupid to see!
>
> Learn about the top secret committee of the world's most powerful men, who meet regularly to determine the course of elections, staffing of gov-ernments, central banks, interest rates, inflation, etc.
>
> Find out how the Clinton Administration is ILLEGALLY granting MIL-LIONS of aliens U.S. Citizenship—knowing that they'll vote for Clinton. Also learn how the ruthless men and women behind "Slick Willie" are keep-ing Clinton in office AT ANY PRICE.[64]

The *Washington Post* once described the *Spotlight* as a "newspaper contain-ing orthodox conservative political articles interspersed with anti-Zionist tracts and classified advertisements for Ku Klux Klan T-shirts, swastika-marked German coins and cassette tapes of Nazi marching songs." That de-scription is actually mild. The *Spotlight* has also celebrated the Nazi Waffen SS, neonazi skinheads, and the apartheid government of South Africa. It regularly promotes the idea that the Nazi genocide of Jews has been exag-gerated by historians. During the mid-1990s the *Spotlight* was said to have had a print run of about 100,000 and claimed a readership of 250,000.[65]

In contrast to the laissez-faire ultraconservative John Birch Society, the

Liberty Lobby is essentially a neofascist organization. It advocates replacing our pluralist system with an authoritarian corporatist system based on a myth of racial nationalist rebirth. During the late 1960s the Liberty Lobby formed a short-lived paramilitary youth organization, the National Youth Alliance.[66]

The most significant political influence on founder Willis Carto's ideology was the book *Imperium*, by Francis Parker Yockey, a "World War II era Nazi sympathizer," whose book Diamond describes as "a classic piece of anti-Jewish propaganda, linking Jews to banking, national indebtedness, and conspiracies behind racial conflict in American society."[67] Yockey, and devotee Carto, synthesized Spengler's theories and arrived at a bloodline-based racial nationalist interpretation, as opposed to Welch's cultural derivation that guided the John Birch Society.[68]

In 1955, Carto, under the pseudonym E. L. Anderson, started the vociferously antisemitic magazine *Right*, which tried to find common ground around the theme of nationalist White supremacy as a way to link segregationists, far-right conspiracist groups, and old Klan and neonazi organizations.[69] Carto later founded the magazine *Western Destiny*, a merger of *Right* and the Nordicist *Northern World*.[70] To edit *Western Destiny* Carto recruited Dr. Roger Pearson, the former editor of *Right*. Pearson went on to recruit former Nazis, fascists, and terrorists into the World Anti-Communist League, and promoted Aryan racial supremacy through the Institute for the Study of Man.[71]

While Carto announced the formation of the Liberty Lobby in 1957, it remained dormant until after he had spent a year (circa 1959) working at the newly established John Birch Society headquarters in Belmont, Massachusetts, picking up organizational and fund-raising skills.[72] As Frank P. Mintz would phrase it, thereafter there was a Liberty Lobby–Birch Society "symbiosis," with the two groups sharing many ideas and personnel but disagreeing over the root conspiracy.[73]

In his history of the Liberty Lobby, Mintz argues that the group reflects three facets of traditional U.S. nativism: racism, conspiracism, and monoculturalism. According to Mintz, the Liberty Lobby clearly voices "racist and anti-Semitic beliefs in addition to conspiracism." As Mintz explains:

> Structurally, the Lobby was a most unusual umbrella organization catering to constituencies spanning the fringes of Neo-Nazism to the John Birch Society and the radical right. It was not truly paramilitary, in the manner of the Ku Klux Klan and Nazis, but was more accurately an intermediary between racist paramilitary factions and the recent right.[74]

Scott McLemee observed that the Liberty Lobby conspiracism seems to consistently scapegoat Jews:

[According to the Liberty Lobby] conspiracies penetrate countless details of everyday life. The American Medical Association is a conspiracy; so are big business, big labor, the educational system, foreign and domestic policy, and the news media. These cabals turn out to be directly connected to the agencies and interests of financial institutions (such as the Federal Reserve and the International Monetary Fund); to individuals whose names tend overwhelmingly to be Jewish; and to Israel and the Anti-Defamation League of B'nai B'rith.[75]

The *Spotlight* frequently rails against "dual-loyalists" or "aliens" in our government when its true target is variously Jews, Zionists, strategic supporters of the nation of Israel, corporate executives, bankers, and human rights advocates, which the *Spotlight* mixes together into an antisemitic stew. Despite all of this, the Liberty Lobby consistently denies that it is the least bit antisemitic, much less neofascist or quasinazi.

The deceptive nature of Liberty Lobby's self-proclaimed populist patriotism is highlighted in the 1982 book *Profiles in Populism*, edited by Carto and published by the Lobby. The introduction to *Profiles in Populism* attacks the "new world order" and seeks to "expose the Establishment's false liberal–conservative dichotomy and focus the attention of political thinkers on the most significant issue in America today: nationalism vs. internationalism."[76] In other writings, however, Carto argues that the real battle in the world is not between capitalism and communism, but "between the white and the colored world."[77] Carto also takes populist themes and, using the producerist paradigm, overlays them with antisemitic themes.

Carto begins *Profiles in Populism* with profiles of Thomas Jefferson, Andrew Jackson, and populist leaders Robert M. LaFollette, Sr., and Tom Watson. Then come some fast shuffles, for which Carto has become legendary. Who is enshrined in the Carto populist pantheon? Henry Ford, for one. The authoritarianism and antisemitism of Ford are simply omitted. Near the end of the book comes a profile of Father Coughlin, who is described as a populist pastor, radio priest, and great patriot. Coughlin's antisemitism and fascist politics are not discussed except to dismiss these historic facts as a smear by allies of the Anti-Defamation League, which in this context is a swipe at Jews.[78]

Carto's book uses the term *populism* to mask an element common to many forms of fascism—namely, an ethnocentric nationalism mobilized against an alleged secret conspiracy of international finance capital. This idea is attributed to many of the men described in *Profiles in Populism*. Carto dubs the internationalist conspirators "mattoids," an archaic term for people whose brilliance is marred by criminal insanity.[79] The book even promotes the quasinazi idea that race, nation, and culture must be synonymous in order for a nation to survive.[80] According to Carto,

The internationalist seeks to mix all races and nations into one homogeneous whole—the whole to accept his own values, of course—thus destroying all national, racial, religious differences. . . . The nationalist, however, loves his own kind as the extension of his family, realizing that universal values are primitive values or no values at all; that men can be free and content only within their native cultural environment.[81]

Thus does Carto invoke the theme of racial nationalism as a type of apartheid fascism—envisioning a world of racially separate nation states. This idea would be promoted later in Europe by the European New Right and the fascist Third Position movement, and in the United States by the right-wing populist nationalism of David Duke and Pat Buchanan.[82]

Both the Liberty Lobby and the John Birch Society backed the 1964 presidential candidacy of Republican Barry Goldwater. *Liberty Lowdown* (an early Liberty Lobby briefing newsletter for donors) headlined one article "Barry Goldwater: Man on the White Horse?" Listed as "imperfections" were Goldwater's order for racial integration of the Arizona Air National Guard and a donation to the NAACP. Still, according to the Lobby, "[The] nomination of Goldwater will . . . mark the divorcement of the GOP from the mongrel, left-wing international banking interests in New York."[83]

Carto assisted in forming and financing Youth for Wallace during the 1968 presidential campaign and then in 1969 assisted the formation of its successor, the National Youth Alliance (NYA) which quickly shifted from states' rights constitutionalism and closet segregationism to a vivid neonazi stance.[84] The NYA planned to use street violence to smash radical student and Black nationalist groups. A faction of NYA survived as the National Alliance, headed by William Pierce, author of *The Turner Diaries*.

In 1978 Carto founded the Institute for Historical Review (IHR), a West Coast–based organization that published the *Journal of Historical Review*, hosted the International Revisionist Conference, and created Noontide Press as a publishing and distribution center. The pseudoscholarly Institute for Historical Review is a "revisionist" research center that claims that the commonly accepted historical account of the Nazi genocide of Jews is based on a hoax.[85] Noontide Press distributed such titles as *Auschwitz: Truth or Lie—An Eyewitness Report*, *Hitler at My Side*, and *For Fear of the Jews*, and reprinted classics by conspiracist antisemites such as Nesta Webster and John Beaty. There is also material praising World War II Nazis, pro-Nazi figures, and World War II battles from the German perspective, including the book *Hitler's Gladiator*, and even an oversized coffee-table book, *Adolf Hitler: The Unknown Artist*.[86]

Carto attempts to shield his antisemitic views from direct public scrutiny, but in a 1983 letter to IHR assistant director Keith Stimely he dismissed the Nazi death camps as an "overall fraud" and described the "Establishment" position on the Nazi genocide as follows:

Their theory, as you know, is that all the allies knew of the extermination policy and took a tolerant attitude toward it. It fits in with the Jews' general approach—everyone hates 'em even if they say they love 'em and we all have to continue to pay for this sin of hypocrisy. When we say we love Jews, we have to *mean* it.[87]

Carto also complains that

Americans, and I guess Germans, too, are just about convinced that the only people who suffered during the war were jews; that nothing else happened during that time other than jew extermination; that the history of the world, literally approved by god, is the history of whatever the ruling jews say it is and nothing else.[88]

In a 1984 letter to Stimely, Carto discussed his ideas for more articles that would show a distinction between the English as an Anglo-Saxon race and Great Britain, which Carto claimed "means primarily the banks which control the corrupt government, with the assistance of the Jews and the Welsh," along with "pro-monarchial propaganda for the suckers so they will keep supporting the criminal British ruling caste."[89] According to Carto:

The British are our main enemy and have been since before the Revolutionary War. Ever since then they have conspired to control this country and pretty well succeeded. . . . The British, using their typically Jewish wiles, have laid down the standard in this country. . . .[90]

Carto cites approvingly *Empire of "The City,"* a tract claiming Jewish bankers run Britain from the London financial district.[91] Among the examples of "British criminality" that Carto explores are:

Abraham Lincoln the warmonger, the murderer of a million whites in a useless, senseless, stupid war. The Republican Party's effort to destroy the white South and build an all-black party in the south and stay in office in perpetuity. The America there might have been if there had been no war.[92]

Carto also wanted to explore the "role of the Masons . . . in fomenting WWII."[93]

Carto and the Liberty Lobby created the Populist Party in 1984, and it quickly became a haven for persons from a variety of Klan, White supremacist, and antisemitic backgrounds.[94] In the spring of 1985 the Populist Party held a major meeting in Chicago where the armed and confrontational activities of racist and antisemitic groups in rural America were saluted as "heroic." Antisemitism at this meeting was so obvious that one group of rural farm activists from the Midwest left the meeting after complaining that too many of the attendees were obsessed with Jews.[95] A series of political and financial schisms soon ended the direct relationship between the Liberty Lobby and the Populist Party.[96]

In late 1993 Carto lost control over his IHR network in a power struggle with staff over the spending of a substantial bequest of money left in a will.[97] Carto was represented in the ensuing lawsuits by conspiracist author and attorney Mark Lane. Carto subsequently created the *Barnes Review* to compete with the IHR publications.

Carto has many other outlets for his views, including Liberty Lobby's weekly three-hour radio program, Radio Free America (RFA), hosted by Tom Valentine. During one December 1996 program that was covered in the *Spotlight* under the headline: "Populist Revolution Explained on RFA," Carto explained that "a one-world government is not possible without free trade and open borders, and free trade is not possible without world government." As usual, a nationalist, conspiracist, and xenophobic spin is put on the story by the *Spotlight* reporter, who explains, "Thus, the powers-that-be . . . must constantly push for so-called free trade and against tight immigration controls."[98]

When the Liberty Lobby opposes free trade, or GATT or NAFTA, as bad for workers and suggests that reasonable restrictions on illegal immigration are sensible, it often attracts support from a broader spectrum of people who are totally unaware of the organization's underlying neofascist worldview. This type of deception extends to a variety of topics. In early 1997 one web page promoting the *Spotlight* highlighted several popular modern variants of the conspiracist and producerist themes of right-wing populism with such headlines as:

"The Trilateral Commission: Planning the New World Order"
"Bilderberg Group: The Rich are building their Global Plantation"
"Federal Reserve System: Tool for manipulating the US Economy. Who benefits? Not you."
"Bill Clinton: Leader of the free world, or common crook?"
"Foreign Military in the US: Why are German and Russian troops training on American soil?"[99]

Again, in this instance, the populist rhetoric was used as bait. Listed under information about the Federal Reserve is the classic essay *Billion$ for the Banker$—Debts for the People* by Sheldon Emry. In this tract, additionally subtitled *The Real Story of the Money-Control Over America*, it might not immediately be obvious that the political ideology Emry espouses is antisemitic. Emry is a Christian Identity minister, a theology that claims Jews and people of color are conspiring to destroy the United States.[100]

In 1999 the *Spotlight* published an English translation of a pamphlet it had produced in Russian for the "grass-roots populist movement in Russia."[101] A quintessential producerist quote from Carto was featured: "Government by the producers and taxpayers of society, not by the plutocratic, tax-free exploiters or the tax-eating, indolent parasites or powerful organized minorities."[102] The three accompanying photographs had the following captions: "The Capitalism of Mayer Rothschild . . . the Communism of Karl Marx . . . and the Zionism of David ben-Gurion . . . can be compared to the three prongs on the devil's pitchfork."[103]

PERMUTATIONS

We have argued that repressive and right-wing populist movements in the United States have promoted many different conspiracy theories, focusing on British oligarchs, manipulative bankers, Jews, the Catholic Church, northern industrialists, and Ivy League intellectuals, among many others. Implicit in both the Freemason and Jewish conspiracy narratives, as they were modified for domestic consumption, is the theme that the United States is essentially a Christian nation threatened with subversion by anti-Christian secret elites with allies in high places. Secular versions of U.S. conspiracism omit the overtly religious references and simply look for betrayal by political and religious leaders.

As the Illuminati, Freemason, and *Protocols* theories intertwined in the United States, multiple variations fanned out to incorporate themes from other sources as well. The charges against the Illuminati, the Freemasons, and Jews at heart embodied a backlash against the Enlightenment.

The Antimasonic books by Robison and Barruel both promote three conspiracist contentions still circulating today, namely, that:

- The Enlightenment themes of equality and liberty undermine respect for private property and the natural social hierarchy;
- There is a secret conspiracy to destroy Christianity; and
- People who encourage free thinking and international cooperation are disloyal cosmopolitans and subversive traitors who are out to destroy national sovereignty, promote moral anarchy, and establish political tyranny.

We discussed in Chapter 2 how the European attack on Freemasonry differed sharply from the Antimasonic movement that flourished in the northern United States in the 1820s and 1830s, although some U.S. Antimasons borrowed ideas from their European counterparts. Only later in the nineteenth century did Robison and Barruel's Illuminati conspiracy theory come to dominate U.S. anti-Freemasonry circles.

Subsequently, the same conspiracist allegations were adapted for use against progressives, communists, internationalists, and secular humanists. The range of scapegoats that gets demonized is vast. At the same time, the dynamics are complex, involving distinct social, political, cultural, and religious movements that frequently overlap. The result is a continuum of conspiracist theories in the United States that range from those stressing secret elite societies that show little influence of antisemitism to those that palpitate with vicious hatred of Jews.

Is the plot run by Moscow Reds, Wall Street plutocrats, British bankers, or the Jews? Issues could have multiple subtexts. For instance, there was concern over the erosion of national sovereignty by the United Nations because it was seen as favoring communist-style collectivism. Right-wing conspiracists expressed the conviction that the United Nations would erode nation-state sovereignty and facilitate intrusive federal intervention on the local level. The concern over federal violations of states' rights was promoted in some cases by libertarians, such as the publishers of the periodical *The Freeman*, but "states' rights" often provided a veneer that masked underlying segregationist and White supremacist sentiments, even if they were unconscious.[104]

Antisemitic conspiracist allegations can come in a variety of guises. Some conspiracist groups that claim not to be antisemitic appear to be unaware when they stray over the line. Others claim not to be antisemitic as a cover for their real hatred of Jews so as not to attract widespread public scrutiny or scare off potential recruits. Coded rhetoric is a key feature in this milieu, with the term "international bankers" often clearly understood by the witting to mean "Jewish bankers."

One derivative theme mixes antisemitism with historic U.S. Anglophobia and contends that the British royal family's intermarriage with Jews resulted in the Rothschild family's exerting total control over the financial center called the City of London, which in turn is alleged to control world finance. Although Anglophobia can exist without antisemitic overtones, the two are often linked, and Anglophobia is often used as an introductory bait to lure people toward later allegations of Jewish influence.

A U.S. corollary is that British and/or Jewish banking families created the Federal Reserve system to extend Jewish/British control over the U.S. economy. Jews have also been accused of creating a culture of "cosmopolitanism," with the attendant worldly secular transnational focus undermining patriotism and sovereignty. This theme often emerges in the lore of various far-right movements such as the Christian Patriot movement, and it is employed in a coded manner by neofascist demagogue and perennial presidential candidate Lyndon LaRouche and his related organizations. Some of the views expressed by Christian Right leader Pat Robertson contain elements of coded Anglophobic antisemitism similar to (although milder than) the worldview of the LaRouchites and the Liberty Lobby.

Some antisemitic versions of the alleged conspiracy reach beyond Christian circles. LaRouche staff collaborate with Nation of Islam staff to promote the claim of an historic Judeo–Freemasonry conspiracy involving

Adam Weishaupt (founder of the Illuminati), Civil War Confederate General Albert Pike, the Ku Klux Klan, organized crime, and the B'nai B'rith.[105] This eclectic collection nonetheless mirrors allegations from the book *Freemasonry*, first published in Arabic in 1980 by the Muslim World League in Saudi Arabia and later in an English translation.[106] The English edition is available in the United States from the Muslim World League offices in New York City or from commercial vendors, including some Islamic and Afrocentric bookstores.

The Freemason conspiracy myth also stretches backward in history, linking the Freemasons to an ancient chain of revealed knowledge secretly provided to chosen followers called adepts. George Johnson charts "the myth of the esoteric tradition" claimed by the Freemasons in this sequence: Egyptian Isis Worshipers, Pythagoreans, Greek Mystery Cults, Gnostics, Cathars, Knights Templar, Rosicrucians, Freemasons.[107] Several critical and uncritical books about Masonic lore cover similar ground. Given this view, it is unsurprising that some fundamentalist Christians see Freemasons as pagans or heretics.

The International Banking Conspiracy

In the United States, theories of an internationalist banking conspiracy may generally be traced back to what is called "The Money Question." Margaret Canovan pointed out that "Between the Civil War and the heyday of Populism in the 1890s, the money question periodically emerged as a political issue. There were, roughly speaking, three distinct view of the subject, those of the Greenbackers, Goldbugs, and Silverites, although all kinds of combinations and qualifications were possible."[108] Should the dollar be linked to the price of gold or silver, or should it be allowed to float without the backing of precious metals? Inflationary Greenback policy in effect reduced loan repayments in terms of the actual value of the payments, so their view was often favored by those with large debts such as farmers. Conversely, persons who held or mined gold or silver had an obvious self-interest, but there were many other factors as well.[109]

Congress demonetized silver in 1873 in what became know as "the Crime of '73" and was "supposedly perpetrated upon the American People by a cabal of English, Jewish, and Wall Street bankers."[110] Thereafter, the three groups of alleged evildoers became the key scapegoats for the conspiracist claim of a struggle between parasitic finance capitalism and productive industrial capitalism. Conspiracist authors that followed developed their own unique versions of the allegations.[111]

Since the creation of the Federal Reserve banking system in 1913, its methods of currency control have been the frequent target of both legitimate criticism and conspiracist theories, inasmuch as these ideas frequently intertwine. In the late 1950s and early 1960s, criticism of the Federal Reserve by Rep. Wright Patman of Texas appeared in both the right-wing populist *American Mercury* and the liberal populist *Texas Observer*. In one article appearing in both publications, Patman heaped scorn on the "fractional reserve system," whereby the "present Federal Reserve banking system is manufacturing money in the bankers' interest and the banks' interest." Patman, arguing that this procedure was robbing the citizenry in broad daylight, traced the practice of reserve banking back to seventeenth-century goldsmiths.[112] These same ideas can be the starting point for conspiracy theories that allege international Jewish control of the banks.

In 1935 two authors amplified the theme of a conspiracy by international financiers. Father Denis Fahey wrote *The Mystical Body of Christ in the Modern World*, an openly antisemitic work that envisioned an organically populist (volkish) Catholic society as ultimately in control. Gertrude Coogan's *Money Creators* contained implicit antisemitic conspiracist allegations linking the Illuminati and the Rothschilds to a secret cabal that created the Federal Reserve.[113] According to Frank P. Mintz, "The Coogan book . . . served as a classic of rightist populism, enjoying a distribution by Liberty Lobby, Gerald L. K. Smith's Christian Nationalist Crusade, and the National States Rights Party in the early 1970s."[114]

The overt British–Jewish conspiracist theory continues to be pursued in many publications, based primarily on tracts "written by British fascists in the 1930's," according to Dennis King, who tracked Lyndon LaRouche's worldview back to this genre.[115] The most energetic purveyor of this theme is Eustace Mullins, antisemitic author of the 1952 book *Mullins on the Federal Reserve* and the 1954 book *The Federal Reserve Conspiracy*. Mullins writes in two styles, one ostensibly focusing on banking practices, the other expressing open and vicious antisemitism.[116]

Elite Planning for Global Domination

One strain of conspiracist interpretation filters out most or all of the obvious antisemitic references and shifts the focus to international groups that foster elite planning for economic and foreign policy matters in countries where the members reside or conduct business. This postulates secret control of the economy and the foreign policy of individual nations by globalists so that sovereignty is eroded and collectivism buttressed. As mentioned earlier, frequent targets in the 1950s and 1960s were the Rockefeller family and the Council on Foreign Relations.[117] A significant work in this genre was the 1952 book by McCarthy supporter Emanuel M. Josephson, *Rockefeller, "Internationalist": The Man Who Misrules the World*. Josephson saw the Council on Foreign Relations as a nest of conspirators carrying out Rockefeller orders on behalf of international finance capital.[118]

Dan Smoot's 1962 *The Invisible Government* introduced Josephson's charges to the Birchite audience.[119] Similarly, Mary M. Davison's 1962 book, *The Secret Government of the United States*, describes the Council on Foreign Relations as "The King-Makers Club which Has Become the Nation's Invisible Government," run by the "international bankers."[120] Carroll Quigley's *Tragedy and Hope*, published in 1966, saw U.S. history after the Civil War as shaped by a power struggle between international finance capital and industrial capitalism. Specifically, Quigley saw British influence, especially Rhodes scholarships, as crucial to understanding the role of foundations and politicians in shaping U.S. policy.[121] Two authors affiliated with the John Birch Society adapted and extended Quigley's work: W. Cleon Skousen self-published *The Naked Capitalist* in 1970, while Gary Allen wrote several books, including *None Dare Call It Conspiracy* (published in 1971), which sold over 5 million copies.[122] According to Mintz, both Skousen and Allen "wedded *Tragedy and Hope* to the tradition of rightist populism of the interwar period and the radical rightist conspiracist literature of the 1950s and 1960s, but avoided the familiar rightist sources as much as possible."[123]

One of the most prolific conspiracists in this category, from the mid-1960s to the mid-1970s, was Phoebe Courtney, who also coauthored several books with her husband, Kent Courtney. The Courtneys and the John ` Birch Society helped spread the antigovernment concept called "constitutionalism," which embodies the claim that secret elites manipulate the economy and the political process, use the Federal Reserve and the Internal Revenue Service as political weapons, and have created a huge federal bureaucracy, all of which violates basic precepts of the original, unamended U.S. Constitution.[124]

Mary M. Davison, in her 1966 booklet *The Profound Revolution*, traced the alleged "New World Order" conspiracy to the creation of the Federal Reserve by international bankers, whom she claimed later formed the Council on Foreign Relations. At the time the booklet was published, "international bankers" would have been interpreted by many readers as a reference to a postulated "international Jewish banking conspiracy." Davison included the standard call for people to rise up against internationalism and rebuild a constitutional form of government—a call echoed later by various right-wing populist groups including the contemporary armed militia movement.[125] Davison later wrote tracts that were tied to Christian Biblical passages and were overtly antisemitic.[126] During the 1960s a great deal of right-wing conspiracist attention also focused on the United Nations as the vehicle for creating the One World Government.

CONCLUSIONS

Individuals assemble their own idiosyncratic package of conspiracy beliefs much in the manner of people selecting food at a smorgasbord. At meetings of conspiracist right wing groups, attendees sit around at meals and breaks discussing the hierarchy of conspirators. In many cases the world-view of the intended reader or listener determines who gets scapegoated by any specific conspiracist narrative. Some people exposed to a conspiracist article or radio program might decide the villains are generic new world order secret elites who are manipulating the government while others might be convinced they are demonic forces of the Antichrist signaling the apocalyptic End Times. Some, inevitably, will blame it all on the Jews. A skillful wordsmith can address all three audiences at once by using coded rhetoric that is opaque to some and transparent to others.

Sometimes the signs of the times are only hinted at. A 1978 brochure with an apocalyptic subtext from Texas Eagle Forum was titled *Christian Be Watchful: Hidden Dangers in the New Coalition of Feminism, Humanism, Socialism, Lesbianism.*[127] Fundamentalists would know to be watchful for End Times signals, while most mainline Protestants and Catholics would have less apocalyptic interpretations. The book *Trilaterals Over Washington* appears to be a secular critique, but it takes on a new dimension when the illustration on the cover is identified as the many-headed beast warned of by the three angels in the book of Revelation. This in turn gives added meaning to the inside graphic with the headline "The Trilateral Commission: The Devil's Triangle of Your Future."[128]

In some cases the audience provides its own philosophical overlay that extrapolates beyond the intended message. For example, C. Wright Mills, G. William Domhoff, and Holly Sklar have written structural and institutional critiques of power that eschew conspiracism.[129] Yet, right-wing populists sometimes cite these works in claiming that more informed research has exposed the nest of secret elites at the source of the conspiracy. Antony C. Sutton's *Wall Street and the Rise of Hitler* even features a chart showing that Sutton names more "conspirators" than Domhoff, which is meant to prove that Sutton has the superior analysis.[130] Both Domhoff and Sklar have expressed exasperation at having their work touted by right-wing conspiracists.[131]

Conspiracism is an attempt to understand the world. Mark Fenster explains that conspiracy theories are all about power and that the central flaw in conspiracism is that it misunderstands how power is exercised.[132] The persons and groups named by various right-wing movements as being behind the alleged conspiracy usually reflect a synergy between ideology, prejudice, and conceptual frames used by leaders to mobilize supporters to collective action. The permutations of the conspiracist scapegoat are probably limitless. Who is scapegoated tells us much about the society where conspiracist scapegoating is tolerated, or even encouraged.

In studying the John Birch Society, J. Allen Broyles identified its appeal as having four dimensions:

- Providing a base for certainty in uncertain times by conveying "simplicity, rigidity, and authority for the ideology";

- Supplying "its members with the gratifying feelings of self-righteous-ness";
- Giving members "a perception of themselves as superior to those on the 'wrong' side"; and
- Justifying ideological conflict and aggression against identified enemies, which "provides for release of frustration."[133]

This model is applicable across the conspiracist Right and holds up well to later sociological theories emphasizing collective identity and conceptual framing.

In the 1970s other branches of right-wing populist conspiracism began to grow, including the Christian Identity religion, the Lyndon LaRouche network, and both secular and religious forms of survivalism. They joined the Birch Society and the Liberty Lobby to spread conspiracist antielitism.

As it coalesced as a political force in the late 1970s the new Christian Right adopted many themes from the Birch Society and subsequently became a major source of conspiracist narrative during the 1980s and 1990s.[134] Conspiracy theories were also evident in portions of the Black community.[135] Following the Iran–Contra scandal, a small but vocal network of leftists adopted the right-wing populist critique of secret elites and circulated it in liberal and progressive communities. The Gulf War facilitated further cross-fertilization of conspiracist narratives across ideological and organizational boundaries.[136]

10

FROM OLD RIGHT TO NEW RIGHT

Godless Communism, Civil Rights, and Secular Humanism

In this chapter we will look at some of the major factors in the shift from the Old Right of the 1950s and early 1960s to the New Right of the 1970s and 1980s. The first half of the chapter traces several major threads of ultraconservative politics during the lean years from Goldwater's defeat in 1964 to the rise of the New Right in the 1970s. Christian anticommunist organizations, by skillfully reframing issues, provided continuity of ideology and expertise and helped keep core constituencies focused on mobilizing to counter domestic subversion. George Wallace's electoral campaigns showed how scapegoating in the form of implicit race-baiting could be coupled with populist antielitism to attract millions of White voters alienated by civil rights liberalism. New organizing drives and theological initiatives began to bring many Protestant evangelicals, long alienated from the electoral arena, back into political activism with a right-wing agenda. These three developments helped ultraconservatism to remain a political player and provided a bridge from the Old Right to the New Right.

The second half of the chapter examines the cluster of social, political, and economic upheavals that created new challenges and opportunities for right-wing populist organizing in the 1970s and 1980s. The rise of social liberation movements, the expansion of the federal government, economic dislocations, and renewed challenges to U.S. global dominance created a widespread sense that the nation was in crisis. Meanwhile, shifts within the business community created a much larger and more powerful bloc of wealthy funders interested in supporting ultraconservative causes. These factors helped emerging New Right organizations to mobilize rapidly and exert major influence on U.S. politics.

THE OLD RIGHT

After World War II the Old Right needed to develop a clear ideology to distinguish itself from fascism. What emerged was "fusionist" conservatism, built around the triad of economic libertarianism, social traditionalism, and militant anticommunism.[1] Himmelstein wrote that "The core assumption that binds these three elements is the belief that American society on all levels has an organic order—harmonious, beneficent, and self-regulating—disturbed only by misguided ideas and policies, especially those propagated by a liberal elite in the government, the media, and the universities."[2] Fusionism's chief architects were William F. Buckley Jr., Frank Meyer, and M. Stanton Evans. Buckley, who had written for the libertarian journal *Freeman*, founded the influential *National Review* in 1955.[3]

Key libertarian influences, according to Himmelstein, came from "leaders of the Old Republican Right like Herbert Hoover and Robert Taft; neoclassical economists like Friedrich Hayek, Ludwig von Mises, and Milton Friedman; and a variety of iconoclastic individualists and objectivists like Albert Jay Nock and Ayn Rand." Social traditionalism was "rooted in natural law, Christian theology, and nineteenth century European conservatism." Influential World War II traditionalists included Leo Strauss, Eric Vogelin, Robert Nisbet, Russell Kirk, and Richard Weaver.[4]

Militant anticommunism in the 1950s and 1960s was spread through a network of interlocking organizations and publications such as *Reader's Digest*, *Human Events*, *National Review*, the National Association of Manufacturers, the Hoover Institution, the Foreign Policy Research Institute, the Foundation for Economic Education, the Intercollegiate Studies Institute, Crusade for Freedom, the American Legion, and the Reserve Officers Association.[5] Groups such as the ultraconservative John Birch Society and the far-right Liberty Lobby carried on McCarthyite themes into the 1960s, as they developed their own constituencies and recruited from more moderate conservative groups.[6]

The 1964 Goldwater presidential campaign was the high point of Old Right fusionism. Most influential Goldwater supporters were not marginal far-right activists, as many liberal academics postulated at the time, but had been Republican Party regulars for years, representing a vocal wing far to the right of most Republican voters. Openly hostile to the moderate Republican establishment centered in the Northeast, the Goldwater campaign lost to Democrat Lyndon Johnson in a landslide, carrying only five Deep South states plus Goldwater's own state of Arizona.

If hard rightists wanted to gain national power, they had to face their image problem and expand beyond their Old Right base. They had to distance themselves (at least publicly) from several problematic sectors. Overt white supremacists and segregationists had to go, as did obvious anti-Jewish bigots. Interventionist William F. Buckley Jr., pronounced the isolationist John Birch Society's conspiracist rhetoric to be unacceptable. At the same time, hard rightists needed to cultivate new and broader sources of popular support.

Christian Anticommunism

Anti-Red conspiracism fed the Cold War witch-hunts and spawned a number of God-fearing anticommunist groups such as: Moral Re-Armament; the Freedoms Foundation at Valley Forge, founded in 1949, which combined free market ideology and religious ecumenism (expressed through its logo of General George Washington kneeling in prayer); the Christian AntiCommunism Crusade, founded in 1955 by Fred Schwarz, which primarily included Protestants but also a handful of Jews; and the Cardinal Mindszenty Foundation, founded in 1958 and run by Eleanor L. Schlafly, which primarily focused on Catholics. Even more militantly anticommunist were the Christian Crusade of the Rev. Billy James Hargis and Rev. Carl McIntire's American Council of Christian Churches, founded in 1941.[7] McIntire's "premature anticommunism" was quickly embraced by some ultraconservative Christians following World War II. His 1946 book *Author of Liberty* warned of Godless communism, linking it to the destructive domestic collectivism encouraged by Roosevelt, and tied it all to the satanic beast prophesied in the book of Revelation.[8]

Anticommunist groups that presented a secular face, such as The Freedoms Foundation at Valley Forge, were nonetheless frequently rooted in Christian social traditionalism and moral orthodoxy. Although often dismissed as marginal, these groups mobilized small but loyal constituencies across the country, using standard outreach such as newsletters, radio, and local public meetings.[9]

Kazin argues that Protestants were not as unified in this campaign as were Catholics. "Catholic organizations constituted the largest and best financed—as well as most uncompromising—battalion in the anti-Communist movement." Church leaders such as Cardinal Spellman in New York and Archbishop Cushing in Boston were active in these movements. According to Kazin, there were pamphlets from the Catholic Information Society, discussion groups with the Knights of Columbus Crusade for the Preservation and Promotion of American Ideals, and organizing through the Catholic War Veterans. Articles in *Our Sunday Visitor* were sent to parishes nationwide.[10]

One Catholic organization, the Cardinal Mindszenty Foundation (CMF), shows the overlap between forerunners of the New Right and Birchite conspiracism.[11] Its original directors included Phyllis Schlafly as research director, J. Fred Schlafly, Jr. (Phyllis's husband), and Eleanor Schlafly (Fred's sister) as executive director, later executive secretary, then president. Attorney Robert Schlafly represented the Foundation with the IRS regarding tax exemption.[12] The politics of the Schlafly family reflect the confluence of Old Right anticommunism and old church orthodoxy, similar to the synthesis of other flag bearers of the Catholic Right such as Pat Buchanan and Paul Weyrich.[13]

The charges against communism in this sector of the Right were often vivid. Fred Schwarz's *You Can Trust the Communists (to be Communists)*, with over one million copies in print by 1965, called communists "paranoics of highly organized delusional patterns . . . so enmeshed in the delusions of Marx-ism–Leninism that they are beyond the scope of rational argument."[14] The assault on America by the forces of godless communism was the central theme in three widely distributed books that were used to mobilize support for the 1964 presidential bid of Arizona Republican Barry Goldwater.[15] The best-known one was Phyllis Schlafly's *A Choice, Not an Echo*, which pro-pounded a conspiracist theory in which the Republican Party was secretly controlled by elitist intellectuals dominated by members of the Bilder-berger banking conference, whose policies were allegedly designed to usher in global communist conquest. The title *A Choice, Not an Echo* became a cam-paign slogan. The book characterized the Goldwater campaign as a revolt of "Grassroots Republicans" against the secret internationalist "kingmakers" al-leged to control both the Democratic and Republican parties.[16] *A Choice, Not an Echo* mainstreamed the conspiracist idea that the shadowy elites behind Wall Street capitalism also propped up Moscow communism.[17] Schlafly, with retired Rear Admiral Chester Ward as coauthor, also wrote *The Grave-diggers*, which was tailored to support the Goldwater campaign and claimed that U.S. military strategy and tactics were actually designed to pave the way for global communist conquest.[18]

Often overlooked because of the publicity surrounding *A Choice, Not an Echo* was John Stormer's *None Dare Call It Treason*, which outlined how the equivocation of Washington insiders might pave the way for global commu-nist conquest.[19] *None Dare Call It Treason* sold over seven million copies, mak-ing it one of the largest-selling paperback books of the day. The back cover summarizes the text as detailing "the communist–socialist conspiracy to en-slave America" and documenting "the concurrent decay in America's schools, churches, and press which has conditioned the American people to accept 20 years of retreat in the face of the communist enemy."

After writing *None Dare Call It Treason* in 1964, John A. Stormer had a Christian renewal experience and wrote the 1965 sequel, *The Death of a Na-tion*, in which he explicitly linked the collectivist conspiracy to destroy America to the work of the Antichrist and discussed signs of the End Times and possible millennial timetables.[20]

WALLACE, NIXON, AND THE RACE CARD

Christian anticommunist groups such as the Cardinal Mindszenty Founda-tion were oriented toward the mostly middle-class Republican Right that had provided Goldwater's organizational core. But the political struggles of the 1960s revealed another large potential pool of support for ultraconservatism: millions of working-class Whites who had traditionally voted Democratic but who opposed the civil rights policies then being endorsed by the national Democratic Party. In the South, this bloc, representing White backlash sentiment, provided the recruiting pool for the terrorist Ku Klux Klan and, among more affluent Whites, for the segregationist Citizens' Councils. In the North, many low-income Whites in cities with large Black populations also joined the anti-civil rights backlash. According to Kazin:

> The rhetoric of white civic groups was full of accusations that "government bureaucrats, many influenced by Communism or socialism . . . misused tax dollars to fund experiments in social engineering for the benefit of pressure groups."
>
> [Politicians like Louise Day Hicks] in Boston and Mario Procaccino in New York echoed this sentiment when they taunted "limousine liberals" for busing children to integrated schools while doing nothing to curb urban crime.
>
> Such talk represented one of the more persistent strains in the populist tradition. The attack on domestic subversion in city hall was new, but the charge that a haughty elite and a rabble of black or yellow hue were ganging up on the industrious Caucasian middle was nearly as old as the republic.[21]

Alabama Governor George Wallace, a major champion of segregation, began to tap this potential in 1964 by making a strong showing in several northern Democratic presidential primaries. Four years later, Wallace ran for president on the American Independent Party ticket. In the most successful third-party showing since that of Teddy Roosevelt in 1912, he received almost ten million votes, or 13.5 percent of the total, and carried five southern states. His campaign appealed to the growing fear and resentment of Black activism and urban rebellions, student radicalism, antiwar demonstrations, sixties counterculture, and the emerging women's movement. Both the John Birch Society and the Liberty Lobby embraced his candidacy.

As a presidential candidate in 1968, Wallace avoided explicit racist attacks. Although open White supremacists played important roles in his campaign, Wallace himself relied on coded racial appeals, moral traditionalism, law-and-order rhetoric, and the fear of centralized government. In opposing "forced" desegregation, he argued that the issue was not racism but federal government interference in people's lives. As Seymour Martin Lipset and Earl Raab point out, Wallace "sought to identify the pressures for Negro equality and integration with the eastern establishment and the intellectual elite."[22]

Despite his stance against an intrusive federal government, Wallace firmly supported many social welfare policies—at least for Whites. While Goldwater was a laissez-faire conservative who attacked popular programs such as Social Security, Wallace oversaw extensive social spending in Alabama, and the American Independent Party's 1968 platform endorsed federal funding for education, job training, unemployment and disability insurance, public works, increases in Social Security and Medicare payments, federal programs to ensure an equitable minimum wage and improve working conditions and hours, and support for collective bargaining. These positions led laissez-faire conservatives such as Goldwater and Buckley to denounce Wallace as a New Deal populist.[23]

Thus, the Wallace campaign was the first major political initiative since Father Charles E. Coughlin's Social Justice movement in the 1930s to combine antielitism, racist appeals, and support for social welfare programs. This combination was tailored to the large bloc of working-class Whites who supported the New Deal system but opposed the social changes of the 1960s. The middle-class suburbanites in and around the John Birch Society tolerated this formula because they liked the rest of Wallace's message, including his antistatism on many issues. Even though Wallace supported the welfare state, he still reinforced many lower-income Whites in their belief that the federal government was their enemy.

Wallace's appeal was not a one-time fluke. In 1972 he again ran in the Democratic presidential primaries. By mid-May, when an assassination attempt left him permanently paralyzed and unable to campaign, he had amassed over 3.3 million votes in state primaries, as compared with 2.2 million for liberal George McGovern, the party's eventual nominee.[24]

Republican strategists well appreciated the strength of the Wallace voting bloc and developed a counterstrategy. According to Kazin:

> Beginning in the late 1960s, conservative activists and politicians—most of whom were Republicans—re-created themselves as the authentic representatives of average white Americans. They learned to harness the same mass resentments (against federal power, left-wing movements, the counterculture, and the black poor) for which George Wallace had spoken but was unable to ride to victory.[25]

To co-opt the Wallace voters in 1972, President Richard Nixon adopted what became known as the "Southern Strategy" based on ideas from Kevin Phillips, who had written a timely book titled *The Emerging Republican Majority*. The Nixon administration employed populist rhetoric to create the idea of a silent majority of middle Americans. In a period of racial tension, it was never necessary to make explicit that this was a White ethnic constituency. According to Dan T. Carter, "Phillips bluntly recognized the critical role fear in general, and white fear of blacks in particular, would play in guaranteeing the emerging Republican majority."[26] After reading the book, Nixon promoted the ideas for his reelection strategy. White House staffer H. R. Haldeman wrote in his notes: "Use Phillips as an analyst—

study his strategy—don't think in terms of old ethnics, go for Poles, Italians, Irish, must learn to understand Silent Majority . . . don't go for Jews and Blacks."[27]

Starting in 1978 with California's Proposition 13, championed by conservative activist Howard Jarvis, a "tax revolt" spread to many states.[28] The conservative Arlington House publishers even issued a guide on running a statewide tax revolt.[29] This movement reflected widespread economic anger, but it was fueled in part by (often unstated) White hostility toward government spending on social welfare programs seen—often incorrectly—as primarily aiding Blacks and Latinos, who were stereotyped as lazy parasites in the producerist narrative framework.

CONSERVATIVE EVANGELICALS MOBILIZE

The Wallace constituency overlapped with another potential source of mass support for ultraconservatism: evangelical Protestants. In the twenty years following Goldwater's defeat, one of the Hard Right's major achievements was to rally millions of evangelicals behind a shared set of political goals and concerns. This meant overcoming evangelicals' traditional aloofness from politics and bitter sectarian infighting. The shift was both political and theological, and had deep historic roots.

Most evangelicals had retreated from political activism after the 1925 Scopes "Monkey" Trial.[30] In this famous Tennessee case the judge ruled that teaching evolution (instead of creationism) was not proper in the public schools. It was a Pyrrhic victory. The case proved to be a substantial public embarrassment not only to fundamentalists but to all evangelicals, who were widely portrayed as ignorant, backward, and irrational. As a result, many evangelicals withdrew from active participation in the electoral and legislative arena.

This separation lasted until an activist (but nonpartisan) Cold War message that Christians should reengage in civic participation brought many evangelical Christians back into the voting booths in the 1950s. The Cold War also saw a resurgence of evangelical fervor, which is best known through the crusades of the Rev. Billy Graham and Oral Roberts. At the same time, fundamentalists, pentecostals, and charismatics moved toward more acceptance and respectability, first within the broadly defined evangelical subculture, then within denominational Protestantism, and then in the larger secular sphere. This process took several decades. By the mid-1970s, with the number of persons identifying themselves as born-again Christians on the rise, both secular and Christian rightists were making a concerted effort to link evangelicals to ultraconservative ideology. Not all evangelicals responded favorably. There is tremendous diversity within the evangelical subculture ranging from progressive to conservative on several dimensions, including theological, economic, and social. In this book we primarily are discussing Protestant Christian evangelicals who are conservative on one or more of these dimensions, and who have been mobilized into political activism by the institutions of the Christian Right.[31]

Dueling Eschatologies

One of the obstacles to mobilizing evangelicals politically had to do with their beliefs about the millennial apocalypse. The theological study of these beliefs is known as *eschatology*. Competing views about the End Times fueled division and conflict among evangelicals; in addition, some eschatological beliefs fostered political passivity.[32]

A remarkable number of myths, metaphors, images, symbols, phrases, and icons in Western culture flow from prophecies in the Bible about apocalyptic confrontations and millennial transformation. The Bible's book of Revelation describes in graphic terms what will happen when an angry God finally intervenes in human affairs at the end of time. These End Times are described as a period of widespread sinfulness, moral depravity, and crass materialism. One way to interpret the central narrative of Revelations is that during the End Times hard-working righteous Christians will be tricked and betrayed by trusted political and religious leaders who are secretly conspiring with Satan while at the same time lazy and sinful human parasites will subversively gnaw away at society from below.

During the End Times Satan's chief henchman will appear in human form as the Antichrist, a popular world leader who secretly harbors sympathy for the Devil. He promises the public peace and unity of all nations under a one world government—but it's a conspiracy. His agents are tracking down and punishing Christians who refuse to abandon their faith. Satan's allies receive a mark—the Mark of the Beast—represented by the number 666. This period of hard times is called "the Tribulations" and culminates in a final cataclysmic doomsday confrontation of massed armies in the Middle East, at a place named Armageddon. Good triumphs over evil at the battle of Armageddon, ushering in a millennium of Christian rule.

Postmillennialists believe that Christ returns *after* a thousand years of reign and rule by godly Christian men, and they urge militant Christian intervention in secular society. Smaller sectors, including preterists and amillennialists, while still anticipating the eventual return of Christ, deemphasize the End Times in favor of more practical considerations affecting daily life.

Most Christian fundamentalists and evangelicals are premillennialists. They believe that Christ's return will *start* the millennial, thousand-year period of Christian rule. Premillennialists disagree about whether faithful Christians will experience no Tribulations, some Tribulations, or all of the Tribulations before Christ's return. This difference is expressed in eschatological timelines called pretribulationalist, midtribulationalist, and posttribulationalist. Furthermore, not all premillennialist Christians believe in "the Rapture"—the temporary protective gathering of Christians up into Heaven while the battle against evil rages on Earth during the Tribulations. If they do believe in the Rapture, there is no agreement on whether or not raptured Christians then return to an Earth purged of evil. The exact sequence of the Rapture, the Tribulations, and the Battle of Armageddon is also disputed.

For many decades, the primary Protestant eschatology was a form of premillennialism called Dispensationalism, an interpretation developed by theologian John Nelson Darby that outlined specific historical epochs (or dispensations) that are preordained by God.[33] In this timeline, Christians are raptured up to heaven before the Tribulations, the sinful are punished, and then Christ returns for a millennium of rule over his loyal flock.

The narrative of Revelation provides important clues for understanding the rhetoric and actions of devout Christians who are influenced by apocalypticism and millennialism. Among Christians belief in an actual coming apocalypse is particularly strong among those fundamentalists who not only read the Bible literally but also consider prophetic biblical text to be a coded timetable or script revealing the future.[34] Those that believe the apocalypse is at hand can act out those theological beliefs in social, cultural, and political arenas.

Many faithful Christians believe they must take on special duties during the End Times. These duties carry the weight of biblical prophecy, and in some cases actions may even be felt to be mandated by God. Revelation's prophecies can thus motivate action, especially on the part of those fundamentalists who combine biblical literalism with a textual timetable.[35] When this worldview intersects with oppressive prejudices, it is easy to prophesy the appearance of demonization, scapegoating, and conspiracism.

Since fundamentalists expect the literal return of Christ in the millennialist End Times, they are watchful for the "Signs of the Times," a phrase used to highlight the possibility that a specific worldly event may fulfill a biblical prophecy and thus be a signal of the End Times, when faithful Christians are expected to engage in appropriate (though highly contested) preparations. Earthquakes, floods, comets, wars, disease, and social unrest are commonly interpreted as such signs.

Some fundamentalists who think they are living in the End Times see those with whom they disagree as agents of the Antichrist. Robert Fuller notes that "Over the last two hundred years, the Antichrist has been repeatedly identified with such 'threats' as modernism, Roman Catholicism, Jews, socialism, and the Soviet Union."[36] Apocalyptic fundamentalists who believe the End Times may have arrived are especially concerned with false prophets and political or business leaders who are seen as subverting God's will and betraying the faithful by urging them to abandon their righteous conduct, especially in terms of sinful sexuality or crass materialism.

For several decades the common evangelical interpretation of premillennialism, including Dispensationalism, encouraged a large sector of the Christian faithful to passively await salvation while remaining aloof from sinful secular society. Premillennialism, however, could be interpreted to promote not just passivity, but political activism, as the country was soon to discover.

THE GOVERNMENT VERSUS GOD

During the 1960s and 1970s a growing number of politically and theologically conservative Protestant evangelicals took a renewed interest in the political process. To many conservative evangelicals, the social and cultural changes of this period, such as the sexual revolution and the rise of feminism and lesbian and gay activism, represented serious threats to the nation's moral fiber. A series of Supreme Court decisions—such as the 1962 and 1963 decisions barring prayer in public schools and several rulings that weakened or overturned obscenity laws—provided ammunition to those who argued that godless—perhaps satanic—forces controlled the federal government. The Court's 1973 decision legalizing abortion further strengthened this viewpoint. Influential Christian ultraconservatives, such as Tim LaHaye, urged evangelicals to set aside their traditional aloofness as well as their theological and eschatological differences and join together as profamily activists. The message was: society is living in sin, and you have to become active to save the country.[37]

Parents in Kanawha County, West Virginia, were among the first to heed the clarion call to the culture wars in 1974 when they protested a new series of textbooks adopted by the local school board.[38] Parents were offended by essays and poems that openly discussed sexuality, or were seen as unpatriotic or blasphemous. There was a clear racial subtext to the Kanawha County battles, and other struggles over culture and family values, as well as a reaction against changing gender roles.[39] The intersection of race, gender, and sexuality also lay beneath Christian conservatives' attacks on modern music in the 1960s and 1970s.[40] Communists were seen as promoting racial unrest, primitive Black "jungle rhythms" in rock music, and rampant teenage sexuality as part of a godless plot to subvert America.[41] And this was before homosexuality was even a public issue. Margaret Quigley explains that "the identification of sexual licentiousness and ´primitive´ music with subversion and people of color is an essential part of the secular humanist conspiracy theory, and one that has been remarkably consistent over time."[42]

Early right-wing think tanks such as the Heritage Foundation, founded in 1973, and the Free Congress Foundation, founded in 1977, gave resources to, and provided a platform for, "profamily" activists. These and other policy institutes would play a role in building the New Right, not only by repackaging conservative ideas for the mass media but also by training activists and grooming them for national leadership roles. For instance, Connie Marshner, who had organized a training seminar for the Kanawha County textbook protesters in 1975, later edited the national newsletter *Family Protection Report* for the Free Congress Foundation.[43]

The Secular Humanist Conspiracy

Secular humanists—pictured as the torchbearers of liberal godlessness, New Deal statism, and globalist collectivism—are scapegoated from a variety of perspectives: economic, antielitist, and moral, as well as religious. The idea of the secular humanist conspiracy buttresses the resurgent libertarian theme that collectivism destroys individual initiative and saps vigor from the free market system. It echoes traditionalist and Old Right concerns over creeping moral decay and the failure of New Deal liberalism. In the view of Christian nationalists, liberal secular humanists are ushering in the globalist New World Order. The congruence of various sectors of the Right, each opposing liberal secular humanism for its own reasons, resulted in some remarkable tactical coalitions over the years, especially surrounding issues of public school curricula and government funding for education.

Secular humanism as a philosophy does exist. It developed in the United States during the late nineteenth century as a descendant of the rationalist philosophies of the Enlightenment. It argues that ethical behavior can flow from the human intellect and a self-conscious conscience. Its attitude toward God and religion ranges from hostile to indifferent. While historically there has been an organized humanist movement in the United States since at least the 1800s, the idea of a large-scale quasireligion called secular humanism is a conspiracist myth.

For the Christian Right, secular humanism represents not only opposition to God but support for evil.[44] According to James Davison Hunter, it was Catholics in the 1950s that first began to criticize the influence of secular humanism on U.S. society.[45] Their refrain was picked up by Protestants, and by the 1990s there were dozens of books and scores of pamphlets decrying the secular humanist menace.[46]

While there are variations and debates, the central theme of a secular humanist conspiracy is promoted by the Christian Coalition, Phyllis Schlafly's Eagle Forum, Beverly LaHaye's Concerned Women for America, her husband Tim LaHaye's American Coalition for Traditional Values, Conservative Caucus, Summit Ministries, the John Birch Society, and the Christian Anti-Communism Crusade. The attack on secular humanism underlies the themes of "traditional values" and "cultural conservatism" as promoted by Paul Weyrich's Free Congress Foundation and others. Sara Diamond observed that Tim LaHaye and other right-wing leaders developed "an elaborate theory on the humanist conspiracy, linking the ACLU, the NAACP, the National Organization for Women, Hollywood movie producers and even Unitarianism to the impending downfall of modern civilization."[47] The solution, according to LaHaye, was for Christian moralists and their allies to take over the government and restore morality.[48] LaHaye even developed a theory of the pretribulation tribulations—caused by secular humanists. In an argument aimed at mobilizing passive premillennialists waiting for the Rapture, LaHaye wrote that resistance to the secular humanist control of government was a Christian duty.[49]

Public Education as Godless Secular Humanist Conspiracy

For decades the public schoolhouse was a popular battle site in the struggle against communist influence. Typifying the many books about purported communist and collectivist influence in public education was Gordon V. Drake's 1968 book *Blackboard Power: NEA Threat to America*. The cover includes the assertion that "Our Children are Being Indoctrinated for a New Collectivist World Government."[50] For those who regard secular humanism as the overarching threat, public education is pivotal.

Conspiracist theocratic rightists assert that the first major push toward secular humanism in the United States occurred in 1805, when the theologically liberal Unitarians took control of Harvard University from the theologically conservative Calvinists. The Calvinists believed that "man" was evil by nature and thus beyond hope of redemption except through the grace of God. The Unitarians, on the other hand, believed that man was good by nature, and evil acts were largely the result of environmental factors such as poverty and lack of education. In this view the proper human manipulation of secular institutions could help to prevent people from committing certain evil acts.

Samuel Blumenfeld's 1984 book *NEA: Trojan Horse in American Education* is one of the key sources for conspiracist theories of secular humanism.[51] As Margaret Quigley observes:

> Blumenfeld is no fringe theorist: his work is cited frequently by other theorists of secular humanism, he has participated in conferences sponsored by the Heritage Foundation and has spoken at the prestigious forums of Hillsdale College, which has positioned itself as a prime source of conservative intellectual theory. He was among the first on the right to attack multiculturalism as a new form of values relativism.[52]

According to the conspiracy theory outlined by Blumenfeld and others, the Unitarians used their new power base at Harvard to push for the idea of free public schools—as part of their conscious plan to convert the

United States from capitalism to the utopian socialism of Robert Owen. Educational reformers such as John Dewey picked up where the Unitarians had left off. Dewey went on to become the father of the "progressive education" movement of the late 1800s.[53]

Dewey is named as a conscious agent of the secular humanist conspiracy because he promoted a secularized version of the previously biblically based McGuffy Readers, thus taking God out of the schools. Dewey is also accused of promoting the Look–Say method of reading, which supposedly led to poor reading habits. This planned illiteracy was part of the communist plot to make the takeover of the United States easier. Blumenfeld argues that the goal of Dewey and other education reformers "was to produce inferior readers with inferior intelligence dependent on a socialist education elite for guidance, wisdom and control."[54]

For right-wing critics of public education, the spread of humanism is interwoven with a frightening growth in the power of government over people's lives. They denounce the state for using taxes to fund education, usurping parents' roles, supplanting the church as moral guide, taking God out of America, and using modern educational techniques (seen as experimental psychological manipulation) in place of traditional rote teaching methods.

The 1976 Heritage Foundation tract titled *Secular Humanism and the Schools: The Issue Whose Time Has Come*, by Onalee McGraw, argued that humanistic education does not focus on "the traditional and generally accepted virtues" stressed by the "Judeo–Christian principles taught by most families at home," but on theories of "moral relativism and situation ethics" that are "based on predominantly materialistic values found only in man's nature itself" and "without regard for the Judeo–Christian moral order, which is based on the existence and fatherhood of a personal God."[55]

According to McGraw, humanistic education led to the "precipitous deterioration of learning achievement in our schools" evidenced by declining SAT scores. She called for federal and state laws barring role playing, sensitivity training, values clarification, moral education, and the teaching of situational ethics. The tract included the text of the Secular Humanism Amendment submitted to Congress in 1976, which sought to ban federal funding of educational programs "involving any aspect of the religion of Secular Humanism."[56]

In 1979 the Carter administration undertook hearings that subsequently led to a White House Conference on Families.[57] Politically active social conservatives sought input but felt rebuffed. Connie Marshner, along with activists such as Phyllis Schlafly, Onalee McGraw of the Heritage Foundation, and Christian Right activists Robert and Bill Billings, formed an informal Pro-Family Coalition.[58] The issues causing the most controversy were the Equal Rights Amendment, abortion, and gay rights.[59] After attempting to get their views greater visibility at the 1980 eastern regional conference in Baltimore, Marshner led a highly publicized walkout.[60]

Soon the profamily activists would not be outsiders.[61] Out of the emerging profamily movement came the periodic Family Forum national conferences, which enabled leaders of dozens of Christian Right groups to network with rank-and-file activists and staff at the growing number of Washington-based conservative think tanks. Family Forum II, held in 1982, was cosponsored by Paul Weyrich's Free Congress Foundation and Jerry Falwell's Moral Majority Foundation. Marshner was the conference co-coordinator. The meeting was held in Washington, DC, and the conference kit included a letter of greetings from President Ronald Reagan. Speakers included a Reagan appointee to the White House Office of Policy Development, Gary L. Bauer, who would later become a major figure in the Christian Right.[62]

Seeking Dominion

While many previously passive sectors of Christianity were being mobilized by right-wing political organizers, a complementary theological movement arose calling for a more "muscular" and interventionist form of Christianity. This movement was influenced by several Christian intellectuals that included popular Christian philosopher Francis A. Schaeffer and theologian Cornelius van Til.[63]

Schaeffer, a right-wing evangelical activist and founder of the L'Abri Fellowship in Switzerland, was the author of *How Should We Then Live?*, a 1976 book and film combination that challenged Christians to take control of a sinful society being destroyed by godless secular humanism.[64] Schaeffer followed up with the 1977 *Whatever Happened to the Human Race?*, coauthored by a pediatric surgeon from Philadelphia named C. Everett Koop, who would later go on to be appointed Surgeon General by President Reagan, in 1982.[65] In *Whatever Happened to the Human Race?* secular humanism was named as the source of godless disregard for what Christian rightists argued was sinful murder of the unborn.[66]

Militant Protestant fundamentalists now had a theological foundation for joining with conservative Catholics in the antiabortion movement and other gender-based activism. Schaeffer's arguments were theocratic and apocalyptic, and they encouraged antiabortion action including civil disobedience, but his argument was not conspiracist.[67] Some of his followers soon remedied what they clearly felt was an oversight, embracing a narrative claiming a vast conspiracy of secular humanists.[68] Whether intellectual or conspiracist, the new emphasis on stopping abortion fit neatly into existing concerns over pornography, sex education, and godless modern curricula. In all of these issues the antagonist was framed as the cosmopolitan liberal elite—in the media, in academia, in federal agencies, and sitting on the Supreme Court.[69]

These theological arguments fit neatly with the secularized theories of the John Birch Society. In 1977 the Birch Society press, Western Islands, published *The SIECUS Circle: A Humanist Revolution* by Claire Chambers. The book was touted as a "convenient guide to the humanist organizations that promote abortion, atheism, forced sex education in the public schools, homosexuality, pornography, and a permissive attitude toward drugs."[70] The book was endorsed by Charles E. Rice, professor of law at Notre Dame Law School.[71]

The ideas of Francis Schaeffer influenced many early Christian Right activists, including Tim LaHaye, John W. Whitehead, and Randall Terry. It was Francis Schaeffer who encouraged televangelist Jerry Falwell to use his broadcasts to urge evangelicals to become politically active. Those influenced by the prolific writings, speeches, and films of Francis A. Schaeffer, his wife Edith, and their son Franky went off in several theological and political directions, but they helped create a broad construct, or category of thought, called dominionism.[72]

Dominion theology is a relatively new current in Christian theology. It argues that, no matter what their view of the End Times, godly men must assert control over secular society. This idea springs from a multistep interpretation of certain biblical passages: if man has been given dominion over the earth, and the New Testament transfers God's covenant to Christians, then Christians owe it to God to seize the reins of secular society.[73] Dominionism frames a common purpose for both premillennial and postmillennial activists.

Much of the New Right's mobilization of grassroots supporters was based on promoting the Christian Right's narrow, exclusionary, and northern European version of traditional biblical values.[74] As Laura Saponara puts it: "The 'deep structure' of New Right rhetoric is rooted in historic and contemporary constructs of Biblical literalism articulated through recurring, polarizing themes of good and evil, personal salvation, evangelism, and the inevitability of apocalypse, among others."[75]

Clearly, some of the Christians mobilized by the New Right felt, and still feel, that they are engaged in "Spiritual Warfare" with satanic forces.[76] The role of biblical apocalyptic thinking within mainstream Christian groups is well documented by academics such as Sara Diamond, Paul Boyer, Robert Fuller, and Charles B. Strozier.

Open discussion of evil and satanic forces is unremarkable within the Christian Right, even among savvy policy analysts and lobbyists. A 1983 booklet from the Free Congress Research and Education Foundation titled *The Morality of Political Action: Biblical Foundations* includes a Bible-based defense of the practice of Christian political activists' misleading or tricking opponents, justified by the higher purpose of the Christian struggle against evil. The author advises that, while opponents may be doing the work of the Devil, it would be wrong to publicly accuse them of being "a card-carrying member of Satan's band"—not because it might be untrue but because it falls under "the scope of the Lord's command: 'Judge not lest ye be judged.'"[77]

COMPONENTS OF A MASSIVE MOBILIZATION

Right-wing populism experienced a dramatic resurgence in the 1970s and 1980s. Building on earlier ultraconservative themes, a "New Right" coalition of political strategists, corporate backers, and grassroots supporters transformed the political climate. New Right political themes and organizational support helped elect Ronald Reagan to the White House in 1980 and 1984. Although President Reagan disappointed ultraconservative hopes on some issues, he skillfully used populist rhetoric to advance policies that primarily benefited wealthy elites. In the remainder of this chapter, we will explore certain external and internal developments that contributed to the New Right's political rise.

Jean Hardisty argues that the confluence of several favorable historical factors assisted the success of the Right: a conservative religious revitalization, the approach of the year 2000 and apocalyptic millennialism, redistribution and economic contraction and restructuring, race resentment and bigotry, backlash and social stress, and a well-funded network of right-wing organizations.

The synergy among these factors is key, explains Hardisty:

> Each of these conditions has existed at previous times in US history. While they usually overlap to some extent, they also can be seen as distinct, identifiable phenomenon. The lightning speed of the right's rise can be explained by the simultaneous existence of all five factors. Further, in this period they not only overlap, but reinforce each other. This mutual reinforcement accounts for the exceptional force of the current rightward swing.[78]

In a similar analysis, Michael Omi and Howard Winant attribute the New Right's mass appeal to a far-reaching crisis that was at once social, political, cultural, and economic. This crisis reflected several factors: the emergence of "new social movements" in the 1960s, the resulting transformation of political culture (especially racial politics), the economic dislocations of the 1970s and 1980s, and the erosion of U.S. global hegemony. In their view these changes:

> portended the collapse of the "American Dream"—the apolitical, perpetually prosperous, militarily invincible, and deeply self-absorbed and self-righteous "mainstream" American culture was, we think, shaken to its foundations by developments over this period. Commonly held concepts of nation, community, and family were transformed, and no new principle of cohesion, no new cultural center, emerged to replace them. New collective identities, rooted in the "new social movements," remained fragmented and politically disunited.[79]

The New Right gained popular support, in large part, because it spoke to the sense of crisis, dislocation, and threat that many people experienced in this period. A rightward shift by large sectors of the business community, coupled with skillful organizing and careful choice and framing of issues, aided the New Right's mass mobilization.

Social Liberation Movements and the Growth of the State

From the mid-1950s to the mid-1970s, social liberation movements gradually broke through the Cold War climate of pervasive repression, passivity, and fear. By about 1970 the traditional order was being challenged by many overlapping movements: antiracist struggles by Blacks, Latinos, American Indians, and Asians; the antiwar movement and the New Left; a revitalized women's movement; groundbreaking struggles by gay men and lesbians; widespread rank-and-file insurgency within labor unions; the environmental movement; and more. After the early 1970s, some of these movements fell apart or stagnated while others continued to grow or rebounded in later years, offering a renewed threat and stimulus to the Right.

The Black liberation movement, including civil rights organizations as well as growing nationalist and revolutionary wings, was the driving force of this upsurge.[80] The civil rights reforms of the mid-1960s broke the back of formal legal discrimination against people of color, and after this time open claims of biological superiority or inferiority for ethnic groups were widely regarded as unacceptable. These changes did not by any means abolish racial oppression or White supremacist attitudes, but brought significant improvements in some areas of society. They also led most defenders of White power and privilege to alter their political arguments and to espouse (at least publicly) equality as a formal goal.[81]

The social liberation movements transformed U.S. political culture in many other ways as well. Millions of people participated for the first time in demonstrations, civil disobedience, local organizing, consciousness raising, and other political activities outside of, and more or less opposed to, official elite-controlled channels. Large numbers of movement activists refused to be red-baited or openly embraced radical politics, and many proclaimed their solidarity with national liberation struggles in Africa, Asia, and Latin America. These developments broke the enforced consensus of anticommunism and patriotism. Feminist, lesbian, and gay activists changed the concept of politics by addressing issues such as the patriarchal family, traditional gender roles, compulsory heterosexuality, sexual violence and harassment, and an inequitable and disempowering health care system. Self-assertion and autonomous organizing by many different oppressed groups challenged the myth of a generic American experience. Campaigns against unsafe working conditions, dangerous consumer products, and environmental hazards widely discredited the myth of capitalist beneficence.

Economic and political elites responded to 1960s social liberation movements with a mixture of co-optation and repression. To some extent these responses reflected strategic disagreements among different factions of the power structure, for example, between the local elite of the Deep South and the more powerful multinationalist-oriented elite based in the North. But co-optation and repression also complemented each other and were sometimes deliberately coordinated. Some movement energy could be channeled into activities that were nonthreatening or useful to elites, while more radical groups could be marginalized and destroyed through programs such as the FBI's COINTELPRO without triggering a large-scale public outcry.

With some exceptions, the Right supported repression of social liberation movements but bitterly opposed reformist concessions. Thus, the political elite's double-edged strategy in the 1960s fostered right-wing ambivalence about the state.

Under popular pressure, political elites expanded and redefined the federal government's role in society. The federal government intervened in the South to protect Black people's right to vote, and banned discrimination in many areas of society based on race, sex, religion, or nationality. The 1965 immigration law established relatively equitable country-of-origin quotas, making it possible for millions of people of color to enter the country in succeeding decades. The administration of President Lyndon Johnson (1963–1969) dramatically broadened social programs with such measures as the War on Poverty, Medicaid, and Medicare. Richard Nixon's administration (1969–1974) reduced social spending in some areas but increased it overall, and oversaw new legislation in such areas as the environment and occupational health and safety, significantly expanding federal regulation of business.[82]

Influenced by the political climate, the U.S. Supreme Court instituted legal reforms, intensifying the Right's hatred of the top judicial body. In 1954 the Court had issued its historic school desegregation decision in *Brown v. Topeka Board of Education*. During the 1960s the Court strengthened the rights of criminal defendants and prisoners, temporarily abolished capital punishment, and broadened eligibility for welfare benefits. In 1973, in *Roe v. Wade*, the court legalized some forms of abortion.[83]

Economic and Geopolitical Crises

Another factor contributing to the right-wing upsurge was a crisis in the New Deal system.[84] Since the 1940s, business had reaped many benefits from the combination of social programs, massive military spending, collective bargaining between big corporations and a bureaucratized labor movement, and U.S. military, political, and economic dominance of the capitalist world. By the 1970s, however, the New Deal system was beginning to unravel. U.S. overseas investments and trade increased during the 1960s and 1970s at the same time that Japan, western Europe, and sections of the Third World were gaining industrial strength. Thus, U.S. companies faced growing foreign competition both abroad and in home markets. Although big military budgets had helped the United States enforce its economic and political primacy since World War II, arms spending became a significant drain on the U.S. economy during the Vietnam War. These factors contributed to the 1971 collapse of the Bretton Woods monetary system, under which the United States had enjoyed certain advantages, with the dollar functioning virtually as an international currency.

Domestic changes also cut into the benefits that major corporate employers reaped from the New Deal system. The long 1960s boom pushed unemployment to unusually low levels at the same time that expansion of social programs provided workers with a somewhat greater cushion against job loss. A reduced threat of unemployment weakened employer leverage over their employees, contributing in the late 1960s to a widespread resurgence of rank-and-file worker militancy and a sharp drop-off in corporate profit rates. In the early 1970s, popular pressure brought a major expansion of government regulation of the environment, occupational health and safety, and consumer protection, forcing business to absorb some of the costs previously passed on to other sectors of society.

The 1974–1975 recession proved to be the most severe downturn since the 1930s, pointing to deep structural problems in the U.S. economy. Several years of stagnation followed the recession. With the long post-1945 boom over, growing sections of the business community turned against New Deal policies and toward aggressive antilabor policies. For millions of working-class people in the industrial Northeast and Midwest, these problems were intensified as capital fled to the Sunbelt in search of low-wage, nonunionized workers, and as old heavy industries such as steel and autos declined in favor of service industries and high-tech fields such as computers.

International confrontations reinforced the sense that U.S. power was in decline. First and foremost was the Vietnam War, in which, as Howard Zinn writes, "the wealthiest and most powerful nation in the history of the world made a maximum military effort, with everything short of atomic bombs, to defeat a nationalist revolutionary movement in a tiny, peasant country—and failed."[85] A mass movement in the United States opposed the war, which killed more than two million people, and such protests helped force a U.S. withdrawal. But to others, the war was shameful because the United States "lost," which they often blamed on "cowardly" protesters or a government unwilling to "let the army win." The Vietnam War was followed by victorious nationalist revolutions in Mozambique, Angola, Nicaragua, and Iran, all of which more or less directly challenged U.S. global power. Oil price increases instituted by the Organization of Petroleum Exporting Countries (OPEC) in the 1970s placed a check on the industrial world's ability to dictate trade terms to raw materials exporters. Many governments in Africa, Asia, and Latin America voiced new levels of hostility toward U.S.-based private banks and the international lending institutions dominated by U.S. capital.[86]

These events represented the first major setback to the steady march of U.S. expansion first across the continent and then around the globe. Manifest Destiny was finally being called into question—at the very same time that serious economic difficulties were beginning to reach upward into White working- and middle-class ranks and that the old hierarchies, under which broad sections of the population had enjoyed significant social privilege, were beginning to be challenged and modified.

The Role of Business Conflict

Lavish procorporate funding was critical to the building of the New Right's organizational infrastructure. Beer mogul Joseph Coors, for example, provided start-up money for the Heritage Foundation and the Committee for the Survival of a Free Congress (later renamed the Free Congress Foundation), both founded in the early 1970s. Major funding also came from Richard Mellon Scaife, an heir to the Mellon family fortune (made through the Mellon Bank and major investments in Gulf Oil and Alcoa).[87] Over the next few years, a large and vigorous network of think tanks, legal foundations, political action committees, and media organs took shape to provide training, conduct research, formulate strategies and tactics, coordinate marketing, prepare legal advice, target electoral races, and promote a sense of political solidarity.

Factional tensions within capitalist elites played an important (though seldom examined) role in the development of the New Right.[88] As we have seen, business nationalists had supported ultraconservative political initiatives from the anti-New Deal drives of the 1930s to Goldwater's 1964 presidential campaign. During the 1960s and 1970s, the weak business nationalist faction, originally centered in the Midwest, was transformed into a larger and more powerful ultraconservative bloc centered in the Sunbelt.

The Sunbelt economy expanded dramatically as Vietnam War contracts spurred industrialization and as capital fled from the Northeast to the antiunion states of the South and West. Major defense contractors and other high-tech Sunbelt companies were more or less multinationalist oriented. But the federally subsidized boom also fostered a new crop of laissez-faire entrepreneurs hostile to the Eastern elite and steeped in a broth of right-wing conspiracism, traditionalist Protestant morality, and cultural nationalism. Unlike the labor-intensive manufacturers who predominated among the old nationalists of the Midwest, these capitalists were concentrated primarily in independent oil and gas, real estate, regional finance, and other service sectors.[89] During the 1970s Sunbelt entrepreneurs based in the heartland of Protestant fundamentalism offered key funding to evangelical Christian and New Right organizations.[90]

Meanwhile, many business multinationalists were moving to the right. For decades this dominant business faction had supported or tolerated New Deal liberalism because it offered a reliable workforce, a large consumer base, a stable economy, privileged access to world markets, and—most important—sustained high profits. In the 1960s many multinationalists endorsed limited concessions to social liberation movements to restore social stability and expand their own political base. But in the 1970s, as the New Deal system faltered, many multinationalists turned to harsher strategies. They sought to reduce labor costs, with efforts ranging from plant relocations to illegal attacks on unions, and pressed for reduced government regulation and cuts in corporate taxes, which had already been cut significantly under both the Kennedy and Johnson administrations.[91]

During the early 1970s the Nixon administration had promoted détente and increased trade with the Soviet Union, as well as increased reliance on "regional surrogates" to police much of Africa, Asia, and Latin America. But détente tended to benefit European companies far more than U.S. ones, and regional surrogates often fell short in enforcing U.S. dictates. For these and other reasons, many multinationalists now supported increased military budgets and more direct aggression in the Third World. Rising competition with Europe and Japan also fueled demands for a more unilateralist foreign policy.

In the mid-1970s, a dwindling liberal–multinationalist wing favored an international strategy centered on economic aid and financial leverage, cooptation of radical Third World movements, and global management in concert with western Europe and Japan. Rightward-moving multinationalists, including many defense contractors, increasingly converged with Sunbelt ultraconservatives around a number of core goals: crank up the Cold War and military spending; dismantle social programs, environmental legislation, and other government regulations on industry; roll back what remained of labor union power; and cut taxes. Both wings of this emerging business coalition channeled hundreds of millions of dollars into the array of New Right organizations pursuing their overall agenda.[92]

Under pressure from this new business coalition, President Jimmy Carter began to implement much of its right-wing program, beginning in 1978. Ronald Reagan's administration (1981–1989), with crucial support from congressional Democrats as well as Republicans, took this process much further.[93] In a massive upward income transfer, the government under Reagan slashed business taxes and personal income taxes for the wealthy while increasing the regressive Social Security tax. Social programs for low-income people were cut dramatically. The administration largely stopped enforcing environmental and health and safety regulations, turned over vast public resources such as timber and offshore oil to private companies at discount rates, tilted the National Labor Relations Board more heavily toward management, and aided the union-busting wave by breaking the pivotal air traffic controllers' strike of 1981. Meanwhile, Reagan's unprecedented peacetime military buildup subsidized military contractors and supported the new Cold War and Third World intervention. It also amounted to the largest application of Keynesian deficit spending in U.S. history, helping to sustain the economic boom of the mid-1980s (thanks to heavy foreign investment in the U.S. bond market) in which profits increased while wages stayed comparatively low.

BUILDING THE NEW RIGHT COALITION

It was in this context that the New Right coalition of the 1970s and 1980s emerged. The New Right "represented a reassertion of the old fusionist blend of anticommunism, traditionalism, and libertarianism," explains Sara Diamond, but with more emphasis on moral traditionalism than 1950s fusionists had placed. The New Right brought together corporate-backed think tanks, political strategists oriented toward the Republican Party, and a mass base largely composed of newly mobilized conservative evangelical Christians.[94]

The New Right rhetoric mobilized a classic backlash movement, rooted in both economic and social grievances. Far from being a fringe movement of the "radical Right," this was mainstream political activism. Diamond's comments about the Christian Right apply to the New Right as a whole:

> There is nothing particularly "radical" about most politically active evangelical Christians. To be "radical" is to seize the roots of a problem and to advocate and work for profound social change. The Christian Right, on the contrary, supports existing conditions that effectively maintain inequality between rich and poor, white and black, men and women. The Christian Right supports capitalism in all its forms and effects and seeks to uphold traditional hierarchies between the genders and, less overtly, between races.[95]

The movement's backlash character was twofold. First, it incorporated the Old Right's effort to roll back New Deal welfarism and state regulation of corporate prerogatives. Second, the New Right harnessed the broader and more recent backlash against the social liberation movements and government reforms of the 1960s and 1970s. The New Right's focus on social and cultural issues reflected this effort to reinforce traditional hierarchies— but also partly masked the anti-New Deal part of the agenda. In some cases the fear of change motivated persons who would obviously benefit from the heightened demands of the social liberation movements—such as women, Blacks, and gays—to join the opposition and defend the status quo.

The New Right frequently used scapegoating—explicit or implicit, conscious or unconscious—against women, gay men and lesbians, people of color, youth, environmentalists, non-Christians, and others. As a right-wing populist movement, the New Right combined such attacks with distorted and manipulative antielite appeals. And the New Right's hard-line anti-communism, calls for increased military spending, and aggressive foreign policy appealed to many who feared a decline in U.S. global power. But, like most movements that mobilize a backlash, the New Right coalition also had its own goals and its own agenda, and it should not be seen as exclusively operating in a reactionary mode.

Seeding the Grassroots

To reach grassroots activists and voters, New Right strategists openly adopted successful organizing, research, and training methods that had been pioneered by the labor and civil rights movements.[96] Old Right activists who had worked on the 1964 Goldwater campaign—including Phyllis Schlafly, Paul Weyrich, and Richard Viguerie—brought into the New Right the strategy of simultaneously building broad political organizations and narrowly focused campaigns based on topical issues. The New Right adopted a more aggressive style of mass mobilization than many traditional conservatives and made skillful use of television, computers, and direct-mail fund-raising and marketing techniques. Most remnants of the Old Right either embraced the trend or at least went along reluctantly.

Rather than directly attack popular New Deal programs, as Goldwater had done, the New Right emphasized social issues such as abortion, education, homosexuality, and crime.[97] An important early example was the successful effort begun in the 1970s to block passage of the Equal Rights Amendment (ERA). Under the leadership of Phyllis Schlafly, the campaign mobilized tens of thousands of women activists by skillfully portraying the ERA as a threat to women's financial security and other interests: "Passage of the Equal Rights Amendment would . . . deprive the American woman of many of the fundamental special privileges we now enjoy, and especially the greatest rights of all: (1) NOT to take a job, (2) to keep her baby, and (3) to be supported by her husband."[98]

During the early 1960s Schlafly's first passion had been aggressive Cold War foreign policy and military strategy, areas in which she developed considerable expertise.[99] Her shift of focus to fighting the ERA indicated the narrow constraints placed on intelligent, capable women within the male-dominated Right—but also the movement's increased attention to domestic social issues.

Fears over the protection of families and children were central themes for the New Right and especially its Christian Right component. Diamond lists the key priorities:

> What people in the Christian Right want is pretty basic. They want laws to outlaw abortion, which they consider a form of infanticide. They want to change the tax code to encourage married mothers to stay home and raise good kids. They want queers to get back in the closet and pretend not to exist. They want high quality schools; they think the public schools are failing not for lack of resources but because kids can't pray or read Genesis in biology class.[100]

Race was another core issue.[101] Following Wallace's example, the New Right used coded racial appeals while avoiding explicit ethnic bigotry. Racism was reframed as concern about specific issues such as welfare, immigration, taxes, or education policies. Movement activists such as Viguerie denounced liberal reformism as an elitist attack on regular working people. In some cases, this antielitism drew directly on the producerist tradition. New Right publisher William Rusher declared that a

> new economic division pits the producers—businessmen, manufacturers, hard-hats, blue-collar workers, and farmers—against the new and powerful class of non-producers comprised of a liberal verbalist elite (the dominant media, the major foundations and research institutions, the educational establishment, the federal and state bureaucracies) and a semipermanent welfare constituency, all coexisting happily in a state of mutually sustaining symbiosis.[102]

The genius of the long-term strategy implemented by savvy organizers such as Weyrich and televangelist Pat Robertson was their method of expanding the base of social conservatives. First, they created a broader Protestant Right that cut across all boundaries separating independent evangelicals, fundamentalists, pentacostals, and charismatics. Second, they issued a challenge to more moderate Protestants. Third, they created a true Christian Right by reaching out to conservative, reactionary, and apocalyptic Catholics. Fourth, they created the illusion of a broader Religious Right by recruiting and promoting their few reactionary allies in the Jewish and Muslim communities. Meanwhile, by disguising some essentially Christian initiatives behind secular organizations and projects, they further enhanced the movement's image of inclusiveness.

A key step in this movement-building process took place in 1979, when Robert Billings of the National Christian Action Council invited rising televangelist Jerry Falwell to a meeting with right-wing strategists Paul Weyrich, Howard Phillips, Richard Viguerie, and Ed McAteer. The main idea was to push the issue of abortion as a way to split social conservatives away from the Democratic Party. This meeting came up with the idea of the "Moral Majority," which Falwell turned into an organization. The New Right coalition really jelled at this point with the creation of a frame of reference with which to mobilize a mass base.[103]

The Moral Majority failed to expand much beyond its Baptist-fundamentalist roots. But as early as 1981, Falwell, Weyrich, and Robertson were working together to build a broader Christian alliance including charismatics, pentacostals, more moderate Protestant denominations, and a few right-wing Catholics. The annual Family Forum national conferences, for example, enabled members of the Reagan Administration to rub shoulders with leaders of dozens of Christian Right groups and share ideas with rank-and-file activists.

This coalition building continued through the Reagan years. According to Kazin, the New Right coalition launched a "multi-issue, multiconstituency offensive" that was very potent on the political scene:

> Conservatives talked like grassroots activists but were able to behave like a counter-elite. Within their coalition were Sunbelt corporations opposed to federal regulation and high taxes; churches mobilized to reverse the spread of "secular humanism"; local groups that protested school busing, sex education, and other forms of bureaucratic meddling in "family issues," and foundations that endowed a new generation of intellectuals and journalists.[104]

Although the New Right became closely associated with the Republican Party, its roots were solidly bipartisan. For example, while it is well known that New Right direct-mail mogul Viguerie got his start in the business with a list of 12,000 contributors to the Goldwater campaign, the fact that he also obtained Wallace's 1972 Democratic primary list of almost 3 million names is rarely noted.[105] In fact, the Republican Party was not the New Right's first choice for an electoral vehicle. In 1976 Viguerie and other New Right leaders tried to take over Wallace's American Independent Party. Only when this attempt failed did they concentrate their efforts on the Republicans.[106]

The New Right quickly allied with the growing neoconservative movement. This was an intellectual network of former Cold War liberals rooted in the Democratic Party, as well as anticommunist social democrats, who were alienated by 1960s social activism and George McGovern's 1972 Democratic presidential candidacy. In contrast to the overwhelmingly Christian New Right, many "neocons" were Jews. Neoconservatives also tended to have a more globalist outlook than many New Rightists and often advocated limited welfare state policies but agreed with the New Right on the need for militaristic anticommunism and, to some extent, moral traditionalism.[107]

How evangelical voting patterns shifted under the guidance of the New Right is complex, and many popular and academic discussions of the phenomenon have conflicting conclusions.

In 1976 unabashed "born-again" evangelical Jimmy Carter attracted many evangelical votes, including votes from those conservative evangelicals disappointed that conservative icon Ronald Reagan had lost to Gerald Ford as the Republican presidential candidate. Better a born-again southern Democrat than a moderate northern Republican. Thus, 56 percent of White Baptist voters picked Carter over Ford, including some Democratic-leaning evangelicals who had not been active voters, as well as evangelicals that usually voted Republican. Noting this trend in 1976 results, the New Right thereafter assiduously used family values rhetoric to pull Republican evangelicals away from Carter. As a result, in 1980 Reagan garnered 56 percent of the White Baptist vote to Carter's 34 percent, and two-thirds of Reagan's ten-point overall margin came from White evangelicals. In addition, some two million new voters had been registered through a variety of religious and secular operations seeking votes for Republican candidates. In 1984 Reagan got 80 percent of the White evangelical vote, and Republican candidates apparently attracted many previously Democratic-leaning evangelicals with promises to halt abortions, reimplement school prayer, fight pornography, beef up defense spending, and pursue more aggressive foreign policies.[108]

Countersubversion Redux

The conspiracist political Right began to reconstruct the congressional countersubversive apparatus soon after Reagan took office.[109] Ultraconservative Strom Thurmond was named head of the Senate Judiciary Committee, which oversaw the work of the newly formed Senate Subcommittee on Security and Terrorism (SST). SST was chaired by ultraconservative Sen. Jeremiah Denton, who quickly began rekindling the Congressional witchhunt. One notable SST staff member was Samuel T. Francis, who, after authoring the security section of the Heritage Foundation's Reagan transition study, became legislative assistant for national security to ultraconservative SST member Senator John P. East.[110]

If there was any doubt that the subcommittee would use McCarthy period and private spying data, it was soon laid to rest by Francis in a 1981 issue of the ultraconservative newspaper *Human Events*. In an article titled "Leftists Mount Attack on Investigative Panel," Francis sought to discredit SST critics by labeling them "far-left, revolutionary, or pro-terrorist." To bolster his charges, Francis reached back to the McCarthy period committees to note that such SST critics as the National Alliance Against Racist and Political Repression and the National Emergency Civil Liberties Committee had been "identified as Communist Party front groups." The National Lawyers Guild, Francis reported, "was cited in 1950 as the 'legal bulwark of the Communist party' by the House Committee on Un-American Activities." The Center for Constitutional Rights was called a "far-left appendage of the National Lawyers Guild," and staff counsel Margaret Ratner was described as "associated with the legal defense of a number of political violence groups and terrorists."[111] Francis also told *Human Events* that the newsletter of a right-wing private spy for the John Birch Society, John Rees, was "authoritative" on the subject of internal subversion.[112]

Early targets of SST included alternative media such as *Mother Jones* magazine and the Pacifica Radio network. As luck would have it, the SST's hearings on the "Red Menace" soon discredited that forum, at least among mainstream journalists, and an attempt to restart the old House Un-American Activities Committee failed. Despite these setbacks, the views of the conspiracist right wing had made serious gains.

President Reagan himself sounded the Red Menace alert in 1982, charging that the nuclear freeze campaign was "inspired by not the sincere, honest people who want peace, but by some people who want the weakening of America and so are manipulating honest and sincere people." Reagan saw freeze activists as dupes of subversives or outright traitors. He later openly criticized those who brought down Joseph McCarthy. A State Department charge that the Women's International League for Peace and Freedom was a "communist front" was retracted when traced to a Western Goals Foundation report by right-wing spy John Rees.[113]

On March 7, 1983, Attorney General William French Smith released "Guidelines on General Crimes, Racketeering Enterprise and Domestic Security/Terrorism Investigations." According to Mitchell Rubin, in *Police Misconduct and Civil Rights Law Report*, "Three authorizations granted to the FBI under the Smith guidelines [included] the FBI's right to conduct surveillance of peaceful public demonstrations, to use informants and infiltrators, and to investigate persons or groups advocating unlawful activities." These were three areas where the FBI had systematically abused constitutional rights in the past and had been restrained under the guidelines issued in 1978 by President Carter's attorney general, Edward Levi.[114]

By late 1983 widespread FBI harassment of Latin American support groups and anti-interventionist organizations began to be reported nationwide. Nearly 100 reports of mysterious break-ins at activists' offices were compiled by the Movement Support Network between 1983 and 1986. According to Ross Gelbspan, these break-ins were largely carried out by agents representing right-wing interests in Central and South America and could only have been carried out with the tacit agreement of U.S. intelligence agencies to look the other way.[115]

There was no mass or elite support for the new witch-hunt, however, and its proponents were isolated by mainstream politicians and the media. Its proponents returned to the anticommunist organizations from which they had emerged, keeping the fires burning for another opportunity.

CONCLUSION

Behind fears of communism, civil rights, Black power, modern curricula, the feminist movement, and gay rights is the classic subversion myth. Joel Kovel talks of the "myth of innocents captured by barbarians" and a process of "diabolization."[116] Christian Right demonization of gays and lesbians mimics the same style as that used in anticommunism and antisemitism.[117] Anna Marie Smith talks about "anxieties about subversion in the broadest sense"—in her example, fears of homosexuality—as being

> located genealogically, within the long tradition of similar representations of subversive social elements and popular anxieties about prostitution, pornography, abortion rights, the provision of contraception to persons under the age of consent, sex education, various diseases, communist infiltration, immigrant populations, crime "waves," drug "crazes," "hooligan" youths and so on.[118]

The New Right superseded the Old Right, but within those sectors using populist rhetoric and the producerist narrative, the dynamic of demonization, scapegoating, and conspiracism remained largely intact.

The continuity between the Old Right and New Right was illustrated by Fred Schwarz in his biweekly *Christian Anti-Communism Crusade* newsletter, sent at the time to 13,000 supporters. As the Reagan Administration was arriving in the nation's capital in January 1981, Schwarz explained why so many pundits were surprised by the election results. In an article titled "Morality, Communism and Politics," Schwarz said poll takers and journalists had underestimated "the role which outraged morality played in the election." According to Schwarz,

> Having long discarded what they often refer to sneeringly as the Puritan Ethic, they feel little or no moral outrage themselves and are incapable of understanding the intensity of the sense of moral outrage many Americans have felt as they have observed a liberal elite dominating the political process and destroying traditional moral values.

Schwarz then discussed five sources of outrage:

Legal slaughter of the unborn;
Compulsory busing for racial integration;
Promotion of venereal disease and illegitimacy disguised as sex education;
Homosexuality, disease, and mass murder; and
The growth of communism.[119]

The New Right benefited from widespread fear, resentment, and uncertainty brought on by the political, cultural, economic, and international upheavals of the 1960s and 1970s. Amid this prolonged period of crisis, a combination of well-funded national infrastructure, strategic leadership, skillful framing of the issues, and energetic grassroots mobilization built the New Right from the ashes of the Old.

By scapegoating big government and liberal elites as the forces behind society's problems, the New Right was able to divert attention away from many important underlying institutional and structural issues. Secular and religious conspiracy theories could be superimposed by some as an additional dimension without disturbing the broader interpretation. Moral traditionalists, anticommunists, and economic conservatives could all agree on a common enemy despite having different views on causation. Meanwhile, the grievances of many White middle- and working-class people—both a legitimate sense of injury and angry scapegoating generated by the erosion of traditional privileges—could be harnessed to benefit wealthy elites and intensify disempowerment and inequality for millions of people.

11

CULTURE WARS
AND POLITICAL SCAPEGOATS

Gender, Sexuality, and Race

The Culture War is a rubric, or umbrella, under which several sectors of the U.S. political Right could criticize modern liberalism. While primarily a rhetorical invention of the Christian Right, the Culture War resonated across multiple political boundaries, picking up support from secular conservatives, neoconservatives, and libertarians. It even allowed well-behaved leaders of the Far Right—those willing to hide their underlying ideologies—to attempt dialogues with more moderate rightists.

The rise of the Christian Right, with its emphasis on "family values," gender roles, and a muted, cultural form of Eurocentric racism, was one of the most significant features of politics in the 1980s and 1990s. The Christian Right opened up new avenues for ultraconservative and Hard Right evangelical women to participate in politics, often in campaigns against the feminist movement and reproductive rights. Another major focus was rolling back the gains of the gay and lesbian movement.

This period saw a shift among many Christian Right leaders from anti-communist scapegoating to a more comprehensive and elastic conspiracy theory centered on a suspected plan by secular humanists to take God out of society.[1] The relatively painless nature of the shift between these scapegoats was due in part to the underlying binary "us/them" apocalyptic paradigm—both religious and secular—which had fed the Cold War and the witch-hunts of the McCarthy period.[2]

The Culture War enabled the New Right coalition to realign itself, but with the Christian Right in command. However, the loss of anticommunist scapegoating as the primary glue holding the various factions together eventually contributed to the breakup of the New Right coalition in the late 1980s and early 1990s. We outline the factional conflicts that emerged and focus particularly on gender and "family values" as themes that transcended these splits.

Despite the spats and factional fights, the New Right has spawned a large number of institutions, such as think tanks and policy institutes, as well as an ongoing infrastructure that in fact is the major legacy of the New Right. The publicity chefs in these institutions have skillfully packaged ideological arguments into tasty morsels fed to the corporate media for use as sound bites and spicy features. This approach has helped to shift popular political discourse in the United States perceptibly to the right.

THE CHRISTIAN RIGHT

Right-wing evangelical Christians formed the bulk of the New Right's activist base. Many social scientists (influenced by "status anxiety" theory or centrist/extremist theory) predicted Christian Right activism would be concentrated among people supposedly cut off from the modern world: those who were low-income, rural, working class, and poorly educated. This approach treated "the Christian Right as the latest attempt by parochial populations to defend status threatened by social change and relieve accompanying anxieties." The reality was quite different. Reviewing extensive data from 1978 and 1988 congressional campaigns, researchers found that "Christian Right activism occurred predominantly in rapidly growing—and relatively prosperous—suburban areas of the South, Southwest, and Midwest." Such activism "drew on higher-status traditionalists confronting modern society directly, rather than their lower-status brethren left behind in the hinterland."

Another study found that members of some Christian Right activist groups, including Focus on the Family and Concerned Women for America, share three related attributes; they are much more likely than the general population to

- depend on religious television, radio, magazines, or direct mail as important sources of information;
- hold relatively intolerant views, believing that most political issues have "one correct Christian view," that should not be compromised; and,
- vote in primary and general elections.[3]

Starting in 1964 with the Goldwater presidential candidacy, Christian Right and secular right activists brought their issues and ideas into the Republican Party, forcing it to the right. After an extensive study of voting patterns from 1960 to 1992, Clem Brooks and Jeff Manza concluded that

The opposition to civil rights and general anti-liberalism of the right-wing of the Republican Party, coupled with strong Republican opposition to the ERA and the increasingly partisan struggle over abortion, appear to have been sufficient to erode the once-dominant Republican alignment of liberal Protestants.

The authors also found little data to support the widely discussed notion that large numbers of Catholics switched their loyalty to the Republican Party, but instead they determined that Catholics became swing-voters in some elections.[4]

Studies that found no major shifts in overall voting habits of Protestants or overall voting habits within denominations missed more subtle patterns. What was happening in the Republican Party was the result of complex and overlapping dynamics. There was a growing number of persons self-identifying as evangelical in the general population, and there was a growing number of voters identifying themselves as evangelical or born-again. Conservative Christian evangelicals were switching from having Democratic to Republican allegiance, but this was over a long period of time starting in the 1960s. As the proportion of self-identified evangelicals voting Republican was growing, there was a receding wave of northern White liberal Protestants (many from mainline denominations). Along with these changes, there was a political mobilization of conservative White evangelical Protestants, many from nonmainline churches or more conservative branches of mainline denominations in the South and Midwest, who gradually were turned into partisan Republican activists by shrewd Christian Right movement leaders. Eventually, the Christian Right activists gained more influence in the Republican Party than their secular partners in the New Right coalition.

Christian Right activism addressed the full range of New Right concerns, from dismantling social welfare programs and government regulation to intensifying anticommunism and the U.S. military buildup. As Sara Diamond has shown, support for counterrevolutionary warfare in southern Africa, the Philippines, and above all Central America played a much greater role in Christian Right activism in the 1980s than has generally been recognized. Through propaganda, lobbying, and direct-supply operations, Christian Right groups worked with the Reagan administration—including Oliver North's secret network—to help "Freedom Fighter" armies in Nicaragua, Angola, and Mozambique, and counterinsurgency operations in El Salvador, the Philippines, and elsewhere. Diamond notes that this cooperation helped keep the Christian Right allied with the Reagan administration despite the movement's growing frustration over the lack of domestic social policy changes.[5]

Although foreign and military policy was a key part of the Christian Right's work, social traditionalism was the core of its mass appeal. Well before the late 1980s, when Free Congress Foundation President Paul Weyrich promoted "cultural conservatism" as the new glue for right-wing mobilization, social traditionalism was the basis for the Culture War.[6] Emboldened by a renewed emphasis on Christian moral absolutism among conservative Christian evangelicals, Culture Warriors championed "traditional values" such as western European culture, private property, and minimum government regulation of business. In the United States there was also particular emphasis on beliefs in individualism, hard work, self-sufficiency, and social mobility. Threats to traditional values included secular humanism, liberalism, collectivism, multiculturalism, environmentalism, and globalism. Also opposed by hard-liners were witchcraft, the occult, Halloween, meditation, values clarification, and anything "New Age."

Diamond explains the dynamic of scapegoating in the Christian Right:

> Average people active in the Christian Right genuinely feel that the country is going to hell in a hand basket, which is true. The problem is that through a long process of ideological formation most have arrived at a distorted view of their own best interests. They look at [what for them was a] stagnant economy and see "illegal aliens," not runaway capitalism, which they generally support. They look at teenage delinquency and then blame teachers' unions instead of the consumer culture that trains young people to shop and not think.[7]

The Christian Right was especially concerned about defending "family values" against such threats as feminism, homosexuality, abortion, divorce, sex outside of marriage, single-parent families, and sex education in schools. In this emphasis the movement broke sharply with its predecessors. The Christian Right of the 1980s was the first right-wing populist movement in U.S. history to place both family structure and sexuality at the center of a major mobilization. Temperance, for example, was a "family values" campaign, but it cut across political lines. The Christian Right's core agenda was the reassertion of heterosexual male dominance and traditional gender roles throughout society.

The Christian Right presented its so-called profamily crusade as a religious imperative, as an answer to social breakdown, and as a defense against liberal and morally corrupt elites out of touch with mainstream America. This crusade helped reinforce a variety of demands. In the Christian Right worldview, communism must be fought, in part, because it promoted sexual immorality and forced women to act like men; social welfare programs for low-income women must be dismantled, in part, because they rewarded sexual irresponsibility and undermined traditional families. But in the 1980s and 1990s, the Christian Right's patriarchal family crusade focused primarily on two fronts: outlawing abortion and suppressing homosexuality. In both campaigns, a populist narrative of average people against cosmopolitan elites was utilized.

Women in the Christian Right

Women have played a key role in the Christian Right's antifeminist campaigns. As Jean Hardisty notes, the Right recognized that women "can don a mantle of legitimacy when speaking and organizing against feminism." Antifeminist activism also provided a way to recruit women for the male-dominated movement's overall social agenda. In the 1980s and 1990s, the largest and most prominent antifeminist women's organizations were Phyllis Schlafly's Eagle Forum, which as of 1996 claimed 80,000 members, and especially Beverly LaHaye's Concerned Women for America (CWA), which claimed between 600,000 and 700,000 members. Although seldom recognized as major players on the Right, these organizations have played important roles in a wide range of right-wing campaigns.[8]

As Andrea Dworkin has argued, the traditionalist Right offered women a sense of meaning, structure, and safety based on a set of predetermined rules. "The Right promises to put enforceable restraints on male aggression, thus simplifying survival for women—to make the world slightly more habitable." If a woman devoted herself to being a good, obedient wife, mother, and homemaker, she would be rewarded with her husband's protection, economic support, and love. In this viewpoint, feminism's assertion of women's autonomy and challenge to traditional structures seemed an invitation to chaos, danger, and isolation, destroying the traditional arrangement under which men followed certain rules. Hardisty notes that additional factors motivating women to embrace antifeminism include a belief that feminist ideology violates God's will, that lesbians control the feminist movement, and a feeling among some that feminism is elitist. "In this view the source of women's oppression is not men, but other women, specifically other women who are inferior morally, but who have influence and power to impose their own twisted, secular priorities."[9]

Yet, even as it vilified feminism, the Christian Right made use of feminist concepts and social gains. For example, the Christian Right organization Women Exploited by Abortion, founded in 1982, "capitalize[d] on the widespread concern for women's well-being that was generated largely by the feminist movement." One CWA staffer borrowed feminist language to explain why she opposed federal support for childcare: "I just think the federal government shouldn't tell us what kind of day care our children should have. I believe women should have a choice." "Contrary to popular stereotypes," wrote Sara Diamond, "Christian Right women are increasingly encouraged to learn administrative skills and pursue advanced degrees." Organizations such as Concerned Women for America also encouraged women to develop self-confidence and assertiveness, to speak publicly and assume leadership—so long as they championed women's traditional roles and did not challenge men's preeminence. LaHaye and her husband, Christian Right leader Tim LaHaye, also wrote a frank sex manual, *The Act of Marriage: The Beauty of Sexual Love*, which declared that (married, heterosexual) women have a right to sexual pleasure—"Your heavenly Father placed [your clitoris] there for your enjoyment"—encouraged women to be active in lovemaking, and even endorsed birth control because it enabled women to enjoy sex more fully.[10]

The Christian Right's balancing act regarding women's roles is rooted in the long history of patriarchy-loyal women's activism in the United States—from the 1840s anti-immigrant movement to the 1920s Women's Klan and the far-right "mothers" movement of 1940–1941. In today's context, the Christian Right's approach means using the expanded opportunities that feminism has won for women since the 1960s in an effort to close off many of those same opportunities. slam the door

The Attack on Abortion Rights

While the U.S. Supreme Court's 1973 *Roe v. Wade* decision legalized many forms of abortion, some feminists have pointed out serious shortcomings in this decision. *Roe* protected abortion based on a right to privacy between a woman and her doctor—not a woman's right to reproductive and sexual freedom, to make decisions about her own body without control by doctors or the government.[11] While noting these deficiencies, Marlene Fried and Loretta Ross highlight how abortion rights was of pivotal importance to many women:

> Without legal abortion, thousands of women died in back alleys, thousands more suffered serious medical complications, and all women's health was threatened. . . . Together with legalizing contraception, abortion legitimized the separation between biology and procreation. This is a necessary step in the struggle for sexual freedom—heterosexual women could choose to have sex and choose not to be pregnant. And by breaking the link between sexuality and reproduction, it opened the door to sexual self-determination for lesbians and gay men.[12]

Opposition to abortion rights was the original focal point for the Christian Right's effort to build an alliance of traditionalist Protestants and Catholics. Many early efforts concentrated on trying to ban abortion through an amendment to the U.S. Constitution.[13] More successful were a gradual series of incremental restrictions that exploited weaknesses in *Roe*'s right-to-privacy framework, such as the 1976 ban on Medicaid funding for abortions (sponsored by Rep. Henry Hyde of Illinois), bans on public funding of abortions by a majority of states, and parental consent or notification laws, all of which have been upheld by the Supreme Court. These and other attacks, note Fried and Ross, "have come first against the most vulnerable women—poor women, young women, women of color."[14]

Christian Right propaganda routinely denounced abortion as "murder" and as a new "holocaust." Calls to oppose proponents of abortion rights often involved violent imagery, such as prayers for the death of proabortion rights Supreme Court justices. Joseph Scheidler of the Pro-Life Action League took special pride in urging on picketers at a women's health clinic by telling them that their protests increased the medical complication rate for those women running the gauntlet and receiving abortions. The 1988 book *A Pro-Life Manifesto* speculated in detail about a campaign of large-scale "armed aggression" to stop abortion, one involving bombings and terrorism, but concluded regretfully that "the zeal is not there."[15]

In the 1980s, influenced by such propaganda, "pro-life" activists conducted hundreds of attacks against women's health clinics, clinic workers, and patients, including stalking, death threats, mass intimidation, vandalism, assaults, kidnappings, firebombings, and even murders.[16] Operation Rescue (OR), founded in 1987–1988, and led for years by Randall A. Terry, organized mass blockades and other direct actions in an effort to shut down clinics, superficially copying civil rights movement language and tactics in a bid for greater legitimacy. Even some Christian Rightists criticized OR's tactics. "To confront an already distraught woman at the door of an abortion clinic and attempt to put her on a ´guilt trip´ for what she is about to do is not the solution," wrote Pentecostal Bishop Earl Paulk.[17]

In the 1990s the militant wing of the antiabortion movement intensified its attacks and targeted abortion providers with concentrated harassment and violence, including several assassinations.[18] Although weakened by splits over such tactics, the movement succeeded in drastically reducing women's access to abortions, especially outside major cities. By 1993, according to the National Abortion Federation, 83 percent of U.S. counties lacked a doctor willing to perform abortions, and only 12 percent of ob-gyn residency programs still taught the procedure.[19]

Feminists countermobilized with a variety of tactics including demonstrations, escorts, and mass clinic defense actions, and their active ranks swelled after the Supreme Court's 1989 *Webster* v. *Reproductive Health Services* decision that further weakened abortion rights. The 1992 March for Women's Lives in Washington, DC, for example, drew an estimated 750,000 people.

Although the federal government had done little to use existing laws to stop clinic violence, some pro-choice organizations sought help through expanding the government's powers to crack down on antiabortion groups. In a federal lawsuit against Operation Rescue and other antiabortion groups, the National Organization for Women won a unanimous 1994 Supreme Court ruling that the Racketeer Influenced and Corrupt Organizations (RICO) Act could be used against members of a "criminal conspiracy" even though no financial motive was involved, as previous interpretations had required. RICO was already a sweepingly repressive law—so broad that even Richard Nixon's Justice Department opposed it—that gave federal prosecutors much more power to bring indictments based on much less evidence than before. As numerous leftists and liberals argued, the 1994 decision offered state forces yet another weapon that can and will be used against nonviolent radical activism and speech.[20]

Antiabortion strategy sparked a fierce debate over the text of the Republican Party platform in 1996, with candidate Bob Dole failing in an effort to offer pro-choice Republicans at least a rhetorical refuge against the dogmatism of the Christian Right ideologues who dominated the party at the grassroots.[21]

The Christian Right shifted from opposing all sex education, to promoting several highly biased abstinence-only sex education curricula—riddled with misinformation and based primarily on fear and guilt. This was an ineffective effort to force young people to abide by the norms of traditionalist Christianity in the era of AIDS. Even when not adopted, abstinence-only curricula have helped erode comprehensive sexuality education nationwide.[22] Most libertarians and even some Republican Party conservatives were uncomfortable with abstinence-only curricula.

The Great Gay Conspiracy

While homophobia is widespread in U.S. culture, the politicization of homophobia was carefully constructed using marketing techniques in a series of media campaigns that began in the right-wing alternative media.[23] Antigay "No Special Rights" themes, for example, were developed over almost a decade of field-testing various slogans before they were used in several state campaigns against equal rights for gays. Like the antiabortion campaign, the Christian Right's focus on homosexuality and AIDS furthered its drive to reimpose the patriarchal nuclear family as the basis for society, and involved an intricate back-and-forth struggle that unwittingly helped galvanize and strengthen antioppression forces.[24]

The Christian Right found allies and opponents in different sectors of the Right. Neoconservatives called for an idealized level playing field for women and people of color, but for heterosexuals only. Meanwhile, some economic libertarians, including a small but vocal group of gay conservatives, criticized the Christian Right for attempting to pass laws curtailing rights based on sexual identity.[25]

Starting in the 1970s, as gay men, and then lesbians, increasingly moved out of the closet, the hyperbolic rhetoric concerning homosexuals in articles in the right-wing alternative press escalated. Early campaigns included Anita Bryant's successful Florida campaign to overturn a local antidiscrimination ordinance, and an unsuccessful California ballot initiative to ban open lesbians and gay men from teaching in the public schools. These initiatives caused a media flurry but could not sustain grassroots momentum.[26]

The Christian Right's major strategic ideological counterattack against gay rights began in 1980 when Free Congress Foundation (FCF) president Paul Weyrich commissioned staff member Father Enrique Rueda to write *The Homosexual Network*, about "the social and political impact of the homosexual movement in America." One jacket blurb writer gushed that Rueda had revealed "the widening homosexual power-grab in our society."[27] Rueda's book, "intended primarily for academics and legislators," according to one FCF memo, was widely quoted in political and religious right-wing publications.[28] Still, interest soon dwindled.

The AIDS crisis offered a new opening to the Christian Right. In 1987 FCF commissioned Rueda and Michael Schwartz to write *Gays, AIDS and You*, after market research indicated demand for a shorter, less expensive book that included information about AIDS.[29] FCF obtained tentative commitments from Jerry Falwell's Moral Majority for 5,000–10,000 copies and from the Conservative Book Club for 6,000–7,000 copies, both "subject to their approval of the manuscript," according to a May 20, 1987, FCF memo.

Gays, AIDS and You popularized many of the myths and slogans later circulated in public homophobic campaigns. The introduction warns: "The homosexual political agenda represents a radical departure from what we as Americans believe . . . a terrible threat—to ourselves, our children, our communities, our country . . . a radical, anti-family agenda."[30] The authors suggest that the movement for homosexual rights is different from movements involving "legitimate" minorities and, using conspiracist phrases, they continue,

> This movement is stronger, more widespread, more skillfully structured than most Americans realize. It reaches into our media, our political institutions, our schools, even into our mainline churches. . . . And now this movement is using the AIDS crisis to pursue its political agenda. This in turn, threatens not only our values but our lives.[31]

An order form for the book includes a picture of a man at a desk, his face in shadows, and the headline: "This Man Wants His 'Freedom' So Bad He's Ready To Let America Die For It." The text added, "Our civilization stands in the path of his fulfillment as a freely promiscuous homosexual."[32]

Underpinning Christian Right antigay activism was the belief that homosexuality was not only sinful, but a monstrous, uncontrollable embodiment of evil. In *Homosexual Politics: Road to Ruin for America*, Dr. Edward Rowe stated, "Homosexual politics is a moral cancer eating at the fabric of America. It is an unholy, satanic crusade. . . . This evil movement must be stopped!" Senator Jesse Helms's introduction to Rowe's book declared: "Homosexual politics continues in fanatical pursuit of its goal of carving out a new 'civil right' based on the sexual appetite of its adherents."[33]

At the same time, movement propaganda often portrayed gay men, like feminists, as a wealthy, privileged elite misusing their power to impose their immoral agenda on society. Such claims turned the targets of homophobic oppression into oppressors, and enabled the Christian Right "to project its own power and influence onto its enemies/victims." (Contrary to myth, gay men actually earned between 10 and 26 percent less income than did hetero-sexual men.)[34]

During the 1980s the Christian Right fomented and exploited an atmo-sphere of hysteria about AIDS by contributing to the widespread scapegoating of gay men (as well as drug users, Haitians, poor women, and prostitutes) for the disease.[35] The Reagan administration also fueled the AIDS panic with irresponsible public statements about the possibility of ca-sual AIDS transmission and through its refusal to fund vastly increased re-search on the disease. Many states enacted or considered repressive mea-sures, often orchestrated by right-wing organizations. In California, for example, the neofascist LaRouche network sponsored a ballot initiative in 1986 and 1988 that called for "quarantining" people with AIDS and manda-tory HIV testing for the general population. The measure was defeated both times after major opposition campaigns spearheaded by lesbian, gay, and AIDS groups, but received first 2 million and then 1.7 million votes.[36] Meanwhile, in 1986, the U.S. Supreme Court ruled in *Bowers* v. *Hardwick* that states could continue to outlaw private, consensual acts of gay or lesbian sex as felonies punishable through long prison terms.

The lesbian and gay community and people with AIDS mobilized in the face of these attacks, for example, holding massive national marches for lesbian and gay rights in Washington in 1987 and 1993. Militant groups such as the predominantly lesbian and gay AIDS Coalition to Unleash Power (ACT UP) helped transform public consciousness about the epi-demic and save lives by changing numerous public and corporate policies. During the late 1980s and 1990s, lesbians and gay men dramatically in-creased their visibility throughout the culture.

In response to these developments, right-wing initiatives escalated, ac-companied by increased antigay and antilesbian violence. Christian rightists led well-funded and centrally coordinated ballot initiative campaigns in sev-eral states to ban laws that prohibited discrimination based on sexual orien-tation, most of which were defeated by a combination of grassroots lesbian and gay organizing and court battles. In 1992, in Colorado, after an infusion of right-wing propaganda and cash, voters narrowly passed Amendment Two, framed as a bill legislating "No Special Rights for Homosexuals" but that actually would have prevented gays, lesbians, and bisexuals from fully exercising their constitutional rights. After a vigorous legal battle, the U.S. Supreme Court eventually ruled that the law should not be implemented. An even more draconian homophobic measure was defeated by voters in Oregon.[37]

These gay-bashing campaigns overlapped with efforts to stop AIDS public health measures such as safer sex education, condom distribution, and needle exchange on grounds that they encouraged immoral behavior. The back-and-forth struggle between the Right and the lesbian and gay movements continued with battles over homophobic discrimination by the military, in 1993, and state-sanctioned marriage, beginning in 1996.

Cultural Racism

The Christian Right's "profamily" agenda was interlaced with cultural racism. This was not the explicit biological White supremacy that has prevailed across most of the political spectrum for most of U.S. history. Many Christian Right groups welcomed those few people of color who shared their ideology. As Jean Hardisty notes, women of color who participate in the Eagle Forum or Concerned Women for America,

> are accepted as worthy because they oppose affirmative action, multiculturalism, and welfare. They are worthy because they believe in individualism, personal responsibility, limited government, and family values. They oppose liberalism, government programs for the needy, secular humanism, and sex education in the schools.[38]

Those who did not share these beliefs, however, or who asserted a distinct cultural identity that challenges the Eurocentric myth of sameness were branded as unworthy of inclusion and acceptance. Claiming that racial discrimination is a thing of the past, the Christian Right routinely blamed its effects on people of color themselves. According to this updated version of scapegoating, says Hardisty,

> though racist stereotypes are not applicable across the board, they are valid when applied to those who are unworthy. Thus, the "welfare queen" or other stereotypes promoted to represent despised members of society are not seen as racist stereotypes but as accurate and honest depictions of unworthiness.[39]

The movement's opposition to "welfare"—selectively interpreted to mean government assistance programs for poor people, especially women and children—highlighted the racism–misogyny synthesis. Different sectors of the Right opposed welfare for different reasons, but for Christian rightists a key issue was the belief that welfare undermined traditional morality by encouraging women, especially teenaged women, to have children out of wedlock and raise families on their own. As Ann Withorn notes, "The real danger is defined as women's ability to *choose* to live without men, not the problem of their being abandoned."[40] This issue struck at the core of the Christian Right's so-called profamily politics,

> for thirty years women have . . . been opening up the secrets of the patriarchal family: the violence, the abuse, the incest. And they have done so not just to name men's sins in order to reform them but to justify the rights of women to live without men. . . . Since right-wingers cannot acknowledge

even to themselves that incest, battering, and rape are the systemic methods that subjugate women, they are in a pickle. But they *can* say that single families are bad, turn children into criminals, and take them away from the "love and discipline" and legitimacy that only a father can bring. They can assert that if such things happen at all it is primarily in families of the "underclass," where bad people have made bad choices while weakened by welfare.[41]

In other words, in the welfare debate the Christian Right used coded racist scapegoating to safeguard its idyllic myth of the traditional patriarchal family. It deflected attention away from widespread domestic brutality and dysfunction by identifying such family problems primarily with low-income communities of color. In this project the movement was aided in an indirect yet parallel manner by members of the Far Right, for whom biological White supremacy remained a core principle. The themes of cultural racism and biological racism reinforced each other in public discourse, further embedding the producerist version of repressive populism, with anger directed up toward sinister elites and discipline directed down toward lazy and sinful parasites, who are pictured by many as people of color.

FROM RED MENACE TO SECULAR HUMANIST CONSPIRACY

The end of the Cold War, with the Soviet bloc's collapse beginning in 1989, had profound implications for right-wing politics in the United States. Having failed to spark another public Red Scare in the opening days of the Reagan administration, the conspiracists in the right wing countersubversion subculture had retreated back to their private sector institutions. They were not idle. Conspiracist ultraconservatives began shifting the focus of their scapegoating from communism to a cluster of other targets: international terrorists, sinful abortion providers, antifamily feminists, homosexual special rights activists, pagan environmentalists, liberal secular humanists and their big government allies, and globalists who plot on behalf of the New World Order. When communism did collapse in Eastern Europe, this sector of the Right was ready.

Liberals as Godless Secular Humanist Traitors

A conference hosted by John Stormer provided a good example of the Christian Right's conspiracist theory in transition, as an obvious attempt to place the collapsing Soviet bloc in the context of a larger struggle against liberalism, secular humanism, and modern egalitarianism. At the February 1989 conference held in Worcester, Massachusetts, Stormer appeared aged but energetic as he told the crowd of 200 that "Communists are running wild in America." The scene could well have been painted by a tipsy Norman Rockwell. There were sex-segregated rows of fresh-faced teenagers from private Christian schools, businessmen in bankers' suits, middle-aged women with henna hair and diamond earrings, gray-haired dowagers shrinking into their furs, young professionals in tweed sports coats and wire-rimmed glasses, craggy couples in L. L. Bean wool shirts and bulky sweaters. Many attendees were recruited through flyers distributed to Christian Right groups and John Birch Society contacts. The conference packet held an issue of the Birch Society magazine, and local Birch activists attended the sessions. The Stormer conference had secular elements but was rooted in ultraconservative Christian evangelical and fundamentalist beliefs.[42]

It is important to place the Stormer conference in historical context. About a year earlier Mikhail Gorbachev had been named 1987's "Man of the Year" by *Time* magazine, which viewed attempts at reform in the Soviet Union as real and significant. According to the *Time* article, "Molded by famine and war, promised a measure of hope after Stalin's demise and then abruptly disillusioned, Gorbachev is not the sort of man who would willingly drag his country back into the dark days of repression, economic hardship and international obloquy."

In November 1989, ten months after the Stormer conference, the Berlin Wall was toppled, soon to be followed by the collapse of Soviet bloc communism. In January 1990 *Time* named Gorbachev "Man of the Decade," trumpeting that

> His commitment to the still elusive goal of perestroika, his effort to make the economy produce what the people want to consume, and glasnost, an end to systematic official lying, have transformed the Soviet Union and made possible a transformation of international relations as well. . . . In the U.S.S.R. the old order is not just passing; it is already on what Leon Trotsky called the trash heap of history.[43]

But for the attendees at the Stormer conference in February of 1989, *perestroika* and *glasnost* were just so much bland borscht dished out to lull Americans into letting their guard down against global communist subversion. The sentiment at the conference was that, even if the Soviet Union retreated from communism, there would still be communist subversives and their secular humanist allies bent on destroying the United States from within.

At his conference Stormer explained the functional link between communism and humanism: "If you have millions of people conditioned to think a certain way by the humanists, it only takes a few communists to manipulate them." He argued that secularists, liberals, humanists, and socialists pave the way for collectivism and communism due to their naive belief that "man" is basically good, when true Christian conservatives know that man is basically evil and finds goodness only through submission to God.

Stormer further argued that, because of their erroneous belief in evolution, all humanists think that communism will eventually evolve in a positive direction. Also, because of the pervasive acceptance of modern psychology, humanists believe man is a product of his environment, the corollary supposedly being that if communists do something bad, it really isn't their fault. Of course, Stormer explained, true Christian conservatives realize that communists are the embodiment of evil.

Treason and conspiracy were the main themes of the conference. Stormer had a revised and updated edition of his book *None Dare Call It Treason* for sale at the conference, and its contents formed the backbone of the presentations. The book's back cover summarized the text as detailing "the communist–socialist conspiracy to enslave America" and documenting "the concurrent decay in America's schools, churches, and press which has conditioned the American people to accept 20 years of retreat in the face of the communist enemy." Oliver North's removal from government service and the prosecution of him for his Iran–Contra involvements were mentioned repeatedly as proof of treason in high places.

Another key theme constantly reiterated at the Stormer conference was that the American intelligence community was so hamstrung by laws, court decisions, federal regulations, and the cabal of traitors that it was not yet able adequately to penetrate subversive political movements in America. This central thesis of the countersubversion network explains why it not only cooperates with the FBI but also establishes parallel private surveillance and data storage institutions.

Howard Phillips, a long-time ultraconservative activist and founder of the Conservative Caucus, conducted several workshops. Phillips shared Stormer's distaste and disdain for the Reagan and Bush administrations, for example, repeatedly referring to the first Bush term as the "third Bush Administration." Phillips asserted that "the Western Alliance is coming apart at the seams" and suggested that the United States should "take back the Panama Canal" and show "support for South Africa as a bulwark against communism." He also spoke on the topic "How U.S. Taxpayers Finance Perversion and Domestic Leftists." According to Phillips, the solution to the nation's problems was to create a new political party capable of overcoming subversives ensconced in the two major parties and in the government. Before long he would do just that.

The audience in Worcester bought most of what Stormer had to say. The only serious discussion in the workshops centered on the pervasiveness of the conspiracy and the relative importance of Trilateralists, Bilderbergers, the Council on Foreign Relations, and Fabian Socialists in trying to induce the nation's downfall.

Completing the Transition

According to George Marsden, the shift in focus to the secular humanist demon

> revitalized fundamentalist conspiracy theory. Fundamentalists always had been alarmed at moral decline within America but often had been vague as to whom, other than the Devil, to blame. The "secular humanist" thesis gave this central concern a clearer focus that was more plausible and of wider appeal than the old mono-causal communist-conspiracy accounts. Communism and socialism could, of course, be fit right into the humanist picture; but so could all the moral and legal changes at home without implausible scenarios of Russian agents infiltrating American schools, government, reform movements, and mainline churches.[44]

As a result of this gradual shift in targets, sectors of the new Christian Right began to join the John Birch Society and the Liberty Lobby as major sources of conspiracist narrative in the United States.

The collapse of communism in Europe prompted a shift in focus to other aspects of the alleged conspiracy—the collectivism and statism promoted by liberalism and secular humanism. The more secular hard-right groups had long contended that behind Moscow Bolshevism and Wall Street capitalism were the same shadowy secret elites with their traitorous allies in Washington. Removing Soviet communists from the alleged secret team still left other dangerous players in the field.

With the collapse of the Cold War, militant anticommunism expanded into a conceptual framework that can usefully be called "militant anti-collectivism," an umbrella for fighting the globalist New World Order, the United Nations, Chinese communism, liberal New Deal Democrats, and the so-called tyranny of political correctness.

For the Right, the term "New World Order" became synonymous with liberal collectivist secular humanism and its drive toward tyrannical globalism. This theme was picked up in the 1990s as the basis for conspiracy theories spread by the Patriot and armed citizens militia movements.

THE NEW RIGHT BREAKS APART

The Reagan presidency was only a mixed success for New Right activists. Brought to power by a broad coalition of various right-wing forces and various sectors of the business community, Reagan set priorities that frustrated and disappointed some of his supporters. Broadly speaking, the administration focused on economic and military issues much more than social policies. Businesses and the wealthy benefited from major cuts in taxes and in environmental, safety, and labor regulations, as well as major increases in military spending. Economic deregulation, an intensified Cold War, and increased military intervention in Central America and elsewhere pleased many libertarians and militarists within the New Right. But many Christian rightists felt betrayed by the failure to deliver on promises to outlaw abortions, sanction prayer in the public schools, and eliminate the Department of Education. In addition, some key hard-right activists such as Phillips and Viguerie denounced Reagan for negotiating with the Soviets over arms reductions, thus joining with militarists (at least temporarily) to drive another wedge into the New Right.[45]

One response was Pat Robertson's 1988 presidential campaign in the Republican primaries, which was marked by populist antielite rhetoric and helped to strengthen the Christian Right's grassroots organizational base. Robertson dropped out of the race after a disappointing showing in the southern primaries, but his campaign laid the basis for the Christian Coalition, founded in 1989, which soon became a major vehicle for gaining influence within the Republican Party (see Chapter 12).[46]

George Bush, widely identified with multinational elites, won the presidency in 1988. This further alienated the Christian Right from mainstream Republicanism, despite Bush's selection of Dan Quayle as a running mate to pacify social traditionalists. The Christian Right briefly kept its ties to the Bush White House through chief of staff John H. Sununu, who worked closely with Paul Weyrich's Free Congress Foundation. The Bush White House also staffed an outreach office to maintain liaison with evangelicals. Eventually, however, pragmatic secular operatives pushed social traditionalists out of the Oval Office.

After the 1988 election the New Right coalition began to break apart. When the Berlin Wall fell in 1989, the glue of anticommunism was no longer strong enough to bind together the voting blocs, organizations, and movements that constituted the New Right.

A particularly sharp fight developed between neoconservatives and self-styled "paleoconservatives."[47] Neoconservatives, including many Jewish and Catholic intellectuals rooted in Cold War liberalism, clustered around publications such as *Public Interest* and *Commentary* and organizations such as the Committee on the Present Danger. They emphasized foreign policy, where they advocated aggressive anticommunism, U.S. global dominance, and international alliances. Although they attacked feminism, gay rights, and multiculturalism, "neocons" often placed less emphasis on social policy issues, and many of them opposed school prayer or a ban on abortion. In addition, many neocons supported limited social welfare programs and nonrestrictive immigration policies.

Paleoconservatives embraced traditionalist Christian morality, Eurocentric monoculturalism, isolationist nationalism, and a complete end to social programs. The Rockford Institute, the Ludwig von Mises Institute, and the Independent Institute were major paleoconservative havens.[48] Paleocons resented the influence of neocons such as Jean Kirkpatrick, Elliott Abrams, and William Bennett within the Reagan and Bush administrations, and they decried a neocon "takeover" of Old Right institutions such as the American Enterprise Institute and the Hoover Institution, as well as influential foundations such as Bradley, Olin, Scaife, and Smith Richardson.[49] Neoconservatives charged, rightly, that the paleocons were tainted with antisemitism and xenophobia.[50]

The neocon–paleocon feud had smoldered since the mid-1980s, but it intensified in 1990 when President Bush massed troops in Saudi Arabia to fight a war with Iraq. Paleocons, as isolationists, generally opposed the action and warned of pro-Israeli "dual-loyalists" exerting too much influence over U.S. foreign policy. Neoconservatives, who were overwhelmingly interventionist and strongly pro-Zionist, supported the war and denounced many of their former partners in Cold War anticommunism as bigots and antisemites. Paleocon Patrick J. Buchanan further highlighted the divisions within the former New Right coalition with his campaigns for the Republican presidential nomination in 1992 and 1996, and his third party aspirations in 2000.

The Free Congress Foundation and the Heritage Foundation, New Right coalition builders, held a sort of middle position in the conflict between neocons and paleocons. Despite their cultural and ideological affinities with the paleocons, these organizations refused to abandon right-wing internationalism or pro-Zionism and leaned overall more to the neocon side of the dispute. Pat Robertson's Christian Coalition also pursued a balancing act between the demands of various constituencies.

From 1988 to 1996 the Christian Right was the most successful of the New Right sectors at building a mass base and pulling together a coalition that dominated much of the Republican Party and much of the country's political and cultural debate.

THE LEGACY OF PACKAGED SCAPEGOATING

That the New Right could break up and spin off several groups that continued to operate with some level of success is in part due to the network of national and statewide institutions that assisted the rise of the New Right and influenced government policy during the Reagan and Bush administrations.[51] A major legacy of this infrastructure was the increased influence of packaged scapegoating—the skillful coding and presentation of scapegoating in forms easily digested by corporate media.

The increased demand for packaged information by reporters and editors with diminishing resources to conduct their own thorough research and investigations has enhanced the ability of ideological groups to slip glib but dubious material directly into the corporate media.

As Lawrence Soley concluded in his article on right-wing foundations and think tanks,

> While the research of conservative think tanks isn't serious, their lobbying efforts on behalf of corporate contributors are. . . . Although information on the shallowness of [conservative] think tank research is available to the news media, reporters appear to have turned their backs on it in order to get easy access to a soundbite or quote. Rather than asking think tank representatives hard questions about their funding and their lobbying efforts, reporters turn to them for their ideologically prefabricated opinions on domestic and foreign affairs. And that's the way the news gets made.[52]

The National Council for Research on Women documented a good example of this process in an analysis of how the false idea that campuses were under siege by radical "PC Police" was constructed.[53]

A tremendous range of right-wing information exchange takes place within traditional and alternative media throughout the United States. Mainstream analysts discount much of this massive information network when calculating the political clout of the Right, and they also overlook an important relationship between right-wing alternative media and corporate media.[54]

Secular conservatives have long molded public opinion in major traditional corporate media, especially in large-circulation publications such as *Reader's Digest*, on conservative talk-radio and talk-TV programs, and even through TV drama series such as *I Led Three Lives*, and *The FBI*. But during the 1980s and 1990s the Right further refined its use of the media, especially direct mail, books, magazines, radio, television, and the Internet.

Ellen Messer-Davidow and others have studied the elaborate apparatus through which the Right manufactures and markets political claims misrepresented as scholarly knowledge.[55] Many of the movement's ideas and proposals are first developed at think tanks funded by right-wing foundations and corporations. After these ideas are sharpened through feedback at conferences and other meetings, they are field-tested within right-wing alternative media, such as small-circulation newsletters, journals, direct-mail appeals, and websites. As popular themes that resonate with conservative audiences emerge, they are moved into more mainstream corporate media through columns by conservative luminaries, press releases picked up as articles in the print media, conversations on radio talk shows, and discussions on TV news roundtables.

As the increasingly refined arguments reach a broader audience, they help mobilize mass constituencies for rightist ideas. This in turn adds to the impression that all fresh ideas are coming from the right, as there is no comparable left infrastructure for the refinement and distribution of ideas.[56] For example, between 1990 and 1993, four influential conservative magazines

(*National Interest, Public Interest, The New Criterion,* and *American Spectator*) received a total of $2.7 million in grants from conservative foundations, while the four major progressive magazines (*The Nation, The Progressive, In These Times,* and *Mother Jones*) received less than 10 percent of that amount, under $270,000 from liberal and left foundations.[57]

Right-wing foundations and funders do provide important start-up money for new organizations and assist the growth and continuity of existing organizations, but the New Right raised most of its funds from solicitations through direct mail and electronic media.

CONCLUSION

Under the banner of the Culture War, Christian Right leaders increasingly focused anxiety over changing sex roles and the unfinished equalization of power between men and women on the convenient scapegoats of the feminist and abortion rights movements. They steered public fears over AIDS toward a vast conspiracy theory of homosexual intrigue. They redirected the legitimate concerns of parents over the quality of education in the public schools to the scapegoats of modern curricula, sex education, materials tolerant of gays, and AIDS awareness programs. They shifted the desperation of unemployment and underemployment to the scapegoat of the well-stereotyped undeserving poor bleeding society through welfare. And they shifted the problem of an unfair economic structure and an overloaded criminal justice system onto the scapegoat of liberal secular humanism and its lack of God-centered morality.

The New Right's partial fragmentation disrupted ultraconservative ranks. But the rise of secular humanist conspiracy theory and the resurgence of White racial nationalism demonstrated ultraconservatives' ability to adapt to the new circumstances that followed the end of the Cold War. The Christian Right also continued to develop new strategies and sought to balance the conflicting pressures of insurgent ideologues, apocalyptic dominionists, and reformist pragmatists.

Meanwhile, a growing infrastructure of think tanks, policy groups, and experts bombarded the media with studies that had the veneer of academic research but lacked substance and did not have to face the scrutiny of true peer review. The result was a political debate sidetracked by dubious statistics, demonization of the poor and weak, and scapegoating of people of color, women, immigrants, and gays and lesbians, among others.

12

DOMINION THEOLOGY
AND CHRISTIAN NATIONALISM

Hard-Line Ideology versus Pragmatism

During the 1980s and 1990s, as the Christian Right became a major political force, a tension developed within the movement between hard-line ideological commitment and the calculated pursuit of power. On the hard-line side was a tendency to reject all forms of secularism and to demand theocratic control over all areas of society. On the pragmatic side was an impulse to cut a deal with the existing power structure—to accept the established political framework in exchange for certain core demands and a role as power broker. These two poles of thought did not define two distinct factions but, rather, interacted in various ways to produce a range of viewpoints and strategic approaches.

Two Christian Right subcultures, in particular, pressured the movement as a whole to reject compromises seen as betraying Christian principles. These subcultures were Protestant Christian Reconstructionism and apocalyptic Catholic traditionalism. They took the lead in shaping *dominionism*—the theocratic idea that Christian men are called upon by God to exercise dominion over sinful secular society by taking control of political and cultural institutions. Dominionism pervaded the Christian Right, either in "hard" form, demanding the literal reimposition of biblical law, or as "soft dominionism," advocating more limited systems of Christian control.[1] A broad dominionist movement spread from independent Protestant evangelical churches and traditionalist Catholic circles to influence theological debates in mainstream Protestantism and Catholicism.

Dominion theology contributed to the growth of hard-line splinter groups and small cells that promoted violent activism. The most militant of the ardent dominionists were behind the increased violence in the antiabortion movement, the nastiest of the attacks on gays and lesbians, and a second wave of battles over alleged secular humanist influence in the public schools. At the same time, soft dominionism influenced electorally oriented mass organizations such as the Christian Coalition.

In this chapter we will outline the core features of Christian Reconstructionism and Catholic traditionalism and will explore dominionist influence within a number of Christian Right organizations. We will focus particularly on Pat Robertson's Christian Coalition as a major organization within which the tension between ideological principle and the quest for power unfolded with particular vividness.

CHRISTIAN RECONSTRUCTIONISM

Christian Reconstructionism is a postmillennial theology that argues that the U.S. Constitution is merely a codicil to Christian biblical law. It is rooted in militant early Calvinism and the idea of America as a Christian redeemer nation. Among the leading Reconstructionist ideologues are R. J. Rushdoony, Gary North, David Chilton, and Greg Bahnsen.[2]

Unlike the majority of evangelicals, Reconstructionists are postmillennialists, who believe "Christ will return to earth only after the Holy Spirit has empowered the church to advance Christ's kingdom in time and history." As Sara Diamond notes, while many premillennialists are concerned with converting as many people as possible before the End Times, postmillennialists are more concerned with long-term structural changes in society.[3]

As Fred Clarkson explains:

> Reconstructionism is a theology that arose out of conservative Presbyterianism (Reformed and Orthodox), which proposes that contemporary application of the laws of Old Testament Israel, or "Biblical Law," is the basis for reconstructing society toward the Kingdom of God on earth.
>
> Reconstructionism argues that the Bible is to be the governing text for all areas of life—such as government, education, law, and the arts, not merely "social" or "moral" issues like pornography, homosexuality, and abortion. Reconstructionists have formulated a "Biblical world view" and "Biblical principles" by which to examine contemporary matters.[4]

Reconstructionist theologian David Chilton explains that "The Christian goal for the world is the universal development of Biblical theocratic republics, in which every area of life is redeemed and placed under the Lordship of Jesus Christ and the rule of God's law."

According to Clarkson:

> More broadly, Reconstructionists believe that there are three main areas of governance: family government, church government, and civil government. Under God's covenant, the nuclear family is the basic unit. The husband is the head of the family, and wife and children are "in submission" to him. In turn, the husband "submits" to Jesus and to God's laws as detailed in the Old

Testament. The church has its own ecclesiastical structure and governance. Civil government exists to implement God's laws. All three institutions are under Biblical Law, the implementation of which is called "theonomy."[5]

The Reconstructionist conception of biblical law includes abolishing the welfare state and all public services, including public schools, as well as labor unions and laws protecting civil rights, the environment, and workplace health and safety. "A radically unfettered capitalism (except in so far as it clashed with Biblical Law) would prevail. . . . Government functions, including taxes, would be primarily at the county level." Only men from biblically correct churches could vote or hold office. The death penalty would be applicable as punishment for homosexuality, adultery, heresy, striking a parent, and, in the case of women, having an abortion or "unchastity before marriage."[6]

Reconstructionism's theocratic vision represents a new form of clerical fascist politics. Like other fascist currents, Reconstructionism aims to rally a mass movement to sweep away pluralist institutions and the evil elites who control them; it calls for totalitarian unity and collective rebirth through the elimination of the demons that it identifies (i.e., scapegoats). Unlike most other fascist currents in the United States, Reconstructionism is not rooted in European traditions such as Mussolini's Italy or Hitler's Germany, and the unity it seeks is based on religion rather than nation or race. Like the Posse Comitatus and some other neonazi groups, Reconstructionists advocate a form of *social totalitarianism*, administered mainly through local governments and private institutions such as the church and the family, rather than the classical fascist goal of a highly centralized nation-state.

The nonprofit Chalcedon Foundation promoted the Reconstructionist ideology of its founder and president, Dr. R. J. Rushdoony. The foundation controlled *The Chalcedon Report*, *The Journal of Christian Reconstruction*, Christian Tape Productions, and a separate tax-exempt publishing entity, Ross House Books. Chalcedon literature bragged that "Newsweek magazine (Feb. 2, 1981) designated us the 'think tank' of the religious right."

Chalcedon supporters included two well-known ultraconservative activists: education activist Samuel L. Blumenfeld and Howard Phillips of the U.S. Taxpayers Party. In a fund-raising letter for Chalcedon, Phillips wrote, "Even as the Twentieth Century, with its extraordinary record of evil, draws to a close, we see all around us signs of Christian reconstructionism—evidence of our belief that God's kingdom will be established on earth as it is in Heaven." Blumenfeld's bylined articles have appeared in *The Chalcedon Report*, and he has praised R. J. Rushdoony as an expert on "constitutional government" in a flyer for Ross House Books, which works cooperatively with Chalcedon and distributes "works by Chalcedon writers." Since most reporters were largely ignorant of the Christian Reconstructionist movement, Blumenfeld and Phillips were seldom asked to defend their antidemocratic ideas.[7]

During the 1990s Christian Reconstructionists played an important role in the most militant wing of the antiabortion movement. Rev. Paul J. Hill, who headed the Pensacola antiabortion group Defensive Action and who murdered Dr. John Britton and clinic escort James Barrett in 1994, was a former minister in the Orthodox Presbyterian Church, many of whose leaders had close ties to Chalcedon. Missionaries to the Preborn, one of the most violent antiabortion groups, was led by three Christian Reconstructionists—Matthew Trewhella, Joseph Foreman, and Gary McCullough.[8] Operation Rescue founder Randall Terry (who joined with Trewhella in supporting Howard Phillips's U.S. Taxpayers Party) echoed Reconstructionism's dominion theology in such statements as "Our goal is a Christian nation. We have a biblical duty, we are called by God to conquer this country."[9]

CATHOLIC MARIANIST APOCALYPTICS

Unlike the Protestant advocates of Christian Reconstructionism, traditionalist Catholics with ties to the Christian Right were generally reactionary rather than fascist. In other words, instead of a totalitarian new order they advocated a return to the "good old days" before the spread of liberalization within the Church and secularism in society at large. Many traditionalist Catholics embraced Marianism, a diverse subculture within the Church that insisted upon special devotion to the Virgin Mary. Some Marianist groups clashed with the Church hierarchy over what the appropriate amount of adoration should be for the Virgin Mary, as compared to Jesus Christ. Some Marianists reported sightings or apparitions of the Virgin Mary, and these were sometimes considered End Times warnings.[10]

The basic message of the Marianist magazine *Fatima Crusader*, for example, was that we are in the apocalyptic End Times and are facing a direct struggle with Satan. Furthermore, the magazine urged that the actions and religious devotions of true Catholics be based on End Times warnings and predictions made in appearances by the Virgin Mary and Jesus Christ before the Catholic faithful.[11]

The Virgin Mary appeared several times before three children in Fatima, Portugal, in 1917, and a shrine to Our Lady of Fatima was built on the site. A key message delivered at Fatima was the need to carry out the consecration and conversion of Russia to Christianity.[12] This mandate, serendipitously benefited the anticommunist movement within Catholicism, a development that in turn had sociopolitical consequences in Europe and the United States.

This task might have seemed less pressing after the collapse of godless communism in Russia. In the worldview of *The Fatima Crusader*, however, Russian tyranny could come in many forms. *The Fatima Crusader*'s editorial position was that the predictions at Fatima referred to the threat of a Russian-style collectivist One World Government ushered in by socialists, liberals, secular humanists, homosexuals, abortionists, and followers of the New Age spirituality movement. Articles in *The Fatima Crusader* also wove in millennialist references to biblical prophecies about the End Times struggles against Satan and the Antichrist.

In the Summer 1994 issue of the Marianist *Fatima Family Messenger*, Charles Martel wrote, in an article on "The Antichrist," that "The Church is in a shambles" characterized by:

- Open rebellion against authority,
- Enthusiasm for abortion, contraception, divorce, etc.,
- Addition of many clerics to Marxism,
- Presence of un-Catholic teachings in seminaries and universities,
- Widespread and well organized homosexual network,
- Acceptance of New Age belief as the latest of ecumenism.[13]

Martel argues that "there is much more indisputable evidence available which indicates that the Antichrist is here and is in command."[14]

Another hard-right Catholic publication with apocalyptic themes was the *Michael Journal*, which included conspiracist articles about the parasitic nature of financial elites that reflected historic antisemitic themes. The *Michael Journal* celebrated the memory of Father Coughlin, the Catholic priest whose national radio programs in the 1930s moved from liberal populism to antisemitism and eventually to fascist demagoguery. The newspaper described Coughlin as a man "who courageously denounced the bankers' debt-money system." According to the *Michael Journal*, "The Illuminati are elite men, those on the top, who control the International Bankers to control, for evil purposes, the entire world." Followers of the *Michael Journal* lobbied against the Massachusetts seat belt law, believing it was a collectivist step toward satanic One World Government. The newspaper featured an article titled "The Beast of the Apocalypse: 666," which proclaimed that "Satan's redoubtable ally" was a "gigantic auto-programming computer" in Brussels at the headquarters of the European Common Market.[15]

Like Reconstructionists, right-wing Catholic Marianists and apocalyptics were a significant force in the militant wing of the antiabortion movement. Human Life International (HLI), a right-wing apocalyptic Catholic group, was a major source of antiabortion materials for such activists. HLI also published and distributed books that blended conspiracist thinking and misogyny, with titles such as *Sex Education: The Final Plague, The Feminist Takeover,* and *Ungodly Rage: The Hidden Face of Catholic Feminism.* HLI also distributed William T. Still's book *New World Order: The Ancient Plan of Secret Societies,* which features anti-Freemason and implicit anti-Jewish themes.[16] In a devastating critique of Human Life International in Planned Parenthood's *Front Lines Research* newsletter, investigative journalists Karen Branan and Frederick Clarkson reviewed in detail how the HLI routinely promoted conspiracist, hard-right, theocratic, and antisemitic ideas.[17]

HLI founder Fr. Paul Marx and other authors published or distributed by HLI made bigoted allegations about Jewish doctors and abortion that drew rebukes for antisemitism from more responsible leaders in the Catholic Church. Msgr. George G. Higgins addressed this issue in a column published in *Catholic New York*:

> Over the years, Human Life International . . . has proven a divisive force within the pro-life movement, frequently attacking the Catholic Hierarchy of the United States both individually and as a conference for what Father Marx viewed as lapses from ideological purity. Alongside this, there has been what I would call a flirtation with anti-Semitism.[18]

Msgr. Higgins notes that the HLI's practice of listing many bishops as advisers created confusion among persons who might have difficulty distinguishing "the preachments of HLI from the official teaching of the Church, which clearly condemns forays into anti-Semitism."[19] Human Life International proudly listed in its publications the regular meetings its leaders had with officials in the Catholic hierarchy across the nation and around the world.[20]

THE REVEREND MOON NETWORK

A different kind of far-right religious organization was Rev. Sun Myung Moon's international network, centered in the Unification Church. With an idiosyncratic version of Christianity that promoted Moon as the successor to Jesus, the Unification Church maintained a dictatorial internal structure to build, in Moon's words, "an automatic theocracy to rule the world." Although not always accepted as a part of the Christian Right, the Moon network cultivated ties with Christian Right and other ultraconservative leaders in the United States, the Reagan administration, the World Anti-Communist League, the Korean CIA, and Japanese organized crime.[21]

THE SPREAD OF SOFT DOMINIONISM

One group that helped elevate soft dominionism within the Christian Right was the Coalition on Revival (COR). Founded in 1982, COR brought together a number of influential Christian Right leaders with the aim of finding theological and political common ground, for example, between pre- and postmillenialists. Militant antiabortion activist Randall Terry, founder of Operation Rescue, wrote for COR's magazine, *Crosswinds*, and signed its "Manifesto for the Christian Church." The text proclaimed that America should "function as a Christian nation" and that the "world will not know how to live or which direction to go without the Church's Biblical influence on its theories, laws, actions, and institutions."[22] The call included a pledge to oppose such "social moral evils" as:

> abortion on demand, infanticide, and euthanasia . . . adultery, fornication, homosexuality, bestiality . . . sexual entertainment . . . state usurpation of parental rights and God-given liberties . . . statist-collectivist theft from citizens through devaluation of their money and redistribution of their wealth . . . atheism, moral relativism, and evolutionism taught as a monopoly viewpoint in the public schools [and] Communism/Marxism, fascism, Nazism and the one-world government of the New Age Movement.[23]

All COR leaders were required to sign "Commitment Sheets" that stated they were "willing to submit to the hierarchical order that God has created in which we are willing to submit as to Christ to employers, civil government and church leaders, and within families, wives to their husbands and children to their parents." A set of core COR tenets called the "25 Articles" stated that everyone, "Jew or Gentile, believer or unbeliever, private person or public official," has a "moral and juridical obligation before God to submit to Christ's Lordship over every aspect of his life in thought, word, and deed."[24]

An action plan issued in 1990 by COR's political arm, the National Coordinating Council (NCC), called for abolishing all public schools, the Internal Revenue Service, and the Federal Reserve by the year 2000. Years before the rise of the armed citizens militia movement, which included so-called common-law courts, NCC called for establishing "county militias" and a system of "Christian" courts.[25]

The COR steering committee included Reconstructionist leaders such as R. J. Rushdoony and Gary North as well as leaders of the "Shepherding" movement, such as Bob Mumford and Dennis Peacocke. Shepherding, a controversial submovement within pentacostal and charismatic churches, required members to submit to the authority of "shepherds" in all areas of life. Under various names such as "discipleship," "cell groups," and "covenant communities," the Shepherding movement established intensely hierarchical chains of control and sought to grow exponentially through continuous recruitment. Many Shepherding networks used secrecy to evade criticism. Shepherding organizations included Christian Growth Ministries and Maranatha Ministries among Protestants, and Sword of the Spirit and People of Praise among Catholic charismatics. Through COR and other organs, there was considerable cross-fertilization between Reconstructionism, with its neofascist vision of the future, and Shepherding, with its hierarchical and totalitarian system of organization. Clarkson wrote in 1994 that "nowhere . . . is Reconstructionism . . . having a more dramatic impact than in Pentacostal and charismatic churches."[26]

THE RUTHERFORD INSTITUTE

Another case study of how soft dominionism influenced a major Christian Right group is the Rutherford Institute, run by attorney John W. Whitehead. Whitehead often described Rutherford in innocuous terms, such as, "a civil liberties organization dedicated to defending religious freedom and the sanctity of human life."[27] Yet, from the beginning, the Rutherford Institute pursued a highly politicized ultraconservative agenda. Whitehead consistently put forward an apocalyptic conspiracist vision of devout Christian activists under concerted attack by corrupt and repressive government officials allied with godless and immoral secular humanism. And, although Whitehead later attempted to minimize his relationship to Reconstructionism, Reconstructionist leader R. J. Rushdoony supported the founding of the Rutherford Institute and was an early board member.[28]

In discussing the Rutherford Institute, Sara Diamond notes that "Christians deserve as much legal protection as anyone else," but she then argues that in much of Rutherford's work "there's a fine line between defending the interests of clients and stepping on the rights of other people":

> In a recent commentary sent to Christian radio stations, Rutherford Institute president John Whitehead argues that workplace seminars on gay rights are a form of "religious discrimination" against employees who are "told to rid themselves of stereotypes about gays and to accept homosexuality as a valid lifestyle choice."
>
> In an odd assertion of victim status, Whitehead claims Christian military personnel may jeopardize their careers if they "speak out against homosexuality. . . . The immediate remedy is for the military to exempt religious people from compelled personal acceptance of homosexuality."[29]

From time to time the Rutherford Institute's magazine carried broad-based articles to buttress its claim that it was just like an American Civil Liberties Union for people of faith. For example, the September 1996 issue, with a cover story on "Politics & Religion: A Recipe for Disaster," included interviews with political commentators such as E. J. Dionne, Jr., and Larry Sabato—and even a column by Barry W. Lynn, executive director of Americans United for Separation of Church and State (AUSCS).

But more in keeping with its conspiracist worldview was the August 1995 special issue, "A Nation on the Edge," with an article claiming that the federal government's response following the Oklahoma City bombing "served to underline many Americans' greatest fear"—namely, a "strong-armed government moving the country toward a dictatorial state."[30] That same issue featured a straight-faced interview with militia demagogue Linda Thompson. The interview raised some soft criticisms but overall served to promote her conspiracist views as at least worthy of consideration.[31]

In the same issue, Free Congress Foundation President Paul Weyrich offered a diatribe against government under President Clinton and his liberal allies. Weyrich portrayed the United States as a country where "God-fearing, law-abiding, taxpaying citizens" live under a statist globalist tyranny. He concluded that a nation with a government that is in opposition to his hard-right view of constitutional and godly laws "will deserve the hatred of God and its people."[32]

In his earlier works, Whitehead saw an atheistic secular humanist plan to subvert America into tyranny by diverting it from a society "operated from a set of presuppositions largely derived from the Christian ethic."[33] He warned that the "loss of traditional values" and the "rise of cosmic secularism" in the United States had created conditions with "ominous parallels to pre-Nazi Germany and the beginning of claims of total ownership by the state."[34] He suggested that the U.S. government had launched a campaign to "circumscribe" and "persecute" the Christian Church.[35] Whitehead urged Christians to resist the secular state through a variety of means, including legislation, litigation, and civil disobedience.[36]

Whitehead's views were deeply influenced by his mentor, Francis A. Schaeffer, a pioneer of dominion theology. In the acknowledgments to his 1987 book *The Stealing of America*, Whitehead declared that "Francis A. Schaeffer's advice and teachings on the essential priorities are reflected in the following pages. Dr. Schaeffer stands as one of the great philosophers of our times." According to Skipp Porteous, Whitehead and the Institute maintained that "courts must place themselves under the authority of God's law" and "all of civil affairs and government, including law, should be based upon principles found in the Bible."[37]

In the late 1990s Whitehead claimed he had changed his earlier views, giving a detailed interview on the subject to *Christianity Today* in December of 1998 and telling *The New York Times* that he had no political motives, only a concern for civil liberties.[38] Yet, Barry Lynn of AUSCS retorted, "Our files on the Institute go back 10 years. After examining the material, we can safely say Whitehead is not being honest in his description of his organization."[39]

CHRISTIAN RIGHT PHOENIX

Dominionism also influenced the Christian Coalition, one of the most prominent and influential Christian Right organizations of the 1990s. A mass organization geared toward winning control of the Republican Party, the Christian Coalition pursued a delicate balancing act between hard-line ideology and pragmatic power politics. The Coalition's leadership mediated in its practices between dominionist principles and interest-group tactics, between New World Order conspiracy theories and policies favorable to multinational business, and between a deep-rooted Christian Euro-centrism and strategic efforts to forge closer ties with right-wing Jews and conservative people of color.

In 1987–1988, the Christian Right was shaken by a highly publicized sex and financial scandal involving prominent televangelist Jim Bakker; this was followed by fellow televangelist Jimmy Swaggart's public confession that he had solicited prostitutes.[40] Many pundits predicted the movement's demise, especially after Pat Robertson lost to George Bush in the 1988 Republican presidential primaries. But those pundits and others who belittled the Christian Right's future overlooked two factors: the huge grassroots constituency that remained connected through an infrastructure of conferences, publications, radio and television programs, videotapes, and audiotapes; and the ideological force of devout religious belief.

The 1988 Robertson campaign organization and mailing list—together with other Robertson-controlled organs such as the Christian Broadcasting Network—provided the basis for the Christian Coalition, which Robertson and organizer Ralph Reed created in 1989. Using seasoned activists in a bid to take over the Republican Party from the ground up, the Christian Coalition moved quickly into the local and state electoral arena and recruited hundreds of thousands of members within a few years. By 1995, the organization claimed 1.5 million donors and supporters and over 1,425 local chapters.[41] The Coalition joined with other Christian Right groups, such as Lou Sheldon's Traditional Values Coalition and Beverly LaHaye's Concerned Women for America to target school boards, public libraries, and state legislatures.

The Christian Coalition marked the Christian Right's shift away from the Moral Majority's national direct-mail approach toward intensive local organizing. The new organization also encompassed a somewhat broader group of right-wing Christians. The Moral Majority appealed almost entirely to fundamentalists, mainly Baptists. But Robertson, as a charismatic, was able to bring in support from many right-wing charismatics and pentacostals as well. (Charismatics had supported Robertson's 1988 campaign much more actively than fundamentalists.)[42] The Christian Coalition also launched an outreach campaign to right-wing Catholics, and even recruited a small number of Jews.

Robertson and his aides were influenced by dominion theology but sought to work within the existing political system. According to Fred Clarkson, "Robertson himself seems to lack the long-term vision of Reconstructionist thinkers, but he is clearly driven by a short-term militant 'dominion' mandate—the mandate that Christians 'Christianize' the country's social and political institutions." Reconstructionist texts were used in courses at the Robertson-controlled Regent University. ("Robertson explained that a 'regent' is one who governs in the absence of a sovereign. And that Regent U. trains students to rule, until Jesus, the absent sovereign, returns.")[43] But, while Christian Coalition leaders sometimes declared openly that "America is a Christian nation"—a claim fundamentally hostile to all non-Christians—at other times they insisted that their aim was to protect religious freedom, not impose their views on anyone.[44] Although this statement was hard to take seriously, the Christian Coalition's support during its early days for virtually all Republican candidates—including pro-choice candidates—made clear that it was more concerned with strategic advantage than ideological purity.[45]

The tension between hard-line ideology and pragmatism also shaped the Christian Coalition's response to paleoconservatism's rise and the breakup of the New Right alliance. Coalition leaders echoed paleocon rhetoric about globalist threats to U.S. sovereignty.[46] As we will detail shortly, Robertson's 1991 book *The New World Order* rehashed Birch Society and Liberty Lobby conspiracy themes. Yet, in the 1992 and 1996 Republican presidential primaries Robertson supported moderate conservatives George Bush and Bob Dole, respectively—not paleocon Pat Buchanan. In 1993, defying many of their own supporters, Christian Coalition leaders initially joined with the multinationalist business community to back the North American Free Trade Agreement (NAFTA), describing its passage as one of the few laudable accomplishments of the Clinton administration.[47]

In addition to ideological factors the Christian Coalition's delicate balancing act reflected conflicting economic and strategic considerations. Robertson's operations, like the Christian Right as a whole, traditionally depended on Sunbelt outsider business forces, who tended to be hostile to the Eastern Establishment and often embraced Birchite conspiracism and isolationism. But, as its political influence grew, the Christian Coalition was concerned not to antagonize more moderate allies, and needed to cultivate friendly relations with at least some business multinationalists if the organization was to stand a chance of winning control of the Republican Party.

In addition, Robertson was himself an international businessman. His nonprofit Christian Broadcasting Network operated on several continents, and his for-profit International Family Entertainment (IFE) business had broadcasting operations in Europe as well as the United States. *Newsweek* noted that Robertson "likes the [NAFTA] treaty's provision protecting intellectual property—including the television shows and movie syndicates."[48] In 1989, Robertson went into partnership with John Malone's Tele-Communications, Inc. (TCI), at that time the largest cable system operator in the United States and a leading member of the multinational business community. Together they formed IFE in order to buy the lucrative Family Channel from the nonprofit Christian Broadcasting Network. Robertson and his son Tim initially invested $183,000 for a majority stake in the new company; in 1997, media tycoon Rupert Murdoch purchased IFE for $1.9 billion. (The following year, AT&T acquired TCI.)[49]

ROBERTSON RESURRECTS THE ILLUMINATI

Pat Robertson's *The New World Order* appeared in September 1991. The book's opening paragraphs sketched the context in terms of global events: the recent collapse of Soviet communism, the Gulf War against Iraq, President Bush's speech proclaiming a "new world order" to justify the war, the imminent formation of the European Union (scheduled for 1992), and the advent of the third millennium of the Christian calendar only eight years away.[50]

This was the appointed time at which one of the Christian Right's leading figures had consciously decided to embrace Birchite conspiracism publicly. Robertson's book was a logical culmination of the U.S. Hard Right's shift of scapegoats—from the Red Menace of old to today's global elites behind the secular humanist conspiracy. At the same time, *The New World Order* was a direct response to the factional clashes among former New Rightists. With *The New World Order*, Robertson moved, consciously or unconsciously, to cover his right flank—to bolster his ideological credentials among conspiracist and paleocon-leaning Christian Rightists—at the same time that the Christian Coalition was developing a strong base, and an inclination for pragmatic power politics. And, because the book received almost no mainstream media criticism for several years, this rightward shift in his appeals and messages initially cost Robertson little.

In *The New World Order* Robertson resuscitated the Freemason conspiracy hinting that its influence was graphically "revealed in the great seal adopted at the founding of the United States" and found on the back of the one dollar bill. The seal, with its pyramid, eye, and Latin motto *Novus Ordo Seclorum*, is widely believed in hard-right circles to show the power of the Freemason conspiracy over the U.S. economy. The Latin motto is frequently (albeit loosely) translated to "New World Order." Robertson then linked this to biblical millennialist prophecy of a "mystery religion designed to replace the old Christian world order of Europe and America"[51]:

> In earlier chapters, we have traced the infiltration of Continental Freemasonry by the new world philosophy of the order of the Illuminati, and its subsequent role in the French revolution. We then were able to find clear documentation that the occultic-oriented secret societies claiming descent from Illuminism and the French Revolution played a seminal role in the thinking of Marx and Lenin.[52]

As both Michael Lind and Jacob Heilbrunn pointed out in separate critiques of the book published in 1995 in *The New York Review of Books*, Robertson moved beyond the Illuminati/Freemason conspiracy, incorporating allegations that originate in antisemitic sources.[53] This happened clearly in one paragraph in particular, where Robertson wrote,

In fact, one historian has asserted that wealthy and influential Europeans with direct roots to Illuminism operated a very secret society out of Geneva, which in fact controlled the Bolshevik movement. We also know that Lord Milner of the British Round Table and Jacob Schiff, of Federal Reserve Board creator Paul Warburg's banking firm, gave the essential seed money to finance the Russian Revolution.[54]

Heilbrunn traced the central themes of Robertson's allegations to three antisemitic works popular on the Far Right: Nesta Webster's *World Revolution: The Plot Against Civilization* and her *Secret Societies and Subversive Movements*, and Eustace Mullins's *Secrets of the Federal Reserve: The London Connection*. As Heilbrunn noted, the claim that Schiff financed the Russian Revolution is false; Schiff actually loaned money to the postczarist Kerensky government that was later toppled by the Bolsheviks, who never repaid the loan.

A number of other notable conspiracist works much closer to the Birch Society line are cited by Robertson.[55] Pondering the possible "link between the Continental Illuminati occultic influences on communism and British and American financial support" of communism, Robertson admitted that there was little evidence of such a link but then stated, "all of the French membership on the Trilateral Commission were members of French Freemasonry. This may just be a coincidence, or it may mean that prominent Frenchmen are also Masons, or it may actually be the missing link tying these sordid elements together."[56]

Robertson appears to have merged the Illuminati conspiracy theory with his own musings about the End Times, asserting that claimed "Members of the Illuminati at the highest levels of the order were atheists and Satanists."[57]

> I believe that the Persian Gulf War has now brought into sharp focus the great cleavage that has existed in the human race since the early beginnings of civilization in the Tigris–Euphrates Valley. On the one side are the beliefs of a portion of humanity that flowed from Abraham to the Jewish race and to the Christians of the world. There are the people of faith, the people who are part of God's world order.
>
> On the other side are the people of Babel—those who build monuments to humanity under the inspiration of Satan. Their successors in Babylon included worshipers of the goddess Astarte and the god Baal. These are the people whose religious rites included the worship of sex with cult prostitutes and cult sodomites, whose temples were adorned with eggs and phallic symbols.[58]

This account skated dangerously close to the antisemitic "good Jew/bad Jew" dichotomy of those, such as the LaRouchites, who claimed that, as rabbinical Judaism developed in Babylon, it included a cabal of evil pagan–satanic–matriarchal forces. The quoted passage also hinted of themes promoted by Christian Identity about two distinct bloodlines of the human race—God's allies and Satan's allies—locked in mortal combat ever since the sons of Abraham chose sides.

Robertson also linked populism and assassination conspiracism with a diatribe of his own against the "European bankers" behind the grand plot:

> The European bankers and money lords of America do not want interest-free government loans, nor do they want to relinquish the power they now hold over the economic and political destiny of America. Lincoln's plan to print interest-free currency, called "greenbacks," during the Civil War—instead of issuing bonds at interest in exchange for bank loans—was so revolutionary that it would have destroyed the monopoly that European bankers exercised over their nation's money. There is no hard evidence to prove it, but it is my belief that John Wilkes Booth, the man who assassinated Lincoln, was in the employ of the European bankers who wanted to nip this American populist experiment in the bud.[59]

Pat Robertson seemed unable to shake his attachment to themes and language historically linked to antisemitism. In a 1995 letter Robertson answered a supporter's question "concerning the United Nations and New World Order" by writing,

> Many people join you in asking, "What can be done?" I believe an informed coalition of evangelicals, pro-family Roman Catholics, Greek Orthodox, and other people who love America and love God can ultimately win control of our government from the small groups of internationalist bankers who have dominated the foreign policy of our nation for some time.[60]

This phraseology demonstrated Robertson's conspiracism and insensitivity to historic antisemitism, despite his claims to the contrary. While Robertson's core conspiracist thesis more resembled that of the John Birch Society than that of the Liberty Lobby, it was entirely appropriate for his critics to first rebuke him for using notorious antisemitic sources and then failing to acknowledge and apologize for doing so until public pressure forced a grudging partial apology from him.

Robertson frequently tied his conspiracist vision to apocalyptic hints that we were in the millennial "End Times," and End Times themes repeatedly appeared on his 700 *Club* television program. On one July 1998 program Robertson hinted that a tsunami in New Guinea coupled with the appearance of asteroids might be signs of the End Times foretold in Bible prophecy. Just after Christmas of 1994, the program carried a feature on new dollar bill designs being discussed to combat counterfeiting. The newscaster then cited Revelation 13 and hinted that, if the Treasury Department put new markings on paper money, the number 666—the satanic Mark of the Beast—might be hidden in the markings, and this might be a sign of the coming End Times.[61]

Robertson's apocalyptic and conspiracist views were not an aberration in the Christian Right. One of Robertson's sources was William T. Still's *New World Order: The Ancient Plan of Secret Societies*.[62] Still's book attacked the Freemasons as part of a conspiracy to control the country through the issuing of paper money, and his references to Rothschild banking interests reflected historic antisemitic theories alleging Jewish control over the economy. The back cover blurb stated that the plan "to bring all nations under one-world government" was actually "the biblical rule of the Antichrist."[63]

D. James Kennedy, senior minister of the Coral Ridge Presbyterian Church, endorsed Still's book in a back cover blurb, declaring that Still "allows the facts to speak for themselves, as he sounds an ominous warning for the 21st Century."[64] Kennedy was an influential figure in the Protestant theocratic Right, and his national conferences drew luminaries from the Republican Party such as former Vice President Dan Quayle. The Catholic antiabortion group Human Life International and other right-wing groups also distributed the Still book. Here we see apocalyptic conspiracism bridging the divide between politically active right-wing Catholics and Protestants.

Fred Clarkson studied how many contemporary Christian Right groups perpetuate the conspiracist charges against the Freemasons, noting that a struggle raged in the late 1990s "to oust the million or more Masons from the largest Baptist denomination."[65] One far-right Protestant ideologue, Gary North, complained that mainstream churches helped undermine the country by "refusing to cast out Freemasons beginning 250 years ago."[66] Some hard-right Catholics also warn of the Illuminati Freemason conspiracy.[67] Anti-Masonic diatribes are easily located on the World Wide Web.

GAINING POWER WITHIN THE REPUBLICAN PARTY

By 1992, owing largely to the Christian Coalition's grassroots organizing, a reconstituted hard-right coalition had gained control over much of the Republican Party's base. This loose alliance included both pragmatic and hard-line Christian Rightists, and smaller contingents of paleocons, business nationalists, and those portions of the Patriot and militia movements and the Far Right still willing to participate in the electoral process. The Hard Right's influence was reflected in the 1992 Republican convention.[68]

Both liberal and conservative pundits condemned the militant apocalyptic rhetoric at the 1992 Republican convention, but there is no evidence that these criticisms had a significant effect on voting outcomes. Contrary to popular opinion, the nasty and divisive convention rhetoric of Pat Buchanan, Pat Robertson, and Marilyn Quayle contributed far less to George Bush's defeat than did the issues of the economy and jobs. As Christian

Right activist Gary Bauer noted, "The fact is that George Bush enjoyed the biggest jump in the polls the morning after Pat Buchanan's speech." The Republicans gained more votes than they lost by stressing social issues and by embracing and elevating the Christian Right.[69]

While the economy was the crucial issue in 1992 for most voters, religious voting blocs were very important, and Christian Right activists helped mobilize their constituency for the Republican ticket. Kellstedt, Green, Guth, and Smidt contend that "the basic building blocs of contemporary American party coalitions are ethnoreligious groups, with their distinct values"; nonetheless, "the voters' response to economic stress is best understood against the baseline of fundamental cultural cleavages." They found that those highly committed in all religious traditions were also more conservative on social issues. They noted a significant "widening gulf between Evangelicals and Seculars," concluding that a new kind of party alignment may be appearing: a division between religious and nonreligious voters, replacing the old ethnoreligious politics based on cleavages between different religious traditions. Other research found these cleavages were not determined by denominational affiliation, but personal religious views and level of religious commitment that varied within denominations.[70]

In 1994 the Republicans regained control of both houses of Congress for the first time in four decades. The Hard Right's control of significant sectors of the party helped to sweep a large number of right-wing politicians into the House of Representatives. Some of them were steeped in apocalyptic demonization and conspiracist scapegoating; a few even echoed the rhetoric of the Patriot and armed citizens militia movements.[71]

Christian Right influence within the Republican Party remained significant. According to Sara Diamond, "Exit poll data indicate that about 25 percent of the people who voted in November 1994 were white evangelical Christians. Among these, about two-thirds voted Republican." And, in 1996,

> against the backdrop of generally low voter turnout, about 29% of those who did vote . . . were self-identified born-again Christians who frequently attended church. Another exit poll indicated that white, self-identified constituents of the Christian Right represented 17% of all voters. Among this 17% bloc, 65% voted for Dole and 26% for Clinton, meaning that Dole would have fared far worse without loyal Christian Right voters.[72]

A thorough study of voting patterns, issues, and constituencies convinced Teixeira and Rogers that manipulation of economic populist themes has been the key factor for predicting voter support for Republican candidates since the 1970s, when the Southern Strategy was implemented.[73] They found that cultural issues were less important than economic concerns for most voters. So, while the Christian Right had become the party activists, most voters (including evangelicals with diverse political and theological allegiances) voted their perception of economic issues. At the same time, many economic issues became highly racialized through being framed as the government's failure to control crime, drugs, welfare, and immigration. This framework lent itself to populist political rhetoric about liberal elites, tax-and-spend liberals, and liberal coddling of the undeserving poor.

A TRUE RAINBOW COALITION?

Alarmed at the Christian Right's growing power within the Republican Party, Democratic leaders and several liberal organizations counterattacked. Using classic centrist/extremist rhetoric, they denounced the "Christian radical Right" as a dangerous fringe force that threatened existent democratic institutions. Sara Diamond notes that this centrist propaganda "served to distract public awareness from the organic relationships between right-wing movements and political elites," and that the term "radical Right" also involved an implicit swipe at the radical Left.[74]

For years, neoconservatives had generally tolerated antisemitism among their Christian Right allies, as well as differences over such issues as school prayer and even abortion. This silence continued after the New Right's breakup and the neocon–paleocon split—primarily because, unlike the anti-Zionist paleocons, most Christian Right leaders strongly supported the Israeli government. But in 1994 some neocons suddenly discovered Christian Right antisemitism. The Anti-Defamation League, which had generally followed a neocon course, issued a report criticizing the Christian Right and citing antisemitism in Robertson's *The New World Order*. In February 1995, three months after the Republicans regained control of Congress, former neocon Michael Lind published his detailed attack on Robertson's "Grand International Conspiracy Theory" in *The New York Review of Books*, which was soon echoed in *The New York Times*. Robertson denied that his book was antisemitic, denied that he referred to the United States as a "Christian nation," and stressed his pro-Zionist stance. He said his organization had attracted Jewish supporters. (In 1996, a Christian Coalition aide said Jews made up two percent of membership.) Leading Jewish neocons such as Irving Kristol, Midge Decter, and Gertrude Himmelfarb also defended the Christian Right, declaring that on "the survival of Israel, the Jews have no more stalwart friends than evangelical Christians."[75]

As the Robertson forces conducted damage control regarding the issue of antisemitism, they also sought to change their image as a movement of and for White people. In 1993 the Christian Coalition announced a campaign to recruit Blacks and Latinos. In 1996, announcing a fund-raising drive for Black and White churches targeted by arsonists, Coalition executive director Ralph Reed declared that "the white evangelical church was

not only on the sidelines but on the wrong side" of the civil rights movement, which he described as "the most central struggle for social justice in
this country." These remarks fit a larger pattern of Christian rightists condemning racism. In 1995 the Southern Baptist Convention, the country's
largest Protestant denomination and one rooted in the proslavery movement, voted overwhelmingly to "repent of racism of which we have been
guilty" and to apologize to "all African Americans."[76]

Reed said that the Christian Coalition was building "a true Rainbow Coalition, one which unites Christians of all races under one banner to take
back this country." The Coalition sought to recruit people of color around
social issues such as shared opposition to abortion, homosexuality, and pornography, and support for school prayer. Other Christian Right groups recruiting people of color included Focus on the Family and the Promise
Keepers (on the latter, see Chapter 16). But while the Christian Coalition
was sometimes able to build tactical alliances with congregations of color
around these issues, few people of color joined Robertson and Reed's
organization. Antiracist words did not erase the Christian Right's long history of racism, or its continuing support for a host of policies that disproportionately hurt people of color.[77]

Even if they were more rhetoric than substance, calls for racial reconciliation put the Christian Coalition· and other mostly White evangelical
groups in sharp contrast to the increasingly explicit racial nationalism
among paleoconservatives and other rightists. For the Christian Coalition,
this was one more shift of weight in the balancing act that marked its drive
for political power.

CONCLUSION

Dominion theology, in its broad definition, provides a frame of reference
that allows different theological outlooks to work together in building a
movement for Christian nationalism. Implicit in this Christian nationalism
are many subtexts of White nationalism, although primarily derived from
cultural rather than biological White supremacy. Biological White supremacists are tolerated in this broad coalition as long as they do not openly promote their views. There is also common agreement that any form of sexual
expression other than heterosexual marriage is sinful or abnormal, and that
ultimately men make the final decisions in family situations. Conspiracy theories that are congruent with these themes are not only tolerated but sometimes openly promoted. All of this neatly fits into the paradigm of
repressive right-wing populism and the producerist narrative.

13

NEW FACES FOR WHITE NATIONALISM

Reframing Supremacist Narratives

While the New Right and Christian Right flourished in the 1970s and 1980s, the Far Right also rebounded, and many groups in this sector used populist themes or rhetoric. Like the New Right, the Far Right responded to the many-sided crisis in U.S. society: the rise of social liberation movements, erosion of the old formal hierarchies such as race and gender, economic hardships and insecurity, expansion of the state, and the decline of U.S. world dominance. The Far Right—encompassing Ku Klux Klan, neonazi, and related organizations—attracted a much smaller following than the New Right, but its influence reverberated in its encouragement of widespread attacks against members of oppressed groups and in broad-based scapegoating campaigns organized around such issues as immigration, welfare, affirmative action, and AIDS. Behind all of this was a drive for White nationalism.

Far rightists developed a variety of political doctrines and strategies in this period. After the 1979 massacre of five militant leftists in Greensboro, North Carolina, by a group of Klansmen and neonazis, neonazi ideologies began to infuse and transform the paramilitary Right, largely supplanting the Klan's old-style segregationism. The new doctrines included Christian Identity, which claimed that Jews were in league with Satan and White Christian Aryans were God's true chosen people; separatism, which called for sovereign national status based on race; and the Third Position, which denounced monopoly capitalism and called on White supremacists to "take the game away from the left."[1]

The Lyndon LaRouche network, an offshoot of the radical student movement that metamorphosed into a fascist organization in the early 1970s, developed an idiosyncratic doctrine and approach quite different from other far-right groups. David Duke led a revival of the Ku Klux Klan in the 1970s and sought to give it a more moderate and telegenic image. Later

Duke recast himself again as a Republican political candidate, presenting himself as an antielite, antiwelfare conservative defending fairness for White middle-class people. As Duke's cryptofascism gained substantial electoral support, both the Republican and Democratic parties shifted to the right to capture his constituency. Meanwhile, political figures ranging from Presidential candidate Patrick Buchanan to rightist intellectual Charles Murray promoted coded and veiled forms of White racial nationalism.

As we discussed in Chapter 12, a new form of clerical fascist ideology also developed within the Christian Right, centered in Christian Reconstructionism and the Shepherding movement.

REINVENTING FASCISM

Visions of collective rebirth in the face of near collapse are central to fascist ideology, and the U.S. social crisis that began in the 1960s created several conditions that fascists could exploit. Military defeat in Vietnam brought cries of betrayal against the U.S. government. Economic dislocations—notably, the farm crisis of the 1980s—increased scapegoating's appeal among sections of the population. The erosion of traditional hierarchies fueled demands to reassert White male heterosexual privilege and power. Newly visible social groups—such as lesbians and gay men, or millions of recent immigrants from Asia, Latin America, and elsewhere—became handy targets for old bigotries. And many people looked for ways to fight back against a growing government apparatus they perceived as bureaucratic, repressive, and answerable to elites rather than ordinary people.

Many of the groups we discuss in this chapter advocated fascism. They embraced racial or cultural supremacy, antielite conspiracism and grassroots mobilization, and hatred of the Left; and they rejected the U.S. pluralist system in favor of an authoritarian new order. At the same time, these organizations were *neofascist* in that they adapted and reinterpreted traditional fascist politics to fit new circumstances. These changes included the rise of new ideological currents—cryptofascism, Third Position, Christian Identity, LaRouchism—as well as political trends that cut across these differences. For example, fascist internationalism increased. Several far-right groups cultivated ties with fascist movements abroad. U.S. fascists significantly aided the distribution of neonazi propaganda in Germany, where most such material is illegal; the LaRouche organization maintained active branches in Europe, Asia, and Latin America. Some neofascists even promoted solidarity with right-wing nationalist movements in the Third World—as part of an apartheid vision of fraternal relations among different nations and races based on separate development.

Traditional explicit racism remained prominent within the movement, upholding the purity and superiority of Whites or "Aryans" (roughly, non-Jews of European descent, sometimes used more narrowly to exclude Mediterranean or eastern European peoples). But race was another area where many neofascists adapted and changed politically. Some, such as David Duke, used coded racism—scapegoating people of color implicitly through symbols, or using pretensions of color blindness to mask de facto racist policies. Others, such as Lyndon LaRouche, celebrated "Western civilization" against "barbarism." This move involved at least a partial shift away from the old biological racism toward a more sophisticated cultural racism, which meant including a few people of color as long as they were loyal to the values of so-called Western civilization. Both the LaRouchites and Tom Metzger's White Aryan Resistance forged active ties with Louis Farrakhan's Nation of Islam.[2]

The context for these maneuvers was not only a political culture and legal system that discouraged explicit bigotry but also a system of racial hierarchy that was becoming more complex and fragmented. Since the 1960s, class and ethnic stratification have increased within Black, Latino, and Asian communities, largely because of the growth of a middle-class minority, increased marginalization of the ghetto poor, and immigration from Asia, Latin America, the Caribbean, and Africa. The system of White supremacy continued to target all people of color, but in more complex and sophisticated ways than previously. For one thing, it fostered social and political conflict among people of color more than ever before—native-born versus immigrant, middle-class versus poor, ethnic group versus ethnic group. Neofascists such as LaRouche and Metzger, among many others, sought to exploit this situation.

To varying degrees, some neofascists also shifted away from traditional fascism's highly centralized approach to political power and toward plans to fragment and subdivide political authority. Many neonazis called for creation of an independent White homeland in the Pacific Northwest, based on the ethnic partitioning of the United States. Posse Comitatus, mostly active in rural areas, repudiated all government authority above the county level. And in the 1990s neonazi leader Louis Beam promoted the influential doctrine of "leaderless resistance." While such decentralist policies may seem incompatible with full-blown fascism, we see them partly as defensive adaptations and partly as expressions of a new social totalitarianism. Industrial-era totalitarianism relied on the nation-state; in the era of outsourcing, deregulation, and global mobility, social totalitarianism looked to local authorities, private bodies (such as churches), and direct mass activism to enforce repressive control.

In the 1970s and 1980s these efforts to reinterpret fascism were not confined to the United States, but took place among neofascists in many industrialized capitalist countries. European, Canadian, and South African neofascists, too, at times advanced the doctrine known as the Third Position, strengthened internationalist ties, used coded racial appeals, advocated ethnic separatism and the breakup of nation-states, and practiced solidarity with right-wing nationalists of color.[3]

Also during this period U.S. neofascists' relationship with government security forces shifted dramatically, from active collaboration to militant opposition. During the 1960s, for example, FBI informers had passed on information about police complicity in planned attacks on civil rights workers, yet the Bureau took no steps to stop the attacks, and those resulted in serious injuries. An FBI informer was in the car carrying the Klansmen who shot to death civil rights worker Viola Liuzzo. These and other incidents at least indirectly helped the Klan in its campaign against civil rights. From 1969 to 1972, the FBI helped to create and funded a right-wing paramilitary group called the Secret Army Organization (SAO), whose activities against the Left included theft, bombings, attempted murder, and kidnappings. The SAO was based in San Diego and claimed branches in eleven western states. In 1979 federal agents and informers from the FBI and the Bureau of Alcohol, Tobacco, and Firearms (BATF) helped to plan the Greensboro massacre, in which a hit squad of neonazis and Klansmen murdered five members of the Communist Workers Party. Federal and state government security agencies did nothing to prevent the shootings even though the group's deadly intent had been reported to authorities.[4]

Many far rightists had maintained ties with (or within) law enforcement.[5] Within a few years of Greensboro, however, neonazi activists were calling for the overthrow of the "Zionist Occupation Government" (often just called ZOG) in Washington or at least the creation of an independent Aryan enclave. In the early 1980s, for the first time since Reconstruction in the 1870s, members of the White supremacist movement "declared war" on the U.S. government and engaged in armed combat with police.

The vision of a White racist revolution against the U.S. government—followed by the extermination of all Jews, people of color, and "race traitors"—was laid out by William Pierce in his 1978 novel *The Turner Diaries*. In the early 1970s, Pierce headed the National Youth Alliance; in 1974 he founded the National Alliance as an independent neonazi organization that published White revolutionary tracts.

The LaRouchites underwent a related shift. During the late 1970s and much of the 1980s, the LaRouche organization passed on information to the Central Intelligence Agency, the FBI, and local police departments, as well as foreign intelligence agencies. But in the late 1980s, the LaRouchites' hostility to government security forces increased sharply. This partly reflected Lyndon LaRouche's 1988 federal conviction for tax evasion and mail fraud conspiracy, but also his organization's renewed effort to position itself as a militant opponent of U.S. military intervention and domestic repression.

Like the Christian Right, most neofascists upheld a traditional form of sexism: men are superior to women by nature and must protect them, the nuclear family must be defended, and sex is for reproduction, not pleasure. For neonazis, racial ideology gave these themes an added intensity: *White* men must control *White* women in order to safeguard racial purity and ensure lots of White babies. Homosexuality, in this framework, threatened the White race's ability to reproduce itself and undermined the gender roles needed for racial dominance.[6]

Many neonazi and Klan groups supported or participated in anti-abortion actions. Pensacola lay preacher John Burt, regional director of Rescue America and a former Klansman, was a close associate of such anti-abortion terrorists as Michael Griffin, Paul Hill, Rachelle Renae Shannon, and others.[7] Aryan Nations security chief Tim Bishop told a reporter, "We fight abortion all the time. . . . Abortion is one of our battlefronts." But he added, "I'm just against abortion for the pure white race. For blacks and other mongrelized [races] abortion is a good idea." White Aryan Resistance leader Tom Metzger declared, "Almost all abortion doctors are Jews. . . . Almost all abortion nurses are lesbians."[8]

More than ever before, fascists also targeted lesbians and gay men. The LaRouchites accompanied their 1986 and 1987 California AIDS quarantine voter initiative campaigns with streams of antigay propaganda. Lyndon LaRouche wrote that, in the face of AIDS, those who lynched gays would perhaps be remembered as the "only force which acted to save the human species from extinction." In January 1987, "former" members of the White Patriot Party murdered three gay men in Shelby, North Carolina, and seriously wounded two others in a carefully planned attack.[9]

THE THIRD POSITION AND WHITE SEPARATISM

The Third Position—which rejects both capitalism and communism—traces its roots to the most "radical" anticapitalist wing of Hitler's Nazi Party. In the 1970s and 1980s, neonazis in several European countries advocated the Third Position.[10] Its leading proponent in the United States was White Aryan Resistance, headed by former California Klan leader Tom Metzger. Metzger, who was a Democratic candidate for Congress in 1980, expounded his philosophy at the 1987 Aryan Nations Congress:

> WAR is dedicated to the White working people, the farmers, the White poor. . . . This is a working class movement. . . . Our problem is with monopoly capitalism. The Jews first went with Capitalism and then created their Marxist game. You go for the throat of the Capitalist. You must go for the throat of the corporates. You take the game away from the left. It's our game! We're not going to fight your whore wars no more! We've got one war, that is right here, the same war the SA fought in Germany, right here, in the streets of America.[11]

Metzger's organization vividly illustrated fascism's tendency to appropriate elements of leftist politics in distorted form. WAR supported "white working-class" militancy such as the lengthy "P-9" labor union strike against Hormel in Minnesota, stressed environmentalism, and opposed U.S. military intervention in Central America and the Persian Gulf. The Aryan Women's League, affiliated with WAR, claimed that Jews invented male supremacy and called for "Women's Power as well as White Power."[12] Metzger's television program, "Race and Reason," was broadcast on cable TV in dozens of cities and aided cooperation among White supremacist groups. Through its Aryan Youth Movement wing, WAR was particularly successful in the 1980s in recruiting racist skinheads, who include thousands of young people clustered in scores of violent pro-Nazi formations. (Not all skinheads are racist and there are antiracist and antifascist skinhead groups.) Metzger and WAR's position in the neonazi movement was weakened in October 1990 when they were fined $12.5 million in a civil suit for inciting three Portland skinheads who murdered Ethiopian immigrant Mulugeta Seraw.[13]

Out of the stew of the Third Position, and the European New Right theories of intellectuals such as Alain de Benoist, came a new version of White Nationalism that championed racially separate nation-states.[14] In the United States this filtered down to White supremacists, who began to call themselves White Separatists.[15] Dobratz and Shanks-Meile believe that "most, if not all, whites in this movement feel they are superior to blacks."[16] Instead of segregation, however, White Separatism called for "geographic separation of the world's races" and in the United States this prompted calls for an Aryan Homeland in the Pacific Northwest.[17]

CHRISTIAN IDENTITY

Christian Identity grew out of an earlier religious movement called British Israelism, whose adherents included Henry Ford publicist William J. Cameron.[18] Based on a racialized view of history and religion, Christian Identity claims the United States is the real promised land and White Christians are the real children of Israel. In its most virulent neonazi form, Identity claims Jews are children of Satan, while African Americans and other people of color are subhuman: they are "pre-Adamic" mud people— "God's failures before perfecting Adam," as Leonard Zeskind explains.[19]

Many Identity adherents believe that Jews, Blacks, communists, homosexuals, and White liberal race traitors have seized control of the United States. They refer to Washington, DC, as the Zionist Occupational Government and read the novel *The Turner Diaries*. Their premillennial script calls for establishing an exclusively White Christian nation through an apocalyptic scenario of antigovernment insurgency in which violent confrontations are considered inevitable.[20] They call the Rapture a hoax and believe a literal battle with evil pits them against Jews and other allies of Satan.[21]

The group most responsible for spreading Christian Identity in the 1980s was the Posse Comitatus, a loose network that merged the Christian Identity teachings of Col. William Potter Gale of California with survivalism.[22] Many survivalists believe the collapse of society is imminent, and thus they may collect weapons, ammunition, food, and water, move to remote locations, and conduct field exercises in reconnaissance or armed self-defense.

The first Posse Comitatus charters were issued in Portland, Oregon, in 1969 by H. L. "Mike" Beach, a former member of William Dudley Pelley's Silver Shirts fascist organization. Gale soon began encouraging the founding of new chapters as well. In 1974, 200–300 supporters attended a national Posse convention in Wisconsin. In 1976, the FBI estimated Posse membership at somewhere between 12,000 and 50,000.[23]

Posse Comitatus is Latin for "power of the county" but is more usefully explained as "to empower the citizenry." This is the legal concept used by sheriffs in Hollywood Westerns to round up a posse and chase criminals. In modern legal terms it means the ability to deputize local citizens to carry out law enforcement functions, and it is also the basis of a U.S. law that traditionally forbade the use of federal military troops in civilian law enforcement without the express consent of the President. Members of Posse Comitatus, however, promoted the unwarranted belief that the Constitution did not authorize any law enforcement powers above the level of county sheriff and that therefore state and federal officials were part of a gigantic conspiracy to deny average citizens their rights.

The most visible and active branch of the Posse for many years was in Wisconsin. The press gave much attention to Wisconsin Posse leader James Wickstrom, although his claim to hold some vague national leadership post was flatly contradicted by the autonomous and decentralist nature of the Posse itself. During the 1980s, significant Posse activity was reported in eighteen states, mostly in the Midwest, Great Plains, Mountain, and Pacific Coast regions, as well as Texas and Pennsylvania.

Following the 1979 Greensboro massacre, a number of previously antagonistic White supremacist groups, including the Posse and various neonazi and Klan factions, began to discuss ideology and joint activities and to establish informal means of communication including computer bulletin boards and cable TV programs. Many of these groups embraced Christian Identity. Gradually, a White racist alliance emerged. Centers of this movement included the Michigan farm of pastor and former Klan leader Robert E. Miles, as well as the Aryan Nations compound in Hayden Lake, Idaho, the site of Identity Pastor Richard Butler's Church of Jesus Christ Christian.

Not all Klan groups accepted the new Identity-based coalition, but those that did began to call themselves the Fifth Era Klan to demarcate what they hoped would be the fifth period of growth by the Klan since its inception. The Fifth Era Klan adherents sought to forge ties with other racist groups across the nation. One concept hotly debated was the idea of a mass migration of White supremacists to the Pacific Northwest, where there were relatively few people of color and a low population density. The idea was to create a racially pure Aryan bastion.

Posse and Identity organizers capitalized on the farm crisis of the 1980s. Rural America faced its worst economic slump in half a century, owing largely to unfair and inequitable policies by the federal government and private banks.[24] While most of society ignored angry and desperate rural families' legitimate grievances, far-right activists urged resistance and offered ready scapegoats, namely, the Jews who supposedly controlled the Internal Revenue Service and the Federal Reserve. In the early 1980s, Posse activists helped to split the influential American Agricultural Movement, while Identity theology and antisemitic conspiracy theories gained an alarming level of acceptance in rural America.[25] One poll in 1985 found that in the farm belt 27 percent of respondents felt that "international Jewish bankers" were responsible for the farm crisis.[26]

In 1983 two federal marshals were killed and several persons were wounded in a mishandled attempt to serve legal papers on Posse farm belt organizer Gordon Kahl. Kahl fled underground and was killed in a shootout with federal officers some months later. Kahl and other White supremacists killed or jailed by the government became martyrs to Posse adherents and other neonazis. After the Gordon Kahl incident, many Posse and Christian Identity activists decided to carry out activities in secret or through front groups.

Also in 1983, an underground organization was recruited out of the Aryan Nations and several other far-right groups. Variously called The Order, Aryan Resistance Movement, White American Bastion, or The Silent Brotherhood, members of The Order were mostly Identity adherents. Led by National Alliance member Robert Mathews, The Order sought to follow the revolutionary script laid out in *The Turner Diaries*. They raised about $5 million through counterfeiting and robberies of banks and armored cars, and murdered Jewish talk show host Alan Berg in Denver.[27] The Order's November 1984 "Declaration of War" against the federal government asserted that "The Capitalists and the Communists pick gleefully at our bones while the vile hook-nosed masters of usury orchestrate our [race's] destruction."[28] The U.S. government cracked down hard on The Order: Mathews was killed in a shootout, and many other members were imprisoned. Of the twenty-three members of The Order convicted in a 1985 trial, according to the *Klanwatch Intelligence Report*, "Five had Klan ties, one had been a Nazi party member, a half-dozen were Aryan Nations, one was a veteran tax protester, four CSA's [Covenant, Sword and Arm of the Lord], five National Alliance members."

Another underground group, the Committee of the States, was founded by Identity leader William Potter Gale in 1984.[29] Each state chapter was supposed to form an "Unorganized Militia."[30] The paramilitary coalition-building efforts of groups such as The Order, Committee of the States, and the Posse Comitatus helped lay the groundwork for the Patriot and armed militia movements of the 1990s.

THE LAROUCHITE SECRET ELITE SYNTHESIS

Though often dismissed as a bizarre political cult, the LaRouche organization and its various front groups are a fascist movement whose pronouncements echo elements of Nazi ideology.[31] Beginning in the 1970s, the LaRouchites combined populist antielitism with attacks on leftists, environmentalists, feminists, gay men and lesbians, and organized labor. They advocated a dictatorship in which a "humanist" elite would rule on behalf of industrial capitalists. They developed an idiosyncratic, coded variation on the Illuminati Freemason and Jewish banker conspiracy theories. Their views, though exotic, were internally consistent and rooted in right-wing populist traditions.

A former Trotskyist, Lyndon H. LaRouche, Jr., founded the National Caucus of Labor Committees (NCLC) in 1968 as an offshoot of the radical student movement. But in the early 1970s, LaRouche engineered a political about-face, using cult pressure tactics to consolidate his grip over the NCLC and initiating a campaign of physical attacks on Communists and Black nationalists, which cut his followers off from the Left. The result was a fascist organization with some unique strengths: a dedicated, full-time cadre of several hundred members, a high proportion of intellectuals with advanced training, familiarity with leftist theory and organizing, and inside information about radical organizations and leaders.

During the 1970s and 1980s, the LaRouchites built an international network for spying and propaganda, with links to the upper levels of government, business, and organized crime. The LaRouchites traded information with intelligence agencies in the United States, South Africa, East Germany, and elsewhere. Their dirty tricks record included harassment campaigns against the United Auto Workers and the United Steelworkers of America in the 1970s. In 1980, they branded George Bush an agent of the Trilateral Commission to help Ronald Reagan win the Republican presidential nomination, and in 1984, they helped Jesse Helms retain his U.S. Senate seat by gay-baiting his opponent. During the 1980s, the LaRouchites raised an estimated $200 million through legal and illegal fund-raising and fielded thousands of candidates for political office in every region of the country. Seeking the George Wallace vote, the LaRouche candidates usually ran in Democratic primaries.[32]

The LaRouchites generally operated under front groups such as Food for Peace and the Schiller Institute, and put out such publications as *New Solidarity* (later *The New Federalist*) and *Executive Intelligence Review.*

In 1976 LaRouche's original electoral arm, the U.S. Labor Party (USLP), published a conspiracist attack on President Jimmy Carter, claiming he was a tool of secret international elites. The Liberty Lobby criticized the report for failing to mention the role of Jewish bankers, and soon LaRouche publications picked up the theme.[33] The Liberty Lobby and the LaRouche group soon began to cooperate closely on projects. When some groups on the right criticized the Liberty Lobby for working with ostensible leftists, meaning the USLP, the Liberty Lobby defended the relationship in 1981: "No group has done so much to confuse, disorient, and disunify the Left as they have. . . . The USLP should be encouraged, as should all similar breakaway groups from the Left, for this is the only way that the Left can be weakened and broken."[34]

In the 1970s, the LaRouchites' anti-Jewish propaganda was relatively explicit, as in LaRouche's 1978 article "New Pamphlet to Document Cult Origins of Zionism," which declared that "The B'Nai B'rith today resurrects the tradition of the Jews who demanded the crucifixion of Jesus Christ, the Jews who pleaded with Nero to launch the ´holocaust´ against the Christians."[35] Gradually the LaRouchites developed increasingly sophisticated ways to invoke antisemitic themes while still maintaining deniability.

The LaRouchites borrowed conspiracist elements from various sources to produce their own Manichean picture of world history. For thousands of years, they argued, the good "humanists" had been locked in a power struggle with a vast conspiracy of evil "oligarchs." In ancient times, the oligarchic conspiracy was centered in Babylon; later it shifted to Venice; in modern times it was centered in Britain's royal House of Windsor. This narrative evoked standard elements of antisemitic doctrine: that Jews had dominated ancient Babylon and that Jewish banking families controlled the British government. Sometimes the LaRouchites highlighted prominent Jews as members of the conspiracy, such as "[Henry] Kissinger's friends, the Rothschild family, and other representatives of Britain's financial power." At other times, they portrayed Jews as unwitting tools of the oligarchs, as for example, "Zionism is that state of collective psychosis through which London manipulates most of international Jewry."[36]

The LaRouchite analysis of British oligarchic control resembles a number of earlier right-wing populist works, such as E. C. Knuth's 1944 tract *The Empire of "The City": alias International Finance, alias the British Empire, alias "ONE WORLD" superstate.* Knuth claimed that the Rothschilds and Sassoons controlled British financial interests, and he cited the International Monetary Fund as proof of their plot for global dominance.

Unlike neonazi groups such as the White Aryan Resistance or the National Alliance, the NCLC has always denied that it is antisemitic and has always included Jewish members (such as LaRouche's longtime security aides

Jeffrey Steinberg and Paul Goldstein). The LaRouchites insisted they were not targeting Jews as a whole, but only the "bad" Jews such as Henry Kissinger, Roy Cohn, the Rothschild banking family, and the Anti-Defamation League.

The LaRouchites seem to have shifted from biological to cultural racism, at least in their public pronouncements. In the 1970s, LaRouche and his followers described the British oligarchs as a separate "species" and often referred to people of color as bestial or subhuman. But in 1995, *New Federalist* editor Nancy Spannaus declared, "We don't believe blood or race has anything to do with determining history. Never fear! It's ideas."[37] LaRouchite ideology has continued to glorify western Christianity and European civilization—especially the classical German culture of Beethoven, Schiller, and Leibniz—over the "barbarism" of non-Europeans. For example, LaRouchites asserted that by bringing Christianity to the Americas, "Columbus' discovery made it possible to liberate the native populations" from "the practices of human sacrifice, cannibalism, and slavery of the Aztec Empire." The LaRouchites vilified jazz and rock music while praising African American spirituals—so long as they conformed to the rules of European classical music.[38]

U.S. right-wing traditions such as business nationalism echoed loudly in the LaRouchites' attacks on Britain, the "liberal Eastern Establishment," homosexuality, globalism, free trade, and international bankers. Producerism, with its problematic distinction between productive industrial capital and parasitic finance capital, was central to LaRouchite economics, as it enabled LaRouche to be procapitalist and "anti-imperialist" at the same time: "Imperialism was not the result of capitalist development; it was the result of the conquest of power over capitalist nations by a usury-oriented rentier–financier interest older than feudalism."[39]

Like traditional fascists of the 1920s and 1930s, but unlike many neonazis and other U.S. rightists today, LaRouchites championed a strong, centralized nation-state as vital to economic and social progress. They declared they were continuing the old Federalist–Whig program of economic protectionism, national control of banking, and government-sponsored infrastructure development to stimulate industrial growth. They attacked both states' rights and laissez-faire conservatism as part of a British plot to undermine the nation-state.[40]

Also, unlike some neonazis, the LaRouchites vilified the environmental movement and nature romanticism while praising high-technology projects such as nuclear power. But here, too, the LaRouchites were partly repackaging earlier conspiracy theories. Their attacks on the Club of Rome, an ecology and population control group, echoed a 1974 article in the rightist *American Mercury* entitled "The Curious Club of Rome," which asked whether the group was "merely a bunch of boring pedants and doom-sayers, or is it a sinister cabal aiming for world control?"[41]

In 1989, LaRouche was sentenced to fifteen years in prison for mail fraud conspiracy, based on illegal and manipulative fund-raising practices, as well as tax evasion. His organization continued to operate while he was in prison, and he was released in early 1994.

LaRouche continued his leadership role in various organizations such as the National Caucus of Labor Committees and the Schiller Institute while in prison, and after his release he resumed his peripatetic speaking circuit, quickly building contacts with a number of groups around the world. His call for new global economic policies in opposition to the International Monetary Fund found favor not only in Europe, but in Africa, Central and South America, and Asia. He spoke at a number of conferences organized in countries previously under Soviet influence or control.

During the 1990s, the LaRouchites once again adopted a more "progressive" guise. They opposed the Gulf War against Iraq and worked to build links with liberal and leftist antiwar groups. They made particular efforts to recruit African Americans. They opposed the death penalty, anti-immigrant racism, and law enforcement agencies' harassment of Black elected officials. They defended social programs against Gingrich–Republican budget cuts. They praised the Israeli–Palestinian negotiations and the Israeli Labor Party while denouncing the rightist Likud Party and the Islamic fundamentalists in Hamas. Starting in 1990, the LaRouchites and Louis Farrakhan's Nation of Islam cultivated friendly ties, sharing articles and praising each other's work.[42]

The LaRouchites set an example of how to package fascist ideology as maverick conservatism, progressive antielitism, or both. In 1986, when LaRouche followers shocked the Illinois Democratic Party by winning the party primaries for lieutenant governor and secretary of state, other far rightists praised their efforts. Some, such as David Duke, looked for lessons in their electoral strategy.[43]

DAVID DUKE'S CODED RACIST RHETORIC

While the paramilitary Right were coaxing nervous populists toward open armed resistance and neofascism, and the LaRouchites were building dirty tricks operations around arcane conspiracy theories, David Duke of Louisiana was pioneering a face-lift for White supremacy in electoral politics. The old racist message had been simply that Black people were biologically inferior and dangerous. The new message was that White people were the victims of large-scale discrimination and that someone had to stand up for straight, White Christians against the liberal, internationalist elites and their parasitic clients in the Black underclass.

Symbolic racism can be used by three groups in the public sphere: (1) persons who really believe people of color are biologically inferior; (2) persons who are culturally racist—willing to accept some people of color as potential equals if they conform to the behavior patterns set by the White majority; and (3) persons who are oblivious to the racialized content of the coded rhetoric and do not consciously advocate biological or cultural racism. Duke clearly used coded symbolic racist rhetoric as a cover for his biological racism, no matter how much he claimed to have reformed his views on race.

Duke worked with various Nazi-affiliated groups in the early 1970s. From 1975 to 1979, he headed the Knights of the Ku Klux Klan (KKKK), which his acumen for managing the media helped build into one of the largest Klan organizations in the country. His assistants included California Grand Dragon Tom Metzger, who later founded White Aryan Resistance, and Louis Beam, head of the Texas KKKK, who later became a key figure within Aryan Nations. In 1980, Duke resigned from the Klan and founded the National Association for the Advancement of White People (NAAWP). The NAAWP claimed to defend Whites against discrimination and to advocate "equal opportunity and equal rights," but it circulated hard-core neonazi articles by such figures as William Pierce, as well as Duke's own proposals for the ethnic partitioning of the United States and a eugenics program to breed genetically superior Whites.

In 1988, Duke ran for president in the Democratic Party's southern primaries. In the general election he ran on the ticket of the Populist Party, a far-right vehicle created by Willis Carto of the Liberty Lobby, and received about 150,000 votes. In February 1989, with fund-raising and organizational help from the Liberty Lobby, Duke was elected to the Louisiana House of Representatives as a Republican.[44]

In 1990, Duke won the Louisiana Republican nomination for U.S. Senate. In the general election, he received 44 percent of the vote—winning 60 percent among White voters. The following year, Duke outpolled the incumbent in the Louisiana governor's race, then lost in a runoff election with 39 percent of the total vote (55 percent of the White vote).[45]

Although running as a Republican, Duke appealed mainly to White working-class Democrats. In his 1989 election as a state representative, he won by converting the vast majority of Democratic voters, but only 20 percent of Republicans, to his cause. During the 1990 Senate race, Duke declared, "I'm the only Republican who can attract a sizable number of the blue-collar, Ronald Reagan, George Wallace voters you need to win."[46]

Journalist Jason Berry wrote that, in the Senate race, "Duke tapped a deep vein of discontent against Washington, crime, and a perception of government favoritism toward blacks." Berry noted that in hard economic times where there were "young white males with poor job prospects [that] a demagogue's quick fix has its appeal."[47]

Berry and others criticized the mainstream media coverage of Duke for repeatedly failing to challenge his claims that he had left his racist and antisemitic past behind. Berry was especially harsh on Boston's respected Ford Hall Forum for inviting Duke to speak at a March 1991 lecture series. Berry wrote that, with the invitation, "the Forum helps legitimize a media huckster whose naked cynicism toward the truth mocks the democracy that guarantees his right to speak."[48] One of the tasks of the Louisiana Coalition Against Racism and Nazism, a multiracial and religiously diverse group that successfully mobilized many voters to oppose Duke's 1990 Senate bid, was to demand that the news media actually report on the evidence that demonstrated that Duke continued to be an apologist for Hitler and continued to promote racism and antisemitism.[49]

In 1989, while Duke was in the Louisiana state legislature, Beth Rickey, a Republican who fought to censure Duke, gained headlines when she revealed she had just purchased books and tapes with overt neonazi, White supremacist, and antisemitic themes from Duke's legislative offices, thus giving the lie to Duke's claims to have reformed.[50]

Many in the human relations community (and the Republican Party) argued that giving Duke any publicity, even negative publicity, would only encourage his supporters. The Center for Democratic Renewal disagreed, citing polls taken before and after the "Nazi books" episode: over three months, Duke's base of support remained unchanged at 23 percent of Louisiana voters, but the number who opposed him rose from 39 to 60 percent.

Duke offered a succinct overview of his cryptofascist message in a speech to the 1988 Populist Party nominating convention in Washington State. Duke warned that, despite "a massive welfare system," the United States was plagued by "25 times more problems," including crime, deteriorating schools, and "a drug epidemic, especially in the ghettos and poor areas." A major reason, Duke argued, was the "illegitimate birthrate" among women on welfare:

> I say it's time for the White middle class or any middle class person in this country that's productive and works hard, it's time for us to say, no, we're not going to finance illegitimate welfare birthrates anymore. Something's wrong in America when hard-working, middle-class, productive people can't afford children of their own . . . while they're being forced to finance massive welfare illegitimacy.[51]

As a state legislator, Duke sponsored a bill to provide cash incentives for welfare recipients who agreed to be temporarily sterilized with Norplant implants. He promoted this measure as solely a means to reduce welfare costs. But many of Duke's supporters undoubtedly viewed this as a eugenicist plan to reduce Black reproduction and preserve the White race. This is another example of coded racial rhetoric.[52]

Duke also employed right-wing populist themes: "We, the people, have so little input anymore. Today it's government by big business, international finance, and organized minorities. . . . It's time we joined together and break this control and give this country back to our people."

Exactly who "our people" are was clear to Duke and his audience: "America is not simply a Constitution and it's not simply a piece of geography. It's far more than that. It's a people. It's a heritage. And our European heritage is what made America possible. And if our European heritage is lost, then we will also lose America."

Duke declared that racial separation was a God-given natural law. "I'm glad that God created different races. I think it offers greater possibilities for mankind. And I want my grandkids and great grandkids to look something like myself and the people that came before me. And I'm proud of that fact."

Duke also invoked classic coded antisemitic rhetoric: "The internationalists want to destroy borders. They want to destroy tariffs. They want to destroy the American middle class and they want to destroy our heritage. [They want to] destroy the vitality, the seed, the spirit, the genetic treasure of this society. . . . That's you and . . . that's our children, our progeny . . ." He argued that "there's no more critical issue than the fact the Zionists control the American media in America." This enabled "the international financial powers" to "dominate our government . . . and the American people." The Zionists were "constantly putting down our heritage, trying to destroy our value system, our faith" while "slavishly" supporting Israel.

Occasionally when speaking to supporters, Duke would expose his rank antisemitism. He told the Populist Party convention that Judaism was "a very vile anti-Christian faith. . . . It doesn't mean all Jews are that way. But I don't respect the Talmud, I think it's a very vicious and vile book and it attacks all Christians and non-Jews in the world."

Robert H. Weems, a former Populist Party chairman, rehashed many of these themes in a 1996 Populist Campaign Fund direct-mail appeal for Duke's Republican Senate primary race. He continued by scapegoating liberals as traitors: "Let's strike a blow for the Constitution and let Bill and Hillary and Dan Rather and Jane Fonda and other such enemies of America know who is REALLY in charge by electing a REAL American to the United States Senate." Weems even invoked anticommunist Red-baiting: "Now you know why the liberal media and their Mercedes Marxist Elitist buddies hate him." So the new coded racism and antisemitism dovetailed with the theme of liberal and secular humanist betrayal.[53]

PATRICK BUCHANAN

Pat Buchanan's 1992 presidential campaign against George Bush, like the paleocon attack on the neoconservatives, echoed the old struggle between business nationalists and multinationalists. The paleocons wanted to revive the anti-interventionist Right that had been led by Midwestern business nationalists half a century before. Thus, Buchanan portrayed Bush as a symbol of the sinister Eastern elite, and declared, "He is a globalist and we are nationalists. He believes in some *Pax Universalis;* we believe in the Old Republic. He would put America's wealth and power at the service of some vague New World Order; we will put America first."[54]

Unfortunately for Buchanan's campaign coffers, not much was left of the business constituency that had backed the Nazi-infested "America First" movement in 1940–1941. He won support from the anti-free-trade U.S. Business and Industrial Council, Birch Society adherent Roger Milliken (representing the protectionist wing of the textile industry), and an assortment of private investors.[55] But too much of the business community— even many Sunbelt ultraconservatives—had developed a stake in an integrated global economy. Like Richard Gephardt in 1988, who campaigned for the Democratic presidential nomination as an economic nationalist, Buchanan found that a direct challenge to free-trade orthodoxy cut him off from major sources of capitalist support.[56]

Despite this limitation, Buchanan appealed to several distinct populist sectors throughout the 1980s and 1990s:

Christian nationalists and theocrats. Buchanan pursued themes that resonated with a large segment of the theocratic wing of the Christian Right, including ultraconservative Catholics and Protestants, as well as a tiny portion of the Jewish community with ultraconservative political views or orthodox religious beliefs. Buchanan's attacks on reproductive rights and gay rights were celebrated among theocrats.[57] Buchanan also raised the issue of the secular humanist conspiracy.[58]

White racial nationalists. Buchanan's racism was often overt, but frequently overlooked in the corporate media. He openly discussed his idea that democracy only worked in monocultural societies and his fear that dark-skinned immigrants were distorting the real America.[59] In one of his syndicated columns he asserted,

> The burning issue here has almost nothing to do with economics, almost everything to do with race and ethnicity. If British subjects, fleeing a depression, were pouring into this country through Canada, there would be few alarms.
>
> The central objection to the present flood of illegals is they are not English-speaking white people from Western Europe; they are Spanish-speaking brown and black people from Mexico, Latin America and the Caribbean.[60]

Racial nationalists are also often concerned with national sovereignty, and they resist the internationalism of major global corporations by calling for protectionism, isolationism, and unilateralism in overseas military involvement. Buchanan's stump speech attacking the implicitly multicultural New World Order attracted support from this sector.

Right-wing economic populists. Buchanan's attack on global elites and Wall Street brokers sounded the alarm for persons who combined repressive populism with isolationism and business nationalism.[61] In 1992, the Birch Society *New American* magazine praised Buchanan as antiestablishment and cited with approval the Buchanan column where he blasted "The Trilateralist, [Council on Foreign Relations], Wall Street–Big Business elite" and those who support a New World Order with its "one-world, collective-security, UN, *uber alles* dream."[62] This is the segment that was most willing to vote for Buchanan in primaries and caucuses.[63]

Authoritarians. Buchanan appealed to the authoritarian impulse among those who blamed dissent and demands for social change on subversive agents stirring up trouble rather than on actual grievances from the dispossessed and impoverished. Buchanan's dismissive comments about democracy and praise for the death squads in Argentina appealed to those who favored swift and strong authoritarian government action against the subversives and their liberal allies.[64]

BIOLOGICAL RACIALISTS VERSUS CULTURAL SUPREMACISTS

The 1990s saw a renewal of the biological determinist claim that genetic racial differences accounted for class inequalities.[65] This focus on race played out in policy debates over street crime, welfare, and immigration.

The work of right-wing political scientist Charles Murray marked the change in political climate. Murray's influential 1984 book *Losing Ground: American Social Policy, 1950–1980* argued that recent social welfare programs created and intensified poverty rather than alleviating it. The book avoided any biological argument: it portrayed poor people, including poor people of color, as rational actors responding intelligently to misguided government policy. But Murray's 1994 book *The Bell Curve*, coauthored with Richard J. Herrnstein, re-embraced biological determinism. *The Bell Curve* argued that most affirmative action and social welfare programs were doomed to failure because Blacks and Latinos were genetically inferior.[66] Much of the underlying research was bankrolled by the Pioneer Fund, which has supported racial IQ studies and research that claims Blacks are genetically inferior to Whites. The Pioneer Fund has financed the research of Dr. Roger Pearson and others whose articles have appeared in the racialist *Journal of Indo-European Studies* and publications from the Institute for the Study of Man, a racialist group that promotes debunked pseudoanthropological claims of a racial Aryanist diaspora similar to those favored by the Nazis.[67] Though sharply criticized by many social scientists, Murray and Herrnstein's book sounded the loudest recent salvo in the battle to make explicit biological racism academically respectable once again.[68]

THE ALIEN OTHER

Short of overt biological determinism, monocultural themes extended well into the mainstream. Samuel Huntington in *The Clash of Civilizations and the Remaking of World Order* argued that the crucial global division in the post-Cold War period was between cultures. Huntington (who once worried about too much democracy in a paper for the Trilateral Commission) now saw ethnoreligious worldviews pitted against one another, with global blocs of Islamic, Orthodox, Japanese, and other cultures battling the beleaguered (heroic, idealized, preferred) Western culture.[69] Noting this paradigm omits consideration of other cleavages, such as between modernists and traditionalists and the haves and have nots, Ronald Steel observed:

> Indeed, the whole "civilization" thesis sometimes seems motivated by a profound distaste for multiculturalism at home, and can be viewed as an elaborate "decadence of the West" alarm that requires battening down the hatches against cultural assaults from within as well as without.[70]

RACIAL NATIONALISM RESURGENT

Buchanan's electoral campaigns, and paleoconservatism's revival, resonated during the 1990s with the broader resurgence of White racial nationalism among ultraconservatives and in mainstream political discourse. Examples included a strong anti-immigrant movement, a burgeoning southern heritage subculture glorifying the Confederacy, and a revival of pseudoscientific claims of Whites' genetic racial superiority. To a much greater extent than the New Right politics of the 1970s and 1980s, such initiatives brought mainstream right-wingers and avowed Klan and neonazi far rightists together.

The attack on immigrants involved an interplay among many forces. Some private employers benefited from restrictive laws and policies that kept a large pool of undocumented immigrants vulnerable to sharply exploitative wages and working conditions. The specter of a mass influx of "illegal aliens" fueled the growth of government agencies such as the Immigration and Naturalization Service (INS) and extensive militarization of the U.S.–Mexico border region, contributing to the overall growth of state repression.[71] Hate groups and unorganized bigots subjected newcomers to verbal abuse and physical violence. Organizations such as the Federation for American Immigration Reform (FAIR), founded in 1979, and the American Immigration Control Foundation (AICF), formed in 1983, conducted propaganda campaigns, lobbying, and electoral initiatives to further limit immigration and immigrants' rights.[72]

In 1994, 59 percent of voting Californians approved Proposition 187, which required teachers, police, social workers, and public health employees to deny undocumented immigrants access to public services (including public education and medical care) and report them to the INS. In 1996, highlighting a steady tightening of federal immigration policy, new federal laws intensified the crackdown against undocumented immigrants and restricted documented residents' access to public services. Several bills were introduced in Congress to partially overturn the Fourteenth Amendment— so that U.S.-born children of undocumented immigrants would be denied citizenship.[73]

Restriction advocates scapegoated immigrants—almost always meaning immigrants of color—for everything from unemployment to environmental deterioration. The California Coalition for Immigration Reform claimed that the Mexican government was using Mexican immigrants in the United States as part of a conspiracy to reconquer territory it had lost in 1848. Some groups tried to recruit Black support by claiming that job competition from immigrants primarily hurt African Americans. But the core attack characterized newcomers from Latin America, Asia, and the Caribbean as a threat to the nation's European cultural heritage. The racism inherent in this claim was stated more or less openly.[74]

Both FAIR and AICF have received hundreds of thousands of dollars from the White racialist Pioneer Fund. Far rightists helped pioneer the new wave of anti-immigrant activism—David Duke and Tom Metzger, for example, organized a "Klan Border Watch" in southern California in the 1970s. Organizers of a number of anti-immigrant groups have been identified as current or former members of the Klan, the Populist Party, and neonazi groups. At the same time, liberal Democrats as well as conservative Republicans jumped on the anti-immigrant bandwagon. U.S. Senator Barbara Boxer (D-CA) called for massing National Guard troops on the Mexico border to repel undocumented immigrants. In 1996, both the Republicans and Democrats included anti-immigrant planks in their party platforms.[75]

Another vehicle for White racial nationalism was the neo-Confederate movement. Although glorification of the slaveholding South goes back to the end of the Civil War, the 1990s saw an upsurge in southern heritage activities, ranging from battlefield reenactments to museums to music to publications all celebrating the Confederacy and its principles. Some neo-Confederates openly advocate a new secession, or explicitly reject the Declaration of Independence pronouncement "all men are created equal" as "deliberate lies" and "egalitarian nonsense." Use of the Confederate battle flag became a point of sharp public controversy in several states. Prominent politicians such as Buchanan, Senate Majority Leader Trent Lott, and House Majority Leader Dick Armey have supported neo-Confederate culture. The movement includes the Council of Conservative Citizens (CCC), the organizational descendant of the White Citizens Councils of the 1960s. The CCC champions use of the Confederate battle flag and includes numerous southern politicians in its ranks.[76]

Columnist and organizer Samuel Francis highlighted the paleoconservatives' pivotal role in building a broad White racial nationalist movement.[77] During the 1980s, Francis worked at the New Right Heritage Foundation and wrote for the *Washington Times*, owned by the Sun Myung Moon network. With the collapse of the Soviet bloc, he shifted from an interventionist foreign policy stance to isolationism and a growing emphasis on promoting White culture as the cornerstone of U.S. national sovereignty. He was forced out of his job at the *Washington Times* after a 1994 speech at an American Renaissance conference in which he declared,

> We as whites under assault need to . . . reassert our identity and our solidarity, and we need to do so in explicitly racial terms, through the articulation of a racial consciousness as whites. . . . The civilization that we as whites created in Europe and America could not have developed apart from the genetic endowments of the creating people.[78]

In the 1990s, Francis maintained a syndicated column in the paleocon Rockford Institute's *Chronicles*, served as cochairman of the American Immigration Control Foundation and as a board member of the Council of Conservative Citizens, and was a contributor to the John Birch Society magazine, *New American*. Leonard Zeskind comments, "Francis still eschews any overt expression of antisemitism and conspiracies are not his style. His white nationalism may thus prove to be more potent than the Aryan variety."[78]

HOW DUKE HELPED THE FAR RIGHT INFLUENCE THE MAINSTREAM

The insurgent Far Right interacts with dissident populist movements, and together they exert a pull on the mainstream electoral system. By reframing the issue of White nationalism, far-right leaders such as David Duke played a role in shaping public policy debates. When asked about the candidacy of David Duke, Vice President Dan Quayle misstated and sanitized Duke's message and then claimed its main themes for the Republican Party. "The message of David Duke is anti-big government, get out of my pocketbook, cut my taxes, put welfare people back to work. That's a very popular message. The problem is the messenger. David Duke, neo-Nazi, ex-Klansman, basically a bad person."[79]

Duke was not the only fascist whose efforts directly influenced more moderate right-wing forces. The LaRouche-sponsored California ballot initiatives in 1986 and 1987 to "quarantine" people with AIDS, which received 2 million and 1.7 million votes, respectively, bolstered Christian Right efforts to exploit the AIDS epidemic in the service of a homophobic agenda.[80] The concept of "populism," was promoted by the Liberty Lobby from 1980 onward as a code word for fascist and quasifascist politics, and at the same time was sanitized and appropriated by New Right leader Richard Viguerie in his 1983 book *The Establishment vs. the People: Is a New Populist Revolt on the Way?*[81]

David Duke's populist electoral campaigns, however, helped to galvanize a whole faction within the fragmented New Right coalition. Self-described paleoconservatives such as Samuel Francis regarded Duke's strong showing in the 1991 race as a "turning point in American history."[82] Coupled with the rise of quasifascist European right-wing populists such as Jean Marie Le Pen and Jörg Haider, Duke's popularity encouraged paleoconservatives to reassert their own version of cultural nationalism. Some paleocons even echoed the concept of ethnic separatism in the claim that democracy works only in ethnically homogeneous cultures. Because they did not share the "baggage" of Duke's past and continuing involvement in neonazi politics, the paleocons could repackage a similar message in a form palatable to a much larger constituency. And, by running in the 1992 Republican presidential primaries, Duke helped fellow candidate Buchanan, a paleocon, by making Buchanan look moderate by comparison.

As the bipartisan attack on welfare illustrates, paleoconservatives and Republicans were not the only ones who repackaged and coded racist appeals in a more mainstream form. Duke's wider impact on issues such as welfare is more difficult to assess. As Lucy Williams notes, "The targeting of welfare dates to the 'Old' Right of the 1960s—the movement headed by Barry Goldwater and identified with the John Birch Society."[83] In the decades that followed, several different sectors of the Right developed the attack in various ways, and Duke was by no means the only prominent figure deploying coded racism against government assistance programs. It is striking that, only one year after southern Democrat-turned-Republican Duke nearly won the Louisiana governorship, another southern Democrat from the neighboring state of Arkansas was elected president after promising to "end welfare as we know it." Bill Clinton's antiwelfare pledge—which he made good four years later by abolishing the long-standing federal program Aid to Families with Dependent Children—was a step no Republican president had dared to take, and it was part of a reverse Southern Strategy designed to recapture the Wallace vote from David Duke's adopted party.

CONCLUSION

From the 1970s on, new doctrines such as the White Rights movement, White Separatism, Christian Identity, Third Position neonazism, and LaRouchite fascism helped revitalize the Far Right. Many fascists moved partly away from explicit biological racism to various forms of coded racism and cultural racism. Meanwhile, sections of the nonfascist Hard Right turned once more to White racial nationalism and even explicit claims of Whites' biological superiority—especially after the end of the Cold War and the splintering of the New Right coalition. These trends fostered increased collaboration between fascists and ultraconservatives and blurred the line between them.

White racism and antisemitism are often portrayed in the media as being mostly limited to agitators from the Far Right—the lunatic fringe. This is the paradigm promoted by centrist/extremist theory, and it is still used by most antiprejudice groups and the U.S. government. But elements of White racial nationalism in the 1990s could be seen not only among neonazis and other sectors of the Far Right, but also in sectors of the Patriot and armed militia movements and the Christian Right, as well as in the mainstream electoral system. Furthermore, most hate crimes are not committed by members of organized hate groups, and attacks on gay men and lesbians were growing at a faster rate in the late 1990s than attacks based on White racism or antisemitism.

James A. Aho points out how easy it is "to dismiss racism and religious bigotry as products of craziness or stupidity," but that such a view is not accurate. According to Aho, "evidence from field research on Pacific Northwest racists and bigots shows that in the main they are indistinguishable from their more conventional peers, intellectually and educationally." Aho also observes that with the exception of those who have engaged in politically motivated murders, the racists and bigots he studied "appear well within the bounds of normal, psychologically."[84]

Not only has the centrist/extremist approach to the racist Right not "abolished the movement, nor diminished racism in general," it "may, in fact, unwittingly support racist beliefs," suggests Abby L. Ferber. "While the focus is on the fringe, mainstream, everyday racism remains unexamined." Ferber argues that a discussion is needed on the "points of similarity between white supremacist discourse and mainstream discourses," especially since "white supremacist discourse gains power precisely because it rearticulates mainstream racial narratives. . . . "

Raphael S. Ezekiel agrees, noting that organized White racism exploits feelings of "lonely resentment." It does this by weaving together ideologies already present in mainstream culture: "white specialness, the biological significance of 'race,' the primacy of power in human relations," and "the feeling of being cheated."[85]

This sense of being cheated undergirds the producerist worldview, and provides a powerful mobilizing framework for right-wing populism. This is true when the system of oppression being bolstered is racism, antisemitism, sexism, homophobia, or class hierarchy—alone or in any combination.

14

BATTLING THE NEW WORLD ORDER

Patriots and Armed Militias

When President Bush announced that his new foreign policy would help build a "new world order," his words surged through the Christian and secular Hard Right like an electric shock. Conspiracists had used the phrase for decades to represent the dreaded collectivist One World Government. A few Christians saw Bush as signaling the End Times betrayal by a world leader. Secular anticommunists saw a bold attempt to smash U.S. sovereignty and impose a tyrannical collectivist system run by the United Nations. Out of this came a resurgence of populist vigilante organizing—the Patriot movement and its armed wing, the citizens militias.[1]

The old feud between business multinationalists and business nationalists was part of the context, building on preexisting antiglobalist sentiments within the Right.[2] So, too, was the paleoconservative attack on neoconservatives, and paleocon Patrick Buchanan's 1992 campaign against George Bush in the Republican presidential primaries. In the December 1991 speech announcing his candidacy, Buchanan trumpeted neoisolationist and xenophobic themes that would soon be embraced by the Patriot movement. Denouncing Bush's New World Order doctrine, Buchanan championed nationalism as "the dynamic force shaping [the post-Cold War] world." "All the institutions of the Cold War," he declared, "from vast permanent U.S. armies on foreign soil, to old alliances against Communist enemies that no longer exist, to billions in foreign aid, must be re-examined." He denounced "the predatory traders of Europe or Asia who have targeted this or that American industry for dumping or destruction," and warned that U.S. sovereignty was threatened "by the rise of a European superstate and a dynamic Asia led by Japan."[3]

Buchanan's portrayal of Bush as a symbol of the sinister Eastern elite added producerist conspiracism to the Patriot backlash against globalization and foreign competition. Buchanan's calls for limiting immigration of Blacks,

Latinos, and Asians continued through 1994 as the Patriot Movement was growing, adding a racist subtext to much of the antiglobalism on the right.[4]

In the early 1990s there were other signs of right wing populist revolt. The dominionist Coalition on Revival (COR) urged the formation of "county militias" and a system of "Christian" courts, and called for abolishing the public schools, the Internal Revenue Service, and the Federal Reserve. In 1992 Conservative Caucus leader Howard Phillips helped launch the U.S. Taxpayers Party (USTP), whose antiglobalism and hostility to the federal government attracted Birchite conspiracists, remnants of George Wallace's American Independent Party, and militant abortion-rights opponents such as Randall Terry.[5]

Populism in the electoral arena clearly heralded its revival in Ross Perot's 1992 third-party candidacy against Republican George Bush and Democrat Bill Clinton. The candidacy began slowly. Jack Gargan, a quintessential angry populist, had an abiding disgust for elected politicians, so he founded the anti-incumbent group, Throw the Hypocritical Rascals Out (THRO). Gargan met with Perot because he thought the wealthy businessman was "the only person who can turn this country around." Perot was equivocal but hinted at interest, which Gargan saw as a signal to launch a full-blown grassroots campaign that eventually pulled Perot onto Larry King's CNN television interview show, and then into the race. Todd Mason captured the dichotomies in Perot the man when he described him as an "Antigovernment patriot, antiunion populist, antimanagement capitalist, loyal boss who sold out twice to GM, [and] billionaire defender of the underdog." Perot's gadfly persona worked in tandem with his populist rhetoric pitting "the people" against the entrenched elites. He also encouraged, in a mild, often implicit, way, the early stirrings of nationalist xenophobia as an antidote to globalization by multinational corporations. Perot racked up close to 20 million votes in the three-way race where he garnered almost 19 percent of the total. But columnist Michael Kelly nailed down the troubling aspects of the candidate when he called Perot "an example of the melding of populism and the paranoid style, of legitimate critic and crackpot, of giving voice to valid grievances and hysterical fears."[6]

PATRIOTS AND MILITIAS

It was in this context of resurgent isolationism and unilateralism that a self-conscious Patriot movement coalesced. It involved some 5 million persons who suspected—to varying degrees—that the government was manipulated by secret elites and planned the imminent imposition of some form of tyranny.[7] This suspicion has been the basic theme of the John Birch Society since the late 1950s.

The Patriot movement was bracketed on the reformist side by the Birch Society and the conspiracist segment of the Christian Right, and on the insurgent side by the Liberty Lobby and groups promoting themes historically associated with White supremacy and antisemitism. A variety of preexisting far-right vigilante groups (including Christian Identity adherents and outright neonazi groups) were influential in helping to organize the broader Patriot movement.[8] The Patriot movement, however, drew recruits from several preexisting movements and networks:

- Militant right-wing gun rights advocates, antitax protesters, survivalists, and far-right libertarians.
- Christian Patriots, and other persons promoting a variety of pseudo-legal "constitutionalist" theories.
- Advocates of "sovereign" citizenship, "freeman" status, and other arguments rooted in a distorted analysis of the thirteenth, fourteenth, and fifteenth Amendments, including those persons who argue that a different or second-class form of citizenship is granted to African Americans through these amendments.
- White racist, antisemitic, or neonazi movement, such as the Posse Comitatus, Aryan Nations, and Christian Identity.
- The confrontational wing of the antiabortion movement.
- Apocalyptic millennialists, including those Christians who believed the period of the "End Times" had arrived and they were facing the Mark of the Beast, which could be hidden in supermarket bar codes, proposed paper currency designs, implantable computer microchips, Internet websites, or e-mail.
- The dominion theology sector of the Christian evangelical right, especially its most militant and doctrinaire branch, Christian Reconstructionism.
- The most militant wings of the antienvironmentalist "Wise Use" movement, county supremacy movement, state sovereignty movement, states' rights movement, and Tenth Amendment movement.

Multiple themes intersected in the Patriot movement: government abuse of power; fears about globalism and sovereignty; economic distress (real, relative, and anticipated); apocalyptic fears of conspiracy and tyranny from above; male identity crisis, backlash against the social liberation movements of the 1960s and 1970s, and more.

Patriot movement adherents who formed armed units became known as armed citizens militias.[9] During the mid-1990s, armed militias were sporadically active in all fifty states, with total membership estimated at between 20,000 and 60,000. Both the Patriot and armed militia movements grew rapidly, relying on computer networks, fax trees, short-wave radio, AM talk radio, and videotape and audiotape distribution. The Patriot and militia movements were arguably the first major U.S. social movements to be organized primarily through overlapping, horizontal, nontraditional electronic media.

The Patriot movement, using conspiracist and producerist rhetoric, identified numerous scapegoats. Each unit, and in some cases each member, could pick and choose from the following list:

- Federal officials and law enforcement officers;
- Jewish institutions;
- Abortion providers and pro-choice supporters;
- Environmentalists and conservation activists;
- Gay and lesbian rights organizers; and
- People of color, immigrants, and welfare recipients.

The movement began to emerge during the Bush administration and continued to grow under Clinton. Both presidents were seen as liberal globalists in the eyes of the Patriot movement. When Clinton cited his old professor Carroll Quigley during the 1992 campaign and in his convention speech, the Patriot movement circulated stories about how Quigley's 1966 book *Tragedy and Hope* and 1981 book *The Anglo-American Establishment: From Rhodes to Cliveden* were really *exposés* about global rule by secret elites. This was seen as proof that Clinton was *part* of the conspiracy allegedly described by Quigley. Coupling Clinton's role in the Anglo-American conspiracy with Bush's previous celebration of a New World Order, the Patriots crafted a conspiracist narrative that the government was planning to impose a globalist UN police state in the near future.

In anticipation of attack by government agents, a small yet significant segment of the Patriot movement embraced survivalism. As a protective maneuver, a number of survivalists withdrew to remote, usually rural, locations or formed small communities for mutual self-defense. This is what led the Weaver family to Ruby Ridge, a remote region of Idaho. Randy Weaver and his wife were survivalists as well as Christian Identity adherents. Had the federal marshals who surrounded their house in 1992 factored these beliefs into their plan for arresting Randy Weaver, the subsequent deadly shoot-out might have been avoided. Federal Marshal William Degan and Weaver's wife Vicki and son Samuel died. Randy Weaver and his friend Kevin Harris were wounded.[10] News of the shoot-out fueled the growth of militias from adherents of the Patriot movement and the Far Right.

In 1993 the Branch Davidian compound in Waco, Texas was functioning as a low-key survivalist retreat. Davidian leader David Koresh was decoding elements of the biblical book of Revelation as an End Times script and preparing for the Tribulations. Some members of the group started attending gun shows to buy and sell arms and survivalist gear, and most likely intersected with the Patriot movement and the early armed militia movement. The government's failure to comprehend the Davidian's apocalyptic millennialist worldview set the stage for the deadly miscalculations by government agents, which cost the lives of 80 Branch Davidians (including 21 children) and four federal agents in April 1993.[11] Television coverage of this incident sent images of fiery apocalypse cascading throughout the society, further inflaming the apocalyptic paradigm within right-wing antigovernment groups, who saw the Weaver family and Branch Davidians as martyrs.[12]

A pattern of legal indictments and abusive government repression against right-wing dissidents had begun in the 1980s. Violent confrontations during standoffs sometimes involved gross misjudgments and the excessive use of force and resulted in deaths including that of Gordon Kahl, a rightist tax protester who became a *Posse Comitatus* organizer, killed in 1983; and Robert Mathews, a leader of the violent White supremacist group The Order, killed in 1984.[13]

There was also the use of questionable legal tactics, such as the 1988 prosecution on charges of seditious conspiracy of White supremacist leaders in Ft. Smith, Arkansas. The witnesses who testified about the alleged conspiracy were so dubious that the case was rejected by jurors, who found the defendants not guilty.[14] During the McCarthy period charges of criminal seditious conspiracy were also used in the political witch-hunt against communism.

When the government announced the sedition trial of White supremacists in Fort Smith, one person to object was Arthur Kinoy, a well-known leftist civil rights attorney and respected constitutional scholar who has argued cases before the U.S. Supreme Court. Kinoy, who had defended persons charged with communist sedition in the 1950s, said the views of the White supremacists in the Ft. Smith case were "disgusting," but, he said, "I'm worried about the charge of sedition against anyone." He noted the historic use of the sedition charge by the government to attack all dissent, especially on the left.[15]

Civil liberties attorney Harvey A. Silverglate agreed,

> I know it is a tricky and emotional issue, but sedition is a very serious charge, and to bring it in the Aryan Nations case at Fort Smith was patently absurd. You can't be cheering when the government brings a charge of sedition against the Aryan Nations crowd and then be complaining when they bring it against your friends.[16]

The fear of government repression prevalent in the Patriot movement and Far Right was not just paranoia. These events shaped new strategies for the Far Right, which began to rely on "leaderless resistance," whereby armed underground cells or individuals took self-directed action against the demonized enemies named by above-ground leaders. This strategy was promoted in a 1983 essay by neonazi leader Louis Beam.[17] This was an adaptation of classic theories of guerrilla struggle and anarchist action. The resulting criminality and violence, in turn, brought about more government raids and confrontations in a cycle that eventually led to the Ruby Ridge and

Waco incidents. Awareness of this history shaped the development of the militia movement out of the Patriot movement.[18] While many in the Patriot movement did not see themselves as part of the Far Right, they *could* see themselves as potential victims of government abuse of power.

Mobilizing gun owners was the first step in building the militia movement out of the Patriot movement. The Ruby Ridge and Waco incidents served as trigger events to galvanize a mobilization in 1993 and 1994 around stopping the Brady Bill and gun control provisions of the Crime Control Act.[19] Some grafted apocalyptic conspiracist fears onto the gun rights campaign, arguing that, if gun rights were restricted, a brutal and repressive government crackdown on gun owners would quickly follow. This interpretation not only existed in the Patriot movement itself but also was promoted by groups such as the National Rifle Association and rightist political leaders such as Pat Buchanan.[20]

The suppression of gun rights was seen by some as merely the opening act in a broader plan of tyranny, with the ultimate goal being UN control of the United States to benefit the global conspiracy of secret elites. While for many this was a secular narrative, an apocalyptic and millennialist End Times overlay was easily added by Christian fundamentalist elements in the movement. Another overlay was overt anti-Jewish conspiracism. The common solution, given these narratives, was to create independent armed defensive units to resist the expected wave of government violence—thus, the armed citizens militias.

The militias were a vigilante force and, like many before them throughout U.S. history, militia members saw themselves as heroes—defending God and country, kith and kin, hearth and home, family and faith. That these were cliches only made the force of the narrative more familiar and powerful. They compared themselves to the brave Minutemen holding the line at Lexington Green and Concord Bridge. They spoke of betrayal in high places and of traitors walking the sacred halls of Congress. They feared plots, so they made plans.

A key early figure in organizing the militia movement (using short-wave radio and the Internet) was Linda Thompson, whose elaborate apocalyptic warnings and conspiracist assertions of government plots were widely believed within the militia movement. In 1994 she called for an armed march on Washington, DC, to punish traitorous elected officials.[21] Her plan was widely criticized as dangerous, probably illegal, and possibly part of a government conspiracy to entrap militia members. Mark Koernke, aka Mark of Michigan, quickly replaced her as the most-favored militia intelligence analyst. Both used secular apoclyptic rhetoric.

Throughout the late 1990s the Patriot and armed militia movements overlapped with a resurgent states' rights movement and a new "county supremacy" movement. There was rapid growth of illegal so-called constitutionalist common-law courts, set up by persons claiming a nonexistent "sovereign" citizenship. These courts claimed jurisdiction over legal matters on the county or state level and dismissed the U.S. judicial system as corrupt and unconstitutional.[22] Constitutionalist legal theory created a two-tiered concept of citizenship in which White people have a superior "natural law" or "sovereign" citizenship. The most doctrinaire constitutionalists argue that only the original U.S. Constitution and Bill of Rights (the first ten amendments) are valid and legally binding, all later amendments are not. Put into effect, this would relegalize slavery, abolish women's right to vote, rescind the right of citizenship now guaranteed to all persons born in the United States, and allow *state* governments to ignore the Bill of Rights itself. Amazingly, many supporters of constitutionalism seem oblivious to the racism and sexism inherent in this construct.

The most publicized incident involving common-law ideology was the 1996 standoff involving the Montana Freemen, who combined Christian Identity, bogus common law legal theories, "debt-money" theories that reject the legality of the Federal Reserve system, and apocalyptic expectation.[23] In another incident, three men suspected of shooting a law enforcement officer while attempting to steal a water truck in Colorado in 1998 had talked to friends about the coming collapse of society, using Patriot-style rhetoric. Two of them reportedly attended meetings of a local Patriot group.[24] Many of the fears over declining sovereignty and imminent tyranny were linked to the idea that "the UN is a critical cornerstone of the New World Order," as one Birch Society publication put it.[25] Opposing the collectivist menace of global government, militia groups invoked metaphors from libertarianism, conspiracist anticommunism, and apocalyptic millennialism.

INSIDE A PATRIOT MEETING

Patriot rhetoric is easy to caricature and dismiss as paranoid ravings, but within the subculture—given certain basic (and flawed) assumptions of the worldview—there is an internal logic and consistency that allows for substantial debate and dialogue. A typical Patriot meeting was held in November 1994 at the high school auditorium in Burlington, Massachusetts, a few miles north of Boston.[26] The seventy-five people who attended the public meeting heard speakers decry the failure of government to meet the needs of average Americans. Several speakers argued that this failure was driven by a vast and even satanic conspiracy. Attendees ranged in age from the early 20s to the late 60s, and they came from Massachusetts and several surrounding states including New Hampshire and Rhode Island.

Leading antiabortion organizer Dr. Mildred Jefferson, an African American woman, began by speaking about problems with the elite medical profession she witnessed as a surgeon. She soon linked the elite medical establishment to what she saw as elite liberal groups such as the National Organization for Women (NOW) and Planned Parenthood, and then she tied them all to proponents of secular humanism dating back to the 1800s. Jefferson was a founder and former officer of the National Right to Life committee and a board member of Massachusetts Citizens for Life. A longtime activist, she appeared in the 1979 antiabortion film by Francis A. Schaeffer and C. Everett Koop that blamed secular humanism for the collapse of morality in America.[27]

Speakers such as Jefferson and Sandra Martinez of the ultraconservative Christian group Concerned Women for America were concerned primarily with the collapse of morality caused by godless secular humanism. Mining the same vein, John Birch Society stalwart Samuel L. Blumenfeld described how public schools did not adequately educate children due to a conspiracy that started with the rise of modern public education curricula.

Others, however, warned about government repression against dissidents. Bruce Chessly of Jews for the Preservation of Firearms Ownership spoke about government violations of civil liberties relating to gun ownership that reminded him of the Nazi era. Ed Brown of the Constitution Defense Militia of New Hampshire passed out brochures offering "Firearms Training, Combat Leadership, Close Combat, and Intelligence Measures."

Scott Stevens from New Hampshire urged those assembled to fight the growing government tyranny he saw resulting from the efforts of the political ruling elite and the financial elite to control the world. Stevens explained how he applied the "dialectic of Hegel" to unravel how the two major parties work together to erode civil liberties. "Liberal Democrats set up a social order that impoverishes people and creates an underclass that becomes criminalized," said Stevens. "Then Republicans get into office and pass laws that put all these people in jail. So then we need more police and more jails, and soon people see police in the streets enforcing laws they don't want to obey."

During the meeting, attendees could browse among three tables of literature brought by Den's Gun Shop in Lakeville, Massachusets. There were instruction manuals for the conversion to automatic firing for several rifles favored by the militia and survivalist movements. Other books contained diagrams on how to build bombs and incendiary devices. One title was *Improvised Weapons of the American Underground*.

You could even purchase the book *Hunter* by neonazi William Pierce, leader of the National Alliance. *Hunter* is a book that describes parasitic Jews destroying America and extols the virtues of armed civilians who carry out political assassinations of Jews and homosexuals to preserve the White race. Pierce's earlier book, *The Turner Diaries*, was the primary sourcebook of racist underground terror organizations such as The Order during the 1980s.

The featured afternoon speaker was Robert K. Spear, a key figure in training armed citizens militias. Spear is the author of *Surviving Global Slavery:*

Living Under the New World Order. According to Spear, we are living in the End Times predicted in the book of Revelation. Spear cited Revelation 13, warning that Christians will be asked to accept the satanic "Mark of the Beast" and reject Christ. True Christians, Spear said, must defend their faith and prepare the way for the return of Christ. Spear believed the formation of armed Christian communities was necessary to prepare for the End Times. The book is dedicated to "those who will have to face the Tribulations."

The rhetoric at the Burlington Patriot meeting was typical of the Patriot genre. What the Weaver family, the Branch Davidians, and the Montana Freemen had in common was the confluence of right-wing populism, conspiracist scapegoating, and apocalyptic End Times millennialism. While these beliefs are often carried in a single package, they can be unbundled. Each person who attended the Burlington Patriot meeting could pick and choose from among various complementary narratives. For instance, Spear made it clear to the audience that, while he was concerned with the End Times and the Tribulations, his advice was equally useful for someone who feared secular forms of economic collapse, social unrest, or government repression.

RACISM AND ANTISEMITISM

The issue of racism and antisemitism in the Patriot and militia movements is complex. Clearly, the narratives of the movement drew from historic antisemitic conspiracy theories, but they also drew from generic claims of secret elites as well, and mingled with accurate assessments of global corporate power and concentration of wealth. The claim of sovereign citizenship derived from the Fourteenth Amendment implicitly regarded Black people as second-class citizens, and there were echoes of segregationist states' rights rhetoric in attacks on the power of the federal government.

Ed Brown, who attended the Burlington Patriot meeting, later assisted a regional speaking tour by Militia of Montana leader John Trochmann, including a speech at Yale University and an appearance at a Patriot meeting outside Sturbridge, Massachusetts. Trochmann frequently interlaced his conspiracy theories with bits and pieces from historic antisemitic conspiracy theories and Christian Identity lore. At the Sturbridge meeting, Brown insisted in a private conversation that the converted Khazar Jews run the banks and the media, but he argued that, since the Khazars were converts, not the covenant Jews of the Bible, his statements were not truly antisemitic. Brown believed he was not being antisemitic while spreading a classic antisemitic story. Yet, this is different from someone who is overtly and consciously bigoted, or someone who hides his bigotry for tactical or strategic reasons, such as easing the tasks of recruitment.

The host of the Sturbridge meeting was Leroy Crenshaw, an African

American. Crenshaw, a hunter since he was a child, was primarily concerned with defending gun ownership rights and other aspects of what he saw as increasing government tyranny. Crenshaw introduced Trochmann by acknowledging that there were differences of opinion in the room about racism and antisemitism. He said he was personally uncomfortable with some of Trochmann's views, but he was more uncomfortable with the views and actions of the government. Crenshaw noted that there were members of the Posse Comitatus present and that he had problems with some of their views, but he welcomed them to hear Trochmann as a matter of courtesy, since Trochmann was being attacked by the same liberal government and media they all opposed. In a private conversation, Crenshaw was asked about his participation in a movement where there was racism and antisemitism that made him uncomfortable. "There is racism and antisemitism wherever I look in our society," replied Crenshaw, "it's no different in this group."[28]

At the Burlington meeting, however, it was made clear from the podium by several speakers that any discussion of racist views or Jewish influence in the conspiracy was unacceptable. Brown accepted those principles of unity for the meeting and remained silent while in the group, only hinting at his views after being pressed during a smoking break.

The principles of unity were different for the two meetings. At Sturbridge, the circle was opened to include those with racist and antisemitic views, although the leader personally distanced himself from those views. At Burlington, racist and antisemitic views were placed outside the circle by the leaders. Although persons with those views were in attendance, they were essentially told to keep silent, although books with racist and antisemitic contents were tolerated at a private display table.

Sometimes people change their views over time. After Scott Stevens was told about the racist roots of the reliance on Fourteenth Amendment claims of sovereign citizenship, he researched the subject. Within several months after the Burlington meeting, he had modified his beliefs about the Fourteenth Amendment basis for sovereign citizenship and had raised the issue of racism among other Patriots.

Activists in the Northwest reported that racism and antisemitism were more pronounced among the militias they encountered. In the Midwest, some militias split into two factions over the issue of racism and antisemitism. Sometimes members with bigoted views were asked to leave by the majority faction. Racism and antisemitism were woven into the Patriot narrative, but in many cases this was unconscious and unintentional. In other cases far-right activists hid their overt racist and antisemitic views to recruit from, or take over, Patriot and militia groups. This complexity led some to indict all militia members as closet neonazis, while others, out of ignorance or expediency, sanitized the movement by trivializing evidence of racism and antisemitism.

Several authors use the idea of "bridging organizations" that ideologically and organizationally serve as links between conservatism and the Far Right.[29] The Patriot and armed citizens militia movements functioned in this manner, as have other right-wing populist groups for generations. After the Oklahoma City bombing, less militant and more reform-oriented members left the militia movement and faded back into the broader Patriot movement. Meanwhile, racists and antisemites, many of them revolutionary rather than reformist, remained active in many militias and even intensified their recruitment and co-optation efforts. As the militia movement began to shrink in size, the proportion of its constituent base that openly espoused bigotry and insurgency rose.

JOHN SALVI: GOD'S PATRIOT

Apocalyptic conspiracy theories intertwined with Patriot mobilization played a role in two recent criminal cases: that of John C. Salvi, III, convicted in the December 1994 murder of two reproductive health center workers and the wounding of five others; and that of Francisco Martin Duran, who sprayed the White House with bullets. Duran listened to a Colorado-based radio talk show hosted by Chuck Baker, who promoted Patriot themes.[30] Both Duran and Salvi showed signs of psychological disturbance. Salvi committed suicide in jail after his conviction.

In the spring of 1994, Salvi joined with 300 antiabortion demonstrators outside the same Planned Parenthood clinic in Brookline, Massachusetts, that he would later attack. Pamphlets circulated at the site by Operation Rescue claimed (falsely) that 18,000 abortions were performed annually at the facility.

Salvi met with a local parish priest and demanded access to the parishioners in church so he could distribute lurid photographs (obtained from Human Life International) of aborted fetuses. Salvi charged that the Catholic Church was not doing enough to stop abortions. He confronted his parish on Christmas Eve 1994 for failing to live up to his interpretation of the Catholic faith and its obligations. He quoted the biblical book of Revelations and told his parents of wanting to confront Satan.

Shortly after his arrest he released a rambling handwritten note alleging conspiracies of Freemasons, conspiracies to manipulate paper currency, and conspiracies against Catholics. He told the court he supported the welfare state, Catholic labor unions, and opposed abortion. He talked about the Vatican printing its own currency and a specific conspiracy of the Ku Klux Klan, the Freemasons, and the Mob. Far from being unique or necessarily symptomatic of mental illness, all of these ideas appeared in apocalyptic right-wing Catholic, Protestant, and secular political publications available in the Boston area.[31] Much of John Salvi's rhetoric about the corrupt money system, for example, echoed themes in the *Michael Journal*, which was distributed by a small group of apocalyptic Catholics in Massachusetts.

Salvi patronized a gun store he may have seen as friendly to the Patriot movement, and generally intersected with the same coalition that were represented at the Burlington meeting. The gun used by Salvi was modified in a way favored by some militia members. Detailed instructions for these modifications were for sale at the Burlington Patriot meeting, as well as in Massachusetts gun stores and gun shows, where Patriot material was easily obtained. According to an article by Sarah Tippit of Reuters,

> While living in Florida in 1992, Salvi talked to a friend about joining a militia and once expressed interest in a particular camping trip with a militia from the Everglades, said his former employer, Mark Roberts of Naples, Florida. "Salvi had mentioned being affiliated with some bivouac thing in the Everglades. They were camping and he wanted to go," said Roberts, who employed Salvi for maintenance work. Shortly before moving to New England in 1992, Salvi stopped at Roberts' house and showed his gun. He had sawed off its barrel and installed a silencer, Roberts said. "He said he was going to shoot cans in the woods, but he didn't want to make any noise," Roberts said. "That worried me."[32]

Magazines found in Salvi's residence included *The New American* and *The Fatima Crusader*, both published by right-wing groups promoting conspiracist theories and vociferously opposing abortion and homosexuality.[33] One issue of *The New American* found in John Salvi's possession contained an article by Charles E. Rice exploring the idea that killing an abortion provider might be morally justified.[34] One does not find issues of *The New American* or *The Fatima Crusader,* or material from Human Life International, at the corner newsstand. They are circulated mainly within a distinctly right-wing conspiracist subculture. This is a subculture where apocalyptic demonization, scapegoating, and conspiracism are rampant. Karen Branan and Frederick Clarkson described the thirteenth annual Human Life International (HLI) conference, held in Irvine, California, in April 1994,

> Attended by 2,000 anti-abortion activists from around the globe, the conference's high point came during Randall Terry's banquet speech when he challenged the crowd to rise up and make America a "Christian Nation" under "Biblical Law," abolish contraception and abortion, take their children out of public schools, and make "dads [the] Godly leaders" of the family, with "the women in submission, raising kids for the glory of God."
>
> Amidst pictures of a weeping Virgin Mary holding a fetus, and banners quoting Pope John Paul II, most of the workshops presented a paranoid message of black-and-white thinking: there's always a plot, a shadow force systematically subverting God's creation. Some mentioned Lucifer or Satan, others gave Lucifer a human form—Bill and Hillary Clinton are popular em-

bodiments this year, as is Margaret Sanger, the founder of Planned Parenthood. For others, the archenemies in this pageant are Freemasons or Jews.[35]

The authors warned that, as HLI's "hate-filled rhetoric" increased, the "impact of this organization . . . will likely be felt in frightening ways."

Some people with a mental illness who carry out acts of violence cannot successfully control their fears and anger and act them out against real targets. Salvi's psychological condition was not demonstrated by his claims about a banking conspiracy, which were commonplace in the Catholic apocalyptic Right, nor was his choice of targets random.[36] Certainly a person like Salvi did not represent the mainstream of Catholicism, the antiabortion movement, or the U.S. political Right, but he expressed the views of a durable subculture with conspiracist views that consciously resorts to scapegoating.

This dynamic of rhetoric triggering violence functions more easily among the mentally ill. But those who are scapegoated can be injured or killed by people—whatever their mental state—who act out their conspiracist beliefs in a zealous manner. The failure of political and religious leaders to take strong public stands against groups and individuals that demagogically spread conspiracist scapegoating theories encourages this dangerous dynamic. Yet, when President Clinton spoke out against the rhetoric of demonization following the Oklahoma City bombing, he was criticized by numerous pundits spanning the whole political spectrum.[37]

Many questions need more study. When does demonizing rhetoric by demagogues motivate action among followers who are not mentally ill? Why and when do sane followers of ideological leaders begin to act out their beliefs through violence? When and how does apocalyptic violence become a mass movement? How and when can it become state policy?

THE FAR RIGHT AND THE OKLAHOMA CITY BOMBING

The conspiracist scapegoating characteristic of right-wing populism, including the Patriot and armed militia movements, creates not only individual acts of violence but also a dynamic where conspiracy theories and scapegoating become routine and seemingly banal. It also provides a handy recruitment device for the Far Right, readily attracting those who need to feel politically superior to others.

Non-Christian neonazis, such as in the pagan Church of the Creator, are sometimes able to work in coalitions with Christian Patriots because of their shared antigovernment sentiments and conspiracism rooted in historic forms of antisemitism. In fact, some conspiracist rhetoric in the Christian Right is virtually indistinguishable from far-right rhetoric. Susan DeCamp found some dozen quotes from Pat Robertson and Christian Identity preacher Pete Peters that when arranged together read like one continuous tract "promoting white nationalism."[38] So, conspiracist antigovernment themes can cross boundaries promiscuously while the various movements and groups working in parallel remain ideologically monogamous.

Thematic similarity, however, does not imply organizational or ideological congruence. The most significant worldview in the Christian Patriot movement was Christian Identity. Yet, Ken Stern makes some important distinctions concerning the Christian Patriot movement:

> Some commentators do not distinguish between Christian Identity and Christian Patriotism because, on the American far right, most who are Identity adherents are also Christian Patriots.
>
> But it is important to distinguish the two. Identity comes from a 19th century belief called "British Israelism." One can be an Identity adherent in Australia, Canada, et cetera. Christian Patriots, on the other hand, only exist in America, and one can be a Christian Patriot without subscribing to Identity religion. For example, James Nichols, brother of accused Oklahoma City-bomber Terry Nichols, is a Christian Patriot who flirted with, but was talked out of, Identity theology by a Methodist friend.[39]

The Gulf War encouraged the Identity adherents in Christian Patriot groups to peddle antisemitic conspiracist theories about Jewish power behind U.S. military involvement. An example was the forty-page newsprint tabloid booklet by Nord Davis, Jr., *Desert Shield and the New World Order*, published in 1990 by his Northpoint Tactical Teams.[40]

Other preexisting Christian Patriot groups quickly reached out to the emerging militia movement with similar propaganda materials. For instance, the Tennessee-based Christian Civil Liberties Association published *The Militia News*, ostensibly a newspaper but actually a catalog of books and other educational resources including guides on how to evade government tracking and surveillance. The opening article, "U.S. Government Initiates Open Warfare Against American People," was a good example of antisemitic Christian Patriot dogma:

> Following the turn of the 20th century, Communism (the Judeo-Bolsheviks of Russia) and other diabolical movements and philosophies—Fabian socialism, materialism, atheism, and secular humanism—would, like malignant parasites, establish themselves in America. Even our presidents, beginning with Franklin Roosevelt, would begin using the resources of this nation to finance and support our foreign enemies, particularly the Communist and Zionist movements.[41]

The article railed against what the author saw as the unconstitutional attack on states' rights by "Court mandated integration and forced busing" in the 1960s and the "systematic de-Christianization of the nation."[42] Warning that this was part of a "satanic conspiracy," the author advised that, for the government to succeed, "the globalists must outlaw and confiscate" firearms.

> Every gun owner who is the least bit informed knows that those who are be-
> hind this conspiracy—who now have their people well placed in political of-
> fice, in the courts, in the media, and in the schools, are working for the total
> disarming of the American people and the surrender of our nation and its sov-
> ereignty. . . . The time is at hand when men and women must decide whether
> they are on the side of freedom and justice, the American republic, and Al-
> mighty God; or if they are on the side of tyranny and oppression, the New
> World Order, and Satan.[43]

Timothy McVeigh, who had moved from conspiracist antigovernment beliefs into militant neonazi ideology, blew up the Oklahoma City federal building on April 19, 1995—the anniversary of the Waco conflagration—to protest government abuse of power that he, and others, believed was but the prelude to a tyrannical New World Order.[44] It is likely that McVeigh hoped that his act of terrorism might push the more defensive and less ideo-logical militias into a more racialized and militant insurgency. Instead, many militia members were shocked by the carnage.

McVeigh's act of terrorism mirrored a similar scenario in William Pierce's *The Turner Diaries*, which McVeigh distributed to friends. Pierce at one point in the novel describes in detail the bombing of a federal building. The novel invokes as its central apocalyptic theme the cleansing nature of ritual violence—a theme reminiscent of German Nazi ideology, which also sought a millenarian Thousand Year Reich.[45]

McVeigh's apparently secular concern that during the Gulf War the government had implanted a microchip into his body echoes familiar re-peated concerns among fundamentalist Christians over the years that the Mark of the Beast might be hidden in electronic devices.

RIPPLES ON THE POND

By 1994 there were local, state, and federal election races where candidates for public office sought to attract voters from the ranks of the Patriot move-ment.[46] On the national level, Mark Pitcavage singled out "Steve Stockman of Texas and Helen Chenoweth of Idaho, freshmen Republicans who in 1994 had no qualms about currying to the militia movement."

Pitcavage noted that, by the 1996 election campaign, "Stockman's close ties to Gun Owners of America leader Larry Pratt, and Chenoweth's videotape hawked by militia members at rallies are just some of the more well-known weaknesses being exploited by their opponents." Still, Pitcavage found that in fifteen state and federal races in 1996, most of the candidates who "courted" the Patriot movement won the election despite public awareness of the connection.[47]

On the state level, the best-known elected officials who articulated Patriot themes were Republican California State Senator Don Rogers and Republican State Senator Charles Duke of Colorado.

In 1996, Rogers was involved in a controversy over his having filed legal documents claiming sovereign citizen status, which is often a prelude to claiming no tax liability.[48] Rogers also spoke at meetings of Jubilee, a Christian Identity group, even after he was told of their bigoted views. Rogers argued that Jubilee was simply a "group of patriotic Americans looking to restore their individual freedoms,"[49] when a more accurate description would be antisemitic and White supremacist conspiracy mongers.

Colorado State Senator Charles Duke claimed taxes were a form of slavery, and defended the Patriot movement. A Duke campaign policy memo issued during his 1996 Republican primary race for the U.S. Senate is revealing:

> The current national interest in restoring power to the states began with a resolution sponsored by Senator Duke when he was a member of the Colorado House of Representatives. Since then [1994], 20 additional states have adopted similar resolutions and laws are being crafted in many state legislatures to further the national movement to restore state sovereignty. Having a grass roots constitutionist, like Senator Duke, in the United States Senate will further the restoration of individual liberty.[50]

Duke lost the 1996 primary election that selected the Republican U.S. Senate candidate for Colorado. Still, in a four-way race he garnered 18 percent of the vote. In 1998, with a year left on his term in office, he resigned his state Senate seat, claiming God had directed him to do so. The next year he announced his interest in returning to politics.

In Montana, human rights activist Christine Kaufmann chronicled how several state legislators pushed the Patriot agenda. She also noted that rightist ideas including "ending affirmative action, asserting states' rights, restricting the rights of non-white immigrants, and making English the official language, are now part of the political mainstream."[51]

Activism on the state level also came from the grassroots of the Patriot movement. The *Spotlight* featured a cover story on how right-wing populists in New Jersey had distributed flyers and faxes opposing a proposed state environmental law. According to the *Spotlight*, "Virtually overnight hundreds of thousands of copies of the flier appeared as if by magic on bulletin boards, store windows and fax machines throughout the state." The flyer was circulated in part through a fax hotline.[52]

There were national campaigns as well.[53] In 1995 several conservative groups and Patriot networks successfully mobilized opposition to a planned

"Conference of the States" that had been supported by the Council of State Governments and National Governors' Association. A conspiracist theory arose that the conference was a secret plot to rewrite the Constitution and specifically eliminate the Second Amendment.

According to *The Right Guide*, there was "strong grassroots opposition from conservative and populist organizations, particularly firearms owners' groups." The *Guide* named the groups most responsible for the campaign: American Pistol and Rifle Association, Conservative Caucus, Constitutionalists United Against a Constitutional Convention, Council on Domestic Relations, Eagle Forum, John Birch Society, and the National Association to Keep and Bear Arms. They also credited Charles Duke, who the *Wall Street Journal* said "spearheaded the opposition."[54] National radio talk show host Michael Reagan also urged listeners to oppose the conference because it was part of the One World Government conspiracy, along with promoting other conspiracist theories.[55]

In 1997 U.S. Rep. Helen Chenoweth of Idaho introduced a bill cosponsored by 43 House members to block a federal plan to designate certain historic waterways "heritage rivers." The primarily symbolic gesture had been attacked by the Patriot movement and the overlapping antienvironmentalist "Wise Use" movement as a federal land grab. Some claimed it was part of a UN-backed New World Order initiative. Conspiracy theories about environmental activists created an atmosphere where confrontations accelerated in rate and intensity.[56]

On the international level, the Biodiversity Treaty was blocked, with a key role being played by a coalition of Patriot, Wise Use and LaRouche network activists who spread misinformation and conspiracist theories.[57]

CONCLUSION

Many commentators have portrayed the Patriot and militia movements as fascist. We believe it is more accurate to describe them as right-wing populist movements with important fascistic tendencies—thus they are quasifascist or protofascist. Like the America First movement of the early 1940s, the Patriot movement and the militias represented a large-scale convergence of committed fascists with nonfascist activists. Such coalitions enable fascists to gain new recruits, increase their legitimacy among millions of people, and repackage their doctrines for mass consumption.

Mary Rupert dubbed the Patriot movement "A Seedbed for Fascism" and suggested that the "major missing piece in looking at the Patriot Movement in relation to fascism is that it does not overtly advance an authoritarian scheme of government. In fact, its emphasis seems to be on protecting individual rights." According to Rupert, there are two "portents of possibility" that could shift this situation: "First is the below-the-surface disposition of the Patriot Movement towards authoritarianism, and second is the way in which Patrick Buchanan . . . picked up and played out the Patriots' grievances."[58] We would add that "individual rights," like states' rights, can also be a cover for the sort of decentralized social totalitarianism promoted by the neofascists of the Posse Comitatus and Christian Reconstructionism—both of which helped lay the groundwork for the Patriot movement itself.

Jim Robinson of the web-based organization Free Republic echoed the basic position of the Patriot movement as it reconstituted itself after the Oklahoma City bombing:

> The federal government has overstepped its Constitutional limits and the complicit media is acting in concert to continue the illegal government expansion and to strengthen its own stranglehold on truth and to continue its agenda of projecting the socialist government propaganda slant on the news.
>
> The government and the corporate media have created, through regulation and policy a liberal propaganda machine whose goal is to continue the expansion of a collective state and to control every aspect of our lives and fortunes.
>
> We, the People, are exercising our Constitutional right to freedom of speech and peaceable assembly to demand that our elected representatives fulfill their Constitutional duty.[59]

The similarity between Patriot movement rhetoric and rhetoric from the right wing of the Republican Party is striking.

15

THE VAST CLINTON
CONSPIRACY MACHINE

The Hard Right on the Center Stage

The roar was visceral—a torrent of sound fed by a vast subconscious reservoir of anger and resentment. Repeatedly, as speaker after speaker strode to the podium and denounced President Bill Clinton, the thousands in the cavernous auditorium surged to their feet with shouts and applause. The scene was the Christian Coalition's annual Road to Victory Conference held in September 1998—three months before the House of Representatives voted to send articles of impeachment to the Senate.

Former Reagan appointee Alan Keyes observed that the country's moral decline had spanned two decades and couldn't be blamed exclusively on Clinton, but when he denounced Clinton for supporting the "radical homosexual agenda," the crowd cheered and gave Keyes one of his several standing ovations. Republican Senator Bob Smith of New Hampshire attacked Clinton's foreign policies, stating that the "globalists of the New World Order" must not be allowed to sell out American sovereignty.

Most attacks on Clinton highlighted his sexual misconduct and subsequent cover-up as proof that he was unfit to remain president, but the full list of complaints was long. When the American Conservative Union distributed a National Impeachment Survey with the type of loaded question typical of the direct-mail genre, it asked, "Which Clinton Administration scandal listed below do you consider to be 'very serious'?" The scandals listed were "Chinagate, Monicagate, Travelgate, Whitewater, FBI 'Filegate,' Cattlegate, Troopergate, Casinogate, [and] Health Caregate." In addition to scandals, those attending the annual conference clearly opposed Clinton's perceived agenda on abortion, gay rights, foreign policy, and other issues.

Several months later, much of the country's attention was focused on the House of Representatives "managers" and their pursuit of having the impeached Clinton removed from office by the Senate. Few people understood the extensive right-wing political machinery that was mobilized to pressure the managers to fight on and never give up.[1] Those gathered at the Road to Victory Conference were naturally inclined to oppose Clinton, but they were "educated" by a large number of relatively unknown right-wing groups and individuals to demonize Clinton not simply as a liberal but as corrupt and immoral, perhaps even as a murderer—the very *embodiment* of evil.

A WIDE COALITION

The anti-Clinton campaign involved an unprecedented mainstreaming of the conspiracist narrative found in right-wing populism. During the 1990s right-wing coalitions increasingly tolerated, or even embraced, the most outlandish and nasty assertions of the conspiracist subcultures—for example, that the president (earlier, while governor of Arkansas) was involved in drug running, bribery—and even numerous murders, to keep word of his crimes from leaking out. Even conservative groups with a more cautious and pragmatic track record appeared more and more open to right-wing conspiracist allegations that became the subtexts of the anti-Clinton campaign.[2] The impeachment struggle demonstrated the extent to which the Republican Party was willing to enlist (or at least accommodate for political gain) sectors of the Right that championed apocalyptic conspiracism—the Christian Right, hard-right ultraconservatives, and the Patriot and militia movements.

Much of the original constituency for the impeachment battle came from the Christian Right, but the Christian Right did not act alone or in isolation. Right-wing attacks on President Clinton flowed from a large and diverse network of individuals and organizations. This was not a vast secret conspiracy against President Clinton but rather a broad loosely knit preexisting coalition among several sectors of the political Right. Business conservatives, neocons, Christian Rightists, hard-right conspiracists, and members of the Patriot movement all shared an anti-Clinton agenda despite wide differences in political outlook, goals, and style. As analyst Russ Bellant explained, "Different sectors on the right didn't have to agree on the person they would choose to replace Clinton; all they had to do was agree that they wanted Clinton to go."[3] It was this convergence of anti-Clinton sentiment across sectors of the Right that accounted for the fervor and depth of the anti-Clinton campaign.

The anti-Clinton drive embodied the Right's fusionist coalition of social traditionalism, economic libertarianism, and anti-collectivism. An extensive review of rightist attacks on Clinton over several years shows that they clustered in familiar fusionist groups emphasizing one or more of the following themes:

- Moral collapse (social traditionalism): gay rights, abortion, feminism, pornography, nontraditional sexuality, and violence.

- Statist intrusion (libertarianism): big government, onerous taxes, government regulations, environment, land use, parental rights, job site safety, and activist judges.

- Collectivist conspiracy: liberal media bias, government tyranny, treason, New World Order globalism, and satanic One World Government.

Conservative business media outlets—such as the *Wall Street Journal* and Rupert Murdoch's *New York Post* and *The Times* of London—played an important role in the impeachment drive. Their editorial proclivities reflected long-standing tensions between Clinton and a business community deeply and increasingly hostile to even small increases in taxes or regulations. Thomas Ferguson argues that "by the middle of its first term, the New Democrat, self-consciously pro-business Clinton Administration was essentially at war with well over half of the largest investors in the United States." Many corporate types were alienated by Clinton's proposals for tax raises, health care reform, gun control, a global warming treaty, and raising the minimum wage. Above all, the administration's call for a large increase in the cigarette tax and the Food and Drug Administration's threat to assume regulatory power over nicotine led tobacco companies to shift their political contributions massively to the Republicans.

Ferguson notes that Kenneth Starr, as a corporate lawyer, represented tobacco firms both before *and during* his tenure as special prosecutor investigating Whitewater and related issues. And he was appointed special prosecutor by a three-judge panel chaired by David Sentelle, a judge from the leading tobacco state of North Carolina. Sentelle's political mentor was ultraconservative and key tobacco advocate Senator Jesse Helms. Helms and fellow North Carolina Senator Lauch Faircloth met with Sentelle shortly before Starr's appointment.[4]

If "big government" was the key issue for many of Clinton's business opponents, for others the key issue was the Culture War. For Christian Rightists and many other ultraconservatives, the impeachment battle embodied the long-standing struggle against liberalism, secularism, cultural change, and even the Enlightenment. For some, it was part of the age-old apocalyptic battle against forces aligned with Satan. Demonization, whether secular or religious, was central to the process. Consider the language with which ultraconservative reporter Christopher Ruddy described the president "Clinton is the quintessential slippery lawyer. Just as a weasel sucks the blood from its prey, so Clinton sucks the ordinary meaning out of words to deceive others. . . . Clinton is a filthy-minded, self-centered man who fits the criteria of a sociopath."[5]

Essayist Ralph Melcher summarized the idea behind such demonization:

> The right wing has succeeded in doing what it set out to do from the beginning . . . to make Bill and Hillary into political monsters. The venomous hatred directed by these people toward the "entire culture" the President represents goes back way before anyone heard of Monica Lewinsky—even before Whitewater (which has all but vanished). I would say that it goes back even before the 60s—all the way to the managed economies of the New Deal and the threat of revolution arising out of the ashes of World War I and later the Great Depression.[6]

As historian Robert Dallek of Boston University put it, "The Republicans are incensed because they essentially see Clinton . . . as the embodiment of the counterculture's thumbing of its nose at accepted wisdoms and institutions of the country."[7] To many on the right, the president's attempt to cover up his sexual relationship with White House intern Monica Lewinsky symbolized his immorality, but it was also sufficient pretext; they hoped to punish Clinton for his suspected larger crimes—much in the tradition of indicting (and convicting) Al Capone for tax evasion rather than mayhem and murder.

The impeachment drive's base of support reflected Christian Right activists' areas of power within the Republican Party. At one point during the Clinton impeachment process, notes journalist David Nyhan, "Nine out of 10 GOP leaders in the two branches hailed from Southern or Western states, where Clinton is unpopular, the religious right controls the party machinery, and right-wing clergymen and talk-show hosts exercise broad sway." Nyhan suggested that impeachment's stronger support in the South and West was partly a legacy of Nixon's 1968 "southern strategy," which at the time accelerated Democrats' loss of control of its once "solid South."[8]

Despite their efforts, anti-Clinton rightists failed to spark a mass movement for impeachment. The use of populist-style rhetoric by elite political leaders does not always spark a grassroots populist movement that grows much beyond its hard-core loyalists. However, contrary to popular punditry, impeachment advocates did succeed in persuading a large majority of the public that Clinton deserved either removal, forced resignation, or censure.[9]

WHY CLINTON?

Although right-wing advocates of impeachment portrayed Clinton as "liberal" and "far left" (as if the two were equivalent), the political gap between the president and themselves was often much narrower than they claimed.

It was Clinton, not his Republican predecessors, who insisted on a two-year cutoff point for welfare benefits and who signed the law abolishing Aid to Families with Dependent Children, a cornerstone of the New Deal system. Clinton fueled attacks on immigrants by massively enlarging the Border Patrol, stepping up militarization of the southern border region, and eroding the legal status of noncitizens. He signed laws that seriously undermined civil liberties protections such as habeus corpus and prisoners' right to appeal. He continued the punitive and ineffective War on Drugs, which heavily discriminated against Black and Latino youth and sharply increased police repression against inner-city neighborhoods. He echoed repressive "law-and-order" politics with his advocacy of the death penalty, mandatory curfews for teens, and prosecuting minors as adults. He endorsed the antigay "Defense of Marriage" Act, which defined marriage as a "union between one man and one woman" and denied same-sex couples access to spousal benefits under federal programs.[10]

Clinton vigorously pushed the North American Free Trade Agreement (NAFTA) and the General Agreement on Tariffs and Trade (GATT), which protected sweatshops and child labor and benefited multinational corporations at the expense of working people in the United States and abroad. He pursued economic sanctions against Iraq that have resulted in hundreds of thousands of civilian deaths. And he was the first president, at least since Richard Nixon, to launch military attacks against four different countries—Iraq, Sudan, Afghanistan, and Yugoslavia—in less than one year.[11]

With the partial exception of the international and military policies, these positions mirrored those of the Right. Precisely because the gap between Clinton and the Right was relatively small, his attackers exaggerated it to monstrous proportions. The commanders of the Culture War demonized Clinton not because he actually represented the antithesis of everything their troops stood for, but because he was highly effective in co-opting right-wing positions and using them to his own advantage.

In the early 1950s Republicans, enraged at President Truman's upset 1948 reelection and his skillful use of anticommunism, backed Joe McCarthy's conspiracist crusade against high government officials. In the late 1990s, Clinton's embrace of Republican positions, and his reelection two years after Republicans gained a majority in Congress, evoked a similar response by the Right.

Clinton's 1996 reelection strategy followed a plan carefully designed by priapic political consultant Dick Morris. Morris told Clinton that Republican strength was based on five "messages": fiscal/economic, foreign/defense, race, crime, and social. He continued: "When Republicans are Reduced to Only Social Message [abortion, antigay sentiment, etc.], they lose." Clinton followed Morris's advice by almost completely adopting Republican positions on the first four messages. He left Republican strategists the "social" issues—the core of the Hard Right's Culture War.[12]

THE ROLE OF THE MEDIA

A symbiotic interplay between right-wing conspiracist subcultures and the conservative mainstream media fueled the anti-Clinton campaign. Conspiracist stories about the president encouraged the small but vocal minority that originally supported Kenneth Starr's investigation of Clinton. Much of the media coverage of Clinton from 1997 through 1999 focused on scandal and impeachment rather than policy, ideological political issues, or electoral politics. This was true not only in alternative right-wing media but also in mainstream corporate media. Reporter Gene Lyons is especially critical of the *New York Times* (and to a lesser degree the *Washington Post*) for devoting so much coverage to the alleged "Whitewater Scandal" over a collapsed land deal, for which no evidence implicating the Clintons in criminal acts has ever been substantiated.[13] Lyons argues that much of the scandal coverage in the mainstream media "rests on ´facts´ that are somewhere between highly dubious and demonstrably false," and he calls it "journalistic malpractice" resulting from a coordinated right-wing "dirty tricks" campaign.[14]

In addition to corporate newspaper and magazine coverage attacking Clinton, there were books, newsletters, fax reports, videotapes, audiotapes, direct mail, Internet sites, and more that spewed out, emanating from tiny one-person operations to international media conglomerates.

British journalist Ambrose Evans-Pritchard, whose mix of investigative reporting and rumor-mongering was an important link in the anti-Clinton propaganda chain, discussed the crucial role played by the Internet:

> In the 1980s our stories would not have gained any traction. Now they are "posted" within hours of publication, and are then perused by the producers of the radio talk shows, who surf the Net in search of avant-garde material. A good scoop may be picked up [and] read on the air by G. Gordon Liddy, Paul Harvey, or Chuck Harder. It might be featured by [columnist] Blanquita Cullum, or by Rush Limbaugh, with his 20 million "ditto heads."[15]

Michael Reagan, the top-rated nighttime talk radio host, has an ultra-conservative worldview but a reputation for being fair and open-minded. Nonetheless, as noted in the previous chapter, Reagan used his nationally syndicated program to promote conspiracy theories emerging from the Patriot movement about a global One World Government and attempts to rewrite the U.S. Constitution. He also pushed various theories claiming that Clinton's deputy White House counsel, Vincent Foster, did not commit suicide but was assassinated. These conspiracist allegations are also in Reagan's 1996 book *Making Waves*, endorsed in back cover blurbs by former U.S. Attorney General Edwin Meese, III, then Republican National Committee Chairman Haley Barbour, and several current and former congresspersons.[16]

The most alarmist attacks on Clinton originated in right-wing alternative media, then spread throughout right-wing information networks, finally appearing in mainstream outlets. This troubling dynamic was described in a 1995 White House memo titled "Communication Stream of Conspiracy Commerce."[17] The memo was widely derided in the corporate media, but it is essentially accurate. Similar contentions about unsubstantiated conspiracy theories fueling anti-Clinton news stories had already appeared in mainstream newspapers and magazines, including the *Columbia Journalism Review*. In early 1995 Mary Ann Mauney of the Center for Democratic Renewal was quoted in a Scripps Howard syndicated news feature discussing how conservative and militia conspiracy theories seemed to be blending together.[18] In addition, a 1998 scholarly book edited by Linda Kintz and Julia Lesage, *Culture, Media, and the Religious Right*, included several chapters that explored how the right-wing alternative media shape issues that are later discussed in the mainstream media.[19]

Matt Drudge was the quintessential example of a rightist interlocutor moving conspiracist scapegoating into the mainstream media. Drudge parlayed an Internet gossip page into international celebrity for himself when he surfaced the Monica Lewinsky story in January 1998. Drudge claimed to have scooped *Newsweek* magazine when he reported rumors that *Newsweek* editors were not running a Lewinsky scandal story that reporter Michael Isikoff had been working on for months.[20] This was less a scoop than an act of scavenging. Actually, *Newsweek* editors were exercising appropriate caution with a story that needed more confirmation. After Drudge "broke" the story, *Newsweek* ran the Isikoff article on the scandal, the first of many such reports.

Conservative sources, including Lucianne Goldberg and Linda Tripp, had fed Isikoff the basics of the story.[21] Isikoff later admitted in his book on the subject that conservative activists were using him, but he was accurate in noting the extensive research he devoted to nailing down the details of the Lewinsky and (during the same period) the Kathleen Willey stories.[22]

Washington Post media critic Howard Kurtz described Matt Drudge as an "Internet gossip-monger," who refused to "play by the rules." According to Kurtz

> Untutored in such basic survival techniques as getting both sides of the story. . . . Drudge seemed to overreach as he moved from titillating fare to serious scandal. . . . Drudge understood how to tap into his self-absorbed audience. By making himself an object of fascination for media types, who love reading about themselves and their political pals, he turned the hype machine to his own advantage.[23]

Tim Cuprisin of the *Milwaukee Journal Sentinel* dubbed Drudge a "cybergossip."[24] But despite his reputation among serious journalists as a media bottom-feeder, Drudge became a hero on the Right. David Horowitz, who with his partner Peter Collier founded the neocon Center for the Study of Popular Culture (CSPC), wrote that he was proud that he and Collier "organized a fund to defend Matt Drudge, the Internet gadfly," and complained:

> Why then the seeming tolerance for the current White House witch-hunt, whose purpose is to smear and destroy its political critics? As anyone can see, there was no conspiracy in the events leading up to the First Lady's accusation. There is no Communist Party of the Right with secret codes and top-down discipline that possesses the ability to give marching orders to anyone.[25]

CSPC's online *FrontPage* magazine website featured a "Matt Drudge Information Center and Defense Fund."[26] For his part, Drudge demanded an apology from his mainstream media critics and compared his own pioneering spirit to that of "Ben Franklin, or a Thomas Edison, or a Henry Ford, or an Einstein. . . . They all leapt so far ahead of the system, shaked it up, changed the balance."[27]

DIVERSITY IN COVERAGE AND FRAMING

The content, tone, and amount of anti-Clinton coverage varied considerably across both the secular and Christian Right. Coverage in the Hard Right was far more consistent in its elaborate conspiracism and apocalyptic tone. Not everyone jumped on the impeachment bandwagon. For instance, Phyllis Schlafly, the *grande dame* of ultraconservative conspiracism, wrote only the occasional column blasting Clinton's morality as symptomatic of decadent liberalism. She spent more space on her perennial issues such as fighting a big federal government, dismantling the Department of Education, opposing the UN, stopping globalism, and calling the nuclear device dropped on two Japanese cities near the end of World War II the "Lifesaver Bomb."[28] Similarly, although D. James Kennedy of Coral Ridge Ministries was embedded in the conspiracist subculture, only one out of thirty of his direct-mail letters reviewed was directly about Clinton—a call for resignation penned by Kennedy in November 1998.[29]

The glossy conservative Christian evangelical magazine *World* featured consistent coverage of Clinton's travails, but, while highly critical of Clinton and liberal politics, the coverage was generally thoughtful and based on solid reporting and interviews. *World* often displayed more professionalism than the *Wall Street Journal* and contained less salacious pandering and self-referential conceit than *Newsweek*.

Some right-wing activists who favored impeaching and removing Clinton had substantial complaints against him and articulated their grievances in a sincere and logical manner. This chapter, nonetheless, focuses not on legitimate criticism of Clinton but on anti-Clinton activism that employed demonization, scapegoating, apocalypticism, millennialism, or conspiracism. To unravel what is a complex scenario, we focus on individuals and groups as a way to show the networking and parallel projects that targeted Clinton.

CASTING CALL

Richard Mellon Scaife

A number of alarming allegations against Clinton came from people funded or encouraged by ultraconservative activist and multimillionaire Richard Mellon Scaife.[30] While his network was not the command center of a vast right-wing conspiracy, his funding was important in sustaining anti-Clinton conspiracism, especially around the case of Clinton's aide Vince Foster, whose suicide early in the Clinton administration was widely regarded as suspicious in the Hard Right.[31] As mentioned earlier, Scaife was an heir to the Mellon family fortune (which was made through the Mellon Bank and investments in Gulf Oil, Alcoa, and other companies).[32] From the 1970s through the 1990s, Scaife was among the top funders of right-wing causes. He was an important political player within the Right partly because he surrounded himself with sophisticated advisers. Both critics and supporters described Scaife's chief aide, Richard M. Larry, as having great influence and autonomy.[33]

Scaife controlled three foundations from his base in Pittsburgh, Pennsylvania: the Sarah Scaife Foundation, with assets of $302 million; the Allegheny Foundation, with $39 million; and the Carthage Foundation, with $24 million. And his children controlled a fourth, The Scaife Family Foundation, with $170 million.[34] These foundations funded numerous right-wing policy think tanks, legal groups, and publications.

Organizations funded by Scaife ranged from GOPAC, the political action committee that Rep. Newt Gingrich used to good effect in rising first to Minority Leader and then Speaker of the House, to the Fully Informed Jury Association, some of whose leaders and members recruited for the Patriot movement. Scaife also funded the Maldon Institute, a right-wing think tank founded in 1985 that studied national security and terrorism from a countersubversive and often conspiracist perspective. Maldon consultant and author John Rees infiltrated the political Left during the 1970s, passing information to groups ranging from the John Birch Society to the FBI.[35]

Scaife-funded organizations included the Western Journalism Center, *American Spectator*, Accuracy in Media, Landmark Legal Foundation, and Judicial Watch—all of which were especially active in the anti-Clinton network. One of Judicial Watch's areas of focus was the "Chinagate" scandal, and the group's claim that "persons in the Asian and Asian-American communities" were involved in illegal fund-raising activities on Clinton's behalf carried a racist and conspiracist subtext. Other anti-Clinton organs supported by Scaife included Brent Bozell's Media Research Center and Paul Weyrich's National Empowerment Television.[36]

As publisher of *The Pittsburgh Tribune-Review*, Scaife hired former *New York Post* reporter Christopher Ruddy to pursue the idea that Vince Foster's death was not a suicide, as well as other stories about Clinton. Fellow journalist Ambrose Evans-Pritchard praised Ruddy and described how he functioned as an activist in a nationwide right-wing network:

> He waged war on the airwaves, broadcasting night after night across the country on the radio talk circuit where he soon became a folk hero. He gave speeches, endlessly. He lobbied on Capitol Hill. He lobbied at the Christian Roundtable meetings in Tennessee. He lobbied wherever people would listen. He built alliances: with Reed Irvine's Accuracy in Media in Washington; with Jim Davidson's Strategic Investment, with the Western Journalism Center in California with Jeremiah Films (which made *The Clinton Chronicles*). He signed up with Richard Scaife, writing about the Foster case for *The Pittsburgh Tribune-Review*. It was a modest little brigade. But it was enough for insurgent warfare.[37]

At the very least, Scaife's funding produced an echo effect that amplified the voices of critics targeting Clinton, creating the illusion that these ideas had widespread support at a time when they did not. Credulous media coverage of scandal mongering then helped create a broader base of support than the original relatively small base in the Christian Right and conspiracist Hard Right. There was much inbreeding. For instance, Scaife funded Gingrich projects, and Gingrich raised questions about the death of Vince Foster, a pet project of Scaife's.[38] Anti-Clinton authors and publications funded by Scaife gave coverage and favorable reviews to other anti-Clinton authors and publications funded by Scaife.[39] Nonetheless, a substantial number of Clinton critics and conspiracy peddlers did not receive funds from Scaife.

The American Spectator

There had been stories about Bill Clinton's sexual affairs in various tabloid media, but an article in the neoconservative *American Spectator* magazine raised the stakes.

The cover of the January 1994 issue of the *American Spectator* featured a caricature of Bill Clinton sneaking down a moonlit alley, with the headline "His Cheatin' Heart: David Brock in Little Rock." Reporter David Brock had already gained a reputation for cutthroat journalism for his March 1992 attack piece "The Real Anita Hill," and he returned to that mode in his

1994 article "Living with the Clintons: Bill's Arkansas bodyguards tell the story the press missed."

The Brock article is long on gossip and hearsay and short on facts corroborated outside the circle of troopers. Several years later, Brock wrote an "open letter" published in *Esquire* magazine in which he apologized for the Troopergate article and said the troopers' greed and anger had motivated their stories.[40] In fact, one trooper later publicly changed his story.[41]

Buried on page 26 of the original Brock article was a paragraph mentioning a "Paula" who allegedly was taken to Clinton's hotel room for a sexual tryst. Neither a date nor a conference name was mentioned. Nonetheless, Paula Jones stepped forward and claimed her reputation had been sullied. The rest is history.

During this period the editor of the *American Spectator* was R. Emmett Tyrrell, Jr., author of *Boy Clinton: The Political Biography*, published by Regnery. Scaife's foundations gave $2.4 million to the American Spectator Education Foundation while it was running anti-Clinton articles. The foundation launched the "Arkansas Project," financing information-gathering operations involving reporters, private investigators, former law enforcement officers, and political operatives.[42] Public tax records of the foundation were obtained by Joe Conason at the *New York Observer*, and he discovered that $1.7 million of the Scaife funds between 1993 and 1996 had been reported as legal fees but apparently were used for the Arkansas Project.[43]

Some $35,000 of these funds ended up with Parker Dozhier, who owns a fishing camp in Arkansas.[44] One witness for Starr, David Hale, "was staying at Dozhier's fishing cabin complex in Hot Springs, Ark., between 1994 and 1996."[45] Two former friends of Dozhier claim he made small cash payments to Hale, but Dozhier denies that claim. Dozhier, however, provided free accommodations to Hale. Dozhier served as a conduit for information on Whitewater from Hale and others to investigators, reporters, and representatives from the *American Spectator*. Theodore Olson, a director at the Spectator Foundation, was Hale's lawyer in 1995 and 1996. Olson is Kenneth Starr's former law partner.[46] A grand jury was seated to investigate potential illegalities.[47]

Scaife gave grants to the Fund for a Living American Government (FLAG), run by attorney William Lehrfeld. Lehrfeld, through FLAG, gave "a secret $50,000 contribution in 1995 to the legal fund of Paula Corbin Jones" while he "simultaneously served as the primary legal counsel" to the Arkansas Project, according to reporters Murray Waas and Jonathan Broder.[48]

Other potential witnesses, reporters, and activists targeting Clinton were in the conservative cash pipeline. Reporter Lynn Sweet of the *Chicago Sun-Times* revealed that conservative fund-raiser Peter W. Smith, a wealthy Chicago investment banker, spent some $80,000 between September 1992 and March 1994 in a secret anti-Clinton campaign. Smith "paid for legal advice on federal campaign finance law; GOP political and public relations consultants; [reporter David Brock's] research expenses, and a gift to two Arkansas state troopers and their lawyer—four months after [Brock's] 'Troopergate' story was published." The troopers each received $6,700.

Brock confirmed to the *Sun-Times* that he had first met Smith in the fall of 1992 in a Washington, DC, meeting where Smith proposed anti-Clinton story ideas including "allegations then swirling around Clinton concerning draft-dodging, womanizing, drugs, the rigging of Arkansas economic statistics, and attempts to cover up indiscreet behavior. Brock recalled another item they discussed: whether Clinton had fathered an illegitimate child." Brock told the *Sun-Times* that at the time he thought that idea was "far-fetched." But the next year, when Smith fed Brock the Arkansas troopers' tales, Brock turned the lead into the Troopergate article in the *American Spectator*.

Sweet outlined Smith's ties to conservative Republican political networks:

> Though nearly invisible on the Chicago and Illinois political scene, Smith, 62, is a wealthy political sophisticate and an activist in national conservative circles. . . . His interest in politics goes back to 1960, when he was studying for an M.B.A. at Syracuse University. Then, Smith was national chairman of the College Young Republicans.
>
> Smith has been one of the leading benefactors of GOPAC, the conservative political action committee once chaired by House Speaker Newt Gingrich. He has given at least $10,000 to the conservative Heritage Foundation and in past years has been a major donor to the Republican National Committee. Smith has personally given GOPAC about $150,000 since 1987 and raised tens of thousands of dollars from others.[49]

Citizens United—Floyd G. Brown

Citizens United is an example of how the players and themes in conspiracist anticommunism shifted easily to conspiracist antiliberalism and joined the campaign to demonize Clinton, pulling their conspiracy theories into the mainstream media and Congress.

The website for Citizens United explained that the group was dedicated to "Reasserting Traditional American Values: limited government, freedom of enterprise, strong families, national sovereignty and security."[50] The group claimed 150,000 members, but that figure most likely included anyone who sent money for projects promoted in frequent direct-mail appeals. The group published a members' newsletter, *Citizens Agenda*, and a specialty periodical, *ClintonWatch*, sent to selected reporters and political activists.[51] *ClintonWatch*, which referred to Clinton's "radical socialist agenda,"[52] reflected the apocalyptic conspiracism commonly found in the Hard Right.

Two senior Citizens United staff were veterans of the conspiracist ultra-conservative subculture with roots in militant anticommunism. Cliff Kincaid, director of the related Citizens United Foundation's American Sovereignty Action Project, had written a 1991 article for the ultraconservative *Human Events* that Red-baited groups protesting the Gulf War and he also authored several conspiracist books and reports attacking the United Nations using claims and arguments common in the Patriot movement.[53] Michael Boos is the Legal Director of the National Citizens Legal Network, a project of the Citizens United Foundation. In a 1982 article for the Young Americans for Freedom magazine *New Guard*, Boos Red-baited the nuclear freeze campaign and the peace movement as a "sinister scheme being directed by the Soviet Union." In 1984 Boos spied on the anti-intervention group CISPES (Committee in Solidarity with the People of El Salvador), and sent an unsolicited copy of his report to the FBI, which promptly distributed it to thirty-two of its field offices and launched official probe of CISPES, based partly on the Boos report.[54]

Citizens United was the project of Floyd G. Brown, who published *"Slick Willie": Why America Cannot Trust Bill Clinton*, a slim paperback book distributed as part of a direct-mail fund-raising effort. The book was a right-wing tirade designed to document Clinton's lack of character.[55] Along with standard attacks on Clinton as a draft dodger and friend to labor unions, Brown asserted that "Bill Clinton's America sees no difference between families of ´homosexual lovers´ and the traditional, monogamous, faithful family. . . . In addition, Mr. Clinton has surrendered completely to the pro-abortion feminists who dominate the Democratic Party."[56] It's no surprise to find citation to *Human Events* and the neoconservative *American Spectator* in *"Slick Willie."*

In 1988, Brown had produced the notorious Willie Horton television ad to assist the George Bush election campaign. Bush was forced to distance himself from the ad. Ten years later, Brown remained proud of the ad, which was widely denounced as racist pandering.[57] In 1992 he attempted to place ads for a $4.99 paid phone call that would play tapes of a telephone conversation between Gennifer Flowers and then-Governor Clinton. The hook was a promise that the conversation probed sexual matters. The incident was so tasteless that the Bush–Quayle campaign was again forced to condemn Brown and his tactics.[58] In 1994 Brown arranged for a reporter a screening of militia leader Linda Thompson's video, *Waco: The Big Lie*, a potage of conspiracy theories attempting to link Clinton to premeditated murder.[59]

Brown and his main researcher, David Bossie, were a significant source for mainstream media coverage of Clinton-related scandals. In 1994 *Chicago Tribune* reporter Carol Jouzaitis found, for example, that "members of the *Wall Street Journal's* editorial board [met] with Brown and examined his pile of information." Following that meeting, "the *Journal* devoted nearly half of its editorial page one day to reprinting" materials obtained from Brown.[60] According to a *Columbia Journalism Review* article by journalist Trudy Lieberman, the *Atlanta Journal-Constitution*, the *Dallas Morning News*, the *Arizona Republic*, the *Boston Globe*, and *Newsday* regularly featured material *ClintonWatch* had highlighted. Lieberman found that when Citizens United repackaged a *Washington Post* story about Vince Foster in more sensationalist form, the number of news organizations covering the story tripled.[61]

Citizens United's Brown and Bossie also had direct links to the anti-Clinton Republicans in the House of Representatives. In 1994, according to Jouzaitis:

> Rep. John Doolittle (R-Calif.) quietly invited Brown to give 10 junior House Republicans his highly partisan take on Whitewater probes. Brown's materials also have wound up in the hands of Rep. Jim Leach (R-Iowa) whose staff also has been doing its own investigation as the congressman presses for hearings into Whitewater. Leach's spokesman, Joe Pinder, declined to say how they got there.[62]

According to an article from the *New York Times* News Service posted on the Patriot-oriented Free Republic web page:

> The dominant staff member of the House committee [investigating campaign finances] is its chief investigator, David N. Bossie. He reports directly to [Rep. Dan] Burton and not through the general counsel. . . . He was an investigator in last year's Whitewater inquiry conducted by Sen. Alfonse D'Amato, R-N.Y.[63]

Speaking from the House floor, Burton, an ultraconservative Republican from Indiana, echoed Citizens United conspiracy theories about Vince Foster's death.[64]

Citizens for Honest Government—Pat Matrisciana

The Clinton Chronicles was probably the best-known video attacking Clinton via spurious conspiracy theories. *The Clinton Chronicles* was presented as a secular investigative narrative, but was produced by Jeremiah Films, which specialized in apocalyptic Christian fundamentalist videos. Jeremiah Films was one of several projects of Pat Matrisciana, who also ran the parent group, Creative Ministries, as well as Citizens for Honest Government, publisher of the newsletter *Citizen's Intelligence Digest*. Matrisciana's operations illustrated the practical linkages between the Republican Party, the conservative Christian Right, Christian Right theocrats, apocalyptic millennialism, and hard-right conspiracism.

Widely distributed by anti-Clinton activists, *The Clinton Chronicles* was circulated in June 1994 to Republican members of the House of Representatives with a cover letter from ultraconservative Illinois Republican Philip M. Crane.[65] Jerry Falwell alone sold more than 60,000 copies of the video.[66] Jeremiah also produced *The Clinton Chronicles Book,* which frequently cited standard ultraconservative sources such as the *Washington Times, Insight,* and *Human Events.* One chapter by ultraconservative Scott Wheeler claimed liberal media conspired to circulate "engineered information" in an "onslaught of manipulated facts" to protect Clinton.[67]

A chapter by Lt. Col. Tom McKenney (retired), titled "Bill Clinton—The Unthinkable Commander in Chief," picked up the theme of treason in high places. McKenney asked: "How could we have a Commander in Chief of the U.S. Armed Forces who holds the military in contempt, who is anti-patriotic, who long ago embraced the dream of world socialism, and who, if he were not President, could not receive a security clearance."

The Clinton Chronicles Book had an appendix that sought to implicate Clinton in "The Mena Airport Drug Smuggling Operation." The appendix included articles based in part on claims by Richard Brenneke, who described details of a vast drug-running conspiracy but who was later discredited for having greatly misrepresented his knowledge.[68] Another article cited was from the neofascist LaRouchite *Executive Intelligence Review,* a font of conspiracist allegations.

Matrisciana spoke at a October 4, 1997, "Take America Back" rally near the U.S. Capitol, a few blocks away from the simultaneous massive Promise Keepers rally, "Stand in the Gap." "Take America Back" turned into a proimpeachment rally. Other speakers included Operation Rescue founder Randall Terry and Alan Keyes, the 1996 and 2000 Republican presidential candidate, radio host, and founder of Black America's PAC.[69] The rally program included a quote from former U.S. Attorney General Edwin Meese, III, praising Citizens for Honest Government.[70]

The January–February 1998 issue of *Citizens Intelligence Digest* featured a posed photograph of John Wheeler, Jr., director of publications for Citizens for Honest Government, handing "The Citizens Presidential Impeachment Indictment" to Rep. Bob Barr at a "Strategy Briefing Breakfast" held in Washington, DC, on November 7, 1998. Flanking the two was Howard Phillips, president of the Conservative Caucus and a leading player in the hard core theocratic wing of the Christian Right. "Contributing Writers" to the newsletter included Clinton-conspiracy mongers Ruddy, Farah, and Evans-Pritchard, as well as ultraconservative Rep. William Dannemeyer, evangelical leader Timothy LaHaye, apocalyptic fundamentalist author Chuck Missler, antigay author Dr. Stanley Monteith, and Hard Right activist Larry Pratt of Gun Owners of America, which is to the right of the National Rifle Association.

Rev. Jerry Falwell

A major distributor of Jeremiah Films' *The Clinton Chronicles* video was Jerry Falwell Ministries and his *Old Time Gospel Hour.* During 1998 Falwell relentlessly harangued against Clinton in TV appearances and radio programs, direct mail, his monthly *National Liberty Journal* newspaper, and *The Falwell Fax*, a chatty memo sent weekly to subscribers.[71]

A review of 1997 and 1998 issues of the *National Liberty Journal* shows the majority of attacks on Clinton centered on scandals involving Monica Lewinsky, Webster Hubbell, Whitewater, Vince Foster, Paula Jones, communist Chinese influence, and impeachment.[72] Sometimes a single issue would contain a front page anti-Clinton scandal article and as many as five additional scandal-oriented articles on inside pages. Many issues contained advertisements for anti-Clinton items such as a book on "The Murder of Vince Foster." Typical headlines included "Many Blacks Wonder Why the Black Caucus Defends Clinton to the Bitter End," and "Clinton Tabs Lesbian Nun for White House Post."[73]

In a December 1998 fund-raising letter for his lobbying organization, the Liberty Alliance, Falwell decried Clinton's "immoral and illegal activities . . . and illegal foreign political fundraising by the President and Vice President." Yet, Falwell, like others in the Christian Right, saw Clinton as just part of the "powerful liberal forces" that are destroying America. Falwell warned that if money didn't soon flow in, "the Clintons, the radical homosexuals, anti-family feminists, Godless atheists, and the liberal media will have won."[74]

Texe Marrs

Many conspiracist attacks on President Bill Clinton originated in the apocalyptic sector of the Christian Right. One example of the more zealous rhetoric is a book penned by Texe Marrs titled *Big Sister Is Watching You: Hillary Clinton And The White House Feminists Who Now Control America—And Tell The President What To Do.* The book alleges a plot by "FemiNazis" and their allies in "subversive organizations whose goal is to end American sovereignty and bring about a global Marxist paradise."[75]

Marrs also posted an April 1998 web article "The Esther Option," with the subtitle: "The Untold Story Of The Secret War For Global Supremacy Between Two Rival Jewish Factions." The article raised old themes of an antisemitic apocalyptic millennialism. A longer audiotape provides the full story "For Your Gift of $10." The teasers read:

> Discover why the future of America and the world may now rest on the shoulders of a giggly, immoral, 24 year old, Jewish woman named Monica Lewinsky—a woman acclaimed by many religious Jews as their new "Queen Esther." [Originally in all caps.]

> Has Vice President Al Gore been chosen by . . . the right-wing Jewish faction to replace Clinton as President of the United States? If and when Gore does take office, will the new President prove more loyal to their cause? Will a prophetic chain of events then lead to the appearance of the antichrist in a rebuilt, great Jewish temple in Jerusalem?[76]

As the year 2000 approached, this type of heated rhetoric became more common.

CONCLUSION

The drive to impeach President Bill Clinton highlighted the fragmented Right's continuing efforts to rally around shared goals. Although the sectors involved varied widely in ideology and methods, they all agreed that Clinton had to go, and they reinforced one another in attacking him. Together they made a formidable machine that was able to keep the attack in the limelight. It is a case study of how a small minority can exert influence far beyond its number if it is organized and its factions collaborate, and frame an issue in populist terms around which multiple constituencies can mobilize.

The Christian Right and its ultraconservative allies scored several successes. Starting with a relatively tiny core group of national strategists and local activists, they mobilized an anti-Clinton coalition that included Republican Party pragmatists and theocratic purists, business conservatives, and hard-right conspiracists. Jointly, they tied up the political process for over a year while continuing to push their legislative agenda at the national and state levels, and they succeeded in giving apocalyptic conspiracy theories an unprecedented degree of legitimacy in mainstream political discourse. Although most citizens still supported President Clinton's job performance, this coalition convinced a majority of Americans that Clinton should resign, be removed, or be censured. While the failure to remove Clinton from office was a setback to this coalition, the Christian Right and its allies continued to exert tremendous influence on the political and social system.

The House managers' (and perhaps the House Judiciary Committee's) mishandling of the impeachment process, which ended in Clinton's acquittal by the Senate, gave breathing room to centrist Republicans and Democrats, who emerged looking comparatively liberal simply because they were not the purist wing of the Christian Right. The Christian Right purists' frustrated fury against the president made it possible to lose sight of how much ultraconservatives had already won, and how far they had succeeded in shifting the whole political spectrum rightward, not least by fixating the nation's attention on a one-year political soap opera. As Clinton himself had shown, earlier and afterward, the Democratic Party often responds to Republican shifts to the right by largely matching them.

Even when right-wing populist movements fail in their stated goals, or do not mobilize broad support in the general population, they can still play a major role in the political, social, or cultural life of the nation.

16

THE NEW MILLENNIUM
Demonization, Conspiracism, and Scapegoating in Transition

As the year 2000 approached, discussions involving apocalyptic and millennialist themes became commonplace, even in the popular media. Yet the actual transition into the twenty-first century was anticlimactic. Since the world did not end, and there were no major disasters, there was a retrospective tendency to forget the amount of activity originally aimed at preparing for the year 2000. These phenomena nevertheless deserve attention because they involved millions of people and shaped the way apocalypticism and millennialism will influence certain right-wing movements in the future.

The dawn of the new millennium saw a renewed wave of populist activism protesting globalization and trade policies benefiting large corporations at the expense of average working people and the environment. The vast majority of protestors were progressive. Yet there was an alarming insensitivity among leaders of national groups protesting globalization to attempts by right-wing populists to insert xenophobia, ultranationalism, conspiracism, and antisemitism into the debate.

Despite schisms, the Christian Right still maneuvered the selection of ultraconservative Dick Cheney as George W. Bush's running mate in the 2000 presidential campaign.

APOCALYPSE AND THE YEAR 2000

Jerry Falwell's millennial speculation turned up the heat in early 1999 when he declared that Christ could return soon, perhaps within ten years, and that the Antichrist was alive and was a Jewish man. According to Falwell,

> Who will the Antichrist be? I don't know. Nobody else knows. . . . Is he alive and here today? Probably. Because when he appears during the Tribulation period he will be a full-grown counterfeit of Christ. Of course he'll be Jewish.

Of course he'll petend to be Christ. And if in fact the Lord is coming soon, and he'll be an adult at the presentation of himself, he must be alive somewhere today.

Falwell seemed surprised that some found his comments offensive, and offered a somewhat ambiguous apology saying he had not intended the comments to be taken as antisemitic. Rabbi James Rudin of the American Jewish Committee said Falwell's statement were part of the "millennial madness" and warned about even the unintentional "unleashing of latent and historical anti-Semitism."[1] Falwell's sense of anticipation was hardly unique. The numerological significance of the year 2000—signaling a new millennium—spawned great excitement around the world, even though it was the year 2000 in only one calendar system based on the Christian era. Any date in any calendar system can be understood as significant given the creativity of those using numerological equations to find justification.[2] Apocalyptic interpretations of the year 2000 came from a variety of Christian, Jewish, Hindu, Buddhist, Muslim, and New Age prophets.[3]

The year 2000 was interpreted by a significant portion of the U.S. population as somehow linked not only to religiously significant events—perhaps even a sign of the Christian End Times—but also to a range of secular ideas of epochal transformation. In the late 1990s, a visit to any large bookstore would have revealed a cornucopia of titles in the religion, prophecy, New Age, and occult sections. Surfing the web would also have produced a pulsating cacophony of multimedia millennial expectation. The topics would have ranged from secular to spiritual and from cataclysmic doom to transcendent rapture in what Michael Barkun has called an "improvisational style" of millennialism and apocalypticism.[4]

The anticipation of a righteous struggle against evil conspiracies has always been a central apocalyptic narrative in our nation's religious, secular, political, and cultural discourse.[5] This is certainly evident in popular culture, where films such as *Armageddon* and *Apocalypse Now* and the TV series *Millennium* named the tradition while mainstreaming the ideas. Films including *Rambo*, *Mad Max*, *Red Dawn*, *Die Hard*, *The Terminator*, and their sequels reinterpreted apocalyptic visions while obscuring their origins.[6] The *X-Files* TV series and subsequent film are quintessential apocalyptic narratives. "Buffy the Vampire Slayer" stomped evil incarnate in her weekly TV series of the same name. Prophetic scripture provided the paradigm for sensational scripts. What was entertainment fodder for some, however, was spiritual and political reality for others.

The varieties of apocalyptic millennialism experienced could be categorized into four related and overlapping tendencies or responses that ranged from the sacred to the secular:

- First in importance, in the view of most Christian fundamentalists, the year 2000 possibly marked the arrival of the apocalyptic millennial

"End Times" or "Last Days" prophesied in Revelation and other books of the Bible;

- Second, it marked for many Christian conservatives and their allies a reason to launch campaigns to "clean up" society.
- Third, for diverse movements across the political spectrum there was manifested a more generic and often secularized apocalyptic world-view which saw an impending crisis, heightened by fears over the Y2K computer problem.
- Fourth, there was a generalized sense of hopeful expectation and possibility for renewal, triggered merely by the approach of the calendar year 2000, because it was a millennial milestone in human recorded history.[7]

There were a variety of small prophetic sects with a kaleidoscope of visions. Conspiracist William Cooper wove an apocalyptic vision out of historic antisemitism and modern UFO lore.[8] The Heaven's Gate group suicides in 1997 were based on a mixture of biblical prophecy, the ancient predictions of Nostradamus, and science fiction.[9] The Order of the Solar Temple also imploded inward, with group suicides in Canada, France, and Switzerland, but the Aum Shinrikyo sect exploded outward, with a gas attack on the Tokyo subway.[10]

As the year 2000 approached, there was an increase in, and a convergence of, apocalyptic thinking, demonization, scapegoating, and conspiracism. This happened in the midst of the longest period of right-wing populist backlash in the United States since the end of Reconstruction.[11]

COUNTDOWN TO THE END TIMES

Author Hal Lindsey reignited Protestant apocalyptic speculation in 1970 with his book *The Late Great Planet Earth*, which sold 10 million copies in English alone.[12] Lindsey argued that the End Times had arrived and that Christians should watch for prophetic signs.[13] Lindsey followed up on his original book with many others, including *Planet Earth—2000 A.D.: Will Mankind Survive?*[14]

Billy Graham also raised expectations in his 1983 book *Approaching Hoofbeats: The Four Horsemen of the Apocalypse*, where he observed that Jesus Christ, "The Man on the white horse...will come when man has sunk to his lowest most perilous point in history." Graham then discussed the terrible state of the world.[15]

The mainstreaming of apocalypticism received an additional boost when, in 1983, Ronald Reagan cited scriptural authority to demonize the Soviet Union as an "evil empire."[16] Grace Halsell wrote in her book *Prophecy and Politics: Militant Evangelists on the Road to Nuclear War* of how some evangelists, including Pat Robertson, Jerry Falwell, and Hal Lindsey, hinted that use of atomic weapons was inevitable as part of the final battle of Armageddon.[17]

Halsell's book and a monograph by Ruth W. Mouly, *The Religious Right and Israel: The Politics of Armageddon*, argued that one reason that certain sectors of the Christian Right mobilized tremendous support for the State of Israel during the Reagan administration was because they believed Jews had to return to Israel before the millennialist prophecies of Revelations could be fulfilled.[18]

Prophecy belief is widespread in the United States. During the Gulf War, 14 percent of one CNN national poll thought that the conflict was the beginning of Armageddon, and, as Lamy notes, at the time "American bookstores were experiencing a run on books about prophecy and the end of the world."[19] In 1993 a *New York Times*/CNN national poll found that 20 percent of the general population thought the second coming of Christ would occur around the year 2000.[20]

Apocalyptic and millennialist ideas circulate in an extensive Christian Right alternative media that addresses a large subculture in our society. This includes far more than magazines and broadcasts. For example, televangelist Jerry Falwell periodically sends material to "162,000 conservative pastors and churches through Pastors' Policy Briefings."[21]

In January 1999 Pat Roberson's 700 *Club* TV program featured a special week-long series of reports on "America's Moral Crisis." Evidence of "America's moral decline" included abortion, euthanasia, homosexuality, and "America's obsession with sex." Viewers with concerns about the moral crises were urged to call the National Counseling Center, part of the CBN Ministry. According to the 700 *Club*, the Center logged 5,000 calls per day.

Paul Boyer argues that Christian apocalypticism must be factored into both Cold War and post-Cold War political equations. He noted that the 1974 prophecy book, *Armageddon, Oil, and the Middle East Crisis* sold three-quarters of a million copies.[22] When it was reissued in connection with the Gulf War, it sold another million copies.[23]

Lee Quinby predicted that the excitement over the year 2000 was unlikely to be good for women.[24] In describing the symbolism in Revelation, one modern Catholic commentary cautions against negative stereotyping of women.[25] This is a needed caution, because antifeminist, misogynist and homophobic interpretations of Revelation are widespread.

Most mainstream Christian religious leaders downplayed or denounced the idea that the year 2000 marked the End Times, some fundamentalist leaders hinted that the date had theological significance, and a few announced that the End Times might have already started. A small but significant number of fundamentalists took the idea seriously and began making preparations.[26]

One Christian publishing house offered a catalog on "Armageddon Books." The 1998 Internet version of the catalog described the publishing house as the "world's largest Bible prophecy bookstore featuring books, videos, and charts on armageddon, antichrist, 666, tribulation, rapture, revelation." Novels with apocalyptic prophecy themes became a surprise hit in the late 1990s, with several titles reaching best-seller status. Among the most popular were the series by Tim LaHaye and J.B. Jenkins, which included *Left Behind: A Novel of the Earth's Last Days, Tribulation Force: The Continuing Drama of Those Left Behind,* and *Nicolae: The Rise of Antichrist.* There was also a young adult series by J.B. Jenkins, Tim LaHaye, and Jen LaHaye. The Left Behind series began in 1995, and by the year 2000, more than 7 million books had been sold. Other authors in this genre included Michael Hyatt, Paul Meier, and Larry Burkett, a Christian financial counselor. Even Pat Robertson penned *The End of the Age: A Novel.*[27]

There were even post-Rapture ministries run by Christians who assumed they would be raptured before the Tribulations, so they created publications, videotapes, and websites to be left behind as a last effort to convert people to Christ. Kurt Seland, on such a website, explained the idea of post-Rapture ministry materials in general:

> To those left behind after the rapture, this is indeed a survival manual. You still have an opportunity to repent and have eternal life. . . . Let me be real frank with you. If you are reading this manual and the rapture has already occurred, then you probably are not going to physically survive; you most likely will die. This manual is about the survival of your soul. You are going to go through terrible suffering. The only question is whether you will go to Heaven or go to hell when you die.

Some authors used an approach that shows more humor, such as Todd Strandberg who wrote an essay titled "Oops, I Guess I Wasn't Ready." Peter and Paul LaLonde produced three dramatic (and not humorous) rapture videos in the Left Behind series in which the Antichrist is shown as the president of the European Union who sends one-world-government agents out after the Rapture to persecute and murder belatedly devout Christians who refuse to obey his dictates.[28]

By some millennialists' reckoning the year 2000 was the start of the seventh millennium since the time God created the earth. This view originally took root in a small movement of apocalyptic Jews around the time the Christian church was forming. They had a theory that the Jewish Messiah would arrive 6,000 years after the Creation. Around A.D. 120 this idea jumped into Christianity. Church scholars decided that, since God took six days to finish creation and to God each day is like one thousand years, then the seventh millennium would bring the return of Christ.[29] This idea still leaves open when the End Times clock starts ticking. Damian Thompson explains that "For millenarians, the world was perpetually on the verge of its 6,000th birthday; for conservatives, that anniversary was always beyond the life expectancy of the current generation."[30] Among Christian fundamentalists in the United States, there was open discussion, but no unanimity of opinion, of whether or not the year 2000 started the seventh millennium.

Sara Diamond has reported that even some Christians who were dubious of "hard" End Times claims were re-energized by a "softer" millennial view of the year 2000 as a time for aggressive evangelism or even "spiritual warfare" against demonic forces.[31] Lee Quinby calls this tendency "coercive purity."[32] Richard K. Fenn argues that popular "rituals of purification" in a society are closely associated with apocalyptic and millennial beliefs.[33]

The broad quest for purity bridged "soft" and "hard" millennial thinking among politically active Christians. It sparked legislative efforts to enforce divisive and narrowly defined biblical standards of morality, homophobic statements by Senate majority leader Trent Lott, and the wave of newspaper advertisements calling on gay men and lesbians to "cure" themselves by turning to Jesus.[34] The most aggressive activists engaged in theologically motivated acts of violence against those seen as sinful, such as abortion providers.

THE PROMISE KEEPERS

The Promise Keepers was a vivid example of soft dominionism and apocalyptic scapegoating in the public sphere. The group's leadership was marked by theocratic tendencies, patriarchal assumptions, hierarchical "shepherding" of its members through discipleship relations with assigned mentors, and tightly organized local membership structures.[35]

Early mass media coverage of the group was often positive to the point of credulousness.[36] In the mainstream press there was little serious discussion of the implicit and explicit antifeminist agenda of the Promise Keepers. The leaders clearly championed a God-inspired patriarchal order in which women must be obedient and submissive to their husbands.[37]

Many of the leaders of the Promise Keepers were tied to Christian Right para-church ministries and conservative legislative campaigns. James Dobson's Focus on the Family published much Promise Keepers' literature, including two key books, *Seven Promises of a Promise Keeper*, a set of essays, and *The Power of the Promise Kept*, a collection of "life stories."[38] In 1995 the Promise Keepers' thirteen major events drew over 700,000 men.[39]

At the massive Promise Keepers "Stand in the Gap" rally on the Washington Mall in October 1997, questions about the approaching End Times elicited eager responses.[40] The Promise Keepers originally scheduled "Vision 2000" rallies at "key population centers and state capitols around the United States," for January 1, 2000.[41] These were later canceled due to concerns over Y2K problems, and fears of low attendance.

Author Russ Bellant noted apocalyptic sentiments among some leaders of Promise Keepers, such as Rev. James Ryle, who "believes Promise Keepers, . . . is the fulfillment of the Biblically prophesied end-time army." He says he has a vision of Promise Keepers purging America of secularism, which he considers "an abortion" of godliness.[42] In 1994 Ryle warned that "America is in the midst of a cultural revolution, which has poised our nation precariously on the brink of moral chaos, which is caused by what I am referring to as the crisis of homosexuality."[43]

While the Promise Keepers is driven in part by millennial expectation, the movement also responds to the need for primarily White men to find a coherent identity in modern culture in the face of issues raised by the civil rights and feminist movements.[44] They certainly have been creative in figuring out a new way to retain control. Men in the Promise Keepers are still considered the spiritual leaders in their families. As Promise Keepers president Randy Phillips said, "We have to listen and honor and respect our wives," but admitted, "we talk about ultimately the decision lying with the man."[45]

Acknowledging the sincere religious devotion and quest for growth of many Promise Keepers men, academic Lee Quinby, who has extensively researched the subject area, nonetheless sees political content in the group's vision of "apocalyptic masculinity," which rejects gender equality and scapegoats homosexuals and feminists "as a threat to the pure community."

Some feminist and progressive groups have criticized the Promise Keepers in harsh ways that exaggerate how much the theocratic leadership dictates followers' behavior and, perhaps inadvertently, have caricatured the average member as a misogynist bully. This rhetoric backfired when most reporters interviewing Promise Keepers members and their wives quickly found that such a description did not fit the people with whom they spoke. Many reporters then overreacted by failing to pursue legitimate questions about the political content of the Promise Keepers agenda.

Members of right-wing populist movements (or any movement) often pick and choose from the statements and dictates of group leaders, devising interpretations that are contradictory, but that provide satisfactory rationalizations and accommodations. This was true for the Promise Keepers movement. Christian Smith has studied the notion of male leadership and submission in the Christian evangelical subculture and found a diversity of interpretations that often mute the overt patriarchal statements issued by leaders in groups such as the Southern Baptist Convention.

The Promise Keepers went through a series of financial crises and organizational restructurings following its 1997 Stand in the Gap rally in Washington, DC, and when the year 2000 arrived its future was uncertain.[46]

JEREMIAH FILMS

Another example of a Christian group engaged in an apocalyptic campaign of millennial ritual purification is Jeremiah Films, named after the Biblical prophet. Jeremiah Films and Jeremiah Books are run by the husband and wife team of Pat and Caryl Matrisciana.

Senate majority leader Trent Lott, who in 1998 pronounced homosexuals not just sinful but sick, had already appeared in Jeremiah's 1993 antigay video *Gay Rights, Special Rights*. The video, used in several statewide legislative campaigns to erode basic rights for gay men and lesbians, also features former attorney general Edwin Meese, III, and former education secretary William J. Bennett, along with notable conspiracists such as David Noebel of Summit Ministries. Lott also stars in Jeremiah's 1993 video *The Crash—The Coming Financial Collapse of America*, which comes in two versions, one with a secular doomsday scenario and another with a special Christian cut featuring discussions of End Times biblical prophecy.

Jeremiah has a large collection of conspiracist videos. Caryl Matrisciana, a leading author of Christian Right books with conspiracist themes, cohosted a thirteen-part video series from Jeremiah titled *Pagan Invasion*. The series includes videos that claim evolution is a hoax, Freemasonry is a pagan religion, Halloween is a tool for satanic abduction, and Mormonism is a cult heresy. The Jeremiah video on Mormons has earned rebukes from mainstream religious commentators for its bigotry toward members of the Church, formally called The Church of Jesus Christ of Latter-day Saints.[47]

One segment of the Jeremiah Films series *Pagan Invasion* was titled "Preview of the Antichrist."[48] It is described in an online Christian Right catalog with the following blurb:

> According to Ancient Hebrew scriptures, in the last days mankind will urgently seek the security of a one-world government. This global desire for a super leader, who will bring peace and safety to a world in chaos, will ultimately leave the human race vulnerable to the beguiling charm and the most intelligent, powerful, and charismatic person of all history. The Bible calls this man the "anti-christ." Ironically, he will dominate the globe and orchestrate society's ultimate destruction.[49]

SATAN'S COMING . . .

Typical of the apocalyptic mood as the year 2000 approached, was a mailing from Prophetic Vision, a small international Christian evangelical outreach ministry, that reported, "Prophecy is moving so fast" and "the Return of Christ is imminent." The mailing went on to declare that the Antichrist "must be alive today waiting to take control!" and then solicited funds for the "end time harvest."

The process of prophecy belief triggering apocalyptic demonization and then leading to searches for the Devil's partners is continuously updated. Paul Boyer points out that those seen as the prophesied agents of Satan girding for End Times battle can be foreign or domestic or both. He notes how in prophetic literature the identity of Satan's allies in the Battle of Armageddon has shifted seamlessly over time, circumstance, and political interest from the Soviet Union to Chinese communists, to Islamic militants; and he warns of an increasing level of anti-Muslim bigotry.[50]

Most Christians, even those who think the End Times are imminent, do not automatically succumb to demonization, scapegoating, and conspiracist thinking. It must be remembered that some politically conservative fundamentalist groups oppose this paradigm and warn against demonization that conflates church and state. For example, the Institute for the Study of Religion in Politics argues that

> if the price of re-establishing a "public Christian culture" in this country means that the church must ostracize its opponents, ghettoize the adherents of other religions and cultures, make enemies of women who choose abortion, demonize homosexuals, etc. as it seeks to gather political power into its hands—maybe, just maybe, the price isn't worth paying.[51]

Yet, in the escalating surge of millennial titles, a surprisingly large number named the agents of the Antichrist or claimed to expose the evil End Times conspiracy.[52]

As the millennium approached, targets of apocalyptic demonization included Jews, Catholics, Mormons, Muslims, Freemasons, New Age devotees, peace activists, environmentalists, feminists, abortion providers, and gay men and lesbians. Members of groups ranging from the Trilateral Commission to the National Education Association were claimed to be suspect—as well as such familiar targets as federal officials and UN troops.

THE Y2K COMPUTER PROBLEM

Christians and non-Christians alike debated the importance of the "Y2K" bug, the technical programming problem that threatened to crash some software and hardware not designed to correctly interpret the dates of years beyond 1999. As in secular circles, Christian responses ranged from cautious preparations to doomsday scenarios that led some to establish rural survivalist retreats.

Among Christians the questions revolved around eschatological timetables. The eschatological differences between premillennialists and postmillennialists significantly influenced how the Y2K bug was interpreted. For premillennialists, a major question was whether or not the Y2K problem was a sign of the End Times? If yes, was the Y2K problem related to the Mark of the Beast? Whatever the eschatology however, the underlying premise was the same—namely that Y2K had the potential for spawning widespread chaos.[53]

Nevertheless, the common belief in the need for survivalist-style preparation allowed people to set aside eschatological debates. Premillennialists, postmillennialists, and amillennialists could interact with secularists in discussions over which water purification filter provided the best value in bacterial protection.[54]

At the Christian Coalition's annual Road to Victory conference in 1998, there was a workshop titled "Y2K: Cough or Catastrophe?"[55] The workshop leaders were Michael Hyatt, author of *The Millennium Bug: How to Survive the Coming Chaos*, and prominent Louisiana Republican Dr. Billy McCormack of the University Baptist Church.[56] It was devoted to outlining the potential seriousness of the problem, then announcing a plan to mobilize churches to provide food, water, shelter, and medical supplies in case the Y2K bug caused widespread societal problems. This mobilization was justified by arguing that the anticipation of resulting disruptions was appropriate no matter what the eschatological viewpoint; and that if there was no serious disruption, the supplies could aid the poor. Special emphasis was placed on the obligation to serve the emergency needs of inner-city poor people.

There was no mention of the End Times in the workshop. This discussion neatly sidestepped the issue of the End Times while allowing those who believe we are in the End Times to work cooperatively with those who do not. Although Hyatt is seen as a secular expert by the media, in the setting of the Christian Coalition meeting he argued that spiritual preparation was the most important aspect, talked about his work with churches, and cited scripture when asked about the possibility of martial law being imposed due to Y2K.[57]

Christian Reconstructionist author Gary North became a much-quoted expert on the Y2K bug with an extensive home page on the Web.[58] North saw much chaos created by Y2K, but as a postmillennialist he dismissed the link to Christ's imminent return. North's apocalyptic predictions about Y2K and the need for survivalist-style preparations echoed his previous stance on surviving nuclear war during the Reagan years, when he cowrote *Fighting Chance: Ten Feet to Survival*.[59] The book, featuring a shovel, a clock, and the Capitol building on its cover, suggested that the way to survive thermonuclear war was to dig a backyard fallout shelter.

Some postmillennialists identified more with the suspicious view of Joseph Farah, quoted in the John Birch Society magazine *New American*: "Much like the Reichstag fire, could the Millennium Bug provide an ambitious President with an opportunity to seize dictatorial powers?"[60] Farah is editor of the WorldNetDaily, an Internet news service.

On December 31, 1999, TV coverage of the stroke of midnight, sweeping around the globe, revealed no great computer catastrophes or Christian cataclysms. The morning after brought little but hangovers that soon faded. Critics of apocalyptic fears and millennial expectation were quick to claim victory. In its February 2000 issue, the glossy magazine *Midnight Call: The Prophetic Voice for the Endtimes*, criticized those who had suggested January 1,

2000, had biblical significance or who made dire predictions about the Y2K computer problem. At the same time, the magazine maintained the editorial position that Christians were still living in the End Times, but argued that the exact dates of specific events in prophecy could not be known. Some, like Jack Van Impe, who had suggested January 1, 2000, had biblical significance, simply reset the countdown to January 1, 2001.[61]

PURISTS, PRAGMATISTS, AND PROPHETS

Campaigns for ritual purification also influenced the role of the Christian Right in electoral politics. There were political and theological debates. Purists argued with pragmatists over litmus test issues for supporting politicians, with abortion and gay rights leading the list.

Decrying pragmatism, Howard Phillips used his U.S. Taxpayers Party (USTP) in an unsuccessful attempt in mid-1996 to lure Pat Buchanan to run for president under the USTP's purist banner after Buchanan lost his bid to become the GOP presidential nominee. Although Buchanan was a paleocon, xenophobic racial nationalist, and a Christian Right theocrat, he was nonetheless (at that point) a team player and pragmatist who remained loyal to the Republican Party. Phillips also approached James Dobson with a plan to have Dobson support the proposed USTP–Buchanan run. Dobson refused the overture. Rebuffed by both Buchanan and Dobson, the USTP dropped the plan for a major third party candidacy. Buchanan and Dobson, however, remained key figures in the theocratic sector of the Christian Right—a sector that urges a hard-line stance rather than pragmatic concession in electoral politics.[62] (In 1999 the USTP became the Constitution Party.)

In 1996 militant Protestants and Catholics unhappy with the pragmatism of the Christian Coalition began to question the legitimacy of electoral politics, the judiciary, and the regime itself. These groups began to push openly theocratic arguments.[63] A predominantly Catholic movement emerged from this sector to suggest that civil disobedience against abortion was mandated by the primacy of natural law over the constitutional separation of powers that allowed the judiciary to protect abortion rights. An example of this theocratic logic can be found in the newspaper *Culture Wars*, with its motto, "no social progress outside the moral order."[64]

Prior to the 1998 elections, Dr. James Dobson led a well-publicized campaign to pull the Republican Party into alignment with Christian Right moral principles. Dobson gave a fiery apocalyptic speech promoting political purity as moral imperative at the meeting of the Council for National Policy in February 1998. This hard-right sector of the Christian Right pushes the Republican Party to the right on issues such as abortion and gay rights.[65]

Dobson's hard-right views are often masked by his professionalism and careful public rhetoric. His writings and endorsements tell a different story. Dobson and his colleague Gary Bauer coauthored *Children at Risk: The Battle for the Hearts and Minds of Our Kids*, which sees an escalating civil war with the forces of Godless secular humanism. Dobson praises Noebel's Summit Ministries, especially its youth training seminars and its high school curriculum that immerse students in apocalyptic conspiracist theories about the secular humanist menace.[66] Dobson's endorsement of Summit is significant because it illustrates how some of the more doctrinaire leaders of the Christian Right are comfortable with or tolerant of conspiracism.

In 1991 David A. Noebel of Summit Ministries, an ultraconservative Christian training center located outside Colorado Springs, Colorado, wrote the 900 page *Understanding the Times* textbook used in 850 Christian schools enrolling a total of over 15,000 students.[67] The book argues that secular humanism has replaced communism as the major anti-Christian philosophy.[68] Among Noebel's previous works are *Communism, Hypnotism and the Beatles*, and *The Homosexual Revolution: End Time Abomination*. Summit Ministries has a long-standing relationship with the conspiracist John Birch Society, placing large ads in the John Birch Society's publications over many years. In at least one instance, in 1983, Summit Ministries appears to have served as a conduit for improperly funneling tax-exempt donations to the Birch Society.[69] Noebel recently absorbed the newsletter of Fred Schwarz's hardright Christian Anti-Communism Crusade.

The continuation of the secular humanist conspiracy thesis was easy to track. Examples abound. For instance, in 1994 Blumenfeld asked, "Is American liberalism—sometimes known as progressivism, socialism, or secular humanism—the latest great 'evil design' guided by Satan himself?"[70] When the Republicans, during the 1996 presidential campaign, invoked opposition to the education reform package known as "Goals 2000" or the curriculum design methodology called "Outcomes Based Education," they were speaking to a constituency that embraces the conspiracist view of secular humanism.

For Christian Right strategist Paul Weyrich, the failure of the drive to impeach President Clinton prompted an exasperated admission of defeat in the electoral arena. In late 1997 Weyrich had been squeezed out of the NET television network he had founded, apparently for his disruptive behavior in attacking GOP pragmatists.[71] Weyrich, dubbed by the *New Republic* the "Robespierre of the Right," was known for his doctrinaire views.[72] In a widely circulated and debated letter, Weyrich promoted a separatist post-impeachment strategy:

> I believe that we probably have lost the culture war. That doesn't mean the war is not going to continue, and that it isn't going to be fought on other fronts. But in terms of society in general, we have lost. This is why, even

when we win in politics, our victories fail to translate into the kind of policies we believe are important.

Therefore, what seems to me a legitimate strategy for us to follow is to look at ways to separate ourselves from the institutions that have been captured by the ideology of Political Correctness, or by other enemies of our traditional culture.

What I mean by separation is, for example, what the homeschoolers have done. Faced with public school systems that no longer educate but instead "condition" students with the attitudes demanded by Political Correctness, they have seceded. They have separated themselves from public schools and have created new institutions, new schools, in their homes.

I think that we have to look at a whole series of possibilities for bypassing the institutions that are controlled by the enemy. If we expend our energies on fighting on the "turf" they already control, we will probably not accomplish what we hope, and we may spend ourselves to the point of exhaustion.[73]

Other Christian Right ideologues such as James Dobson rejected Weyrich's call.[74] A debate quickly ensued among Christian Right leaders, with comments and roundtable essays appearing in the evangelical media. Weyrich clarified his meaning in several printed responses where he said he never meant to suggest giving up. In the influential conservative evangelical magazine *World* he wrote, "The question is not whether we should fight, but how. . . . In essence, I said that we need to change our strategy. Instead of relying on politics to retake the culturally and morally decadent institutions of contemporary America, I said that we should separate from those institutions and build our own."[75]

Weyrich was proposing parallel institutions such as "schools, media, entertainment, universities" from which to create "a new society within the ruins of the old."[76] This strategy also surfaced at the 1998 Christian Coalition "Road to Victory" conference. The workshop on education included two panelists, Marty Angell and Marshall Fritz, who argued in favor of expanding separate, parallel Christian school systems. Fritz even blasted the idea of any state-funded public schools.[77]

Moving in a slightly different direction, conservative evangelicals Cal Thomas and Ed Dobson wrote a book, *Blinded by Might: Can the Religious Right Save America?*, suggesting that evangelicals had compromised their piety by pushing too far into electoral politics.[78] Instead of separatism, however, they suggested returning to the basic evangelical idea of saving souls.

APOCALYPTIC VIOLENCE AND THE FAR RIGHT

Several incidents of hate violence in 1999 seemed influenced by apocalyptic ideologies heated up by millennial expectation. In Illinois and Indiana, Benjamin Nathaniel Smith went on a shooting rampage in July of 1999, killing a Black man and a Korean man, as well as wounding six Orthodox Jews and a man of Taiwanese descent. He then killed himself. Smith was a member of the Church of the Creator, which espoused a crude neonazi theology cobbled together from odd bits of Celtic paganism, Odinism, the theories of Nietzsche, and Aryanist White supremacy.[79]

Several other attacks appear to have been motivated by Christian Identity, the antisemitic theology in which the End Times battle is a race war for White control, and in which anything that challenges heterosexual patriarchy is a target. Californians James "Tyler" Williams and Benjamin "Matthew" Williams, whose ideas echoed Christian Identity beliefs, were charged with slaying a gay couple, arson attacks on three synagogues, and the firebombing of a reproductive health clinic in June and July 1999.[80] In August 1999 Buford O'Neal Furrow, Jr., is alleged to have opened fire on adults and children in a California Jewish community center and, while fleeing the scene of the crime, gunned down a Filipino American postal worker.[81] When arrested, Furrow told reporters what he had done was a "wake-up call to America to kill Jews." Furrow had been involved with Christian Identity for years.[82]

Suspected terrorist Eric Rudolph also appears to have followed Christian Identity; thus his alleged choice of bombing targets in the Atlanta area in 1996–1997 were an Olympic-related event (race-mixing, internationalism), a reproductive health clinic (women in control of their bodies, the killing of White babies), and a gay bar (sinful and unnatural sexuality).[83]

The media dubbed this series of slayings and attacks the "Lone Wolf" phenomenon, since the actions were carried out by persons influenced by race and hate ideology but who were not acting under the direct orders of a specific group or leaders—a technique suggested by Louis Beam's restatement of guerilla principles in his essay on leaderless resistance.[84] Although these attacks received prominent attention, hate crime data collected by the federal government between 1995–1998 actually showed no major overall increase in incidents or a major shift in targets. The most significant trends appeared to be a small decrease in attacks on Whites and a small increase in attacks on gay men and lesbians. During this period the brutal murders of Matthew Shepard and James Byrd, Jr., gained national headlines and raised awareness of hate crimes.[85]

In early November of 1999 both the FBI and the Anti-Defamation League (ADL) distributed reports about the potential for apocalyptic violence at a meeting of the International Association of Chiefs of Police in North Carolina.[86] The ADL report contained an important discussion of Far Right groups such as Christian Identity and Church of the Creator, and the FBI report showed a new understanding of the role of apocalyptic thinking and the complexity of its operation in various dissident movements. But both documents contained important misconceptions as well.

The FBI report had a poorly written discussion of Christian apocalypticism based on Catholic interpretations of the Bible, which was not helpful since the Catholic Church officially discourages apocalyptic interpretations of the book of Revelation. It is Protestant fundamentalist interpretations of prophecy and their secular doppelgangers that influence the apocalyptic dynamic in the United States. The few references in the FBI report to Prostestant fundamentalist influences were limited and inadequate. The FBI also foolishly named its report *Project Megiddo,* after the plain in the Middle East where the battle of Armageddon is fought. Since the FBI is characterized in some Hard Right circles as in league with the Antichrist, the outcome was entirely predictable: portions of the Hard Right saw *Project Megiddo* as a drift toward the imposition of martial law in the End Times.

The ADL report, *Y2K Paranoia: Extremists Confront the Millennium,* lumped together under the rubric "extremists" a wide range of political and religious groups. While it tried to make some distinctions regarding Christian apocalyptic thought, it was easy to read the report as implying that all evangelical Christians who believed in a conspiracy of world leaders during the End Times were potential terrorists. The ADL report's discussion of cults represented a narrow and controversial view challenged by scholars of new religious movements. The ADL report also lacked any footnotes or references, an omission that seriously weakened its arguments.[87]

The way most media covered the reports further amplified their flaws and in some cases misrepresented their contents through uninformed reporting. The FBI report was leaked to the press before its official release, and articles were rushed into print that conflated numerous groups and issues. The FBI was even forced to issue a press release to correct the impression left by a story on its report in *USA Today.*[88] Coming so close to the end of the year, the reports and press coverage had the unintended outcome of fueling the fears of Far Right, Patriot, and armed militia groups, and some militant Christian Right movements. In addition, while both reports focused on racism and antisemitism, there was almost no discussion of potential attacks on feminists, reproductive rights activists, and gay men and lesbians.

Some conservative groups complained (with a degree of justification) that the FBI report left the impression "that members of the Religious Right in America are lunatics who are a danger to society," that "anyone who believes in the end of the world and the Second Coming of Christ also fits that description," and that "religious people, specifically Christians of all denominations, are ´extremists´ and should be watched."[89] This stance echoed complaints from civil libertarians and leftists that some watchdog groups, especially the ADL and the Southern Poverty Law Center, circulated claims about the threat from right-wing "extremists" in a way that erodes civil liberties and encourages government repression of dissidents.[90] Other critics questioned the reliance of these groups on outdated social science models such as centrist/extremist theory. The ADL was criticized for repeatedly calling for increased government powers to conduct surveillance and send informers into "extremist" dissident groups.[91] A related perspective that also cut across political lines even questioned the effectiveness and appropriateness of hate crimes legislation, although supporters of the legislation responded with new research and counter arguments.[92]

GLOBALIZATION, ECONOMIC POPULISM, AND PATRICK BUCHANAN

In 1999 Patrick Buchanan finally bolted from the Republican Party and sought the presidential nomination for the 2000 race from the Reform Party, causing internal dissent and forcing a rift between supporters of Buchanan's nomination by the party and H. Ross Perot, the party's founder, godfather, funder, and former candidate.[93] Buchanan had hinted at this move in a 1998 speech to the Chicago Council on Foreign Relations:

> The day is not too distant when economic nationalism will triumph. Several events will hasten that day. The first is the tidal wave of imports from Asia about to hit these shores. When all those manufactured goods pour in, taking down industries and killing jobs, there will arise a clamor from industry and labor for protection. If that cry goes unheeded, those who turn a stone face to the American workers will be turned out of power. In the Democratic Party or the Republican Party or the Reform Party or some new party, economic nationalism will find its vehicle and its voice. Rely upon it.[94]

In previous campaign rhetoric Buchanan had juggled demonization, scapegoating, conspiracism, apocalyptic and millennialist metaphors, and a crude populist antielitism. In the year 2000, Buchanan sought to broaden his base by reaching out to self-described leftist Lenora Fulani, who ran for president as an independent in 1988 and 1992 and was the first African American woman to be put on the ballot in all 50 states.[95] Fulani, along with her mentor Fred Newman, led a small national group that operated under numerous names, including the New Alliance Party, which dissolved in 1994. The Newmanites have been widely denounced for manipulative organizing tactics, the use of therapy to recruit and discipline members, and a dictatorial philosophy influenced by a 1970s alliance with neofascist Lyndon LaRouche.[96] As early as 1996, Fulani praised Buchanan as an unfairly demonized populist who "has tapped into the anti-government, anti-big business, pro-people sentiments of a significant portion of the American people."[97]

Bruce Shapiro explained the coalition between Buchanan and Fulani,

> Both are nationalists, albeit in different arenas. And both Buchanan and the Newmanites enjoy provoking Jewish outrage with rhetoric that steps up to the threshold of anti-Semitism. Buchanan's well-known sins in this area, enough to persuade William F. Buckley of his fellow conservative's Jew-bait-

ing streak, have their parallel with Fulani and the Jewish Newman, whose writings and speeches over the years have described post-Holocaust Jews as "stormtroopers of decadent capitalism" and used other choice epithets. The political identity of both is rooted in declared reverence for deeply authoritarian institutions: In the case of Buchanan, the most reactionary faction of the Catholic Church, which is nostalgic for the days before women could read from the altar or deliver Communion; in the case of Fulani, her "guru" Newman and a system of psychotherapy famous for giving Newman personal control of the most intimate aspects of clients' lives. Right or left, Buchanan and Fulani offer variations on the same nationalist, scapegoating and authoritarian impulses.[98]

Buchanan may have hoped that Fulani's support would provide a screen for his own racism, but the only noticeable supporters of the alliance were some right-wing populists and a handful of White social democrats.[99] Fulani and Buchanan later parted ways.

Business nationalism and xenophobia have been part of organizing against corporate multinationalist globalization since the first campaigns against the alphabet soup of international treaties such as NAFTA, GATT, WTO, and MAI.[100] Conspiracist analysis of globalization even reached into the U.S. Congress where congresswoman Helen Chenoweth-Hage (R-ID) worked openly with the John Birch Society. Senator Bob Smith (R-NH) briefly quit the Republican Party to run for president on the antiglobalist U.S. Taxpayers Party ticket, but later returned to the fold.[101]

Some ultraconservatives even cultivated ties with liberal antiglobalists such as Public Citizen founder Ralph Nader. Doug Henwood noted that Nader's "twin themes, the hypertrophy of corporate power and the monetary perversion of democracy," are the "core themes of any broad 'progressive' mobilization," but they largely had been appropriated by the "populist right."[102] Consider the statement of John Talbott, the Reform Party spokesperson in New Hampshire:

> If you close your eyes, it is difficult to hear much of a difference between Ralph Nader on the left and Pat Buchanan on the right when they talk about corruption in government, the excesses of corporate welfare, the devastating effect of free international trade on the American worker and a desire to clean big money and special-interests out of Washington. There's a reason for this; 91 percent of the American people consider themselves middle class or working class. The time is now for a new political party that is neither right nor left, neither conservative nor liberal, but created and built to represent the hard-working average American in reforming our government.
>
> If we all pull together, put our prejudices behind us, and ignore traditional labeling such as liberal or conservative, we can join together to fight the battle of our lives against the collaboration of big business and big government, break the two-party monopoly, and return control of our government to the true owners of this country—the American people.[103]

This is an example of repressive populism in the service of nationalist business interests, because it calls on "the people" in the middle to attack the internationalist elites while ignoring the racist and xenophobic policies of Buchanan, who in August 2000 was selected by one faction of the split Reform Party as their presidential hopeful.

Nader and his colleagues worked closely with a business nationalist brain trust financed by right-wing textile magnate Roger Milliken. The strategists included Milliken's lobbyist, Jock Nash; Alan Tonelson of the ultraconservative U.S. Business and Industrial Council; and Pat Choate of the Manufacturing Policy Project. According to Ryan Lizza, it was Choate, the 1996 Reform Party vice–presidential candidate, who "orchestrated Buchanan's flight from the Republican Party."[104] The Naderites and other antiglobalization forces frequently cited books and reports by authors such as Charles Derber, David C. Korten, Jerry Mander, Edward Goldsmith, and William Greider. In thousands of pages these authors denounce large multinational corporations, global finance capital, international banking interests, powerful elites, and the betrayal by corrupt politicians. Only in Greider is there a serious (albeit brief) discussion of how these historic themes have been woven into right-wing populist conspiracy theories.[105]

Despite important differences, many liberal critics of corporate globalization share certain assumptions with right-wing conspiracy theorists. Both argue that the greedy and power-hungry have corrupted the U.S. political and economic system, but both portray the underlying system as essentially just and democratic, which is also the conventional view. As Henwood notes, "quasiradical" antiglobalists such as David Korten denounce large corporations and financial speculation while claiming that private enterprise and the market economy fostered community values in some vaguely defined past. By contrast, genuinely radical critiques see the multinational corporation as only the current logical expression of the underlying capitalist economic system—not as the basic problem in itself. Thus it is not radical analysis, but conventional mainstream illusions, that make left-leaning antiglobalists vulnerable to right-wing conspiracist overtures. The same is true of other progressive movements.[106]

CONSPIRACIST ANALYSIS SPREADS

Right-wing conspiracy theories made inroads into sections of the Left during the Iran–Contra scandal in the late 1980s with the help of Danny Sheehan and his Christic Institute. Sheehan's theory of a "secret team" hijacking U.S. foreign policy drew freely from the LaRouchites and from the Liberty Lobby's *Spotlight* newspaper, and at one point Christic developed a close relationship with Patriot movement leader James "Bo" Gritz. During the Gulf War the nationalist Right continued to recruit from the Left around shared opposition to the U.S. intervention.[107] By the mid-1990s, a few activists in alternative, green, and left subcultures defended the militias, or spread conspiracy theories about the bombing of the federal building in Oklahoma City.[108]

In a lengthy article on snowballing conspiracism in *The New Yorker*, Michael Kelly dubbed this left/right phenomenon "fusion paranoia." Applying a centrist/extremist model, Kelly argued that "both the far right and the far left" have long posited "that sinister, antidemocratic forces have wormed their way into the inner workings of the government and have subverted it to serve not the interests of the nation but those of a powerful few."[109] But this conspiracist idea assumes that the government used to be democratic and at some point served "the interests of the nation"—which is a conventional mainstream view, not a radical one. A truly radical critique sees the U.S. political system as inherently undemocratic from the beginning.

The ease with which anyone can post information on the Internet and reach a potential audience of millions has facilitated the spread of conspiracism, but it can be found in any type of media and across the culture.[110] Even *UFO* magazine felt compelled to run a two-part series denouncing conspiracy theories that had fascist and antisemitic roots.[111] Conspiracist ideas were popularized by the militias in the mid-1990s, and carried forward by Hard Right groups into the new millennium.[112] But as the militia movement faded as a social movement following the Oklahoma City bombing, populist right-wing conspiracism still flourished in other movements. Far-right antisemitism, such as the Internet attacks on Democratic vice-presidential pick Joe Lieberman, also continued.

Conspiracy theories gained popularity in the Black community, assisted in part by television personality Tony Brown, host of *Tony Brown's Journal*. In his 1998 book *Empower the People: Overthrow the Conspiracy That Is Stealing Your Money and Freedom*, Brown exceeded Robertson in the use of antisemitic sources and claims about the Illuminati, and wove them together with material from the conspiracist Christian Right, Patriot movement, LaRouchites, and other segments of the Far Right.[113] The back cover of his book featured a quote from Newt Gingrich: "Tony Brown is a genuine historic figure—and he is going to continue to make history."

In the 1990s, some African Americans embraced unsubstantiated claims that the AIDS epidemic was the result of a deliberate U.S.-government policy of biowarfare. Birchers and LaRouchites were among those promoting these claims, which also circulated among prison inmates. David Gilbert argues that such conspiracy theories divert attention from a racist system of health care and the need for risk reduction measures to interrupt the spread of HIV.[114]

One popular author bringing right-wing antisemitism into left and alternative subcultures was David Icke.[115] A former soccer player and sports commentator, Icke was removed as spokesperson of the Green Party in Britain for antisemitic conspiracism in his book *The Robot's Rebellion*.[116]

Critics of conspiracism quickly emerged in a number of progressive alternative movements.[117] In the social ecology newsletter *Green Perspectives,* Janet Biehl warned that "antistatism has been adopted by a movement of insurgent hate," and that made it even more important for leftists to understand that they have "nothing to learn from paranoid racists, no matter how psychedelic their conspiracies may be."[118] As one report from a progressive watchdog group argued, "There is a vast gulf between the simplistic yet dangerous rhetoric of elite cabals, Jewish conspiracies and the omnipotence of 'international finance' and a thoughtful analysis of the deep divisions and inequities in our society."[119]

LEFT–RIGHT COALITIONS AND ANTIGLOBALISM

A handful of right-wing activists, including some Third Position neonazis and fans of David Icke, took part in the large and dramatic Seattle protests against globalization in early December 1999.[120] As a result, the Southern Poverty Law Center used the Seattle protests to anchor a report titled "Neither Left Nor Right: The Spreading Battle against the Forces of Economic Globalism Is Shaping the Extremism of the New Millennium."[121] The report contained a detailed discussion of the rise of Third Position fascist movements and their call for Left/Right unity to smash capitalism. But since the report relied heavily on centrist/extremist analysis, it was read by some as implying that fascist forces played a major role in Seattle, which was false. In addition, the report appears to have played a role in law enforcement circles where countersubversive hard-liners lumped "extremists" of the Right and the Left together. They falsely asserted that antiglobalist protests were a cover for neonazis and anarchists to engage in terrorism.[122] When the Washington, DC, protests against the World Bank were staged in mid-April 2000, police engaged in a number of repressive preemptive maneuvers and there were numerous reports of excessive use of force.[123]

At the same time, mainstream "Free Trade" supporters opportunistically pointed out the xenophobia in Buchanan's antiglobalization rhetoric as a way to tarnish the larger movement. For example *New York Times* columnist Thomas L. Friedman wrote,

> during the recent anti-I.M.F. protests in Washington . . . hate-mongering isolationist Pat Buchanan joined forces with the Teamsters and their boss James Hoffa. Mr. Buchanan told cheering Teamsters that as president he would tell the Chinese to either shape up or "you guys have sold your last pair of chopsticks in any mall in the United States," and that he would appoint Mr. Hoffa as America's top trade negotiator.[124]

Progressive antiglobalists were susceptible to being tarnished by association with the likes of Buchanan because the liberal, labor, and consumerist groups framing the issues on behalf of middle-class constituents were reluctant to criticize the right-wing populists in their coalition.[125] J. Sakai noted, "The anti-WTO movement is extraordinarily broad, ranging from the revolutionary left to the centrist liberals and social-democrats who manage it all the way over to the neo-fascists and Far-Right." He argued that nationalist, right-wing opposition to the WTO was a powerful and dangerous force because it spoke to the "old middle classes" in the United States. These classes' relative economic privilege was threatened by corporate globalization, and they were "maneuvering with desperation against classes above and below" them, the classic producerist paradigm.[126]

Progressive groups began to object to uncritical coalitions of left-wing and right-wing populists. In June 1999, the Dutch antifascist group De Fabel van de Illegaal (The Myth of Illegality), quit a coalition of European groups organizing against the Multilateral Agreement on Investment (MAI), and the WTO, warning that the reigning political analysis encouraged unprincipled coalitions with right-wing nationalists and bigots.[127] Also in 1999, an "anti-free-trade group called Peoples Global Action amended its manifesto to specifically reject any alliances with right-wing WTO opponents. That was partly out of fear that far-right groups in India and in Europe were infiltrating liberal anti-WTO groups."[128] In early 2000, Pressebüro Savanne in Zurich set up a website "Right-Left—A Dangerous Flirt," to prompt an international discussion of the problem.[129]

CONCLUSIONS

Apocalyptic and millennial themes remained durable components in the toolkit of right-wing populism as the new millennium began, but with a much lower level of excitement than that exhibited during the prelude to the year 2000. New recruits and new versions of old conspiracy claims will continue to shape right-wing populism for many years.

The Christian Right split into three main camps: Christian purist separatists, electoral pragmatists, and spiritual proselytizers, yet this did not signal the end of the Christian Right as a force in U.S. politics, merely a new phase.[130] Meanwhile, liberal stereotyping of conservative Christian evangelicals came under increasing criticism by scholars.[131]

Confusion over populism continued. There was support among liberals, Democrats, and independents for the populist mystique of Republican presidential contender John McCain and the populist mission of wealthy celebrity Arianna Huffington to "Overthrow the Government."[132] Carl Boggs sees this as a response by people "increasingly alienated from a political system that is commonly viewed as corrupt, authoritarian, and simply irrelevant to the most important challenges of our time."[133] Lauren Langman agrees, additionally noting that "today many of those marginalized in the new globalized system, like many previous generations of the alienated, disempowered, humiliated and outraged, tend to gravitate" toward various right-wing movements and leaders such as Buchanan and Perot in the United States, Jean-Marie LePen in France, and Silvio Berlesconi in Italy.[134] Martin A. Lee says voting patterns in Europe demonstrate that far-right opportunists are riding the crest of a populist backlash against globalization. According to Lee this is "a product of democratic decay." He says, "radical right-wing populism and its current fascist manifestations . . . vary from country to country [but] only thrive in situations where social injustice is prevalent."[135]

Valerie Scatamburlo points out that while the Right has successfully understood the interrelationships between cultural, social, political, and economic concerns in popular discussions, many progressives have failed to do likewise. Meanwhile, left-wing intellectuals too often use "inaccessible and overly cryptic" language; or they simply dismiss the Right as "bigoted malcontents" without assisting activists by engaging in public debates over reactionary and oppressive policies.[136]

Adolph Reed, Jr., says the experience of being Black in the United States has made him aware that a "simplistically majoritarian notion of democracy" prevents activists from considering the "underside of populist rhetoric in segregationism and opposition to civil rights," and the fact that "a lot of nastiness can lie under labels like 'the people.'" Reed warns, "We have to recognize that not every popular movement is progressive just because it arises from the grassroots."[137]

Commenting on Jörg Haider, Joel Kovel observes that people "call attention, correctly, to his fascist past and potentials, but do not sufficiently draw the implication that Haider (like Hitler) is also a genuinely populist politician, combining charisma and the ability to mobilize mass hostility to a corrupt regime." Kovel briefly challenged Ralph Nader for the nod from the Green Party as their 2000 presidential candidate. He argued that "There is no question that much good has come out of populism (for example, it played an important role in the passage of anti-trust legislation early in the last century), and that many good people have been, and continue to be, attracted to its banner." He warned, however, that

> Populism builds on resentment and anger against abusive power. . . . The politics of resentment can easily turn into the politics of exclusion, scapegoating and demagoguery. That is why, along with the many virtuous people who have marched under the populist banner, have come more than a fair share of dubious characters who . . . combine populist virtues with various malignant tendencies. . . . So long as [activists] remain populist, they cannot rise above the implications of its basic method, which is to personalize politics. The racism and scapegoating can be restrained, but the need to focus upon some personification of evil remains.

According to Kovel, the "prevailing populist mythology" is the notion that "the People against Corporations comprises the main ground of contemporary struggle" when a more complex systemic analysis is required.[138]

CONCLUSIONS

At the beginning of the twenty-first century, right-wing populist movements remain an important part of politics in the United States. These movements are deeply rooted in U.S. political traditions and are a response to the tensions and inequities of U.S. society. Rather than dismiss right-wing populists as paranoid or fanatical extremists—or romanticize them as "the people" resisting tyranny—we need to recognize these movements as both complex and dangerous: complex, because they speak to a combination of legitimate and selfish grievances; dangerous, because they channel people's hopes and fears into misguided rebellions that only serve to heighten inequality and oppression.

Our conclusions focus on several issues we believe are central to understanding right-wing populism.

- These are movements engaged in real power struggles.
- They target both elites and subordinate groups.
- People find a real sense of effectiveness and community within these movements.
- Unfair social and economic relations fuel populist resentments, especially when mainstream politicians are indifferent to or ineffective in challenging this inequality.
- Different demographic groups join right-wing populist movements.
- Resentments can be mobilized using demonization, scapegoating, and conspiracism especially in a narrative package called producerism.
- The resulting dynamics are complex, placing populist dissidents in a tug-of-war between the Far Right and centrist politicians, and prompting situations that can generate both vigilante bullying and violence, as well as improper government surveillance and political repression.

Since the 1820s, repressive and right-wing populist movements have played an almost continual role in U.S. political life. Why? In the broadest terms, structural inequalities have continually fueled social, political, cultural, and economic tensions of one kind or another. These in turn have provided numerous openings for repressive populist movements to develop.

345

Second, the United States has experienced almost constant upheaval since its founding, between wars, conquest and expansion, mass immigration, industrial growth and change, economic cycles, geographic and social mobility, and antioppression struggles. Third, as the country has expanded and developed (and given its decentralized political system), older elites based along the Atlantic seaboard and in the Northeast have repeatedly been challenged by newer, outsider factions of the elite based in other regions.[1] These outsiders have sometimes used antielite conspiracism to rally grassroots support. Fourth, the United States was one of the first countries to establish mass-based electoral politics—largely through the work of repressive populist movements themselves. In this context politicians quickly established a tradition of demagogic appeals to "the people" against "the establishment."

Why do people join right-wing populist movements? Looking at recent history, we can identify several general factors that seem significant, including:

- anxiety over social, cultural, and political change;
- fears of losing privilege and status, as traditional social hierarchies have been challenged and become more fragmented;
- a sense of disempowerment in the face of massive bureaucratic institutions, both public and private, over which ordinary people have little influence;
- economic hardships and dislocations connected to globalization and other factors;
- disillusionment with mainstream political choices;
- the weakness or nonexistence of leftist radical alternatives that speak effectively to many people's concerns.

In Chapter 10 ("From Old Right to New Right"), we outlined what Michael Omi and Howard Wynant called "the collapse of the ´American Dream,´" under pressure from social liberation movements, economic disruptions and upheavals, and the apparent decline of U.S. global power in the wake of setbacks such as the Vietnam War. For many people drawn to right-wing populist movements, this sense of a many-sided national crisis persists even today.

Holly Sklar, too, has written of "The Dying American Dream." Her analysis highlights soaring economic inequality, growing poverty, inadequate real wages, the disappearance of union jobs, global corporate restructuring, the shredding of social programs, the growth of prisons, and the shift toward "a cheaper, more disposable workforce of temporary workers, part-timers, and other ´contingent workers.´" These trends disproportionately hurt people of color, but they also affect large numbers of White people, who form the vast majority of right-wing populism's supporters. Many

workers find little in their lives that confirms headlines boasting of a booming economy or low unemployment. Sklar underscores that as "the American Dream has become more impossible for more people, scapegoating is
being used to deflect blame from the economic system and channel anger
to support reactionary political causes." Democrats as well as Republicans,
liberals as well as conservatives, have been complicit in this process.[2]

The effect of globalization on the economy is hardly an analysis limited
to the Left. Consider this quote from *Business Week*:

> The Darwinian demands of global competition have led to waves of corpo-
> rate downsizing. Real median incomes haven't moved much for two decades,
> while the earnings gap between the richest and the poorest Americans has
> widened. This has heightened workers' economic insecurity and sown doubts
> about the future.[3]

Other writers have noted the bankruptcy of conventional politics for
addressing social problems. Conservative analyst Kevin Phillips wrote:
"The sad truth is that frustration politics has built to a possibly scary level
precisely because of the unnerving weakness of the major parties and their
prevailing philosophies." Phillips cited both Republicans and Democrats
for "ineptness and miscalculation." After decrying liberal elitism and arro-
gance, Phillips condemned Republican politicians who have "periodically
unleashed the anti-black and anti-Israel messages they now complain about
in more blunt politicians as 'bigotry.'"

According to Phillips, "If Patrick Buchanan is to be put in a 1930-some-
thing context, so should the second-rate conservatives and liberals responsible for the economic and social failures from which he and other outsiders
have drawn so many angry votes."[4] For a growing portion of the population
in the 1990s, neither the Democrats nor the Republicans offered hope for
redress of grievances. This in part explains the Perot phenomenon and the
Reform Party.

Which right-wing populist themes attract which groups of supporters?
Serious statistical research in the United States is scarce, but Hans-Georg
Betz, in his study *Radical Right-Wing Populism in Western Europe*, noted one frequent theme was xenophobia and racist scapegoating of immigrants and asy-
lum seekers in an electoral context. Betz's review of voting demographics in
Europe reveals that right-wing populist parties attract a disproportionate
number of men, persons employed in the private sector, and younger
voters.

In terms of social base, two versions of secular right-wing populism
have emerged: one centered around "get the government off my back" economic libertarianism coupled with a rejection of mainstream political parties
(more attractive to the upper middle class and small entrepreneurs); the
other based on xenophobia and ethnocentric nationalism (more attractive

to the lower middle class and wage workers).[5] These different constituencies unite behind candidates that attack the current regime since both constituencies identify an intrusive and incompetent government as the cause of their grievances. Anecdotal evidence suggests a similar constituency for right-wing populists in the United States.[6]

A third version of right-wing populism unique to the United States has a social base of politically mobilized ultraconservative Christian evangelicals. Persons in the Christian Right are motivated primarily by cultural and religious concerns. Women play a significant role in this sector. A *Washington Post* survey of Promise Keepers attending the Stand in the Gap rally in Washington, DC, showed they most had solidly middle-class income levels. This squares with the finding by Green, Guth, and Hill that Christian Right activism from 1978 through 1988 was concentrated primarily in relatively prosperous suburban areas.[7]

In contrast, it seems persons in the more secular Patriot movement are primarily motivated by economic and social concerns. A study by Deborah Kaplan found members of a Patriot group in California had good reasons to fear downward mobility: "Many of the adherents here did suffer reversals, . . . as a direct result of corporate restructuring strategies. As many as 49.3 percent, compared to 28.0 percent in a national news survey, said they had been 'personally affected' by business downsizing."[8]

More research is needed to draw clearer conclusions, but one tendency that muddles many analyses is the conflation of social movements, political movements, voting blocs, political campaigns, coalitions, and topical projects. While they generally overlap, they are not identical.[9]

As these tentative thoughts indicate, we are not in a position to offer a general theory about the dynamics of right-wing populist movements. What we can say is that the old theory—that "these people are crazy"—does not work.[10] Right-wing populist claims are no more and no less irrational than conventional claims that presidential elections express the will of the people, that economic health can be measured by the profits of multibillion-dollar corporations, or that U.S. military interventions in Haiti or Somalia or Kosovo or wherever are designed to promote democracy and human rights.

Right-wing populists develop narratives about themselves and their society: who's good and who's bad, who has power and who doesn't, who is one of us and who isn't. These narratives may be wrong, but they are important, and they reflect real conflicts, fears, and longings. They are a means by which millions of people make sense of their world and decide how to act on their perceptions.[11]

Producerism is one of the most basic frameworks for right-wing populist narratives in the United States. Producerism posits a noble hard-working middle group constantly in conflict with lazy, malevolent, or sinful parasites at the top and bottom of the social order. The characters and details in this story have changed repeatedly, but its main outlines have remained the same for some two hundred years. See Appendix B.

Producerism, in the forms we have examined, reflects a national culture that has long glorified individual hard work as the key to success and upward mobility. This tradition set Henry Ford's antisemitic philosophy apart from czarist Russia's *The Protocols of the Elders of Zion*, which was rooted in an ethos of rigid class deference and inherited rank. But U.S. producerism also reflects the rigidities of a racial caste system and the interests of middle- and working-class Whites, concerned with defending their privileges over people of color, yet resenting the powerful elites above them.

Producerism has been interwoven with other narratives in the right-wing populist storybook, such as apocalyptic themes about an End Times battle between good and evil. Apocalypticism reflects the influence of Bible-believing Christianity—not only within the Right, but as a major force shaping U.S. politics and culture since the colonial period. Apocalyptic biblical narratives have also shaped both religious and secular fears of betrayal by political leaders plotting a repressive global regime. In recent decades, the theme of defending the traditional family against immoral, elitist feminists and homosexuals has also taken on a new centrality. Far from being irrational, this reflects a predictable effort to bolster heterosexual male power and privilege in the face of major movements demanding equality.

But most people in right-wing populist movements don't get up in the morning and say to themselves, "I'm going to victimize some oppressed groups today to get more power and privilege." What they are more likely to say is, "I want to get my fair share." They embrace narratives that portray themselves as victims and that depict the people they target as either more powerful than they are, being given an unfair advantage, or being immoral. This was true in 1676, when Nathaniel Bacon declared that a corrupt governor was unfairly favoring Indians against English settlers. And it was equally true in the 1990s, when right-wing populists demanded an end to "racial discrimination against white people" and "no special rights for homosexuals." Such claims are a form of scapegoating in defense of social inequality.

Right-wing and repressive populist movements relate to the established order in contradictory ways. They challenge us to go beyond binary models of power and resistance. It is oversimplified and wrong to treat such movements simply as attack dogs for bigoted elites. It is also a serious mistake to gloss over these movements' oppressive politics just because they challenge certain kinds of elite interests. And the reverse is also true: it is a serious mistake to gloss over the established order's oppressive politics—as centrist/extremist theory does—just because right-wing populists want to impose something that could be worse.

It is the dynamic interplay between the Right and the Center, and between right-wing populist insurgency and established institutions, that is particularly dangerous. As we noted in Chapter 15, Bill Clinton often responded to Republican attacks largely by embracing right-wing positions, in a pattern that Democratic politicians have followed repeatedly. As Holly Sklar notes, "Views once considered extremist far right are now considered ordinary, views once considered centrist are now considered ultraliberal, and views genuinely to the left are largely absent in the mass media."[12]

Right-wing populists have scored major successes in helping to shift the political spectrum to the right, and this influence must be combated. But actual Christian theocracy or Aryanist fascism in the United States is purely hypothetical, whereas a political system dominated by enormously wealthy elites is real—in fact, it is what we live under now. Rightists promote nightmare visions of the death penalty to help reinforce patriarchal families, or the formation of a "racially pure" White Christian republic; meanwhile, in our existing society, millions of women face sexual assault or domestic violence daily, and millions of people of color are relegated to rural and inner-city areas of rampant unemployment, poverty, violence, and state repression.

The growth of state repression is not simply a function of right-wing initiatives. It is fundamentally a mechanism for political and economic elites to protect their own power. The Cold War produced a consensus among liberals, conservatives, reactionaries, and fascists on the need for a national security state to crush threats from the Left both inside and outside the United States. This consensus was challenged in the 1960s and 1970s, as many liberals, under pressure from the Left, criticized and sought to limit the most glaring abusive and illegal practices by government agencies. During the following years, ultraconservative organizations played a pivotal role in helping the security establishment circumvent such limits by shifting certain operations into private channels.

Since the 1970s, well-publicized rightist-backed initiatives—the War on Drugs, crackdowns against "illegal aliens," and campaigns against "terrorism"—have been used to promote massive expansion of the security establishment, as well as serious attacks on civil liberties, especially against people of color. At the same time, the repressive apparatus has also grown through quieter measures such as expanded identification systems, increased ties between police and community organizations, and greater coordination between local, state, federal, and international police bodies.[13]

During the 1990s, government forces also used the growth of right-wing paramilitarism—such as the armed militias—as a rationale for further expanding state repression, which in turn fueled greater right-wing insurgency. This is a vicious cycle in which each side scapegoats the other— what Girard calls mimetic scapegoating.[14] Here it is not simply the Right, or forces outside the Right, but also elite-sponsored *opposition* to the Right, that feeds authoritarian tendencies. To an alarming extent, liberal and even leftist antiracists and antifascists—following centrist/extremist theory—have contributed to this vicious cycle by denouncing only right-wing paramilitarism while ignoring the much more powerful repressive forces of the state itself—or worse, by directly urging a government crackdown as the way to fight the Right. Government abuse of power to silence dissent should be opposed regardless of the target group's political pedigree. History reveals, however, that while the state's repressive apparatus will sometimes go after right-wing insurgents, in the long run its main targets are oppressed groups and the Left.

Centrist/extremist theory glorifies the U.S. political system as democratic and glosses over its oppressive, antidemocratic features. It suggests that "irrational" dissidents of the Left and the Right are to blame for stirring up trouble. It implies that when leftists organize to demand equality and human rights it is the disruptive moral equivalent of right-wing campaigns to defend inequality and privilege. Whose interests does this analytical model serve?

We see a need for a dual strategy in combating right-wing populism, On one hand, there is a need for broad antirightist alliances to defend access to abortion, affirmative action, gay rights, immigration, and more. Confronting rightist groups involves rationally refuting their scapegoating, addressing legitimate grievances, and exposing the lies and prejudices their most fanatical members spew.

Such a strategy was used, with partial success, to confront the Posse Comitatus in the early 1980s. At that time the Posse blamed the collapsing farm economy on a conspiracy of Jewish bankers manipulating subhuman people of color. In response, a coalition led by the Center for Democratic Renewal in Atlanta organized against scapegoating, offered assistance to groups voicing legitimate economic grievances, and assisted people in reintegrating into the economy.

Teams went county by county through Posse strongholds. Black Baptist ministers talked about antisemitism; Jews talked about racism; Lutherans talked about healing; and farm organizers gave economic advice. The American Jewish Committee hosted a conference in Chicago to call national attention to both antisemitism in the farm belt and social and economic injustice in rural America.[15]

This coalition had more to do with beating back the Posse than armed law enforcement attacks, criminal trials, or civil litigation. What the coalition's educational work could not do, however, was uproot the underlying social and economic problems that made the Posse, and later the Patriot movement, attractive to large numbers of people.

Along with such coalitions, we also see a need for radical initiatives to highlight the links between right-wing populism and institutionalized oppression and to address centrism and liberalism's inadequate plans for resolving society's problems. This approach means exploring new political options when Republican and Democratic politicians are both representing narrow wealthy interests. It means opposing both antiabortion terrorism and FBI repression. It means defending social welfare programs against rightist attack while also pointing out the paternalistic, abusive, and inadequate nature of many such programs. It means combating the fake radicalism and scapegoating characteristic of conspiracy theories by articulating systemic analyses of elite power. It means joining and supporting movements for social change that are based on equality and social justice, not scapegoating and illusions of supremacy.

NOTES

Some periodical articles, primarily those on side issues or narrow details, appear only in the notes and have been omitted from the bibliography.

A large number of LaRouchite authors and publications are in the notes to Chapter 13. The publications are the *New Federalist*, *Executive Intelligence Review*, and *The Campaigner*.

A large number of Patrick Buchanan's columns and articles are in the notes to Chapter 13. The publications are the *Washington Inquirer*, *Human Events*, the *Boston Herald*, and *From the Right* (Buchanan's newsletter).

Several references to articles in the Nation of Islam's *Final Call* newspaper are in the notes to Chapter 13.

Notes to Introduction

1. Neiwert, *In God's Country*; Joel Dyer, *Harvest of Rage*; Stern, *Force Upon the Plain*; Burghart and Crawford, *Guns and Gavels*.

2. Canovan, *Populism*, pp. 13, 128–138.

3. Ibid., pp. 289, 293, 294; Canovan notes that there are "a great many interconnections" among her seven forms of populism, and that "many phenomena—perhaps most—belong in more than one category." She adds that "given the contradictions" between some of the categories, "none could ever satisfy all the conditions at once."

4. Kazin, *Populist Persuasion*. See also Harrison, *Of Passionate Intensity*.

5. Sara Diamond, *Roads to Dominion*, p. 9.

6. Kazin, *Populist Persuasion*, p. 35.

7. Our conception of producerism is derived from Alexander Saxton's discussion of the "Producer Ethic" as an ideology of the early White labor movement that "emphasized an egalitarianism reserved for whites" (Saxton, *Rise and Fall of the White Republic*, p. 313). See also p. 298; and *Indispensable Enemy*, pp. 21–22, 52, 265–269.

Our conception is also deeply influenced by Moishe Postone's discussion of how modern antisemitism draws a false dichotomy between "productive" industrial capital and "parasitic" finance capital. See Postone, "Anti-Semitism and National Socialism," especially pp. 106–113.

We use the term producerism in a different way than Catherine McNicol Stock does in her book *Rural Radicals*. Stock portrays producerism simply as a form of populist antielitism, separate from (though sometimes coinciding with) attacks on socially oppressed groups. In our view, producerism intrinsically involves a dual-edged combination of antielitism and oppression (in the U.S. setting, usually in the form of racism or antisemitism, but also sexism and homophobia) and it is precisely this combination that must be addressed.

8. Hardisty, *Mobilizing Resentment.*

9. Aho, "Phenomenology of the Enemy," pp. 107–121. See also Young-Bruehl, *Anatomy of Prejudices;* and Noël, *Intolerance, A General Survey.*

10. Pagels, *Origin of Satan,* p. 182.

11. Carus, *History of the Devil,* pp. 70–72.

12. Allport, *Nature of Prejudice,* p. 244. On the ritualized transference and expulsion of evil in a variety of cultures, see Frazier, *Golden Bough,* pp. 624–686. On the process and social function of scapegoating in historic persecution texts of myth and religion, see Girard, *Scapegoat.*

13. Landes, "Scapegoating," p. 659. In contrast to our approach, Franz Neumann has argued against using the term scapegoating when discussing conspiracist movements. See Neumann, "Anxiety in Politics," p. 255.

14. Allport, *Nature of Prejudice,* p. 350. For other early studies, see Dollard, Doob, Miller, Mowrer, and Sears, *Frustration and Aggression;* Adorno, Frenkel-Brunswick, Levinson, and Sanford, *Authoritarian Personality;* and Rokeach, *Open and Closed Mind;* Hoffer, *True Believer.*

15. Conversation with Susan M. Fisher, MD (clinical professor of psychiatry at University of Chicago Medical School and Faculty, Chicago Institute for Psychoanalysis), 1997. For an interesting approach linking Jungian psychology to interventions against scapegoating in dysfunctional small organizations and groups, see Colman, *Up from Scapegoating.*

16. See Allport, *Nature of Prejudice,* pp. 243–260; Girard, *Scapegoat.*

17. Conversation with Herman Sinaiko, professor of humanities, University of Chicago, 1997.

18. Fenster, *Conspiracy Theories,* pp. 67, 74. For additional views of the cultural context of conspiracism, see Dean, *Aliens in America;* Nancy Lusignan Schultz, ed., *Fear Itself;* and Marcus, ed., *Paranoia within Reason;* Melley, *Empire of Conspiracy.*

19. Cumings, *Origins of the Korean War: Vol. 2,* p. 767. See also Albert, "Conspiracy? . . . Not!"; "Conspiracy? . . . Not, Again."

20. Hofstadter, "Paranoid Style in American Politics," pp. 37–38.

21. Donner, *Age of Surveillance,* p. 11.

22. This analysis of apocalyptic demonization and millennialism is drawn primarily from the following sources:

For apocalypticism: Paul Boyer, *When Time Shall Be No More;* Strozier, *Apocalypse;* O'Leary, *Arguing the Apocalypse;* Fuller, *Naming the Antichrist;* Lamy, *Millennium Rage;* Damian Thompson, *End of Time;* Fenn, *End of Time.*

For Christian critiques of conspiracist apocalyptics: Camp, *Selling Fear;* Abanes, *End-Time Visions;* and Sine, *Cease Fire.*

For a progressive challenge to apocalyptic thinking: Quinby, *Anti-Apocalypse.*

For apocalyptic demonization: Pagels, *Origin of Satan;* and Cohn, *Cosmos, Chaos and the World to Come;* Aho, *This Thing of Darkness.*

23. The word *apocalypse* comes from the Greek, "*apokalypsis*" which means unveiling hidden information or revealing secret knowledge concerning unfolding human events. The word "revelation" is another way to translate the idea of *apokalypsis.* Thus, the words "apocalypse," "revelation," and "prophecy" are closely related. Prophets, by definition, are apocalyptic. See LaHaye, *Revelation,* p. 9.

24. Devout Christians in Salem, Massachusetts, and other towns sought to expose witches and their allies as conspiring with the Devil (Fuller, *Naming the Antichrist*, pp. 56–61, 63). Modern scholarship has shown that persons accused of being witches were disproportionately women who did not conform to societal expectations, and that there was frequently an economic dimension to the charge, such as a disputed inheritance. See Karlsen, *Devil in the Shape of a Woman*, pp. 46–116.

25. This can be found in a wide range of sources; see O'Sullivan, "Satanism Scare"; Victor, "Search for Scapegoat Deviants"; Zeskind, "Some Ideas on Conspiracy Theories"; Blee, "Engendering Conspiracy"; Harrington, "Conspiracy Theories and Paranoia"; Stern, "Militias and the Religious Right"; Price, "Antichrist Superstar"; and Stix, "Apocalypse, Shmapocalypse"; Daniels, ed., *Doomsday Reader*.

26. See, for example, Paul Boyer, *When Time Shall Be No More*, pp. 254–339; Strozier, *Apocalypse*, pp. 108–129; O'Leary, *Arguing the Apocalypse*, pp. 134–193; Fuller, *Naming the Antichrist*, pp. 165–190; Frances FitzGerald, "American Millennium"; Halsell, *Prophecy and Politics*; Harding, "Imagining the Last Days; Sara Diamond, *Not by Politics Alone*, pp. 197–215; *Spiritual Warfare*, pp. 130–136; and "Political Millennialism"; Clarkson, *Eternal Hostility*, pp. 125–138; Kintz, *Between Jesus and the Market*, pp. 8–9, 134–139, 266–267; Herman, *Antigay Agenda*, pp. 19–24, 35–44, 125–128, 171–172.

27. Landes, "On Owls, Roosters, and Apocalyptic Time."

28. David G. Bromley, "Constructing Apocalypticism"; and Wessinger, "Millennialism With and Without the Mayhem."

29. Cohn, *Pursuit of the Millennium*.

30. Paul Boyer, *When Time Shall Be No More*, pp. 80–85.

31. See, generally, Cohn, *Cosmos, Chaos and the World to Come*.

32. Damian Thompson, *End of Time*, p. 307.

33. The word millennium refers to a span of 1,000 years, but also has many deeper meanings. It has come to mean the point at which one period of a thousand years ends and the next begins, and for some this has important religious, social, or political significance. This was certainly the case as the year 2000 approached. All millennial movements are apocalyptic in some sense, even when positive and hopeful; but not all apocalyptic movements are millennial.

34. See, for example, Berrigan, *Ezekiel*; Gomes, *Good Book*; Camp, *Selling Fear*.

35. We reject narrow definitions of what constitutes a social movement applied by some academics. Challenges to centrist/extremist theory by social scientists who study the Right include Rogin, *Intellectuals and McCarthy*, pp. 261–282; Curry and Brown, eds., "Introduction," pp. xi–xii; Ribuffo, *Old Christian Right*, pp. 237–257; Canovan, *Populism*, pp. 46–51, 179–190; Himmelstein, *To the Right*, pp. 1–5, 72–76, 152–164; Sara Diamond, *Roads to Dominion*, pp. 5–6, 40–41; Kazin, *Populist Persuasion*, pp. 190–193. Hixson, in *Search for the American Right Wing*, analyzes Rogin's criticisms.

36. For reviews of social movement theory in transition, see Buechler, *Social Movements in Advanced Capitalism*, pp. 3–57; and Garner and Tenuto, *Social Movement Theory and Research*, pp. 1–48. See also, note 133 for Chapter 16.

37. Christian Smith, "Correcting a Curious Neglect," p. 3.

38. Aho, *This Thing of Darkness*.

39. The Anti-Defamation League (ADL) is a prime example of centrist/extremist theory being used to help rationalize collaboration with state repression. On the ADL's spying against progressive organizations and collaboration with U.S., South African, and Israeli espionage agencies, see Friedman, "Enemy Within"; Dennis King and Chip

Berlet, "A.D.L. Under Fire"; "ADLgate"; Jane Hunter, "Who was the ADL spying for?"; Jabara, "Anti-Defamation League."

40. An example of leftist romanticization of the militia movement is James Murray, "Chiapas & Montana." For a critique of this type of portrayal, see Biehl, "Militia Fever"; and Biehl and Staudenmaier, *Ecofascism.*

41. See Berlet, *Right Woos Left.*

42. Domhoff, *Powers That Be; Who Rules America?;* Mills, *Power Elite.*

43. For an overview of business conflict analysis in comparison with other theories of politics, see Gibbs, *Political Economy of Third World Intervention,* ch. 1. For other examples of business conflict analysis, see Thomas Ferguson and Joel Rogers, *Right Turn;* Thomas Ferguson, *Golden Rule;* Cumings, *Origins of the Korean War: Vol. 2,* chs. 2 and 3; Mike Davis, *Prisoners of the American Dream,* pp. 167–176; Ansell, "Business Mobilization and the New Right"; Bodenheimer and Gould, *Rollback!;* Ronald W. Cox, *Power and Profits;* Matthew N. Lyons, "Business Conflict and Right-Wing Movements."

44. Matthew N. Lyons, "What is Fascism?"

The literature on fascism is vast. A few general discussions we have found particularly useful are Roger Griffin, *Nature of Fascism;* Payne, *Fascism;* Eley, "What Produces Fascism," pp. 69–99; and Mayer, *Dynamics of Counterrevolution in Europe.*

Notes to Chapter 1

1. Washburn, *Governor and the Rebel,* pp. 70–71.

2. On Bacon's Rebellion, see Washburn, *Governor and the Rebel;* Edmund S. Morgan, *American Slavery, American Freedom,* ch. 13; and Breen, "Changing Labor Force," pp. 3–25, collected in Breen, *Shaping Southern Society.*

3. Theodore W. Allen, *Invention of the White Race: Vol. 1,* p. 18.

4. Sakai, *Settlers,* p. 13.

5. Washburn, *Governor and the Rebel,* p. 38.

6. Lens, *Radicalism in America,* p. 14; Theodore W. Allen, *Invention of the White Race: Vol. 1,* pp. 214–215.

7. Theodore W. Allen, " '. . . They Would Have Destroyed Me, '" p. 44.

8. Ibid.

9. Edmund S. Morgan, *American Slavery, American Freedom,* p. 269.

10. Paine, *Common Sense.*

11. Gunderson, "Independence, Citizenship, and the American Revolution," p. 77, quoted in Kerber, " 'I Have Don . . . much, '" p. 233. On patriots' equation of slavery with blackness, see Burrows and Wallace, "American Revolution," p. 198; Roediger, *Wages of Whiteness,* p. 28; Okoye, "Chattel Slavery as the Nightmare," pp. 3–28.

12. See Zinn, *People's History,* ch. 4.

13. Gutman, ed., *Who Built America?,* pp. 122–125.

14. On the farmers' riots, see Allen Taylor, "Agrarian Independence," pp. 221–245; on New York tenant farmers, see Kulikoff, "American Revolution," pp. 95, 97.

15. David Brion Davis, *Problem of Slavery,* p. 262.

16. Eric Williams, *Capitalism and Slavery,* p. 120.

17. See Jennings, "Indians' Revolution"; Friedenberg, *Life, Liberty and the Pursuit of Land,* chs. 14–16.

18. Fuller, *Naming the Antichrist,* pp. 68–69.

19. Friedenberg, *Life, Liberty and the Pursuit of Land,* pp. 149–150.

20. Sakai, *Settlers*, pp. 8–9.

21. Friedenberg, *Life, Liberty and the Pursuit of Land*, p. 152.

22. Kulikoff, "American Revolution"; Taylor, "Agrarian Independence"; Alfred F. Young, "Afterword," p. 343.

23. Zinn, *People's History*, p. 83.

24. Friedenberg, *Life, Liberty and the Pursuit of Land*, pp. 183–185; Blackburn, *Overthrow of Colonial Slavery*, p. 116.

25. Calloway, *American Revolution in Indian Country*, pp. 26–34, especially p. 31.

26. Quoted in Drinnon, *Facing West*, p. 331.

27. Calloway, *American Revolution in Indian Country*, pp. 47–55.

28. This discussion of Black people's relationship with the American Revolution benefited from a conversation with Clinton Cox, author of *Come All You Brave Soldiers*.

29. Between 1777 and 1784, Massachusetts, New Hampshire, and Vermont outlawed slavery, while Pennsylvania, Rhode Island, and Connecticut enacted gradual emancipation laws. Meanwhile, between 1782 and 1790, Virginia, Maryland, and Delaware repealed laws against private manumission, further increasing the number of free Black people. In 1787, the Continental Congress passed the Northwest Ordinance, which banned the importation of slaves into the territories north of the Ohio and east of the Mississippi rivers (but included no mechanism to emancipate the small number of slaves already present in the area). Many states, including Virginia, also prohibited slave imports, before Congress banned the slave trade permanently in 1808. David Brion Davis, *Problem of Slavery*, pp. 25–27; Nash, *Race and Revolution*, pp. 7–19; Freehling, "Founding Fathers," p. 22; Kolchin, *American Slavery*, p. 79.

30. See, for example, Nash, *Race and Revolution*. For an overview of historians' differing views about the American Revolution's significance for slavery and for Black people, see Egerton, "Black Independence Struggles," pp. 95–116.

31. Freehling, "Founding Fathers," p. 13.

32. Peter H. Wood, "'Liberty is Sweet,'" p. 152. Wood also challenges the assumption widespread among historians that "the most radical ideas of the American Revolution—especially the core concept of personal liberty—for the most part trickled *downward* through colonial society from the top." As he argues, "it may well be that, during the generations preceding 1776, African Americans thought longer and harder than any other sector of the colonial population about the concept of liberty, both as an abstract ideal and as a tangible reality" (pp. 151, 152).

33. On Black resistance efforts from 1765 to 1775, see Peter H. Wood, "'Liberty is Sweet,'" pp. 158–168; Frey, *Water from the Rock*, pp. 53–54, 59, 61–62, 64. On Black offers to fight for Britain against rebel colonists, see Wood, "'Liberty is Sweet,'" pp. 160, 163–164.

34. Frey, *Water from the Rock*, pp. 56–66, 147–149. See also Quarles, *Negro in the American Revolution*, pp. 123–130.

35. Frey, *Water from the Rock*, pp. 66, 86–87, 114, 118–120, 167–169; Walker, "Blacks as American Loyalists," pp. 53–55; on the Charleston harbor strike, see Peter H. Wood, "'Liberty is Sweet,'" p. 170.

36. Walker, "Blacks as American Loyalists," pp. 53–57.

37. Washington quoted in Peter H. Wood, "'Liberty is Sweet,'" p. 170. On U.S. recruitment of Black soldiers, see Frey, *Water from the Rock*, pp. 77–79; Franklin and Moss, *From Slavery to Freedom*, pp. 72–79. Blackburn, *Overthrow of Colonial Slavery* (p. 114) estimates that 4,000 Blacks served in the Continental Army; Walker, "Blacks as American Loyalists" (p. 55) says 5,000; and Egerton, "Black Independence Struggles" (p. 97)

states that "three times as many black Americans found liberty in the armies of King George than they did in patriot forces." Philip S. Foner gives the figures of 65,000 Blacks with the British military, and 5–8,000 with the Continental Army (Foner, *Labor and the American Revolution*, p. 184).

38. Frey, *Water from the Rock*, pp. 89–92, 106–107, 113–114, 119–123, 130–131, 141, 155–156, 170; Walker, "Blacks as American Loyalists," pp. 59–61, 65.

39. Frey, *Water from the Rock*, p. 211. On Blacks' resettlement see Frey, ch. 6; Walker, "Blacks as American Loyalists," pp. 61–66.

40. Frey, *Water from the Rock*, pp. 226–227; Mullin, "British Caribbean and North American Slaves," pp. 240–241.

41. The percentage of Blacks in New England and Pennsylvania is derived from statistics in Franklin and Moss, *From Slavery to Freedom*, p. 85. On northern emancipation, see Blackburn, *Overthrow of Colonial Slavery*, pp. 117–120; Egerton, "Black Independence Struggles," p. 102–104. On New York slaves sold southward, see Freehling, "Founding Fathers," p. 18. Egerton and Freehling note that emancipation in New Jersey was so slow that the state still had a few slaves on the eve of the Civil War.

42. Egerton, "Black Independence Struggles," p. 105; Frey, *Water from the Rock*, pp. 213–215.

43. Finkelman, "Color of Law," pp. 937–991, especially pp. 969–974; Blackburn, *Overthrow of Colonial Slavery*, pp. 122–126. On slave imports from 1788 to 1808, see Kolchin, *American Slavery*, p. 79.

44. Haney López, *White by Law*, pp. 42–43.

45. Paine, p. 49; see also Peter H. Wood, "'Liberty is Sweet,'" pp. 161, 171.

46. Quoted in Donovan, *Mr. Jefferson's Declaration*, p. 86.

47. Calloway, *American Revolution in Indian Country*, pp. 281–286, quote is from p. 293.

48. Quoted in ibid., pp. 86–87.

49. On Jefferson's ambivalence about slavery, see for example David Brion Davis, *Problem of Slavery*, pp. 165–184.

50. Quoted in Burrows and Wallace, "American Revolution," pp. 215, 292, 268, 202.

51. Quoted in ibid., pp. 215, 287. Seeing circumcision as emasculating also carried an antisemitic subtext.

52. See Kerber, "'History Can Do It No Justice,'" especially pp. 10–25; Young, "Women of Boston," especially pp. 194–209.

53. Wilson, "Illusions of Change." New Jersey permitted some women to vote until 1807. See also Kathleen M. Brown, *Good Wives, Nasty Wenches*.

54. On Abigail Adams, see Young, "Women of Boston," pp. 181–183; "an outpouring" is quoted from Young, "Women of Boston," p. 217. On Judith Sargent Murray, see Kerber, "'I Have Don . . . much,'" pp. 238–244.

55. Norton, *Liberty's Daughters*, p. 298; see also Kerber, *Women of the Republic*.

56. Cornell, Saul, (1999), *The Other Founders*, Chapel Hill, NC: University of North Carolina Press; Lens, *Radicalism in America*; Starkey, Marion L. (1955), *A Little Rebellion*, New York: Alfred A. Knopf; Szatmary, David P. (1980), *Shays' Rebellion*, Amherst MA: University of Massachusetts Press; Zinn, *People's History*.

Notes to Chapter 2

1. Lipset and Raab, *Politics of Unreason*, pp. 39–61; Bennett, *Party of Fear*, pp. 32–35.

2. Lipset and Raab, *Politics of Unreason*, p. 40.

3. Franklin and Moss, *From Slavery to Freedom*, pp. 86–88, 110–113.

4. Rogin, *Fathers and Children*, p. 252.

5. Thomas Ferguson, *Golden Rule*, p. 59.

6. Ignatiev, *How the Irish Became White*, pp. 116, 140.

7. Lerner, "Lady and the Mill Girl"; Baker, "Domestication of Politics," pp. 71–72.

8. Pessen, *Jacksonian America*, pp. 157–162.

9. Saxton, *Rise and Fall of the White Republic*, pp. 95–100.

10. Goodman, *Towards a Christian Republic*, pp. 3, 12, 41.

11. David Brion Davis, ed., "Some Themes of Countersubversion," in *Fear of Conspiracy*, pp. 9–22.

12. Robison, *Proofs of a Conspiracy*.

13. Barruel, *Memoirs Illustrating the History of Jacobinism*.

14. Ibid., p. 396; Robison, *Proofs of a Conspiracy*, pp. 11–56; Johnson, *Architects of Fear*, pp. 43–50.

15. David Brion Davis, ed., editor's comments in *Fear of Conspiracy*, pp. 35–37; Johnson, *Architects of Fear*, pp. 47–50; Robison, *Proofs of a Conspiracy*, p. 9.

16. Robison's first edition appeared just as Barruel's third volume, first edition, was going to press; but Robison had not yet seen Barruel's work. In their second editions, both authors acknowledge each other, and Barruel engages in some criticism of Robison's informal treatment of quotes. See Barruel, *Memoirs Illustrating the History of Jacobinism*, pp. 396–398.

17. Ratner, *Antimasonry*, pp. 6, 24–25. For further discussion of the Illuminati conspiracy theory, see Chapter 9. See also Moss, *Life of Jedidiah Morse*.

18. Other Antimasonry supporters who became leading antislavery activists included Lewis Tappan, Gerrit Smith, William Seward, Salmon P. Chase, and former president John Quincy Adams (Goodman, *Towards a Christian Republic*, pp. 160–161, 239–240, 294).

19. Eric Foner, *Reconstruction*, p. 42.

20. Formisano and Kutolowski, "Antimasonry and Masonry," pp. 139–165.

21. Holt, *Political Parties*, pp. 91–92.

22. Giddens, *Account of the Savage Treatment*, p. 1.

23. Goodman, *Towards a Christian Republic*, pp. 7–8, 27.

24. Ibid., pp. 94, 239–243.

25. See ibid., pp. vii–ix, for an overview of this debate.

26. Ibid., p. 157, see also pp. 124–125, 201–202.

27. Ibid., pp. 185, 36.

28. Saxton, *Rise and Fall of the White Republic*, p. 73n16; Holt, *Political Parties*, pp. 38–42.

29. Takaki, *Iron Cages*, pp. 95–96.

30. Wallace, *Long, Bitter Trail*, pp. 53–54; Rogin, *Fathers and Children*, p. 165.

31. Rogin, *Fathers and Children*, p. 206.

32. Wallace, *Long, Bitter Trail*, pp. 97–101.

33. Saxton, *Rise and Fall of the White Republic*, p. 146.

34. Ibid., pp. 67–72, quotes from p. 70.

35. Ibid., pp. 148–151.

36. Litwack, *North of Slavery*, pp. 74–93; Roediger, *Wages of Whiteness*, p. 57.

37. Saxton, *Rise and Fall of the White Republic*, p. 151; Litwack, *North of Slavery*, pp. 64–74, 100–102; Ignatiev, *How the Irish Became White*, p. 97.

38. Ignatiev, *How the Irish Became White*, pp. 69, 74, 79, 106–121; Roediger, *Wages of Whiteness*, pp. 73–87.

39. Saxton, *Rise and Fall of the White Republic*, p. 132; Mike Davis, *Prisoners of the American Dream*, p. 14; Hugins, *New York Workingmen*, pp. 63–64.

40. Roediger, *Wages of Whiteness*, p. 50; Ignatiev, *How the Irish Became White*, p. 74; Takaki, *Iron Cages*, p. 105.

41. Baker, "Domestication of Politics," p. 71.

42. Martha May, "Bread before roses," pp. 5, 4–5.

43. Hugins, *New York Workingmen*, pp. 199–200; see also Saxton, *Rise and Fall of the White Republic*, pp. 142–144.

44. Rogin, *Fathers and Children*, pp. 253, 282; Hugins, *New York Workingmen*, pp. 200, 233–234.

45. Jackson quoted in Takaki, *Iron Cages*, p. 104; Van Buren quoted in Rogin, *Fathers and Children*, p. 290.

46. Rogin, *Fathers and Children*, pp. 294–295; Burch, *Elites in American History: Vol. 1*, pp. 150–152.

47. Hammond, *Banks and Politics in America*, p. 353.

48. Benson, *Concept of Jacksonian Democracy*, p. 56; see also pp. 47–56.

49. Hammond, *Banks and Politics in America*, p. 329.

50. Rogin, *Fathers and Children*, p. 277; Thomas Ferguson, *Golden Rule*, pp. 59–60; Richard B. Morris, "Andrew Jackson, Strikebreaker."

51. Roediger, *Wages of Whiteness*, p. 141.

52. Ignatiev, *How the Irish Became White*, pp. 1, 6–31, 161; Acuña, *Occupied America*, p. 16.

53. Holt, *Political Parties*, pp. 116–117.

54. Ignatiev, *How the Irish Became White*, p. 41; on English oppression of Ireland and its relevance to racial oppression in the United States, see Theodore W. Allen, *Invention of the White Race: Vol. 1*, especially chs. 2–5. On the key privileges reserved for Whites, see Theodore W. Allen, *Invention of the White Race: Vol. 1*, p. 184.

55. Billington, *Origins of Nativism*, pp. 301–302; Holt, *Political Parties*, p. 119; on Irish anticolonialist republicanism, see Mike Davis, *Prisoners of the American Dream*, p. 23.

56. Billington, *Origins of Nativism*, e.g., pp. 80–96, 463–473.

57. Ibid., pp. 151–168.

58. Bennett, *Party of Fear*, pp. 50–59; Benson, *Concept of Jacksonian Democracy*, pp. 120–122; Holt, *Political Parties*, p. 212.

59. Ignatiev, *How the Irish Became White*, p. 159.

60. Tabachnik, *Origins of the Know-Nothing Party*, pp. 150–153, 160–161, 243–245.

61. Ibid., pp. 91, 147, 176.

62. Ibid., pp. 191–201, 220–221, 243–244.

63. Hales, "'Co-Laborers in the Cause'"; Tabachnik, *Origins of the Know-Nothing Party*, pp. 81–83.

64. Mulkern, *Know-Nothing Party in Massachusetts*, p. 76; Holt, *Political Parties*, pp. 112–114, 147.

65. Hutchinson, *Startling Facts for Native Americans*, p. vii.

66. Holt, *Political Parties*, pp. 116–123.

67. Ibid., pp. 134–137.

68. Mulkern, *Know-Nothing Party in Massachusetts*, pp. 88–89, 103, 108–111.

69. Saxton, *Rise and Fall of the White Republic*, pp. 249–253.

70. Ibid., pp. 154, 85.

71. Quoted in Litwack, *North of Slavery*, p. 269.

72. See Ignatiev, *How the Irish Became White*, p. 85; Saxton, *Rise and Fall of the White Republic*, pp. 82, 153–154.

Notes to Chapter 3

1. See Du Bois, *Black Reconstruction*, p. 61.

2. See Du Bois, *Black Reconstruction*, chs. 4, 5; Ignatiev, "White Worker and the Labor Movement," pp. 105–107; Michael W. Fitzgerald, "Poor Man's Fight," pp. 14–17.

3. Fuller, *Naming the Antichrist*, pp. 88–92.

4. Richard O. Boyer, *Legend of John Brown*, p. 86; Theodore W. Allen, *Invention of the White Race: Vol. 1*, p. 189; Eric Foner, *Reconstruction*, p. 32; Ignatiev, *How the Irish Became White*, pp. 99–100.

5. On Reconstruction, see Du Bois, *Black Reconstruction*; Eric Foner, *Reconstruction*; Theodore W. Allen, *Invention of the White Race: Vol. 1*, pp. 139–144; Sakai, *Settlers*, pp. 38–41.

6. Eric Foner, *Reconstruction*, pp. 470–472.

7. Saxton, *Indispensable Enemy*, p. 36.

8. Du Bois, *Black Reconstruction*, p. 217; see also pp. 353, 367.

9. Northern business supporters of the Democrats included textile manufacturers, many merchants and bankers, and some railroads (Burch, *Elites in American History: Vol. 2*, pp. 31, 59n95).

10. On the Sand Creek Massacre, see Dee Brown, *Bury My Heart at Wounded Knee*, pp. 84–91; Saxton, *Rise and Fall of the White Republic*, ch. 12, especially pp. 276–280. Sherman quoted in Drinnon, *Facing West*, p. 329; see also Eric Foner, *Reconstruction*, pp. 70–71, 462–463; on western lands, see Foner, *Reconstruction*, p. 467.

11. Eric Foner, *Reconstruction*, pp. 461–469; Goldstein, *Political Repression in Modern America*, pp. 6–9; Saxton, *Rise and Fall of the White Republic*, pp. 252–253.

12. Goldstein, *Political Repression in Modern America*, p. 26.

13. On the anti-Reconstruction backlash, including the Ku Klux Klan, see Forest G. Wood, *Black Scare*; Wade, *Fiery Cross*, chs. 1–3; Eric Foner, *Reconstruction*, pp. 342–344, 425–444.

14. Wade, *Fiery Cross*, p. 107; Philip S. Foner, *Organized Labor*, p. 42.

15. Hodes, *White Women, Black Men*, pp. 5, 147–148, 157–158, 199.

16. Ibid., pp. 174, 166–167.

17. Sommerville, "Rape Myth in the Old South," pp. 481–518; Angela Y. Davis, *Women, Race & Class*, ch. 11, especially pp. 187, 189, 191.

18. Hodes, *White Women, Black Men*, pp. 161–162; Wade, *Fiery Cross*, pp. 69–71; Blee, *Women of the Klan*, p. 16.

19. Wade, *Fiery Cross*, p. 107.

20. Roger Griffin, *Nature of Fascism*, p. 38 (italics in original).

21. Wade, *Fiery Cross*, p. 59; on anti-Klan resistance, see Eric Foner, *Reconstruction*, pp. 435–437.

22. Sakai, *Settlers*, p. 44.

23. Philip S. Foner, *Organized Labor*, pp. 19, 25–26; Roediger, *Wages of Whiteness*, p. 180.

24. NLU quoted in Philip S. Foner, *History of the Labor Movement: Vol. 1*, p. 399; Philip S. Foner, *Organized Labor*, pp. 18–45; Sakai, *Settlers*, pp. 43–44.

25. Du Bois, *Black Reconstruction*, pp. 353, 700.

26. Zinn, *People's History*, pp. 240–246; Eric Foner, *Reconstruction*, pp. 583–586; Goldstein, *Political Repression in Modern America*, pp. 30–33.

27. Roediger, *Wages of Whiteness*, pp. 167–169; Saxton, *Rise and Fall of the White Republic*, pp. 296–297.

28. Goldstein, *Political Repression in Modern America*, pp. 9–19.

29. Ibid., pp. 24–60; Donner, *Protectors of Privilege*, pp. 12–14; Higham, *Strangers in the Land*, p. 54.

30. Saxton, *Rise and Fall of the White Republic*, pp. 300–303, 313.

31. Fink, *Workingmen's Democracy*, ch. 6; Philip S. Foner, *Organized Labor*, ch. 4.

32. On the Populists, see Goodwyn, *Democratic Promise*; on their racial politics, see Robert L. Allen with Pamela P. Allen, *Reluctant Reformers*, ch. 3; Acuña, *Occupied America*, p. 37; Saxton, *Rise and Fall of the White Republic*, pp. 362–364.

33. Saxton, *Rise and Fall of the White Republic*, p. 304.

34. Destler, *American Radicalism*, pp. 25–28, 50–76; Nugent, *Tolerant Populists*, pp. 102–121; Lipset and Raab, *Politics of Unreason*, pp. 92–95.

35. Philip S. Foner, *Women and the American Labor Movement*, ch. 4; Mari Jo Buhle, *Women and American Socialism*, pp. 83–91; Flexner, *Century of Struggle*, pp. 177, 223–224; Hymowitz and Weissman, *History of Women in America*, p. 186.

36. Philip S. Foner, *Organized Labor*, p. 34.

37. On the anti-Chinese crusade, see Saxton, *Indispensable Enemy*; Takaki, *Iron Cages*, ch. 10; Herbert Hill, "Anti-Oriental Agitation"; Mink, *Old Labor and New Immigrants*, ch. 3; Lyman, "Strangers in the City," pp. 163–166, 170–175.

38. Acuña, *Occupied America*, ch. 5.

39. Saxton, *Indispensable Enemy*, pp. 3–10; Sakai, *Settlers*, p. 33; Amott and Matthaei, *Race, Gender, and Work*, pp. 199–202.

40. Takaki, *Iron Cages*, p. 236; Herbert Hill, "Anti-Oriental Agitation," p. 44; Saxton, *Indispensable Enemy*, p. 76.

41. Saxton, *Rise and Fall of the White Republic*, p. 310; Takaki, *Iron Cages*, pp. 216–220; George quoted in Saxton, *Indispensable Enemy*, p. 102; labor newspaper quoted in Saxton, *Indispensable Enemy*, p. 244.

42. George quoted in Saxton, *Indispensable Enemy*, p. 102; Gompers quoted in Mink, *Old Labor and New Immigrants*, p. 96; Yu, "World of Our Grandmothers," p. 35; *Gazeteer* quoted in Saxton, *Indispensable Enemy*, p. 18.

43. Saxton, *Indispensable Enemy*, p. 81.

44. Takaki, *Iron Cages*, pp. 236–239.

45. Saxton, *Indispensable Enemy*, p. 260.

46. Ibid., p. 81.

47. Herbert Hill, "Anti-Oriental Agitation," pp. 47, 48–51.

48. Saxton, *Rise and Fall of the White Republic*, p. 310; Saxton, *Indispensable Enemy*, p. 237; Higham, *Strangers in the Land*, p. 346n13; Ginger, *Eugene V. Debs*, p. 131.

49. Saxton, *Indispensable Enemy*, pp, 148–150.

50. Mazumdar, "General Introduction," p. 4.

51. Saxton, *Indispensable Enemy*, p. 234.

Notes to Chapter 4

1. Dowd, *Twisted Dream*, p. 65; Zinn, *People's History*, pp. 342–343.

2. Burch, *Elites in American History: Vol. 2*, pp. 131–135; Philip S. Foner, *History of the Labor Movement: Vol. 2*, pp. 369–370.

3. Kolko, *Triumph of Conservatism*, pp. 2–14.

4. Fredrickson, *White Supremacy*, pp. 200–201.

5. Abramovitz, *Regulating the Lives of Women*, p. 185; Evans, *Feminists*, pp. 53–55; Baker, "Domestication of Politics," pp. 75–76.

6. Angela Y. Davis, *Women, Race & Class*, chs. 7–8; Giddings, *When and Where I Enter*, pp. 90–117, 123–127, 159–160; Amott and Matthaei, *Race, Gender, and Work*, p. 164.

7. Robert L. Allen with Pamela P. Allen, *Reluctant Reformers*, pp. 88–89.

8. Abramovitz, *Regulating the Lives of Women*, p. 182.

9. Kolko, *Triumph of Conservatism*, p. 14.

10. Mink, *Old Labor and New Immigrants*, pp. 168–184; Goldstein, *Political Repression in Modern America*, p. 63.

11. Thomas Ferguson, *Golden Rule*, pp. 71–75.

12. On romanticism, see Bernal, *Black Athena*, pp. 28, 204–205; on palingenetic nationalism, see Roger Griffin, *Nature of Fascism*, pp. 32–33, 37–38.

13. Roosevelt quoted in G. Edward White, *Eastern Establishment*, p. 83.

14. G. Edward White, *Eastern Establishment*, pp. 153–158, 161, 166–167; Robert L. Allen with Pamela P. Allen, *Reluctant Reformers*, p. 95; William Loren Katz, *Black West*, pp. 272–280.

15. Quoted in Drinnon, *Facing West*, p. 232.

16. Ibid., p. 314.

17. Ibid., pp. 307–313; Roosevelt quoted in ibid., p. 299.

18. LaFeber, *Panama Canal*, pp. 35, 52–53.

19. Robert L. Allen with Pamela P. Allen, *Reluctant Reformers*, pp. 94–96; Thomas G. Dyer, *Theodore Roosevelt and the Idea of Race*, ch. 5.

20. Quoted in Leuchtenburg, "Introduction," p. 11.

21. Linda Gordon, *Woman's Body, Woman's Right*, pp. 156–157.

22. Ibid., p. 134.

23. Roosevelt, *New Nationalism*, p. 143; Roosevelt quoted in Linda Gordon, *Woman's Body, Woman's Right*, p. 136; Gordon, p. 142.

24. Abramovitz, *Regulating the Lives of Women*, pp. 182, 185; see also Kessler-Harris, *Out to Work*, pp. 152–158, 180–214; Charlotte Baum, Paula Hyman, and Sonya Michel, *Jewish Woman in America*, pp. 144–145.

25. Linda Gordon, *Woman's Body, Woman's Right*, p. 140.

26. Macleod, *Building Character in the American Boy*, p. 58.

27. Ibid., pp. 136–137, 39–49, 58.

28. Ibid., pp. 148, 178–180.

29. Bernal, *Black Athena*, p. 208.

30. Macleod, *Building Character in the American Boy*, p. 100.

31. Turner quoted in Takaki, *Iron Cages, Iron Cages*, p. 263; G. Edward White, *Eastern Establishment*, p. 172.

32. Barry Weisberg, *Beyond Repair*, pp. 23–24; Kolko, *Triumph of Conservatism*, pp. 110–111; G. Edward White, *Eastern Establishment*, ch. 8, especially pp. 172–181.

33. Roosevelt quoted in Irving Greenberg, *Theodore Roosevelt and Labor*, p. 350; Burch, *Elites in American History: Vol. 2*, pp. 146–161, 165; Kolko, *Triumph of Conservatism*, pp. 194–195, 199–204.

34. Burch, *Elites in American History: Vol. 2*, p. 156.

35. Mink, *Old Labor and New Immigrants*, p. 162; see also Payne, *Fascism*, pp. 24–25; Cannistraro, ed., *Historical Dictionary of Fascist Italy*, pp. 138–140.

36. Mink, *Old Labor and New Immigrants*, pp. 172–178; Burch, *Elites in American History: Vol. 2*, p. 164.

37. Mink, *Old Labor and New Immigrants*, pp. 199–203.

38. On racism and nativism in the Socialist Party, see Paul Buhle, "Debsian Socialism and the 'New Immigrant' Worker," pp. 249–277; Mink, *Old Labor and New Immigrants*, pp. 228–235; Riddell, ed., *Lenin's Struggle*, pp. 3–20, especially pp. 16–17.

39. Mink, *Old Labor and New Immigrants*, pp. 194–196; Higham, *Strangers in the Land*, pp. 114–115.

40. Roosevelt quoted in Thomas G. Dyer, *Theodore Roosevelt and the Idea of Race*, p. 131.

41. Thomas G. Dyer, *Theodore Roosevelt and the Idea of Race*, ch. 6; Mink, *Old Labor and New Immigrants*, pp. 214, 219–222; Higham, *Strangers in the Land*, pp. 112, 128–129, 149, 190, 198–199.

42. Mink, *Old Labor and New Immigrants*, pp. 184–186.

43. Kolko, *Triumph of Conservatism*, pp. 196–198; Roosevelt quoted in Kolko, p. 199.

44. Ibid., p. 199; Mink, *Old Labor and New Immigrants*, p. 219; see also Beede, "Foreign Influences on American Progressivism," pp. 541–542.

45. Roger Griffin, *Nature of Fascism*, pp. 56–60, 202–204, 212–213; Payne, *Fascism*, pp. 22–41; De Grand, *Italian Nationalist Association*; Laqueur, *Black Hundred*; Whiteside, *Socialism of Fools*; Mosse, *Crisis of German Ideology*, especially ch. 12.

46. Ledeen, *Universal Fascism*, p. 5.

Notes to Chapter 5

1. On people of color's migration to the North, see Marks, *Farewell—We're Good and Gone*; Acuña, *Occupied America*, pp. 174–181; Amott and Matthaei, *Race, Gender, and Work*, p. 169. On women's movement into paid work, see Amott and Matthaei, pp, 126–127.

2. Ridgeway, *Blood in the Face*, p. 34.

3. On suffragist picketers, see Flexner, *Century of Struggle*, pp. 284–285; Stevens, *Jailed for Freedom*. On German Americans, see Higham, *Strangers in the Land*, pp. 207–211.

4. Higham, *Strangers in the Land*, pp. 209–210, 227; Kornweibel, "Seeing Red," p. 5.

5. Donner, *Age of Surveillance*, pp. 32–33, 44, 47; Kornweibel, "Seeing Red," pp. 4–16; Higham, *Strangers in the Land*, pp. 211–212.

6. Vaughn, *Holding Fast the Inner Lines*, especially pp. 30–31, 43–45, 47, 141, 202.

7. Socialist Party quoted in Richard O. Boyer and Herbert M. Morais, *Labor's Untold Story*, p. 198. On the Socialist Party and immigrant workers, see Paul Buhle, "Debsian Socialism and the 'New Immigrant' Worker," pp. 267–268; Kolko, *Main Currents in Modern American History*, pp. 181–184.

8. IWW quoted in Pencak, *For God and Country*, p. 149. See also Higham, *Strangers in the Land*, pp. 219–220; Sakai, *Settlers*, pp. 68–69; Zinn, *People's History*, pp. 360–364; Philip S. Foner, *History of the Labor Movement: Vol. 4*.

9. Preston, *Aliens and Dissenters*; Post, *The Deportations Delirium*.

10. Donner, *Age of Surveillance*, pp. 36–39; Richard O. Boyer and Herbert M. Morais, *Labor's Untold Story*, pp. 212–215.

11. Donner, *Age of Surveillance*, p. 15.

12. On the American Legion, see Pencak, *For God and Country*. On the American Legion's praise for Mussolini, see Pencak, p. 21.

13. Marsden, *Understanding Fundamentalism*, pp. 9–61; Fuller, *Naming the Antichrist*, pp. 108–133.

14. Kovel, *Red Hunting in the Promised Land*, pp. 76–79, 123–132, 215–218.

15. Donner, *Age of Surveillance,* pp. 47–48.

16. Szajkowski, *Jews, Wars and Communism: Vol.* 2, pp. 149–158; Hall quoted in Singerman, "Jew as Racial Alien," p. 115.

17. Kornweibel, *"Seeing Red,"* pp. 1–2, 7, 11, 20, 23, 40–41.

18. On the PLM, see MacLachlan, *Anarchism and the Mexican Revolution;* Acuña, *Occupied America,* pp. 149–151; Sakai, *Settlers,* p. 71. On the call for an uprising in the United States, see Sandos, *Rebellion in the Borderlands.* On anti-Mexican violence in the United States, see Acuña, *Occupied America,* pp. 158–164. See also Coerver and Hall, *Texas and the Mexican Revolution,* ch. 4.

19. Higham, *Strangers in the Land,* p. 265.

20. Curran, *Xenophobia and Immigration,* p. 137; Marks, *Farewell—We're Good and Gone,* pp. 148–150; Justice Department quoted in Donner, *Age of Surveillance,* pp. 43–44.

21. See Judith Stein, *World of Marcus Garvey,* pp. 46–60; Marable, "A. Philip Randolph," pp. 61–74; Tani and Sera, *False Nationalism False Internationalism,* pp. 79–82.

22. See Judith Stein, *World of Marcus Garvey;* Tony Martin, *Race First;* Giddings, *When and Where I Enter,* pp. 193–195; Pinckney, *Red, Black, and Green,* ch. 3. (We note that Tony Martin's later work embraced antisemitism.)

23. See Kornweibel, *"Seeing Red."* On the federal campaign against Marcus Garvey, see Kornweibel, ch. 6.

24. Ludmerer, "Genetics, Eugenics," p. 375.

25. Madison Grant, *Passing of the Great Race,* pp. 32–33.

26. Ibid., pp. 91, 77, 87–88.

27. Laborer quoted in Pavolko, "Racism and the New Immigration," p. 61; attorney quoted in Sakai, *Settlers,* p. 63; miner quoted in Curran, *Xenophobia and Immigration,* p. 115; senator quoted in Sakai, *Settlers,* p. 63.

28. Bearlieu quoted in Singerman, "Jew as Racial Alien," p. 107; test result quoted in Pavolko, "Racism and the New Immigration," p. 65.

29. Madison Grant, *Passing of the Great Race,* pp. 50–51.

30. Reilly, *Surgical Solution,* pp. 26–27, 45–48, 88, 97.

31. Ibid., pp. 106–109; Kühl, *Nazi Connection.*

32. Linda Gordon, *Woman's Body, Woman's Right,* p. 279. Although the association with Nazism sharply discredited eugenics after the 1930s, the U.S. medical establishment continued to promote sterilization extensively until at least the 1980s as a way to limit subordinate populations—with collusion or active support from government agencies. The main targets after World War II were poor women and women of color, who were frequently manipulated, misinformed, or pressured into sterilization despite some weak federal efforts to check such abuse, beginning in the 1970s. During one four-year period in the 1970s, for example, the federal Indian Health Service sterilized at least 3,000 Native women without proper consent forms. By the 1970s, over 35 percent of childbearing-age women in Puerto Rico had been sterilized. See Hartmann, *Reproductive Rights and Wrongs,* pp. 240–241; Trombley, *Right to Reproduce,* pp. 176–179, 198–202, 224–226; Angela Y. Davis, *Women, Race & Class,* pp. 217–219.

33. Linda Gordon, *Woman's Body, Woman's Right,* pp. 275–276; Reilly, *Surgical Solution,* p. 77; see also Margaret Quigley, "Roots of the IQ Debate," pp. 210–222, available as a monograph with footnotes from Political Research Associates.

34. Reilly, *Surgical Solution,* pp. 22–24.

35. Yung, "Appendix," pp. 425–426.

36. On European immigration under the 1924 act, see Higham, *Strangers in the Land*, pp. 202–203, 311, 319. On Asian immigration, see Yung, "Appendix," p. 426; Amott and Matthaei, *Race, Gender, and Work*, p. 240.

37. Ludmerer, "Genetics, Eugenics," pp. 370, 381; Higham, *Strangers in the Land*, p. 317; Acuña, *Occupied America*, pp. 185–188.

38. The 1924 Immigration Act became law one year after the U.S. Supreme Court's 1923 decision in *United States v. Thind*, a landmark case on the question of who was a "white person" eligible for citizenship under the 1790 naturalization law. In a series of cases beginning in 1909, federal courts had issued conflicting rulings on the Whiteness of citizenship applicants from Syria and India. These cases hinged on a split between popular conceptions of Whiteness and anthropologists' emerging "scientific" schema. Scientists' racial category of "Caucasian"—generally equated with White—included not only light-skinned Europeans and their descendants but also peoples of North Africa, the Middle East, South Asia, and Polynesia—many of them darker-skinned—whom most European Americans did not consider to be White. In *Thind*, the Supreme Court declared that Asian Indians were not White, and that the phrase "white persons" should "be interpreted in accordance with the understanding of the common man"—not anthropologists' broader concept of Caucasian. In later rulings, this same principle was applied to Arabians and Afghanis. In other words, the U.S. government endorsed racial science when it served to *narrow* the boundaries of racial privilege (as in the 1924 Immigration Act) but rejected racial science when it threatened to *broaden* the boundaries of racial privilege. See Haney López, *White By Law*, pp. 3–8, 204–208, and chs. 3 and 4, especially pp. 88–92. On repression, see Preston, *Aliens and Dissenters*.

39. Dixon's *The Clansman* was first pubished in 1905 by Doubleday, Page & Company. Later reissued 1907 with pencil illustrations by A. Wessels Company; and after 1915 by Grosset & Dunlap with "Reproductions of Scenes from the Photo-Play of 'The Birth of a Nation.'" See also Dixon's earlier work, *Leopard's Spots*.

40. Watson on Jews quoted in Grosser and Halperin, *Anti-Semitism*, pp. 246–247; Watson on the Ku Klux Klan quoted in Jackson, *Ku Klux Klan in the City*, p. 257n4.

41. Wade, *Fiery Cross*, p. 146.

42. Ibid., p. 149.

43. Jackson, *Ku Klux Klan in the City*, p. 7; Wade, *Fiery Cross*, pp. 149–150.

44. Fox, *Mirror Makers*, p. 79.

45. Wade, *Fiery Cross*, pp. 153–157.

46. Chalmers, *Hooded Americanism*, p. 298.

47. Wade, *Fiery Cross*, pp. 160–166.

48. Ibid., p. 165.

49. Wade, *Fiery Cross*, pp. 196–197, 201–202, 235–237, 239–247, 253; Jackson, *Ku Klux Klan in the City*, p. 236; Chalmers, *Hooded Americanism*, p. 291; Blee, *Women of the Klan*, pp. 27–30; William Loren Katz, "People vs. the Klan in Mass Combat," pp. 96–100; Lay, "Conclusion," p. 221.

50. This discussion of historical reinterpretations of the Klan is largely based on Leonard J. Moore, "Historical Interpretations," pp. 17–38; and other articles in the same volume. See also Blee, *Women of the Klan*, and the list of works cited in Moore's article.

51. Leonard J. Moore, *Citizen Klansmen*, p. 10.

52. Leonard J. Moore, "Historical Interpretations," p. 24.

53. Ibid., p. 34.

54. Leonard J. Moore, *Citizen Klansmen*, p. 23.

55. Lay, "Conclusion," p. 222.

56. On southern dailies, see Lay, "Introduction," p. 14n14; on Indiana, see Leonard J. Moore, *Citizen Klansmen*, p. 12; on Georgia, see Pencak, *For God and Country*, p. 108. Other references: Goldberg, *Hooded Empire*, pp. 121, 129; Lay, "Imperial Outpost," pp. 67–95; Toy, "Robe and Gown," p. 178; Gerlach, "Battle of Empires," p. 131.

57. Chalmers, *Hooded Americanism*, pp. 51, 145, 156–157.

58. David A. Horowitz, "Order, Solidarity, and Vigilance," pp. 195–196; Lipset and Raab, *Politics of Unreason*, pp. 127–128; Lila Lee Jones, *Ku Klux Klan in Eastern Kansas*, p. 33.

59. On the United Mine Workers, see Zerzan, "Rank-and-file Radicalism," p. 52. On the Colorado strike, see Goldberg, *Hooded Empire*, p. 146.

60. Goldberg, *Hooded Empire*, pp. 80, 134; Leonard J. Moore, *Citizen Klansmen*, p. 96; Zerzan, "Rank-and-file Radicalism," p. 52; Lipset and Raab, *Politics of Unreason*, p. 128.

61. Acuña, *Occupied America*, p. 154; Sakai, *Settlers*, pp. 73–74; Noel Ignatin, "Golden Bridge," p. 64.

62. Zerzan, "Rank-and-file Radicalism," p. 51.

63. Ibid.

64. The following discussion of women and the Klan is based on Blee, *Women of the Klan*.

65. Wade, *Fiery Cross*, p. 150.

66. Blee, *Women of the Klan*, pp. 23–27.

67. Ibid., pp. 103–104; Stanton quoted in Andolsen, *"Daughters of Jefferson,"* p. 31; Angela Y. Davis, *Women, Race & Class*, especially ch. 7; Blee, *Women of the Klan*, pp. 29–30, 116.

68. Blee, *Women of the Klan*, pp. 57–65, 147–153, 40–41.

69. Ibid., pp. 80, 83, 49–51.

70. Ibid., pp. 51–52.

71. Ibid., pp. 72–76.

72. Durham, "Gender and the British Union of Fascists"; see also Durham, *Women and Fascism*.

Notes to Chapter 6

1. See, for example, Gelderman, *Henry Ford*, pp. 220, 242; Higham, *Strangers in the Land*, pp. 282–283; Hofstadter, *Age of Reform*, p. 81.

2. Schonbach, *Native American Fascism*, p. 68; Lipset and Raab, *Politics of Unreason*, pp. 111, 135; Gelderman, *Henry Ford*, pp. 223, 224. For a general discussion of Ford's antisemitic campaign, see Ribuffo, "Henry Ford and *The International Jew*," pp. 437–477.

3. Higham, *Strangers in the Land*, pp. 161, 278; Sacks, "How Did Jews Become White Folks?," p. 84.

4. George Mosse states that the *Protocols* "were forged in France in the midst of the Dreyfus affair, with the assistance of the Russian secret police, probably between 1894 and 1899" (Mosse, *Toward the Final Solution*, p. 117). Captain Alfred Dreyfus was a Jewish officer in the French army convicted of treason in 1894 and later exonerated; his case became a focal point for resurgent antisemitism in France and western Europe.

5. Szajkowski, *Jews, Wars and Communism: Vol. 2*, p. 162.

6. Ribuffo, "Henry Ford and *The International Jew*," p. 447.

7. *International Jew: Vol. 1*, p. 47.

8. Ibid., p. 45.

9. Ibid., pp. 53, 21–22.

10. Ibid., p. 228, 229.

11. Cumings, *Origins of the Korean War: Vol. 2*, pp. 83–84; Nugent, *Tolerant Populists*, pp. 102–121.

12. *International Jew: Vol. 1*, p. 30.

13. Szajkowski, *Jews, Wars and Communism: Vol. 2*, pp. 174–176.

14. Webster, *World Revolution*, and *Secret Societies and Subversive Movements*. For this and other such works, see Singerman, *Antisemitic Propaganda*.

15. Singerman, *Antisemitic Propaganda*, entry 0101, p. 29, citing Holmes, *Anti-Semitism in British Society*, pp. 147–150; Cohn, *Warrant for Genocide*, pp. 168–170.

16. Ribuffo, *Old Christian Right*, pp. 16–17, 167, 196–197, 211; Bennett, *Party of Fear*, p. 269. Dilling engaged in racist and antisemitic red-baiting from the Patriotic Research Bureau in Chicago. See Dilling, *Red Network*, and *Roosevelt Red Record and its Background*. See also the excerpt from Dilling's *Roosevelt Red Record and its Background* in David Brion Davis, ed., *Fear of Conspiracy*, pp. 273–276. Human rights activist Susan DeCamp traced some current conspiracist theories circulating in Montana and other Rocky Mountain states back to Dilling's books in *Conspiracy, Identity & the Religious Right*, a lecture presented at the Northwest Coalition Against Malicious Harassment Symposium, Eugene, Oregon, October 1998. A more overtly antisemitic tract was Dilling, *New Dealers in Office*, a booklet consisting of a list of Roosevelt appointees with supposedly Jewish-sounding names. The cover sports the slogan "Keep America Christian." In this milieu, Roosevelt was thought to be a secret Jew hiding his real name, often alleged to be "Rosenfeld." For background on popular antisemitism during this period, see Dinnerstein, *Antisemitism in America*, pp. 105–149.

17. Higham, *Strangers in the Land*, p. 285; Gelderman, *Henry Ford*, pp. 235–241.

18. On Cameron, see Barkun, *Religion and the Racist Right*, ch. 3; on Spanknoebel, see Schonbach, *Native American Fascism*, p. 123; on Coughlin, see Kahn, *High Treason*, pp. 183–185; on Ford's decoration, see Gelderman, *Henry Ford*, p. 240.

19. Hitler quoted in Carlson [Avedis Derounian], *Under Cover*, p. 210; Gelderman, *Henry Ford*, pp. 225–227.

20. Nevins and Hill, *Ford: Expansion and Challenge*, pp. 4–5.

21. Ibid.; Rothschild, "Fordism and Sloanism," pp. 276–277.

22. Dowd, *Twisted Dream*, p. 93.

23. Rothschild, "Fordism and Sloanism," p. 279.

24. Ibid.; David L. Lewis, *Public Image of Henry Ford*, p. 160.

25. Gelderman, *Henry Ford*, p. 51; Donald Finlay Davis, *Conspicuous Production*, p. 122.

26. David L. Lewis, *Public Image of Henry Ford*, p. 213.

27. Rothschild, "Fordism and Sloanism," p. 277.

28. Nevins and Hill, *Ford: Expansion and Challenge*, p. 459.

29. Ibid., pp. 126–128; Higham, *Strangers in the Land*, p. 284.

30. Lipset and Raab, *Politics of Unreason*, pp. 111, 141; Nevins and Hill, *Ford: Expansion and Challenge*, pp. 301–305.

31. Lipset and Raab, *Politics of Unreason*, p. 138; Nevins and Hill, *Ford: Expansion and Challenge*, p. 508.

32. Ford with Crowther, *Today and Tomorrow*, p. 151; Costigliola, *Awkward Dominion*, p. 156.

33. *Today and Tomorrow* was the second of three books that Crowther wrote with Ford. Nevins and Hill comment: "Company executives recognized the basic ideas of

the Ford–Crowther writings as essentially Henry's, demurring only that Crowther made them seem too fixed; actually Ford was always revising them, always pushing ahead. But of course the literary dress was almost entirely Crowther's" (Nevins and Hill, *Ford: Expansion and Challenge*, p. 613).

34. Ford with Crowther, *Today and Tomorrow*, p. 27.

35. Ibid., pp. 29, 8, 150, 90.

36. Quoted in Donald Finlay Davis, *Conspicuous Production*, p. 127.

37. Ford with Crowther, *Today and Tomorrow*, p. 24.

38. The first quote is from Ford with Crowther, *My Life and Work*, pp. 156–157; the second is from *Today and Tomorrow*, pp. 26–27.

39. Ford with Crowther, *Today and Tomorrow*, pp. 27–28.

40. Kele, *Nazis and Workers*, p. 143.

41. Donald Finlay Davis, *Conspicuous Production*, pp. 146–150; Trescott, *Financing American Enterprise*, p. 171; Donald Finlay Davis, *Conspicuous Production*, pp. 130–131; Higham, *Strangers in the Land*, p. 283.

42. Thomas Ferguson, *Golden Rule*, p. 138.

43. David L. Lewis, *Public Image of Henry Ford*, p. 219; Trescott, *Financing American Enterprise*, pp. 169, 176–192.

44. Lipset and Raab, *Politics of Unreason*, p. 138.

45. Karl Marx, *Capital: Vol. 1*, p. 409.

46. Ford with Crowther, *My Life and Work*, pp. 158–159.

47. Ford with Crowther, *Today and Tomorrow*, pp. 167, 160.

48. Braverman, *Labor and Monopoly Capital*, pp. 146–150; Donald Finlay Davis, *Conspicuous Production*, p. 143.

49. Nevins and Hill, *Ford: Expansion and Challenge*, ch. 20.

50. Nevins with Hill, *Ford: The Times, the Man, the Company*, pp. 561–562.

51. NLRB quoted in Kahn, *High Treason*, p. 170; Ibid., pp. 176–189; Gelderman, *Henry Ford*, pp. 329–332, 343–347.

52. Company policy quoted in John R. Lee, "Ford's Personnel Manager," p. 191; Martha May, "Historical Problem of the Family Wage," p. 284; Nevins and Hill, *Ford: Expansion and Challenge*, pp. 333–334.

53. Gelderman, *Henry Ford*, p. 57.

54. Nevins and Hill, *Ford: Expansion and Challenge*, p. 337.

55. Martha May, "Historical Problem of the Family Wage," pp. 281, 284–285.

56. Ibid., p. 277; Koonz, *Mothers in the Fatherland*, pp. 388–389; De Grazia, *How Fascism Ruled Women*, pp. 5–6, 9.

57. Ford with Crowther, *Today and Tomorrow*, p. 159; *My Life and Work*, p. 129.

58. Higham, *Strangers in the Land*, pp. 247–248.

59. Pavolko, "Racism and the New Immigration," pp. 71–72; Higham, *Strangers in the Land*, p. 244.

60. Ewen and Ewen, *Channels of Desire*, p. 33; Fox, *Mirror Makers*, p. 101.

61. Northrup, "Blacks in the United Automobile Workers Union," p. 158.

62. Meier and Rudwick, *Black Detroit and the Rise of the UAW*, pp. 7–9; Northrup, "Blacks in the United Automobile Workers Union," p. 157.

63. Meier and Rudwick, *Black Detroit and the Rise of the UAW*, p. 14.

64. Ibid., p. 12.

65. Ibid., p. 14.

66. Ibid., pp. 9–11, 18; Northrup, "Blacks in the United Automobile Workers Union," pp. 161–163.

67. On the Ford Foundation, see Robert L. Allen, *Black Awakening in Capitalist America*, especially pp. 71–77. On the FBI, see Churchill and Vander Wall, *Agents of Repression*.

68. Quote is from Gelderman, *Henry Ford*, p. 243; see also pp. 281, 289; Nevins and Hill, *Ford: Expansion and Challenge*, pp. 485–492.

69. *Dearborn Independent* quoted in Ridgeway, *Blood in the Face*, pp. 40–41.

70. Postone, "Antisemitism and National Socialism," pp. 97–115, especially pp. 106–112. On early Christian antisemitism, see Oberman, *Roots of Antisemitism*.

71. David L. Lewis, *Public Image of Henry Ford*, pp. 162–163; Heuser, "Was grün begann endete blutigrot"; Bramwell, *Blood and Soil*, pp. 158, 173; Nevins and Hill, *Ford: Expansion and Challenge*, pp. 228–230.

Notes to Chapter 7

1. Leuchtenburg, *Franklin D. Roosevelt*, p. 28.

2. Roosevelt quoted in Chernow, *House of Morgan*, p. 357; Charles E. Coughlin, *Eight Discourses on the Gold Standard*, pp. 54–55.

3. Leuchtenburg, *Franklin D. Roosevelt*, p. 80.

4. Thomas Ferguson, *Golden Rule*, p. 149.

5. Leuchtenburg, *Franklin D. Roosevelt*, p. 69. On the NRA's debt to Theodore Roosevelt, see Kolko, *Main Currents in Modern American History*, p. 127.

6. Leuchtenburg, *Franklin D. Roosevelt*, p. 147.

7. Burk, *Corporate State*, p. 158; Scholnick, *New Deal and Anti-Semitism*, pp. 89–90, 68–69.

8. Archer, *Plot to Seize the White House*; Schonbach, *Native American Fascism*, pp. 233–236; Burk, *Corporate State*, pp. 159–162; Pencak, *For God and Country*, p. 317.

9. Burk, *Corporate State*, p. 162; committee quoted in Archer, *Plot to Seize the White House* p. 192.

10. Archer, *Plot to Seize the White House* p. 198.

11. Kane, *Huey Long's Louisiana Hayride*, pp. 112–113; Badger, "Huey Long and the New Deal," pp. 70–72.

12. Jeansonne, *Gerald L. K. Smith*, p. 34; Brinkley, *Voices of Protest*, pp. 28–30.

13. Lipset and Raab, *Politics of Unreason*, p. 197; Long quoted in Brinkley, *Voices of Protest*, p. 32; Long quoted in Scholnick, *New Deal and Anti-Semitism*, p. 72.

14. Smith quoted in Jeansonne, *Gerald L. K. Smith*, p. 39; Brinkley, *Voices of Protest*, pp. 32–33; Badger, "Huey Long and the New Deal," p. 74; *The Crisis* quoted in Brinkley, *Voices of Protest*, p. 34.

15. Long quoted in Brinkley, *Voices of Protest*, p. 59; Brinkley, *Voices of Protest*, pp. 77–78.

16. Long quoted in Badger, "Huey Long and the New Deal," p. 90; Long, *Kingfish to America*, pp. 108–110, 128–129; Brinkley, *Voices of Protest*, pp. 72–73; Badger, "Huey Long and the New Deal," p. 81.

17. Brinkley, *Voices of Protest*, p. 74.

18. Jeansonne, *Gerald L. K. Smith*, p. 36.

19. Badger, "Huey Long and the New Deal," pp. 94–95.

20. Brinkley, *Voices of Protest*, pp. 70–71; Mencken quoted in Jeansonne, *Gerald L. K. Smith*, p. 39; Jeansonne, *Gerald L. K. Smith*, p. 40; Badger, "Huey Long and the New Deal," p. 96; Brinkley, *Voices of Protest*, p. 193.

21. Brinkley, *Voices of Protest*, pp. 207–208, 284–286; Badger, "Huey Long and the New Deal," p. 97; Jeansonne, *Gerald L. K. Smith*, p. 40.

22. Jeansonne, *Gerald L. K. Smith*, p. 57; Carlson [Avedis Derounian], *Under Cover*, p. 33; Jeansonne, *Gerald L. K. Smith*, p. 105; Scholnick, *New Deal and Anti-Semitism*, p. 90.

23. Leuchtenburg, *Franklin D. Roosevelt*, pp. 132–133, 150–166, 245–249, 264; Thomas Ferguson, *Golden Rule*, p. 151.

24. Stokes, "FDR's Class Coalition," p. 152.

25. This and the following two paragraphs are based on Mike Davis, *Prisoners of the American Dream*, pp. 53–74; and Zinn, *People's History*, pp. 390–393.

26. Burch, *Elites in American History: Vol. 3*, p. 43; Sakai, *Settlers*, p. 79.

27. Leuchtenburg, *Franklin D. Roosevelt*, p. 188; Sakai, *Settlers*, p. 81.

28. Zinn, *People's History*, pp. 393–394; Elaine Tyler May, *Homeward Bound*, pp. 48–50; Abramovitz, *Regulating the Lives of Women*, pp. 222–224, 248–266.

29. Sakai, *Settlers*, pp. 109–110; Amott and Matthaei, *Race, Gender, and Work*, p. 129; Acuña, *Occupied America*, p. 199; Sakai, *Settlers*, p. 83; Leuchtenburg, *Franklin D. Roosevelt*, pp. 185–186.

30. *Kourier* quoted in Wade, *Fiery Cross*, p. 268; ibid., pp. 268–272.

31. Schonbach, *Native American Fascism*, pp. 315–319.

32. Ribuffo, *Old Christian Right*, pp. 116, 118.

33. Strong, *Organized Anti-Semitism in America*, pp. 75–77.

34. Ribuffo, *Old Christian Right*, pp. 64, 66; Strong, *Organized Anti-Semitism in America*, pp. 49–50; membership profile quoted in Ribuffo, *Old Christian Right*, p. 65.

35. Ribuffo, *Old Christian Right*, pp. 67–70; Lipset and Raab, *Politics of Unreason*, p. 164.

36. Chart from William Dudley Pelley's *Liberation*, August 21, 1938; as cited in Singerman, *Antisemitic Propaganda*, p. xxx.

37. Schonbach, *Native American Fascism*, pp. 220–221; Sander A. Diamond, *Nazi Movement*, pp. 204–205, 213, 233.

38. Schonbach, *Native American Fascism*, pp. 187–188, Sander A. Diamond, *Nazi Movement*, pp. 21, 150, 234; Strong, *Organized Anti-Semitism in America*, pp. 32–34.

39. Sander A. Diamond, *Nazi Movement*, pp. 67–70.

40. Wade, *Fiery Cross*, pp. 269–270; Ribuffo, *Old Christian Right*, p. 73; Carlson [Avedis Derounian], *Under Cover*, p. 25.

41. Deloria and Lytle, *Nations Within*, pp. 173–174, 180. On the 1934 Indian Reorganization Act, see also Ismaelillo and Wright, eds., *Native Peoples in Struggle*, pp. 90, 102, 122; Sakai, *Settlers*, p. 100; Amott and Matthaei, *Race, Gender, and Work*, pp. 49–50.

42. Schonbach, *Native American Fascism*, pp. 217–220; Carlson [Avedis Derounian], *Under Cover*, pp. 160–161.

43. See Jeansonne, *Women of the Far Right*.

44. Carlson [Avedis Derounian], *Under Cover*, pp. 211–217; Schonbach, *Native American Fascism*, pp. 334–335; Dilling, *Roosevelt Red Record and its Background*, pp. 143–144.

45. Quoted in Schonbach, *Native American Fascism*, pp. 247–248.

46. Kahn, *High Treason*, pp. 190–191.

47. Sander A. Diamond, *Nazi Movement*, p. 194; Schonbach, *Native American Fascism*, p. 325; Kahn, *High Treason*, p. 192n; Sander A. Diamond, *Nazi Movement*, pp. 261–266, 286–301.

48. Strong, *Organized Anti-Semitism in America*, p. 78; Earle quoted in Kahn, *High Treason*, pp. 210–211; Lipset and Raab, *Politics of Unreason*, p. 159.

49. Jeansonne, *Gerald L. K. Smith*, pp. 65–67; Ribuffo, *Old Christian Right*, pp. 147, 152.

50. Jeansonne, *Gerald L. K. Smith*, p. 70.

51. Brinkley, *Voices of Protest*, pp. 83, 97.

52. Ibid., p. 120.

53. Ibid., pp. 111–112; Tull, *Father Coughlin*, p. 53; Brinkley, *Voices of Protest*, p. 121.

54. Charles E. Coughlin, *New Deal in Money*, p. 118.

55. Charles E. Coughlin, *Driving Out the Money Changers*, p. 105.

56. Ibid., pp. 38–39.

57. Charles E. Coughlin, *Eight Lectures on Labor, Capital and Justice*, pp. 119–120.

58. Charles E. Coughlin, *Series of Lectures on Social Justice*, pp. 33, 32.

59. Charles E. Coughlin, *Driving Out the Money Changers*, p. 39.

60. Ibid., pp. 58–59.

61. Charles E. Coughlin, *Series of Lectures on Social Justice*, pp. 15, 22, 147, 21.

62. Ibid., p. 23; Brinkley, *Voices of Protest*, pp. 187–188, 206–207, 179.

63. Quoted in Tull, *Father Coughlin*, p. 52; Charles E. Coughlin, *Series of Lectures on Social Justice*, p. 124; quoted in Tull, *Father Coughlin*, p. 52.

64. Charles E. Coughlin, *Series of Lectures on Social Justice*, pp. 27, 28; Kele, *Nazis and Workers*, p. 87.

65. Tull, *Father Coughlin*, p. 55; Schonbach, *Native American Fascism*, p. 289.

66. Brinkley, *Voices of Protest*, pp. 209–215.

67. Jeansonne, *Gerald L. K. Smith*, p. 60.

68. Brinkley, *Voices of Protest*, p. 259; Charles E. Coughlin, *Series of Lectures on Social Justice*, pp. 144–145.

69. Brinkley, *Voices of Protest*, pp. 140–141, 200–201; Tull, *Father Coughlin*, pp. 177–178.

70. Lipset and Raab, *Politics of Unreason*, p. 170; Coughlin quoted in Scholnick, *New Deal and Anti-Semitism*, pp. 123–125.

71. Coughlin quoted in Schonbach, *Native American Fascism*, p. 294; Strong, *Organized Anti-Semitism in America*, pp. 66–69; Scholnick, *New Deal and Anti-Semitism*, pp. 140–142; Schonbach, *Native American Fascism*, pp. 298–299.

72. Schonbach, *Native American Fascism*, pp. 293, 298; Lipset and Raab, *Politics of Unreason*, p. 171; Brinkley, *Voices of Protest*, p. 267; Strong, *Organized Anti-Semitism in America*, p. 65.

73. Tull, *Father Coughlin*, pp. 192–193, 230–231; Schonbach, *Native American Fascism*, pp. 300–301.

74. Schonbach, *Native American Fascism*, pp. 300–301; Brinkley, *Voices of Protest*, p. 268.

75. Lipset and Raab, *Politics of Unreason*, pp. 171–176.

76. Brinkley, *Voices of Protest*, pp. 201–202.

77. Kocka, *White Collar Workers in America*, p. 240.

78. Sakai, *Settlers*, p. 92.

79. Zinn, *People's History*, pp. 398–416; Wyman, *Abandonment of the Jews*; Dower, *War Without Mercy*; Kolko, *Politics of War*; Sakai, *Settlers*, pp. 90–98; Alperovitz, "Why the United States Dropped the Bomb," pp. 23–35.

80. C. L. R. James, George Breitman, Edgar Keemer, et al., *Fighting Racism in World War II*, p. 42.

81. Glaberman, *Wartime Strikes*, p. 74; Cantor, *Divided Left*, pp. 148–149; Glaberman, *Wartime Strikes*, pp. 67–68.

82. Adams, "Three Faces of Midwestern Isolationism," pp. 36–38.

83. Cole, "Gerald P. Nye," pp. 1–10; Doenecke, "Isolationism of General Robert E. Wood," pp. 11–22; Adams, "Three Faces of Midwestern Isolationism," pp. 35–44.

84. Wood quoted in Doenecke, "Isolationism of General Robert E. Wood," pp. 13, 15–16.

85. Cole, *Roosevelt & the Isolationists*, pp. 379–381; Jeansonne, *Women of the Far Right*, pp. 43, 50, 87.

86. Cole, *Roosevelt & the Isolationists*, p. 380; Jeansonne, *Gerald L. K. Smith*, p. 82; Schonbach, *Native American Fascism*, p. 16.

87. Schonbach, *Native American Fascism*, pp. 258, 257, 336, 260; Carlson [Avedis Derounian], *Under Cover*, pp. 304–305, 256; Jeansonne, *Gerald L. K. Smith*, p. 84. The fascist Laura Ingalls is not to be confused with children's book author Laura Ingalls Wilder.

Generally speaking, left-wing anti-interventionists steered well clear of right-wing anti-interventionists. One exception was Norman Thomas, head of the Socialist Party, who spoke at several America First events, including a rally in May 1941. Avedis Derounian (John Roy Carlson) reported that a Nazi speaker on the West Coast adopted the Communist slogan "The Yanks Are Not Coming," but we have found no evidence that the Communists ever reciprocated such gestures (Schonbach, *Native American Fascism*, p. 15; Cantor, *Divided Left*, p. 148; Carlson [Avedis Derounian], *Under Cover*, p. 245).

88. Shirer, *Rise and Fall of the Third Reich*, p. 986n; Lindbergh quoted in Chernow, *House of Morgan*, p. 444.

89. Schonbach, *Native American Fascism*, pp. 285–286.

90. Scholnick, *New Deal and Anti-Semitism*, p. 154; Dennis King, *Lyndon LaRouche and the New American Fascism*, pp. 281–282; Schonbach, *Native American Fascism*, pp. 346–350, 352–353, 356–357.

91. Schonbach, *Native American Fascism*, pp. 353–356; Cole, *Roosevelt & the Isolationists*, pp. 471–474.

92. Cole, *Roosevelt & the Isolationists*, pp. 534, 548.

93. Jeansonne, *Gerald L. K. Smith*, p. 142.

94. Kocka, *White Collar Workers in America*, p. 242.

95. For connections between populism and Nazism from a historical perspective, see Fritzsche, *Rehearsals for Fascism*, and *Germans into Nazis*.

Notes to Chapter 8

1. Ribuffo, *Old Christian Right*, p. xiii.

2. Sander A. Diamond, *Nazi Movement*, pp. 324–328; Brenner, *Zionism in the Age of the Dictators*, pp. 180–182. We find that some of Brenner's later work is insensitive to stereotypes of Jewish power.

3. Sander A. Diamond, *Nazi Movement*, pp. 157–158; Schonbach, *Native American Fascism*, pp. 147, 88, 108, 149–150.

4. Leuchtenburg, *Franklin D. Roosevelt*, p. 280; Wade, *Fiery Cross*, pp. 272–274; Ribuffo, *Old Christian Right*, p. 182.

5. Wade, *Fiery Cross*, pp. 273–274; Sander A. Diamond, *Nazi Movement*, pp. 323–324, 310n, 333.

6. Sander A. Diamond, *Nazi Movement*, p. 309.

7. Wade, *Fiery Cross*, p. 273.

8. On the American Legion, see Pencak, *For God and Country*, pp. 237–250. On gov-

ernment repression of the German-American Bund, see Schonbach, *Native American Fascism*, pp. 369, 372–373; Sander A. Diamond, *Nazi Movement*, pp. 307–308, 333, 346–349. For a detailed study of one state, see Philip Jenkins, *Hoods and Shirts*.

9. Theoharis and Cox, *Boss*, pp. 148–152; Donner, *Age of Surveillance*, pp. 57–58.

10. Theoharis and Cox, *Boss*, pp. 148–149; Donner, *Age of Surveillance*, p. 86.

11. Donner, *Age of Surveillance*, p. 61.

12. Chafee quoted in Schonbach, *Native American Fascism*, p. 412; Schonbach, *Native American Fascism*, pp. 413, 411.

13. Donner, *Age of Surveillance*, p. 61; Schonbach, *Native American Fascism*, p. 411; Ribuffo, *Old Christian Right*, p. 183, 193–211; Caute, *Great Fear*, p. 178.

14. Donner, *Age of Surveillance*, pp. 62–63.

15. Theoharis and Cox, *Boss*, p. 155; Donner, *Age of Surveillance*, pp. 61–62.

16. Theoharis and Cox, *Boss*, pp. 157, 171, 193–198; Pencak, *For God and Country*, pp. 312–315; Theoharis and Cox, *Boss*, pp. 172–175.

17. Amott and Matthaei, *Race, Gender, and Work*, p. 228; Hosokawa, "Cherishing of Liberty," p. 218; Dower, *War Without Mercy*, pp. 79–82; Sakai, *Settlers*, pp. 96–97. See also Weglyn, *Years of Infamy*; Matsumoto, "Nisei Women and Resettlement"; Armor and Wright, *Manzanar*.

18. See Ribuffo, *Old Christian Right*, ch. 5.

19. Carlson [Avedis Derounian], *Under Cover*; Ribuffo, *Old Christian Right*, pp. 189–193; Schonbach, *Native American Fascism*, p. 227n.

20. See Goldfield, "Recent Historiography," pp. 315–358; Mike Davis, *Prisoners of the American Dream*, pp. 57, 62–64, 72, 79–80; Sakai, *Settlers*, p. 126; Campbell, "'Black Bolsheviks'"; Skotnes, "Communist Party"; Tani and Sera, *False Nationalism False Internationalism*, chs. 3 and 4.

21. Theoharis and Cox, *Boss*, pp. 221–222.

22. Klehr and Haynes, *American Communist Movement*, pp. 100–102; Schrecker, "McCarthyism," p. 124.

23. Ribuffo, *Old Christian Right*, p. 227.

24. Caute, *Great Fear*, pp. 38–39, 253, 230; Acuña, *Occupied America*, p. 269.

25. Donner, *Age of Surveillance*, pp. 98–105; Theoharis and Cox, *Boss*, pp. 203–221.

26. Caute, *Great Fear*, pp. 112–114, 115, 354; Theoharis and Cox, *Boss*, pp. 215–219.

27. Caute, *Great Fear*, pp. 115–116, 181–183, 245–250; Schrecker, "McCarthyism," p. 124. See generally O'Reilly, *Hoover and the Un-Americans*.

28. Richard O. Boyer and Herbert M. Morais, *Labor's Untold Story*, pp. 344, 347–348; Mike Davis, *Prisoners of the American Dream*, p. 86; MacShane, *International Labour*, p. 112; Oshinsky, *Senator Joseph McCarthy*, p. 63; Mike Davis, *Prisoners of the American Dream*, pp. 120–121.

29. Caute, *Great Fear*, p. 116; D'Emilio, *Sexual Politics, Sexual Communities*, p. 46.

30. Mike Davis, *Prisoners of the American Dream*, p. 92.

31. D'Emilio, *Sexual Politics, Sexual Communities*, ch. 3.

32. Bérubé, "Dignity for All." On the MCS, see also Philip S. Foner, *Organized Labor*, especially pp. 285–287. Foner does not mention the role of gay men in the union or the use of gay-baiting against it.

33. Marable, *Race, Reform, and Rebellion*, ch. 2; Acuña, *Occupied America*, pp. 270–272, 293–294; Cockcroft, *Outlaws in the Promised Land*, p. 74.

34. D'Emilio, *Sexual Politics, Sexual Communities*, pp. 75–87.

35. Acuña, *Occupied America*, pp. 266–268; Cockcroft, *Outlaws in the Promised Land*, pp. 73–78; Dunn, *Militarization of the U.S.–Mexico Border*, pp. 14–17.

36. Abramovitz, *Regulating the Lives of Women*, pp. 323–327.

37. Caute, *Great Fear*, pp. 253–254; Carey quoted in Simpson, *Blowback*, p. 126.

38. On the U.S. recruitment of Nazis, see Simpson, *Blowback*. On Puerto Rico see Sakai, *Settlers*, pp. 130–132. On the Philippines, see Drinnon, *Facing West*, pp. 389–401; Kolko, *Confronting the Third World*, pp. 63–65.

39. Cumings, *Origins of the Korean War: Vol. 2*, p. 111. In this chapter we are especially indebted to Cumings's work, which first introduced us to business conflict analysis. Portions of this chapter appeared in different form in Matthew N. Lyons, "Business Conflict and Right-Wing Movements," pp. 80–102.

40. Rogin, *Intellectuals and McCarthy*, p. 247; see also p. 215.

41. This discussion of business conflict and the New Deal is based on Thomas Ferguson, *Golden Rule*, chs. 2 and 4; Thomas Ferguson and Joel Rogers, *Right Turn*; Schurmann, *Logic of World Power*, pp. 48–60; Cumings, *Origins of the Korean War: Vol. 2*, chs. 2 and 3; and Mike Davis, *Prisoners of the American Dream*, pp. 163–167.

42. Thomas Ferguson and Joel Rogers, *Right Turn*, pp. 46, 47–48.

43. Ibid., p. 48.

44. Schurmann, *Logic of World Power*, p. 58.

45. Jeansonne, *Gerald L. K. Smith*, p. 65; Ribuffo, *Old Christian Right*, p. 147.

46. Crowther, *American Self-Contained*, pp. 87, 238.

47. Cumings, *Origins of the Korean War: Vol. 2*, pp. 89–90; Leuchtenburg, *Franklin D. Roosevelt*, p. 311.

48. Mike Davis, *Prisoners of the American Dream*, p. 85.

49. McCarthy quoted in Caute, *Great Fear*, p. 46.

50. Burch, *Elites in American History: Vol. 3*, p. 121n.

51. On business ties with Nazism, see Kolko, "American Business and Germany," pp. 713–728. For examples of U.S. capitalist sympathy with European fascism, see Chernow, *House of Morgan*, pp. 403, 405–407.

52. Caute, *Great Fear*, pp. 350, 369, 114, 269.

53. Goldman, *Crucial Decade—And After*, p. 134; *Chicago Tribune* quoted in Caute, *Great Fear*, p. 42.

54. On MacArthur and anti-New Deal politics, see Cumings, *Origins of the Korean War: Vol. 2*, pp. 97, 102–104; Drinnon, *Facing West*, pp. 318, 383–384.

55. Cumings, *Origins of the Korean War: Vol. 2*, pp. 103, 107–109.

56. Ibid., p. 109; Goldman, *Crucial Decade—And After*, p. 144; Caute, *Great Fear*, p. 310; Cumings, *Origins of the Korean War: Vol. 2*, pp. 109, 112.

57. McCarthy quoted in Goldman, *Crucial Decade—And After*, p. 144.

58. McCarthy quoted in Caute, *Great Fear*, pp. 43, 106; Jeffreys-Jones, *CIA and American Democracy*, pp. 74–75.

59. Other businessmen cited as strong McCarthy supporters included Joseph Kennedy, Charles R. Hook (Armco Steel), Tom Coleman (president of Madison–Kipp, an oil systems and die castings firm); Walter Harnischfeger (president of Harnischfeger Corp. of Wisconsin), and Frank J. Sensenbrenner (Kimberly-Clark Corp.). See Cumings, *Origins of the Korean War: Vol. 2*, pp. 91–92; Reeves, *Life and Times of Joe McCarthy*, pp. 203, 347, 442–444, 447; Burch, "NAM as an Interest Group," p. 118n; Burch, *Elites in American History: Vol. 3*, p. 149; Murphy, "McCarthy and the Businessman," especially p. 184; Murphy, "Texas Business and McCarthy," pp. 100–101, 208, 211–216.

60. Cumings, *Origins of the Korean War: Vol. 2*, pp. 112, 90.

61. I. F. Stone, *Haunted Fifties*, pp. 18, 25–30; Theoharis and Cox, *Boss*, pp. 74, 296–298, 311; Thomas Ferguson, *Golden Rule*, pp. 142, 168n67.

62. Caute, *Great Fear*, p. 47; McCarthy quoted in Lipset and Raab, *Politics of Unreason*, p. 239; Rogin, *Intellectuals and McCarthy*, pp. 236–238.

63. Scher, *Cold War on the Home Front*.

64. See McAuliffe, *Crisis on the Left*, especially pp. 75–88.

65. I. F. Stone, *Haunted Fifties*, p. 69.

66. A founding text of centrist/extremist theory was Daniel Bell's 1955 anthology *New American Right*, which was published in revised form as Daniel Bell, ed., *Radical Right*.

67. Burch, *Elites in American History: Vol. 3*, pp. 127–140.

68. Theoharis and Cox, *Boss*, pp. 293–299; Caute, *Great Fear*, pp. 49, 108; Lipset and Raab, *Politics of Unreason*, p. 236. Senator Flanders was a trustee of the Committee for Economic Development and a former vice-chairman of the Business Advisory Council, perhaps the two most important business multinationalist organizations. See Burch, *Elites in American History: Vol. 3*, pp. 149, 165n.

69. Bodenheimer and Gould, *Rollback!*, p. 24; Kolko, *Confronting the Third World*, p. 52; Cumings, *Origins of the Korean War: Vol. 2*, p. 101.

70. Ribuffo, *Old Christian Right*, p. 226.

71. Cashman, *African-Americans and the Quest for Civil Rights*, p. 89; Acuña, *Occupied America*, pp. 275–295; Harris, *Harder We Run*, p. 131; Marable, *Race, Reform, and Rebellion*, ch. 2, especially pp. 25, 38; Giddings, *When and Where I Enter*, p. 239.

72. Jeansonne, *Gerald L. K. Smith*, pp. 97, 142.

73. Cashman, *African-Americans and the Quest for Civil Rights*, p. 102.

74. Caute, *Great Fear*, p. 225.

75. Sachar, *History of the Jews in America*, pp. 634–637; Gabriner, "Rosenberg Case," p. 176.

76. Amott and Matthaei, *Race, Gender, and Work*, pp. 231, 210.

77. House resolution quoted in Debo, *History of the Indians of the United States*, p. 304; Amott and Matthaei, *Race, Gender, and Work*, pp. 50–51; Marable, *Race, Reform, and Rebellion*, p. 36; Debo, *History of the Indians of the United States*, pp. 301–318.

78. For a thorough debunking of the Khazar myth and its relationship to antisemitism, see Barkun, *Religion and the Racist Right*, pp. 136–142.

79. Beaty, *Iron Curtain over America*, especially pp. 37–43.

80. Beaty, *Iron Curtain over America*. Mintz in *Liberty Lobby* has an extensive discussion of Beaty, pp. 51–59.

81. Goff, *One World a Red World*, pp. 56–57, 62.

82. Goff, *Reds Promote Racial War*, pp. 13–16, 25–33.

83. Thayer, *Farther Shores*, pp. 73–74.

84. See, for example, issues of *The Councilor*, a newspaper of the Citizens Council of Louisiana, especially July 16, 1964; September 14, 1964; April 9, 1965; April 30, 1965; October 6, 1965; August 15, 1966. Similar conspiracist rhetoric is analyzed by Chang, "*According to Rumors.*"

85. Caute, *Great Fear*, pp. 146–157; Theoharis and Cox, *Boss*, pp. 312–313.

Notes to Chapter 9

1. Mintz, *Liberty Lobby*, pp. 3–10, 141–162; Sara Diamond, *Roads to Dominion*, pp. 140–142.

2. For a detailed study of producerism that nonetheless maintains its allegiance to the classical centrist/extremist theory, see Stock, *Rural Radicals*, pp. 15–86.

3. Sara Diamond, *Roads to Dominion*, pp. 140–160. For the classical view, see Bennett, *Party of Fear*, pp. 48–182.

4. For a very different view of antigovernment conspiracism in the United States, see Billig, *Fascists*, p. 296.

5. Scher, *Cold War on the Home Front*, p. 2.

6. For background, see Mintz, *Liberty Lobby*, pp. 141–162; Diamond, *Roads to Dominion*, pp. 52–59; 140–141; 147–148; Grupp, "Political Perspectives of Birch Society Members."

7. See, for example, Gary Allen with Larry Abraham (1983), *None Dare Call It Conspiracy*, p. 125. See pp. 140–141 in the 1983 edition.

8. Portions of this chapter first appeared in Matthew N. Lyons, "Business Conflict and Right-Wing Movements."

9. For more detail, see William V. Moore, *John Birch Society*; McNall, *Career of a Radical Rightist*; Grove, *Inside the John Birch Society*; Thayer, *Farther Shores*, pp. 174-216; Epstein and Forster, *Radical Right*.

10. Welch, *Blue Book*, twenty-first printing. The *Blue Book* was originally self-published by Welch in Belmont, Massachusetts, in 1959. Note that in various printings text is dropped or added, and footnoted comments shift numbers. The 1961 twenty-first printing is cited here unless otherwise noted because it is indexed, has complete pagination, and is often available in used book stores. Notes from earlier editions are included.

11. Welch, *Blue Book*, pp. 20–24, 113.

12. Welch, *Blue Book*, biographical notes for the second printing, pp. 167–168; and G. Edward Griffin, *Life and Words of Robert Welch*, pp. 105–107, 112, 144–146. The NAM booklet, however, defended the free expression of diverse ideas, whereas Welch, after founding the Birch Society, demonized liberal ideas as subversive. See Bunzel, *Anti-Politics in America*, p. 75.

13. G. Edward Griffin, *Life and Words of Robert Welch*, pp. 148, 158–159, 164.

14. Ibid., pp. 168–171.

15. Ibid., pp. 189–197. Welch, *Blue Book*, pp. 145–146.

16. Welch, *Blue Book*, biographical notes for the second printing, pp. 167–168.

17. Burch, "NAM as an Interest Group," pp. 121–130.

18. On business interests and the John Birch Society, see ibid., pp. 97–130, especially pp. 120–129.

19. Welch, *Blue Book*, pp. 38–39.

20. Hayek, *Road to Serfdom*, pp. 13, 24; Himmelstein, *To the Right*, pp. 43–60; Sara Diamond, *Roads to Dominion*, pp. 19–36.

21. Sara Diamond, *Roads to Dominion*, p. 55.

22. Welch, *Blue Book*, pp. 33–38; Broyles, *John Birch Society*, p. 141; Spengler, *Decline of the West: Vol. 1, Vol. 2*. Spengler, *Hour of Decision* is more openly racist.

23. Welch, *Blue Book*, p. 129.

24. De Koster, *Citizen and the John Birch Society*.

25. John Birch Society, *White Book*, p. 14.

26. Broyles, *John Birch Society*, pp. 107–111.

27. Welch, *Blue Book*, pp. 28–29.

28. G. Edward Griffin, *Life and Words of Robert Welch*, pp. 10, 44, 197, 275–278.

29. Our thanks to Ernie Lazar for sending documentation for these figures with addi-

tional material from the archives of the University of Wyoming American Heritage Center. Letter from Welch to National Council members dated September 14, 1960.

30. Welch, "Postscript for the Fifth Printing, March 15, 1961," *Blue Book*, p. 163.

31. Sara Diamond, *Roads to Dominion*, pp. 55, 324n87. Broyles, *John Birch Society*, p. 167. For context, see Schoenberger, ed., *American Right Wing*.

32. Broyles, *John Birch Society*, p. 167.

33. Welch, "Footnotes for the Fourth Printing," *Blue Book*, p. 97n11.

34. Broyles, *John Birch Society*, p. 166.

35. Josephson, *Rockefeller*, *"Internationalist"*; Smoot, *Invisible Government*.

36. Smoot, *Invisible Government*, page following p. 244.

37. Ibid., p. 141.

38. McManus, *Insiders*, p. 20.

39. Welch, *New Americanism*, pp. 126–132. Author Berlet has attended numerous Birch Society meetings over a twenty-five-year period and has heard many discussions concerning the role of the Freemasons and the Illuminati in the conspiracy. On Eisenhower, see Broyles, *John Birch Society*, p. 7; Welch, *Politician*, p. 279.

40. Welch, "Footnotes for the Fourth Printing," *Blue Book*, p. 101n19.

41. Sara Diamond, *Roads to Dominion*, pp. 62–64; see also, Edwards, *Goldwater*.

42. On the Goldwater campaign, see Thomas Ferguson and Joel Rogers, *Right Turn*, p. 53; Burch, "NAM as an Interest Group" pp. 115n39, 120n124, 126–127; Burch, *Elites in American History: Vol. 3*, p. 224n98; and Schlafly, *Choice Not an Echo*.

43. John Birch Society, *White Book*, January, pp. 3–14.

44. Ibid., p. 20.

45. Ibid., p. 20.

46. John Birch Society, *White Book*, February, p. 6.

47. Letter on file at Political Research Associates.

48. Stang, *It's Very Simple*, see especially pp. 209–214.

49. Kayyem, " . . . Need Not Apply"; Berlet, "Trashing the Birchers."

50. Mintz, *Liberty Lobby*, pp. 172–173.

51. Gary Allen with Larry Abraham (1972), *None Dare Call It Conspiracy*, p. 125.

52. Ibid., p. 39.

53. Mintz, *Liberty Lobby*, p. 149.

54. Gary Allen, *Rockefeller*. A similar theme was promoted by the Lyndon LaRouche network; see: Dennis King, *Lyndon LaRouche*, pp. 38–40, 125.

55. Webster and Sutton are both in the *American Opinion Book List* spring catalog, 1988; Sutton is in the *American Opinion Book Service* winter catalog, 1996. Webster and Sutton are both recommended reading in "Conspiracy for Global Control," a special issue of *The New American*, September 16, 1996, "An Annotated Bibliography," pp. 73–75.

56. Letter on file at Political Research Associates.

57. Documents, including correspondence between Welch, his aide, and a donor outlining the procedure, are on file at Political Research Associates.

58. Kraft, *Preliminary Socio-Economic & State Demographic Profile*.

59. Lamy, *Millennium Rage*, pp. 17–19.

60. Estimates based on printing and subscription data reported in Birch Society magazines to comply with Post Office regulations, as well as conversations with Birch Society staff members and chapter organizers.

61. O'Keeffe and Daley, "Checking the Right."

62. There are few serious studies of Carto and the Liberty Lobby network. We rely primarily on Mintz, *Liberty Lobby*. See also Sara Diamond, *Roads to Dominion*, pp. 140–160; Johnson, *Architects of Fear*, pp. 114–120, 125–126; and McLemee, "Spotlight on the Liberty Lobby," pp. 23–32.

63. Liberty Lobby founder Willis Carto has even defined populism as government by producers, not exploiters; see Carto, ed., *Profiles in Populism*, p. 192.

64. *Spotlight* home page, New World Order text, http://www.spotlight.org/order.html, February 22, 1997.

65. The indicated ratio between print run and implied readership is well within the norm for alternative newspapers.

66. Mintz, *Liberty Lobby*, pp. 93–94, 171.

67. Sara Diamond, *Roads to Dominion*, p. 150; Kevin Coogan, *Dreamer of the Day*, pp. 515–522; Ulick Varange [pseudonym for Francis Parker Yockey], *Imperium*.

68. Mintz, *Liberty Lobby*, pp. 24–27

69. Ibid., pp. 71–80; Sara Diamond, *Roads to Dominion*, pp. 85–87.

70. Revilo P. Oliver, letter to Colonel Dall, dated December 17, 1970. From Special Collections, Knight Library, University of Oregon; Sara Diamond, *Roads to Dominion*, pp. 85, 157.

71. Sara Diamond, *Roads to Dominion*, p. 157; Bellant, *Old Nazis, the New Right*, pp. 60–65.

72. Mintz, *Liberty Lobby*, pp. 81, 85–86; Oliver letter; Sara Diamond, *Roads to Dominion*, pp. 86–87.

73. Mintz, *Liberty Lobby*, pp. 141–162; Sara Diamond, *Roads to Dominion*, p. 86.

74. Mintz, *Liberty Lobby*, pp. 5, 198.

75. McLemee, "Spotlight on the Liberty Lobby," p. 24.

76. Carto, ed., *Profiles in Populism*, p. x.

77. Sara Diamond, *Roads to Dominion*, p. 86, citing Carto, "Right Line," p. 1. See the discussion of Carto's White supremacy in *Roads to Dominion*, pp. 85–87.

78. Carto, ed., *Profiles in Populism*, pp. 153, 161–165.

79. Ibid., pp. 191, 203.

80. Ibid., pp. ix–xvi, 189–197.

81. Ibid., p. 195.

82. Martin A. Lee, *Beast Reawakens*, pp. 204–220, 251–267, 367–374; Antonio, *Reactionary Tribalism*.

83. *Liberty Lowdown*, June 1963, p. 1.

84. Mintz, *Liberty Lobby*, pp. 128–131; Oliver letter.

85. Collette, "Encountering Holocaust Denial," pp. 246–265; .

86. *Noontide Press*, book catalog, 1989 and 1995.

87. Willis Carto, letter to Keith Stimely on IHR stationery, dated April 17, 1983. From Special Collections, Knight Library, University of Oregon. Emphasis, punctuation, and spelling in the original.

88. Ibid.

89. Willis Carto letter to Keith Stimely on IHR stationery, dated November 23, 1984. From Special Collections Knight Library, University of Oregon.

90. Ibid.

91. Ibid.

92. Ibid.

93. Ibid.

94. Sara Diamond, *Roads to Dominion*, pp. 262–265; Crawford, Gardner, Mozzochi, and Taylor, *Northwest Imperative*; Novick, "Front Men for Fascism."

95. Interviews with attendees, 1985.

96. Sara Diamond, *Roads to Dominion*, pp. 263–264.

97. McLemee, "Spotlight on the Liberty Lobby," p. 27.

98. *Spotlight*, January 13, 1997, p. 23.

99. *Spotlight* subscription page, http://webbindustries.com/spotlight/index.html, February 21, 1997.

100. Zeskind, *"Christian Identity" Movement*; Emry, *Billion$ for the Banker$*.

101. *Spotlight*, "Liberty Lobby Describes Populist Perspectives for Russians" March 8, 1999, pp. A2–A3 of the special wrap-around section sent to members of the Board of Policy.

102. Ibid., citing Carto's *Populism v. Plutocracy: The Universal Struggle*.

103. Ibid., p. A3.

104. See, for example, the implicit anti-Black prejudice in Stang, *It's Very Simple*, especially pp. 209–214.

105. Editors of *Executive Intelligence Review*, *Ugly Truth about the ADL* (Washington, DC: Executive Intelligence Review, 1992).

106. Muhammad Safwat al-Saqqa Amini and Sa'di Abu Habib, *Freemasonry*, Arabic version (Makkah al-Mukarramah, Saudi Arabia: The Muslim World League, 1980); English version (New York: The Muslim World League, 1982), pp. 4–15.

107. Johnson, *Architects of Fear*, p. 41.

108. Canovan, *Populism*, p. 23.

109. Destler, *American Radicalism*, pp. 32–77, 222–254.

110. Ibid., p. 23

111. The best discussion of the important authors in this genre is in Mintz, *Liberty Lobby*, pp. 47–64. An excellent review of the British–Jewish genre is Dennis King, *Lyndon LaRouche*, pp. 274–292.

112. "How New Money Is Created," *American Mercury*, August 1961, pp. 71–76; condensed from the *Texas Observer*.

113. Mintz, *Liberty Lobby*, pp. 17–22; Fahey, *Mystical Body of Christ*; Gertrude Coogan, *Money Creators*. On the creative myths of antisemitism, see David Norman Smith, "Social Construction of Enemies."

114. Mintz, *Liberty Lobby*, p. 17.

115. Dennis King, *Lyndon LaRouche*.

116. One book mixes the themes: Eustace Mullins, *Federal Reserve Conspiracy*. See also Mullins, *Mullins on the Federal Reserve*; *World Order: Our Secret Rulers*; *Secret Holocaust*. See also the listings on Mullins in Singerman, *Antisemitic Propaganda*, including Eustace Mullins, *Biological Jew*; "Jews Mass Poison American Children," p. 11; *Impeach Eisenhower!* Similarly, John Coleman wrote pamphlets for the far-right Christian Defense League, but wrote a milder book, *Conspirators Hierarchy*. Dennis King suggests that some of Coleman's work echoes the LaRouchites, and notes that Mullins, friendly to the LaRouchites, was a contributing editor for Coleman's former periodical *World Economic Review*; see King, *Lyndon LaRouche*, p. 283. Coleman now publishes *World in Review* magazine.

117. Mintz, *Liberty Lobby*, pp. 47–64; Johnson, *Architects of Fear*, pp. 78–80, 135–136.

118. Josephson, *Rockefeller, "Internationalist."* See Mintz, *Liberty Lobby*, pp. 61–64, 82–83. See also Merta, *Birth of a Conspiracy Theory*, unpublished paper following the trail of the conspiracist view of the Council on Foreign Relations. On file at Political Research Associates.

119. Smoot, *Invisible Government*.

120. Davison, *Secret Government*, pp. 1–5. For a study of the role of 1950s conservative women in battling globalism, see Scher, *Cold War on the Home Front*.

121. Carroll Quigley, *Tragedy and Hope*; Mintz, *Liberty Lobby*, pp. 145–146.

122. Skousen, *Naked Capitalist*. Skousen's subtitle is *A Review and Commentary on Dr. Carroll Quigley's Book: Tragedy and Hope—A History of the World in Our Time*. See also Gary Allen with Larry Abraham, *None Dare Call It Conspiracy*, paperback ed., reissued revised in hardcover as Gary Allen and Larry Abraham, *None Dare Call It Conspiracy*, and revised and expanded as a sequel in Larry Abraham, *Call It Conspiracy*. The last volume featured a prologue by Christian Reconstructionist Gary North.

123. Mintz, *Liberty Lobby*, pp. 147–148.

124. See, for example, Phoebe Courtney, *Beware Metro and Regional Government!*.

125. Davison, *Profound Revolution*, pp. 1–18, 26–28, 84, 86–87. Davison went on to help form the Council for Statehood, similar in ideology to the Committee of the States.

126. Davison, *Twentieth Century Snow Job*.

127. Frierson and Garlock, *Christian Be Watchful*.

128. Sutton and Wood, *Trilaterals Over Washington*; the graphic is in the back coupon section.

129. Mills, *Power Elite*; Domhoff, *Higher Circles*; *Powers That Be*; *Who Rules America Now*; Sklar, ed., *Trilateralism*; Sklar, *Reagan, Trilateralism and the Neoliberals*; *Chaos or Community?*

130. Sutton, *Wall Street and the Rise of Hitler*, pp. 170–171.

131. Author Berlet's conversations with Domhoff and Sklar at academic conference panels on power structure research. One presumes Mills would have objected, as well. Domhoff discusses this problem in *Higher Circles*, pp. 279–308.

132. Fenster, *Conspiracy Theories*.

133. Broyles, *John Birch Society*, pp. 151–153.

134. Sara Diamond, *Spiritual Warfare*.

135. Turner, *I Heard It Through the Grapevine*.

136. Berlet, *Right Woos Left*; "Friendly Fascists"; Ramos, "Feint to the Left," pp. 13, 18.

Notes to Chapter 10

1. Himmelstein, *To the Right*, p. 14.

2. Ibid. Himmelstein's discussion of the practical problems of uniting the three strands into a conservative movement is especially useful See pp. 43–60.

3. Ibid., pp. 43–44. This section appeared in Berlet, "Following the Threads."

4. Ibid., pp. 46, 49. Himmelstein cites the key works of conservative thinkers in his footnotes.

5. Sara Diamond, *Roads to Dominion*, pp. 37–65, 95–106; Kovel, *Red Hunting in the*

Promised Land, pp. 64–166; Navasky, *Naming Names*; Caute, *Great Fear*, Bellant, *Old Nazis*, pp. 33–38; Simpson, *Blowback*, p. 219; Cogley, *Report on Blacklisting*, Vols. 1 & 2; Donner, *Age of Surveillance*, pp. 416–429.

6. Forster and Epstein, *Danger on the Right*; Epstein and Forster, *Radical Right*; Mintz, *Liberty Lobby*, pp. 65–105; Thayer, *Farther Shores*, pp. 147–216; Jeansonne, *Women of the Far Right*, pp. 165–178; Sara Diamond, *Roads to Dominion*, pp. 52–58, 140–141; Bellant, *Old Nazis*, pp. 38–39.

7. William Martin, *With God on Our Side*, pp. 35–38; Sara Diamond, *Roads to Dominion*, pp. 92–106; Bellant, *Coors Connection*, p. 125. See, as examples of anticommunist literature, American Business Consultants, *Red Channels*; Bundy, *How the Communists Use Religion*; Philbrick, *I Led 3 Lives*; Romerstein, *Communism and Your Child*.

8. McIntire, *"Author of Liberty."*

9. Thayer, *Farther Shores*, pp. 217–261; Kovel, *Red Hunting in the Promised Land*, pp. 117–123. For a different perspective, see Heale, *American Anticommunism*; *McCarthy's America*.

10. Kazin, *Populist Persuasion*, p. 174. See, for example, Richard Cardinal Cushing, *Red Menace* pamphlet, based on a speech to Massachusetts state employees (Boston: Knights of Columbus State Council, 1959).

11. This paragraph is adapted from a previously published article: Berlet, "Cardinal Mindszenty."

12 According to an investigation by the Washington-based Group Research, Inc., report on file at Political Research Associates.

13. Weyrich belongs to a church closer to old Roman Catholic orthodoxy and liturgy; his goal is to pull the Roman Catholic Church and U.S. politics far to the right.

14. Schwarz, *You Can Trust the Communists*, p. 7. See also Schwarz, *Beating the Unbeatable Foe*.

15. This discussion is adapted from Berlet and Quigley, "Theocracy & White Supremacy."

16. Schlafly, *Choice Not an Echo*, pp. 111–121.

17. Scher, *Cold War on the Home Front*, pp. 300–301; Schlafly's husband, Fred, her early political mentor, had lectured at Schwarz's local Christian Anti-Communism Crusade traveling schools. Forster and Epstein, *Danger on the Right* p. 271; Berlet, "Cardinal Mindszenty." See also letters, *St. Louis Journalism Review*, June, July 1988.

18. Schlafly and Ward, *Gravediggers*. The two authors went on to pen *Strike from Space*, which anticipated the Right's call for the Star Wars program to defend against Soviet missile attack. See also Schlafly and Ward, *Strike from Space*. Ward, a member of the National Strategy Committee of the American Security Council, was also a lecturer at the Foreign Policy Research Institute, which formulated many benchmark Cold War anticommunist strategies. See Bellant, *Old Nazis*, pp. 35, 37.

19. Stormer, *None Dare Call It Treason*.

20. Ibid. The book sold over 7 million copies, according to later editions. See also Stormer, *Death of a Nation*, pp. 152–174; on religious renewal experience, see "About the Author," page preceding the table of contents.

21. Kazin, *Populist Persuasion*, p. 227, citing several sources.

22. Lipset and Raab, *Politics of Unreason*, p. 364. See also Omi and Winant, *Racial Formation*, p. 123; Ansell, *New Right, New Racism*, pp. 74–76. For background on the forces against integration, see Cook, *Segregationists*; Thayer, *Farther Shores*, pp. 85–124; Sara Diamond, *Roads to Dominion*, pp. 66–91; Nelson, *Terror in the Night*.

23. Lipset and Raab, *Politics of Unreason*, pp. 346–348.

24. Carter, *Politics of Rage*, p. 427.

25. Kazin, *Populist Persuasion*, p. 246.

26. Carter, *Politics of Rage*, p. 379.

27. Ibid., p. 380, citing Haldeman notes from Nixon presidential archives.

28. Lo, *Small Property versus Big Government*; Jarvis, *I'm Mad as Hell*.

29. Engelmayer and Wagman, *Tax Revolt 1980*. See also Brinkley, "Reagan's Revenge."

30. William Martin, *With God on Our Side*, pp. 25–46.

31. Marsden, *Understanding Fundamentalism and Evangelicalism*, pp 60, 147, 163; Marsden, *Fundamentalism and American Culture*, pp. 153–230; William Martin, *With God on Our Side*, pp. 14–15; Christian Smith, *American Evangelicalism*, pp. 1–19; Himmelstein, *To the Right*, pp. 114–128; Wilcox, *Onward Christian Soldiers*, pp. 25–33; Lienesch, "Prophetic Neo-Populists"; Moen, "Changing Nature of Christian Right Activism: 1970s-1990s."

Smith divides Protestantism into four subcategories: evangelical, fundamentalist, mainline Protestant, and theologically liberal Protestant (*American Evangelicalism*, p. 19). Using Marsden's criteria, we use the term "evangelical" to describe Protestants who affirm "(1) the Reformation doctrine of the final authority of the Bible, (2) the real historical character of God's saving work recorded in Scripture, (3) salvation to eternal life based on the redemptive work of Christ, (4) the importance of evangelism and missions, and (5) the importance of a spiritually transformed life." A "fundamentalist" is an evangelical "who is militant in opposition to liberal theology in the churches or changes in cultural values or mores" that are seen as denigrating a God-centered society (Marsden, *Understanding Fundamentalism and Evangelicalism*, pp. 1–6).

Diamond describes the term "born-again" as signifying a Christian who has had an experience "in which the believer surrenders [their] life to Jesus Christ." "Born-again" Christians believe that only people who believe that Christ is their personal "savior" will have eternal life after death (Sara Diamond, *Spiritual Warfare*, p. 237). According to Diamond, "Gallup polls between 1976 and 1979 found, variably, that one-third to one-fifth of the U.S. adult population reported having a 'born again' conversion" (*Roads to Dominion*, p. 163).

People of faith have sometimes been described in patronizing caricature or dismissed as ignorant, irrational, or even mentally ill. This careless bigotry and stereotyping by many liberal and left commentators is objectionable on both moral and factual grounds. There also has been a tendency among some social scientists to overlook the influence of sincere and devout religious belief on political action. In recent years, a number of researchers have attempted to analyze in a serious and respectful way a variety of religiously motivated social movements, and we emphasize their work. See discussions of this in Brinkley, *Liberalism and Its Discontents*, pp. 266–276; Harvey Cox, "Warring Visions of the Religious Right"; Wilcox, *Onward Christian Soldiers*, pp. 96–101; Gomes, *Good Book*, pp. 4–52, 129–135, 161–162, 246–250, 348–353; and, generally, Christian Smith, *American Evangelicalism* and *Disruptive Religion*.

32. Holy Bible, Revelation 20:22; Fuller, *Naming the Antichrist*, pp. 6–7; Marsden, *Understanding Fundamentalism and Evangelicalism*, pp. 40, 112–114; Sara Diamond, *Spiritual Warfare*, pp. 130–138, 240; Barkun, *Religion and the Racist Right*, pp. 75–79, 104–105, 213.

33. Paul Boyer, *When Time Shall Be No More*, pp. 80–112.

34. Johnson, *Fire in the Mind*, pp. 308–313.

35. See Schalit and Bertsch, "Millennial Revelations." A post-Rapture ministry creates evangelical outreach materials to be "left behind" after the authors are Raptured up into heaven; see Peter and Paul Lalonde's work, including the popular video, *Apocalypse: Caught in the Eye of the Storm;* and the website articles, "Oops, I Guess I Wasn't Ready," http://www.novia.net/~todd/rap49.html; and Kurt Seland, "The Post Rapture Survival Guide," http://www.novia.net/~todd/rap34.html.

36. Fuller, *Naming the Antichrist,* p. 5.

37. For general background, see Himmelstein, *To the Right;* Sara Diamond, *Roads to Dominion;* William Martin, *With God on Our Side;* and Klatch, *Women of the New Right.*

38. William Martin, *With God on Our Side,* pp. 117–143; Moffett, *Storm in the Mountains.*

39. William Martin, *With God on Our Side,* pp. 117–121.

40. See, for example, Noebel, *Communism, Hypnotism and the Beatles; Rhythm, Riots and Revolution; Marxist Minstrels.*

41. Berlet and Quigley, "Theocracy & White Supremacy," pp. 33–37.

42. Ibid., p. 36.

43. William Martin, *With God on Our Side,* p. 175; Viguerie, *New Right,* pp. 39–131. The newsletter began when the organization was called the Free Congress Research and Education Foundation, which replaced the Committee for the Survival of a Free Congress.

44. Klatch, *Women of the New Right,* pp. 55–83; Marsden, *Understanding Fundamentalism and Evangelicalism,* pp. 108–109. Portions of this section are adapted from Berlet and Quigley, "Theocracy & White Supremacy."

45. James Davison Hunter, *Culture Wars,* p. 202.

46. See, for example, in chronological order González Ruiz, *Atheistic Humanism and the Biblical God;* Barbara M. Morris, *Why Are You Losing Your Children?;* LaHaye, *Battle for the Mind;* Thomson, *Withstanding Humanism's Challenge;* Francis A. Schaeffer, *Christian Manifesto;* Franky Schaeffer, *Time for Anger;* Hitchcock, *What Is Secular Humanism?;* LaHaye, *Battle for the Family;* Schlafly, ed., *Child Abuse in the Classroom;* Whitehead, *Stealing of America;* Dobson and Bauer, *Children at Risk.*

47. Sara Diamond, *Spiritual Warfare,* pp. 84–87.

48. Ibid., p. 85; LaHaye, *Battle for the Mind,* pp. 177–185, 225–237.

49. LaHaye, *Battle for the Mind,* pp. 217–223. See the discussion in Harding, "Imagining the Last Days."

50. Drake, *Blackboard Power.*

51. Blumenfeld, *N.E.A.: Trojan Horse.*

52. "Multiculturalism: A Prescription for Moral Anarchy," *Blumenfeld Education Newsletter,* September 1986; Quigley quote from the working draft of Berlet and Quigley, "Theocracy & White Supremacy."

53. Other examples of this theory can be found in Barbara M. Morris, *Change Agents in the Schools,* pp. 16–47; and *Your Child's New Teacher,* pp. 4–8.

54. Blumenfeld, *N.E.A.: Trojan Horse,* pp. 106–107.

55. Onalee McGraw, *Secular Humanism and the Schools.*

56. For more on secular humanism, see "Credulity, Superstition, and Fanaticism," special issue, *The Humanist,* September–October 1992, including Berlet, "Great Snark Hunt," where portions of this section first appeared. For a view inside the private Christian school classroom, see Menendez, *Visions of Reality.*

57. Sara Diamond, *Roads to Dominion,* p. 232.

58. William Martin, *With God on Our Side*, p. 181.

59. Ibid., p. 177.

60. Ibid., pp. 181–185; Viguerie, *New Right*, pp. 206–207.

61. Sara Diamond, *Roads to Dominion*, pp. 231–233; Viguerie, *New Right*, pp. 195–225.

62. Conference booklet, "Traditional Values Work! Family Forum II, July 27–July 29, 1982," on file at Political Research Associates.

63. On early Schaeffer, see William Martin, *With God on Our Side*, pp. 159–161; on van Til, see Clarkson, *Eternal Hostility*, pp. 79–80. An excellent discussion Francis A. Schaeffer and the apocalyptic basis for this shift is Harding, "Imagining the Last Days." See also O'Leary, *Arguing the Apocalypse*, pp. 178–179.

64. William Martin, *With God on Our Side*, p. 195.

65. Ibid., pp. 238–240.

66. Francis A. Schaeffer and C. Everett Koop, *Whatever Happened to the Human Race?*

67. Francis A. Schaeffer, *Christian Manifesto*, pp. 117–130; see also his son, Franky Schaeffer, *Time for Anger*, pp. 15–25, 76–78.

68. See, for example, conspiracism in LaHaye, *Battle for the Mind*, pp. 141–179; for a milder rendition, see Whitehead, *Stealing of America*, pp. 31–59, 82–106.

69. William Martin, *With God on Our Side*, pp. 194–197; Blanchard, *Anti-Abortion Movement*, p. 97. This discussion is drawn from Berlet, "Right Rides High."

70. Chambers, *SIECUS Circle*, back cover.

71. Ibid., first page.

72. William Martin, *With God on Our Side*, pp. 196–197; Sara Diamond, *Roads to Dominion*, pp. 246–248; Clarkson, *Eternal Hostility*, p. 93; Risen and Thomas, *Wrath of Angels*, pp. 121–127.

73. Clarkson, *Eternal Hostility*, pp. 77–96. An excellent survey of dominionism and Christian Reconstructionism is Barron, *Heaven on Earth?*.

74. Berlet and Quigley, "Theocracy & White Supremacy," pp. 15–43.

75. Saponara, "Ideology at Work," p. 27.

76. See, generally, Sara Diamond, *Spiritual Warfare*.

77. Marshner and Rueda, *Morality of Political Action*, pp. 35–48.

78. Hardisty, "Resurgent Right," pp. 1–13; see also, Hardisty, *Mobilizing Resentment*, pp. 9–36.

79. Omi and Winant, *Racial Formation*, pp. 121–122.

80. On the Black liberation movement, see Marable, *Race, Reform, and Rebellion*; Carson, Garrow, Gill, Harding, and Clark, *Eyes on the Prize*; Branch, *Parting the Waters*; *Pillar of Fire*; and Tani and Sera, *False Nationalism, False Internationalism*, chs. 5, 6, and 8. On FBI repression, see O'Reilly, *"Racial Matters."*

81. See Omi and Winant, *Racial Formation*, pp. 96, 117–118.

82. On Nixon and the welfare state, see Thomas Ferguson and Joel Rogers, *Right Turn*, pp. 69–70.

83. See Burch, *Elites in American History: Vol. 3*, p. 212; Abramovitz, *Regulating the Lives of Women*, p. 335; Baehr, *Abortion Without Apology*, p. 4.

84. On the economic and geopolitical crises, see Bowles, Gordon, and Weisskopf, *After the Waste Land*, pp. 63–95; Thomas Ferguson and Joel Rogers, *Right Turn*, pp. 79–83; Kolko, *Anatomy of a War*, pp. 283–290; and Omi and Winant, *Racial Formation*, pp. 114–116.

85. Zinn, *People's History*, p. 460.

86. Kolko, *Confronting the Third World*, ch. 19; Marchak, *Integrated Circus*, p. 8.

87. Rothmyer, "Citizen Scaife," pp. 41–50; Warner four-part series "Scaife" in the *Pittsburgh Post-Gazette.*

88. Another version of this section appears in Matthew N. Lyons, "Business Conflict and Right-Wing Movements."

89. This discussion of ultraconservative Sunbelt capital is based on Mike Davis, *Prisoners of the American Dream*, pp. 167–176, and Thomas Ferguson and Joel Rogers, *Right Turn*, pp. 91–92.

90. See Bellant, *Coors Connection*, p. 2; and Sara Diamond, *Spiritual Warfare*, pp. 13, 53.

91. This discussion of the changes that pulled many multinationalists to the right is based on Marchak, *Integrated Circus*, especially pp. 3–14; Thomas Ferguson and Joel Rogers, *Right Turn*, ch. 3; and Peschek, *Policy-Planning Organizations*, especially pp. 46–72. On the cuts in corporate taxes under Kennedy and Johnson, see Ferguson and Rogers, *Right Turn*, pp. 52, 100; and Burch, *Elites in American History: Vol. 3*, p. 188.

92. On corporate funding for right-wing organizations and campaigns in this period, see Morgan, "Conservatives," pp. A1, A14; Institute for Southern Studies' Campaign Finance Project, "Jesse Helms," pp. 17, 21; Peter H. Stone, "Counter-Intelligentsia," pp. 14–19; Hatfield and Waugh, "Where think tanks get their money," pp. A1–A14; Messer-Davidow, "Manufacturing the Attack"; "Who (Ac)Counts and How"; Callahan, "Liberal Policy's Weak Foundations," *$1 Billion for Ideas*; Schulman, "Foundations for a Movement," p. 11; Soley, "Right-Think Inc.," p. 10, and generally, Soley, *Leasing the Ivory Tower.*

93. This discussion of Reagan administration actions is based on Thomas Ferguson and Joel Rogers, *Right Turn*, ch. 4. See also Sara Diamond, *Roads to Dominion*, pp. 212–227; and Mike Davis, *Prisoners of the American Dream*, pp. 138–143.

94. Himmelstein, *To the Right*, p. 8. See also Viguerie, *New Right.*

95. Sara Diamond, "Christian Right Seeks Dominion," p. 49. See also Diamond, "How 'Radical' Is The Christian Right?"; "Shifting Alliances on the Right."

96. One of the best organizing books published in 1968 was by two conservative activists, Lee and Anne Edwards, *You Can Make the Difference*. On how the organizing worked, see Green, *Understanding the Christian Right.*

97. Mike Davis, *Prisoners of the American Dream*, pp. 170–171.

98. *The Phyllis Schlafly Report*, May 1973, p. 1, quoted in Sara Diamond, *Roads to Dominion*, p. 169.

99. Scher, *Cold War on the Home Front*, pp. 300–301.

100. Sara Diamond, "Christian Right Seeks Dominion," p. 47.

101. Ansell, *Race and Reaction.*

102. Rusher, *Making of a New Majority Party*, p. 14, also quoted in Omi and Winant, *Racial Formation*, p. 127. Rusher then urges readers to consult Kevin Phillips, *Mediacracy.*

103. D'Souza, *Falwell*, pp. 105–118; William Martin, *With God on Our Side*, pp. 200–201; Sara Diamond, *Spiritual Warfare*, pp. 49–63.

104. Kazin, *Populist Persuasion*, p. 247.

105. Lesher, *George Wallace*, pp. 463–464; Viguerie, *New Right*, pp. 26–27. Viguerie credits Morris Dees, who handled direct mail for Democratic candidate George McGovern in 1972, for suggesting to the Wallace campaign that he (Viguerie) be hired to raise funds to retire Wallace's 1972 presential campaign debt (p. 33).

106. Himmelstein, *To the Right*, pp. 80–94; Sara Diamond, *Roads to Dominion*, pp. 127–138; Kazin, *Populist Persuasion*, pp. 255–260; William Martin, *With God on Our Side*, p. 88; Lesher, *George Wallace*, pp. 463–464; Bellant, *Coors Connection* p. 44; Viguerie, *The New Right*, p. 116.

107. Dorrien, "Inventing an American Conservatism"; Sara Diamond, *Roads to Dominion*, ch. 8. In the United States, the neoconservatives are a specific sector, and not identical to the "neoliberals."

108. Flaws in this analysis of voting patterns are our own responsibility, but we base our conclusions on the following sources: Sara Diamond, *Spiritual Warfare*, pp. 55–56; *Roads to Dominion*, pp. 172–177, 209–210, 231–233; *Not by Politics Alone*, pp. 67–69; Himmelstein, *To the Right*, pp. 122–123; Green, Guth, and Hill, "Faith and Election"; William Martin, *With God on Our Side*, pp. 148–159, 197–220; Brooks and Manza, "Religious Factor."

Viguerie estimated that between 5 million and 7.5 million "born-again Christians voted for Nixon or Wallace in 1968 and for Nixon in 1972, but switched to Carter in 1976," and that he and his allies in the New Right set out to win them back to vote for Reagan in 1980 (Viguerie, *New Right*, pp. 155–174, quote from p. 156). This figure is probably unrealistically high, but the belief in those numbers helped shape the New Right election strategy.

Diamond credits the addition of 2 million new voters in 1980 to "the combined efforts of Moral Majority, Christian Voice, and New Right electoral vehicles" like Howard Phillips's Conservative Caucus and Paul Weyrich's Free Congress Foundation (*Roads to Dominion*, p. 233).

109. This section is based on Berlet, *Hunt for Red Menace*; "Frank Donner." See also Pell, *Big Chill*; Curry, ed., *Freedom at Risk*. The most extensive coverage at the time was in *The Nation* magazine.

110. Francis, ed., "Intelligence Community."

111. Francis, "Leftists Mount Attack on Investigative Panel," pp. 10–12.

112. Ibid., p. 12. For more on Rees, see Berlet, *Hunt for Red Menace*; and Birch, "Master of the Politics of Paranoia."

113. Donner, "Campaign to Smear the Nuclear Freeze Movement"; Seth Rosenfeld, "Spy Who Came Down on the Freeze."

114. Rubin, "FBI and Dissidents" (Parts I and II). Quote is from Part 1, p. 158.

115. Gelbspan, *Break-Ins, Death Threats and the FBI*.

116. Kovel, *Red Hunting in the Promised Land*, pp. 206, 213.

117. Herman, *Antigay Agenda*. See also Hardisty, "Constructing Homophobia"; Arlene Stein, *When the Culture War Comes to Town*; and "Whose Memories? Whose Victimhood?"; Khan, *Calculated Compassion*.

118. Anna Marie Smith, *New Right Discourse*, pp. 198–199.

119. *Christian Anti-Communism Crusade*, newsletter, vol. 2, no. 1, January 1, 1981, pp. 1–4.

Notes to Chapter 11

1. Johnson, *Architects of Fear*, pp 169–173; Sara Diamond, *Spiritual Warfare*, pp. 84–87, 233; Berlet and Quigley, "Theocracy & White Supremacy," pp. 32–33.

2. Kovel, *Red Hunting in the Promised Land*; Herman, *Antigay Agenda*, pp. 19–24, 35–44, 125–128, 170–172.

3. Quotes are from Green, Guth, and Hill, "Faith and Election," pp. 81, 85. For more criticism of status discontent theories and Christian activism, see Christian Smith, *American Evangelicalism*, pp. 83–84. On media, voting, and intolerance, see Smidt, Kellstedt, Green, and Guth, "Characteristics of Christian Political Activists," pp. 148–

152. On shifts in the political orientation and activism of Protestant clergy, see Guth, Green, Smidt, Kellstedt, and Poloma, *Bully Pulpit*.

4. Brooks and Manza, "Religious Factor." See also Green, Smidt, Kellstedt, and Guth, "Bringing in the Sheaves," pp. 75–91.

5. Sara Diamond, *Roads to Dominion*, pp. 222–223, 228–229, 237–241.

6. Berlet and Quigley, "Theocracy & White Supremacy," pp. 30–35.

7. Sara Diamond, "Christian Right Seeks Dominion," p. 47.

8. Hardisty, "Kitchen Table Backlash," pp. 106, 114. See also Luker, *Abortion and the Politics of Motherhood*; Klatch, *Women of the New Right*, pp. 119–153.

9. Dworkin, *Right-Wing Women*, ch. 1, quote from p. 21; Hardisty, "Kitchen Table Backlash," pp. 119–121, quote from p. 121.

10. On the group Women Exploited by Abortion, see Sara Diamond, *Spiritual Warfare*, pp. 97–98. On child care, see Faludi, *Backlash*, p. 255. On learning administrative skills, see Sara Diamond, *Spiritual Warfare*, p. 105. On developing self-confidence, and the LaHaye sex manual, see Faludi, *Backlash*, pp. 250–252. See also Wessinger, *Religious Institutions and Women's Leadership*; and Brasher, *Fundamentalism and Female Power*.

11. Baehr, *Abortion Without Apology*; see also Fried and Ross, "Reproductive Freedom," pp. 94–96.

12. Fried and Ross, "Reproductive Freedom," p. 84.

13. Luker, *Abortion and the Politics of Motherhood*, pp. 128–131, 216, 234–240. See also Paige, *Right to Lifers*; Ginsburg, *Contested Lives*; Risen and Thomas, *Wrath of Angels*; Faludi, *Backlash*, pp. 400–460; Sara Diamond, *Not by Politics Alone*, pp. 131–155.

14. Fried and Ross, "Reproductive Freedom," p. 92.

15. Sara Diamond, "No Place to Hide," pp. 39–40. Scheidler's book, *Closed: 99 Ways to Stop Abortion*, has a foreword by Franky Schaeffer.

16. This and the following two paragraphs are based partly on comments by Tom Burghardt of the Bay Area Coalition for Our Reproductive Rights (BAYCORR). See also Solotoroff, "Surviving the Crusades"; Sara Diamond, *Roads to Dominion*, pp. 170–172, 250—252, 302–304; Hairston, "Killing Kittens, Bombing Clinics"; and Barbara Barnett, "Of Babies & Ballots."

17. Paulk cited in Sara Diamond, *Spiritual Warfare*, p. 92. See also Terry, *Accessory to Murder*.

18. Blanchard, *Anti-Abortion Movement*.

19. Solotoroff, "Surviving the Crusades," p. 60. See also Center for Reproductive Law and Policy, *Tipping the Scales*.

20. See, for example, "A Sub-Zero Blast Against Conscientious Protest," paid advertisement, *The New York Times*, March 27, 1994, p. 17. On the Nixon Justice Department and RICO, see Dan Baum, *Smoke and Mirrors*, p. 38.

21. Rosin, "Walking the Plank," pp. 16–20; Judis, "Republican Splintering," p. 35.

22. Burlingame [with Children's Express], *Sex, Lies, and Politics*.

23. See, for instance, Monteith, *AIDS*; LaHaye, *Unhappy Gays*; Noebel, *Homosexual Revolution*. See also various pamphlets and reprints from the John Birch Society, including "The Truth About AIDS," *The New American*, August 31, 1987, and "What they are not telling you about AIDS," a pamphlet reprinting articles from the January 19, 1987, issue of *The New American*.

24. On homophobia, see Hardisty, "Constructing Homophobia"; Herman, *Antigay Agenda*; Sara Diamond, *Not by Politics Alone*, pp. 156–172.

25. Khan, "Gay Conservatives," pp. 1–10.

26. Hardisty, "Constructing Homophobia."

27. Rueda, *Homosexual Network*, p. xv. Portions of this section first appeared in Berlet, "Re-framing Dissent" and "Marketing the Religious Right's Anti-Gay Agenda."

28. All FCF memos and letters to FCF mentioned throughout this chapter were obtained from a source close to FCF and are on file at Political Research Associates.

29. Rueda and Schwartz, *Gays, AIDS and You*.

30. Ibid., p. vii.

31. Ibid., p. viii.

32. Ad for *Gays, AIDS and You*, from Free Congress Foundation, circa 1988, as reproduced in Bellant, *Coors Connection*, p. 65.

33. Rowe, *Homosexual Politics*, back cover, p. 4.

34. Quote is from Sara Diamond, "Christian Right's Anti-Gay Agenda," p. 33; see also Anna Marie Smith, "Why Did Armey Apologize?," pp. 157, 152.

35. This and the following three paragraphs are based primarily on discussions with Bob Lederer and John Riley of ACT UP New York.

36. Dennis King, *Lyndon LaRouche*, pp. 139–144.

37. Herman, *Antigay Agenda*, pp. 137–169; Hardisty, "Constructing Homophobia"; Arlene Stein, *When the Culture War Comes to Town*, "Whose Memories? Whose Victimhood?"

38. Hardisty, "Kitchen Table Backlash," p. 122.

39. Ibid., p. 123.

40. Withorn, "Fulfilling Fears and Fantasies," p. 136.

41. Ibid., pp. 136–137. See also Lucy A. Williams, "Right's Attack."

42. Author Berlet attended the Stormer conference; quotes are based on his notes.

43. *Time*, January 4, 1988. Bruce W. Nelan, "Catalyst for reform from Moscow to Bucharest, Gorbachev has transformed the world," *Time*, January 1, 1990, p. 46.

44. Marsden, *Understanding Fundamentalism and Evangelicalism*, p. 109. See also Sara Diamond, *Roads to Dominion*, pp. 246–248; William Martin, *With God on Our Side*, pp. 194–198, 331–333, 344–347); Damian Thompson, *End of Time*, pp. 310–312.

45. Sara Diamond, *Roads to Dominion*, pp. 233–237, 261–262; Thomas Ferguson, *Golden Rule*, pp. 243–251.

46. On Robertson's 1988 campaign, see Sara Diamond, *Spiritual Warfare*, pp. 72–76. On parallels with the presidential campaign of civil rights activist Rev. Jesse Jackson, see Hertzke, *Echoes of Discontent*.

47. On the paleocon–neocon feud and overall fragmentation of the right-wing coalition, see Sara Diamond, *Roads to Dominion*, ch. 12.

48. Pavlik, "Review of Gottfried's *Conservative Movement*." Note that the Independent Institute and the Independence Institute are separate entities.

49. Ibid., pp. 36—37.

50. Bernstein, "Magazine Dispute"; see, for example, the June 1992 *Rothbard–Rockwell Report*, which defends the paleocons. For a look at the neocon view of Buchanan and the Rockford crowd, see the May 1992 issues of *First Things*, published by Neuhaus ("The Year That Conservatism Turned Ugly") and *Commentary* ("Buchanan and the Conservative Crackup").

51. Comprehensive documentation of this network and its power in Burch, *Reagan, Bush, and Right-Wing Politics*; and *American Right Wing at Court and in Action*.

52. Soley, "Right-Think Inc.," p. 10. See also Soley, *Leasing the Ivory Tower*.

53. Debra L. Schultz, *To Reclaim a Legacy of Diversity*.

54. Kintz and Lesage, eds., *Media, Culture, and the Religious Right;* this source includes a chapter by Berlet, "Who's Mediating the Storm?," from which some material in this section is taken. Detailed articles on the general topic of right-wing media may be found in *Afterimage* (Visual Studies Workshop, Rochester, NY), special issue on "Fundamentalist Media," vol. 22, nos. 7 and 8 (February–March 1995); *Extra!* (Fairness and Accuracy in Reporting), special issue on "The Right-Wing Media Machine," March–April 1995; and Danky and Cherney, "Beyond Limbaugh."

55. Messer-Davidow, "Manufacturing the Attack"; "Who (Ac)Counts and How."

56. Callahan, "Liberal Policy's Weak Foundations."

57. Schulman, "Foundations for a Movement," p. 11. Calling *The New Republic* a leftist magazine these days will be met with laughter.

Notes to Chapter 12

1. Sara Diamond, *Spiritual Warfare,* pp. 136–139; *Roads to Dominion,* pp. 246–249. Some analysts use the term *dominionism* solely to refer to forms of Reconstructionism, but others use it as we do here, in the broader sense of exclusionary Christian nationalism.

2. Clarkson, *Eternal Hostility,* pp. 77–123. See also the excellent Barron, *Heaven on Earth?*

3. Quote from Sandlin, "Creed of Reconstructionism"; Sara Diamond, *Spiritual Warfare,* p. 137.

4. Clarkson, "Christian Reconstructionism," pp. 60–61.

5. Ibid.

6. Ibid., pp. 62–63, 67–68; the quote is from p. 67.

7. "Dear Friend" letter on Chalcedon letterhead citing *Newsweek* beginning, "We at Chalcedon thank you for your interest," no date, on file at Political Research Associates; Howard Phillips letter on behalf of Chalcedon, dated October 7, 1994, on file at Political Research Associates; Blumenfeld articles in *The Chalcedon Report,* December 1994 and May 1996; flyer for Ross House Books, "The Foundation of the Christian Education," no date, on file at Political Research Associates.

Blumenfeld's 1994 article blames declining education standards on satanic influences. Blumenfeld and Howard Phillips both are cited as experts by the John Birch Society. There seems to be a growing cooperation between the Birch Society and dominion theorists. Between 1988 and 2000 the online dominionist journal *Studies in Reformed Theology* featured dominion theologians Greg Bahnsen, Gary North, and David H. Chilton, as well as featuring, between March 1997 and March 2000, numerous persons on the staff list of the Birch Society magazine *The New American.* These include the magazine's publisher, John F. McManus; senior editors, William F. Jasper and William Norman Grigg; editor Gary Benoit; contributor, Samuel L. Blumenfeld; and researcher, Thomas A. Burzynski. Compiled from http://www.reformed-theology.org, various sub pages, March 28, 2000; and various issues of *The New American.*

On March 28, 2000 the *Studies in Reformed Theology* web page also featured a sponsors box flipping between the slogan "Get US Out of UN" and an ad for a John Birch Society information packet available for $5 by calling (800) JBS-USA1 (http://www.reformed-theology.org).

8. Burghardt, "Anti-Abortion Terror Continues," p. 4.

9. Covino, "Grace Under Pressure," p. 19; Goetz, "Randall Terry and the U.S. Tax-payers Party," p. 1.

10. An exceptional and detailed survey of Catholic apocalypticism may be found in Cuneo, *Smoke of Satan*. See also Damian Thompson, *End of Time*, pp. 175–190. Useful overviews of key right-wing Catholic groups are in Askin, *New Rite*.

11. *The Fatima Crusader*, Summer 1992, p. 2.

12. Martel, "Why Sr. Lucia Went Public," pp. 2–4, 44–48.

13. Martel, "Antichrist," pp. 6–9.

14. Ibid., p. 9.

15. "Father Coughlin, a great apostle of social justice who courageously denounced the bankers' debt-money system," the *Michael Journal*, May–June 1995, p. 10; and various undated *Michael Journal* reprints handed out in the Boston area from 1995 to 1998, on file at Political Research Associates.

16. Still, *New World Order*.

17. Branan and Clarkson, "Extremism in Sheep's Clothing."

18. Higgins, "Forays into Anti-Semitism," p. 10.

19. Ibid.

20. Various HLI publications on file at Political Research Associates.

21. Sara Diamond, *Spiritual Warfare*, pp. 70, 78–79, 195; Scott Anderson and Jon Lee Anderson, *Inside the League*, pp. 64–69, 105–106, 123–130, 255; Junas, *Rising Moon*.

22. The Coalition on Revival, "Manifesto for the Christian Church," *Crosswinds*, Winter 1992, pp. 111–122.

23. Ibid., p. 117.

24. Clarkson, "HardCOR," pp. 9–12; Sara Diamond, *Not by Politics Alone*, pp. 212–213; Clarkson, *Eternal Hostility*, pp. 97–103.

25. Ibid., p. 10. On the militia movement's common-law courts, see Burghart and Crawford, "Vigilante Justice," pp. 27–32.

26. Sara Diamond, *Spiritual Warfare*, pp. 111–130, 138–139; Clarkson, "Christian Reconstructionism," p. 71.

27. John W. Whitehead, "God's Love Through Christ," tract, no date, on file at Political Research Associates.

28. Clarkson, *Eternal Hostility*, pp. 16, 93–94. Whitehead distances himself from Rushdoony and Reconstructionism in Olsen, "Dragon Slayer," pp. 39–40.

29. Sara Diamond, *Facing the Wrath*, pp. 110–111.

30. Chuvala, "Nation on the Edge?," p. 9.

31. "Corrupt and Criminal," interview with Linda Thompson, *Rutherford* magazine, pp. 14–15, 17.

32. Weyrich, "Fear & Oppression," p. 16.

33. Whitehead, *Stealing of America*, p. 31.

34. Ibid., pp. 30–31.

35. Ibid., p. 100.

36. Ibid., pp. 106–127; John W. Whitehead, *Engaging the Culture*, pamphlet, The Rutherford Institute, circa 1993.

37. Porteous, "Special profile: The Rutherford Institute."

38. Olsen, "Dragon Slayer"; Neil A. Lewis, "Group Behind Paula Jones," p. 18.

39. Americans United for Separation of Church and State, "Rutherford Institute, Other Religious Right Groups Have Long Track Record of Vicious Attacks on Bill and

Hillary Clinton, Says Church–State Watchdog Group," News Media Backgrounder, January 1988.

40. Sara Diamond, *Spiritual Warfare*, pp. 29–33.

41. "Christian Right Profile," *NCFE Bulletin*, Spring 1995, p. 6; published by the National Campaign for Free Expression.

42. Wilcox, "Christian Right in Twentieth Century America," pp. 671–672.

43. Clarkson, "Christian Reconstructionism," pp. 73, 74.

44. Pat Robertson, for example, made both statements at "Faith and Freedom '94: Conference and Strategy Briefing," an annual gathering of the Christian Coalition of New York, Niagara Falls, New York, June 11, 1994.

45. Sara Diamond, "It's Political Power, Stupid!," p. 32.

46. See, for example, "New World Order Threat: Keyes Warns Americans Against Complacency," interview with Alan Keyes by John Wheeler, *Christian American*, January 1994, pp. 10–11.

47. On the 1992 endorsement of Bush, see Conason, "Religious Right's Quiet Revival," p. 553. On NAFTA, see Martin Mawyer, "A Rift in the Ranks of the Christian Right," *Washington Post*, National Weekly Edition, October 4–10, 1993, p. 24; and Seib, "Christian Coalition Hopes to Expand." The Christian Coalition later waffled on NAFTA.

48. Fineman, "God and the Grassroots."

49. See Sara Diamond, *Spiritual Warfare*, pp. 12–22; "Family Cable Channel Switches Signals," *Wall Street Journal*, September 24, 1990, pp. 1–2; "An Empire on Exemptions?" *Washington Post*, February 13, 1994, pp. H1, H5; and Geraldine Fabrikant, "Murdoch Set to Buy Family Cable Concern," *The New York Times*, June 12, 1997, pp. D1, D4; Grover and Siklos, "Malone: TV's New Uncrowned King?"

50. Robertson, *New World Order*, pp. 3–14.

51. Ibid., p. 36.

52. Ibid., pp. 177–178.

53. Lind, "Rev. Robertson's Grand International Conspiracy Theory," "On Pat Robertson"; Heilbrunn, "On Pat Robertson."

54. Robertson, *New World Order*, pp. 177–178.

55. Sutton, *Wall Street and the Bolshevik Revolution*; Perloff, *Shadows of Power*; Schlafly and Ward, *Kissinger on the Couch*; Skousen, *Naked Capitalist*; and two favorites of conspiracist analysts, Carroll Quigley, *Anglo-American Establishment*, and Quigley, *Tragedy and Hope*.

56. Robertson, *New World Order*, p. 178

57. Ibid., p. 183.

58. Ibid., p. 257.

59. Ibid., p. 265.

60. Robertson letter dated April 20, 1995, on file at Political Research Associates.

61. *700 Club*, July 23, 1998 and December 27, 1994, author Berlet's notes made while watching programs.

62. Robertson, *New World Order*, pp. 181, 274.

63. Still, *New World Order*, introduction; pp. 140–141, 148–149; back cover.

64. Ibid., back cover.

65. Clarkson, *Eternal Hostility*, pp. 132–135.

66. Ibid., p. 133.

67. Cuneo, *Smoke of Satan*, pp. 83, 88–89, 96, 109–110, 133, 156. An entire book on the subject of the Freemason/Illuminati conspiracy, written by a hard-right Catholic

priest, and published by the John Birch Society, is Clarence Kelly, *Conspiracy against God and Man.*

68. Berlet and Quigley, "Theocracy & White Supremacy," pp. 28–29, 34; Sara Diamond, *Roads to Dominion*, pp. 292–299; "Christian Right Seeks Dominion," pp. 44–49.

69. Barabak, "Gary Bauer," interview. Bauer's claim is supported by Kellstedt, Green, Guth, and Smidt, *Religious Voting Blocs in the 1992 Election*, pp. 1–2; and Green, "Religion, Social Issues, and the Christian Right," pp. 2–3, 27.

70. Kellstedt, Green, Guth, and Smidt, *Religious Voting Blocs in the 1992 Election;* quotes are from pp. 1–3. Brooks and Manza, "Religious Factor."

71. Balz and Brownstein, *Storming the Gates*, pp. 19–245; Green, Smidt, Kellstedt, and Guth, "Bringing in the Sheaves," pp. 75–88; Dionne, *They Only Look Dead*, pp. 193–230; Teixeira and Rogers, "Mastering the New Political Arithmetic," pp. 231–242; Wilcox, *Onward Christian Soldiers?*, pp. 61–151; Watson, *Christian Coalition;* Stan, "Power Preying"; Stern, *Force Upon the Plain*, pp. 77–78, 174–175, 210–220.

72. Sara Diamond, *Not by Politics Alone*, p. 4.

73. Teixeira and Rogers, "Mastering the New Political Arithmetic," pp. 230–237.

74. Sara Diamond, *Roads to Dominion*, p. 306.

75. Ibid., p. 305; Lind, "Rev. Robertson's Grand International Conspiracy Theory"; Rich, "Bait and Switch"; Niebuhr, "Pat Robertson Says He Intended," p. 10; Decter, "ADL vs. the 'Religious Right.'" Quote from neocons is from "Should Jews Fear the 'Christian Right'?" advertisement, *The New York Times*, August 2, 1994, p. A21. On the Christian Coalition's Jewish membership percentage, see Nixon, "All God's Children?," p. 35.

76. "Christian Coalition starts drive to recruit blacks and Hispanics," *The Virginian Pilot and Ledger-Star*, September 10, 1993, p. A4; DeParle, "Christian Right Confesses Sins of Racism." Reed quoted in Sack, "Penitent Christian Coalition," p. A19. On Southern Baptists, see Niebuhr, "Baptist Group Votes to Repent Stand on Slaves," p. A1.

77. Nixon, "All God's Children?" pp. 34–38; quote is from p. 35.

Notes to Chapter 13

1. Tom Metzger, quoted in "Metzger Begins Move to the Top," *The Monitor*, January 1988, p. 5.

2. On the LaRouchite–Nation of Islam connection, see Magida, "Evil Twins"; Benjamin, "La Rouche, Nation of Islam Team Up"; Marable, "No Compromise." For examples, see "'We Must Accept the Responsibility of Freedom': An interview with Minister Louis Farrakhan," *New Federalist*, June 12, 1995, pp. 5–7; Dennis Speed, "LaRouche, Farrakhan, Chavis Mobilize Against Nazi Economics," *New Federalist*, July 15, 1996, pp. 1, 4. On Metzger's links with the Nation of Islam, see Wayne King, "White Supremacists Voice Support of Farrakhan"; Southern Poverty Law Center, "Klan leader attends Farrakhan rally," *Klanwatch*, Winter 1985.

The beginnings of the alliance between the LaRouchites and the Nation of Islam track back to the early 1990s. The Nation of Islam's *Final Call* newspaper ran an article by LaRouchite Carlos Wesley on Panama in its issue of May 31, 1990, p. 10. It was credited as a reprint from the LaRouchite *Executive Intelligence Review*. The LaRouchite *New Federalist* ran several articles praising the political work of Nation of Islam spokesman Dr. Abdul Alim Muhammad (including articles on September 14, 1990, p. 1; and September 28, 1990, p. 10); and his speech at a LaRouchite Schiller Institute meeting in Paris was reported in the Nation of Islam's *Final Call* on December 24, 1990, p. 3. The Schiller Institute-Food for Peace Anti-War Teach In, December 15–16, 1990, featured Abdul Wali Muhammad, Editor of the *Final Call* newspaper as a speaker; the meeting program is on file at Political Research Associates. By 1992 joint campus appearances by representatives of *Executive Intelligence Review,* The Nation of Islam, and The Schiller Institute, featured attacks on the Anti-Defamation League (ADL); flyers are on file at Political Research Associates. This evolved into publications and speeches claiming the ADL was part of a conspiracy involving the Freemasons and the Ku Klux Klan, featuring a campaign to remove the statue of Confederate General Albert Pike from its pedestal in Washington, DC; see, for example, Marianna Wertz, "Pike Issue Before Congress," *New Federalist,* May 17, 1993, p. 1, which featured comments by the 1960s civil rights leader the Rev. James L. Bevel, an African American who has worked with the LaRouchites for many years. See also Brackman, *Farrakhan's Reign of Historical Error.*

3. Roger Griffin, *Nature of Fascism,* pp. 166–172. For general background, see Jeffrey Kaplan and Leonard Weinberg, *Emergence of a Euro-American Radical Right;* Jeffrey Kaplan and Tore Bjørgo, eds., *Nation and Race;* Martin A. Lee, *Beast Reawakens;* Cheles, Ferguson, and Vaughan, eds., *Far Right in Western and Eastern Europe;* Merkl and Weinberg, eds., *Encounters with the Contemporary Radical Right;* Hockenos, *Free to Hate;* Michael Schmidt, *New Reich;* Golsan, ed., *Fascism's Return.* On philosophical aspects of neofascist and ethnonationalist ideology, see Antonio, "After Postmodernism." On occult roots of some neofascist movements, see Spielvogel and Redles, "Hitler's Racial Ideology."

4. Donner, *Age of Surveillance,* pp. 440–446, 204–208; *Protectors of Privilege,* pp. 360–362. Churchill and Vander Wall, *Agents of Repression,* pp. 55, 182, 181; for Greensboro background generally, see Wheaton, *Code Name Greenkil;* for the legal battle, see G. Flint Taylor, "Waller v. Butkovich."

5. Donner, *Age of Surveillance,* pp. 426–446; Novick, *White Lies, White Power,* ch. 4.

6. Segrest and Zeskind, *Quarantines and Death,* pp. 23–29.

7. Ross, "Anti-Abortionists and White Supremacists"; Novick, *White Lies, White Power,* pp. 134–140; Flanders, "Far-Right Militias."

8. Charles Allen, Jr., "Pro-Life Hate," p. 155.

9. Dennis King, *Lyndon LaRouche,* p. 143; Segrest, "Deadly New Breed."

10. See, for example, the magazines *The Third Way* and *Scorpion.*

11. "Metzger Begins Move to the Top," *The Monitor,* January 1988, p. 5. See also Lawrence, "Klansmen, Nazis, Skinheads," p. 33. On antecedents, see Schmaltz, *Hate.*

12. Monique Wolfing (leader of the Aryan Women's League), discussion with Tom Metzger on "Race and Reason," aired on San Francisco public access television, May 1989. See also Zia, "Women in Hate Groups."

13. "What Next For Metzger & WAR," *The Monitor,* March 1991, p. 9. For background on the skinhead subculture see Hamm, *American Skinheads.*

14. On de Benoist, see Martin A. Lee, *Beast Reawakens,* pp. 208–215; on convergence between continents, see Jeffrey Kaplan and Tore Bjørgo, eds., *Nation and Race;* on Third Position and racially separate nation-states, see Antonio, "After Postmodernism."

15. Dobratz and Shanks-Meile, *"White Power, White Pride!"*

16. Ibid., p. 124. See also Dobratz and Shanks-Meile, "Ideology and the Framing Process."

17. Ibid., pp. 89–107.

18. The most extensive discussion is in Barkun, *Religion and the Racist Right;* see also Katz and Popkin, *Messianic Revolution,* pp. 170–204; Minges, *Apocalypse Now!* For early

examples of British Israelism being adapted to America, see J. H. Allen, *Judah's Sceptre and Joseph's Birthright*; and Mackendrick, *Destiny of Britain and America*.

19. Zeskind, *"Christian Identity" Movement*, p. 7; interview with author Berlet, 1992.

20. Weinberg, "American Radical Right," pp. 202–203.

21. Zeskind, *"Christian Identity" Movement*, p. 33; Barkun, *Religion and the Racist Right*, pp. 249–253.

22. Corcoran, *Bitter Harvest*; Levitas, "Antisemitism and the Far Right," pp. 187–188, 197–198.

23. Ridgeway, *Blood in the Face*, p. 115.

24. Davidson, *Broken Heartland*; Ridgeway, *Blood in the Face*, pp. 186–187.

25. Center for Democratic Renewal, *When Hate Groups Come to Town*, pp. 118–125; Sara Diamond, *Roads to Dominion*, pp. 259–260; Ridgeway, *Blood in the Face*, pp. 186–187.

26. Levitas, "Antisemitism and the Far Right," pp. 200–201.

27. Flynn and Gerhardt, *Silent Brotherhood*.

28. Aryan Resistance Movement, "Declaration of War," November 25, 1984; flyer on file at Political Research Associates.

29. Seymour, *Committee of the States*.

30. Ibid., p. 271.

31. See Dennis King, *Lyndon LaRouche*.

32. Ibid., p. 89.

33. Ibid., pp. 39–40.

34. *Spotlight*, March 2, 1981, p. 20.

35. Lyndon H. LaRouche, "New Pamphlet to Document Cult Origins of Zionism," *New Solidarity*, December 8, 1978, quoted in Dennis King, *Nazis Without Swastikas*, p. 9.

36. "Zionism Is Not Judaism," editorial, *The Campaigner*, December 1978.

37. *New Federalist*, June 19, 1995, p. 10.

38. William F. Wertz, Jr., "Fidelo Magazine Refutes Slanderers of Columbus," *New Federalist*, June 29, 1992, p. 11; Dennis Speed, "African-American Spiritual and the Resurrection of Classical Art," *New Federalist*, October 9, 1995, pp. 6–7.

39. "Imperialism . . . " quoted in LaRouche, *Power of Reason*, p. 191. "Kissinger's friends . . . " quote in Christopher White, "George Bush's Countdown to Middle East War."

40. In the early 1980s, LaRouche described himself as "an American Whig by family ancestry stretching back into the early 19th century, born a New Hampshire Whig, and a Whig Democrat by profession today," Lyndon LaRouche, "Is Republican George Bush a 'Manchurian Candidate'?" issued by Citizens for LaRouche, Manchester, New Hampshire, January 12, 1980; as cited in Tarpley and Chaitkin, *George Bush: The Unauthorized Biography*, online at http://www.tarpley.net/bush16.htm. LaRouche briefly explains how one can be a modern Federalist Whig Democrat in Lyndon H. LaRouche, Jr., *A Program for America* (Washington, DC: The LaRouche Democratic Campaign, 1995), pp. 315–332.

On rapid growth economic and industrialization policies, see LaRouche, *The Case for Walter Lippman: A Presidential Strategy* (New York: Campaigner Publications/University Editions, 1977), especially pp. 164–167; LaRouche, *There Are No Limits to Growth* (New York: New Benjamin Franklin House, 1983); and LaRouche, *Program for America*, especially ch. 4, "LaRouche's Proposals for Economic Reform," pp. 37–120, including subtitles "Great Projects versus Kissinger Genocide," and "The United States Under President Reagan's 'Hoover' Recovery"; and ch. 8, "The Pathway to a U.S. Economic Recovery," pp. 263–313, including the subtitle "Reopen America's Steel Plants Now!"

On a LaRouchite critique of the 1995 Republican Contract with America proposed by Newt Gingrich, see "How the Conservative Revolution Crowd Plans to Destroy America," pamplet, Leesburg, Virginia, *New Federalist*, March 1995.

On British conspiracy against the United States, see LaRouche, "Foreword," in *The Trilateral Conspiracy Against the U.S. Constitution: Fact or Fiction?* ([EIR Special Report] Washington, DC: Executive Intelligence Review, 1985), in which the Trilateral Commission is identified as "merely one of numerous ventures, launched by the same Anglo-American Liberal Establishment which created the New York Council on Foreign Relations (CFR)," p. 2; and Christopher White, "The Socialist One-World Conspiracy," *The Campaigner*, April 1981, pp. 2–3.

A large amount of LaRouchite conspiracist anti-British material was found at the American Almanac website, http://members.tripod.com/~american_almanac/britspt. htm (April 1, 2000) including an entire section titled "'Winds of Change'—The Sun Never Sets on the New British Empire—Financial Control and the Destabilization of Governments." Another website containing material illustrating several of our points was "LaRouche's Major Writings," at http://www.larouchepub.com/major_writings. html (April 1, 2000).

41. *American Mercury*, Fall 1974, p. 16.

42. See the following articles from the *New Federalist*: Marianna Wertz, "American Opposition Is Growing to the Use of the Death Penalty," June 29, 1992, p. 12; Edward Spannaus, "Supreme Court Upholds Limits on Death Row Prisoners' Habeas Petitions," July 15, 1996, p. 12; Stuart Lewis, "Anti-Immigration Fanatics Assess Efficacy of Efforts Against Mexico," June 12, 1995, p. 3; Debra Hanania Freeman, "National Scandal," June 12, 1995, p. 4; Marianna Wertz, "Clinton and Democrats Fight GOP's Budget Gouging," May 29, 1995, p. 12; Anton Chaitkin, "President Rejects 'Crush the Poor' Welfare Plan," June 19, 1995, p. 2; Richard Freeman, "Privatization," June 19, 1995, p. 11; Dean Andromidas, "Likud, GOP Out to Wreck Mideast Peace," May 29, 1995, p. 3. See also Caryle Murphy, "LaRouche Sentenced to 15 Years in Prison," *The Washington Post*, January 28, 1989; Associated Press, "Supreme Court Upholds LaRouche Convictions," *The Washington Post*, June 12, 1990; Peter Pae and Leef Smith, "LaRouche, Paroled After 5 Years in Prison, Returns to Loudoun," *The Washington Post*, January 27, 1994.

On LaRouche's postjail activities, see the following articles from the *New Federalist*: "LaRouche: Accepting Gingrich Nazi Policies Means Doom for the U.S.," February 26, 1996, p. 1; Rachel Douglas, "LaRouche Urges U.S.–Russian Cooperation Against British," May 6, 1996, p. 1; Nancy Spannaus, "The World Depression Has Arrived," February 24, 1997, p. 1.

On LaRouchite continued Anglophobic conspiracism, see the following articles from the *New Federalist*: Jeffrey Steinberg, "Scandals Shake British Throne," October 31, 1994; Jeffrey Steinberg, "Prince Phillip's Eco-Terrorists Make Death Threats vs. Clinton, Chirac," September 4, 1995, p. 1.

43. Dennis King, *Lyndon LaRouche*, pp. 103, 119.

44. Sara Diamond, *Roads to Dominion*, p. 264; Berry, "David Duke's Role Model?"

45. "Biographical Chronology of David Duke," in Louisiana Coalition Against Racism and Nazism, *Resource Packet: The Politics and Background of State Representative David Duke* (New Orleans: Author, 1991); Diamond, *Roads to Dominion*, p. 271.

46. Ridgeway, "White Blight," p. 18; quote in Peter Applebome, "Ex-Klan Leader Facing First Test in Senate Bid," *The New York Times*, December 8, 1989, p. A20.

47. Berry, "Huckster Who Mocks Democracy."

48. Ibid.

49. See especially Lance Hill, "Nazi Race Doctrine"; and Rickey, "Nazi and the Republicans."

50. "Sugar-Coated White Supremacy in Louisiana, Developing a Response," *The Monitor* (Center for Democratic Renewal), December 1989.

51. This and subsequent Duke quotes transcribed from video of state of Washington Populist Party nominating convention, recorded July 23, 1988, transcript on file at Political Research Associates.

52. "Report on Louisiana House Bill No. 1584: The Duke Sterilization Plan," in Louisiana Coalition Against Racism and Nazism, *Resource Packet*.

53. Populist Campaign Fund direct-mail appeal dated April 12, 1996 and signed by Robert H. Weems.

54. Patrick J. Buchanan, "Why I Am Running for President," *Human Events*, December 28, 1991, p. 11. This is the text of Buchanan's December 10, 1991, speech announcing his candidacy.

55. Milliken's "Visa" fabric has been promoted in expensive full-page full-color ads in Birch Society publications for over a decade.

56. On the Buchanan and Gephardt campaigns, see Thomas Ferguson, *Golden Rule*, pp. 334*n*28, and 260–262, respectively.

57. Patrick J. Buchanan, "Gays Are Aggressors in Culture War," *Boston Herald*, September 14, 1994, p. 23; "Feminism and Abortion," *Washington Inquirer*, August 24, 1984, p. 7; "America's Soul Under Siege," *From the Right*, April 20, 1990, p. 6; "Mainstreaming Satanism," *From the Right*, October 22, 1990, p. 6.

58. Patrick J. Buchanan, "Behind the School Prayer Fight? *Washington Inquirer*, March 9, 1984, p. 5.

59. Patrick J. Buchanan, "Out of Place in 1990s America," *From the Right*, August 1991, p. 3; "High Court Assaults WASPs" *Washington Inquirer*, July 8, 1988, p. 5; "Today Canada, Tomorrow USA," *Washington Inquirer*, July 6, 1990, p. 5; "Manifest Destiny—North to the Pole?" *Washington Inquirer*, April 27, 1990, p. 5.

60. Patrick J. Buchanan, "Immigration Reform or Racial Purity? *Washington Inquirer*, June 15, 1984, p. 5. See also Naurekas and Jackson, "It's the Mexicans, Stupid."

60. Patrick J. Buchanan, "America First—A Foreign Policy for the Rest of Us," *From the Right*, November 1991, pp. 1–4; "Towards a Non-Suicidal Foreign Policy," *Washington Inquirer*, June 10, 1988, p. 5; "Abolish the Income Tax" *Washington Inquirer*, April 26, 1991, p. 5; "Declawing the Union Beast" *Washington Inquirer*, July 28, 1989, p. 5.

62. McManus, "Taking on the Giant," p. 5.

63. Yemma, "Populist Pitch on Worker Insecurity"; Stark, "Right Wing Populist"; Dionne, "Class Issues"; Kevin Phillips, "Right Makes Fright"; *Business Week*, America's New Populism."

64. Patrick J. Buchanan, "Worship Democracy? A Dissent," *From the Right*, January 25, 1991, p. 6; "Death Squads and No-Win Wars," *Washington Inquirer*, February 3, 1984, p. 4; "Police Brutality, Popular Reaction," *From the Right*, March 22, 1991, p. 5.

65. Sara Diamond, *Roads to Dominion*, p. 310.

66. Charles A. Murray, *Losing Ground*; Herrnstein and Murray, *Bell Curve*.

67. DeParle, "Daring Research," p. 48; on the Pioneer Fund, see Lane, "Tainted Sources of 'The Bell Curve'"; Bellant, *Old Nazis*, pp. 60–64; Bellant, *Coors Connection*, pp. 38–39, 54, 75; Miller, "Professors of Hate." For more background on eugenics and academic racism, see Mehler, "Foundation for Fascism"; "In Genes We Trust"; Margaret Quigley, "Roots of the I.Q. Debate." A dubious map and chart adapted from the

Aryanist *Journal of Indo-European Studies* are used in Riane Eisler, *Chalice and the Blade, Our History, Our Future*, pp. 249, 251.

68. For critical responses to *Bell Curve*, see Kincheloe, Steinberg, and Gresson, eds., *Measured Lies*. See also the informative reviews of other books critical of *Bell Curve* in *Contemporary Sociology*, May 1997, vol. 26, no. 3, pp. 311–316.

69. Huntington, *Clash of Civilizations*. See Holly Sklar's discussion of Huntington's elitism in Sklar, *Trilateralism*, pp. 3, 35–43.

70. Steel, "Hard Questions," p. 25. See also Gaddis Smith, "Dividing a Single World."

71. Dunn, *Militarization of the U.S.-Mexico Border*; Silko, "Border Patrol State."

72. Crawford and Rybovich, "Lady Liberty No More"; Conniff, "War on Aliens."

73. Kadetsky, "Bashing Illegals in California"; Brugge, "Pulling Up the Ladder," pp. 203–204; Pfitsch and Jung, "Immigration Enforcement's Little Secret"; Neil A. Lewis, "Bill Seeks to End."

74. Conniff, "War on Aliens" p. 24; Crawford and Rybovich, "Lady Liberty No More," pp. 18–19; Kadetsky, "Bashing Illegals in California," pp. 420–421; Muwakkil, "Color Bind."

75. Crawford and Rybovich, "Lady Liberty No More," pp. 18–19; Kadetsky, "Bashing Illegals in California," pp. 418, 421; Novick, *White Lies, White Power*, ch. 7. Perea, *Immigrants Out!*

76. Britt, "Neo-Confederate Culture"; Prague, "Neo-Confederate Movement." A vast collection of documents critical of the neo-Confederate movement is at the Temple of Democracy website: http://www.mindspring.com/~newtknight/index.htm.

77. Berlet and Quigley, "Theocracy & White Supremacy," p. 18; Berlet, "Following the Threads," p. 34.

78. Zeskind with Hunt, "Sam Francis," p. 24; Crawford and Rybovich, "Lady Liberty No More."

79. Berlet and Quigley, "Theocracy & White Supremacy," pp. 20–21.

80. Dennis King, *Lyndon LaRouche*, p. 143.

81. Viguerie, *Establishment vs. the People*. See Sara Diamond, *Roads to Dominion*, pp. 261–262.

82. Sara Diamond, *Roads to Dominion*, p. 272.

83. Lucy A. Williams, "Right's Attack."

84. Aho, "Library of Infamy," citing his then forthcoming book, *The Politics of Righteousness: Idaho Christian Patriotism*.

85. Ferber, "Reconceptualizing the Racist Right," p. 121; Ezekiel, *Racist Mind*, p. 321.

Notes to Chapter 14

1. Portions of this chapter first appeared in Berlet and Lyons, "Militia Nation"; Berlet, "Armed and Dangerous"; "Violence of Right-Wing Populism"; "Clinic Violence, The Religious Right"; and "Who's Mediating the Storm?" We also relied on Junas, "Rise of Citizen Militias"; McLemee, "Public Enemy"; Stern, *Force Upon the Plain*; and Hamm, *Apocalypse in Oklahoma*.

2. Mark Rupert, *Globalization and the Reconstruction of Common Sense*. See also Rupert's Web page, "A Virtual Guided Tour of Far Right Anti-Globalist Ideology," URL:http://www.maxwell.syr.edu/maxpages/faculty/merupert/far-right.

3. Patrick J. Buchanan, "Why I Am Running for President," *Human Events*, December 28, 1991, p. 11.

4. Patrick J. Buchanan, "We need to Call a Time-Out on Immigration," *Conservative Chronicle*, November 9, 1994.

5. On COR, see Clarkson, *Eternal Hostility*, pp. 97–104; for the COR 1990 action plan, see p. 103. On the USTP, see pp. 104–106, 117–119, 152–155.

6. On Gargan and King, see Germond and Witcover, *Mad as Hell*, pp. 211–223; Posner, *Citizen Perot*, pp. 1–8; Todd Mason, *Perot*, p. 5; Michael Kelly, "Road to Paranoia." For a detailed election analysis, see Menendez, *Perot Voters*.

7. The figure is an estimate arrived at by adding up various subscription reports, rally and meeting attendance, book sales, vote totals for Patriot-leaning candidates, program viewership and listenership, etc., and then reducing the total substantially to account for overlap and weak support. This is an imperfect system, but several other analysts who monitor the Right have arrived at similar estimates using the broadest definition of the Patriot movement.

8. Stern, *Force Upon the Plain*; Lamy, *Millennium Rage*.

9. Most of the early serious coverage of the militia movement appeared in the progressive alternative press, including the previously cited articles by Junas and McLemee, and Hawkins, "Patriot Games." See also Hazen, Smith, and Triano, eds., *Militias in America*.

10. Walter, *Every Knee Shall Bow*, pp. 64–87.

11. Tabor and Gallagher, *Why Waco?*; Reavis, *Ashes of Waco*; Katz and Popkin, *Messianic Revolution*, pp. 142–169; Samples, de Castro, Abanes, and Lyle, *Prophets of the Apocalypse*. See also Alan A. Stone, *Concerning the Handling of Incidents*, an expert report for the Justice Department. See also Stone's critical commentary on the video "Waco: The Rules of Engagement," http://bostonreview.mit.edu/BR22.5/stone.html. Ammerman, expert report for the Justice Department, *Report to the Justice and Treasury Departments*.

12. Quinby, *Anti-Apocalypse*, pp. 155–162; Damian Thompson, *End of Time*, pp. 278–321; Hamm, *Apocalypse in Oklahoma*; O'Leary, *Arguing the Apocalypse*, pp. 225–228; Lamy, *Millennium Rage*, pp. 253–267; Jeffrey Kaplan, *Radical Religion*, pp. 164–177.

13. Stern, *Force Upon the Plain*, pp. 50–56.

14. Ezekiel, *Racist Mind*, pp. 28–29; Dobratz and Shanks-Meile, "*White Power, White Pride!,*" p. 185.

15. Interview with Arthur Kinoy, 1989. A study devoted to this dynamic of state repression against White supremacists is Ziegenhorn, "No Rest for the Wicked."

16. Interview with Harvey A. Silverglate, 1989.

17. Beam, "Leaderless Resistance," reprint of the 1983 essay that was posted by Beam on racist computer bulletin board systems (BBSs) in the late 1980s and was available on the Internet even throughout the 1990s (see http://www.louisbeam.com/leaderless.htm, April 15, 2000).

18. Hamm, *Apocalypse in Oklahoma*, pp. 1–33, Abanes, *American Militias*, pp. 43–62; Dobratz and Shanks-Meile, "*White Power, White Pride!,*" pp. 184–185.

19. Halpern and Levin, *Limits of Dissent*, pp. 2–4, 42–52; Stern, *Force Upon the Plain*, pp. 107–118, 135–138; Abanes, *American Militias*, pp. 22, 43–71.

20. Rand, *Gun Shows in America*, pp. 33–35.

21. Vest, "Spooky World of Linda Thompson."

22. Burghart and Crawford, *Guns & Gavels*.

23. Daniels, "Another Standoff," pp. 1–4; Pitcavage, "Every Man a King"; Jean Rosenfeld, "Justus Freeman Standoff"; "Brief History of Millennialism."

24. Unruh, "Authorities Speculate Fugitives"; Associated Press, "Authorities Track-

ing Two People," July 10, 1998, online archive; Foster, "Vast Manhunt Comes up Empty"; Burton, "Cop Killing."

25. Letter from the Birch Society's American Opinion Book Services, in promotional catalog of anti-UN materials, August 1998, on file at Political Research Associates.

26. Author Berlet attended the Burlington, Massachusetts, Patriot meeting and took notes. Portions of this discussion also appeared in Berlet and Lyons, "Militia Nation," and Berlet, "Violence of Right-Wing Populism."

27. Dr. Koop later was named Surgeon General by President Reagan. See Francis A. Schaeffer and C. Everett Koop, "Whatever Happened to the Human Race?" five episodes, video. Muskegon, MI: Gospel Films, 1979, Franky Schaeffer, V Productions. Carol Mason helped sort out these links.

28. Author Berlet attended the Sturbridge meeting at the invitation of Crenshaw, and took notes of the meeting and spoke with Crenshaw privately.

29. Mintz, *Liberty Lobby*; Barkun, *Religion and the Racist Right*; Dobratz and Shanks-Meile, *"White Power, White Pride!"*; Hardisty, *Mobilizing Resentment*.

30. Leslie Jorgensen, a freelance reporter in Colorado, first reported Duran's tie to militia-oriented talk radio. In her article "AM Armies" she discusses the Chuck Baker program in detail. William E. Clayton, Jr., "Colorado Man Charged with Trying to Kill Clinton," *Houston Chronicle*, November 18, 1994, p. 1.

31. This section appeared previously, in Berlet, "Armed and Dangerous"; "Clinic Violence"; "Violence of Right-Wing Populism."

32. A collection of this material from the Burlington meeting is on file at Political Research Associates.

33. *The New American* is published by the John Birch Society, based in Appleton, Wisconsin. *The Fatima Crusader* is published by the National Committee for the National Pilgrim Virgin of Canada and is distributed in the United States by the Servants of Jesus and the Mary Fatima Center in Constable, New York. On Salvi and the Florida militia, see Tippit, "Chilling New Link Suspected."

34. Rice, "Death Penalty Dilemma." Rice, in another publication, suggests heeding a biblical passage interpreted by some Christians as sanctioning death for homosexuality.

35. Branan and Clarkson, "Extremism in Sheep's Clothing."

36. Author Berlet was subpoenaed and questioned as an expert by the defense in the Salvi trial but was never called to testify. This discussion is based in part on a conversation with a mental health professional who had analyzed Salvi's psychological status for the court case.

37. Jacob Weisberg, "Playing with Fire."

38. DeCamp, "Locking the Doors to the Kingdom."

39. Stern, "Militias and the Religious Right," footnote 4. See also Maxell and Tapia, "Guns and Bibles."

40. Nord Davis, Jr., *Desert Shield and the New World Order*.

41. *The Militia News* (Afton, TN: Christian Civil Liberties Association, 1994), p. 1.

42. Ibid., p. 2.

43. Ibid., p. 3.

44. Author Berlet's review of documents admitted into evidence in the Timothy McVeigh and Terry Nichols trials. Berlet was subpoenaed and questioned as an expert by the defense in the Nichols trial but never called to testify. McVeigh adopted neonazi beliefs while Terry Nichols, on the other hand, appears to be more of a generic constitutionalist. See also Hamm, *Apocalypse in Oklahoma*; and Joel Dyer, *Harvest of Rage*.

45. Andrew Macdonald [pseudonym of William Pierce], *Turner Diaries*.

46. Joel Dyer, *Harvest of Rage*; Neiwert, *In God's Country*; Pitcavage, "Extremism and the Electorate."

47. Pitcavage, "Extremism and the Electorate." See also Pitcavage, "Welcome."

48. Steve Lawrence, "Rogers' Comments No Cause For Sanctions, Officials Say," Associated Press, April 26, 1996; press release from office of Don Rogers, "Rogers Hails Counsel Opinion Re Legislative Status," April 25, 1996, circulated online.

49. As cited in Crawford, Gardner, Mozzochi, and Taylor, *Northwest Imperative*, pp. 3, 20. On the nature of Christian Identity, see Chapter 13.

50. Based on Charles Duke 1996 U.S. Senate campaign documents from his website, now offline, on file at Political Research Associates. The state sovereignty legislation introduced by Charles Duke was House Joint Resolution 94-1035. On Duke's political fortunes, see Fred Brown, "Allard Gets Ballot Top Line: Let Race Begin, Norton Says," *The Denver Post*, June 9, 1996 p. B1; Associated Press, "Duke, now a truck driver, wants back into politics," from the *Gazette* (Colorado), October 1, 1999, online in the Northern Light collection, http://library.northernlight.com. For a detailed look at Patriot movement involvement in Colorado state politics, see the Colorado Citizens Project online newsletter, *Freedom Watch*, at http://citproj.ppages.com/freedom.htm, especially Leslie Jorgensen, "Preaching the Patriot Gospel," October 1996. See also Loretta J. Ross, "The Militia Movement—in Their Own Words and Deeds," Congressional Testimony, July 11, 1995, online at http://webdev.maxwell.syr.edu/merupert/Research/far-right/cdr_militias.htm.

51. Kaufmann, "From the Margins to the Mainstream," pp. 32–36.

52. *Spotlight*, December 11, 1995, p. 1.

53. Dale Russakoff, "No-Name Movement Fed by Fax Expands."

54. "Postponement of the 'Conference of the States,'" supplement to *The Right Guide*, May 31, 1995.

55. Michael Reagan with Jim Denney, *Making Waves*, pp. 121–133.

56. Burke, "Wise Use Movement"; Ramos, "Regulatory Takings and Private Property Rights"; Helvarg, *War Against the Greens*; Rowell, *Green Backlash*; Switzer, *Green Backlash*.

57. Barry and Cook, *How the Biodiversity Treaty Went Down*, p. 1.

58. Mary Rupert, "Patriot Movement and the Roots of Fascism," p. 96.

59. Free Republic home page, http://www.freerepublic.com/about.htm, April 15, 2000.

Notes to Chapter 15

1. As this book goes to press, several books on the Clinton controversies have recently been published. The most useful for studying right-wing movement influences is Conason and Lyons, *Hunting of the President*, especially pp. 67–182, 308–322. The book includes considerable detail about the Federalist Society, Jeremiah Films, Citizens United and other rightist groups. Legal maneuvering and conservative politics is the theme of Toobin, *Vast Conspiracy*. Both books include sources and indexes. Another book, by Susan Schmidt and Michael Weisskopf, *Truth at Any Cost*, lacks historical and political acumen, highlighting personality at the expense of context. The authors argue that charges against Starr by Clinton's supporters were hyperbolic and politically motivated, but they fail to explore Starr's demonstrable ties to and support from conservatives and the Hard Right. Two earlier books worth examining are Gene Lyons and the

editors of *Harpers, Fools for Scandal;* and Retter, *Anatomy of a Scandal.* We relied on the list of players at http://www.msnbc.msn.com/news/158930.asp. A more detailed study of right-wing networks involved in attacking Clinton, by author Berlet, with additional material by Fred Clarkson, is available from Political Research Associates: *Clinton, Conspiracism, and the Continuing Culture War: What Is Past Is Prologue,* revised and expanded from an article in the *Public Eye* magazine.

2. The importance of studying common vernacular and rhetoric in popular culture, especially in terms of purveying apocalyptic and millennialist forms of scapegoating and conspiracism, has been explored in books and papers by Gow, *Jewish Shock-Troops of the Apocalypse, Medieval Racism?;* Landes, "On Owls, Roosters, and Apocalyptic Time"; Carol Mason, *Fetal Legislation,* "Cracked Babies and the Partial Birth of a Nation"; Quinby, *Anti-Apocalypse, Millennial Seduction;* and Redles, *"Day Is Not Far Off," Final War, Final Solution.* These authors discussed their ideas at symposia held by the Center for Millennial Studies at Boston University attended by author Berlet who was influenced by their ideas.

3. Interview with Russ Bellant, 1999.

4. Thomas Ferguson, "Smoke in Starr's Chamber"; Waas, "Starr Minds the Bar." Kenneth Starr was listed in the February 1997 *The Federalist Paper,* the newsletter of the right-wing libertarian Federalist Society for Law and Public Policy Studies, as a founding member of the group's James Madison Club, composed of $1,000 donors. Other donors included the Kirkland & Ellis Foundation, Theodore Olson, C. Boyden Gray, and Alfred Regnery. In 1997 the board of trustees of the Federalist Society included Robert H. Bork, Orrin G. Hatch, Holland H. Coors, C. Boyden Gray, Lois Haight Herrington, Donald Paul Hodel, Harvey C. Koch, Edwin Meese, III, Hugh R. Overholt, and Wm. Bradford Reynolds. Judge David Sentelle, who appointed Starr, was a member of the Federalist Society and spoke at their events. For more details, see Van Natta and Abramson, "Shadow Legal Team." These and other articles outline the cooperative organic network of right-wing political activists with ties to Starr's former Washington law firm Kirkland & Ellis, conservative Republicans, and the Federalist Society.

5. Christopher Ruddy subscription letter for *Vortex,* received on January 5, 1999, on file at Political Research Associates.

6. Melcher, "Culture Wars."

7. Pertman, "Partisan Drama Will Lack Heroes."

8. Nyhan, "Sun Belt Senators Could Get Burned."

9. Ladd, "Why Reporting of the Polls," p. 37.

10. Fitch, "New Poor Laws," p. 29; Christian Parenti, "Crossing Borders"; Lena Williams, "Law Aimed at Terrorists Hits Legal Immigrants"; Martinez, "It's a Terrorist War on Immigrants"; Gage, "Lie"; Lusane, "Lie"; Anthony Lewis, "Crime and Politics"; Purdum, "Clinton Backs Plan to Deter Youthful Violence"; Lawton, "Clinton Signs Law Backing Heterosexual Marriage." Congress later blunted some of the worst features of the 1996 welfare "reform"—especially in regard to immigrants.

11. David Corn, "Wag the Elephant," *American Politics Journal* online, Loyal Opposition column, December 23, 1998, http://www.american-politics.com/122398Corn.html. On NAFTA, see Thea Lee, "Happily Never NAFTA," *Dollars & Sense,* no. 183 (January/February 1993), pp. 12–15; Sarah Anderson, John Cavanagh, and David Ranney, "NAFTA," pp. 26–29. On international treaties, globalization, corporate power, and the World Trade Organization, see Martin Khor, "Colonialism Redux," *The Nation,* vol. 263, no. 3 (July 15/22, 1996), pp. 18–20. On the Balkans, see Jacob Heilbrunn and Mi-

chael Lind, "Third American Empire," *The New York Times,* January 2, 1996, p. A15; On attacks on Afghanistan, Iraq, and the Sudan, see Art Pine, "U.S. Bombs Terrorists: The Surprise Missile Attacks at Sites in Afghanistan and Sudan Are Aimed at the Prime Suspects in Recent U.S. Embassy Bombings," Los Angeles Times News Service, *Portland Press Herald,* August 21, 1998, p. A1, online at Northern Light; Tim Weiner and James Risen, "Decision to Strike Factory in Sudan Based on Surmise," *The New York Times,* September 21, 1998, online at http://www.library.cornell.edu/colldev/mideast/shifa.htm; Tyler Marshall, "More Bombs, Another Bombshell: Missiles Hit Armed Sites For 2nd Day," Los Angeles Times News Service, *Morning Star* (Wilmington, NC), December 18, 1998, online at Northern Light. For a conservative anti-interventionist view, see Andrew J. Bacevich, "Policing Utopia: The Military Imperatives of Globalization," *The National Interest,* Summer 1999, no. 56, p. 5, online at Northern Light. See also Nader, "Greens & the Presidency," pp. 18–19; Joy Gordon, "Sanctions as Siege Warfare."

12. Schell, "Master of All He Surveys."

13. See, generally, Gene Lyons and the Editors of *Harpers, Fools for Scandal.*

14. Ibid., pp. 4–5.

15. Evans-Pritchard, *Secret Life of Bill Clinton,* p. 202.

16. Michael Reagan with Jim Denney *Making Waves.* On One World Government, see pp. 135–147; on proposed Constitutional Convention, see pp. 121–133; on Vince Foster, see pp. 81–118.

17. Memo prepared in 1995 by the White House counsel's office, with attachments, "Communication Stream of Conspiracy Commerce," obtained from the White House Press Office First revealed by editorial writer Micah Morrison in *Wall Street Journal,* January 6, 1997. See ultraconservative criticism of the memo in "Who's Shooting the Messenger Now?" *Media Watch,* March 1997.

18. Hoffman, "Whitewater and Oklahoma City."

19. See Kintz and Lesage, eds., *Media, Culture, and the Religious Right,* which includes a chapter by author Berlet, "Who's Mediating the Storm?," from which some material in this section is taken. See Perkins, *Logic and Mr. Limbaugh,* for dubious nature of some information.

20. Robert Manning, "Dancing With Snakes."

21. This section on Drudge is based largely on the reporting of Shephard, "Scandal Unfolds."

22. Isikoff, *Uncovering Clinton.*

23. Kurtz, "When Cyber-Gossip Meets Stodgy Old Libel Laws."

24. Cuprisin, "This Drudge muck won't stick either."

25. David Horowitz, "Drudge Affair and Its Ripple Effect."

26. http://cspc.org/drudge/mdinfo.htm, January 1, 1999.

27. Matt Drudge, "The Media Should Apologize," address before the Wednesday Morning Club, September 10, 1998, http://www.frontpagemag.com/archives/drudge/wmcspeech.htm, January 1, 1999.

28. Review of archives of Schlafly's columns online at http://www.eagleforum.org/column/, "Lifesaver Bomb," August 10, 1995.

29. Kennedy direct mail on file at People for the American Way, Washington, DC.

30. Michelmore, "Right Wingers Claim"; Gullo, "Wealthy Clinton Foe Lets His Money Do the Talking."

31. Weiner, "One Source, Many Ideas in Foster Case."

32. Rothmyer, "Citizen Scaife"; Warner, "Scaife."

33. Kaiser and Chinoy, "How Scaife's Money Powered a Movement."

34. Ibid.

35. On GOPAC, see Nurith Aizenman, *Washington Monthly*, July–August 1997, p. 28. On the Jury Association, see Crawford, Gardner, Mozzochi, and Taylor, *Northwest Imperative*, pp. 2.11–2.19. On the Maldon Institute, see Birch, "Master of the Politics of Paranoia."

36. PFAW online, citing the *Washington Post*, March 16, 1997. On Judicial Watch and Chinagate, see "Clinton-Battling Lawyer Loses Case," Associated Press, October 5, 1998, online; Judicial Watch direct-mail fund-raising letter, received January 29, 1999, on file at Political Research Associates.

37. Evans-Pritchard, *Secret Life of Bill Clinton*, p. 210.

38. Ball, "Newt Has Doubts." Associated Press, "Gingrich 'Not Convinced' White House Aide's Death Was Suicide," July 25, 1995, online.

39. For example, *Human Events* promoted Ann Coulter's book from Regnery, and the Western Journalism Center promoted Ruddy's work.

40. Brock, "Confessions of a Right-Wing Hit Man."

41. Rempel, "Trooper Changes His Story."

42. This story was broken by Joe Conason, Karen Gullo, Murray Waas, and Jonathan Broder; see below. For summaries, see John Mintz, "A Cloud Over Starr Witness," *Washington Post*, April 19, 1998, p. A1, http://www.washingtonpost.com/wp-srv/politics/special/clinton/stories/arkansas041998.htm; Robert Scheer, "Now It's Starr Who Needs to Be Investigated," Online Journalism Review, http://ojr.usc.edu/indexf.htm?/sections/editorial/98_stories/commentaries_scheer_033198.htm.

43. Early articles by Joe Conason, who obtained the public tax records documenting the Arkansas Project, appeared in *The New York Observer*. On tax records, see Conason, "Scaife Paid $1.7 in *Spectator* 'Legal Fees.'" See also Joe Conason with Murray Waas, "Richard Scaife Paid for Dirt on Clinton in 'Arkansas Project,'" *New York Observer*, February 9, 1998, p. 1. Online, Conason's work can be found at *Salon* magazine, sometimes coauthored with Jonathan Broder or Murray Waas. See Jonathan Broder and Joe Conason, "The American Spectator's Funny Money," June 8, 1998; and "A Clinton Critic's Tax-exempt Lifestyle," June 9, 1998, at http://www.salonmagazine.com/news/special/clinton/date.html.

44. Karen Gullo, "Key Whitewater Witness Wooed By Conservatives," Associated Press, in *The Columbian* online, March 5, 1998; "Starr Gets OK To Probe Whether Whitewater Witness Received Money," Associated Press online, April 10, 1998; Michael Haddigan, "On the Trail of Trapper Dozhier: Another strange tale from the wilds of Whitewater," *Arkansas Times*, May 22, 1998.

45. Jonathan Broder and Murray Waas, "Road to Hale," *Salon* magazine, 3/17/98 http://www.salonmagazine.com/news/1998/03/cov_17news.html.

46. Farrell, "Whitewater Is Taking a Twist Against Starr."

47. Joe Conason, "Now Clinton's Foes Could Be Disgraced," *The New York Observer*, August 31, 1998, p. 5, online at http://www.vcol.net/democrat/ny.htm; Karen Gullo, "Whitewater Tampering Probe Begins," Associated Press, online, August 21, 1998.

48. Scaife-related foundation records, online at the *Washington Post*, http://www.washingtonpost.com/wp-srv/politics/special/clinton/stories/scaife050299.htm; Waas and Broder, "Ties That Bind."

49. Sweet, "Chicago Man Paid Clinton Troopers." See also Farrell, "Whitewater Is Taking a Twist against Starr."

50. http://www.citizensunited.org/, March 13, 1999.

51. Lieberman, "Churning Whitewater." Francis Shane is technically the publisher of Citizens United's specialty political periodical, *ClintonWatch*.

52. Jouzaitis, "From The Folks Who Brought You."

53. On Kincaid's biography, see http://www.citizensunited.org/about/bios/cliffkincaid.html. On Patriot support, see http://www.freedomlaw.com/PatrMedia.html, 3/13/99; http://www.rightbooks.net, May 1, 2000; http://www.radioliberty.com/books.htm, May 1, 2000. Kincaid's books include *Global Taxes for World Government* and *Global Bondage* His online reports include *Report on the International Criminal Court* and *The Pan Am 103 Terrorism Trial*, http://www.usasurvival.org, May 1, 2000. For more on Kincaid, see Berlet, *Hunt for Red Menace*. Kincaid, "Far Left Sparks Anti-War Protests," *Human Events*, February 9, 1991, p. 4.

54. http://www.citizensunited.org/about/bios/michaelboos.html. For more information on Boos, see Berlet, *Hunt for Red Menace*.

55. Floyd G. Brown, *"Slick Willie."*

56. Ibid., p. 76.

57. Bio including cite to the Horton ad from http://www.citizensunited.org/about/bios/floydbrown.html, March 13, 1999. On Horton, see David C. Anderson, *Crime and the Politics of Hysteria*. Willie Horton, a Black man, was a convicted murderer imprisoned in Massachusetts who in 1987 escaped during a routine 48-hour furlough. Horton traveled to Maryland where he assaulted a White couple in their suburban home, brutally raping the woman while the man was tied up in the basement. During the 1988 presidential campaign, Brown produced a vivid ad using racist images that essentially blamed the rape on Massachusetts Governor Michael Dukakis and his liberal policies. Democrat Dukakis was facing Republican Bush in the presidential race. In fact, the furlough program had been implemented during the administration of a Republican governor, and had been shown to reduce recidivism among released prisoners.

58. Floyd G. Brown, *"Slick Willie,"* pp. 87–88, 99–107.

59. Andrew Ferguson, "You Won't Believe This."

60. Jouzaitis, "From the Folks Who Brought You."

61. Lieberman, "Churning Whitewater."

62. Jouzaitis, "From the Folks Who Brought You."

63. http://www.freerepublic.com/forum/a1001605.htm, citing New York Times News Service, "House and Senate panels have different agendas in their fund-raising inquiries," April 7, 1997.

64. Clines, "Rep. Dan Burton."

65. Matrisciana, ed., *Clinton Chronicles Book*, appendix 32.

66. Weiner and Abramson, "Clinton Foes Have Ties."

67. Matrisciana, ed., *Clinton Chronicles Book*, pp. 141–142.

68. Berlet, "Big Stories, Spooky Sources"; Snepp, "Brenneke Exposed." See also, Snepp, "Last Rites." For a view from the Right, "'October Surprise' Unravels: Nightline and Frontline Caught in Hoax," *Mediawatch*, November 1991, p. 1, online archive.

69. For more on Terry, see Corn, "Contract on Bill."

70. Ibid., p. 2. *Citizens Intelligence Digest*, 4809 Phoenix Dr., Chesapeake, VA, 23321.

71. Falwell material on file at Americans United for Separation of Church and State, Washington, DC.

72. In addition, there were a few articles critical of specific Clinton administration policies, particularly on gays and abortion, and a few articles critical of the Democratic Party.

73. *National Liberty Journal*, December 1998 (on the Black Caucus); and November 1997 (on the "Lesbian Nun").

74. Falwell fund-raising letter, December 1998, on file at Political Research Associates.

75. Marrs, *Big Sister Is Watching You.*

76. http://www.texemarrs.com/archive/may98/esther.htm. See also "Monica A Modern Queen Esther?" *Jewish Week*, January 13, 1998, online.

Notes to Chapter 16

1. Sonja Barisic, "Falwell: Antichrist May Be Alive," Associated Press, January 16, 1999, online at Northern Light; "Falwell Claims Anti-Christ Probably Alive Today," Evangelical Press News Service, no date, posted on *Maranatha Christian Journal*, http://www.mcjonline.com/news/news3013.htm.

2. Gould, *Questioning the Millennium.* Gould also examines the difference between "millenarian" groups and "millennial" expectation.

3. Yemma, "Countdown to Catastrophe," citing research by Richard Landes of Boston University and Charles B. Strozier, professor of history at John Jay College in New York.

4. Barkun, "Politics and Apocalypticism."

5. On background of apocalypticism, see note 22 for the Introduction. For apocalypticism and antiabortion violence, see Carol Mason, *Fundamental Opposition; Fetal Legislation, Killing for Life*, "Minority Unborn," "Cracked Babies and the Partial Birth of a Nation," and "From Protest to Retribution."

6. Lamy, *Millennium Rage*, pp. 86–88.

7. For ongoing detailed coverage of these diverse forms see the quarterly *Millennial Prophecy Report*, Millennium Watch Institute, POB 34021, Philadelphia, PA 19101-4021.

Useful introductory anthologies are Robbins and Palmer, eds., *Millennium, Messiahs, and Mayhem*; and Strozier and Flynn, *The Year* 2000.

For handy guides, see Clouse, Hosack, and Pierard, *New Millennium Manual*; and Gould, *Questioning the Millennium*. See also "On the Millennium," a collection of articles in *Deolog*, Feb. 1997, online, http://www.stealth.net/~deolog/297.html.

Discussions at the Center for Millennial Studies in 1998 focused on the following topics: authorities in Israel are making plans for dealing with devout Christians expected to flock to Jerusalem and other sites to await (or perhaps encourage) the second coming of Christ; apocalyptic Christians, Muslims, and Jews covet the Temple Mount; and messianic Jews are looking for the flawless "red heifer" of ancient prophecy.

8. Cooper, *Behold a Pale Horse.*

9. O'Leary, "Heaven's Gate and the Culture of Popular Millennialism." Nostradamus was a sixteenth-century prophet who utilized astrological charts and visions in writing a prehistory of the world, making predictions about events centuries in advance. The text, written in quatrains, is obscure and ambiguous. There are many published commentaries claiming to unravel their meaning. One major prediction was the arrival of a great comet. His predictions do not go beyond the year 2000. On the renewed popularity of Nostradamus, see, for example, Roberts, *Complete Prophesies of Nostradamus*; Paulus, *Nostradamus 1999*; and de Fontbrune, *Nostradamus: Countdown to Apocalypse*. A contemporary treatment of the comet prophecy is Kay, *When the Comet Runs.*

10. Damian Thompson, *End of Time*; Jeffrey Kaplan, *Radical Religion in America*.

11. See, for example, Herman, *Antigay Agenda*; Males, *Scapegoat Generation*; Debra L. Schultz, *To Reclaim a Legacy of Diversity*; Messer-Davidow "Manufacturing the Attack"; Kelsey and Texeira, "*Scapegoating at the End of the Millennium*.

12. Lindsey with Carlson, *Late Great Planet Earth*.

13. See the analysis of Lindsey in O'Leary, *Arguing the Apocalypse*, pp. 134–171; and Katz and Popkin, *Messianic Revolution*, pp. 205–216.

14. Lindsey, *Planet Earth—2000 A.D.*

15. Graham, *Approaching Hoofbeats*, pp. 222–224.

16. Johnson, *Architects of Fear*, pp. 28–29; Knelman, *Reagan, God and the Bomb*, pp. 175–190; Paul Boyer, *When Time Shall Be No More*, p. 162.

17. Halsell, *Prophecy and Politics*. For a Christian manual on how to survive the nuclear Armageddon through bomb shelters, see Robinson and North, *Fighting Chance*.

18. Mouly, *Religious Right and Israel*.

19. Lamy, *Millennium Rage*, p. 155. See also Paul Boyer, *When Time Shall Be No More*, pp. 327–331; Daniels, ed., *Doomsday Reader*.

20. Sara Diamond, "Political Millennialism," p. 210.

21. December 1998 Falwell fund-raising letter, on file at Political Research Associates.

22. Paul Boyer, *When Time Shall Be No More*, pp. 148–149, 327; referencing Walvoord, *Armageddon, Oil And The Middle East Crisis*.

23. Sara Diamond, *Not by Politics Alone*, pp 200–201.

24. Quinby, symposium presentation, "The Millennial Cusp: Western Cultures at 1000, 1500, 2000 and Beyond," sponsored by the Center for Millennial Studies, Boston, October 12, 1996. In the classic science fiction film *Five Million Years to Earth* an ancient Martian spaceship is unearthed at the aptly named Hobbes End Underground station in London. When its passenger comes to life, it appears as the Devil, complete with little horns. A women falls under its spell and, using superhuman powers supplied by the Devil, attempts to stop the male heroes planning to block the fiery apocalypse using logic and science.

25. *Catholic Study Bible*, commentary on Revelation, p. 399.

26. See, generally, Camp, *Selling Fear*.

27. "Armageddon Books," Cliffside Publishing House, General Catalog, Fall/Winter 1996; http://www.armageddonbooks.com, November 13, 1998. The first book in the Left Behind series is LaHaye and Jenkins, *Left Behind: A Novel of the Earth's Last Days: Vol. 1*. Other novels are Mike Hyatt and George Grant, *Y2K, the Day the World Shut Down*; Paul D. Meier, *The Third Millennium: A Novel* (Nashville, TN: Thomas Nelson, 1993); Paul D. Meier and Robert L. Wise, *The Fourth Millennium: The Sequel* (Nashville, TN: Thomas Nelson, 1996); Larry Burkett, *The Illuminati: A Novel* (Nashville, TN: Thomas Nelson, 1991); Burkett, *The Thor Conspiracy: The Seventy-Hour Countdown to Disaster* (Nashville, TN: Thomas Nelson, 1996); and Pat Robertson, *The End of the Age: A Novel* (Dallas: Word Publishing, 1995).

28. On Seland, http://www.raptureready.com/rap34.html; on Stranberg, http://www.novia.net/~todd/rap49.html; both retrieved August 1999. On the LaLondes' Apocalypse videos, http://www.cloudtenpictures.com/, retrieved May 6, 2000.

29. Damian Thompson, *End of Time*, p. 29.

30. Ibid.

31. Sara Diamond, "Political Millennialism," pp. 206–210.

32. Quinby, "Coercive Purity," pp. 154–156.

33. Fenn, *End of Time*, pp. 127–149.

34. Khan, *Calculated Compassion*.

35. Conversations with Fred Clarkson, Russ Bellant, and Al Ross shaped this discussion.

36. Solomon, "Mass Media are Boosting Promise Keepers."

37. Novosad, "God Squad"; Pharr, "Match Made in Heaven."

38. Janssen and Weeden, eds., *Seven Promises of a Promise Keeper* ; Gregg Lewis, *Power of the Promise Kept*.

39. Berkowitz, "Promise Keepers."

40. Ferrini Productions, *10.4.97 Promise Keepers*, video; interviews by author Berlet at Promise Keepers Mall rally.

41. "Vision 2000: Frequent Questions," and related updates, official PK web site, www.promisekeepers.org, July 17, 1998.

42. Bellant, "Promise Keepers."

43. Ibid.

44. Gardiner, "Promises to Keep"; Kintz, *Between Jesus and the Market*, pp. 111–139; Connie Anderson, *Visions of Involved Fatherhood*. Some of this discussion is based on the roundtable on the Promise Keepers, with papers presented by Mary Stricker, Amy Schindler, and Jennifer Carrol Lena; R. Lorraine Bernotsky and Joan M. Bernotsky, with discussion leader Jennifer Reich, at the annual meeting, American Sociological Association, San Francisco, 1998.

45. Interview with Promise Keepers leader Randy Phillips on *Late Edition*, CNN, October 5, 1997, from transcript, p. 9.

46. Quinby, "Coercive Purity," pp. 154–156. On how conservative evangelical women can find spheres of influence and agency within the constraints of submission, see Brasher, *Fundamentalism and Female Power*. Morin and Wilson, "Men Were Driven to 'Confess Their Sins'"; Christian Smith, *Christian America?*, pp. 160–191. This section of Smith's book was written with Melinda Lundquist. For a feminist critique that dismisses the political content of the Promise Keepers movement, see Judith Newton, "White Guys," *Feminist Studies*, vol. 24, no. 3, Fall, 1998, p. 572. On the larger issue of women in Christian subcultures, see Wessinger, *Religious Institutions and Women's Leadership*. On broad liberal misconceptions about evangelicals and conservatives, see Brinkley, *Liberalism and Its Discontents*, pp. 266–297.

Christian Right demonization of gays and lesbians in much the same style as anticommunism and anti-Semitism demonization is described in Herman, *Antigay Agenda*. See also Hardisty, "Constructing Homophobia," pp. 86–104; Arlene Stein, *When the Culture War Comes to Town*, and "Whose Memories? Whose Victimhood?"; and Khan, *Calculated Compassion*.

47. Find charges and response at URL: http://www.saintsalive.com/mormonism/nccj.htm.

48. This is the same Jeremiah Films that made the *Clinton Chronicles* video.

49. Church on the Web, Video List, URL: http://www.churchontheweb.com/bookshop/paganinvasion/8.html.

50. Paul Boyer, lecture and seminar, Boston University, November 12, 1998.

51. ISRP web page, URL: http://www.isrp.org/welcome.html, October 6, 1998.

52. Hunt, *Global Peace and the Rise of Antichrist*; Peter LaLonde, *One World Under Anti-*

Christ; William T. James and others, eds., *Foreshocks of Antichrist*; Froese, *How Democracy Will Elect the Antichrist*.

53. Cover story and series of articles on Y2K from a Christian perspective by Joel Belz, Roy Manard, Chris Stamper, and Lynn Vincent, in *World* (God's World Publications), August 22, 1998. See also: "Y2K: Playing the Millennium Card," *Culture Watch* (The DataCenter), September 1998, for a very useful roundup on the topic.

54. Berlet, "Y2K and Millennial Pinball"; Southern Poverty Law Center, "Y2Kaos."

55. Author Berlet attended the workshop.

56. Michael S. Hyatt, *Millennium Bug*.

57. Michael S. Hyatt's website had a special message for Christians as part of a promotional strategy, http://www.michaelhyatt.com/christians.htm. Jerry Falwell, Pat Robertson, Larry Burkett, Jack Van Impe, and many other Christian evangelical leaders added apocalyptic fuel to the Y2K furnace; see, for example, Falwell's video, *Y2K: A Christian's Guide to the Millennium Bug*, online, http://www.otgh.org/otgh_site/offers/y2k.html; see also the site maintained by the Inspiration Network, http://www.insp.org/y2k/.

58. http://www.garynorth.com.

59. Robinson and North, *Fighting Chance*.

60. Behreandt, "Millennium Mayhem"; Froese, "Great Y2K Hoax."

61. Clarkson, "Out on the Fringes."

62. Rosin, "God's Hit Man," p. 118. See also Alexander-Moegerle, *James Dobson's War on America*. This paragraph appeared in Berlet, "Following the Threads."

63. Heilbrunn, "Neocon v. Theocon."

64. See for example, E. Michael Jones, "Summer of '65." On ultratraditionalist Catholics, see Cuneo, *Smoke of Satan*; on ultratraditionalist Protestants, especially the influence of Bob Jones University, see Dalhouse, *Island in the Lake of Fire*; on the nationalist tradition in Protestantism, see Vinz, *Pulpit Politics*. An early glimpse of this trend is in Stan, "Power Preying."

65. Rosin, "God's Hit Man," pp. 118–119; Clarkson, *Eternal Hostility*, pp. 33, 104–106, 117–119, 153.

66. Author Berlet purchased curricular materials during a tour of Summit Ministries in 1997, which are on file at Political Research Associates.

67. *Christian Anti-Communism Crusade*, newsletter, April 1, 1998, p. 2.

68. Noebel, *Understanding the Times*.

69. Documentation, including correspondence between Welch, his aide, and a donor outlining the procedure, at Political Research Associates in the file "John Birch Society, Nonprofit Funding Conduits." See Degette, "Devil Inside."

70. Blumenfeld, "Strange, Irrational World."

71. "Conservative TV Network Fires Founder Weyrich," *The Boston Sunday Globe*, November 9, 1997.

72. Grann, "Robespierre of the Right"; Heilbrunn, "Neocon v. Theocon."

73. Letter by Paul Weyrich, dated February 16, 1999, posted online at http://www.freecongress.org/fcf/specials/weyrichopenltr.htm.

74. See the symposium with Weyrich, Dobson, and Pate, "Q: Should conservatives refocus their energies away from politics?" in *Insight*, March 26, 1999, pp. 24–27.

75. Weyrich, "Creating a New Society." George W. Bush advisor Mavin Olasky is editor of *World* magazine where he promotes compassionate conservatism.

76. Weyrich, "Creating a New Society."

77. Author Berlet attended the workshop.

78. Thomas and Dobson, *Blinded by Might;* see http://www.zondervan.com/blindedbymight/index.htm.

79. Sally Macdonald and Carol M. Ostrom, "How White Supremacists See It." See also Kirsten Scharnberg, Evan Osnos, and David Mendell, "The Making of a Racist," *Chicago Tribune,* July 25, 1999; Douglas Holt, "State panel charges [Matt] Hale endorsed hate shootings," *Chicago Tribune,* October 30, 1999; Kirsten Scharnberg, "Smith's Legacy of Hate, Fear Emerge," *Chicago Tribune,* January 3, 2000; online archive. See also the books by Church of the Creator founder Ben Klassen.

80. Stacy Finz, "Brothers Charged in Slaying of Gay Couple," *San Francisco Chronicle,* July 20, 1999; Lynda Gledhill, "Shasta Brothers Indicted in Synagogue Fires," *San Francisco Chronicle,* March 18, 2000, online at Northern Light. Associated Press, "Supremacists Accused of Synagogue Arsons," March 18, 2000, in the *Salt Lake Tribune,* online.

81. Vivienne Walt, "L.A. Killer's 'Wake-Up Call to America to Kill Jews,'" *Salon* online, August 11, 1999.

82. Sally Macdonald and Carol M. Ostrom, "How White Supremacists See It," cited above.

83. Hoag Levins and David Eberhart, *The Hunt for Eric Rudolph: An Enigma and Bomb Suspect Disappears,* APBnews.com, May 6, 2000, http://207.87.13.63/newscenter/majorcases/rudolph/index.html. Federal indictment of Eric Rudolph.

84. Jo Thomas, "New Face of Terror Crimes: 'Lone Wolf' Weaned on Hate," *New York Times,* August 16, 1999, online archive.

85. Based on an analysis of government statistics that first appeared as Berlet, "Countering Genocidal and Hate Movements." On Byrd and Shephard, see Rich "Road to Laramie."

86. FBI Report, *Project Megiddo,* http://www.fbi.gov/library/megiddo/publicmegiddo.pdf; ADL Report, *Y2K Paranoia: Extremists Confront the Millennium,* http://www.adl.org/frames/front_y2k.html. Both retrieved in December 1999. "ADL Report on Y2K Made Available to Meeting of International Association of Chiefs of Police," U.S. Newswire, November 1, 1999, online at Northern Light. There were reporters who wrote accurately on the two reports; see, for example, Brad Knickerbocker, "FBI turns watchful eye to doomsday cults," *Christian Science Monitor,* November 5, 1999, online.

87. In an academic setting the ADL report would be considered plagiarism of work by Norman Cohn, Robert Fuller, Paul Boyer, Philip Lamy, Damian Thompson, the Southern Poverty Law Center, and others.

88. Kevin Johnson, "FBI: Militias a threat at millennium," *USA Today,* October 20, 1999, online archive; FBI press release dated October 20, 1999.

89. "'Project Megiddo' Report," Memoranda from the Free Congress Foundation, dated November 17, 1999, with 31 signatures, online at http://www.freecongress.org/centers/technology/memo991117.htm.

90. Jeffrey Kaplan, *Radical Religion in America,* pp. 127–163; Berlet and Lyons, "One Key to Litigating"; Berlet, "Three Models for Analyzing"; de Armond, "Time for New Beginnings." These are serious critiques, not to be confused with the charges made by the John Birch Society, Laird Wilcox, and others on the Hard Right; see William Norman Grigg, "Propagandizing the Police," *The New American,* vol. 15, no. 23, November 8, 1999, pp. 16–23, online at http://www.thenewamerican.com/tna/1999/11-08-99/vo15no23_police.htm; Robert Stacy McCain, "Researcher says hate 'fringe' isn't as crowded as claimed, *The Washington Times,* May 9, 2000, online edition. Other groups

criticized include the American Jewish Committee, Center for Democratic Renewal, and Political Research Associates, which employs author Berlet.

91. Berlet and Lyons, "One Key to Litigating"; Berlet, "Three Models for Analyzing." On government surveillance, see David Cole, "Spying on Hate," *Cal Law*, September 1, 1999, online at http://www.callaw.com/weekly/last906.html; For other examples, see Daniel Kurtzman, "Behind the headlines: Amtrak Derailment Prompts New Calls For Anti-Terror Laws," Jewish Telegraphic Agency, 10-11-1995, online at Electric Library; "ADL Commends Reno and Freeh for Vigilance in Fight against Extremism on Anniversary of Oklahoma City Bombing and Waco Tragedy and Urges Expanded Role for Anti-Terrorism Task Forces," press release, Anti-Defamation League, April 16, 1998, online at http://206.3.178.10/PresRele/Militi_71/3142_71.html; "ADL Applauds Guilty Verdict in Mcveigh Trial Calls for Legislation to Protect against Terrorism on Our Soil," press release, Anti-Defamation League, June 2, 1997, online at http://206.3.178.10/PresRele/Militi_71/2991_71.html.

92. See, for example, both sides of the debate in Winters, *Hate Crimes*; and a good short overview, James Corcoran, "Monitoring Hate Groups," *Encarta Encyclopedia 99*; online update. From a libertarian perspective, see Jacobs and Potter, *Hate Crimes*; and Andrew Sullivan, "What's So Bad About Hate?," *New York Times Magazine*, September 26, 1999, pp. 50–57+. From a left perspective, see Janet R. Jakobsen, "Why Hate Crimes Legislation Won't Work," *Sojourner*, August 1999; Richard Kim, "The Truth about Hate Crimes Laws," *The Nation*, July 12, 1999, p. 20. For background, see Jenness and Broad, *Hate Crimes*; Altschiller, *Hate Crimes*; Jenness, Ferber, Grattet, with Short, "Hate in America: What Do We Know?" Defenders of hate crimes laws include Brian Levin, "Hate Crimes: Worse by Definition"; Herek and Berrill, eds., *Hate Crimes*; and Jack Levin and Jack McDevitt, *Hate Crimes*.

93. Associated Press, "Perot May Not Address Reform Party," *The New York Times*, online, May 8, 2000. Minnesota Governor Jesse Ventura left the Reform Party citing the internal battles; see Maria Recio, "Fractured Reform Party at crossroads: Perot, Ventura factions create a 'circuslike atmosphere,'" *The Fort Worth Star-Telegram*, January 18, 2000, online at Northern Light.

94. Patrick J. Buchanan, speech to the Chicago Council on Foreign Relations, Chicago, November 18, 1998, online.

95. Joe Conason, "Invasion of the body snatchers," *Salon* online, November 16, 1999, http://www.salon.com/news/col/cona/1999/11/16/fulani/index.html; David Grann, "What You Don't Know about Lenora Fulani Could Hurt You," *New Republic*, December 13, 1999, http://www.tnr.com/121399/coverstory121399.html; Thomas B. Edsall, "The Leftists in the Center: Reform Party's Fulani, Newman Rise to Prominence by Supporting Buchanan's Bid," *Washington Post*, March 15, 2000, p. A6.

96. Berlet, *Clouds Blur the Rainbow*.

97. Lenora Fulani, "Black Empowerment: What Does The New Populism Mean For African-Americans?," originally posted online circa February 1996, http://www.publiceye.org/Sucker_Punch/Fulani_2.html.

98. Bruce Shapiro, "Buchanan-Fulani: New Team? *The Nation*, November 1, 1999, online archive.

99. Charles Barron, "Black Folk, Reject Fulani and Buchanan!," The Black World Today, November 22, 1999, http://www.tbwt.com/views/feat/feat1628.asp.

100. Allen Hunter, "Globalization from Below?"; Mark Rupert, "Globalization and the Reconstruction of Common Sense."

101. In 1999 the Patriot-oriented Chenoweth married Nevada rancher Wayne Hage, a right-wing "Sagebrush Rebellion," activist who opposed federal land regulations. See Pat Murphy, "The Perfect Couple," *Idaho Mountain Express*, July 7–13, 1999, http://www.mtexpress.com; "American Jewish Committee Urges Rep. Chenoweth-Hage to Withdraw Invitation to John Birch Society," press release, American Jewish Committee, February 01, 2000, U. S. Newswire, online at Northern Light; Helen Chenoweth-Hage, "Don't Give Up the Canal!" *The New American*, vol. 15, no. 25, December 6, 1999, online archive. On Smith, see Holly Ramer, "GOP Defector Smith Seeks Taxpayers Party Nod," Associated Press, *Boston Globe*, August 11, 1999, p. A13.

102. Doug Henwood, "1.75 cheers for Ralph," *Left Business Observer*, no. 74, October 1996, online archive. On right/left populism see Boggs, *End of Politics*, pp. 123–165; and, in Canada, Harrison, *Of Passionate Intensity*, pp. 250–260.

103. Talbot comments posted on http://www.primarydiner.com retrieved on September 27, 1999.

104. Ryan Lizza, "Silent Partner"; Conniff, "Left-Right Romance."

105. Derber, *Corporation Nation*; Korten, *When Corporations Rule the World*; Mander and Goldsmith, eds., *Case Against the Global Economy*; Greider, *Secrets of the Temple*; *Who Will Tell the People*. Author Berlet challenged Nader and Derber (panelists at the American Sociological Association annual meeting, August 2000, Washington, DC) to publicly speak out against the xenophobia and racial nationalism of the Buchananites, and they did not.

106. Doug Henwood, "Antiglobalization," *Left Business Observer*, no. 71, January 1996, online at http://www.panix.com/~dhenwood/Globalization.html; Kovel, "Beyond Populism."

107. Berlet, *Right Woos Left*, "Friendly Fascists," *Fascism's Franchises*, *Mad as Hell*; Ramos, "Feint to the Left"; Mozzochi and Rhinegard, *Rambo, Gnomes and the New World Order*; Novick, "Front Man for Fascism."

108. James Murray, "Chiapas & Montana"; Adam Parfrey, "Finding Our Way Out of Oklahoma," *Alternative Press Review*, Winter 1996, pp. 60–67, especially pp. 63, 67 (reprinted from Adam Parfrey, ed., *Cult Rapture* [Portland, OR: Feral House, 1995]).

109. Michael Kelly, "Road to Paranoia," pp. 62–63. For an example, see Art Bell and Jennifer L. Osborne, *Quickening*. See Michael Parenti, *Dirty Truths*, for a defense of conspiracy analysis.

110. Berlet, "Who's Mediating the Storm?;" Alter, "Age of Conspiracism"; Yemma, "Science vs. Fiction"; Rosen, "What's Behind the Obsession with Conspiracies?" For an interesting treatment of hoax documents and internet conspiracism, see the discussion in *Perforations* 2 at http://www.pd.org/topos/theory/perf-frame.html.

111. "Conspiracy Theories," *UFO: A Forum on Extraordinary Theories and Phenomena*, special two-part series of articles, vol. 7, no. 3, 1992; vol. 7, no. 4, 1992.

112. See Ward, ed., *Conspiracies*. This discussion was informed by de Armond, *Out on an Alleged, Conspiracy Theorists take a Leap of Faith*. For a very conservative view of conspiracism, see Pipes, *Hidden Hand*, and *Conspiracy*.

113. Tony Brown, *Empower the People*, pp. 230, 241–242.

114. Gilbert, "AIDS"; Karen Grigsby Gates, "Is it Genocide?"

115. Kalman and Murray, "Icke Man Cometh"; Damian Thompson, "Gaia Anti-Christ and the Ex-Files: A Trawl through the Cultic Milieu," lecture, Kingston University, March 5, 1997, http://www.kingston.ac.uk/cusp/Lectures/Thompson.htm; Derek Wall, "Darker Shades of Green," *Red Pepper*, no date, online archive, http://www.redpepper.org.uk/cularch/xdkgreen.html; Will Offley, "David Icke and the Politics of

Madness: Where the New Age Meets the Third Reich," online essay, February 29, 2000, http://www.publiceye.org/Icke/IckeBackgrounder.htm.

116. "David Icke—Anti-Semitic or Just Naive?" *Green World*, British Green Party, 1995 statement reproduced by Green Party of Ontario at http://www.flora.org/flora.action-forum/742, retrieved May 1, 2000; "Greens to Protest David Icke at Hart House Theatre, October 6," press release, Green Party of Ontario; "David Icke: Part of the Problem, Not the Solution," leaflet produced by Green Party Anti-Racist and Anti-Fascist Network; both online at http://www.flora.org/flora.action-forum/742, retrieved May 1, 2000. See also Biehl and Staudenmaier, *Ecofascism*.

117. In addition to those cited above (Berlet of Political Research Associates; Ramos, of the Western States Center; Mozzochi and Rhinegard of the Coalition for Human Dignity; and Novick of People Against Racist Terror), a number of progressive voices were raised against the growing recruitment within the Left by the Right, including author Sara Diamond; researcher Richard Hatch; Erwin Knoll, editor of the *Progressive*; author Holly Sklar; journalist David Barsamian, of Alternative Radio; Tom Burghardt of the Bay Area Coalition for Our Reproductive Rights; Hank Roth of the online Progressive News and Views; Michael Albert of *Z Magazine*; and columnist Joel Bleifus of *In These Times*; among others. See also Barsamian, "Militias and Conspiracy Theories"; Givel, "Progressive Populism and Conspiracy Theories," "Conspiracy Thinking, Part II"; Albert, "Conspiracy? . . . Not!," "Conspiracy? . . . Not, Again."

118. Biehl, "Militia Fever," citing Alexander Cockburn, "Who's Left? Who's Right?" Beat the Devil column, *Nation*, June 12, 1995, p. 820; and Jason McQuinn, "Conspiracy Theory vs. Alternative Journalism?" *Alternative Press Review*, Winter 1996, p. 2.

119. Mozzochi and Rhinegard, *Rambo, Gnomes and the New World Order*, p. 1.

120. Michael Paulson, "WTO Meets Amid Real Splits Opponents Outside, Divisions Within Promise Raucous Week," *Seattle Post-Intelligencer*, November 30, 1999, p. A1; "Violent Images Tarnish Orderly WTO Protesters," editorial, *Seattle Post-Intelligencer*, January 10, 2000, p. A5; online at Newslibrary.

121. Southern Poverty Law Center, "'Neither Left Nor Right.'"

122. The report did not make these claims, and in fact carried a number of cautions and caveats apparently ignored by many readers, but author Berlet heard the report interpreted incorrectly by several law enforcement officials and their consultants.

123. John Ward Anderson, "Poor Nations' Leaders Back Washington Protesters; Group Says IMF and World Bank Policies 'Stabilized Poverty,'" *Washington Post*, April 16, 2000, p. A31; Henry Allen, "That Was Then, This Is Now; In Today's Revolution, Internet Takes the Place of Leadership," *Washington Post*, Friday, April 14, 2000, p. C1, online archive. On police abuse, see Terry J. Allen, "Breaking Law to Keep Order."

124. Thomas L. Friedman, "America's Labor Pains" *The New York Times*, online, May 9, 2000.

125. An example of this was Lizza, "Silent Partner."

126. J. Sakai, "Aryan Politics & Fighting the W.T.O." from *Review of Anti-Fascism*, May, 2000, online at http://www.savanne.ch/right-left-materials/sakai-aryanwto.html.

127. "De Fabel van de illegaal quits Dutch anti-MAI campaign," posted July 1999, and archived at http://www.savanne.ch/right-left-materials/no-more-anti-mai.html.

128. David Postman, "Buchanan on same side as liberals," *Seattle Times*, November 29, 1999, online archive. See also Mark S., "The Progressive Left's Dirty Little Secret: Public Citizen, IFG and the Far Right," http://www.tao.ca/~resist/theleftsdirtylittlesecret.html, retrieved May 1, 2000.

129. http://www.savanne.ch/right-left.html, May 1, 2000; see also the similar site maintained by author Berlet for Political Research Associates at http://www.publiceye.org/Sucker_Punch/Clueless.html.

130. This continuity and other trends were in part predicted by Rozell and Wilcox, eds., in *God at the Grassroots*, pp. 253–262. See, generally, Sara Diamond, *Not by Politics Alone;* Wilcox, *Onward Christian Soldiers;* Oldfield, *Right and the Righteous;* Smidt and Penning, *Sojourners in the Wilderness.*

131. Brinkley, *Liberalism and Its Discontents*, pp. 277–297; Christian Smith, *Christian America?*, pp. 193–196.

132. David Nyhan, "Yes I'm Voting for McCain," *The Boston Globe*, February 16, 2000, p. A23; Huffington, *How to Overthrow the Government*, excerpted online at http://www.overthrowthegov.com/home.htm.

133. Boggs, *End of Politics*. For an extensive treatment of the alienation of men in America, see Faludi, *Stiffed*.

134. Langman, "Fascism and the Feast of Fools," p. 12.

135. Lee, "Fascist Response To Globalization." For more on the political Right in Europe and elsewhere, see Betz, *Radical Right-wing Populism in Western Europe;* Betz and Immerfall, eds., *New Politics of the Right*. For books on neofascism, see note 3 for Chapter 13.

136. Scatamburlo, *Soldiers of Misfortune*, p. 229. There are many creative responses to right-wing populism by progressive writers. See, for example, Albelda, Folbre, and the Center for Popular Economics, *War on the Poor: A Defense Manual;* Collins, Leondar-Wright, and Sklar, *Shifting Fortunes: The Perils of the Growing American Wealth Gap;* Cowan and staff of the Center for Campus Organizing, *Uncovering the Right on Campus;* Hardisty, *Mobilizing Resentment;* Pharr, *In the Time of the Right;* Reed, *Class Notes;* Sklar, *Chaos or Community?: Seeking Solutions, Not Scapegoats for Bad Economics;* Political Research Associates, *Defending Public Education.*

137. Reed, *Class Notes*, p. 67. This argument is similar to critiques of majoritarianism by Lani Guinier and Derrick A. Bell.

138. Kovel, "Beyond Populism."

Notes to Conclusions

1. Mike Davis, *Prisoners of the American Dream*, pp. 163–164.

2. Sklar, "Dying American Dream"; quote is from p. 115. This article is in part based on Sklar, *Chaos or Community?*

3. "The New Populism," *Business Week*, March 13, 1995, p. 73.

4. Phillips, "Politics of Frustration."

5. Betz, *Radical Right-Wing Populism in Western Europe*, pp. 106–108, 174; "America's New Populism," *Business Week*, cover story, March 13, 1995. This section first appeared in Berlet, "Following the Threads."

6. "Portrait of an Anxious Public," in special report on "The New Populism," *Business Week*, March 13, 1995, p. 80; Manza and Brooks, *Social Cleavages and Political Change*, pp. 217–230.

7. Morin and Wilson, "Men Were Driven"; "Promise Keepers Poll," Religion Column, *Washington Post*, October 11, 1997, p. C7; Green, Guth, and Hill, "Faith and Election," Guth and Green, "Moralizing Minority"; Green, "Look at the 'Invisible Army.'"

8. Deborah Kaplan, *Republic of Rage*, p. 33. See also Van Dyke and Soule, *Mobilizing Effect of Social Strain.*

9. See Sara Diamond, "Personal Is Political," pp. 41–43, for her discussion of how cultural projects interact with social movements and electoral politics.

10. This is not to suggest that there are no psychological factors in any of these phenomena. See, for example, the arguments in Altemeyer, *Authoritarian Specter*; Klandermans, *Social Psychology of Protest*; Robins and Post, *Political Paranoia*; Strozier, *Apocalypse*; Milburn and Conrad, *Politics of Denial*; Kramer and Alstad, *Guru Papers*; David Norman Smith, "Social Construction of Enemies." An excellent review of the psychosocial aspects of authoritarianism and the Frankfurt School theories is in *Social Thought & Research*, vol. 21, nos. 1, 2, 1998. See also the classic works of Arendt, *Origins of Totalitarianism*, and *Eichmann in Jerusalem*.

11. A number of sociologists have moved beyond centrist/extremist theory. Dobratz and Shanks-Meile, in *"White Power, White Pride!,"* suggest that to understand right-wing movements (or any movement) it is necessary to consider "socioeconomic conditions, changing political opportunities, resources, consciousness, labeling, framing, interpretations of reality, boundaries, and negotiation of the meaning of symbols" (p. 32).

For an introduction to these sociological concepts, see Boggs, *Social Movements and Political Power*; Buechler, "Beyond Resource Mobilization?"; *Social Movements in Advanced Capitalism*; Buechler and Cylke, eds., *Social Movements*; J. Craig Jenkins and Bert Klandermans, eds., *Politics of Social Protest*; Johnston and Klandermans, eds., *Social Movements and Culture*; Lofland, *Social Movement Organizations*; McAdam, *Political Process and the Development of Black Insurgency*; McAdam, McCarthy, and Zald, eds., *Comparative Perspectives on Social Movements*; McCarthy and Zald, "Resource mobilization and Social Movements"; Morris and Mueller, eds., *Frontiers in Social Movement Theory*; Oberschall, *Social Conflict and Social Movements*; Skocpol and Campbell, eds., *American Society and Politics*; Tarrow, *Power in Movement*.

Useful sociological studies with a more narrow focus include Gamson, "Constructing Social Protest"; Klandermans, *Social Psychology of Protest*; Gary T. Marx, "External Efforts to Damage or Facilitate Social Movements"; Mueller, *Building Social Movement Theory*; Piven and Cloward, *Poor People's Movements*; Sara Diamond, "Personal Is Political."

The framing of issues by movement leaders is a specialized area of sociological study. See, for example, Johnston, "Methodology for Frame Analysis"; Snow and Benford, "Ideology, Frame Resonance, and Participant Mobilization," and "Master Frames and Cycles of Protest"; Snow, Rochford, Worden, and Benford, "Frame Alignment Process, Micromobilization, and Movement Participation"; Zald, "Culture, Ideology, and Strategic Framing."

12. Sklar, "Dying of the American Dream," p. 133.

13. Lawrence, *New State Repression*; Churchill and Vander Wall, *Agents of Repression*, and *COINTELPRO Papers*; Gelbspan, *Break-Ins, Death Threats and the FBI*; Dempsey and Cole, *Terrorism and the Constitution*.

14. Girard, *Scapegoat*.

15. Many people were involved in the farm-belt organizing, but special mention should be made of the Rev. C. T. Vivian, Lyn Wells, the Rev. Mac Charles Jones, and Leonard Zeskind of the National Anti-Klan Network (which became the Center for Democratic Renewal); the Rev. David Ostendorf and Daniel Levitas of PrairieFire Rural Action, Merle Hanson of the North American Farm Alliance, and Jonathan Levine of the American Jewish Committee. The analytical debates of the antiprejudice groups that grew out of these efforts can be found in Ward, *Conspiracies*; *Second Revolution*; and *American Armageddon*.

APPENDIX A

SECTORS OF THE U.S. RIGHT ACTIVE IN THE YEAR 2000

There is much overlap and sectors are not mutually exclusive. Populist, apocalyptic, and conspiracist styles can be found in several sectors. Methodologies range from cautious moderation, to activism, to insurgency, to violence. Forms of oppression—racism, sexism, homophobia, antisemitism—vary in each sector.

CONSERVATIVES

Secular Right

Corporate Internationalists   Nations should control the flow of people across borders, but not the flow of goods, capital, and profit. Sometimes called the "Rockefeller Republicans." Globalists.

Business Nationalists   Multinational corporations erode national sovereignty; nations should enforce borders for people, but also for goods, capital, and profit through trade restrictions. Enlists grassroots allies among Regressive Populists. Antiglobalists.

Economic Libertarians   The state disrupts the perfect harmony of the free market system. Modern democracy is essentially congruent with capitalism.

National Security Militarists   Support U.S. military supremacy and unilateral use of force to protect U.S. national security interests around the world. A major component of Cold War anticommunism.

Neoconservatives   The egalitarian social liberation movements of the 1960s and 1970s undermined the national consensus. Intellectual oligarchies and political institutions preserve democracy from mob rule.

Christian Right

Christian Nationalists   Biblically defined immorality and sin breed chaos and anarchy. America's greatness as God's chosen land has been undermined by liberal secular humanists, feminists, and homosexuals. Purists want litmus tests for issues of abortion, tolerance of gays and lesbians, and prayer in schools. Includes some non-Christian cultural conservatives. Overlaps somewhat with Christian theocracy.

THE HARD RIGHT

Christian Theocrats   Christian men are ordained by God to run society. Eurocentric version of Christianity based on early Calvinism. Intrinsically Christian ethnocentric, treating non-Christians as second-class citizens. Implicitly antisemitic. Includes soft dominionists and hard-line Reconstructionists.

Xenophobic Right

Paleoconservatives   Ultraconservatives and reactionaries. Natural financial oligarchies preserve the republic against democratic mob rule. Usually nativist (White Racial Nationalist), sometimes antisemitic or Christian nationalist. Elitist emphasis is similar to the intellectual conservative revolutionary wing of the European New Right. Often libertarian.

Regressive Populist Patriots   Secret elites control the government and banks. The government plans repression to enforce elite rule or global collectivism. The patriot and armed militia movements are one response from this sector. Americanist. Often support Business Nationalism due to its isolationist emphasis. Antiglobalists, yet support noninterventionist national security militarism.

White Nationalists   Alien cultures make democracy impossible. Cultural Supremacists argue different races can adopt the dominant (White) culture; Biological Racists argue the immutable integrity of culture, race, and nation. Segregationists want distinct enclaves, Separatists want distinct nations. Americanist. Tribalist emphasis is similar to the race-is-nation wing of the European New Right.

Far Right   Militant forms of revolutionary right ideology and separatist ethnocentric nationalism. Reject pluralist democracy for an organic oligarchy that unites the homogeneic nation. Conspiracist views of power that are overwhelmingly antisemitic. Home to overt fascists, neonazis, Christian Identity, Church of the Creator.

THE PRODUCERIST NARRATIVE USED IN RIGHT-WING POPULISM

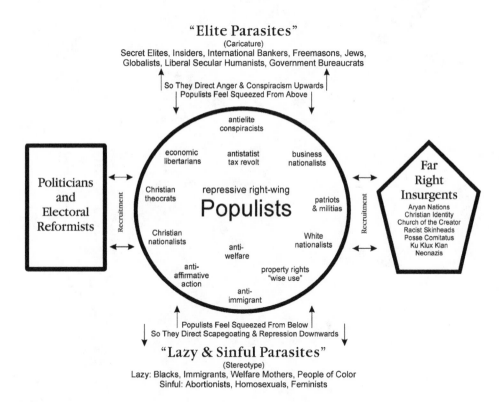

"Elite Parasites"
(Caricature)
Secret Elites, Insiders, International Bankers, Freemasons, Jews,
Globalists, Liberal Secular Humanists, Government Bureaucrats

So They Direct Anger & Conspiracism Upwards
Populists Feel Squeezed From Above

antielite
conspiracists

economic
libertarians

antistatist
tax revolt

business
nationalists

Christian
theocrats

repressive right-wing
Populists

patriots
& militias

Christian
nationalists

White
nationalists

anti-
welfare

anti-
affirmative
action

property rights
"wise use"

anti-
immigrant

**Politicians
and
Electoral
Reformists**

Recruitment

Recruitment

**Far
Right
Insurgents**
Aryan Nations
Christian Identity
Church of the Creator
Racist Skinheads
Posse Comitatus
Ku Klux Klan
Neonazis

Populists Feel Squeezed From Below
So They Direct Scapegoating & Repression Downwards

"Lazy & Sinful Parasites"
(Stereotype)
Lazy: Blacks, Immigrants, Welfare Mothers, People of Color
Sinful: Abortionists, Homosexuals, Feminists

BIBLIOGRAPHY

Abanes, Richard. (1996). *American Militias: Rebellion, Racism & Religion*. Downers Grove, IL: InterVarsity Press.

Abanes, Richard. (1998). *End-Time Visions: The Road to Armageddon?* New York: Four Walls Eight Windows.

Abraham, Larry. (1985). *Call it Conspiracy*. Seattle, WA: Double A Publications.

Abramovitz, Mimi. (1988). *Regulating the Lives of Women: Social Welfare Policy from Colonial Times to the Present*. Boston: South End Press.

Acuña, Rodolfo. (1988). *Occupied America: A History of Chicanos*. 3rd ed. New York: Harper & Row.

Adams, Frederick. (1981). "Three Faces of Midwestern Isolationism: Comments." In John N. Schacht (Ed.), *Three Faces of Midwestern Isolationism: Gerald P. Nye, Robert P. Wood, John L. Lewis*. Iowa City, IA: The Center for the Study of the Recent History of the United States.

Adorno, Theodor W., Else Frenkel-Brunswick, Daniel J. Levinson, and R. Nevitt Sanford. (1950). *The Authoritarian Personality*. New York: Harper & Row.

Aho, James A. (1989). "A Library of Infamy." *Idaho Librarian*, vol. 41, no. 4, pp. 86–88.

Aho, James A. (1990). *The Politics of Righteousness: Idaho Christian Patriotism*. Seattle: University of Washington Press.

Aho, James A. (1994). *This Thing of Darkness: A Sociology of the Enemy*. Seattle: University of Washington Press.

Albelda, Randy, Nancy Folbre, and the Center for Popular Economics. (1966). *The War on the Poor: A Defense Manual*. New York: The New Press.

Albert, Michael. (1992). "Conspiracy? . . . Not!" Venting Spleen column. *Z Magazine*, January, pp. 17–19.

Albert, Michael. (1992). "Conspiracy? . . . Not, Again." Venting Spleen column. *Z Magazine*, May, pp. 86–88.

Alexander-Moegerle, Gil. (1997). *James Dobson's War on America*. Amherst, NY: Prometheus Books.

Allen, Charles, Jr. (1994). "Pro-Life Hate: Violence in the Name of God." *Reform Judaism*, Summer, pp. 12–17, 76–77.

Allen, Gary. (1974 [circa]). *Rockefeller: Campaigning for the New World Order*. Pamphlet. No date. Reprint of an article in the John Birch Society magazine, *American Opinion*, February.

Allen, Gary, with Larry Abraham. (1972 [1971]). *None Dare Call It Conspiracy*. Rossmoor, CA; Seal Beach, CA: Concord Press. Self-published in 1971.

Allen, Gary, and Larry Abraham. (1983). *None Dare Call It Conspiracy*. Revised and expanded. Seattle, WA: Double A Publications.

Allen, J. H. (1917 [1902]). *Judah's Sceptre and Joseph's Birthright*. 15th ed. Haverhill, MA: Destiny Publishers.

Allen, Robert L. (1970). *Black Awakening in Capitalist America: An Analytic History*. Garden City, NY: Anchor Books, Doubleday & Company, Inc.

Allen, Robert L., with Pamela P. Allen. (1974). *Reluctant Reformers: Racism and Social Reform Movements in the United States.* Washington, DC: Howard University Press.

Allen, Terry J. (2000). "Breaking Law To Keep Order." *In These Times,* May 29, 2000, online at http://www.inthesetimes.com/allen2413a.html.

Allen, Theodore W. (1975). "´ . . . They Would Have Destroyed Me´: Slavery and the Origins of Racism." *Radical America,* vol. 9, no. 3, May–June, pp. 41–63.

Allen, Theodore W. (1994). *The Invention of the White Race: Vol. 1. Racial Oppression and Social Control.* New York: Verso.

Allport, Gordon W. (1954). *The Nature of Prejudice.* Cambridge, MA: Addison-Wesley.

Alperovitz, Gar. (1990). "Why the United States Dropped the Bomb." *Technology Review,* vol. 93, no. 6, August–September, pp. 23–25.

Altemeyer, Bob. (1996). *The Authoritarian Specter.* Cambridge, MA: Harvard University Press.

Alter, Jonathan. (1997). "The Age of Conspiracism." *Newsweek,* March 24, p. 47.

Altschiller, Donald. (1999). *Hate Crimes: A Reference Handbook.* Denver, CO: ABC-CLIO.

American Business Consultants. (1950). *Red Channels: The Report of Communist Influence in Radio and Television.* New York: Counterattack.

Amini, Muhammad Safwat al-Saqqa, and Sa'di Abu Habib. (1982). *Freemasonry,* English version, New York City: The Muslim World League. Arabic version, Makkah al-Mukarramah, Saudi Arabia: The Muslim World League, 1980.

"America's New Populism," *Business Week,* cover story, March 13, 1995, pp. 1, 72–80.

Ammerman, Nancy T. (1993). *Report to the Justice and Treasury Departments regarding law enforcement interaction with the Branch Davidians in Waco, Texas.* Submitted September 3. Recommendations of Experts for Improvements in Federal Law Enforcement After Waco. Washington, DC: U.S. Department of Justice and U.S. Department of the Treasury. Online at http://www.jehovah.to/freedom/ammerman.htm.

Ammerman, Nancy T. (1998). "North American Protestant Fundamentalism." In Linda Kintz and Julia Lesage (Eds.), *Culture, Media, and the Religious Right* (pp. 55–113). Minneapolis: University of Minnesota Press.

Amott, Teresa L., and Julie A. Matthaei. (1991). *Race, Gender, and Work: A Multicultural Economic History of Women in the United States.* Boston: South End Press.

Anderson, Connie. (1997). *Visions of Involved Fatherhood: Pro-Feminists and "Promise Keepers."* Paper, annual meeting, American Sociological Association, Toronto.

Anderson, David C. (1995). *Crime and the Politics of Hysteria: How the Willie Horton Story Changed American Justice.* New York: Times Books.

Anderson, Scott, and Jon Lee Anderson. (1986). *Inside the League: The Shocking Exposé of How Terrorists, Nazis, and Latin American Death Squads Have Infiltrated the World Anti-Communist League.* New York: Dodd, Mead & Company, Inc.

Andolsen, Barbara Hilkert. (1986). *"Daughters of Jefferson, Daughters of Bootblacks": Racism and American Feminism.* Macon, GA: Mercer University Press.

Andrew, John A., III. (1997). *The Other Side of the Sixties: Young Americans for Freedom and the Rise of Conservative Politics.* New Brunswick, NJ: Rutgers University Press.

Ansell, Amy Elizabeth. (1992). *Race and Reaction: New Right Ideology in Britain and the United States.* Ph.D. diss., Cambridge University.

Ansell, Amy Elizabeth. (1996). "Business Mobilization and the New Right: Currents in U.S. Foreign Policy." In Ronald W. Cox (Ed.), *Business and the State in International Relations.* Boulder, CO: Westview Press.

Ansell, Amy Elizabeth. (1997). *New Right, New Racism: Race and Reaction in the United States and Britain.* New York: New York University Press.

Ansell, Amy E. (Ed.). (1998). *Unraveling the Right: The New Conservatism in American Thought and Politics.* Boulder, CO: Westview.

Antonio, Robert. (2000). "After Postmodernism: Reactionary Tribalism." *American Journal of Sociology,* vol. 106, no. 1, pp. 40–87.

Applebome, Peter. (1989). "Ex-Klan Leader Facing First Test in Senate Bid." *The New York Times*, December 8, p. A20.

Archer, Jules. (1973). *The Plot to Seize the White House*. New York: Hawthorn Books, Inc..

Arendt, Hannah. (1963). *Eichmann in Jerusalem: A Report on the Banality of Evil*. New York: Penguin Books.

Arendt, Hannah. (1973 [1951]). *The Origins of Totalitarianism*. New York: Harcourt Brace Jovanovich.

Armageddon Books. (1996). *General Catalog*. Cliffside Publishing House, Fall/Winter. Online at: http://www.armageddonbooks.com, November 13.

Armor, John, and Peter Wright. (1988). *Manzanar*. Commentary by John Hersey, photographs by Ansel Adams. New York: Times Books, Random House, Inc.

Askin, Steve. (1994). *A New Rite: Conservative Catholic Organizations and Their Allies*. Washington, DC: Catholics for Free Choice.

Badger, Anthony J. (1985). "Huey Long and the New Deal." In Stephen W. Baskerville and Ralph Willett (Eds.), *Nothing Else to Fear: New Perspectives on America in the Thirties*. Dover, NH: Manchester University Press.

Baehr, Ninia. (1990). *Abortion Without Apology: A Radical History for the 1990s*. Pamphlet no. 8. Boston: South End Press.

Baker, Paula. (1990). "The Domestication of Politics: Women and American Political Society, 1780–1920." In Ellen Carol DuBois and Vicki L. Ruiz (Eds.), *Unequal Sisters: A Multicultural Reader in U.S. Women's History* (pp. 67–91). New York: Routledge, Chapman & Hall.

Ball, Karen. (1995). "Newt Has Doubts Foster Killed Self." *New York Daily News*, July 26.

Balz, Daniel J., and Ronald Brownstein. (1996). *Storming the Gates: Protest Politics and the Republican Revival*. Boston: Little, Brown.

Barabak, Mark Z. (1998). "Gary Bauer." Interview with Gary Bauer, *Los Angeles Times*, September 13. Online archive, http://www.latimes.com.

Barkun, Michael. (1994). *Religion and the Racist Right: The Origins of the Christian Identity Movement*. Chapel Hill: University of North Carolina Press.

Barkun, Michael. (1998). "Politics and Apocalypticism." In Stephen J. Stein (Ed.), *The Encyclopedia of Apocalypticism*, Volume 3 (pp. 442–460). New York: Continuum.

Barnett, Barbara. (1990). "Of Babies & Ballots." *Southern Exposure*, vol. 18, no. 2, pp. 20–23.

Barron, Bruce. (1992). *Heaven on Earth? The Social & Political Agendas of Dominion Theology*. Grand Rapids, MI: Zondervan.

Barruel, Abbé Augustin. (1995 [1797–1798]). *Memoirs Illustrating the History of Jacobinism*. 2nd ed., revised and corrected. English translation by Robert Clifford. Reprint, reissued in one volume. Fraser, MI: Real-View-Books.

Barry, Daniel J., and Kenneth A. Cook. (1994). *How the Biodiversity Treaty Went Down: The Intersecting Worlds of "Wise Use" and Lyndon LaRouche*. Washington, DC: Environmental Working Group.

Barsamian, David. (1995). "Militias and Conspiracy Theories." An Interview with Chip Berlet and Holly Sklar. *Z Magazine*, September, pp. 29–35.

Bates, Karen Grigsby. (1990). "Is it Genocide?" *Essence*, vol. 21, no. 5, September, p. 76.

Baum, Charlotte, Paula Hyman, and Sonya Michel. (1976). *The Jewish Woman in America*. New York: The Dial Press.

Baum, Dan. (1996). *Smoke and Mirrors: The War on Drugs and the Politics of Failure*. Boston: Little, Brown and Company.

Beam, Louis. (1992 [1983]). "Leaderless Resistance." *Seditionist*, no. 12, February. Online at various sites, including http://www.louisbeam.com/leaderless.htm.

Beaty, John O. (1951). *The Iron Curtain Over America*. Dallas, TX: Wilkinson Publishing. Reprint. Los Angeles, CA: Noontide Press, no date. Reprint is cited.

Beede, Benjamin R. (1983). "Foreign Influences on American Progressivism." *The Historian*, vol. 65, no. 4, August, p. 541.

Behreandt, Dennis. (1998). "Millennium Mayhem." *The New American*, September 14, p. 14.

Bell, Art, and Jennifer L. Osborne. (1997). *The Quickening: Today's Trends, Tomorrow's World.* New Orleans: Paper Chase Press.

Bell, Daniel (Ed.). (1964). *The Radical Right: "The New American Right" Expanded and Updated.* Garden City, NY: Anchor Books/Doubleday.

Bellant, Russ. (1991 [1988]). *Old Nazis, the New Right and the Reagan Administration: The Role of Domestic Fascist Networks in the Republican Party and Their Effect on U.S. Cold War Policies.* Boston, MA: South End Press and Political Research Associates.

Bellant, Russ. (1991 [1988]). *The Coors Connection: How Coors Family Philanthropy Undermines Democratic Pluralism.* Boston: South End Press and Political Research Associates.

Bellant, Russ. (1995). "Promise Keepers: Christian Soldiers for Theocracy." In Chip Berlet (Ed.), *Eyes Right! Challenging the Right Wing Backlash* (pp. 81–85). Boston: South End Press.

Benjamin, Caren. (1994). "LaRouche, Nation of Islam Team Up." *Washington Jewish Week*, April 21.

Bennett, David H. (1995 [1988]).*The Party of Fear: The American Far Right from Nativism to the Militia Movement*, revised. New York: Vintage Books.

Benson, Lee. (1961). *The Concept of Jacksonian Democracy: New York as a Test Case.* Princeton, NJ: Princeton University Press.

Berkowitz, Bill. (1996). "Promise Keepers: Brotherhood and Backlash." *Culture Watch*, September.

Berlet, Chip. (1987). *Clouds Blur the Rainbow: The Other Side of the New Alliance Party.* Somerville, MA: Political Research Associates.

Berlet, Chip. (1988). "Cardinal Mindszenty: Heroic Anti-Communist or Anti-Semite or Both?" *The St. Louis Journalism Review*, April, pp. 10–11, 14.

Berlet, Chip. (1989). "Trashing the Birchers: Secrets of the Paranoid Right." *Boston Phoenix*, July 20, pp. 10, 23.

Berlet, Chip. (1992). "Friendly Fascists." *The Progressive*, June, pp. 16–20.

Berlet, Chip. (1992). "The Great Right Snark Hunt: Some Notes on the Secular-Humanist Conspiracy for World Domination." *The Humanist*, September–October, pp. 14–17, 36.

Berlet, Chip. (1992). "Re-framing Dissent as Criminal Subversion," *CovertAction Quarterly*, no. 41, Summer, pp. 35–41.

Berlet, Chip. (1993). "Big Stories, Spooky Sources." *Columbia Journalism Review*, May–June, pp. 67–71.

Berlet, Chip. (1993 [1987]). *Hunt for Red Menace: How Government Intelligence Agencies and Private Right-wing Countersubversion Groups Forge Ad Hoc Covert Spy Networks that Target Dissidents as Outlaws.* Monograph. Somerville, MA: Political Research Associates.

Berlet, Chip. (1993). "Marketing the Religious Right's Anti-Gay Agenda." *CovertAction Quarterly*, Spring, pp. 46–47.

Berlet, Chip. (1994). "The Right Rides High." *The Progressive*, October, pp. 22–24, 26–29.

Berlet, Chip. (1994 [1990]). *Right Woos Left: Populist Party, LaRouchian, and Other Neo-fascist Overtures to Progressives and Why They Must Be Rejected.* Cambridge, MA: Political Research Associates.

Berlet, Chip. (1995). "Armed and Dangerous." Op-Ed. *The Boston Globe*, January 6, p. 23.

Berlet, Chip. (1995). "Clinic Violence, The Religious Right, Scapegoating, Armed Militias, and the Freemason Conspiracy." *The Body Politic.* In two parts, vol. 5, no. 2, February, pp. 12–16; and vol. 5, no. 3, March, pp. 15–16.

Berlet, Chip (Ed.). (1995). *Eyes Right! Challenging the Right Wing Backlash.* Boston: South End Press.

Berlet, Chip. (1995). "Frank Donner: An Appreciation." *CovertAction Quarterly*, Summer, pp. 17–19.

Berlet, Chip. (1995). "The Violence of Right-Wing Populism." *Peace Review*, vol. 7, no. 4, pp. 283–288.

Berlet, Chip. (1996). "Three Models for Analyzing Conspiracist Mass Movements of the Right." In Eric Ward (Ed.), *Conspiracies: Real Grievances, Paranoia, and Mass Movements* (pp. 47–75). Seattle: Northwest Coalition Against Malicious Harassment, Peanut Butter Publishing.

Berlet, Chip. (1997). *Fascism's Franchises: Stating the Differences from Movement to Totalitarian Government*. Paper, annual meeting, American Sociological Association, Toronto.

Berlet, Chip. (1998). "Following the Threads." In Amy E. Ansell (Ed.), *Unraveling the Right: The New Conservatism in American Thought and Politics* (pp. 17–40). Boulder, CO: Westview.

Berlet, Chip. (1998). *The Ideological Weaponry of the American Right: Dangerous Classes and Welfare Queens* (L'arsenal idéologique de la droite américaine: «classes dangereuses» et «welfare queens»). Paper, international symposium, The American Model: An Hegemonic Perspective for the End of the Millennium? (Le «modèle américain»: une perspective hégémonique pour la fin du millénaire?), Group Regards Critiques, University of Lausanne, Switzerland, May 12.

Berlet, Chip. (1998). *Mad as Hell: Right-Wing Populism, Fascism, and Apocalyptic Millennialism*. Paper, 14th World Congress of Sociology, International Sociological Association, Montreal, Quebec, Canada.

Berlet, Chip. (1998). "Who's Mediating the Storm? Right-Wing Alternative Information Networks." In Linda Kintz and Julia Lesage, eds., *Culture, Media, and the Religious Right* (pp. 249–273). Minneapolis: University of Minnesota Press.

Berlet, Chip. (1998). *Y2K and Millennial Pinball: How Y2K Shapes Survivalism in the US Christian Right, Patriot and Armed Militia Movements, and Far Right*. Paper, symposium, Center for Millennial Studies at Boston University, December.

Berlet, Chip. (1999). *Clinton, Conspiracism, and the Continuing Culture War: What is Past is Prologue*. Monograph. Somerville, MA: Political Research Associates. Revised and expanded from an article in the *Public Eye* magazine.

Berlet, Chip. (2000). "Countering Genocidal and Hate Movements in the Unites States." *The ISG Newsletter* (Institute for the Study of Genocide), no. 24, Winter, pp. 12–17.

Berlet, Chip, and Joel Bellman. (1989). *Lyndon LaRouche: Fascism Wrapped in an American Flag*. Report. Somerville, MA: Political Research Associates.

Berlet, Chip, and Matthew N. Lyons. (1995). "Militia Nation." *The Progressive.*, June, pp. 22–25.

Berlet, Chip, and Matthew N. Lyons. (1998). "One Key to Litigating Against Government Prosecution of Dissidents: Understanding the Underlying Assumptions." *Police Misconduct and Civil Rights Law Report* (West Group). In two parts, vol. 5, no. 13, January–February, and vol. 5, no. 14, March–April.

Berlet, Chip, and Margaret Quigley. (1995). "Theocracy & White Supremacy: Behind the Culture War to Restore Traditional Values." In Chip Berlet (Ed.), *Eyes Right! Challenging the Right Wing Backlash* (pp. 15–43). Boston: South End Press.

Bernal, Martin. (1987). *Black Athena: The Afroasiatic Roots of Classical Civilization: Vol. 1. The Fabrication of Ancient Greece 1785–1985*. New Brunswick, NJ: Rutgers University Press.

Bernstein, Richard. (1989). "Magazine Dispute Reflects Rift on U.S. Right." *The New York Times*, May 16, p. 1.

Berrigan, Daniel. (1997). *Ezekiel: Vision in the Dust*. Maryknoll, New York: Orbis Books.

Berry, Jason. (1991). "David Duke's Role Model?" *Gambit* (New Orleans Weekly), September 3, p. 15.

Berry, Jason. (1991). "A Huckster Who Mocks Democracy." *Boston Globe*, March 24.

Bérubé, Alan. (1995). "Dignity for All: 'Queer Work' and Gay Activism in the Marine Cooks and Stewards Union, 1930s to 1950s." Slide show presentation, Ithaca, New York, February 10.

Betz, Hans-Georg. (1994). *Radical Right-wing Populism in Western Europe.* New York: St. Martin's Press.

Betz, Hans-Georg, and Stefan Immerfall (Eds.). (1998). *The New Politics of the Right: Neo-Populist Parties and Movements in Established Democracies.* New York: St. Martin's Press.

Biehl, Janet. (1996). "Militia Fever: The Fallacy of 'Neither Left nor Right,'" *Green Perspectives, A Social Ecology Publication,* no. 37, April. Online at http://www.nwcitizen.com/publicgood/reports/milfev2.html.

Biehl, Janet, and Peter Staudenmaier. (1995). *Ecofascism: Lessons from the German Experience.* San Francisco: AK Press.

Billig, Michael. (1978). *Fascists: A Social Psychological View of the National Front.* New York: Harcourt Brace Jovanovich.

Billig, Michael. (1989). "The Extreme Right: Continuities in Anti-Semitic Conspiracy Theory in Post-War Europe." In Roger Eatwell and Noël O'Sullivan (Eds.), *The Nature of the Right: American and European Politics and Political Thought Since 1789* (pp. 146–166). Boston: Twayne Publishers.

Billington, Ray Allen. (1974[1933]). *The Origins of Nativism in the United States 1800–1844.* New York: Arno Press.

Birch, Doug. (1998). "Master of the Politics of Paranoia." *The Baltimore Sun,* June 5, magazine, pp. 24–27.

Blackburn, Robin. (1998). *The Overthrow of Colonial Slavery, 1776–1848.* New York: Verso.

Blanchard, Dallas A. (1994). *The Anti-Abortion Movement and the Rise of the Religious Right: From Polite to Fiery Protest.* New York: Twayne Publishers.

Blee, Kathleen M. (1991). *Women of the Klan: Racism and Gender in the 1920s.* Berkeley: University of California Press.

Blee, Kathleen M. (1996). "Engendering Conspiracy: Women in Rightist Theories and Movements." In Eric Ward (Ed.), *Conspiracies: Real Grievances, Paranoia, and Mass Movements* (pp. 91–112). Seattle: Northwest Coalition Against Malicious Harassment, Peanut Butter Publishing.

Blee, Kathleen M. (Ed.). (1998). *No Middle Ground: Women and Radical Protest.* New York: New York University Press.

Blumenfeld, Samuel L. (1984). *N.E.A.: Trojan Horse in American Education.* Boise, ID: The Paradigm Company.

Blumenfeld, Samuel L. (1994). "The Strange, Irrational World of American Primary Education." *Chalcedon Report,* December, p. 31.

Blumenthal, Sidney. (1986). *The Rise of the Counter-Establishment: From Conservative Ideology to Political Power.* New York: Random House.

Bodenheimer, Thomas, and Robert Gould. (1989). *Rollback! Right-wing Power in U.S. Foreign Policy.* Boston: South End Press.

Boggs, Carl. (1986). *Social Movements and Political Power: Emerging Forms of Radicalism in the West.* Philadelphia: Temple University Press.

Boggs, Carl. (2000). *The End of Politics: Corporate Power and the Decline of the Public Sphere.* New York: Guilford Press.

Bowles, Samuel, David M. Gordon, and Thomas E. Weisskopf. (1990). *After the Waste Land: A Democratic Economics for the Year 2000.* Armonk, NY: M. E. Sharpe, Inc.

Boyer, Paul. (1992). *When Time Shall Be No More: Prophecy Belief in Modern American Culture.* Cambridge, MA: Belknap/Harvard University Press.

Boyer, Richard O. (1973). *The Legend of John Brown: A Biography and a History.* New York: Alfred A. Knopf.

Boyer, Richard O., and Herbert M. Morais. (1980). *Labor's Untold Story.* 3rd ed. New York: United Electrical, Radio and Machine Workers of America.

Brackman, Harold. (1992). *Farrakhan's Reign of Historical Error: The Truth Behind the Secret Relationship Between Blacks and Jews.* Los Angeles: Simon Wiesenthal Center.

Bramwell, Anna. (1985). *Blood and Soil: Richard Walther Darré and Hitler's "Green Party."* Bourne End, UK: The Kensal Press.

Branan, Karen, and Frederick Clarkson. (1994). "Extremism in Sheep's Clothing: A Special Report on Human Life International." *Front Lines Research*, June.

Branch, Taylor. (1988). *Parting the Waters: America in the King Years, 1954–63.* New York: Simon and Schuster.

Branch, Taylor. (1998). *Pillar of Fire: America in the King Years, 1963–65.* New York: Simon and Schuster.

Brasher, Brenda E. (1998). *Godley Women: Fundamentalism and Female Power.* New Brunswick, NJ: Rutgers University Press.

Braverman, Harry. (1974). *Labor and Monopoly Capital: The Degradation of Work in the Twentieth Century.* New York: Monthly Review Press.

Breen, T. H. (1973). "A Changing Labor Force and Race Relations in Virginia 1660–1710." *Journal of Social History*, vol. 7, no. 1, Fall, pp. 3–25. Collected in Breen, *Shaping Southern Society.*

Breen, T. H. (1976). *Shaping Southern Society: The Colonial Experience.* New York: Oxford University Press.

Brenner, Lenni. (1983). *Zionism in the Age of the Dictators.* Westport, CT: Lawrence Hill & Company.

Brinkley, Alan. (1982). *Voices of Protest: Huey Long, Father Coughlin, and the Great Depression.* New York: Alfred A. Knopf.

Brinkley, Alan. (1994). "Reagan's Revenge: As Invented by Howard Jarvis." *The New York Times Magazine*, June 19, pp. 36–37.

Brinkley, Alan. (1998). *Liberalism and Its Discontents.* Cambridge, MA: Harvard University Press.

Britt, Brian. (1996). "Neo-Confederate Culture: A Culture of Pride and Bigotry." *Z Magazine*, vol. 9, no. 12, December, pp. 26–30.

Brock, David. (1997). "Confessions of a Right-Wing Hit Man." *Esquire*, July, p. 52.

Broder, Jonathan, and Murray Waas. (1998). "The Road to Hale." *Salon* magazine, March 17. Online at http://www.salonmagazine.com/news/1998/03/cov_17news.html. See other articles by Broder and Waas in notes to Chapter 15.

Bromley, David G. (1997). "Constructing Apocalypticism." In Thomas Robbins and Susan J. Palmer (Eds.), *Millennium, Messiahs, and Mayhem: Contemporary Apocalyptic Movements* (pp. 31–45). New York: Routledge.

Brooks, Clem, and Jeff Manza. (1996). "The Religious Factor in U.S. Presidential Elections, 1960–1992." Paper, annual meeting, American Sociological Association, New York, NY. Revised and included in Jeff Manza and Clem Brooks, *Social Cleavages and Political Change: Voter Alignment and U.S. Party Coalitions* (pp. 85–127). Oxford, UK: Oxford University Press, 1999.

Brown, Dee. (1971). *Bury My Heart at Wounded Knee: An Indian History of the American West.* Bantam Books.

Brown, Floyd G. (1993). *"Slick Willie": Why America Cannot Trust Bill Clinton.* Annapolis, MD: Annapolis–Washington Book Publishers.

Brown, Kathleen M. (1996). *Good Wives, Nasty Wenches, and Anxious Patriarchs: Gender, Race, and Power in Colonial Virginia.* Chapel Hill, NC: University of North Carolina Press, for the Omohundro Institute of Early American History and Culture, Williamsburg, VA.

Brown, Tony. (1998). *Empower the People: Overthrow the Conspiracy That Is Stealing Your Money and Freedom.* New York: William Morrow; Quill.

Broyles, J. Allen. (1964). *The John Birch Society: Anatomy of a Protest.* Boston: Beacon Press.

Brugge, Doug. (1995). "Pulling Up the Ladder: The Anti-Immigrant Backlash." In Chip Berlet (Ed.), *Eyes Right! Challenging the Right Wing Backlash* (pp. 191–209). Boston: South End Press.

Buchanan, Patrick J. (1990 [1988]). *Right from the Beginning*. Washington, DC: Regnery Gateway.

Buchanan, Patrick J. (1998). *The Great Betrayal: How American Sovereignty and Social Justice are being Sacrificed to the Gods of the Global Economy*. New York: Little, Brown.

Buechler, Steven M. (1997). "Beyond Resource Mobilization? Emerging Trends In Social Movement Theory." In Steven M. Buechler and F. Cylke, Jr. (Eds.), *Social Movements: Perspectives and Issues* (pp. 193–210). Mountain View, CA: Mayfield.

Buechler, Steven M. (2000). *Social Movements in Advanced Capitalism: The Political Economy and Cultural Construction of Social Activism*. New York: Oxford University Press.

Buechler, Steven M., and F. Kurt Cylke, Jr. (Eds.). (1997). *Social Movements: Perspectives and Issues*. Mountain View, CA: Mayfield.

Buhle, Mari Jo. (1981). *Women and American Socialism, 1870–1920*. Urbana: University of Illinois Press.

Buhle, Paul. (1973). "Debsian Socialism and the 'New Immigrant' Worker." In William L. O'Neill (Ed.), *Insights and Parallels: Problems and Issues of American Social History* (pp. 249–277). Minneapolis: Burgess Publishing Company.

Bundy, Edgar C. (1966). *How the Communists Use Religion*. New York: Devin-Adair.

Bunzel, John H. (1970 [1967]). *Anti-Politics in America*. New York, Vintage.

Burch, Philip H., Jr. (1973). "The NAM as an Interest Group." *Politics and Society*, vol. 4, no. 1.

Burch, Philip H., Jr. (1980). *Elites in American History: Vol. 3. The New Deal to the Carter Administration*. New York: Holmes & Meier.

Burch, Philip H., Jr. (1981). *Elites in American History: Vol. 1. The Federalist Years to the Civil War*. New York: Holmes & Meier.

Burch, Philip H., Jr. (1981). *Elites in American History: Vol. 2. The Civil War to the New Deal*. New York: Holmes & Meier.

Burch, Philip H., Jr. (1997). *Reagan, Bush, and Right-Wing Politics: Elites, Think Tanks, Power, and Policy: Part A. The American Right Wing Takes Command: Key Executive Appointments*. Supplement 1, Vol. 16, Research in Political Economy, Paul Zarembka (Ed.). Greenwich: CT: JAI Press.

Burch, Philip H., Jr. (1997). *Reagan, Bush, and Right-Wing Politics: Elites, Think Tanks, Power, and Policy: Part B. The American Right Wing at Court and in Action: Supreme Court Nominations and Major Policymaking*. Supplement 1, Vol. 16, Research in Political Economy, Paul Zarembka (Ed.). Greenwich, CT: JAI Press.

Burghardt, Tom. (1994). "Anti-Abortion Terror Continues: Missionaries to the Preborn." *Turning the Tide* (People Against Racist Terror), vol. 7, no. 6, December, p. 4.

Burghart, Devin, and Robert Crawford. (1996). "Vigilante Justice: Common Law Courts." *CovertAction Quarterly*, no. 57, Summer, pp. 27–32.

Burghart, Devin, and Robert Crawford. (1996). *Guns & Gavels: Common Law Courts, Militias & White Supremacy*. Portland, OR: Coalition for Human Dignity.

Burk, Robert F. (1990). *The Corporate State and the Broker State: The du Ponts and American National Politics, 1925–1940*. Cambridge: Harvard University Press.

Burke, William Kevin. (1995). "The Wise Use Movement: Right-Wing Anti-Environmentalism." In Chip Berlet (Ed.), *Eyes Right! Challenging the Right Wing Backlash* (pp. 135–145). Boston: South End Press.

Burlingame, Phyllida [with Children's Express]. (1997). *Sex, Lies, and Politics: Abstinence-Only Curricula in California Public Schools*. Oakland, CA: Applied Research Center.

Burrows, Edwin G., and Michael Wallace. (1972). "The American Revolution: The Ideology and Psychology of National Liberation." In Donald Fleming and Bernard Bailyn (Eds.), *Perspectives in American History: Vol. 6*. Cambridge, MA: Harvard University Press.

Burton, Greg. (1998). "Cop Killing: A Meeting of Radicalism, Religion." *Salt Lake City Tribune*, June 21. Online at http://www.sltrib.com/199August jun/0621199August utah/39732.htm.

Callahan, David. (1995). "Liberal Policy's Weak Foundations: Fighting the 'Bell Curve,'" *The Nation*, November 13, pp. 568–572.

Callahan, David. (1999). *$1 Billion for Ideas: Conservative Think Tanks in the 1990s*. Washington, DC: National Committee for Responsive Philanthropy, March.

Calloway, Colin G. (1995). *The American Revolution in Indian Country: Crisis and Diversity in Native American Communities*. Cambridge, UK: Cambridge University Press.

Camp, Gregory S. (1997). *Selling Fear: Conspiracy Theories and End-Times Paranoia*. Grand Rapids, MI: Baker Books.

Campbell, Susan. (1994). "'Black Bolsheviks' and Recognition of African-America's Right to Self-Determination by the Communist Party USA." *Science & Society*, vol. 58, no. 4, pp. 440–470.

Cannistraro, Philip V. (Ed.). (1982). *Historical Dictionary of Fascist Italy*. Westport, CT: Greenwood Press.

Canovan, Margaret. (1981). *Populism*. New York: Harcourt Brace Jovanovich.

Cantor, Milton. (1978). *The Divided Left: American Radicalism, 1900–1975*. New York: Hill and Wang; Farrar, Straus and Giroux.

Carlson, John Roy (pseudonym of Avedis Derounian). (1943). *Under Cover: My Four Years in the Nazi Underworld of America—The Amazing Revelation of How Axis Agents and Our Enemies Within Are Now Plotting to Destroy the United States*. New York: Dutton.

Carmines, Edward G., and James A. Stimson. (1989). *Issue Evolution: Race and the Transformation of American Politics*. Princeton, NJ: Princeton University Press.

Carson, Clayborne, David J. Garrow, Gerald Gill, Vincent Harding, and Darlene Clark (Eds.). (1991). *The Eyes on the Prize Civil Rights Reader: Documents, Speeches, and Firsthand Accounts from the Black Freedom Struggle, 1954–1990*. New York: Penguin Books.

Carter, Dan T. (1995). *The Politics of Rage: George Wallace, the Origins of the New Conservatism, and the Transformation of American Politics*. New York: Simon and Schuster.

Carter, Dan T. (1996). *From George Wallace to Newt Gingrich: Race in the Conservative Counterrevolution, 1963–1994*. Baton Rouge: Louisiana State University Press.

Carto, Willis A. (Ed.). (1982). *Profiles in Populism*. Old Greenwich, CT: Flag Press.

Carto, Willis A. (Ed.). (1998 [1982]). *Populism vs. Plutocracy: The Universal Struggle*. Update of Carto's *Profiles in Populism*.

Carus, Paul. (1996 [1900]). *The History of the Devil and the Idea of Evil*. New York: Gramercy/Random House. Originally published Chicago: Open Court.

Cashman, Sean Dennis. (1991). *African-Americans and the Quest for Civil Rights, 1900–1990*. New York: New York University Press.

Catholic Study Bible. (1990). Includes *New American Bible*. Donald Senior, General Editor. New York: Oxford University Press.

Caute, David. (1978). *The Great Fear: The Anti-Communist Purge Under Truman and Eisenhower*. New York: Simon and Schuster.

Center for Democratic Renewal. (1992). *When Hate Groups Come to Town: A Handbook of Effective Community Responses*. 2nd ed. revised and updated. Multiple editors and contributors. Atlanta, GA: Center for Democratic Renewal.

Center for Reproductive Law and Policy. (1998). *Tipping the Scales: The Christian Right's Legal Crusade Against Choice*. New York: By the author.

Chalmers, David M. (1965). *Hooded Americanism: The First Century of the Ku Klux Klan, 1865–1965*. Garden City, NY: Doubleday & Company.

Chambers, Claire. (1977). *The SIECUS Circle: A Humanist Revolution*. Belmont, MA: Western Islands.

Chanes, Jerome A. (1995). *Antisemitism in America Today: Outspoken Experts Explode the Myths*. New York: Birch Lane Press/Carol Publishing.

Chang, Perry. (1994). *"According to Rumors it is Communists Stirring this Trouble": The Christian Anti-Communism of the Civil Rights Movements' Southern White Opposition*. Paper, meeting, Social Science History Association, Atlanta, GA.

Chang, Perry. (1999). *Frame Integration as Countermovement Innovation: Examples from the Anti-Civil Rights and Anti-Abortion Movements.* Paper, annual meeting, American Sociological Association, Chicago, IL.

Cheles, Luciano, Ronnie Ferguson, and Michalina Vaughan (Eds.). (1995). *The Far Right in Western and Eastern Europe.* 2nd ed. New York: Longman.

Chernow, Ron. (1990). *The House of Morgan: An American Banking Dynasty and the Rise of Modern Finance.* New York: Atlantic Monthly Press.

Church on the Web. (1999). *Video Catalog.* Online at: http://www.churchontheweb.com/bookshop/paganinvasion/8.html, October 20.

Churchill, Ward, and Jim Vander Wall. (1988). *Agents of Repression: The FBI's Secret Wars Against the Black Panther Party and the American Indian Movement.* Boston: South End Press.

Churchill, Ward, and Jim Vander Wall. (1989). *The COINTELPRO Papers: Documents from the FBI's Secret Wars Against Domestic Dissent.* Boston: South End Press.

Chuvala, Bob. (1995). "A Nation on the Edge?" *Rutherford* magazine, August, p. 9.

Clarkson, Frederick. (1991). "HardCOR." *Church & State,* vol. 44, no. 1, January, pp. 9–12.

Clarkson, Frederick. (1995). "Christian Reconstructionism: Theocratic Dominionism Gains Influence." In Chip Berlet (Ed.), *Eyes Right! Challenging the Right Wing Backlash* (pp. 59–80). Boston: South End Press. Revised and included in Clarkson, *Eternal Hostility.*

Clarkson, Frederick. (1996). "Out on the Fringes." *In These Times,* September 16, pp. 24–26.

Clarkson, Frederick. (1997). *Eternal Hostility: The Struggle Between Theocracy and Democracy.* Monroe, ME: Common Courage.

Clines, Francis X. (1997). "Rep. Dan Burton: A 'Pit Bull' Gets His Chance to Charge." *The New York Times,* March 9, p. 22.

The Clinton Chronicles. (1994). Video. Jeremiah Films, Hemet, CA. See also: Matrisciana, Pat.

Clouse, Robert G., Robert N. Hosack, and Richard V. Pierard. (1999). *The New Millennium Manual: A Once and Future Guide.* Grand Rapids, MI: Baker Books.

Coates, James. (1995 [1987]). *Armed and Dangerous: The Rise of the Survivalist Right.* New York: Hill and Wang.

Cockcroft, James D. (1986). *Outlaws in the Promised Land: Mexican Immigrant Workers and America's Future.* New York: Grove Press.

Coerver, Don M., and Linda B. Hall. (1984). *Texas and the Mexican Revolution: A Study in State and National Border Policy, 1910–1920.* San Antonio, TX: Trinity University Press.

Cogley, John. (1956). *Report on Blacklisting: Vol. 1. Movies.* New York: The Fund for the Republic.

Cogley, John. (1956). *Report on Blacklisting: Vol. 2. Radio-Television.* New York: The Fund for the Republic.

Cohn, Norman. (1970 [1957]). *The Pursuit of the Millennium.* New York: Oxford University Press.

Cohn, Norman. (1993). *Cosmos, Chaos and the World to Come: The Ancient Roots of Apocalyptic Faith.* New Haven: Yale University Press.

Cohn, Norman. (1996 [1967]). *Warrant for Genocide: The Myth of the Jewish World Conspiracy and the Protocols of the Elders of Zion.* London: Serif.

Cole, Wayne S. (1981). "Gerald P. Nye and Agrarian Bases for the Rise and Fall of American Isolationism." In John N. Schacht (Ed.), *Three Faces of Midwestern Isolationism: Gerald P. Nye, Robert P. Wood, John L. Lewis* (pp. 1–10). Iowa City: The Center for the Study of the Recent History of the United States.

Cole, Wayne S. (1983). *Roosevelt & the Isolationists, 1932–45.* Lincoln: University of Nebraska Press.

Coleman, John. (1997). *The Conspirators' Hierarchy: The Committee of 300.* 4th ed. Carson City: NV: World in Review.

Collette, Lin (1995). "Encountering Holocaust Denial." In Chip Berlet (Ed.), *Eyes Right! Challenging the Right Wing Backlash* (pp. 246–265). Boston: South End Press.

Collins, Chuck, Betsy Leondar-Wright, and Holly Sklar. (1999). *Shifting Fortunes: The Perils of the Growing American Wealth Gap.* Boston: United for a Fair Economy.

Colman, Arthur D. (1995). *Up From Scapegoating: Awakening Consciousness in Groups.* Wilmette, IL: Chiron.

Conason, Joe. (1992). "The Religious Right's Quiet Revival." *The Nation,* April 27, p. 553.

Conason, Joe. (1998). "Scaife Paid $1.7 in *Spectator* 'Legal Fees.'" *New York Observer,* February 23, p. 1. See other articles by Conosan in notes to Chapter 15.

Conason, Joe, and Gene Lyons. (2000). *The Hunting of the President: The Ten-Year Campaign to Destroy Bill and Hillary Clinton.* New York: St. Martin's Press.

Conniff, Ruth. (1993). "The War on Aliens: The Right Calls The Shots." *The Progressive,* October, pp. 22–29.

Conniff, Ruth. (2000). "Left-Right Romance." Word from Washington column. *The Progressive,* May 2000, pp. 12–15.

Coogan, Gertrude. (1935). *Money Creators: Who Creates Money? Who Should Create It?* Chicago: Sound Money Press.

Coogan, Kevin. (1999). *Dreamer of the Day: Francis Parker Yockey and the Postwar Fascist International.* Brooklyn, NY: Autonomedia.

Cook, James Graham. (1962). *The Segregationists: A Penetrating Study of the Men and the Organizations Active in the South's Fight Against Integration.* New York: Appleton-Century-Crofts.

Cooper, Milton William. (1991). *Behold a Pale Horse.* Sedona, AZ: Light Technology Publishing.

Corcoran, James. (1995 [1990]). *Bitter Harvest: The Birth of Paramilitary Terrorism in the Heartland.* Revised. New York: Viking Penguin.

Corn, David. (1994). "Contract on Bill." *The Nation,* December 12, p. 714.

Costigliola, Frank. (1984). *Awkward Dominion: American Political, Economic, and Cultural Relations with Europe, 1919–1933.* Ithaca, NY: Cornell University Press.

Coughlin, Charles E. (1933). *Driving Out the Money Changers.* Royal Oak, MI: The Radio League of the Little Flower.

Coughlin, Charles E. (1933). *Eight Discourses on the Gold Standard and Other Kindred Subjects.* Royal Oak, MI: The Radio League of the Little Flower.

Coughlin, Charles E. (1933). *The New Deal in Money.* Royal Oak, MI: The Radio League of the Little Flower.

Coughlin, Charles E. (1934). *Eight Lectures on Labor, Capital and Justice.* Royal Oak, MI: The Radio League of the Little Flower.

Coughlin, Charles E. (1935). *A Series of Lectures on Social Justice.* Royal Oak, MI: The Radio League of the Little Flower.

Coughlin, Paul T. (1999). *Secrets, Plots and Hidden Agendas: What You Don't Know About Conspiracy Theories.* Downers Grove, IL: InterVarsity Press.

Courtney, Phoebe. (1973). *Beware Metro and Regional Government!* Littleton, CO: The Independent American Newspaper.

Covington, Sally. (1997). *Moving A Public Policy Agenda: The Strategic Philanthropy of Conservative Foundations.* Washington, DC: National Committee for Responsive Philanthropy, July.

Covino, Marghe. (1994). "Grace Under Pressure: The World According to Rev. R. J. Rushdoony." *Sacramento News & Review,* October 20, p. 19.

Cowan, Rich, and staff of the Center for Campus Organizing. (1997). *Uncovering the Right on Campus: A Guide to Resisting Conservative Attacks on Equality and Social Justice.* Cambridge, MA: Center for Campus Organizing.

Cox, Clinton. (1999). *Come All You Brave Soldiers: Blacks in the Revolutionary War.* New York: Scholastic Press.

Cox, Harvey. (1995). "The Warring Visions of the Religious Right." *Atlantic Monthly,* November, pp. 59–69.

Cox, Ronald W. (1994). *Power and Profits: U.S. Policy In Central America*. Lexington: The University Press of Kentucky.

Crawford, Robert, and Terre Rybovich. (1999). "Lady Liberty No More: The Anti-Immigrant Movement in the USA." *Searchlight*, May, p. 18.

Crawford, Robert, S. L. Gardner, Jonathan Mozzochi, and R. L. Taylor. (1994). *The Northwest Imperative: Documenting a Decade of Hate*. Portland, OR: Coalition for Human Dignity; Seattle, WA: Northwest Coalition Against Malicious Harassment.

Crowther, Samuel. (1933). *American Self-Contained*. Garden City, NY: Doubleday, Doran & Company.

Cumings, Bruce. (1990). *The Origins of the Korean War: Vol. 2. The Roaring of the Cataract, 1947–1950*. Princeton, NJ: Princeton University Press.

Cuneo, Michael W. (1997). *The Smoke of Satan: Conservative and Traditionalist Dissent in Contemporary American Catholicism*. New York: Oxford University Press.

Cuprisin, Tim. (1999). "This Drudge Muck Won't Stick Either." *The Milwaukee Journal Sentinel*, February 2. Online at Northern Light.

Curran, Thomas J. (1975). *Xenophobia and Immigration, 1830–1930*. Boston: Twayne Publishers, G. K. Hall.

Curry, Richard O. (Ed.). (1988). *Freedom at Risk: Secrecy, Censorship, and Repression in the 1980´s*. Philadelphia: Temple University Press.

Curry, Richard O., and Thomas M. Brown. (1972). "Introduction." In Richard O. Curry and Thomas M. Brown (Eds.), *Conspiracy: The Fear Of Subversion In American History* (pp. vii-xi) New York: Holt, Rinehart and Winston.

Curry, Richard O., and Thomas M. Brown (Eds.). (1972). *Conspiracy: The Fear of Subversion in American History*. New York: Holt, Rinehart and Winston.

Dalhouse, Mark Taylor. (1996). *An Island in the Lake of Fire: Bob Jones University, Fundamentalism, and the Separatist Movement*. Athens, GA: The University of Georgia Press.

Daniels, Ted (Ed.). (1999). *A Doomsday Reader: Prophets, Predictors, and Hucksters of Salvation*. New York: New York University Press.

Daniels, Ted. (1996). "Another Standoff: The Montana Freeman." *Millennial Prophecy Report*, April, pp. 1–4.

Danky, Jim, and John Cherney. (1996). "Beyond Limbaugh: The Hard Right's Publishing Spectrum." *Reference Services Review*, Spring, pp. 43–56.

Davidson, Osha Gray. (1996 [1990]). *Broken Heartland: The Rise of America's Rural Ghetto*. Expanded ed. Iowa City: University of Iowa Press.

Davis, Angela Y. (1983). *Women, Race & Class*. New York: Random House, Vintage Books.

Davis, David Brion (Ed.). (1971). *The Fear of Conspiracy: Images of Un-American Subversion from the Revolution to the Present*. Ithaca, NY: Cornell University Press.

Davis, David Brion. (1975). *The Problem of Slavery in the Age of Revolution, 1770–1823*. Ithaca, NY: Cornell University Press.

Davis, Donald Finlay. (1988). *Conspicuous Production: Automobiles and Elites in Detroit, 1899–1933*. Philadelphia: Temple University Press.

Davis, Mike. (1986). *Prisoners of the American Dream: Politics and Economy in the History of the US Working Class*. London: Verso.

Davis, Nord, Jr. (1990). *Desert Shield and the New World Order*. Topton, NC: Northpoint Tactical Teams.

Davison, Mary M. (1966). *The Profound Revolution*. Omaha, NE: The Greater Nebraskan.

Davison, Mary M. (1970 [circa]). *Twentieth Century Snow Job*. Lighthouse Point, FL: Council for Statehood.

Davison, Mary M. (1962). *The Secret Government of the United States*. Omaha, NE: The Greater Nebraskan.

Dean, Jodi. (1998). *Aliens in America: Conspiracy Cultures from Outerspace to Cyberspace*. Ithaca, NY: Cornell University Press.

de Armond, Paul. (1999). "A Time for New Beginnings (or This Singular Epidemic Among the Sheep)." *Studies in Conflict and Terrorism*, vol. 22, no. 2, April–June.

de Armond, Paul. (1999). *Out on an Alleged: Conspiracy Theorists take a Leap of Faith.* Unpublished paper provided by the author.

de Armond, Paul. (1999). "Right Wing Terrorism and Weapons of Mass Destruction: Motives, Strategies and Movements." Public Good Project. Online at: http://www.nwcitizen.com/publicgood/.

Debo, Angie. (1970). *A History of the Indians of the United States.* Norman: University of Oklahoma Press.

DeCamp, Susan. (1998). "Locking the Doors to the Kingdom: An Examination of Religion in Extremist Organizing and Public Policy." In Eric Ward (Ed.), *American Armageddon: Religion, Revolution and the Right* (pp. 30–34). Seattle, Northwest Coalition Against Malicious Harassment, Peanut Butter Publishing.

Decter, Midge. (1994). "The ADL vs. the 'Religious Right.'" *Commentary*, September.

Dees, Morris, with James Corcoran. (1996). *Gathering Storm: America's Militia Threat.* New York: HarperCollins.

de Fontbrune, Jean-Charles. (1985 [1980]). *Nostradamus: Countdown to Apocalypse.* New York: Henry Holt.

DeGette, Cara. "The Devil Inside." *The Colorado Springs Independent*, August 19–25, pp. 13–17.

De Grand, Alexander J. (1978). *The Italian Nationalist Association and the Rise of Fascism in Italy.* Lincoln: University of Nebraska Press.

De Grazia, Victoria. (1992). *How Fascism Ruled Women: Italy, 1922–1945.* Berkeley: University of California Press.

De Koster, Lester. (1967). *The Citizen and the John Birch Society.* A *Reformed Journal* monograph. Grand Rapids, MI: William B. Eerdmans.

Deloria, Vine, Jr., and Clifford M. Lytle. (1984). *The Nations Within: The Past and Future of American Indian Sovereignty.* New York: Pantheon Books.

D'Emilio, John. (1983). *Sexual Politics, Sexual Communities: The Making of a Homosexual Minority in the United States, 1940–1970.* Chicago: The University of Chicago Press.

Dempsey, James X., and David Cole. (1999). *Terrorism and the Constitution: Sacrificing Civil Liberties in the Name of National Security.* 3rd printing. Los Angeles: First Amendment Foundation.

DeParle, Jason. (1994). "Daring Research or 'Social Science Pornography'?" *New York Times Magazine*, October 9, p. 48.

DeParle, Jason. (1996). "The Christian Right Confesses Sins of Racism." *The New York Times*, August 4. Online archive.

Derber, Charles. (1998). *Corporation Nation: How Corporations Are Taking Over Our Lives And What We Can Do About It.* New York: St. Martin's Press.

Derounian, Avedis. See pseudonym: Carlson, John Roy.

Destler, Chester McCarthur. (1966 [1946]). *American Radicalism 1865–1901: Essays and Documents.* Chicago: Quadrangle.

Diamond, Sander A. (1974). *The Nazi Movement in the United States 1924–1941.* Ithaca, NY: Cornell University Press.

Diamond, Sara. (1989). *Spiritual Warfare: The Politics of the Christian Right.* Boston: South End Press.

Diamond, Sara. (1993). "No Place to Hide." Watch on the Right column. *The Humanist*, vol. 53, no. 5, September–October, pp. 39–41. Collected in Diamond, *Facing the Wrath*.

Diamond, Sara. (1993). "Shifting Alliances On The Right." Opposition Research Column. *Z Magazine*, November.

Diamond, Sara. (1994). "The Christian Right's Anti-Gay Agenda." Watch on the Right column. *The Humanist*, vol. 54, no. 4, July–August.

Diamond, Sara. (1994). "How 'Radical' Is The Christian Right?" Watch on the Right column. *The Humanist*, vol. 54, no. 2, March–April, pp. 32–34.

Diamond, Sara. (1995). "It's Political Power, Stupid!" *Z Magazine*, January, p. 32.

Diamond, Sara. (1995). "The Christian Right Seeks Dominion: On the Road to Political Power & Theocracy." In Chip Berlet (Ed.), *Eyes Right! Challenging the Right Wing Backlash* (pp. 44–49). Boston: South End Press.

Diamond, Sara. (1995). *Roads to Dominion: Right-Wing Movements and Political Power in the United States.* New York: Guilford Press.

Diamond, Sara. (1996). *Facing the Wrath: Confronting the Right in Dangerous Times.* Monroe, ME: Common Courage Press.

Diamond, Sara. (1997). "Political Millennialism within the Evangelical Subculture." In Charles B. Strozier and Michael Flynn (Eds.), *The Year 2000: Essays on the End* (pp. 206–216). New York: New York University Press.

Diamond, Sara. (1998). *Not by Politics Alone: The Enduring Influence of the Christian Right.* New York: Guilford Press.

Diamond, Sara. (1998). "The Personal Is Political: The Role of Cultural Projects in the Mobilization of the Christian Right." In Amy E. Ansell (Ed.), *Unraveling the Right: The New Conservatism in American Thought and Politics* (pp. 41–55). Boulder, CO: Westview.

Dilling, Elizabeth. (1934). *The Red Network: A "Who's Who" and Handbook of Radicalism for Patriots.* Chicago: By the author.

Dilling, Elizabeth. (1936). *The Roosevelt Red Record and its Background.* Kenilworth, IL: By the author.

Dilling, Elizabeth. (1941 [circa]). *New Dealers in Office.* Indianapolis: The Fellowship Press.

Dinnerstein, Leonard. (1994). *Anti-Semitism in America.* New York: Oxford University Press.

Dionne, E. J., Jr. (1996). "Class Issues: Lurking, Not Gone." *Washington Post*, July 26, online archive.

Dionne, E. J., Jr. (1996). *They Only Look Dead: Why Progressives Will Dominate the Next Political Era.* New York: Simon and Schuster.

Dixon, Thomas, Jr. (1902). *The Leopard's Spots: a Romance of the White Man's Burden, 1865–1900.* New York: Grosset & Dunlap.

Dixon, Thomas, Jr. (1905). *The Clansman: An Historical Romance of the Ku Klux Klan.* New York: Doubleday, Page & Company.

Dobratz, Betty A., and Stephanie L. Shanks-Meile. (1996). "Ideology and the Framing Process in the White Separatist/Supremacist Movement in the United States." *Quarterly Journal of Ideology*, vol. 19, nos. 1–2, pp. 3–29.

Dobratz, Betty A., and Stephanie L. Shanks-Meile. (1997). *"White Power, White Pride!" The White Separatist Movement in the United States.* New York, Twayne Publishers.

Dobson, James, and Gary L. Bauer. (1990). *Children at Risk: The Battle for the Hearts and Minds of Our Kids.* Dallas: Word Publishing.

Doenecke, Justus D. (1981). "The Isolationism of General Robert E. Wood." In John N. Schacht (Ed.), *Three Faces of Midwestern Isolationism: Gerald P. Nye, Robert P. Wood, John L. Lewis.* Iowa City: The Center for the Study of the Recent History of the United States.

Dollard, John, Ned E. Miller, Leonard W. Doob, O. H. Mowrer, and Robert R. Sears. (1939). *Frustration and Aggression.* New Haven, CT: Yale University Press.

Domhoff, G. William. (1979). *The Powers That Be: Processes of Ruling Class Domination in America.* New York: Vintage Books.

Domhoff, G. William. (1986 [1983]). *Who Rules America Now: A View for the '80's.* New York: Touchstone, Simon and Schuster.

Domhoff, G. William. (1970). *The Higher Circles: The Governing Class in America.* New York: Random House.

Domhoff, G. William. (1998). *Who Rules America? Power and Politics in the Year 2000.* Mountain View, CA: Mayfield Publishing.

Donner, Frank J. (1980). *The Age of Surveillance: The Aims and Methods of America's Political Intelligence System*. New York: Alfred A. Knopf.

Donner, Frank J. (1982). "The Campaign to Smear the Nuclear Freeze Movement." *The Nation*, November 6, pp. 456–465.

Donner, Frank J. (1990). *Protectors of Privilege: Red Squads and Police Repression in Urban America*. Berkeley: University of California Press.

Donovan, Frank. (1968). *Mr. Jefferson's Declaration: The Story Behind the Declaration of Independence*. New York: Dodd, Mead & Company.

Dorrien, Gary. (1998). "Inventing an American Conservatism: The Neoconservative Episode." In Amy E. Ansell (Ed.), *Unraveling the Right: The New Conservatism in American Thought and Politics* (pp. 56–79). Boulder, CO: Westview.

Dowd, Douglas F. (1974). *The Twisted Dream: Capitalist Development in the United States Since 1776*. Cambridge, MA: Winthrop Publishers.

Dower, John W. (1986). *War Without Mercy: Race and Power in the Pacific War*. New York: Pantheon Books.

Drake, Gordon V. (1968). *Blackboard Power: NEA Threat to America*. Tulsa, OK: Christian Crusade Publications.

Drinnon, Richard. (1990 [1980]). *Facing West: The Metaphysics of Indian-Hating and Empire-Building*. New York: Schocken Books.

D'Souza, Dinesh. (1984). *Falwell, Before the Millennium: A Critical Biography*. Chicago: Regnery Gateway.

Du Bois, W. E. B. (1992 [1935]). *Black Reconstruction in America, 1860–1880*. New York: Atheneum.

Dunn, Timothy J. (1996). *The Militarization of the U.S.–Mexico Border, 1978–1992: Low-Intensity Conflict Doctrine Comes Home*. Austin, TX: Center for Mexican American Studies, University of Texas at Austin.

Durham, Martin. (1992). "Gender and the British Union of Fascists." *Journal of Contemporary History*, vol. 27, pp. 513–529.

Durham, Martin. (1998). *Women and Fascism*. London: Routledge.

Dworkin, Andrea. (1983). *Right-Wing Women*. New York: Coward-McCann.

Dyer, Joel. (1998). *Harvest of Rage: Why Oklahoma City is Only the Beginning*. Revised. Boulder, CO: Westview.

Dyer, Thomas G. (1980). *Theodore Roosevelt and the Idea of Race*. Baton Rouge: Louisiana State University Press.

Eatwell, Roger, and Noël O'Sullivan (Eds.). (1989). *The Nature of the Right: American and European Politics and Political Thought Since 1789*. Boston: Twayne Publishers.

Eco, Umberto. (1995). "Ur-Fascism." *New York Review of Books*, June 22. Reprinted as "Eternal Fascism: Fourteen Ways of Looking at a Blackshirt." *Utne Reader*, no. 72, November–December 1995, pp. 57–59.

Editors of Executive Intelligence Review. (1992). *The Ugly Truth about the Anti-Defamation League*. Washington, DC: Executive Intelligence Review.

Edwards, Lee. (1995). *Goldwater: The Man Who Made a Revolution*. Washington, DC: Regnery Publishing.

Edwards, Lee, and Anne Edwards. (1968). *You Can Make the Difference*. New Rochelle, NY: Arlington House. Rewritten and published as Lee Edwards, *You Can Make the Difference*, Westport, CT: Arlington House, 1980.

Egerton, Douglas R. (1998). "Black Independence Struggles and the Tale of Two Revolutions: A Review Essay." *The Journal of Southern History*, vol. 64, no. 1, February, pp. 95–116.

Eisler, Riane. (1987). *The Chalice and the Blade: Our History, Our Future*. New York: Harper and Row.

Eley, Geoff. (1989). "What Produces Fascism: Preindustrial Traditions or a Crisis of the Capitalist State?" In Michael N. Dobkowski and Isidor Walliman (Eds.), *Radical Perspectives* on the Rise of Fascism in Germany, *1919–1945* (pp. 69–99). New York: Monthly Review Press.

Emry, Sheldon. (1982). *Billion$ for the Banker$, Debts for the People: The Real Cause of Inflation.* Pamphlet, 32pp. Phoenix, AZ: Lord's Covenant Church/America's Promise.

Engelmayer, Sheldon D., and Robert J. Wagman. (1980). *Tax Revolt 1980: A How-To Guide.* Wesport, CT: Arlington House. Originally published under the title *The Taxpayer's Guide to Effective Tax Revolt,* Dale Books, 1978.

Epstein, Benjamin R., and Arnold Forster. (1966). *The Radical Right: Report on the John Birch Society and Its Allies.* New York: Vintage Books.

Evans, Richard J. (1977). *The Feminists: Women's Emancipation Movements in Europe, America and Australasia 1840–1920.* Totowa, NJ: Barnes & Noble Books.

Evans-Pritchard, Ambrose. (1997). *The Secret Life of Bill Clinton: The Unreported Stories.* Washington, DC: Regnery Publishing.

Ewen, Stuart, and Elizabeth Ewen. (1992). *Channels of Desire: Mass Images and the Shaping of American Consciousness.* 2nd ed. Minneapolis: University of Minnesota Press.

Ezekiel, Raphael S. (1995). *The Racist Mind: Portraits of American Neo-Nazis and Klansmen.* New York: Viking.

Fahey, Denis. (1935). *Mystical Body of Christ in the Modern World.* Dublin: Browne and Nolan.

Faludi, Susan. (1992). *Backlash: The Undeclared War Against American Women.* New York: Doubleday.

Faludi, Susan. (1999). *Stiffed: The Betrayal of the American Man.* New York: William Morrow.

Falwell, Jerry. (1998). *Y2K: A Christian's Guide to the Millennium Bug.* Video. Lynchburg, VA: Liberty Broadcasting Network.

Farrell, John Aloysius. (1998). "Whitewater Is Taking A Twist Against Starr." *Boston Globe,* April 13, p. A1. Online archive.

Federici, Michael P. (1991). *The Challenge of Populism: The Rise of Right-Wing Democratism in Postwar America.* New York: Praeger.

Fenn, Richard K. (1997). *The End of Time: Religion, Ritual, and the Forging of the Soul.* Cleveland: Pilgrim Press.

Fenster, Mark. (1999). *Conspiracy Theories: Secrecy and Power in American Culture.* Minneapolis: University of Minnesota Press.

Ferber, Abby L. (1996). Reconceptualizing the Racist Right. In E. Ward (Ed.), *Conspiracies: Real Grievances, Paranoia, and Mass Movements* (pp. 113–126). Seattle: Northwest Coalition Against Malicious Harassment, Peanut Butter Publishing.

Ferber, Abby L. (1998). *White Man Falling: Race, Gender, and White Supremacy.* Lanham, MD: Rowman & Littlefield.

Ferguson, Andrew. (1994). "You Won't Believe This." *Washingtonian Magazine,* May.

Ferguson, Thomas. (1995). *Golden Rule: The Investment Theory of Party Competition and the Logic of Money-Driven Political Systems.* Chicago: The University of Chicago Press.

Ferguson, Thomas. (1999). "Smoke in Starr's Chamber (Impeachment: The Sequel)." *The Nation,* March 8. Online archive.

Ferguson, Thomas, and Joel Rogers. (1986). *Right Turn: The Decline of the Democrats and the Future of American Politics.* New York: Hill and Wang.

Ferrini Productions. (1997). *10.4.97 Promise Keepers.* Video. Produced for the Center for Millennial Studies, Boston.

Fine, Melinda. (1995). *Habits of Mind: Struggling Over Values in America's Classrooms.* San Francisco: Jossey-Bass.

Fineman, Howard. (1993). "God and the Grassroots." *Newsweek,* November 8, p. 45.

Fink, Leon. (1983). *Workingmen's Democracy: The Knights of Labor and American Politics.* Urbana: University of Illinois Press.

Finkelman, Paul. (1993). "The Color of Law." Review of *The Color-Blind Constitution* by Andrew Kull. *Northwestern Law Review,* vol. 87, no. 3, Spring.

Fitch, Robert. (1995). "The New Poor Laws: How Mr. Gingrich Brought Back Tiny Tim." *Village Voice*, January 10, p. 29.

FitzGerald, Frances. (1985). "The American Millennium." *The New Yorker*, November 11, pp. 105–196.

Fitzgerald, Michael W. (1990). "Poor Man's Fight." *Southern Exposure*, vol. 18, no. 1, Spring, pp. 14–17.

Flanders, Laura. (1995). "Far-Right Militias and Anti-Abortion Violence: When Will Media See the Connection?" *Extra!* (Fairness and Accuracy in Reporting), July/August. Online archive.

Flexner, Eleanor. (1974 [1959]). *Century of Struggle: The Woman's Rights Movement in the United States*. New York: Atheneum.

Flynn, Kevin, and Gary Gerhardt. (1989). *The Silent Brotherhood: Inside America's Racist Underground*. New York: Free Press.

Foner, Eric. (1988). *Reconstruction: America's Unfinished Revolution, 1863–1877*. New York: Harper & Row, Publishers.

Foner, Philip S. (1955). *History of the Labor Movement in the United States: Vol. 2. From the Founding of the American Federation of Labor to the Emergence of American Imperialism*. New York: International Publishers.

Foner, Philip S. (1965). *History of the Labor Movement in the United States: Vol. 4. The Industrial Workers of the World, 1905–1917*. New York: International Publishers.

Foner, Philip S. (1976). *Labor and the American Revolution*. Westport, CT: Greenwood Press.

Foner, Philip S. (1976). *Organized Labor and the Black Worker 1619–1973*. New York: International Publishers.

Foner, Philip S. (1978). *History of the Labor Movement in the United States: Vol. 1. From Colonial Times to the Founding of the American Federation of Labor*. New York: International Publishers.

Foner, Philip S. (1979). *Women and the American Labor Movement: From the First Trade Unions to the Present*. New York: Free Press.

Ford, Henry, in collaboration with Samuel Crowther. (1923). *My Life and Work*. Garden City, NY: Doubleday, Page & Company.

Ford, Henry, in collaboration with Samuel Crowther. (1926). *Today and Tomorrow*. Garden City, NY: Doubleday, Page & Company.

Formisano, Ronald P., and Kathleen Smith Kutolowski. (1977). "Antimasonry and Masonry: The Genesis of Protest, 1826–1827." *American Quarterly*, vol. 29, no. 2, Summer, pp. 139–165.

Forster, Arnold, and Benjamin R. Epstein. (1964). *Danger on the Right: The Attitudes, Personnel and Influence of the Radical Right and Extreme Conservatives*. New York: Random House, Anti-Defamation League.

Foster, David. (1998). "Vast Manhunt Comes up Empty." *Associated Press*, August 8.

Fox, Stephen. (1984). *The Mirror Makers: A History of American Advertising and Its Creators*. New York: William Morrow.

Francis, Samuel T. (Ed.). (1981). "The Intelligence Community." In Charles L. Heatherly (Ed.), *Mandate for Leadership: Policy Management in a Conservative Administration* (pp. 903–953). Washington, DC: Heritage Foundation.

Francis, Samuel T. (Sam). (1981). "Leftists Mount Attack on Investigative Panel." *Human Events*, July 11, pp. 10–12.

Franklin, John Hope, and Alfred A. Moss, Jr. (1994). *From Slavery to Freedom: A History of African Americans*. 7th ed. New York: McGraw-Hill.

Frazier, Sir James George. (1922). *The Golden Bough: A Study in Magic and Religion*. Abridged. New York: Macmillan.

Fredrickson, George M. (1982). *White Supremacy: A Comparative Study in American and South African History*. New York: Oxford University Press.

Freehling, William W. (1994). "The Founding Fathers, Conditional Antislavery, and the

Nonradicalism of the American Revolution." In *The Reintegration of American History: Slavery and the Civil War* (pp. 13–33). New York: Oxford University Press.

Frey, Sylvia R. (1991). *Water from the Rock: Black Resistance in a Revolutionary Age.* Princeton, NJ: Princeton University Press.

Fried, Marlene, and Loretta Ross. (1993). "Reproductive Freedom: Our Right to Decide." In Greg Ruggiero and Stuart Sahulka (Eds.), *Open Fire: The Open Magazine Pamphlet Series Anthology* (pp. 94–96). New York: The New Press.

Friedenberg, Daniel M. (1992). *Life, Liberty and the Pursuit of Land: The Plunder of Early America.* Buffalo, NY: Prometheus Books.

Friedman, Robert I. (1993). "The Enemy Within." *The Village Voice*, May 11, pp. 27–32.

Frierson, Vicki, and Ruthanne Garlock. (1978). *Christian Be Watchful: Hidden Dangers in the New Coalition of Feminism, Humanism, Socialism, Lesbianism.* Pamphlet. Dallas: Texas Eagle Forum. On file at PRA.

Fritzsche, Peter. (1990). *Rehearsals for Fascism: Populism and Political Mobilization in Weimar Germany.* New York: Oxford University Press.

Fritzsche, Peter. (1998). *Germans into Nazis.* Cambridge, MA: Harvard University Press.

Froese, Arno. (1997). *How Democracy Will Elect the Antichrist: The Ultimate Denial of Freedom, Liberty and Justice According to the Bible.* West Columbia, SC: Olive Press.

Froese, Arno. (2000). "The Great Y2K Hoax." *Midnight Call: The Prophetic Voice for the Endtimes* (magazine), February, pp. 18–19.

Fuller, Robert C. (1995). *Naming the Antichrist: The History of an American Obsession.* New York: Oxford University Press.

Gabriner, Vicki. (1977). "The Rosenberg Case: We Are All Your Children." In Steven Lubet, Jeffry (Shaye) Mallow, Adar Rossman, Susan Schechter, Robbie (Sholem) Skeist, and Miriam Socoloff (Eds.), *Chutzpah: A Jewish Liberation Anthology* (pp. 173–180). San Francisco: New Glide Publications.

Gage, Kit. (1996). "Lie: The Anti-Terrorism Bill Only Targets Terrorists." *CovertAction Quarterly*, no. 57, Summer, pp. 8–9.

Gage, Kit. (1996). "The Terrorism Bill: The Threat it Poses." *The Right to Know & the Freedom to Act* (National Committee Against Repressive Legislation, Washington, DC), January–February, pp. 1–6.

Gamson, William. A. (1995). "Constructing Social Protest." In Hank Johnston and Bert Klandermans (Eds.), *Social Movements and Culture: Vol. 4. Social Movements, Protest, and Contention* (pp. 85–106). Minneapolis: University of Minnesota Press.

Gardiner, Steven L. (1996). "Promises to Keep: the Christian Right Men's Movement." *Dignity Report*, vol. 3, no. 4, Fall.

Gardiner, Steven L. (1998). "Through the Looking Glass and What the Christian Right Found There." In Linda Kintz and Julia Lesage (Eds.), *Culture, Media, and the Religious Right* (pp. 141–158). Minneapolis: University of Minnesota Press.

Garner, Roberta, and John Tenuto. (1997). *Social Movement Theory and Research: An Annotated Guide.* Magill Bibliographies. Lanham, MD: Scarecrow Press, Pasadena, CA: Salem Press.

Gates, Henry Louis, Jr. (1992). "Black Demagogues and Psuedo-Scholars." Op-ed. *The New York Times.* July 20, p. A15.

Gelbspan, Ross. (1991). *Break-Ins, Death Threats, and the FBI: The Covert War Against the Central America Movement.* Boston: South End Press.

Gelderman, Carol. (1981). *Henry Ford: The Wayward Capitalist.* New York: St. Martin's Press.

Gerlach, Larry R. (1992). "A Battle of Empires: The Klan in Salt Lake City." In Shawn Lay (Ed.), *The Invisible Empire in the West: Toward a New Historical Appraisal of the Ku Klux Klan of the 1920s* (pp. 121–152). Urbana: University of Illinois Press.

Germani, Gino. (1978). *Authoritarianism, Fascism, and National Populism.* New Jersey: Transaction Books.

Germond, Jack W., and Jules Witcover. (1993). *Mad as Hell: Revolt at the Ballot Box, 1992*. New York: Warner Books.

Gibbs, David N. (1991). *The Political Economy of Third World Intervention: Mines, Money, and U.S. Policy in the Congo Crisis*. Chicago: The University of Chicago Press.

Gibson, James William. (1994). *Warrior Dreams: Paramilitary Culture in Post-Viet Nam America*. New York: Hill and Wang.

Giddens, Edward. (1996 [1829]). *An Account of the Savage Treatment of Captain William Morgan, in Fort Niagara*. Reprint. Montague, MA: Acacia Press. Original edition Boston: Anti-Masonic Bookstore, 1829.

Giddings, Paula. (1985). *When and Where I Enter: The Impact of Black Women on Race and Sex in America*. New York: Bantam Book.

Gilbert, David. (1996). "AIDS: Conspiracy or Unnatural Disaster? Tracking the Real Genocide," *CovertAction Quarterly*, no. 58, Fall, pp. 55–64.

Ginger, Ray. (1977 [1949]). *Eugene V. Debs: A Biography*. New York: Collier Books. Originally published as *The Bending Cross*.

Gingrich, Newt. (1995). *To Renew America*. New York: HarperCollins.

Ginsburg, Faye D. (1989). *Contested Lives: The Abortion Debate in an American Community*. Updated Edition. Berkeley: University of California Press.

Girard, René. (1986). *The Scapegoat*. Baltimore: Johns Hopkins University Press.

Givel, Michael. (1998). "Conspiracy Thinking, Part II: Where Do We Go from Here?" Fair Comment. *The Alliance Reports*, vol. 2, no. 5, May, pp. 2, 16.

Givel, Michael. (1998). "Progressive Populism and Conspiracy Theories." Fair Comment. *The Alliance Reports*, vol. 2, no. 3, March, pp. 2–3.

Glaberman, Martin. (1980). *Wartime Strikes: The Struggle Against the No-Strike Pledge In the UAW During World War II*. Detroit: Bewick Editions.

Goetz, John. (1994). "Randall Terry and the U.S. Taxpayers Party." *Front Lines Research* (Planned Parenthood Federation of America), vol. 1, no. 2, August, pp. 1, 3, 6.

Goff, Kenneth. (1952). *One World a Red World*. Pamphlet. Englewood, CO: By the author.

Goff, Kenneth. (1958). *Reds Promote Racial War*. Pamphlet. Englewood, CO: By the author, under the imprint Soldiers of the Cross.

Goldberg, Robert Alan. (1981). *Hooded Empire: The Ku Klux Klan in Colorado*. Urbana: University of Illinois Press.

Goldfield, Michael. (1985). "Recent Historiography of the Communist Party U.S.A." In M. Davis, F. Pfeil, and M. Sprinker (Eds.), *The Year Left: An American Socialist Yearbook* (pp. 315–358). London: Verso, New Left Books.

Goldman, Eric F. (1960). *The Crucial Decade—And After: America, 1945–1960*. New York: Random House, Inc., Vintage Books.

Goldstein, Robert Justin. (1978). *Political Repression in Modern America, From 1870 to Present*. Boston, G. K. Hall, Cambridge, MA: Schenkman.

Golsan, Richard J. (Ed.). (1998). *Fascism's Return: Scandal, Revision, and Ideology since 1980*. Lincoln: University of Nebraska Press.

Gomes, Peter J. (1996). *The Good Book: Reading the Bible with Mind and Heart*. New York: William Morrow.

González Ruiz, José María. (1969). *Atheistic Humanism and the Biblical God*. Translated by Amado José Sandoval, S.J. Milwaukee: Bruce Publishing.

Goodman, Paul. (1988). *Towards a Christian Republic: Antimasonry and the Great Transition in New England, 1826–1836*. New York: Oxford University Press.

Goodwyn, Lawrence. (1976). *Democratic Promise: The Populist Moment in America*. New York: Oxford University Press.

Goodwyn, Lawrence. (1978). *The Populist Moment: A Short History of the Agrarian Revolt in America*. New York: Oxford University Press. An abridged version of Goodwyn, *Democratic Promise*.

Gordon, Joy. (1999). "Sanctions as Siege Warfare." *The Nation*, March 22, pp. 18–22.

Gordon, Linda. (1976). *Woman's Body, Woman's Right: A Social History of Birth Control in America*. New York: Viking Press, Grossman Publishers.

Gould, Stephen Jay. (1997). *Questioning the Millennium: A Rationalist's Guide to a Precisely Arbitrary Countdown*. New York: Harmony Books.

Gow, Andrew. (1997). *Jewish Shock-Troops of the Apocalypse*. Paper, symposium, Center for Millennial Studies, Boston University.

Gow, Andrew. (1999). *Medieval Racism? The Red Jews and Dehumanization in Popular Medieval Apocalypticism*. Paper, symposium, Center for Millennial Studies, Boston University.

Graham, Billy. (1983). *Approaching Hoofbeats: The Four Horsemen of the Apocalypse*. Minneapolis, MN: Grason.

Grann, David. (1997). "Robespierre of the Right: Paul Weyrich and the Conservative Quest for Purity." *New Republic*, October 27.

Grant, George. (1996). *Buchanan: Caught in the Crossfire*. Nashville: Thomas Nelson Publishers.

Grant, Madison. (1923). *The Passing of the Great Race: or The Racial Basis of European History*. 4th ed. New York: Charles Scribner's Sons.

Green, John C. (1993). *Religion, Social Issues, and the Christian Right*. Paper, presented at "The Religious New Right and the 1992 Campaign: An Assessment," Ethics and Public Policy Center, Washington, DC, December 9–10.

Green, John C. (1996). "A Look at the 'Invisible Army': Pat Robertson's 1988 Activist Corps." In John C. Green, James L. Guth, Corwin E. Smidt, and Lyman A. Kellstedt (Eds.), *Religion and the Culture Wars: Dispatches from the Front* (pp. 44–61). Lanham, MD: Rowman & Littlefield.

Green, John C. (1996). *Understanding the Christian Right*. Booklet. New York: The American Jewish Committee.

Green, John C., James L. Guth, and Kevin Hill. (1993). "Faith and Election: The Christian Right in Congressional Campaigns 1978–1988." *The Journal of Politics*, vol. 55, no. 1, February, pp. 80–91.

Green, John C., James L. Guth, Corwin E. Smidt, and Lyman A. Kellstedt. (1996). *Religion and the Culture Wars: Dispatches from the Front*. Lanham, MD: Rowman & Littlefield.

Green, John C., Corwin E. Smidt, Lyman A. Kellstedt, and James L. Guth. (1997). "Bringing in the Sheaves: The Christian Right and White Protestants, 1976–1996." In Corwin E. Smidt and James M. Penning (Eds.), *Sojourners in the Wilderness: The Christian Right in Comparative Perspective: Religious Forces in the Modern Political World* (pp. 75–91). Lanham, MD: Rowman & Littlefield.

Greenberg, Irving. (1988). *Theodore Roosevelt and Labor: 1900–1918*. New York: Garland Publishing.

Greider, William B. (1987). *Secrets of the Temple: How the Federal Reserve Runs the Country*. New York: Simon and Schuster.

Greider, William B. (1992). *Who Will Tell the People: The Betrayal of American Democracy*. New York: Simon and Schuster.

Griffin, G. Edward. (1975). *The Life and Words of Robert Welch: Founder of the John Birch Society*. Thousand Oaks, CA: American Media.

Griffin, Roger. (1991). *The Nature of Fascism*. New York: St. Martin's Press.

Grosser, Paul E., and Edwin G. Halperin. (1979). *Anti-Semitism: The Causes and Effects of a Prejudice*. Secaucus, NJ: Citadel Press, Lyle Stuart.

Grove, Gene. (1961). *Inside the John Birch Society*. Greenwich, CT: Fawcett.

Grover, Ronald, and Richard Siklos. (1998). "Malone: TV's New Uncrowned King?" *Business Week*, October 5, p. 118.

Grupp, Fred W., Jr. (1969). "The Political Perspectives of Birch Society Members." In Robert A. Schoenberger (Ed.), *The American Right Wing: Readings in Political Behavior* (pp. 83–118). New York: Holt, Rinehart & Winston.

Guillaumin, Colette. (1995). *Racism, Sexism, Power and Ideology*. London: Routledge.

Gullo, Karen. (1998). "Wealthy Clinton Foe Lets His Money Do The Talking." Associated Press, in *The Record* (Bergen County, New Jersey), June 10. Online archive.

Gullo, Karen. (1998). "Whitewater Tampering Probe Begins." Associated Press, August 21. Online archive. See other articles by Gullo in notes to Chapter 15.

Gunderson, Joan. (1987). "Independence, Citizenship, and the American Revolution." *Signs*, vol. 13, no. 1, pp. 59–77.

Guth, James L., and John C. Green. (1996). "The Moralizing Minority: Christian Right Support among Political Contributors." In John C. Green, James L. Guth, Corwin E. Smidt, and Lyman A. Kellstedt (Eds.), *Religion and the Culture Wars: Dispatches from the Front* (pp. 30–43). Lanham, MD: Rowman & Littlefield.

Guth, James L., John C. Green, Corwin E. Smidt, Lyman A. Kellstedt, and Margaret M. Poloma. (1997). *The Bully Pulpit: the Politics of Protestant Clergy*. Studies in Government and Public Policy. Lawrence: University Press of Kansas.

Gutman, Herbert G. (Ed.). (1989). *Who Built America? Working People and the Nation's Economy, Politics, Culture, and Society: Vol. 1*. New York: Pantheon Books.

Habermas, Jürgen. (1973). *Legitimation Crisis*. Translated by Thomas McCarthy. Boston: Beacon Press.

Harding, Susan Friend. (2000). *The Book of Jerry Falwell: Fundamentalist Language and Politics*. Princeton, NJ: Princeton University Press.

Hairston, Julie B. (1990). "Killing Kittens, Bombing Clinics." *Southern Exposure*, vol. 18, no. 2, Summer, pp. 15–18.

Hales, Jean Gould. (1994). "'Co-Laborers in the Cause': Women in the Ante-bellum Nativist Movement." In Nancy F. Cott (Ed.), *History of Women in the United States: Historical Articles on Women's Lives and Activities: Vol. 18. Women and Politics, Part 1* (pp. 77–96). Munich: K. G. Saur Verlag.

Halff, Charles. (1997). *The End Times Are Here Now*. Springdale, PA: Whitaker House.

Halpern, Thomas, and Brian Levin. (1996). *The Limits of Dissent: The Constitutional Status of Armed Civilian Militias*. Amherst, MA: Aletheia Press.

Halsell, Grace. (1986). *Prophecy and Politics: Militant Evangelists on the Road to Nuclear War*. Westport, CT: Lawrence Hill.

Hamm, Mark S. (1994). *American Skinheads: The Criminology and Control of Hate Crime*. Westport, CT: Praeger.

Hamm, Mark S. (1997). *Apocalypse in Oklahoma: Waco and Ruby Ridge Revenged*. Boston: Northeastern University Press.

Hammond, Bray. (1957). *Banks and Politics in America: From the Revolution to the Civil War*. Princeton, NJ: Princeton University Press.

Haney López, Ian F. (1996). *White by Law: The Legal Construction of Race*. New York: New York University Press.

Harding, Susan. (1994). "Imagining the Last Days: The Politics of Apocalyptic Language." In Martin E. Marty and R. Scott Appleby (Eds.), *Accounting for Fundamentalisms: Vol. 4. The Fundamentalism Project* (pp. 57–78). Chicago: University of Chicago Press.

Hardisty, Jean V. (1995). "Constructing Homophobia: Colorado's Right-Wing Attack on Homosexuals." In Chip Berlet (Ed.), *Eyes Right! Challenging the Right Wing Backlash* (pp. 86–104). Boston: South End Press. Revised and included in Hardisty, *Mobilizing Resentment*.

Hardisty, Jean V. (1995). "The Resurgent Right: Why Now?" *The Public Eye*, Fall–Winter. Revised and included in Hardisty, *Mobilizing Resentment*.

Hardisty, Jean V. (1998). "Kitchen Table Backlash: The Antifeminist Women's Movement." In Amy E. Ansell (Ed.), *Unraveling the Right: The New Conservatism in American Thought and Politics*, (pp. 105–125). Boulder, CO: Westview. Revised and included in Hardisty, *Mobilizing Resentment*.

Hardisty, Jean V. (1999). *Mobilizing Resentment: Conservative Resurgence from the John Birch Society to the Promise Keepers*. Boston: Beacon.

Hargis, Billy James. (1986 [1960]). *Communist America . . . Must It Be?* Arizona: New Leaf Press.

Harrington, Evan. (1996). "Conspiracy Theories and Paranoia: Notes from a Mind-Control Conference." *Skeptical Inquirer*, September–October, pp. 35–52.

Harris, William H. (1982). *The Harder We Run: Black Workers since the Civil War*. New York: Oxford University Press.

Harrison, Trevor. (1995). *Of Passionate Intensity: Right-Wing Populism and the Reform Party of Canada*. Toronto: University of Toronto Press.

Hartmann, Betsy. (1987). *Reproductive Rights and Wrongs: The Global Politics of Population Control and Contraceptive Choice*. New York: Harper & Row.

Hatfield, Larry D., and Dexter Waugh. (1992). "Where Think Tanks Get Their Money." *San Francisco Examiner*, May 26, pp. A1, A14.

Hawkins, Beth. (1994). "Patriot Games: The Armed Right and the Religious Right are Joining Together to Form Militias Across the Country." *Detroit Metro Times*, October 12. Reprinted *Detroit Metro Times*, April 26–May 2, 1995, and collected in Hazen, Smith, and Triano (Eds.), *Militias in America 1995*.

Hayek, Friedrich A. (1960 [1944]). *The Road to Serfdom*. Chicago: University of Chicago Press.

Hazen, Don, Larry Smith, and Christine Triano (Eds.). (1995). *Militias in America 1995: A Book of Readings & Resources*. San Francisco: Institute for Alternative Journalism.

Heale, M. J. (1990). *American Anticommunism: Combating the Enemy Within, 1830–1970*. Baltimore, MD: Johns Hopkins University Press.

Heale, M. J. (1998). *McCarthy's Americans: Red Scare Politics in State and Nation, 1935–1965*. Athens: University of Georgia Press.

Heider, Ulrike. (1994). *Anarchism: Left, Right, and Green*. Translated by Danny Lewis and Ulrike Bode. San Francisco: City Lights Books. Original edition in German, 1992.

Heilbrunn, Jacob. (1995). "On Pat Robertson: His Anti-Semitic Sources." *The New York Review of Books*, April 20, pp. 68–70.

Heilbrunn, Jacob. (1996). "Neocon v. Theocon." *The New Republic*, December 30, pp. 20–24.

Helvarg, David. (1994). *The War Against the Greens: The "Wise-Use" Movement, The New Right, and Anti-Environmental Violence*. San Francisco: Sierra Club Books.

Herek, Gregory M., and Kevin T. Berrill (Eds.). (1992). *Hate Crimes: Confronting Violence Against Lesbians and Gay Men*. Newbury Park, CA: Sage.

Herman, Didi. (1997). *The Antigay Agenda: Orthodox Vision and the Christian Right*. Chicago: University of Chicago Press.

Herrnstein, Richard J., and Charles Murray. (1994). *The Bell Curve: Intelligence and Class Structure in American Life*. New York: Free Press.

Hertzke, Allen D. (1993). *Echoes of Discontent: Jesse Jackson, Pat Robertson, and the Resurgence of Populism*. Washington, DC: Congressional Quarterly Press.

Heuser, Marie-Luise. (1991). "Was grün begann endete blutigrot: Von der Naturromantik zu den Reagrarisierungs- und Entvölkerungsplänen der SA und SS." In Dieter Hassenpflug (Ed.), *Industrialismus und Ökoromantik: Geschichte und Perspektiven der Ökolgisierung*. Wiesbaden: Deutsche-Universitäts-Verlag.

Higgins, George G. (1995). "Forays Into Anti-Semitism." *Catholic New York*, March 9, p. 10.

Higham, John. (1972 [1955]). *Strangers in the Land: Patterns of American Nativism 1860–1925*. New York: Atheneum.

Hill, Herbert. (1973). "Anti-Oriental Agitation and the Rise of Working-Class Racism." *Society*, January–February, pp. 43–54.

Hill, Lance. (1992). "Nazi Race Doctrine in the Political Thought of David Duke." In Douglas D. Rose (Ed.), *The Emergence of David Duke and the Politics of Race*. Chapel Hill: University of North Carolina Press.

Hilliard, Robert L., and Michael C. Keith. (1999). *Waves of Rancor: Tuning in the Radical Right*. Armonk, NY: M.E. Sharpe.

Himmelstein, Jerome L. (1990). *To the Right: The Transformation of American Conservatism*. Berkeley: University of California Press.

Himmelstein, Jerome L. (1998). *All But Sleeping with the Enemy: Studying the Radical Right Up Close*. Paper, annual meeting, American Sociological Association, San Francisco.

Historical Research Department. (1991). *The Secret Relationship Between Blacks and Jews*. Chicago, IL: Nation of Islam.

Hitchcock, James. (1982). *What is Secular Humanism?* Ann Arbor, MI: Servant Books.

Hixson, William B., Jr. (1992). *Search for the American Right Wing: An Analysis of the Social Science Record, 1955–1987*. Princeton, NJ: Princeton University Press.

Hoberman, J. (1986). "The Fascist Guns in the West." *American Film*, March, pp. 42–48.

Hockenos, Paul. (1993). *Free to Hate: The Rise of the Right in Post-Communist Europe*. New York: Routledge.

Hodes, Martha. (1997). *White Women, Black Men: Illicit Sex in the Nineteenth-Century South*. New Haven, CT: Yale University Press.

Hoffer, Eric. (1951). *The True Believer: Thoughts on the Nature of Mass Movements*. New York: Harper.

Hoffman, Lisa. (1995). "Whitewater and Oklahoma City Get Linked as Conspiracy." Scripps Howard News Service, April 28.

Hofstadter, Richard. (1955). *The Age of Reform: From Bryan to F.D.R.* New York: Vintage Books.

Hofstadter, Richard. (1965). *The Paranoid Style in American Politics and Other Essays*. New York: Knopf.

Holmes, Colin. (1979). *Anti-Semitism in British Society, 1876–1939*. New York: Holmes and Meier.

Holt, Michael F. (1992). *Political Parties and American Political Development: from the Age of Jackson to the Age of Lincoln*. Baton Rouge: Louisiana State University Press.

Holy Bible. (1984). New International Version, International Bible Society. Grand Rapids, MI: Zondervan.

Holy Bible. (1996). King James Version. Grand Rapids, MI: Zondervan.

Horowitz, David A. (1992). "Order, Solidarity, and Vigilance: The Ku Klux Klan in La Grande, Oregon." In Shawn Lay (Ed.), *The Invisible Empire in the West: Toward a New Historical Appraisal of the Ku Klux Klan of the 1920s* (pp. 185–216). Urbana: University of Illinois Press.

Horowitz, David A. (1997). "The Drudge Affair and Its Ripple Effect." *Salon*, February 23. Online at http://www.frontpagemag.com/dh/mccarthy.htm.

Hosokawa, Bill. (1971). "The Cherishing of Liberty: The American Nisei." In Amy Tachiki, Eddie Wong, Franklin Odo, with Buck Wong (Eds.), *Roots: An Asian American Reader* (pp. 215–220). Los Angeles: UCLA Asian American Studies Center.

Howell, Leon. (1995). *Funding the War of Ideas*. Cleveland, OH: United Church Board for Homeland Ministries.

Hsia, R. Po-chia. (1988). *The Myth of Ritual Murder: Jews and Magic in Reformation Germany*. New Haven, CT: Yale University Press.

Hugins, Walter Edward. (1958). *The New York Workingmen and Jacksonian Democracy, 1829–1837*. Ph.D. diss., Columbia University, New York, NY.

Hunt, Dave. (1990). *Global Peace and the Rise of Antichrist*. Eugene, OR: Harvest House.

Hunter, Allen. (1995). "Globalization from Below? Promises and Perils of the New Internationalism." *Social Policy*, vol. 25, no. 4, pp. 6–13. Online at http://www.publiceye.org/Sucker_Punch/Hunter.htm.

Hunter, James Davison. (1991). *Culture Wars: The Struggle to Define America*. New York: Basic Books.

Hunter, Jane. (1993). "Who was the ADL Spying For?" *Israeli Foreign Affairs*, vol. 9, no. 4, May 11, pp. 1–2, 5–8.

Huntington, Samuel P. (1997). *The Clash of Civilizations and the Remaking of World Order*. New York: Touchstone.

Hutchinson, E. (1855). *Startling Facts for Native Americans called "Know-Nothings": or a Vivid Presentation of the Dangers to American Liberty, to be Apprehended from Foreign Influence*. New York: By the author.

Hyatt, Michael S. (1998). *The Millennium Bug: How to Survive the Coming Chaos*. Washington, DC: Regnery.

Hyatt, Mike, and George Grant. (1998). *Y2K: The Day the World Shut Down*. Nashville, TN: Word Publishing.

Hymowitz, Carol, and Michaele Weissman. (1978). *A History of Women in America*. New York: Bantam Books.

Ignatiev, Noel. (1994). "The White Worker and the Labor Movement in Nineteenth-Century America." *Race Traitor*, no. 3, Spring, pp. 99–107.

Ignatiev, Noel. (1995). *How the Irish Became White*. New York: Routledge.

Ignatin, Noel. (1980). "A Golden Bridge: A New Look at William Z. Foster, the Great Steel Strike, and the 'Boring-from-Within' Controversy." *Workplace Papers*. Chicago: Sojourner Truth Organization.

Institute for Southern Studies' Campaign Finance Project. (1985). "Jesse Helms: The Meaning of His Money." *Southern Exposure*, vol. 13, no. 1, January–February, pp. 14–23.

The International Jew: The World's Foremost Problem. (1976 [1920]). Vols. 1–4. Republished. Reedy, WV: Liberty Bell Publications, 1976. Originally published Dearborn, MI: The Dearborn Publishing Company, 1920. Primarily consists of reprints of a series of articles from the *Dearborn Independent* in book form.

Irvine, Janice M. (1994). "Birds, Bees and Bigots." *The Women's Review of Books*, vol. 11, nos. 10–11, July, p. 23.

Isikoff, Michael. (1999). *Uncovering Clinton, A Reporter's Story*. New York: Crown Books.

Ismaelillo, and Robin Wright (Eds.). (1982). *Native Peoples in Struggle*. Bombay, NY: E.R.I.N. Publications.

Jabara, Abdeen. (1993). "The Anti-Defamation League: Civil Rights and Wrongs." *CovertAction Quarterly*, no. 45, Summer, pp. 28–35.

Jackson, Kenneth T. (1967). *The Ku Klux Klan in the City 1915–1930*. New York: Oxford University Press.

Jacobs, James B., and Kimberly Potter. (1998). *Hate Crimes: Criminal Law & Identity Politics*. New York: Oxford University Press.

Jaher, Frederic Cople. (1994). *A Scapegoat in the New Wilderness: The Origins and Rise of Anti-Semitism in America*. Cambridge, MA: Harvard University Press.

James, C. L. R., George Breitman, Edgar Keemer, et al. (1980). *Fighting Racism in World War II*. New York: Monad Press.

James, William T. (Ed.). (1997). *Foreshocks of Antichrist*. Eugene, OR: Harvest House.

James, William T., and others (Eds.). (1996). *Raging Into Apocalypse: Essays in Apocalypse IV*. Green Forest, AK: New Leaf Press.

Janssen, Al, and Larry K. Weeden (Eds.). (1994). *The Seven Promises of a Promise Keeper*. Colorado Springs, CO: Focus on the Family Publishing.

Jarvis, Howard, with Robert Pack. (1979). *I'm Mad as Hell: The Exclusive Story of the Tax Revolt and its Leader*. New York: Times Books/Quadrangle.

Jeansonne, Glen. (1988). *Gerald L. K. Smith: Minister of Hate*. New Haven, CT: Yale University Press.

Jeansonne, Glen. (1996). *Women of the Far Right: The Mothers' Movement and World War II*. Chicago: University of Chicago Press.

Jeffrey, Grant R. (1994). *Apocalypse: The Coming Judgement of Nations*. New York: Bantam.

Jeffreys-Jones, Rhodri. (1989). *The CIA and American Democracy*. New Haven, CT: Yale University Press.

Jenkins, J. Craig, and Bert Klandermans (Eds.). (1995). *The Politics of Social Protest: Comparative Perspectives on States and Social Movements: Vol. 3. Social Movements, Protest, and Contention*. Minneapolis: University of Minnesota Press.

Jenkins, Philip. (1997). *Hoods and Shirts: The Extreme Right in Pennsylvania, 1925–1950*. Chapel Hill: University of North Carolina Press.

Jenness, Valerie, and Kendal Broad. (1997). *Hate Crimes: New Social Movements and the Politics of Violence*. Hawthorne, NY: Aldine de Gruyter.

Jenness, Valerie, Abby Ferber, Ryken Grattet, with James Short. (1999). "Hate in America: What Do We Know?" Press briefing packet, annual meeting, American Sociological Association, Chicago. Online at http://www.publiceye.org/hate/Hate99ASA_toc.htm.

Jennings, Francis. (1976). "The Indians' Revolution." In Alfred F. Young (Ed.), *The American Revolution*.

John Birch Society. (1964). *The White Book of the John Birch Society for 1964*. Belmont, MA: John Birch Society.

Johnson, George. (1983). *Architects of Fear: Conspiracy Theories and Paranoia in American Politics*. Los Angeles: Tarcher/Houghton Mifflin.

Johnson, George. (1995). "The Conspiracy That Never Ends." *The New York Times*, April 30.

Johnson, George. (1995). *Fire in the Mind: Science, Faith, and the Search for Order*. New York: Knopf.

Johnston, Hank. (1995). "A Methodology for Frame Analysis: From Discourse to Cognitive Schemata." In Hank Johnston and Bert Klandermans (Eds.), *Social Movements and Culture: Vol. 4. Social Movements, Protest, and Contention* (pp. 217–246). Minneapolis: University of Minnesota Press.

Johnston, Hank, and Bert Klandermans (Eds.). (1995). *Social Movements and Culture*. Minneapolis: University of Minnesota Press.

Jones, E. Michael. (1996). "The Summer of '65: Or, How Contraceptives Cause Drive-by Shootings." *Culture Wars*, vol. 1, no. 9, February, pp. 1, 12–15.

Jones, Lila Lee. (1975). "The Ku Klux Klan in Eastern Kansas during the 1920's." *The Emporia State Research Studies*, vol. 23, no. 3, Winter.

Jorgensen, Leslie. (1995). "AM Armies." *Extra!* (Fairness and Accuracy in Reporting), March–April, pp. 20–22.

Josephson, Emanuel M. (1968). *The "Federal" Reserve Conspiracy & the Rockefellers: Their "Gold Corner."* New York: Chedney Press.

Josephson, Emanuel M. (1952). *Rockefeller, "Internationalist": The Man Who Misrules the World*. New York: Chedney Press.

Jouzaitis, Carol. (1994). "From The Folks Who Brought You Willie Horton, Here's Whitewater." *Chicago Tribune*, March 27. Online archive.

Judis, John B. (1988). *William F. Buckley, Jr.: Patron Saint of the Conservatives*. New York: Simon and Schuster.

Judis, John B. (1996). "The Republican Splintering: A Preview of the San Diego Zoo." *The New Republic*, August 19 & 26, pp. 32–36.

Junas, Daniel. (1989). *Rising Moon: The Unification Church's Japan Connection*. Working Paper No. 5. Seattle, WA: Institute for Global Security Studies.

Junas, Daniel. (1995). "The Rise of Citizen Militias: Angry White Guys with Guns." *CovertAction Quarterly*, Spring. Citation to reprint in Don Hazen, Larry Smith, and Christine Triano (Eds.), *Militias in America 1995: A Book of Readings and Resources*. San Francisco: Institute for Alternative Journalism, 1995.

Kadetsky, Elizabeth. (1994). "Bashing Illegals in California." *The Nation*, vol. 259, no. 12, October 17.

Kah, Gary H. (1991). *En Route to Global Occupation*. Lafayette, LA: Huntington House Publishers.

Kahn, Albert E. (1950). *High Treason: The Plot Against the People.* Croton-on-Hudson, NY: The Hour Publishers.

Kaiser, Robert G., and Ira Chinoy. (1999). "How Scaife's Money Powered a Movement." *Washington Post*, May 2, p. A1.

Kalman, Matthew, and John Murray. (1995). "The Icke Man Cometh." *New Moon*, November, pp. 24–27.

Kane, Harnett T. (1990 [1941]). *Huey Long's Louisiana Hayride: The American Rehearsal for Dictatorship 1928–1940.* Gretna, LA: Pelican Publishing.

Kaplan, Deborah. (1998). *Republic of Rage: A look inside the patriot movement.* Paper, annual meeting, American Sociological Association, San Francisco.

Kaplan, Jeffrey. (1997). *Radical Religion in America: Millenarian Movements from the Far Right to the Children of Noah.* Syracuse, NY: Syracuse University Press.

Kaplan, Jeffrey, and Tore Bjørgo (Eds.). (1998). *Nation and Race: The Developing Euro-American Racist Subculture.* Boston: Northeastern University Press.

Kaplan, Jeffrey, and Leonard Weinberg. (1998). *The Emergence of a Euro-American Radical Right.* New Brunswick, NJ: Rutgers University Press

Karlsen, Carol F. (1998). *The Devil in the Shape of a Woman: Witchcraft in Colonial New England.* New York: Norton.

Katz, David S., and Richard H. Popkin. (1998). *Messianic Revolution: Radical Religious Politics to the End of the Second Millennium.* New York: Hill and Wang.

Katz, William Loren. (1980). "The People vs. the Klan in Mass Combat." *Freedomways*, vol. 20, no. 2, pp. 96–100.

Katz, William Loren. (1987). *The Black West.* 3rd ed. Seattle: Open Hand Publishers.

Kaufmann, Christine. (1999). "From the Margins to the Mainstream: Montana 'Patriots' in the Political Arena." *The Provocateur*, Montana Human Rights Network, Spring.

Kay, Tom. (1997). *When the Comet Runs: Prophecies for the New Millennium.* Charlottesville, VA: Hampton Roads.

Kayyem, Juliette. (1989). " . . . Need Not Apply." *The Boston Phoenix*, July 14–20.

Kazin, Michael. (1995). *The Populist Persuasion: An American History.* New York: Basic Books.

Kele, Max H. (1972). *Nazis and Workers: National Socialist Appeals to German Labor, 1919–1933.* Chapel Hill: The University of North Carolina Press.

Keller, Catherine. (1996). *Apocalypse Now and Then: A Feminist Guide to the End of the World.* Boston: Beacon Press.

Kellner, Douglas. (1990). *Television and the Crisis of Democracy.* Boulder, CO: Westview.

Kellstedt, Lyman A., John C. Green, James L. Guth, and Corwin E. Smidt. (1993). *Religious Voting Blocs in the 1992 Election: The Year of the Evangelical?* Paper, annual meeting, American Political Science Association. Collected in Green, Guth, Smidt, and Kellstedt, *Religion and the Culture Wars.*

Kelly, Clarence. (1974). *Conspiracy against God and Man.* Belmont, MA: Western Islands.

Kelly, Michael. (1995). "The Road to Paranoia." *The New Yorker*, June 19, pp. 60–75.

Kelsey, Mary E., and Mary Thierry Texeira. (1998). "Scapegoating at the End of the Millennium: Symbolic Legislation and the Crisis of Capitalism." Paper, annual meeting, American Sociological Association, San Francisco.

Kerber, Linda K. (1980). *Women of the Republic: Intellect and Ideology in Revolutionary America.* Chapel Hill: The University of North Carolina Press.

Kerber, Linda K. (1989). " 'History Can Do It No Justice': Women and the Reinterpretation of the American Revolution." In Ronald Hoffman and Peter J. Albert (Eds.), *Women in the Age of the American Revolution.* Charlottesville: The University Press of Virginia.

Kerber, Linda K. (1990). " 'I Have Don . . . much to Carrey on the Warr': Women and the Shaping of Republican Ideology after the American Revolution." In Harriet B. Applewhite and Darline G. Levy (Eds.), *Women and Politics in the Age of the Democratic Revolution.* Ann Arbor: The University of Michigan Press.

Kessler-Harris, Alice. (1982). *Out to Work: A History of Wage-Earning Women in the United States.* New York: Oxford University Press.

Khan, Surina. (1996). "Gay Conservatives: Pulling the Movement to the Right." *The Public Eye*, vol. 10, no. 1, Spring.

Khan, Surina. (1998). *Calculated Compassion: How the Ex-Gay Movement Serves the Right's Attack on Democracy.* Somerville, MA: Political Research Associates.

Kincaid, Cliff. (1995). *Global Bondage: The U.N. Plan to Rule the World.* Lafayette, LA: Huntington House; Vital Issues Press.

Kincaid, Cliff. (1997). *Global Taxes for World Government.* Lafayette, LA: Huntington House; Vital Issues Press.

Kincheloe, Joe, Shirley R. Steinberg, and Aaron D. Gresson, III (Eds.). (1996). *Measured Lies: The Bell Curve Examined.* New York: St. Martin's Press.

King, Dennis. (1982). *Nazis Without Swastikas: The Lyndon LaRouche Cult and Its War on American Labor.* New York: League for Industrial Democracy.

King, Dennis. (1989). *Lyndon LaRouche and the New American Fascism.* New York: Doubleday.

King, Dennis, and Chip Berlet. (1993). "ADLgate." *Tikkun* magazine, vol. 8, no. 4.

King, Dennis, and Chip Berlet. (1993). "The A.D.L. Under Fire." Op-ed. *The New York Times*, May 28.

King, Wayne. (1985). "White Supremacists Voice Support of Farrakhan." *The New York Times*, October 12, p. 12.

Kintz, Linda. (1997). *Between Jesus and the Market: The Emotions that Matter in Right-Wing America.* Durham, NC: Duke University Press.

Kintz, Linda, and Julia Lesage (Eds.). (1998). *Media, Culture, and the Religious Right.* Minneapolis: University of Minnesota Press.

Klandermans, Bert. (1997). *The Social Psychology of Protest.* Cambridge, MA: Blackwell.

Klasen, Thomas G. (1988). *A Pro-Life Manifesto.* Westchester, IL: Crossway Books, Good News Publishers.

Klassen, Ben. (1992 [1973]). *Nature's Eternal Religion.* Milwaukee: The Milwaukee Church of the Creator.

Klassen, Ben. (1992 [1981]). *The White Man's Bible.* Milwaukee: The Milwaukee Church of the Creator.

Klassen, Ben. (1993). *On the Brink of a Bloody Racial War: With the White Race Targeted for Extermination.* Niceville, FL: The Church of the Creator.

Klatch, Rebecca E. (1987). *Women of the New Right.* Philadelphia, PA: Temple University Press.

Klatch, Rebecca E. (1999). *A Generation Divided: The New Left, the New Right, and the 1960s.* Berkeley: University of California Press.

Klehr, Harvey, and John Earl Haynes. (1992). *The American Communist Movement: Storming Heaven Itself.* New York: Twayne Publishers.

Knelman, F. H. (1985). *Reagan, God and the Bomb: From Myth to Policy in the Nuclear Arms Race.* Buffalo, NY: Prometheus Books.

Kocka, Jürgen. (1980). *White Collar Workers in America 1890–1940: A Social–Political History in International Perspective.* Translated by Maura Kealey. Beverly Hills, CA: Sage.

Kolchin, Peter. (1993). *American Slavery, 1619–1877.* New York: Hill and Wang.

Kolko, Gabriel. (1962). "American Business and Germany, 1930–1941." *The Western Political Quarterly*, vol. 15, no. 4, December, pp. 713–728.

Kolko, Gabriel. (1963). *The Triumph of Conservatism: A Re-interpretation of American History, 1900–1916.* New York: The Free Press of Glencoe.

Kolko, Gabriel. (1968). *The Politics of War: The World and United States Foreign Policy, 1943–1945.* New York: Random House.

Kolko, Gabriel. (1976). *Main Currents in Modern American History.* New York: Harper & Row.

Kolko, Gabriel. (1985). *Anatomy of a War: Vietnam, the United States, and the Modern Historical Experience.* New York: Pantheon Books.

Kolko, Gabriel. (1988). *Confronting the Third World: United States Foreign Policy, 1945–1980.* New York: Pantheon Books; Random House.

Koonz, Claudia. (1987). *Mothers in the Fatherland: Women, the Family, and Nazi Politics.* New York: St. Martin's Press.

Kornweibel, Theodore, Jr. (1998). *"Seeing Red": Federal Campaigns Against Black Militancy, 1919–1925.* Bloomington: Indiana University Press.

Korten, David C. (1995). *When Corporations Rule the World.* West Hartford, CT: Kumerian Press and San Francisco: Berrett-Koehler Publishers.

Kovel, Joel. (1994). *Red Hunting in the Promised Land: Anticommunism and the Making of America.* New York, Basic Books.

Kovel, Joel. (2000). "Beyond Populism." Memo No. 2, To the Greens. Circulated February 2000. Online at http://www.publiceye.org/Sucker_Punch/Kovel.htm.

Kraft, Charles Jeffrey. (1992). *A Preliminary Socio-Economic and State Demographic Profile of the John Birch Society.* Cambridge, MA: Political Research Associates.

Kramer, Joel, and Diana Alstad. (1993). *The Guru Papers: Masks of Authoritarian Power.* Berkeley, CA: Frog, Ltd.

Kühl, Stefan. (1994). *The Nazi Connection: Eugenics, American Racism, and German National Socialism.* New York: Oxford University Press.

Kulikoff, Allen. (1993). "The American Revolution, Capitalism, and the Formation of the Yeoman Classes." In Alfred F. Young (Ed.), *Beyond the American Revolution: Explorations in the History of American Radicalism* (pp. 80–119). DeKalb, IL: Northern Illinois University Press.

Kurtz, Howard. (1997). "When Cyber-Gossip Meets Stodgy Old Libel Laws: The Web's Rule-Ignoring Matt Drudge May Have Gone Too Far With His Blumenthal Story." *Washington Post* (Weekly Edition), August 25.

Ladd, Everett Carll. (1998). "Why Reporting of the Polls Has Consistently Understated the Drop in Clinton's Support." *The Public Perspective,* The Roper Center, University of Connecticut, vol. 9, no. 6, October–November, pp. 35–37.

LaFeber, Walter. (1978). *The Panama Canal: The Crisis in Historical Perspective.* New York: Oxford University Press.

LaHaye, Tim. (1975). *Revelation: Illustrated and Made Plain.* Grand Rapids, MI: Zondervan.

LaHaye, Tim. (1978). *The Unhappy Gays: What Everyone Should Know about Homosexuality.* Wheaton, IL: Tyndale House Publishers.

LaHaye, Tim. (1980). *The Battle for the Mind.* Old Tappan, NJ: Fleming H. Revell.

LaHaye, Tim. (1982). *The Battle for the Family.* Old Tappan, NJ: Fleming H. Revell.

LaHaye, Tim, and Jerry B. Jenkins. (1995). *Left Behind: A Novel Of The Earth's Last Days.* Vol. 1, *Left Behind* series. Wheaton, IL: Tyndale House Publishers. For more apocalyptic novels by LaHaye and others, see Chapter 16, note 27.

LaLonde, Peter. (1991). *One World Under AntiChrist: Globalism, Seducing Spirits and Secrets of the New World Order.* Eugene, OR: Harvest House.

LaLonde, Peter, and Paul LaLonde. (1988). *Apocalypse: Caught in the Eye of the Storm.* Niagara Falls, NY: This Week in Bible Prophecy. Also produced as a video.

Lamy, Philip. (1996). *Millennium Rage: Survivalists, White Supremacists, and the Doomsday Prophecy.* New York: Plenum.

Landes, Richard. (1994). "Scapegoating." In Peter N. Stearn (Ed.), *Encyclopedia of Social History.* New York: Garland.

Landes, Richard. (1996). "On Owls, Roosters, and Apocalyptic Time: A Historical Method for Reading a Refractory Documentation." *Union Seminary Quarterly Review,* vol. 49, nos. 1–2, pp. 165–185.

Lane, Charles. (1994). "The Tainted Sources of 'The Bell Curve.'" *The New York Review,* December 1, pp. 14–19.

Langer, Elinor. (1990). "The American Neo-Nazi Movement Today." Special Report. *The Nation,* July 16–23.

Langer, Lawrence L. (1995). *Admitting the Holocaust: Collected Essays*. New York: Oxford University Press.

Langman, Lauren. (1998). "Fascism and the Feast of Fools." Paper, 14th World Congress of Sociology (XIVe Congrès Mondial de Sociologie), International Sociological Association, Montreal, Quebec, Canada.

Laqueur, Walter. (1993). *Black Hundred: The Rise of the Extreme Right in Russia*. New York: HarperCollins Publishers.

LaRouche, Lyndon H., Jr. (1987). *The Power of Reason, 1988: An Autobiography*. Washington, DC: Executive Intelligence Review.

Lasch, Christopher. (1995). *The Revolt of the Elites: and the Betrayal of Democracy*. New York: Norton.

Lawrence, Ken. (1985). *The New State Repression*. Chicago: International Network Against New State Repression.

Lawrence, Ken. (1989). "Klansmen, Nazis, Skinheads: Vigilante Repression." *CovertAction Quarterly*, no. 31, Winter, pp. 29–33.

Lawton, Kim A. (1996). "Clinton Signs Law Backing Heterosexual Marriage." *Christianity Today*, October 28.

Lay, Shawn. (1992). "Conclusion: Toward a New Historical Appraisal of the Ku Klux Klan of the 1920s." In Shawn Lay (Ed.), *The Invisible Empire in the West: Toward a New Historical Appraisal of the Ku Klux Klan of the 1920s* (pp. 217–222). Urbana: University of Illinois Press.

Lay, Shawn. (1992). "Imperial Outpost on the Border: El Paso's Frontier Klan No. 100." In Shawn Lay (Ed.), *The Invisible Empire in the West: Toward a New Historical Appraisal of the Ku Klux Klan of the 1920s* (pp. 67–96). Urbana: University of Illinois Press.

Lay, Shawn. (1992). "Introduction: The Second Invisible Empire." In Shawn Lay (Ed.), *The Invisible Empire in the West: Toward a New Historical Appraisal of the Ku Klux Klan of the 1920s* (pp. 1–15). Urbana: University of Illinois Press.

Lay, Shawn (Ed.). (1992). *The Invisible Empire in the West: Toward a New Historical Appraisal of the Ku Klux Klan of the 1920s*. Urbana: University of Illinois Press.

Lea, Henry Charles. (1961). *The Inquisition of the Middle Ages*. Abridged. New York: Macmillan.

Ledeen, Michael Arthur. (1972). *Universal Fascism: The Theory and Practice of the Fascist International, 1928–1936*. New York: Howard Fertig.

Lee, John R. (1964). "Ford's Personnel Manager Describes the Five-Dollar Day and Other Labor Programs at Ford." In Alfred Dupont Chandler (Ed.), *Giant Enterprise: Ford, General Motors, and the Automobile Industry: Sources and Readings*. New York: Harcourt, Brace & World.

Lee, Martin A. (1997). *The Beast Reawakens*. Boston: Little, Brown.

Lee, Martin A. (1999). "The Fascist Response To Globalization." Op-ed. *Los Angeles Times*, November 28. Online archive.

Lens, Sidney. (1969). *Radicalism in America*. New updated ed. New York: Thomas Y. Crowell Company.

Lerner, Gerda. (1979). "The Lady and the Mill Girl: Changes in the Status of Women in the Age of Jackson." In *The Majority Finds Its Past: Placing Women in History*. New York: Oxford University Press.

Lesage, Julia. (1998). "Christian Coalition Leadership Training." In Linda Kintz and Julia Lesage (Eds.), *Culture, Media, and the Religious Right* (pp. 295–325). Minneapolis: University of Minnesota Press.

Lesher, Stephan. (1994). *George Wallace: American Populist*. Reading, MA: Addison-Wesley.

Leuchtenburg, William E. (1961). "Introduction." In Theodore Roosevelt, *The New Nationalism*. New ed. Englewood Cliffs, NJ: Prentice-Hall.

Leuchtenburg, William E. (1963). *Franklin D. Roosevelt and the New Deal, 1932–1940*. New York: Harper & Row.

Levin, Brian. (1999). "Hate Crimes: Worse by Definition." *Journal of Contemporary Criminal Justice*, vol. 15, no. 1, February, pp. 6–21.

Levin, Jack, and Jack McDevitt. (1993). *Hate Crimes: The Rising Tide of Bigotry and Bloodshed.* New York: Plenum Press.

Levitas, Daniel. (1995). "Antisemitism and the Far Right: 'Hate' Groups, White Supremacy, and the Neo-Nazi Movement." In Jerome A. Chanes (Ed.), *Antisemitism in America Today: Outspoken Experts Explode the Myths.* New York: Birch Lane Press, Carol Publishing.

Lewis, Anthony. (1997). "Crime and Politics." *The New York Times*, May 19, p. A15.

Lewis, David L. (1978). *The Public Image of Henry Ford: An American Folk Hero and His Company.* Detroit: Wayne State University Press.

Lewis, Gregg. (1995). *The Power of the Promise Kept.* Colorado Springs, CO: Focus on the Family Publishing.

Lewis, Neil A. (1995). "Bill Seeks to End Automatic Citizenship for All Born in the U.S." *The New York Times*, December 14, p. A26.

Lewis, Neil A. (1998). "Group Behind Paula Jones Gains Critics as Well as Fame." *The New York Times*, January 18, p. 18.

Lieberman, Trudy. (1994). "Churning Whitewater." *Columbia Journalism Review*, May–June. Online archive.

Lienesch, Michael. (1998). "Prophetic Neo-Populists: The New Christian Right and Party Politics in the United States." In Hans-Georg Betz and Stefan Immerfall (Eds.), *The New Politics of the Right: Neo-Populist Parties and Movements in Established Democracies.* New York: St. Martin's Press.

Lind, Michael. (1995). "On Pat Robertson: His Defenders." *The New York Review of Books*, April 20, pp. 67–68.

Lind, Michael. (1995). "Rev. Robertson's Grand International Conspiracy Theory." *The New York Review of Books*, vol. 42, no. 2, February 2, pp. 21–25.

Lindsey, Hal. (1994). *Planet Earth—2000 A.D.: Will Mankind Survive?* Palos Verdes, CA: Western Front.

Lindsey, Hal. (1997). *Apocalypse Code.* Palos Verdes, CA: Western Front.

Lindsey, Hal, with C. C. Carlson. (1970). *The Late Great Planet Earth.* Grand Rapids, MI: Zondervan.

Lipset, Seymour Martin, and Earl Raab. (1970). *The Politics of Unreason: Right-Wing Extremism in America, 1790–1970.* New York: Harper & Row.

Litwack, Leon F. (1961). *North of Slavery: The Negro in the Free States, 1790–1860.* Chicago: The University of Chicago Press.

Lizza, Ryan. (2000). "Silent Partner: The Man Behind the Anti-Free Trade Revolt." *The New Republic*, January 10, 2000. Online archive.

Lo, Clarence Y. H. (1995). *Small Property Versus Big Government: Social Origins of the Property Tax Revolt.* Berkeley: University of California Press.

Lofland, John. (1996). *Social Movement Organizations: Guide to Research on Insurgent Realities.* New York: Aldine de Gruyter.

Long, Huey P. (1985). *Kingfish to America, Share Our Wealth: Selected Senatorial Papers of Huey P. Long.* Edited by Henry M. Christman. New York: Schocken Books.

Louisiana Coalition Against Racism and Nazism. (1991). "Report on Louisiana House Bill No 1584: The Duke Sterilization Plan." In Resource Packet. New Orleans, LA: Louisiana Coalition Against Racism and Nazism.

Ludmerer, Kenneth M. (1991). "Genetics, Eugenics, and the Immigration Restriction Act of 1924." In George E. Pozzetta (Ed.), *Nativism, Discrimination, and Images of Immigrants* New York: Garland Publishing.

Luker, Kristin. (1984). *Abortion and the Politics of Motherhood.* Berkeley: University of California Press.

Lusane, Clarence. (1996). "Lie: The Drug War is Color-Blind and We Can Prove It." *CovertAction Quarterly*, no. 57, Summer, pp. 9–11.

Lyman, Stanford. (1971). "Strangers in the City: the Chinese in the Urban Frontier." In Amy Tachiki, Eddie Wong, Franklin Odo, with Buck Wong (Eds.), *Roots: An Asian American Reader* (pp. 159–187). Los Angeles: UCLA Asian American Studies Center.

Lyons, Gene, and the editors of Harpers Magazine. (1996). *Fools for Scandal: How the Media Invented Whitewater.* New York: Franklin Square Press.

Lyons, Matthew N. (1992). *Parasites and Pioneers: Anti-Semitism in White Supremacist America.* Unpublished paper.

Lyons, Matthew N. (1992). *Tracing the Roots of Conspiracy Thinking.* Unpublished paper.

Lyons, Matthew N. (1995). "What is Fascism? Some General Ideological Features." In Chip Berlet (Ed.), *Eyes Right! Challenging the Right Wing Backlash* (pp. 244–245). Boston: South End Press.

Lyons, Matthew N. (1998). "Business Conflict and Right-Wing Movements." In Amy E. Ansell (Ed.), *Unraveling the Right: The New Conservatism in American Thought and Politics* (pp. 80–102). Boulder, CO: Westview.

Macdonald, Andrew (pseudonym of William Pierce). (1978). *The Turner Diaries.* Washington, DC: National Alliance Books.

Macdonald, Sally, and Carol M. Ostrom. (1999). "How White Supremacists See It." *The Seattle Times*, August 12, online archive.

Mackendrick, W. G. (The Roadbuilder). (1922). *The Destiny of Britain and America.* Revised ed. Toronto: McClelland & Stewart.

MacLachlan, Colin M. (1991). *Anarchism and the Mexican Revolution: The Political Trials of Ricardo Flores Magón in the United States.* Berkeley: University of California Press.

Macleod, David I. (1983). *Building Character in the American Boy: The Boy Scouts, YMCA, and Their Forerunners, 1870–1920.* Madison: University of Wisconsin Press.

MacShane, Denis. (1992). *International Labour and the Origins of the Cold War.* Oxford: Clarendon Press.

Magida, Arthur J. (1994). "Evil Twins: LaRouche and Farrakhan operatives offered—with no proof." *Baltimore Jewish Times*, April 22, online archive.

Males, Mike A. (1996). *The Scapegoat Generation: America's War on Adolescents.* Monroe, ME: Common Courage Press.

Mander, Jerry, and Edward Goldsmith (Eds.). (1996). *The Case Against the Global Economy: And for a Turn Toward the Local.* San Francisco: Sierra Club Books.

Manning, Christel J. (1999). *God Gave Us the Right: Conservative Catholic, Evangelical Protestant, and Orthodox Jewish Women Grapple with Feminism.* New Brunswick, NJ: Rutgers University Press.

Manning, Robert. (1999). "Dancing With Snakes: In Digging Out The Clinton–Lewinsky Story, Reporter Michael Isikoff Became Part Of It." *Boston Globe*, April 4, Books section, p. L1.

Manza, Jeff, and Clem Brooks. (1999). *Social Cleavages and Political Change: Voter Alignment and U.S. Party Coalitions.* New York: Oxford University Press.

Marable, Manning. (1980). "A. Philip Randolph: A Political Assessment." In *From the Grassroots: Essays Toward Afro-American Liberation* (pp. 59–85). Boston: South End Press.

Marable, Manning. (1991). *Race, Reform, and Rebellion: The Second Reconstruction in Black America, 1945–1990.* 2nd ed. Jackson: University Press of Mississippi.

Marable, Manning. (1997). "No Compromise: Farrakhan, Chavis and Lyndon LaRouche." *Amsterdam News*, February 1, pp. 13, 22.

Marchak, M. Patricia. (1991). *The Integrated Circus: The New Right and the Restructuring of Global Markets.* Montreal & Kingston: McGill-Queen's University Press.

Marcus, George E. (Ed.). (1999). *Paranoia Within Reason: A Casebook on Conspiracy Explanation.* Chicago, University of Chicago Press.

Mardsen, Victor E. See: *Protocols of Zion.*

Marks, Carole. (1989). *Farewell—We're Good and Gone: The Great Black Migration.* Bloomington: Indiana University Press.

Marrs, Texe W. (1993). *Big Sister Is Watching You: Hillary Clinton And The White House Feminists Who Now Control America—And Tell The President What To Do.* Austin, TX: Living Truth Publishers.

Marsden, George M. (1982). *Fundamentalism and American Culture: The Shaping of Twentieth Century Evangelicalism, 1870–1925.* New York: Oxford University Press.

Marsden, George M. (1991). *Understanding Fundamentalism and Evangelicalism.* Grand Rapids, MI: William B. Eerdmans Publishing Co.

Marshner, William H., and Enrique T. Rueda. (1983). *The Morality of Political Action: Biblical Foundations.* Washington, DC: Free Congress Research and Education Foundation.

Martel, Charles. (1992). "Why Sr. Lucia Went Public." *Fatima Family Messenger,* April–June, pp. 2–4, 44–48.

Martel, Charles. (1994). "The Antichrist." *The Fatima Crusader,* Summer, pp. 6–9.

Martin, Tony. (1976). *Race First: The Ideological and Organizational Struggles of Marcus Garvey and the Universal Negro Improvement Association.* Westport, CT. Greenwood Press.

Martin, William. (1996). *With God on Our Side: The Rise of the Religious Right in America.* New York: Broadway Books.

Martinez, Elizabeth. (1997). "It's a Terrorist War on Immigrants." *Z Magazine,* vol. 10, nos. 7–8, July–August, pp. 29–36.

Marx, Gary T. (1997). "External Efforts to Damage or Facilitate Social Movements: Some Patterns, Explanations, Outcomes, and Complications." In Steven M. Buechler and F. Kurt Cylke, Jr. (Eds.), *Social Movements: Perspectives and Issues* (pp. 360–384). Mountain View, CA: Mayfield Publishing.

Marx, Karl. (1978 [1867]). *Capital: Vol. 1.* In Robert C. Tucker (Ed.), *The Marx–Engels Reader,* 2nd ed. New York: Norton.

Mason, Carol. (1996). *Fundamental Opposition: Feminism, Narrative and the Abortion Debate.* Ph.D. dissertation, University of Minnesota.

Mason, Carol. (1998). *Fetal Legislation: The Partial Birth of a Nation?* Paper, symposium, Center for Millennial Studies, Boston University.

Mason, Carol. (1999). *Killing for Life.* Unpublished book manuscript provided by author.

Mason, Carol. (1999). "Minority Unborn." In Lynn M. Morgan and Merideth W. Michaels (Eds.), *Fetal Subjects, Feminist Positions.* Philadelphia: University of Pennsylvania Press.

Mason, Carol. (2000). "Cracked Babies and the Partial Birth of a Nation: Millennialism and Fetal Citizenship." *Cultural Studies,* vol. 14, no. 1, pp. 35–60.

Mason, Carol. (2000). "From Protest to Retribution: The Guerilla Politics of Pro-Life Violence. *New Political Science,* vol. 22, no. 1, pp. 11–29.

Mason, Todd. (1990). *Perot: An Unauthorized Biography.* Homewood, IL: Business One Irwin.

Matrisciana, Patrick (Ed.). (1994). *The Clinton Chronicles Book.* 4th ed. Hemet, CA: Jeremiah Books.

Matsumoto, Valerie. (1989). "Nisei Women and Resettlement during World War II." In Asian Women United of California (Eds.), *Making Waves: An Anthology of Writings By and About Asian American Women* (pp. 115–126). Boston: Beacon Press.

Mawyer, Martin. (1993). "A Rift in the Ranks of the Christian Right." *The Washington Post,* National Weekly Edition, October 4–10, p. 24.

Maxwell, Joe, and Andrés Tapia. (1995). "Guns And Bibles: Militia Extremists Blend God And Country Into A Potent Mixture." *Christianity Today,* vol. 39, no. 7, June 19, pp. 34–37.

May, Elaine Tyler. (1988). *Homeward Bound: American Families in the Cold War Era.* New York: Basic Books.

May, Martha. (1990). "The Historical Problem of the Family Wage: The Ford Motor Company and the Five Dollar Day." In Ellen Carol DuBois and Vicki L. Ruiz (Eds.), *Unequal*

Sisters: A Multicultural Reader in U.S. Women's History. New York: Routledge; Chapman & Hall.

May, Martha. (1991). "Bread Before Roses: American Workingmen, Labor Unions And The Family Wage." In Ruth Milkman (Ed.), *Women, Work and Protest: A Century of US Women's Labor History*. London: Routledge; Chapman and Hall.

Mayer, Arno J. (1971). *Dynamics of Counterrevolution in Europe, 1870–1956: An Analytic Framework*. New York: Harper & Row, Publishers.

Mazumdar, Sucheta. (1989). "General Introduction: A Woman-Centered Perspective on Asian American History." In Asian Women United of California (Eds.), *Making Waves: An Anthology of Writings By and About Asian American Women* (pp. 1–22). Boston: Beacon Press.

McAdam, Doug. (1985). *Political Process and the Development of Black Insurgency, 1930–1970*. Chicago: University of Chicago Press. Originally published 1982.

McAdam, Doug, John D. McCarthy, and Mayer N. Zald (Eds.). (1996). *Comparative Perspectives on Social Movements: Political Opportunities, Mobilizing Structures, and Cultural Framings*. Cambridge, UK: Cambridge University Press.

McAlvany, Donald S. (1990). *Toward a New World Order: The Countdown to Armageddon*. Oklahoma City, OK: Hearthstone Publishing, Southwest Radio Church of the Air.

McAuliffe, Mary Sperling. (1978). *Crisis on the Left: Cold War Politics and American Liberals, 1947–1954*. Amherst: The University of Massachusetts Press.

McCarthy, John D., and Mayer N. Zald. (1977). "Resource Mobilization and Social Movements: A Partial Theory." *American Journal of Sociology*, vol. 82, no. 6, May, pp. 1212–1241.

McGraw, Onalee. (1976). *Secular Humanism and the Schools: The Issue Whose Time has Come*. Pamphlet. Washington, DC: Heritage Foundation.

McIntire, Carl. (1963 [1946]). "*Author of Liberty*." 2nd ed. Collingswood, NJ: *Christian Beacon*/20th Century Reformation Hour. Originally published 1946.

McLemee, Scott. (1994). "Spotlight on the Liberty Lobby." *CovertAction Quarterly*, Fall, pp. 23–32.

McLemee, Scott. (1995). "Public Enemy." *In These Times*, May 15, pp. 14–19.

McManus, John F. (1983). *The Insiders*. Belmont, MA: John Birch Society.

McManus, John F. (1992). "Taking on the Giant: How Dare Pat Buchanan Defy the Establishment!" *The New American*, April 20, p. 5.

McMath, Robert C. Jr. (1993). *American Populism: A Social History 1877–1898*. New York: Hill and Wang; Farrar, Straus & Giroux.

McNall, Scott G. (1975). *Career of a Radical Rightist: A Study in Failure*. Port Washington, NY: Kennikat Press/National University Publications.

Mehler, Barry. (1989). "Foundation for Fascism: The New Eugenics Movement in the United States." *Patterns of Prejudice*, vol. 23, no. 4, pp. 17–25.

Mehler, Barry. (1994). "In Genes We Trust: When Science Bows to Racism." *Reform Judaism*, vol. 23, pp. 10–13, 77–79.

Mehler, Barry. (1999). "Race and 'Reason': Academic Ideas a Pillar of Racist Thought. *Intelligence Report* (Southern Poverty Law Center), Winter, pp. 27–32.

Meier, August, and Elliott Rudwicke. (1979). *Black Detroit and the Rise of the UAW*. New York: Oxford University Press.

Melcher, Ralph. (1998). "Culture Wars." *Ctheory* (an international journal of theory, technology and culture), September 15. Online at http://www.ctheory.com/e66.html.

Melley, Timothy. (1999). *Empire of Conspiracy: The Culture of Paranoia in Postwar America*. Ithaca, NY: Cornell University Press.

Menendez, Albert J. (1993). *Visions of Reality: What Fundamentalist Schools Teach*. Buffalo, NY: Prometheus Books.

Menendez, Albert J. (1996). *The Perot Voters & the Future of American Politics*. Amherst, NY: Prometheus Books.

Merkl, Peter H., and Leonard Weinberg (Eds.). (1993). Encounters with the Contemporary Radical Right. Boulder, CO: Westview.

Merta, Ed. (1998 [circa]). Birth of a Conspiracy Theory. Unpublished paper provided by author, written while at Department of History, Harvard University. Traces the roots of the conspiracist view of the Council on Foreign Relations.

Messer-Davidow, Ellen. (1993). "Manufacturing the Attack on Liberalized Higher Education." Social Text, Fall, pp. 40–80.

Messer-Davidow, Ellen. (1994). "Who (Ac)Counts and How." MMLA (The Journal of the Midwest Modern Language Association), vol. 27, no. 1, Spring, pp. 26–41.

Michelmore, David L. (1995). "Right Wingers Claim Clinton Lawyer's Death is a Cover-up." Pittsburgh Post Gazette, April 30, p. A1.

Milburn, Michael A., and Sheree D. Conrad. (1996). The Politics of Denial. Cambridge, MA: MIT Press.

Miller, Adam. (1994). "Professors of Hate." Rolling Stone, October 20.

Mills, C. Wright. (1956). The Power Elite. New York: Oxford University Press.

Minges, Patrick. (1994). Apocalypse Now! The Realized Eschatology of the "Christian Identity" Movement. Paper, Mid-Atlantic Conference, American Academy of Religion. Online at http://www.publiceye.org/rightist/aarlong.html.

Mink, Gwendolyn. (1986). Old Labor and New Immigrants in American Political Development: Union, Party, and State, 1875–1920. Ithaca, NY: Cornell University Press.

Mintz, Frank P. (1985). The Liberty Lobby and the American Right: Race, Conspiracy, and Culture. Westport, CT: Greenwood Press.

Moen, Matthew C. (1997). "The Changing Nature of Christian Right Activism: 1970s–1990s." In Corwin E. Smidt and James M. Penning (Eds.), Sojourners in the Wilderness: The Christian Right in Comparative Perspective: Religious Forces in the Modern Political World (pp. 21–37). Lanham, MD: Rowman & Littlefield.

Moffett, James. (1988). Storm in the Mountains: A Case Study of Censorship, Conflict, and Consciousness. Carbondale: Southern Illinois University Press.

Monteith, Dr. Stanley. (1991). AIDS: The Unnecessary Epidemic—America Under Seige. Sevierville, TN: Covenant House Books.

Moore, Leonard J. (1991). Citizen Klansmen: The Ku Klux Klan in Indiana, 1921–1928. Chapel Hill: The University of North Carolina Press.

Moore, Leonard J. (1992). "Historical Interpretations of the 1920s Klan: The Traditional View and Recent Revisions." In Shawn Lay (Ed.), The Invisible Empire in the West: Toward a New Historical Appraisal of the Ku Klux Klan of the 1920s (pp. 17–38). Urbana: University of Illinois Press.

Moore, William V. (1981). The John Birch Society: A Southern Profile. Paper, annual meeting, Southern Political Science Association, Memphis, TN.

Morgan, Dan. (1981). "Conservatives: A Well-Financed Network." The Washington Post, January 4, p. A1.

Morgan, Edmund S. (1975). American Slavery, American Freedom: The Ordeal of Colonial Virginia. New York: Norton.

Morgan, Lynn M., and Merideth W. Michaels (Eds.). (1999). Fetal Subjects, Feminist Positions. Philadelphia, University of Pennsylvania Press.

Morin, Richard, and Scott Wilson. (1997). "Men Were Driven to 'Confess Their Sins': In Survey, Attendees Say They Also Are Concerned About Women, Politics." Washington Post, October 5; p. A1.

Morris, Aldon D., and Carol McClurg Mueller (Eds.). (1992). Frontiers in Social Movement Theory. New Haven, CT: Yale University Press.

Morris, Barbara M. (1976). Why Are You Losing Your Children? Revised. Upland, CA: The Barbara Morris Report.

Morris, Barbara M. (1979). Change Agents in the Schools: Destroy Your Children, Betray Your Country. Upland, CA: The Barbara M. Morris Report.

Morris, Richard B. (1949). "Andrew Jackson, Strikebreaker." *The American Historical Review*, vol. 55, no. 1, October, pp. 54–68.

Moss, Richard J. (1995). *The Life of Jedidiah Morse: A Station of Peculiar Exposure*. Knoxville, TN: University of Tennessee Press.

Mosse, George L. (1964). *The Crisis of German Ideology: Intellectual Origins of the Third Reich*. New York: Grosset & Dunlap.

Mosse, George L. (1985). *Toward the Final Solution: A History of European Fascism*. Madison, WI: University of Wisconsin Press.

Mouly, Ruth W. (1987). *The Religious Right and Israel: The Politics of Armageddon*. Chicago: Midwest Research (now Political Research Associates).

Mozzochi, Jonathan, and L. Events Rhinegard. (1991). *Rambo, Gnomes and the New World Order: The Emerging Politics of Populism*. Portland, OR: Coalition for Human Dignity.

Mueller, Carol McClurg. (1992). "Building Social Movement Theory." In Aldon. D. Morris and Carol McClurg Mueller (Eds.), *Frontiers in Social Movement Theory* (pp. 3–25). New Haven, CT: Yale University Press.

Muhammad, Abdul Alim. (1990). "Making America the Nation She Was Intended To Be." *New Federalist*, September 28, p. 10. See other cites to Nation of Islam interaction with LaRouchites in Chapter 13.

Mulkern, John R. (1990). *The Know-Nothing Party in Massachusetts: The Rise and Fall of a People's Movement*. Boston: Northeastern University Press.

Mullin, Michael. (1978). "British Caribbean and North American Slaves in an Era of War and Revolution, 1775–1807." In Jeffrey J. Crow and Larry E. Tise (Eds.), *The Southern Experience in the American Revolution* (pp. 235–265). Chapel Hill: University of North Carolina Press.

Mullins, Eustace. (1952). *Mullins on the Federal Reserve*. Also titled *A Study of the Federal Reserve*. New York: Kaspar and Horton.

Mullins, Eustace. (1954). *The Federal Reserve Conspiracy*. 2nd ed. Union, NJ: Christian Educational Association.

Mullins, Eustace. (1955 [circa]). *Impeach Eisenhower!* Chicago: *Women's Voice*, no date.

Mullins, Eustace. (1955). "Jews Mass Poison American Children." *Women's Voice* (Chicago), June, p. 11.

Mullins, Eustace. (1968 [circa]). *The Biological Jew*. Staunton, VA: Faith and Service Books, no date.

Mullins, Eustace. (1985? [circa]). *The Secret Holocaust*. Pamphlet. No date. Various published editions including Word of Christ Mission, Sons of Liberty, and apparently by the author.

Mullins, Eustace. (1992). *The World Order: Our Secret Rulers*. 2nd ed. Staunton, VA: Ezra Pound Institute of Civilization.

Murphy, Charles J. V. (1954). "McCarthy and the Businessman." *Fortune*, vol. 44, no. 4, April, pp. 156–158, 180–194.

Murphy, Charles J. V. (1954). "Texas Business and McCarthy." *Fortune*, vol. 44, no. 5, May, pp. 100–101, 208–216.

Murray, Charles A. (1984). *Losing Ground: American Social Policy, 1950–1980*. New York: Basic Books.

Murray, James. (1998). "Chiapas and Montana: Tierra Y Libertad." *Race Traitor*, no. 8, Winter, pp. 39–50.

Muwakkil, Salim. (1995). "Color Bind." *In These Times*, March 6, pp. 15–17.

Nader, Ralph. (1999). "The Greens & the Presidency: A Voice, Not an Echo," *The Nation*, July 8, pp. 18–19.

Nash, Gary B. (1990). *Race and Revolution*. Madison, WI: Madison House.

Naurekas, Jim, and Janine Jackson. (1996). "It's the Mexicans, Stupid: The Phony Populism of Pat Buchanan. *Extra!* (Fairness and Accuracy in Reporting), May–June, pp. 8–10.

Navasky, Victor S. (1980). *Naming Names*. New York: The Viking Press.

Neiberger, Ami. (1996). "Promise Keepers: Seven Reasons You Should Watch Out." *Freedom Writer*, September.

Neiwert, David A. (1999). *In God's Country: The Patriot Movement and the Pacific Northwest.* Pullman: Washington State University Press.

Nelson, Jack. (1993). *Terror in the Night: The Klan's Campaign Against the Jews.* New York: Simon and Schuster.

Neumann, Franz. (1972). "Anxiety in Politics." In Richard O. Curry and Thomas M. Brown (Eds.), *Conspiracy: The Fear of Subversion in American History.* New York: Holt, Rinehart and Winston.

Nevins, Allan, with the collaboration of Frank Ernest Hill. (1954). *Ford: The Times, the Man, the Company.* New York: Charles Scribner's Sons.

Nevins, Allan, and Frank Ernest Hill. (1957). *Ford: Expansion and Challenge: 1915–1933.* New York: Charles Scribner's Sons.

Niebuhr, Gustav. (1995). "Baptist Group Votes to Repent Stand on Slaves." *The New York Times*, June 21, p. A1.

Niebuhr, Gustav. (1995). "Pat Robertson Says He Intended No Anti-Semitism in Book He Wrote Four Years Ago." *The New York Times*, March 4, p. 10.

Nixon, Ron. (1996). "All God's Children?" *Southern Exposure*, vol. 24, no. 1, Spring, pp. 34–38.

Noebel, David A. (1965). *Communism, Hypnotism and the Beatles.* Tulsa, OK: Christian Crusade Publications.

Noebel, David A. (1966). *Rhythm, Riots and Revolution.* Tulsa, OK: Christian Crusade Publications.

Noebel, David A. (1974). *Marxist Minstrels: A Handbook on Communist Subversion of Music.* Tulsa, OK: American Christian College Press.

Noebel, David A. (1977). *The Homosexual Revolution.* Tulsa, OK: American Christian College Press.

Noebel, David A. (1992). *Understanding the Times: The Story of the Biblical Christian, Marxist/Leninist and Secular Humanist Worldviews.* Manitou Springs, CO: Summit Ministries Press.

Noël, Lise. (1994). *Intolerance: A General Survey.* Translated by Arnold Bennett. Montreal: McGill-Queen's University Press.

Northrup, Herbert R. (1971). "Blacks in the United Automobile Workers Union." In John H. Bracey, Jr., August Meier, and Elliott Rudwick (Eds.), *Black Workers and Organized Labor.* Belmont, CA: Wadsworth Publishing Company.

Norton, Mary Beth. (1980). *Liberty's Daughters: The Revolutionary Experience of American Women, 1750–1800.* Boston: Little, Brown and Company.

Novick, Michael. (1995). "Front Man for Fascism: Bo Gritz and the Racist Populist Party." In Michael Novick, *White Lies, White Power.* Monroe: ME: Common Courage Press.

Novick, Michael. (1995). *White Lies White Power: The Fight Against White Supremacy and Reactionary Violence.* Monroe: ME: Common Courage Press.

Novosad, Nancy. (1996). "God Squad: The Promise Keepers Fight For A Man's World." *The Progressive*, August, pp. 25–27.

Nugent, Walter T. K. (1962). *The Tolerant Populists: Kansas Populism and Nativism.* Chicago: University of Chicago Press.

Nyhan, David. (1999). "Sun Belt Senators Could Get Burned." *Boston Globe*, January 8, p. A19.

Oberman, Heiko A. (1984 [1981]). *The Roots of Anti-Semitism: In the Age of Renaissance and Reformation.* Translated by James I. Porter. Philadelphia: Fortress Press. Original edition in German, 1981.

Oberschall, Anthony. (1973). *Social Conflict and Social Movements.* Englewood Cliffs, NJ: Prentice-Hall.

O'Keeffe, Michael, and Kevin Daley. (1993). "Checking The Right: Rightist Backlash Against The Environmental Movement." *Buzzworm*, May.

Okoye, F. Nwabueze. (1980). "Chattel Slavery as the Nightmare of the American Revolutionaries." *William and Mary Quarterly*, vol. 37, January, pp. 3–28.

Olasky, Marvin N. (2000). *Compassionate Conservatism: What It Is, What It Does, and How It Can Transform America*. New York: Free Press.

Oldfield, Duane Murray. (1996). *The Right and the Righteous: The Christian Right Confronts the Republican Party*. Lanham, MD: Rowman & Littlefield.

O'Leary, Stephen D. (1994). *Arguing the Apocalypse: A Theory of Millennial Rhetoric*. New York: Oxford University Press.

O'Leary, Stephen D. (1998). "Heaven's Gate and the Culture of Popular Millennialism." *Millennial Stew* (newsletter of the Center for Millennial Studies), Winter.

Olsen, Ted. (1998). "The Dragon Slayer." *Christianity Today*, December 7, pp. 36–42.

Omi, Michael, and Howard Winant. (1994). *Racial Formation in the United States: From the 1960s to the 1990s*. 2nd ed. New York: Routledge.

O'Reilly, Kenneth. (1983). *Hoover and the Un-Americans: The FBI, HUAC and the Red Menace*. Philadelphia, PA: Temple University Press.

O'Reilly, Kenneth. (1988). *"Racial Matters": The FBI's Secret File on Black America, 1960–1972*. New York: Free Press.

Oshinsky, David M. (1976). *Senator Joseph McCarthy and the American Labor Movement*. Columbia: University of Missouri Press.

O'Sullivan, Gerry. (1991). "The Satanism Scare." *Postmodern Culture*, vol. 1, no. 2, January.

Pagels, Elaine. (1996). *The Origin of Satan*. New York: Vintage.

Paige, Connie. (1983). *The Right to Lifers: Who They Are, How They Operate, Where They Get Their Money*. New York: Summit Books.

Paine, Thomas. (1984). *Common Sense, the Rights of Man, and Other Essential Writings of Thomas Paine*. New York: Meridian, New American Library.

Parenti, Christian. (1998). "Crossing Borders." *In These Times*, March 22, pp. 15–17.

Parenti, Michael. (1996). *Dirty Truths: Reflections on Politics, Media, Ideology, Conspiracy, Ethnic Life and Class Power*. San Francisco: City Lights.

Paulus, Stefan. (1997). *Nostradamus 1999: Who Will Survive?* St. Paul, MN: Llewellyn Publications.

Pavlik, Gregory. (1993). Review of Gottfried's *The Conservative Movement*, revised. *Conservative Review*, vol. 4, no. 5, September–October, p. 37.

Pavolko, Ronald M. (1980). "Racism and the New Immigration: A Reinterpretation of the Assimilation of White Ethnics in American Society." *Sociology and Social Research*, vol. 65, no. 1.

Payne, Stanley G. (1980). *Fascism: Comparison and Definition*. Madison, WI: The University of Wisconsin Press.

Pell, Eve. (1984). *The Big Chill: How the Reagan Administration, Corporate America, and Religious Conservatives are Subverting Free Speech and the Public's Right to Know*. Boston: Beacon Press.

Pencak, William. (1989). *For God and Country: The American Legion, 1919–1941*. Boston: Northeastern University Press.

People for the American Way. (1996). *Buying a Movement: Right-Wing Foundations and American Politics*. Washington, DC: People for the American Way.

Perea, Juan F. (1997). *Immigrants Out! The New Nativism and the Anti-Immigrant Impulse in the United States*. New York: New York University Press.

Perkins, Ray, Jr. (1995). *Logic and Mr. Limbaugh*. Chicago: Open Court.

Perloff, James. (1988). *Shadows of Power: The Council on Foreign Relations and the American Decline*. Appleton, WI: Western Islands.

Pertman, Adam. (1998). "Partisan Drama will Lack Heroes, Scholars Agree." *Boston Globe*, December 16, p. A41.

Peschek, Joseph G. (1987). *Policy-Planning Organizations: Elite Agendas and America's Rightward Turn*. Philadelphia: Temple University Press.

Pessen, Edward. (1969). *Jacksonian America: Society, Personality, and Politics*. Homewood, IL: The Dorsey Press.

Pharr, Suzanne. (1988). *Homophobia: A Weapon of Sexism*. Inverness, CA: Chardon Press.

Pharr, Suzanne. (1996). "A Match Made in Heaven: Lesbian Leftie Chats with a Promise Keeper." *The Progressive*, August, pp. 28–29.

Pharr, Suzanne. (1996). *In the Time of the Right: Reflections on Liberation*. Berkeley, CA: Chardon Press.

Philbrick, Herbert A. (1952). *I Led 3 Lives: Citizen, "Communist," Counterspy*. New York: McGraw-Hill.

Phillips, Howard. (1983). *The New Right at Harvard*. Vienna, VA: The Conservative Caucus.

Phillips, Kevin P. (1969). *The Emerging Republican Majority*. New Rochelle, NY: Arlington House.

Phillips, Kevin P. (1975). *Mediacracy: American Parties and Politics in the Communications Age*. Garden City, NY: Doubleday.

Phillips, Kevin P. (1982). *Post-Conservative America: People, Politics, and Ideology in a Time of Crisis*. New York: Random House.

Phillips, Kevin P. (1990). *The Politics of Rich and Poor: Wealth and the American Electorate in the Reagan Aftermath*. New York: Random House.

Phillips, Kevin. (1992). "The Politics of Frustration." *The New York Times Magazine*. April 12, pp. 38–42.

Phillips, Kevin P. (1993). *Boiling Point: Republicans, Democrats, and the Decline of Middle-Class Prosperity*. New York: Random House.

Phillips, Kevin P. (1994). *Arrogant Capital: Washington, Wall Street, and the Frustration of American Politics*. Boston: Little, Brown.

Phillips, Kevin. (1995). "Right Makes Fright." Commentary, *San Jose Mecury News*, May 10, NewsLibrary online archive.

Phillips, Randy. (1997). "Late Edition." Television program. October 5. CNN. Interviews, from transcript, p. 9.

Pierce, William. See pseudonym: Macdonald, Andrew.

Pinckney, Alphonso. (1976). *Red, Black, and Green: Black Nationalism in the United States*. New York: Cambridge University Press.

Pipes, Daniel. (1997). *Conspiracy: How the Paranoid Style Flourishes and Where it Comes From*. New York: The Free Press.

Pipes, Daniel. (1998). *The Hidden Hand: Middle East Fears of Conspiracy*. New York: St. Martin's Press.

Pitcavage, Mark. (1996). "Every Man a King: The Rise and Fall of the Montana Freemen." Monograph. The Militia Watchdog. Online at http://www.militia-watchdog.org/freemen.htm.

Pitcavage, Mark. (1996). "Extremism and the Electorate: Campaign '96 and the 'Patriot' Movement." Special Report. The Militia Watchdog. Online at http://www.militia-watchdog.org/elect96.htm.

Pitcavage, Mark. (1999). "Welcome." The Militia Watchdog. Online at http://www.militia-watchdog.org/welcome.htm.

Piven, Francis Fox, and Richard A. Cloward. (1978). *Poor People's Movements: Why They Succeed, How They Fail*. New York: Vintage.

Podhoretz, Norman. (1979). *Breaking Ranks: A Political Memoir*. New York: Harper & Row.

Political Research Associates. (1999). *Defending Public Education: An Activist Resource Kit*. Cambridge, MA: By the author.

Porteous, Skipp. (1994). "Special profile: The Rutherford Institute." *The Freedom Writer*, June.

Posner, Gerald. (1996). *Citizen Perot: His Life and Times*. New York: Random House.

Post, Louis F. (1923). *The Deportations Delirium of Nineteen-Twenty*. Chicago: Charles H. Kerr.

Postone, Moishe. (1980). "Anti-Semitism and National Socialism: Notes on the German Reaction to 'Holocaust.'" *new german critique*, no. 19, Winter, pp. 97–115.

Prague, Emil Greenhalgh. (1996). "The Neo-Confederate Movement" *Turning the Tide*, vol. 9, no. 2, Summer, pp. 43–47.

Preston, William, Jr. (1963). *Aliens and Dissenters: Federal Suppression of Radicals, 1903–1933*. New York: Harper Torchbooks.

Price, Robert M. (1997). "Antichrist Superstar and the Paperback Apocalypse: Rapturous Fiction and Fictitious Rapture." In special report, "On the Millennium." *Deolog* (online journal), January–February. Online at http://www.stealth.net/~deolog/Price297.html.

The Protocols of Zion. (1934 [1905]). Full inside title: *The Protocols of the Meetings of the Learned Elders of Zion with Preface and Explanatory Notes*. Includes the 1905 Nilus version translated from the Russian text by Victor E. Mardsen. Dearborn, MI: *Dearborn Independent*. Note that there are many variations on the title, including *The Protocols of the Learned Elders of Zion*.

Purdum, Todd S. (1996). "Clinton Backs Plan to Deter Youthful Violence." *The New York Times*, May 31, p. A20.

Quarles, Benjamin. (1961). *The Negro in the American Revolution*. Chapel Hill: The University of North Carolina Press.

Quigley, Carroll. (1981). *The Anglo-American Establishment: From Rhodes to Cliveden*. New York: Books in Focus.

Quigley, Carroll. (1992? [1966]). *Tragedy and Hope: A History of the World in Our Time*. Republished, Rancho Palos Verdes, CA: GSG Associates, no date, circa 1992. Originally published New York: Macmillan, 1966.

Quigley, Margaret. (1995). "The Roots of the I.Q. Debate: Eugenics & Social Control." In Chip Berlet (Ed.), *Eyes Right! Challenging the Right Wing Backlash* (pp. 210–222). Boston: South End Press. Expanded, footnoted monograph available from Political Research Associates.

Quinby, Lee. (1994). *Anti-Apocalypse: Exercises in Genealogical Criticism*. Minneapolis: University of Minnesota Press.

Quinby, Lee. (1997). "Coercive Purity: The Dangerous Promise of Apocalyptic Masculinity." In Charles B. Strozier and Michael Flynn (Eds.), *The Year 2000: Essays on the End*. New York: New York University Press.

Quinby, Lee. (1999). *Millennial Seduction: A Skeptic Confronts Apocalyptic Culture*. Ithaca, NY: Cornell University Press.

Ramos, Tarso Luís. (1991). "Feint to the Left: The Growing Popularity of Populism." *Portland Alliance* (Oregon), December, pp. 13, 18.

Ramos, Tarso Luís. (1995). "Regulatory Takings & Private Property Rights." In Chip Berlet (Ed.), *Eyes Right! Challenging the Right Wing Backlash* (pp. 146–154). Boston: South End Press.

Rand, Kristen. (1996). "Gun Shows in America: Tupperware® Parties for Criminals." Washington, DC: Violence Policy Center.

Ratner, Lorman (Comp.). (1969). *Antimasonry: The Crusade and the Party*. Englewood Cliffs, NJ: Prentice-Hall.

Reagan, Michael, with Jim Denney. (1996). *Making Waves*. Nashville: Thomas Nelson.

Reagan, Ronald. (1984). *Abortion and the Conscience of the Nation*. Nashville, TN: Thomas Nelson.

Reavis, Dick J. (1995). *The Ashes of Waco: An Investigation*. New York: Simon and Schuster.

Redles, David. (1998). *"The Day Is Not Far Off": The Millennial Reich and the Induced Apocalypse*. Paper, symposium, Center for Millennial Studies, Boston University.

Redles, David. (1999). *Final War, Final Solution: WWII and the Holocaust as Eschatological Conceptions*. Paper, symposium, Center for Millennial Studies, Boston University.

Reed, Adolph, Jr. (2000). *Class Notes: Posing as Politics and Other Thoughts on the American Scene*. New York: The New Press.

Reeves, Thomas C. (1982). *The Life and Times of Joe McCarthy: A Biography*. New York: Stein and Day, Publishers.

Reilly, Philip R. (1991). *The Surgical Solution: A History of Involuntary Sterilization in the United States*. Baltimore: The Johns Hopkins University Press.

Rempel, William C. (1998). "Trooper Changes His Story, New Account Helps Clinton." *Chicago Sun-Times*, March 22. Online archive.

Retter, James D. (1998). *Anatomy of a Scandal: An Investigation Into the Campaign to Undermine the Clinton Presidency*. Los Angeles: General Publishing Group.

Ribuffo, Leo P. (1980). "Henry Ford and *The International Jew*." *American Jewish History*, vol. 69, no. 4, June, pp. 437–477.

Ribuffo, Leo P. (1983). *The Old Christian Right: The Protestant Far Right from the Great Depression to the Cold War*. Philadelphia: Temple University Press.

Rice, Charles E. (1994). "The Death Penalty Dilemma." *New American*, April 4.

Rich, Frank. (1995). "Bait and Switch." Column. *The New York Times*, March 2.

Rich, Frank. (1998). "The Road to Laramie." *The New York Times*, October 14, online archive.

Rickey, Elizabeth. (1992). "The Nazi and the Republicans: An Insider View of the Response of the Republican Party to David Duke." In Douglas D. Rose (Ed.), *The Emergence of David Duke and the Politics of Race*. Chapel Hill: University of North Carolina Press.

Riddell, John (Ed.). (1984). *Lenin's Struggle for a Revolutionary International: Documents 1907–1916, The Preparatory Years*. New York: Monad Press, Pathfinder Press.

Ridgeway, James. (1989). "White Blight: David Duke Worms Ahead" *The Village Voice*, July 4, pp. 18, 22.

Ridgeway, James. (1991). *Blood in the Face: The Ku Klux Klan, Aryan Nations, Nazi Skinheads, and the Rise of a New White Culture*. New York: Thunder's Mouth Press.

Riker, William H. (1988 [1982]). *Liberalism Against Populism: A Confrontation Between the Theory of Democracy and the Theory of Social Choice*. Prospect Heights, IL: Waveland Press.

Risen, James, and Judy L. Thomas. (1998). *Wrath of Angels: The American Abortion War*. New York: Basic Books.

Robbins, Thomas, and Susan J. Palmer (Eds.). (1997). *Millennium, Messiahs, and Mayhem: Contemporary Apocalyptic Movements*. New York: Routledge.

Roberts, Henry C. (1994 [1947]). *The Complete Prophesies of Nostradamus*. Translated, edited, and interpreted, by Henry C. Roberts. Re-edited by Lee Roberts Amsterdam and Harvey Amsterdam. Updated by Robert Lawrence. New York: Crown Publishers.

Robertson, Pat. (1991). *The New World Order*. Dallas: Word Publishing.

Robins, Robert S., and Jerrold M. Post. (1997). *Political Paranoia: The Psychopolitics of Hatred*. New Haven, CT: Yale University Press.

Robinson, Arthur, and Gary North. (1986). *Fighting Chance: Ten Feet to Survival*. Cave Junction, OR: Oregon Institute of Science and Medicine.

Robison, John. (1967 [1798]). *Proofs of a Conspiracy—against All the Religions and Governments of Europe, carried on in the secret meetings of Freemasons, Illuminati and Reading Societies*. 4th ed. with postscript. Boston: Western Islands.

Roediger, David R. (1991). *The Wages of Whiteness: Race and the Making of the American Working Class*. New York: Verso.

Rogin, Michael Paul. (1967). *The Intellectuals and McCarthy: The Radical Specter*. Cambridge, MA: MIT Press.

Rogin, Michael Paul. (1976). *Fathers and Children: Andrew Jackson and the Subjugation of the American Indian*. New York: Vintage Books.

Rokeach, Milton. (1960). *The Open and Closed Mind*. New York: Basic Books.

Romerstein, Herbert. (1962). *Communism and Your Child*. New York: The Bookmailer.

Roosevelt, Theodore (1961 [1910]). *The New Nationalism*. Englewood Cliffs, NJ: Prentice-Hall. Originally published in 1910 as Theodore Roosevelt and Ernest Hamlin Abbott, *The New Nationalism*. New York: The Outlook Company.

Rose, P. I. (1974). *They and We: Racial and Ethnic Relations in The United States*. 2nd ed. New York: Random House.

Rosen, James. (1997). "What's Behind the Obsession with Conspiracies?" *The News and Ob-*

server (North Carolina), August 17. Online at http://www.news-observer.com/daily/1997/08/17/qq00.html, August 13, 1999.

Rosenfeld, Jean E. (2000). "A Brief History of Millennialism and Suggestions for a New Paradigm for Use in Critical Incidents." In Catherine Wessinger (Ed.), *Millennialism, Persecution, and Violence: Historical Cases.* Syracuse, NY: Syracuse University Press.

Rosenfeld, Jean E. (2000). "The Justus Freeman Standoff: The Importance of the Analysis of Religion in Avoiding Violent Outcomes." In Catherine Wessinger (Ed.), *Millennialism, Persecution, and Violence.* Syracuse, NY: Syracuse University Press.

Rosenfeld, Seth. (1983). "The Spy Who Came Down on the Freeze: Rees, Reagan, and the Digest Smear." *Village Voice,* August 16.

Rosin, Hanna. (1997). "Walking the Plank: Henry Hyde's Abortion Problem." *The New Republic,* August 19.

Rosin, Hanna. (1999). "God's Hit Man." GQ, January, p. 118.

Ross, Loretta J. (1994). "Anti-Abortionists and White Supremacists Make Common Cause." *The Progressive,* vol. 58, no. 10, October.

Rothmyer, Karen. (1981). "Citizen Scaife." *Columbia Journalism Review,* July–August.

Rothschild, Emma. (1974). "Fordism and Sloanism." In Alan S. Brown, John T. Houdek, and John H. Yzenbaard (Eds). *Michigan Perspectives: People, Events, and Issues.* Dubuque, IA: Kendall, Hunt Publishing Company.

Rowe, Ed. (1984). *Homosexual Politics: Road to Ruin for America.* Herndon, VA: Growth Book and Tape Company; Church League of America, Washington, DC, office.

Rowell, Andrew. (1996). *Green Backlash: Global Subversion of the Environmental Movement.* New York: Routledge.

Rozell, Mark J., and Clyde Wilcox (Eds.). (1995). *God at the Grassroots: The Christian Right in the 1994 Elections.* Lanham, MD: Rowman & Littlefield.

Rubin, Mitchell S. (1986). "The FBI and Dissidents: A 1st Amendment Analysis of Attorney Gen. Smith's 1983 FBI Guidelines on Domestic Security Investigations." Parts I & II. *Police Misconduct and Civil Rights Law Report,* vol. 1, nos. 14–15, March–April, May–June.

Rueda, Enrique T. (1982). *The Homosexual Network: Private Lives and Public Policy.* Old Greenwich, CT: The Devin-Adair Company.

Rueda, Enrique T., and Michael Schwartz. (1987). *Gays, AIDS and You.* Old Greenwich, CT: The Devin-Adair Company.

Rupert, Mark. (1997). "Globalization and the Reconstruction of Common Sense in the US." In Stephen Gill and James H. Mittelman (Eds.), *Innovation and Transformation in International Studies.* New York: Cambridge University Press.

Rupert, Mary. (1997). "The Patriot Movement and the Roots of Fascism." In Susan Allen Nan et al. (Eds.), *Windows to Conflict Analysis and Resolution: Framing our Field.* Fairfax, VA: Institute for Conflict Analysis and Resolution.

Rusher, William. (1975). *The Making of the New Majority Party.* Ottawa, IL: Greenhill Publications.

Russakoff, Dale. (1995). "No-Name Movement Fed by Fax Expands." *The Washington Post,* August 20.

Sachar, Howard M. (1992). *A History of the Jews in America.* New York: Alfred A. Knopf.

Sack, Kevin. (1996). "A Penitent Christian Coalition Offers Aid to Burned Churches." *The New York Times,* June 19, p. A19.

Sacks, Karen Brodkin. (1994). "How Did Jews Become White Folks?" In Steven Gregory and Roger Sanjek (Eds.), *Race* (pp. 78–102). New Brunswick, NJ: Rutgers University Press.

Sakai, J. (1983). *Settlers: The Mythology of the White Proletariat.* 2nd ed. Chicago: Morningstar Press.

Saloutos, Theodore (Ed.). (1978). *Populism: Reaction or Reform?* New York: Robert E. Kieger Publishing Company.

Samples, Kenneth, Erwin de Castro, Richard Abanes, and Robert Lyle. (1994). *Prophets of the Apocalypse: David Koresh and Other American Messiahs*. Grand Rapids, MI: Baker Books.

Sandlin, Andrew. (1996). "The Creed of Reconstructionism." *Chalcedon Report*, no. 369, April.

Sandos, James A. (1992). *Rebellion in the Borderlands: Anarchism and the Plan of San Diego, 1904–1923*. Norman: University of Oklahoma Press.

Saponara, Laura Elizabeth. (1997). "Ideology at Work: Deciphering the Appeal of New Right Discourse." Masters thesis. University of Texas at Austin.

Saxton, Alexander. (1971). *The Indispensable Enemy: Labor and the Anti-Chinese Movement in California*. Berkeley: University of California Press.

Saxton, Alexander. (1990). *The Rise and Fall of the White Republic: Class Politics and Mass Culture in Nineteenth-Century America*. New York: Verso.

Scatamburlo, Valerie L. (1998). *Soldiers of Misfortune: The New Right's Culture War and the Politics of Political Correctness*. Counterpoints series, Vol. 25. New York: Peter Lang.

Schacht, John N. (Ed.). (1981). *Three Faces of Midwestern Isolationism: Gerald P. Nye, Robert P. Wood, John L. Lewis*. Iowa City: The Center for the Study of the Recent History of the United States.

Schaeffer, Francis A. (1980 [circa]). *Plan for Action: An Action Alternative Hanbook for Whatever Happened to the Human Race?* Old Tappan, NJ: Fleming H. Revell.

Schaeffer, Francis A. (1981 [circa]). *A Christian Manifesto*. Westchester, IL: Crossway Books.

Schaeffer, Francis A. (1982). *A Christian Manifesto*. Revised. Westchester, IL: Crossway Books.

Schaeffer, Francis A., and C. Everett Koop. (1979). *Whatever Happened to the Human Race*. Old Tappan, NJ: Fleming H. Revell Co.

Schaeffer, Franky. (1982). *A Time for Anger: The Myth of Neutrality*. Westchester, IL: Crossway Books.

Schalit, Joel, and Charlie Bertsch. (1997). "Millennial Revelations: Religious Extremism and the Preparations For a Secular Apocalypse." In special report, "On the Millennium." *Deolog* (online journal), January–February. Online at http://www.stealth.net/~deolog/SchalitBertsch297.html.

Schapiro, Mark. (1994). *Who's Behind the Culture War?: Contemporary Assaults on Freedom of Expression*. New York: Nathan Cummings Foundation.

Scheidler, Joseph M. (1985). *Closed: 99 Ways to Stop Abortion*. Westchester, IL: Crossway Books.

Schell, Jonathan. (1999). "Master of All He Surveys." Review of *The New Prince: Machiavelli Updated for the Twenty-First Century* and *Behind the Oval Office: Getting Reelected Against All Odds*, both by Dick Morris. *The Nation*, June 21, pp. 25–30.

Scher, Abby. (1995). *Cold War on the Home Front: Middle Class Women's Politics in the 1950's*. Ph.D. diss., New School for Social Research, New York, NY.

Schlafly, Phyllis. (1964). *A Choice Not An Echo*. Alton, IL: Pere Marquette Press.

Schlafly, Phyllis (Ed.). (1984). *Child Abuse in the Classroom*. Alton, IL: Pere Marquette Press.

Schlafly, Phyllis, and Chester Ward. (1964). *The Gravediggers*. Alton, IL: Pere Marquette Press.

Schlafly, Phyllis, and Chester Ward. (1966). *Strike from Space*. Revised and expanded. Alton, IL: Pere Marquette Press.

Schlafly, Phyllis, and Chester Ward. (1975). *Kissinger on the Couch*. New Rochelle, NY: Arlington House.

Schmaltz, William H. (1999). *Hate: George Lincoln Rockwell and the American Nazi Party*. Washington, DC: Brassey's.

Schmidt, Michael. (1993). *The New Reich: Violent Extremism in Unified Germany and Beyond*. Translated by Daniel Horch. New York: Pantheon Books.

Schmidt, Susan, and Michael Weisskopf. (2000). *Truth at any Cost: Ken Starr and the Unmaking of Bill Clinton*. New York: HarperCollins.

Schoenberger, Robert A. (Ed.). (1969). *The American Right Wing: Readings in Political Behavior.* New York: Holt, Rinehart & Winston.

Scholnick, Myron I. (1990). *The New Deal and Anti-Semitism in America.* New York: Garland Publishing.

Schonbach, Morris. (1985 [1958]). *Native American Fascism During the 1930s and 1940s: A Study of Its Roots, Its Growth and Its Decline.* New York: Garland Publishing. Ph.D. diss., University of California at Los Angeles, 1958.

Schrecker, Ellen. (1993). "McCarthyism and the Decline of American Communism, 1945–1960." In Michael E. Brown, Randy Martin, Frank Rosengarten, and George Snedeker (Eds.), *New Studies in the Politics and Culture of U.S. Communism.* New York: Monthly Review Press.

Schulman, Beth. (1995). "Foundations for a Movement: How the Right Wing Subsidizes its Press." *Extra!* (Fairness and Accuracy in Reporting), special issue on "The Right-Wing Media Machine," March–April, p. 11.

Schultz, Debra L. (1993). *To Reclaim a Legacy of Diversity: Analyzing the "Political Correctness" Debates in Higher Education.* New York: National Council for Research on Women.

Schultz, Nancy Lusignan. (1999). *Fear Itself: Enemies Real & Imagined in American Culture.* West Lafayette, IN: Purdue University Press.

Schurmann, Franz. (1974). *The Logic of World Power: An Inquiry into the Origins, Currents, and Contradictions of World Politics.* New York: Random House, Inc.; Pantheon Books.

Schwarz, Fred. (1965 [1960]). *You Can Trust the Communists (to be Communists).* Paperback. Long Beach, CA: Christian Anti-Communism Crusade. Original hardcover published New York: Prentice Hall.

Schwarz, Fred. (1996). *Beating the Unbeatable Foe: One Man's Victory over Communism, Leviathan, and the Last Enemy.* Washington, DC: Regnery.

Segrest, Mab. (1989). "A Deadly New Breed." *Southern Exposure,* Spring, pp. 57–60.

Segrest, Mab, and Leonard Zeskind. (1989). *Quarantines and Death: The Far Right's Homophobic Agenda.* Booklet. Atlanta, GA: Center for Democratic Renewal.

Seib, Gerald F. (1993). "Christian Coalition Hopes to Expand by Taking Stands on Taxes, Crime, Health Care and NAFTA." *The Wall Street Journal,* September 7, p. A18.

Seymour, Cheri. (1991). *Committee of the States: Inside the Radical Right.* Mariposa, CA: Camden Place Communications.

Shapiro, Bruce. (1992). "Doctor Fulani's Snake-Oil Show: The New Alliance Party." *The Nation,* May 4, pp. 585–594.

Shapiro, Bruce. (1999). "Buchanan-Fulani: New Team?" *The Nation,* November 1, online archive.

Shephard, Alicia C. (1998). "A Scandal Unfolds." *American Journalism Review,* March, online.

Shirer, William L. (1960). *The Rise and Fall of the Third Reich: A History of Nazi Germany.* Greenwich, CT: Fawcett Publications.

Silko, Leslie Marmon. (1994). "The Border Patrol State." *The Nation,* vol. 259, no. 12, October 17, pp. 412–416.

Simon, William E. (1978). *A Time for Truth.* New York: Reader's Digest Press, McGraw Hill.

Simpson, Christopher. (1988). *Blowback: America's Recruitment of Nazis and Its Effects on the Cold War.* New York: Macmillan Publishing Company, Collier Books.

Sine, Tom. (1995). *Cease Fire: Searching for Sanity in America's Culture Wars.* Grand Rapids, MI: William B. Eerdmans.

Singerman, Robert. (1982). *Antisemitic Propaganda: An Annotated Bibliography and Research Guide.* New York: Garland Publishing.

Singerman, Robert. (1986). "The Jew as Racial Alien: The Genetic Component of American Anti-Semitism." In David A. Gerber (Ed.), *Anti-Semitism in American History.* Urbana: University of Illinois Press.

Sklar, Holly (Ed.). (1980). *Trilateralism: The Trilateral Commission and Elite Planning for World Management.* Boston: South End Press.

Sklar, Holly. (1986). *Reagan, Trilateralism and the Neoliberals: Containment and Intervention in the 1980s.* Pamphlet No. 4. Boston: South End Press.

Sklar, Holly. (1995). *Chaos or Community?: Seeking Solutions, Not Scapegoats for Bad Economics.* Boston: South End Press.

Sklar, Holly. (1995). "The Dying American Dream and the Snake Oil of Scapegoating." In Chip Berlet (Ed.), *Eyes Right! Challenging the Right Wing Backlash* (pp. 113–134). Boston: South End Press.

Skocpol, Theda, and John L. Campbell (Eds.). (1995). *American Society and Politics: Institutional, Historical, and Theoretical Perspectives.* New York: McGraw-Hill.

Skotnes, Andor. (1996). "The Communist Party, Anti-Racism, and the Freedom Movement: Baltimore, 1930–1934." *Science & Society,* vol. 60, no. 2, Summer, pp. 164–194.

Skousen, W. Cleon. (1970). *The Naked Capitalist: A Review and Commentary on Dr. Carroll Quigley's Book: Tragedy and Hope—A History of the World in Our Time.* Salt Lake City, UT: self published under imprint Reviewer.

Smelser, Neil J. (1971). *Theory of Collective Behavior.* New York: Free Press.

Smidt, Corwin E., and James M. Penning (Eds.). (1997). *Sojourners In The Wilderness: The Christian Right In Comparative Perspective.* Lanham, MD: Rowman & Littlefield.

Smidt, Corwin E., Lyman Kellstedt, John Green, and James Guth. (1994). "The Characteristics of Christian Political Activists: An Interest Group Analysis." In William R. Stevenson (Ed.), *Christian Political Activism at the Crossroads.* Lanham, MD: University Press of America.

Smith, Anna Marie. (1994). *New Right Discourse on Race and Sexuality: Britain, 1968–1990.* New York: Cambridge University Press.

Smith, Anna Marie. (1998). "Why Did Armey Apologize? Hegemony, Homophobia, and the Religious Right." In Amy E. Ansell (Ed.), *Unraveling the Right: The New Conservatism in American Thought and Politics* (pp. 148–172). Boulder, CO: Westview.

Smith, Christian. (1996). "Correcting a Curious Neglect, or Bringing Religion Back In." In Christian Smith (Ed.), *Disruptive Religion: The Force of Faith in Social-Movement Activism.* New York: Routledge.

Smith, Christian (Ed.). (1996). *Disruptive Religion: The Force of Faith in Social-Movement Activism.* New York: Routledge.

Smith, Christian. (2000). *Christian America? What Evangelicals Really Want.* Berkeley: University of California Press.

Smith, Christian, with Sally Gallagher, Michael Emerson, Paul Kennedy, and David Sikkink. (1998). *American Evangelicalism: Embattled and Thriving.* Chicago: University of Chicago Press.

Smith, David Norman. (1996). "The Social Construction of Enemies: Jews and the Representation of Evil." *Sociological Theory,* vol. 14, no. 3, November, pp. 203–240.

Smith, Gaddis. (1996). "Dividing a Single World into Many Cultural Spheres." *Boston Globe,* December 22, p. N20. A review of Samuel P. Huntington, *The Clash of Civilizations and the Remaking of World Order.* New York: Simon and Schuster.

Smith, James Allen. (1991). *The Idea Brokers: Think Tanks and the Rise of the New Policy Elite.* New York: The Free Press.

Smith, Rogers M. (1999 [1997]). *Civic Ideals: Conflicting Visions of Citizenship in U.S. History.* New Haven, CT: Yale University Press.

Smoot, Dan. (1977 [1962]). *The Invisible Government.* Boston: Western Islands.

Snepp, Frank. (1991). "Brenneke Exposed." *Village Voice,* September 10, pp. 27–31.

Snepp, Frank. (1993). "Last Rites: The Implications of the Final Debunking (We Hope) of October Surprise, *Village Voice,* February 2, p. 36.

Snow, David A., and Robert D. Benford. (1988). "Ideology, Frame Resonance, and Participant Mobilization." In Bert Klandermans, Hanspeter Kriesi, and Sidney Tarrow (Eds.), *From Structure to Action: Comparing Social Movements Across Cultures: Vol. 1. International Social Movement Research* (pp. 197–217). Greenwich, CT: JAI Press.

Snow, David A., and Robert D. Benford. (1992). "Master Frames and Cycles of Protest." In Aldon D. Morris and Carol McClurg Mueller (Eds.), *Frontiers in Social Movement Theory*. New Haven, CT: Yale University Press.

Snow, David A., E. B. Rochford, Jr., S. K. Worden, and Robert D. Benford. (1986/1997). Frame alignment process, micromobilization, and movement participation. *American Sociological Review* 51, August 1986, pp. 464–481. Reprinted 1997 in Steven M. Buechler and F. Kurt Cylke, Jr. (Eds.), *Social Movements: Perspectives and Issues* (pp. 211–228). Mountain View, CA: Mayfield Publishing.

Soley, Lawrence C. (1990). "Right-Think Inc." *City Pages* (Minneapolis, MN), October 31.

Soley, Lawrence C. (1995). *Leasing the Ivory Tower: The Corporate Takeover of America*. Boston: South End Press.

Solomon, Normon. (1996). "Mass Media are Boosting Promise Keepers," syndicated column, August 1. Online archive.

Solotoroff, Paul. (1993). "Surviving the Crusades." *Rolling Stone*, October 14, pp. 57–62.

Sommerville, Diane Miller. (1995). "The Rape Myth in the Old South Reconsidered." *The Journal of Southern History*, vol. 61, no. 3, August, pp. 481–518.

Southern Poverty Law Center. (1998). "Y2Kaos." *Intelligence Report*, Fall.

Southern Poverty Law Center. (2000). "'Neither Left Nor Right.'" *Intelligence Report*, Winter 2000, pp. 40–47.

Spengler, Oswald. (1934). *The Hour of Decision*. Translated by Charles Francis Atkinson. New York: Alfred A. Knopf.

Spengler, Oswald. (1992 [1926]). *The Decline of the West: Vol. 1. Form and Actuality*. Translated by Charles Francis Atkinson. New York: Knopf.

Spengler, Oswald. (1992 [1928]). *The Decline of the West: Vol. 2. Perspectives of World History*. Translated by Charles Francis Atkinson. New York: Knopf.

Spielvogel, Jackson, and David Redles. (1986). "Hitler's Racial Ideology: Content and Occult Sources." *Simon Wiesenthal Center Annual*, vol. 3. Los Angeles, Simon Wiesenthal Center.

Stan, Adele. (1995). "Power Preying." *Mother Jones*, November–December.

Stanford, Peter. (1996). *The Devil: A Biography*. New York: Henry Holt.

Stang, Alan. (1965). *It's Very Simple: The True Story of Civil Rights*. Boston: Western Islands.

Stark, Steven. (1996). "Right Wing Populist." *The Atlantic Monthly*, February, online archive.

Steel, Ronald. (1996). "The Hard Questions: Paradigm Regained." *New Republic*, December 30, p. 25. A review of Samuel P. Huntington, *The Clash of Civilizations and the Remaking of World Order*. New York: Simon and Schuster.

Stefancic, Jean, and Richard Delgado. (1996). *No Mercy: How Conservative Think Tanks and Foundations Changed America's Social Agenda*. Philadelphia: Temple University Press.

Stein, Arlene. (1998). *When the Culture War Comes to Town: An Ethnography of Contested Sexuality in Rural Oregon*. Paper, annual meeting, American Sociological Association, San Francisco.

Stein, Arlene. (1998). "Whose Memories? Whose Victimhood? Contests for the Holocaust Frame in Recent Social Movement Discourse." *Sociological Perspectives*, vol. 41, no. 3.

Stein, Judith. (1986). *The World of Marcus Garvey: Race and Class in Modern Society*. Baton Rouge: Louisiana State University Press.

Stern, Kenneth S. (1996). *A Force Upon the Plain: The American Militia Movement and the Politics of Hate*. New York: Simon and Schuster.

Stern, Kenneth S. (1996). "Militias and the Religious Right." *Freedom Writer*, Institute for First Amendment Studies, October.

Stevens, Doris. (1976 [1920]). *Jailed for Freedom*. New York: Schocken Books.

Stevenson, William R. (Ed.). (1994). *Christian Political Activism at the Crossroads*. Lanham, MD: University Press of America.

Still, William T. (1990). *New World Order: The Ancient Plan of Secret Societies*. Lafayette, LA: Huntington House.

Stix, Nicholas. (1997). "Apocalypse, Shmapocalypse: You Say You Want a Revolution." In special report, "On the Millennium." *Deolog* (online journal), January–February. Online at http://www.stealth.net/~deolog/297.html.

Stock, Catherine McNicol. (1996). *Rural Radicals: Righteous Rage in the American Grain.* Ithaca, NY: Cornell University Press.

Stokes, Thomas L. (1940). *Chip Off My Shoulder.* Princeton, NJ: Princeton University Press.

Stokes, Thomas. (1968). "FDR's Class Coalition." In William E. Leuchtenburg (Ed.), *The New Deal: A Documentary History.* New York: Harper & Row.

Stone, Alan A., M.D. (1993). *Concerning the Handling of Incidents Such As the Branch Davidian Standoff in Waco Texas.* Submitted November 10. Recommendations of experts for improvements in federal law enforcement after Waco. Washington, DC: U.S. Department of Justice and U.S. Department of the Treasury. Online at http://www.pbs.org/wgbh/pages/frontline/waco/stonerpt.html.

Stone, I. F. (1963). *The Haunted Fifties.* New York: Random House.

Stone, Peter H. (1979). "The Counter-Intelligentsia: The 'Free-Enterprise' Think Tanks and the Holy War on Government." *The Village Voice,* October 22, pp. 14–19.

Stormer, John A. (1964). *None Dare Call It Treason.* Florissant, MO: Liberty Bell Press.

Stormer, John A. (1968). *The Death of a Nation.* Florissant, MO: Liberty Bell Press.

Strong, Donald S. (1941). *Organized Anti-Semitism in America: The Rise of Group Prejudice During the Decade 1930–40.* Washington, DC: American Council on Public Affairs.

Strozier, Charles B. (1994). *Apocalypse: On the Psychology of Fundamentalism in America.* Boston: Beacon Press.

Strozier, Charles B., and Michael Flynn (Eds.). (1997). *The Year 2000: Essays on the End.* New York: New York University Press.

Sutton, Antony C. (1974). *Wall Street and the Bolshevik Revolution.* New Rochelle, NY: Arlington House.

Sutton, Antony C. (1976). *Wall Street and the Rise of Hitler.* Seal Beach, CA: '76 Press.

Sutton, Antony C., and Patrick M. Wood. (1979). *Trilaterals Over Washington.* Scottsdale, AZ: The August Corporation.

Sweet, Lynn. (1998). "Chicago Man Paid Clinton Troopers: On Mission To Air Sex Tales." *Chicago Sun-Times,* March 31. Online at Northern Light.

Switzer, Jacqueline Vaughn. (1997). *Green Backlash: The History and Politics of the Environmental Opposition in the U.S.* Boulder, CO: Lynne Rienner.

Szajkowski, Zosa. (1974). *Jews, Wars and Communism: Vol 2. The Impact of the 1919–20 Red Scare on American Jewish Life.* New York: Ktav Publishing House.

Tabachnik, Leonard. (1973). *Origins of the Know-Nothing Party: A Study of the Native American Party in Philadelphia, 1844–1852.* Ph.D. diss., Columbia University.

Tabor, James D., and Eugene V. Gallagher. (1995). *Why Waco? Cults and the Battle for Religious Freedom in America.* Berkeley: University of California Press.

Takaki, Ronald. (1990). *Iron Cages: Race and Culture in 19th-Century America.* New York: Oxford University Press.

Tani, E., and Kaé Sera. (1985). *False Nationalism False Internationalism: Class Contradictions in the Armed Struggle.* Chicago: Seeds Beneath the Snow.

Tarpley, Webster Griffin, and Anton Chaitkin. (1992). *George Bush: The Unauthorized Biography.* Washington, DC: Executive Intelligence Review.

Tarrow, Sidney. (1994). *Power in Movement: Social Movements, Collective Action and Politics.* New York: Cambridge University Press.

Taylor, Allen. (1993). "Agrarian Independence: Northern Land Rioters after the Revolution." In Alfred F. Young (Ed.), *Beyond the American Revolution: Explorations in the History of American Radicalism* (pp. 221–245). DeKalb, IL: Northern Illinois University Press.

Taylor, G. Flint. (1986). "Waller v. Butkovich: Lessons in Strategy and Tenacity for Civil Rights Legislators." *Police Misconduct and Civil Rights Law Report,* vol. 1, no. 13, January–February. New York: Clark Boardman.

Terry, Randall A. (1991). *Accessory to Murder: The Enemies, Allies, and Accomplices to the Death of our Culture.* Brentwood, TN: Wolgemuth and Hyatt Publishers.

Terry, Randall A. (1993). *Why Does a Nice Guy Like Me Keep Getting Thrown in Jail?* Lafayette, LA: Huntington House Publishers.

Teixeira, Ruy A., and Joel Rogers. (1998). "Mastering the New Political Arithmetic: Volatile Voters, Declining Living Standards, and Non-College-Educated Whites." In Amy E. Ansell (Ed.), *Unraveling the Right: The New Conservatism in American Thought and Politics* (pp. 228–247). Boulder, CO: Westview.

Thayer, George. (1967). *The Farther Shores of Politics: The American Political Fringe Today.* New York: Simon and Schuster.

Theoharis, Athan. (1978). *Spying on Americans: Political Surveillance from Hoover to the Huston Plan.* Philadelphia, Pa: Temple University Press.

Theoharis, Athan G., and John Stuart Cox. (1988). *The Boss: J. Edgar Hoover and the Great American Inquisition.* Philadelphia: Temple University Press.

Thomas, Cal, and Ed Dobson. (1999). *Blinded by Might: Can the Religious Right Save America?* Grand Rapids, MI: Zondervan.

Thompson, Damian. (1996). *The End of Time: Faith and Fear in the Shadow of the Millennium.* Great Britain: Sinclair-Stevenson.

Thompson, Jerry. (1982). *My Life in the Klan.* New York: G.P. Putnum's Sons.

Thomson, Rosemary. (1981). *Withstanding Humanism's Challenge to Families: Anatomy of a White House Conference.* Morton, IL: Traditional Publications.

Tippit, Sarah. (1995). "Chilling New Link Suspected Among Anti-Abortion Activists." Reuters News Agency, transmitted January 13, 1995.

Toobin, Jeffrey. (1999). *A Vast Conspiracy: The Real Story of the Sex Scandal that Nearly Brought Down a President.* New York: Random House.

Toy, Eckard V. (1992). "Robe and Gown: The Ku Klux Klan in Eugene, Oregon." In Shawn Lay (Ed.), *The Invisible Empire in the West: Toward a New Historical Appraisal of the Ku Klux Klan of the 1920s* (pp. 153–184). Urbana: University of Illinois Press.

Trescott, Paul B. (1963). *Financing American Enterprise: The Story of Commercial Banking.* New York: Harper & Row, Publishers.

Trombley, Stephen. (1988). *The Right to Reproduce: A History of Coercive Sterilization.* London: George Weidenfeld and Nicholson Limited.

Tull, Charles J. (1965). *Father Coughlin and the New Deal.* Syracuse, NY: Syracuse University Press.

Turner, Patricia A. (1993). *I Heard it Through the Grapevine, Rumor in African-American Culture.* Berkeley: University of California Press.

Unruh, Robert. (1998). "Authorities Speculate Fugitives May Have Slipped Away—Again." *Associated Press,* June 5.

Van Dyke, Nella, and Sarah A. Soule. (2000). *The Mobilizing Effect of Social Strain: Explaining the Variation in Levels of Patriot and Militia Organizing.* Paper, annual meeting, American Sociological Association, Washington, DC.

Van Impe, Jack. (1996). *2001: On the Edge of Eternity.* Dallas: Word Publishing.

Van Natta, Don, Jr., and Jill Abramson. (1999). "Shadow Legal Team for Jones Lawyers Worked Behind the Scenes to Keep Case Alive." *The New York Times,* January 2. Online archive.

Varange, Ulick (pseudonym of Francis Parker Yockey). (1962 [1948]). *Imperium: The Philosophy of History and Politics.* Costa Mesa, CA: Noontide Press.

Vaughn, Stephen. (1980). *Holding Fast the Inner Lines: Democracy, Nationalism, and the Committee on Public Information.* Chapel Hill: The University of North Carolina Press.

Vest, Jason. (1995). "The Spooky World of Linda Thompson." *Washington Post.* May 11, p. D1.

Victor, Jeffrey. (1992). "The Search for Scapegoat Deviants." *The Humanist,* September–October, pp. 10–13.

Viguerie, Richard A. (1980). *The New Right: We're Ready to Lead.* Falls Church, VA: The Viguerie Company.

Viguerie, Richard A. (1983). *The Establishment vs. the People: Is a New Populist Revolt on the Way?* Chicago, IL: Regnery Gateway.

Vinz, Warren Lang. (1997). *Pulpit Politics: Faces of American Protestant Nationalism in the Twentieth Century.* Albany: State University of New York Press.

Waas, Murray. (1997). "Starr Minds the Bar." *The Nation,* March 17, pp. 6–7. See other articles by Waas in notes to Chapter 15.

Waas, Murray, and Jonathan Broder. (1998). "The Ties that Bind." *Salon,* March 18. Online at http://www.salonmagazine.com/news/1998/03/18newsb.html. See other articles by Waas and Broder in notes to Chapter 15.

Wade, Wyn Craig. (1987). *The Fiery Cross: The Ku Klux Klan in America.* New York: Simon and Schuster.

Walker, James W. St. G. (1989). "Blacks as American Loyalists: The Slaves' War for Independence." In Paul Finkelman (Ed.), *Slavery, Revolutionary America, and the New Nation* (pp. 447–463). New York: Garland Publishing.

Wallace, Anthony F. C. (1956). "Revitalization Movements." *American Anthropologist,* vol. 58, no. 2, April, pp. 264–281.

Wallace, Anthony F. C. (1993). *The Long, Bitter Trail: Andrew Jackson and the Indians.* New York: Hill and Wang.

Walter, Jess. (1995). *Every Knee Shall Bow: The Truth and Tragedy of Ruby Ridge and the Randy Weaver Family.* New York: Regan Books.

Walvoord, John F. (1990 [1974]). *Armageddon, Oil And The Middle East Crisis. What The Bible Says About The Future Of The Middle East And The End Of Western Civilization.* Grand Rapids, MI: Zondervan.

Ward, Eric (Ed.). (1996). *Conspiracies: Real Grievances, Paranoia, and Mass Movements.* Seattle: Northwest Coalition Against Malicious Harassment, Peanut Butter Publishing.

Ward, Eric (Ed.). (1997). *The Second Revolution: States Rights', Sovereignty, and Power of the County.* Seattle: Northwest Coalition Against Malicious Harassment, Peanut Butter Publishing.

Ward, Eric (Ed.). (1998). *American Armageddon: Religion, Revolution and the Right.* Seattle: Northwest Coalition Against Malicious Harassment, Peanut Butter Publishing.

Warner, David. (1981). "Scaife." Four-part series in the *Pittsburgh Post-Gazette,* including, "Scaife: Financier of the Right," April 20; "Scaife the Man: His Impact on Western Pa." April 21; "Scaife the Publisher: His Favorite Role," April 22.

Warren, Donald I. (1976). *The Radical Center: Middle Americans and the Politics of Alienation.* Notre Dame, IN: University of Notre Dame Press.

Washburn, Wilcomb E. (1972 [1957]). *The Governor and the Rebel: A History of Bacon's Rebellion in Virginia.* New York: Norton.

Watson, Justin. (1997). *The Christian Coalition: Dreams of Restoration, Demands for Recognition.* New York: St. Martin's Press.

Webber, David. (1997). "Cyberspace: The Beast's Worldwide Spiderweb." In William T. James (Ed.), *Foreshocks of Antichrist* (pp. 125–162). Eugen OR: Harvest House.

Weber, Max. (1999 [1930]). *The Protestant Ethic and the Spirit of Capitalism.* Translated by Talcot Parsons. New York: Routledge.

Webster, Nesta H. (1921). *World Revolution: The Plot Against Civilization.* London: Constable.

Webster, Nesta H. (1924). *Secret Societies and Subversive Movements.* London: Boswell Printing.

Weglyn, Michi. (1976). *Years of Infamy: The Untold Story of America's Concentration Camps.* New York: William Morrow.

Weinberg, Leonard. (1993). "The American Radical Right: Exit, Voice, and Violence." In Peter H. Merkl and Leonard Weinberg (Eds.), *Encounters with the Contemporary Radical Right.* Boulder, CO: Westview.

Weiner, Tim. (1995). "One Source, Many Ideas in Foster Case." *The New York Times*, August 13, p. 19.

Weiner, Tim, and Jill Abramson. (1998). "Clinton Foes Have Ties, But They Deny They Are Acting In Concert." *New York Times News Service*, January 27. Online archive. Also appears as "The President Under Fire: The Actors; In the Case Against Clinton, Some Links to Conservatives." *The New York Times*, January 28, 1998. Online archive.

Weisberg, Barry. (1971). *Beyond Repair: The Ecology of Capitalism*. Boston: Beacon Press.

Weisberg, Jacob. (1995). "Playing with Fire." *New York* magazine, May 8, pp. 30–35.

Welch, Robert. (1961). *The Blue Book of the John Birch Society*. 21st printing. Boston: John Birch Society.

Welch, Robert. (1964). The Politician. Revised, 5th printing, hardcover. Belmont MA: Belmont Publishing.

Welch, Robert. (1966). *The New Americanism and Other Speeches*. Boston: Western Islands.

Wessinger, Catherine L. (1996). *Religious Institutions and Women's Leadership: New Roles Inside the Mainstream*. Columbia, SC: University of South Carolina Press.

Wessinger, Catherine. (1997). "Millennialism With and Without the Mayhem." In Thomas Robbins and Susan J. Palmer (Eds.), *Millennium, Messiahs, and Mayhem: Contemporary Apocalyptic Movements* (pp. 47–59). New York: Routledge.

Wessinger, Catherine (Ed.). (2000). *Millennialism, Persecution, and Violence: Historical Cases*. Religion and Politics Series, Michael Barkun (Ed.). Syracuse, NY: Syracuse University Press.

Weyrich, Paul. (1995). "Fear and Oppression: American Birthright?" *Rutherford* magazine, August, p. 16.

Weyrich, Paul. (1999). "Creating a New Society." *World* magazine, May 15, pp. 22–23.

Wheaton, Elizabeth. (1987). *Code Name GREENKIL: The 1979 Greensboro Killings*. Athens, GA: University of Georgia Press.

White, Christopher. (1991). "George Bush's Countdown to Middle East War." *New Federalist*, extra edition, January.

White, G. Edward. (1968). *The Eastern Establishment and the Western Experience: The West of Frederic Remington, Theodore Roosevelt, and Owen Wister*. New Haven, CT: Yale University Press.

Whitehead, John W. (1987). *The Stealing of America*. Westchester, IL: Crossway Books.

Whiteside, Andrew G. (1975). *The Socialism of Fools: Georg Ritter von Schönerer and Austrian Pan-Germanism*. Berkeley: University of California Press.

Wilcox, Clyde. (1988). "The Christian Right in Twentieth Century America: Continuity and Change." *The Review of Politics*, vol. 50, no. 4, Fall, pp. 659–681.

Wilcox, Clyde. (1996). *Onward Christian Soldiers?: The Religious Right in American Politics*. Boulder, CO: Westview.

Williams, Eric. (1966 [1944]). *Capitalism and Slavery*. New York: Capricorn Books.

Williams, Lena. (1996). "A Law Aimed at Terrorists Hits Legal Immigrants." *The New York Times*, July 17, pp. A1, B5.

Williams, Lucy A. (1996). "The Right's Attack on Aid to Families with Dependent Children." *The Public Eye*, vol. 10, nos. 3–4, Fall–Winter. Expanded into Lucy A. Williams, *Decades of Distortion*.

Williams, Lucy A. (1997). *Decades of Distortion*. Somerville, MA: Political Reserach Associates.

Wilson, Joan Hoff. (1976). "The Illusions of Change: Women and the American Revolution." In Alfred F. Young (Ed.), *The American Revolution*. DeKalb, IL: Northern Illinois University Press.

Winters, Paul A. (Ed.). (1996). *Hate Crimes*. Current Controversies Series. San Diego, CA: Greenhaven Press.

Wistrich, Robert. (1985). *Hitler's Apocalypse: Jews and the Nazi Legacy*. New York: St. Martin's Press.

Withorn, Ann. (1998). "Fulfilling Fears and Fantasies: The Role of Welfare in Right-Wing Social Thought and Strategy." In Amy E. Ansell (Ed.), *Unraveling the Right: The New Conservatism in American Thought and Politics* (pp. 126–147). Boulder, CO: Westview.

Wood, Forest G. (1970). *Black Scare: The Racist Response to Emancipation and Reconstruction.*
Berkeley: University of California Press.

Wood, Peter H. (1993). "'Liberty is Sweet': African-American Freedom Struggles in the
Years before White Independence." In Alfred F. Young (Ed.), *Beyond the American Revo-
lution: Explorations in the History of American Radicalism* (pp. 149–184). DeKalb: Northern
Illinois University Press.

Worrell, Mark P. (1999). "The Veil of Piacular Subjectivity: Buchananism and the New
World Order." *Electronic Journal of Sociology* vol. 4, no. 3. Online at http://www.sociol-
ogy.org/content/vol004.003/buchanan.html.

Wyman, David S. (1984). *The Abandonment of the Jews: America and the Holocaust, 1941–1945.* New
York: Random House; Pantheon Books.

Yemma, John. (1996). "Countdown to Catastrophe: Doomsday Visions Abound as Millennium Approaches." *Boston Sunday Globe,* December 29, p. 1.

Yemma, John. (1996). "Populist Pitch on Worker Insecurity Hits Home with the Lesser-Edu-
cated." *The Boston Globe,* February 29, online archive.

Yemma, John. (1997). "Science vs. Fiction." *The Boston Globe Magazine,* April, 13. Online archive.

Yockey, Francis Parker. See pseudonym: Varange, Ulick.

Young, Alfred F. (Ed.). (1976). *The American Revolution.* DeKalb: Northern Illinois University
Press.

Young, Alfred F. (1990). "The Women of Boston: 'Persons of Consequence' in the Making
of the American Revolution, 1765–76." In Harriet B. Applewhite and Darline G. Levy
(Eds.), *Women and Politics in the Age of the Democratic Revolution.* Ann Arbor: The University of Michigan Press.

Young, Alfred F. (1993). "Afterword: How Radical Was the American Revolution?" In Alfred F. Young (Ed.), *Beyond the American Revolution: Explorations in the History of American
Radicalism.* DeKalb, IL: Northern Illinois University Press.

Young, Alfred F. (Ed.). (1993). *Beyond the American Revolution: Explorations in the History of American Radicalism.* DeKalb, IL: Northern Illinois University Press.

Young-Bruehl, Elisabeth. (1996). *The Anatomy of Prejudices.* Cambridge, MA: Harvard University Press.

Your Child's New Teacher: The Federal Government in the Classroom. (no date). Pamphlet published
in several versions during the 1990s by Concerned Women for America in Washington, D.C.

Yu, Connie Young. (1989). "The World of Our Grandmothers." In Asian Women United of
California (Eds.), *Making Waves: An Anthology of Writings By and About Asian American
Women* (pp. 33–42). Boston: Beacon Press.

Yung, Judy. (1989). "Appendix: A Chronology of Asian American History." In Asian
Women United of California (Eds.), *Making Waves: An Anthology of Writings By and
About Asian American Women* (pp. 423–431). Boston: Beacon Press.

Zahner, Dee. (1994). *The Secret Side of History: Mystery Babylon and the New World Order.*
Hesperia, CA: LTAA Communications.

Zald, Mayer N. (1996). "Culture, Ideology, and Strategic Framing." In Doug McAdam, John
D. McCarthy, and Mayer N. Zald (Eds.), *Comparative Perspectives on Social Movements: Political Opportunities, Mobilizing Structures, and Cultural Framings* (pp. 261–274). Cambridge, UK: Cambridge University Press.

Zerzan, John. (1993). "Rank-and-file Radicalism within the Ku Klux Klan of the 1920s." *Anarchy: A Journal of Desire Armed,* no. 37, Summer, pp. 48–53.

Zeskind, Leonard. (1987). *The "Christian Identity" Movement.* Atlanta, GA: Center for Democratic Renewal; New York: Division of Church and Society, National Council of Churches.

Zeskind, Leonard. (1996). "Some Ideas on Conspiracy Theories for a New Historical Period." In Eric Ward (Ed.), *Conspiracies: Real Grievances, Paranoia, and Mass Movements* (pp. 11–33). Seattle: Northwest Coalition Against Malicious Harassment, Peanut Butter Publishing.

Zeskind, Leonard. (2000). "White Nationalists Just Love Buchanan." *Los Angeles Times*, July 30, online archive.

Zeskind, Leonard, with Keith Hunt. (1999). "Sam Francis: General from MARs." *Searchlight*, May, p. 24. (Note correction: Francis resigned from the *Washington Times*.)

Zia, Helen. (1991). "Women in Hate Groups." *Ms. Magazine*, March–April.

Ziegenhorn, William Karl. (1995). "No Rest for the Wicked: The FBI Investigations of White Supremacist Groups, 1983–1988." Masters Thesis, Department of History, San Jose State University.

Zinn, Howard. (1980). *A People's History of the United States*. New York: HarperCollins.

INDEX

ABOUT THE AUTHORS

Chip Berlet has written about right-wing movements for over twenty years, with bylines in *The New York Times*, the *Boston Globe*, *The Progressive*, and scores of other publications. He is senior analyst at Political Research Associates in Somerville, Massachusetts, and editor of *Eyes Right!: Challenging the Right Wing Backlash* (South End Press, 1995). He has contributed articles and chapters to several scholarly books and journals and his media appearances and cites as an expert include *Newsweek*, National Public Radio, and *Nightline*.

Matthew N. Lyons is a historian, activist, and writer whose work has focused on systems of oppression and social movements. He is research associate for the Hansberry–Nemiroff Archival, Educational, and Cultural Fund, and author of *The Grassroots Network: Radical Nonviolence in the Federal Republic of Germany, 1972–1985* (Cornell University Center for International Studies, 1989).